OUTDOOR RECREATION

ENRICHMENT FOR A LIFETIME

4TH EDITION

KATHLEEN A. CORDES

Professor Emerita, San Diego Miramar College

GARRETT A. HUTSON

Associate Professor, Brock University

SAGAMORE
PUBLISHING

Publishers: Joseph J. Bannon and Peter L. Bannon
Sales and Marketing Managers: Misti Gilles and Emily Wakefield
Director of Development and Production: Susan M. Davis
Production Coordinator: Amy S. Dagit
Cover Designer: Marissa Willison
Interior Photos: Jane Lammers

ISBN print edition: 978-1-57167-777-8
ISBN e-book: 978-1-57167-778-5
Library of Congress Control Number: 2015939589

Printed in the United States

1807 N. Federal Dr.
Urbana, IL 61801
www.sagamorepublishing.com

To the Brownies: Ann, Irene, Jennifer, Kit,
Patty, Stefani, Stevie, and Sue

K.C.

To my parents: Darryl Hutson and Carol Siano

G.H.

Contents

Kathleen Cordes, professor emerita, served as chair at Whittier and Miramar colleges and Honors Director of the San Diego Community College District. Other than teaching courses in leisure, recreation, physical education, and interdisciplinary offerings, she served as one of the first female directors of men and women's athletics, the first female varsity coach at the University of Notre Dame, the first athletic director of Saint Mary's College (Notre Dame, Indiana), and a visiting professor at the University of Zulia and the University of the Andes (Venezuela).

As interim executive director for the American Association for Leisure/Recreation (AALR), Cordes represented AAHPERD on the White House Green Ribbon Panel and authored *America's Millennium Trails Pathways for the 21st Century,* an official project of the White House Millennium Council. AALR recognized her with its Outstanding Achievement Award and the Merit Service Award for Distinguished Service to Recreation.

Cordes, also author of *America's National Historic Trails* and *America's National Scenic Trails* (University of Oklahoma Press), is author of other college textbooks including *Applications in Recreation and Leisure* (Sagamore Publishing) and *Parks, Recreation, and Leisure Service Management* with Hilmi Ibrahim (Eddie Bowers).

The President's Council on Fitness, Sports, and Nutrition selected Cordes as a 2014 Lifetime Achievement Award winner. The American Alliance of Health, Physical Education, Recreation, and Dance (AAHPERD) recognized her with its national, district, and state honor awards. She was inducted into SHAPE America's North American Society for Health, Physical Education, Recreation, Sport, and Dance Professionals (2015); elected American Leisure Academy Senior Fellow; honored with Indiana University's 2014 Anita Aldrich Distinguished Alumni Award; and honored with the California Legislative Assembly Recognition Award (2014) for dedication to the promotion of innovative teaching and learning in physical education across the country. The past president of California's AHPERD, Cordes is the recipient of its highest recognition, the Verne Landreth Award. Cordes serves on the board of directors for California's Santa Rosa Plateau Nature Education Foundation, is news editor for SHAPE America's southwest district, and is listed in *Who's Who in America* and *Who's Who in the World.*

Garrett Hutson, PhD, is an associate professor of recreation and leisure studies at Brock University in St. Catharines, Ontario, Canada. He has done considerable work exploring the topics of outdoor recreation, outdoor leadership, and person–place relationships. His current research projects explore how human dimensions of place can inform sustainable outdoor recreation practices and resource management. He is also a member of a research team that explores how sense of community evolves and changes during organized wilderness trip experiences.

Hutson's work appears in the *Journal of Leisure Research, Controversial Issues in Adventure Programming, Landscapes of Leisure: Space, Place, and Identities,* and within the environmental studies curriculum of the National Outdoor Leadership School (NOLS). Hutson also serves as co-editor of the peer-reviewed journal, *Research in Outdoor Education.*

Prior to academic life, Hutson worked full time as a ski patroller helping to launch one of the first ski areas ever to operate on U.S. Bureau of Land Management lands in Southwest Colorado. Additionally, he worked as a NOLS instructor in Wyoming, Alaska, and the Yukon Territory and as a climbing guide for organizations accredited by the American Mountain Guides Association in both Oregon and Colorado. He currently facilitates collaborative research and management efforts between the Ontario Rock Climbing Access Coalition, the Ontario Ministry of Natural Resources and Forestry, and the Niagara Parks Commission. Hutson most often experiences leisure through time spent with loved ones, rock climbing, trail biking, writing, and exploring the city of Toronto, which he now calls home.

Acknowledgements

It is such a pleasure to work with Sagamore Publishing. We would like to thank Joe Bannon for his encouragement and enthusiasm for this project. Thank you Peter Bannon for always being so supportive. Thanks to Susan Davis and William Anderson for your help and ideas. We are appreciative of our stellar editor, Amy Dagit, especially for her skills and perseverance. Thank you! We are grateful to Hilmi Ibrahim for his many contributions to the prior editions of this manuscript. You are missed, Hilmi. His wife Cynthia was so helpful, too, and will always be a part of this book. Finally, a very special thank-you goes to Jane P. Lammers for sharing her expressive photographs and always being willing to lend a helping hand when needed.

We wish to extend our thanks as well to our reviewers, whose comments improved various editions. They are:

Brenda K. Blessing,
    Missouri Western State University
Lowell Caneday
    Oklahoma State University
Craig Kelsey,
    University of New Mexico
Phyllis Ford,
    Greenbough Programs
Wayne Allison,
    Lock Haven University
O. J. Helvey,
    Cumberland College
Jack B. Frost,
    California Polytechnic University-
        Pomona

K.C.
G.H.
April 2015

Introduction

This book was written with a number of objectives in mind. Most important, it tries to avoid duplicating other books on outdoor recreation. This book attempts to look at outdoor pursuits first as a sub-phenomenon of the larger recreation and leisure phenomenon, but with an added touch, that of the natural element, with its psychological influence and social significance. These two points will be elaborated on in Part One.

Part One provides two views of nature. The first is based on the experiences and values of the original inhabitants of the New World. The second is based on the values of Western society transplanted into the New World after discovery and colonization. These two views are not necessarily incompatible. For despite the exploitation of nature that began with the early European settlers, there were, and still are, those whose love of nature is evident in their writing, advocacy, and leadership. The early transcendentalists, naturalists, and practitioners were ahead of their time. Today, the field of psychology shows us why nature is so appealing and soothing to human beings. Because we need nature for our well-being, effective management of our natural resources is a must. Psychology aside, effective managers should be equipped with managerial skills and also a thorough understanding of the socioeconomic factors that

have a direct bearing on outdoor recreational pursuits.

Part Two provides the reader with a description of the resources available to the outdoor adventurer. There are four categories of resources: federal, state, local, and private. These categories prevail in the United States, and Canada has a similar arrangement. In part, this edition highlights, the Canadian outdoor recreation identity, which has been shaped by Canada's landscapes, weather patterns, rich cultural history, the emergence of federal and provincial parks, and the mystique and wild nature of "the North."

Part Three is devoted to examining the management of outdoor resources as well as outdoor education and activities. Future managers and recreation participants would definitely benefit from knowing the policies, procedures, and even the problems of outdoor recreation management and the environment.

An epilogue is provided that expresses our hopes for a bright and prosperous future for outdoor recreation. The appendices provide pertinent information such as a list of federal and state agencies dealing with outdoor recreation, as well as professional and voluntary associations concerned with outdoor pursuits. Finally, an index is provided for the reader.

Part One

The Fundamentals of Outdoor Recreation

The first part of this book is devoted to examining the foundations of outdoor recreation, which include the historical, spiritual, social, psychological, and economic factors that led to its rise in the Western world, particularly in the United States and Canada. In Chapter 1, we give an overview of these foundations. Chapter 2 is focused on the spiritual attitudes of Americans toward the outdoors. In Chapter 3, we examine the influence of some of the outdoor recreation movement's most important leaders and teachers. Chapter 4 includes a discussion of the psychology of the natural environment, and in Chapter 5, we discuss the social aspects of outdoor experiences. In Chapter 6, we discuss the economics of outdoor recreation.

Chapter 1

Foundations of Outdoor Recreation

In this book, we use the term *outdoor recreation* to encompass the organized free-time activities participated in for their own sake and where there is an interaction between the participant and an element of nature. Surfing is an outdoor recreational activity where there is interaction between the participant and water, an element of nature. Football is not an outdoor recreational activity under our definition, for although it is an organized recreational activity, nature plays a minimal role in it. Nature plays a more important role in mountain climbing or cross-country skiing than it does in football.

Although predicated on play and part of the growing sphere of leisure activities, recreation is different from both play and leisure in that it is basically organized and takes place mainly in groups. At the core of recreation is play, and at the core of outdoor recreation is involvement with the natural environment. On the other hand, leisure is defined as the state of mind that allows an individual to participate in certain activities, and availability of free time is an important contributor to both recreation and outdoor recreation.

Recent studies have shown that ritual among humans played, and still plays, an important role, not only in establishing social order but also as a vehicle of creativity and expression. Ritual seems to have added to the importance and significance of both leisure and recreation. Elaboration on play, ritual, and outdoor recreation follows.

HUMANS, PLAY, AND RITUAL

Hardly anyone disagrees that humans tend to play. Some may argue that play is witnessed among the young of the human race only, but empirical evidence negates such a claim: Some adult activities that may not be considered as play by everyone are in fact play activity, albeit somewhat sophisticated play. Such sophistication results from both the maturation of the individual and the complexity of modern societies. Studies show that many of the original activities of adults in some primal societies were very similar to children's play (Blanchard & Cheska, 1985; Roth 1902; Wood, 1871). Complexity in many activities provides people with much of today's recreation (Turner, 1982).

Outdoor recreation—the activities that are the main focus of this volume—is practiced by most members of complex, modern urbanized and industrial societies. Most Americans and Canadians camp, ski, and go on organized picnics. In previous societies, only the well-to-do could afford to do so. Their value system not only allowed but also encouraged enjoyment of picnics, camping, and skiing. The reasons for the shift that allows everyone to recreate are societal, be they economic or political, but the reason for participation, by wealthy and nonwealthy alike, is based on the tendency of humans to play and, to a great extent, to ritualize.

Play

Some researchers have claimed that the tendency to play may have a deeper niche in human behavior than was once believed. Humans share this propensity with the upper mammals (deVore, 1965; Lancaster 1975; Marano, 1999), and there may be a genetic imprint, or a chemical code, that propels people in this direction (Eisen, 1988). To understand this tendency, an explanation of the structure of the human brain and its evolution is a must.

The simple elementary brain, which is labeled the reptilian brain, is surrounded by a more complicated brain known as the limbic system, or the old mammalian brain. The elementary brain handles basic functions of self-preservation and preservation of the species through hunting, homing, mating, fighting, and territoriality, and the old mammalian brain is identified with mothering, audiovocal communication, and play. Experiments have shown that when the limbic system was severed in some small animals, they reverted to reptilian behavior, which is void of play (Ibrahim, 1991).

The third brain, called the new mammalian brain or the neocortex, surrounds the old mammalian brain and is divided into two hemispheres, each responsible for the opposite side of the body. According to Ornestein and Thompson (1984), hemispheric specialization occurred when humans were becoming bipedal and beginning to use their front limbs in tool making. With the enlarged brain, more complicated processes occurred, including the construction and storage of symbols. Mental processes using the two hemispheres can be roughly divided into two groups: processes that help in maintaining order in everyday activities such as language and others that pertain to insight, imagination, and artistic expression. Sagan (1977) as-

serted that the left hemisphere is responsible for the first group and the right hemisphere is responsible for the second.

In the early 1940s, brain research led to the assumption that a drive for arousal in both humans and animals helps to avoid boredom (Berlyne, 1960). Others today are advocating that a "hormonal code" or "genetic programming" initiates, propels, and, to a lesser degree, regulates play (Eisen, 1988). The evidence comes from observation of animals and humans. In the case of animals, it is evident that the higher the animal on the evolutionary scale, the greater the time devoted to play, at least among the young. Among humans, Sutton-Smith suggested that neuroimaging studies of the brain may reveal a ludic center located somewhere in the frontal lobe (Marano, 1999).

Although play varies among primate species, Lancaster (1975) indicated that field observers were impressed with the amount of time and energy spent in play by their juveniles. For instance, young chimpanzees spend over 50% of their waking hours in play. Play behavior is first seen in the early morning and last seen before young baboons retire. The same has been observed among young howlers and bonnet macaques (de Vore, 1965).

Evidence of a biological base for play among young humans comes from the forms and sequence of children's play, regardless of social or cultural background. The sequence of manipulative, repetitive, relational, make-believe, and rule-governed play is remarkably stable across diverse populations, which points toward a possible universal blueprint for play (Wolf, 1984). Others have found similar regularities (Edwards, 2000).

But play is not the only element in the rise of organized recreational activities among the members of a given society. Ritual plays an important role as well. The first scholar to bring to attention the link between play and ritual is historian Johan Huizinga. He believed that play is the basis of culture and that ritual assisted in the process of bringing about civilized life.

Now in myth and ritual the great instinctive forces of civilized life have their origin:

law and order, commerce and profit, craft and art, poetry, wisdom, and science. All are rooted in the primeval soil of play (Huizinga, 1950).

At the time of Huizinga's (1950) writing, the concept of instinctive play was not palatable to many scholars of play. The idea that ritual might also be instinctive was equally unacceptable. In the last few decades, however, research on the brain has lent some credence to Huizinga's advocation that some biological basis seems to exist for both play and ritual (Marano, 1999). For a recent discussion on the topic of play, see Stuart Brown's (2008) TED Talk about the important links between play, human intelligence and development, and creativity at http://www.ted.com/talks/stuart_brown_says_play_is_more_than_fun_it_s_vital.html. In his talk, Brown highlighted scientific findings, which strongly suggest that human play is integral to human health and survival.

In between these two extremes—biological nature versus cultural orientation—are theories in which play is explained in terms of psychology and sociology. These theories underscore the multifaceted nature of play.

Ritual

Scholars are just now beginning to understand the role of ritual in human life. Ritual is a set or series of acts, with a sequence established by tradition and stemming from the life of a people. Thanksgiving dinner in America, for example, is a tradition with an original purpose that some may have forgotten, yet it is celebrated year after year (with a new element added, a televised football game). Although the original meaning of the activity may be forgotten, humans ritualistically repeat the activity with great passion. Some scholars believe that it is the repetitiveness that matters and not the activity itself, on the assumption that ritualization has a biological basis in humans and animals.

Ritualization is the stylized, repeated gestures and posturing of humans or animals. Ritualization is based on rhythmicity and formation, biological principles that are essential for survival. Rhythmicity is observed in the alteration of systole and diastole (higher reading and lower reading of blood pressure, respectively) and in the cycle of wakefulness and sleep. Formalization is the tendency to stabilize inner compulsions as well as output by putting things in order—a tendency that paves the way for the act called ritualization. Rhythmic, formalized, and ritualistic activity give life stability not only for the young, but also for the adult.

Simple ritualization evolved into complex rituals, which in turn expanded to five modes as proposed by Grimmes (1982). Although decorum, magic, and liturgy are not usually connected with outdoor activities, ceremony and celebration can be. A ceremony is a ritual that requires that one surrender to the demands of authority. Examples of nature ceremonies in many societies will be provided in Chapter 2. Celebration is the ritual most related to play. Here one participates for the sake of participation and not for an external end. Celebration has permeated human life since early times, including the celebration of nature, as will be seen in the examples given in Chapter 2.

Deegan (1989) stated that participatory ritual is deeply rooted in social interaction in America. Participatory rituals exhibit three common characteristics:

1. Require participation and face-to-face contact.
2. Have a matrix of roles, statuses, and culture.
3. Are organized by a set of rules for ritual action.

For our purposes, we want to know, for instance, what propels a person to go fishing or hunting year after year during the long weekend designed to celebrate the birth of a president? Is it the tendency to play? Or is it the tendency to ritualize? If the tendencies to play and to ritualize are biologically based, why is it that not all Americans of the same age and sex go fishing on that occasion? Another person may spend the long weekend alone watching nature programs on television, and a third may spend it hiking in the woods. A presentation of two more concepts that affect the outdoor experience is important at this point: leisure and recreation.

LEISURE OR RECREATION

When it comes to adult behavior during free time, analyzing the situation becomes complicated. For instance, when camping, is the individual playing, recreating, or at leisure? One does not hear or see terms such as *outdoor leisure* or *therapeutic play*, yet the American and Canadian lifestyle is full of outdoor recreation, community recreation, and therapeutic recreation. What is the difference? Conceptual differentiation among the definitions for play, recreation, and leisure is necessary at this point. In this work, play is activities of the young partaken by choice. On the other hand, recreation is an organized activity in which an adult participates during free time. The emphasis in leisure is on the state of mind that allows the adult to participate in an activity of his or her choice during the time free from work or civil or familial obligations.

This state of mind, by itself and in itself, is not easily discernible to the casual observer, but engagement in a recreational activity is. Recreation gained greater attention at the start of the 20th century in the United States and Canada because it revolved around the most easily observed feature of the leisure phenomenon, the activity. The other two elements—the state of mind and free time—were not essential in recreational programs. The activity became central to the thinking of social reformers such as Jane Addams, who advocated that the lack of these activities led to social ills such as delinquency and truancy. In fact, there are still attempts in that direction, recreation as rehabilitation, not only where adolescents are concerned (Mahoney & Stattin, 2000) but also for people with disabilities (Pati et al.,1997).

The philosopher Aristotle, who paid serious attention to the leisure phenomenon "qua," a phenomenon and not as a method to combat social ills, may help people understand the nature of leisure. Aristotle believed that leisure encompasses contemplative, recreative, and amusive activities. Leisure can be seen as a pyramid, the bottom third of which encompasses amusive activities, on top of which are recreative activities, which is topped by contemplative activities (see Figure 1.1).

In outdoor settings, all three levels can be achieved. On the first level, people would

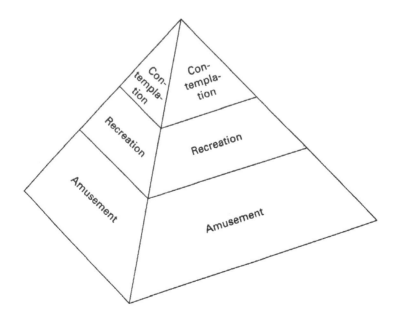

Figure 1.1. Hierarchy of leisure.

enjoy watching animals as they go about their lives. On the second level, backpacking and hiking are pursued. On the third level, the study of nature is an important aspect of contemplation. One of the elements in pushing for the building of America's first city park, Central Park of New York City, was the concept of contemplation (Taylor, 1999).

THE EMERGENCE OF OUTDOOR RECREATION

Contemplation is only one form of leisure that Americans came to enjoy, the other forms being recreation and amusement. Although the new settlers of North America had more free time, that free time did not transform into leisure easily. Leisure, as a state of being, was protested vigorously by the strict Calvinists of colonial America. Puritan requirements led the colonists to live without the "mispence of time," adhering strictly to the observance of the Sabbath. They tolerated no pagan festivities, no licentious plays and spectacles, and no violations of the Sabbath.

Outdoor recreation can inspire contemplation. Courtesy of Garrett Hutson.

Available open space was used as commons, pastureland, or training grounds in hunting. The term *commons* describes a piece of land to be shared and enjoyed by all members of the community. By the mid-1700s, open space was being used for recreational pursuits and other amusements. Some Dutch settlers in New York, who were less restrained in their religious beliefs, organized a few recreational activities after the Sunday service over the objection of church leaders. Also, wealthy Southerners began to socialize and to recreate on the Lord's Day. By the middle of the 1700s, the American lifestyle included many recreational activities, among which were pursuits in natural settings such as hunting, fishing, skating, sleighing, and tobogganing. Resorts became fashionable among the wealthy of that era.

Despite the proposal to the Continental Congress of 1774 to prohibit extravagance and dissipation such as horse racing, gaming, and cockfighting, outdoor recreation increased steadily after the Revolutionary War, particularly on the frontiers. With America's westward expansion, the frontier people found in hunting, horse racing, rail tossing, and tomahawk hurling a needed release from a life of hard work and isolation. These were also occasions for get-togethers where ritualistic activities, such as husking and quilting bees, took place.

In the meantime, American cities were growing, and the need for open space was obvious. A site in Chicago was preserved for outdoor recreation near Fort Dearborn in 1839, but it was in New York that the first city park was built in 1853. Central Park was designed by Frederick Law Olmsted and Calvert Vaux. According to Taylor (1999), Central Park was a source of conflict between the elite, the middle class, and the working class. The first group sought the park as a tool of social control; the second group looked at it as a place for art, nature, and beauty; and the third group wanted active leisure. Olmsted later planned San Francisco's Golden Gate Park, Philadelphia's Fairmount Park, Boston's Franklin Park, and the District of Columbia's Rock Creek Park. Olmstead will be discussed in more detail later in the book.

The second half of the 19th century witnessed a surge in organized sports such as baseball, basketball, and football and in outdoor recreational pursuits such as hunting and fishing. Wildlife depletion became a concern, and in 1887, two prominent sportsmen, Theodore Roosevelt and George Bird Grinnell, editor of *Forest and Stream Magazine,* formed the Boone and Crockett Club to deal with conservation issues on the national level.

Conquering the wilderness during the western expansion meant the destruction of many of America's forests, to which Franklin B. Hough, head of the 1870 census, sounded the alarm. In 1876, the U.S. Congress authorized him to study the issue, and his reports led to the creation of the Division of Forestry in the U.S. Department of Agriculture in 1881—the forerunner of today's U.S. Forest Service, U.S. Department of Agriculture.

Meanwhile, many of the states on the eastern seaboard began to establish game preserves. Deer parks were established to preserve this popular game animal. The concept of preservation reached its pinnacle in 1872 with the establishment of America's first national park.

Although there were two earlier precedents for national preserves, at Hot Springs, Arkansas, in 1832 and Yosemite Valley, California, in 1864, the concept of a national park was born with Yellowstone in 1872. The significance of this event was in the change in public policy from allowing private exploitation of America's natural resources to the setting aside of public land for protection and public enjoyment. In 1890, a bill was passed in the U.S. Congress creating Yosemite National Park. Two years later, naturalist John Muir formed the Sierra Club to explore, preserve, and enjoy the mountains of the west coast of the United States.

The concept of preservation spilled over into America's forests when President Harrison created a 13 million-acre forest preserve in 1891 to which President Cleveland added 20 million acres in 1897. Gifford Pinchot enhanced human knowledge of forests as the first American to study forest management in Europe. In 1896, the Division of Biological Survey was created in the U.S. Department of Agriculture to administer wildlife refuges. It became the forerunner of the U.S. Fish and Wildlife Service, Department of the Interior, when it was combined with the Bureau of Fisheries, U.S. Department of Commerce, in 1940.

President Theodore Roosevelt appointed a National Conservation Commission in 1908, which put together an inventory of America's natural resources. He also took executive actions to preserve vast federal lands as forest preserves, wildlife refuges, and national monuments. Eight years later, in 1916, the National Park Service was established, and in 1924, the first wilderness area was designated in the Gila National Forest. The same year witnessed the first national conference on outdoor recreation. Three years earlier, Appalachian Trail opened, ushering in a new concept in outdoor recreation. Illinois became the first state to establish a state park system in 1909, followed by Indiana in 1919. The first national conference on state parks occurred in 1921, and 5 years later the Federal Recreation Act made some public domain lands available to states for parks.

During the Depression years, and despite the economic conditions, Americans saw the opening of their first scenic parkway, the Blue Ridge Parkway. The Tennessee Valley Authority was created to provide the needed energy to vitalize the region and to control floods, but it also created many opportunities for outdoor recreational pursuits.

In the 1940s, the Bureau of Land Management was formed to control most federal real estate. The Flood Control Act of 1944 charged the U.S. Army Corps of Engineers with providing recreation on many of the reservoirs it built. A 1948 amendment to the 1944 Surplus Property Act provided for the transfer of surplus federal lands at 50% of fair market value for use as state and local parks and recreational areas.

The Outdoor Recreation Resources Review Commission and the resultant Bureau of Outdoor Recreation were created in the 1950s. Motivated by the ORRRC report, many state and local governments passed laws for bond issues to acquire more open space. In

1962, the National Park Service began a 10-year renovation program. The U.S. Forest Service began Operation Outdoors for the purpose of revitalizing its offerings.

The 1960s witnessed the passage of many federal acts, the impact of which is felt today on outdoor recreation. Among these is the Multiple-Use Sustained-Yield Act, which formalized multiple use in national forests and added outdoor recreation to the statutory list of activities provided on these lands. Other federal legislation passed in the 1960s included the Land and Water Conservation Act, the National Wilderness Preservation System Act, and the Federal Water Project Recreation Act, all of which provided significant funds for federal grants to be matched by equal state and local funds for outdoor recreational areas. The National Trails System Act and the National Wild and Scenic Rivers Act embodied new and significant concepts for outdoor recreation in America.

Significant acts for outdoor recreation were passed in the 1970s, too. The Volunteers in the Park Act authorized the National Park Service to use volunteers in its system. Also of significance was the Youth Conservation Corps Act, which employed youth in the National Park Service and the U.S. Forest Service. A new approach was tested at that time, which was the addition of urban recreational areas to the National Park Service, for example, the Gateway National Recreation Area in New York City and the Golden Gate National Recreation Area in San Francisco. Revenue-sharing programs of the 1970s helped with the establishment of many state and local parks.

According to Clawson (1985), a major development at that time was the expansion of privately owned, privately financed, and privately operated outdoor facilities. These included ski areas, water sport areas, amusement parks, campgrounds, and resorts in outdoor settings. Another important development was the application of new technologies to outdoor settings, the results of which were the modern activities of scuba diving, snowmobiling, and recreational vehicle camping. Today, thanks to the insight of a few persons and to the foresight of America's

legislators, Americans are enjoying a lifestyle that includes many opportunities for active and contemplative recreation in outdoor settings.

A parallel movement for the provision of outdoor recreational areas occurred in Canada (see Chapter 11 for the history of outdoor recreation in Canada). Canada and the United States and, to some extent, Australia led the world in this movement. It took the rest of the world almost another 100 years to try to catch up with these three countries. Leisure and recreation (including outdoor pursuits) are becoming an important part in the lifestyles of many countries today. The following factors have led to this development.

Leisure and Recreation: A Human Right

In 1948, the General Assembly of the United Nations adopted the Universal Declaration of Human Rights. The member nations at that time agreed to the following principle:

> Every citizen has the right to rest and leisure, including reasonable limitation of working hours, and periodic holidays with pay . . . and . . . the right to freely participate in the cultural life of the community, to enjoy the arts. . . . (United Nations, 1978)

This statement by the United Nations represents the culmination of many human endeavors to achieve such a right. It may have begun with the Sixth Right, which evolved among the Ancient Israelites. The first five rights were the Right to Live, the Right of Possession, the Right to Work, the Right to Clothing, and the Right to Shelter. The Sixth Right included a provision for a Sabbath. Although the Sabbath was originally for rest and worship, it provided the opportunity for recreational activities that took place at later dates among the Israelites (Ibrahim & Shivers, 1979).

The ancient Greeks were also interested in the idea of leisure. The free men among them took it seriously and sent their offspring to *schole*, the institution where the young would learn the arts of graceful living, music, philosophy, art, and gymnastics. As mentioned earlier, it was their philosopher, Aristotle, who underscored leisure as an important ingredient of the good life.

Ibn Khaldun, the Arab philosopher of the 14th century, went as far as claiming the desire for leisure as the fifth layer of a five-layer schema of human desires, the first of which is bodily appetites, followed by the desire for safety and calm, the desire for companionship, and the desire for superiority (Ibrahim, 1988). The fifth and last of these desires would be satisfied with the United Nations resolution. Many nations are working to provide the same right. But the resolution alone did not contribute to the rise of leisure pursuits in today's world.

Increased Free Time

Although time free from civic and familial obligations began with the rise of the leisure class, as suggested by Veblen (1953), leisure in its "pure" form, as a state of being, did not materialize until recently. The Sabbath was observed as a day of rest from labor among the Israelites and early Christians, albeit as a day devoted to worship. Labor time was measured by the day that started at sunrise and ended at sundown, leaving little or no free time. Conditions became worse with the coming of the Industrial Revolution, which initially emphasized production over human happiness.

The movement to reduce work hours among labor began in the United States when, in the early 1800s, Boston machinist Ira Stewart formed the Grand Eight-Hour League of Massachusetts (Viau, 1939). Much later, the World Labor Organization passed a bill for 40-hour workweeks and a 12-day annual vacation in 1966. Both France and Great Britain adopted a 40-hour workweek in 1919, which became the standard for many industrialized nations.

The standard for paid annual vacation adopted in most of the industrialized nations was 2 weeks initially, and it has reached 4 weeks in some of these nations today (Samuel, 1986). Recently, France decreed a 5-week vacation for its citizens. Adding to free time is the sometimes compulsory retirement from work. Paid retirees are now a fact of life in most countries, not only among those who served in industry but also in services and trade. Productivity in industry, services, and trade continues at a high level, thanks to the increased use of machines in the 20th century, which has made even more free time available to people. Assisting in the increase of free time are industrialization and automation. Although some scholars have decried the decline of leisure (Schor, 1991), the demand for more free time continues (Boggis, 2001).

Industrialization and Automation

Initially, the Industrial Revolution created unsafe, unpleasant working conditions for many workers. Emigration to industrial centers led to crowded conditions in the cities of western Europe and North America. These slum dwellers included many children who worked long hours. Even when the conditions improved, industrialization revolved around tedious and repetitive tasks for the individual worker, and the need for outlets became apparent. A need for outlets that "would exercise the workers' creative energy and provide a sense of achievement and accomplishment became pressing for people" (MacLean, Peterson, & Martin, 1985, p. 44). Recreation, including outdoor pursuits, provided the required outlets. Many social reformers worked on providing facilities and programs of recreation. The Playground Association of America was organized in 1906. It was renamed the Playground and Recreation Association of America in 1911, became the National Recreation Association in 1930, and merged with other associations in 1965 to become the National Recreation and Park Association. The association published *Playground Magazine,* now *Parks and Recreation.* The need for such an organization grew as the world's population shifted from the countryside to urban cities.

Urbanization

In the mid-1800s, there were 85 cities in the United States. Most people lived in the country. By 1910, the number of American cities with populations over 100,000 increased to 50. In Canada there were 20 communities with populations over 5,000 by the mid-1800s; by the turn of the century, there were 62. The trend is not limited to North America or Europe. Today, there are 83 cities in the world with populations over 1 million. Only 18 are in Europe, and nine are in North America. There are 39 in Asia, seven in what used to be the Soviet Union, seven in South America, and three in Africa.

Urban life itself may have increased the need for recreational outlets, including outdoor ones. More important is the role that urbanization plays in modernizing, meaning not only economic growth, but also cultural and social changes. Services such as education, both formal and informal, are easier to provide in urban centers. Improved literacy rates lead to more sophisticated demands, one of which is the demand for recreational outlets. As will be shown in Chapter 5, the higher the education acquired, the more the demand for recreation, for outdoor pursuits in particular. There are calls today for the provision of recreational activities, particularly in the outdoors, for the urban centers of the world (Griffiths, 2001). But because most outdoor facilities are located away from urban centers, those who are interested in partaking of an outdoor pursuit must find not only the time but also the means to get there.

Transportation

The railroad and steamboat had tremendous impact on recreation in North America and abroad. The railroad encouraged outdoor recreation on a large scale. The Train Excursion of 1844 provides a good example of the role of mass transportation in outdoor pursuits. The excursion, from London to the seaside resort of Brighton, created popular excitement in Great Britain (Lowerson & Myerscough, 1977). In the United States, the steamboat carried people and horses to racing centers along the Mississippi River in the antebellum era. After the Civil War ended, the railroad helped transport people to the growing athletic events, on both the intercollegiate level and the professional level. The same was occurring in Canada.

But it was the invention of the internal combustion engine that contributed to the expansion of outdoor recreation. In the last decade of the 19th century, the automobile was introduced, and Henry Ford converted it into a means of popular transportation. Outdoor facilities require space and were often built outside urban centers, and the masses finally had transportation to get to golf courses, ski resorts, campgrounds, fishing spots, and hunting lodges.

Not until World War I did the air become commercialized. Today, it has become means of transportation for millions of people seeking rest and recreation in remote spots that in times past were frequented only by the privileged few. Tourism has become an important international business. Within the United States and Canada, another important means of recreational travel has evolved: the RV (recreational vehicle). Its sales peaked in 1972, at 540,000 a year in the United States and then leveled off and saw a drastic drop until 1985 when sales began to pick up again (Barker, 1986). Also, pleasure boats have seen a surge in popularity. They may represent a status in life that indicates prestige. This is a function of social mobility.

Mobility

The purchase of a vehicle such as an RV or a boat does not automatically mean that its owner will visit a park or engage in an outdoor pursuit. Mobility has a psychological dimension as well as a social dimension. The social dimension is the movement of an individual from one status to another. Upward mobility leads to improvement in status, downward mobility moves a person to a lower status, and horizontal mobility leads to a new and different status that is similar to the old one. Mobility is a phenomenon that is seen in open societies, the ones that allow for changes in one's status. This creates a psychological dimension that not only allows but also prompts the individual to go after the benefits to be accrued from the new, upward status, such as the type of recreation and the lifestyle enjoyed by the members of the desired "class." People seek higher pay, longer vacations, and the ability to afford an RV and/or a pleasure boat for psychological and social reasons. Perhaps the article in *Transportation Quarterly* is the testimony that travel associated with leisure activities has become increasingly important (Lawson, 2001).

RECENT TRENDS IN OUTDOOR RECREATION

Two publications were authored under the same principal investigator (Cordell, 1999, 2004). The author concluded that both supply and demand for outdoor recreation, in both the public and private sectors, kept pace with population growth in the 20th century. In the public sector, the increase in resources was seen basically in land-based facilities at federal, state, and local governmental levels. Trail resources grew substantially and acreage of lakes and reservoirs increased only slightly. In the private sector, downhill ski areas increased their capacities in all regions of the country. The studies show that recreational activities that took place on land, rather than water, snow, or ice, constituted the largest single category in outdoor recreation. The investigators suggested that trail, street, and road activities; viewing and learning activities; camping; hunting; hiking; and some forms of social activities dominate land-based outdoor recreation.

Among land-based activities, camping seemed to be the one that grew substantially during the 20th century. Also, bird-watching increased 155% compared with 93% in hiking and 73% in backpacking. Downhill skiing and cross-country skiing increased about 50% and 176%, respectively. Developed camping grew by 42%, and most surprisingly "primitive" camping grew at 72%. Although bicycling saw a dramatic rise during the 1980s and the 1990s, the investigators described that increase as faddish rather than a trend in long-term growth. Nonetheless mountain biking has seen an increase. On the other hand, hunting began to decline as an outdoor recreational activity, perhaps due to the increasing difficulty of gaining access to land or water areas suitable for that activity (The Elusive Hunter, 2006).

During the last few years of the 20th century, water-based activities were dominated by motor boating followed by wind-powered boating and muscle-powered boating. Fishing, which used to be a popular outdoor recreational activity in the United States, declined and so did sailing. The data revealed that snorkeling and scuba diving, along with viewing water areas and learning about them, became important aspects of water-based outdoor recreational activities in this country. Participation in the vigorous activities of swimming, canoeing, and kayaking increased as did white-water recreational activities.

Furthermore, the data revealed that about 94% of the U.S. population participated in some form of outdoor recreation over 1 year. The investigators used the term *enthusiasts* to describe the men and women who constituted the bulk of participants, accounting for 70% to 89% of participation. It is estimated that 21.4% of enthusiasts were keen on walking, followed by 19.7% who were beachgoers, 17.4% sightseeing fans,

Rock climbing is an excellent form of outdoor recreation that people choose to participate in during free time. Courtesy of Garrett Hutson.

and 11.8% visitors to historic sites. Kayaking fans account for only .02% of outdoor participants, and windsurfers account for mere .03% and migratory bird-watchers for .06%.

Among the participants in outdoor recreation in the United States, demographic changes took place. For instance the percentage of women participating in walking dropped from 60% to 53%, and the percentage of male participants increased from 40% to 47%. When it comes to ethnicity, 28% of Native Americans participated in camping compared to 21% of Hispanic Americans and 18% of Asian Americans. Native Americans participated more in hunting than did the other ethnic groups. Participation in outdoor recreational activities increased among persons with disabilities, with sightseeing being their most favored activity, followed by developed camping and visiting nature centers.

The longitudinal comparisons among the different generations of Americans were included in the data. The investigators used such terms as the G.I. generation for those born between 1901 and 1924, the silent generation (1925–1942), the boom generation (1943–1960), the 13th generation (1961–1981) and the millennial generation (1982–2004). Participation in outdoor recreation has increased among most of the members of these five generations thanks to industrialization and automation, urbanization, transportation, and mobility. Cordell (2008) continues to suggest that this increase is likely to continue and "between 2000 and 2007, the total number of people who participated in one or more outdoor recreational activities increased by 4.4 percent, from an estimated 208 million to 217 million." The continued increase in participation in outdoor recreation may be attributed to all of the mentioned reasons, but perhaps most important, the increase will be sustained by the global principle that leisure and recreation (including outdoor recreation) are human rights.

SUMMARY

In this work, outdoor recreation is defined as organized, free-time activities participated in for their own sake and where there is an interaction between the participant and an element of nature. Such activities are predicated on the tendencies to play and to ritualize. Both of these tendencies have biological roots as well as evolutionary dimensions. Observation of play among animals, particularly the higher forms, along with the studies of the human brain show how profound the tendency to play is. Meanwhile, the tendency to ritualize is seen in ceremonies and celebration of many human societies. Also, outdoor recreational pursuits are affected by a recent phenomenon, leisure, which describes the state of mind that allows a person to participate in an activity solely for the sake of that activity during a time free from civic and familial obligations.

The need for recreational outlets overcame the objection of those who considered such pursuits as wasteful, if not sinful, among the early European settlers of the New World. Open spaces that were allocated for meeting, grazing, and training of hunters evolved into parks. Fear of wanton destruction of the vast yet limited natural resources on this continent led to the rise of a preservation movement, which led to the establishment, for the first time in human history, of natural areas allocated for the enjoyment of present and future generations. The concept of federally designated national parks, born in the United States with the establishment of Yellowstone National Park, is adopted by many nations today.

Expansion of outdoor recreational opportunities required the establishment of many agencies at the federal, state, and local levels. This was in response to demands that were accelerated by (a) the adoption of the Universal Declaration of Human Rights by the General Assembly of the United Nations in 1948, which includes the right to leisure and recreation; (b) an increase in free time for almost every citizen in many countries regardless of social class and lifestyle; (c) the advent of industrialization and automation, which allowed for more free time; (d) an increase in urbanization with the resultant increase in the need for outdoor recreational outlets; (e) the provision of adequate means of transportation that takes the desiring person to the spot of his or her choice; and 6) mobility with its social as well as psychological dimensions that, in the case of upward mobility, drives one to seek recreational pursuits that correspond to the newly acquired status.

The 20th century saw changes in outdoor pursuits such as increases in hiking, backpacking, and both cross-country and downhill skiing versus a decreases in hunting and road bicycling. Also, the number of minority group members participating in outdoor recreational activities increased.

REFERENCES

Barker, R. (1986, February 24). On the road to recovery: RV makers rev up for a strong year. *Barons, 15,* 28–30.

Berlyne, D. E. (1960). *Conflict, arousal and curiosity.* New York, NY: McGraw-Hill.

Blanchard, K., & Cheska, A. (1985). *The anthropology of sport: An introduction.* South Hadley, MA: Bergin and Garvey.

Boggis, J. J. (2001). The eradication of leisure. *New Technology, Work and Employment, 16*(2), 188–129.

Brown, S. (2008). Stuart Brown: Play is more than fun [Video file]. Retrieved June 27, 2013, from http://www.ted.com/talks/stuart_brown_says_play_is_more_than_fun_it_s_vital.html

Clawson, M. (1985). Outdoor recreation: Twenty-five years of history, twenty-five years of projection. *Leisure Sciences, 7*(l), 73–99.

Cordell, H. K. (1999). *Outdoor recreation in American life: A national assessment of demand and supply demands.* Champaign, IL: Sagamore.

Cordell, H. K. (2004). *Outdoor recreation for 21st Century America. A report to the nation: The national survey on recreation and the environment.* State College: Venture.

Cordell, H. K. (2008). The latest in trends in nature-based outdoor recreation. *Forest History Today, 2008,* 4–10.

Deegan, M. J. (1989). *American ritual dramas: Social rules and culture meanings.* Westport, CT: Greenwood Press.

deVore, I. (1965). *Primate behavior.* New York, NY: Holt, Reinhart and Winston.

Edwards, C. P. (2000). Children's play in cross cultural perspective. *Cross Cultural Research, 34*(4), 318.

Eisen, G. (1988). Theories of play. In G. Gerson et al. (Eds.), *Understanding leisure.* Dubuque, IA: Kendall-Hunt.

The elusive hunter. (2006). *Newsweek, 148*(23), 50–53.

Griffiths, J. (2001). Playing for time: The importance of recreation in society. *The Ecologist, 31*(4), 52.

Grimmes, R. (1982). *Beginnings in ritual studies.* Landham, MD: University Press of America.

Huizinga, J. (1950). *Homo ludens.* New York, NY: The Beacon.

Ibrahim, H. (1988). Leisure, idleness and Ibn Khaldun. *Leisure Studies, 7,* 51–58.

Ibrahim, H. (1991). *Leisure and society: A comparative approach.* Dubuque, IA: Wm. C. Brown.

Ibrahim, H., & Shivers, J. (1979). *Leisure: Emergence and expansion.* Los Alamitos, CA: Hwong.

Lancaster, J. B. (1975). *Primate behavior and the emergence of human culture.* New York, NY: Holt, Rinehart, and Winston.

Lawson, C. T. (2001). Leisure travel/activity decision: Time and location differences. *Transportation Quarterly, 55*(3), 51.

Lowerson, J., & Myerscough, J. C. (1977). *Time to spare in Victorian England.* Hassocks, England: Harvester Press.

MacLean, J., Peterson, J., & Martin, W. D. (1985). *Recreation and leisure: The changing scene.* New York, NY: Macmillan.

Mahoney, J. L., & Stattin, H. (2000). Leisure activities and adolescent antisocial behavior: The role of structure and social context. *Journal of Adolescence, 23*(2), 113.

Marano, H. E. (1999). The power of play. *Psychology Today, 32,* 36.

Ornestein, R., & Thompson, R. (1984). *The amazing brain.* New York, NY: Houghton-Mifflin.

Pati, A. B. et al. (1997). Recreation/leisure interest of inpatients rehabilitation clients. *Physical Therapy, 79*(5), 78.

Roth, W. C. (1902). *Games, sports and amusements*. Brisbane, Australia: G. A. Vaughan, Government Printer.

Sagan, C. (1977). *The dragons of Eden*. New York, NY: Random House.

Samuel, N. (1986). Free time in France: A historical & sociological survey. *International Social Science Journal, 38*, 49–63.

Schor, J. B. (1991). *The overworked Americans: The unexpected decline of leisure*. New York, NY: Basic Books.

Taylor, D. E. (1999). Central Park as a model for social control: Urban parks, social class and leisure behavior in nineteenth century America. *Journal of Leisure Research, 31*(4), 420.

Turner, V. (1982). *From ritual to theatre: The human seriousness of play*. New York, NY: Performance Arts Journal Publication.

United Nations. (1978). *Human rights: A compilation of international instruments*. New York, NY: Author.

Veblen, T. (1953). *The theory of leisure class*. New York, NY: New American Library.

Viau, J. (1939). *Hours and wages in American organized labor*. New York, NY: George Putnam and Sons.

Wolf, D. D. (1984). Repertoire, style, and format: Notions worth borrowing from children's play. In P. Smith (Ed.), *Play in animals and humans*. Oxford, England: Basil Blackwell.

Wood, J. (1871). *The uncivilized races of man*. Hartford, CT: J.B. Burr.

Chapter 2

Nature and the Spiritual Life

One aspect of American outdoor recreation is a person's respect for, and, in some cases, reverence for, nature. This reverence is characteristic of some of the early leaders who laid the foundation for preservation of federal lands. In this chapter, we will explore American Indian reverence for nature and address other Western attitudes toward nature.

Historically, respect for nature was challenged by American cultural values as embodied by the Industrial Revolution during the late 19th century and 20th century. In more recent years, there has been a movement toward a renewed reverence for nature due to the influence of the ecology and health movements and spiritual reawakening. The origins of modern reverence for nature are traced to the philosopher Jean-Jacques Rousseau, who popularized the notion that the world in its natural state is closer to the truth (Clark, 1969). Contemporary writers such as Thomas Berry in *The Great Work* (2000) and *The Dream of the Earth* (1990), George Sessions in *Deep Ecology for the 21st Century* (1995), and former Vice President Al Gore in *Earth in the Balance: Ecology and the Human Spirit* (1992) and *Inconvenient Truth* (2006) have advocated a spirituality that includes a fresh respect for the universe and a more harmonious relationship with nature.

As North Americans have rekindled a sense of spiritual interest, the study of recreation's connections with the spiritual has begun to emerge. This area of research surfaced during a 1990s multiperspective focus session when public land managers and other experts discussed the use of public lands to refresh the human spirit (Zuefle, 1999). The study of spiritual connections with natural places is important in achieving a complete and balanced view of the diversity inherent in the outdoor recreational experience.

Three broad trends have reawakened people's awareness of the connection between nature and the human spirit. First, there has been a shift to a faster paced life in urban areas where there is a perceived loss of predictability and control; second, there is a widespread orientation toward physical activity, nutrition, and the nurturance of more satisfying relationships aimed at a sense of fitness and inner peace; and third, there is an increased concern for the natural environment and the contribution that environment makes to the quality of life (Driver, Dustin, Baltic, Elsner, & Peterson, 1996). Practitioners and visionaries alike have called for an expanded land management ethic that adds to the foundation set by Aldo Leopold, discussed in the next chapter. For many, this expanded base includes the deeper spiritual and psychological meanings of land.

A SPIRITUAL RELATIONSHIP TO NATURE

The origins of the relationship of nature and the spirit have been tracked by archeologists and anthropologists to the dawn of human civilization when much of the world was predicated on the worship of a single earth goddess who communicated a sense of harmony among all living things (Gore, 1992). When the focus is on American history as it relates to nature, the spiritual emphasis plays an interesting role, particularly in regard to the leisure experience. The first stage was an early relationship with nature. American Indians celebrated and ritualized nature, making efforts to achieve harmony and continuity with its many forces and its animal and plant life. The second stage occurred with the arrival of the pioneers. Eager to begin a new life in a new country, the pioneers felt compelled to conquer nature. The third stage was a time of dualities. The wilderness was less threatening, and with more leisure time available, transcendentalists began a philosophical movement back to nature. But during this stage, industrialization resulted in the exploitation of American lands. Fortunately, foresighted citizens sought the protection of significant public lands, which today provide a setting for a reawakening of the process of spiritual refreshment.

Spirituality

Spirituality, often mistakenly used interchangeably with *religion,* can be thought of as a personal belief in, or a search for a reason for one's existence; a greater or ultimate reality; or a sense of connection with God, nature, or other living beings. This is different from *religion,* which is commonly perceived as organized and institutional in nature, a group experience with accepted beliefs and traditions (Zuefle, 1999). When the two become entangled, authors often err by using the term *religion* to describe both activities. It is imperative that public park and recreation professionals understand the difference. Outdoor programs that include spiritual benefits, for example, involve individuals with and without specific religious faiths, whereas programs that are focused on specific religious practices may be in violation of federal and state constitutions. Some experts agree that in more recent years physical wellness has been emphasized, and they are now in the early stages of realizing that individuals have spiritual wellness needs that pertain to the out-of-doors experience and that people are actively seeking inner peace at special places. Spiritual resources that can be found in the nature experience provide a route-finding system that enables people to navigate life's journey. Certainly bookshelves in bookstores do not lack in ways to begin that search, with many references to experiences in nature as gateways to the inner life and the spiritual journey.

Leisure offers time for contemplation and meditation in which human values can be established and enriched. Educator and leader in the profession Jay B. Nash (1886–1965) deemed the highest form of recreational participation to be activities in which the participant is most fully involved emotionally, physically, and creatively. The spiritual aspect of life, according to one specialist in the field (Kaplan, 1979), "opens us to the interdisciplinary, fusionary, holistic prospect of leisure that invites emotional, unforced, free adventuresome levels of experience" (p. 190). Another authority (Kraus, 1984) found that

> leisure provides the arena in which personal values are shaped and in which the individual may reach the highest potential of which he or she is capable. Beyond the purely practical and purposeful goals that characterize work, it [leisure] offers a vision of life carried on for its own sake, in celebration of all that is vital and generous in people.

William R. H. Stevens, a writer on leisure and religion, found that the essential spirit of leisure is that of celebration: ". . .Real joy is a condition of the spirit deeper than the mere fleeting experience of pleasurable sensation" (Kaplan, 1979, p. 187).

Spiritual forms or aspects of leisure, then, are not limited to special philosophies or church programs. One of the most significant outcomes of the camp experience is the development of spiritual feelings and values. In this sense, Meier and Mitchell (1993) defined *spiritual* as connoting a keen appreciation of nature as well as a kinship with one's fellow beings and an orderly universe. *Religious* groups have used camps for spiritual settings for years, but *spiritual* experiences do not necessarily occur at formally arranged times or in specifically designated places. These experiences may occur when the senses are unusually heightened, such as when immersed in the wilderness, where the scent of pines, the fragrance of wildflowers, the dazzle of soft light at sunset, or the caress of a gentle wind that rustles through the trees provide opportunities to experience the deep beauty and complexity of life's mysteries and mystique.

There are two sides to the spiritual or sacred life: the personal, ecstatic side that individuals are at a loss of words to adequately describe and the communal part, which may be celebrated year after year through oral histories, rituals, ceremonies, and customs (Beck & Walters, 1988). The camp experience can nurture both sides of this spiritual life. A person can have a peak experience in which the wholeness of life is experienced in a mystical fashion while making an arduous ascent to the top of a mountain or while feeling the refreshing mist of a cascading waterfall. Group members may have a communal experience around the blazing campfire in which a unity of spirit and connectivity with others is achieved that elevates the group to a more intense spiritual experience. In each case, something of the mystery of life is revealed, albeit for a brief moment.

American Indians experience a rich spiritual life that permeates their entire life, both individually and communally. Their experience is germane to outdoor recreationists in that they live close to nature and spend much of their lives in the out-of-doors. They, too, sense the mystical in nature that hikers and backpackers, as will be discussed later,

refer to as some of life's most profound experiences.

American Indians and the Native American Experience

American Indians view themselves as part of a delicate and balanced universe, not as its masters. In their world view, all life forms and natural elements are connected in that they interrelate and interplay: No part of nature is considered more important than another. They further believe, generally, that only humans can upset this balance on earth. Everything is naturally alive, and ceremonies serve to maintain harmony with the pervasive powers of nature, stressing the relationship of people with the cosmos. Chief Luther Standing Bear of the Oglala Sioux found that

> only to the white man was nature a wilderness and only to him was the land infested with wild animals and savage people. To us it was tame. Earth was bountiful and we were surrounded with the blessings of the Great Mystery. (Stegner, 1990, p. 35)

Most American Indians have two common beliefs that play significant roles in their sacred practices: a belief in a knowledge of unseen powers and a belief in the knowledge that all things in the universe are dependent on each other. Unseen powers might be worshiped in elaborate ceremonial dances. The mysterious powers of nature, such as the way the seasons change, are often marked by collective rituals and ceremonials that recognize the spirits of the seasons and the good they bring. The rituals provide order and systematize the way in which the society, the natural environment, and the unseen worlds meet and come together. The rituals provide a physical expression of a mystical experience. In this manner, the participants come closer to understanding the mysteries of life. Historically, the American Indian ritual cycle has contained many celebrations and liturgies that are focused on harmony with nature.

Harmony With Nature

By living in harmony with nature, American Indians seek unity with a fundamental life force inherent in everything. For Hopi Traditionalists, it is referred to as *Techqua Ikachi*, which means "blending with the land and celebrating life" (Mails, 1997, p. 1). Ceremonies, rites, and songs serve as aids. Rituals transform the mysterious into something more tangible. It is glorified and celebrated rather than explained. Rituals are not simple, crude, or barbaric; they are complex, pervasive, remarkable human processes that are central to life. Whether as straightforward as prescribing how meals are shared or as intricate as how major events are marked, rituals give people ways to be playful or explore their lives. They provide people with ways of dealing with forces that seem beyond comprehension and control, and they help people make connections and transitions (Imber-Black & Roberts, 1997).

For example, puberty ceremonies among the Sioux are closely linked to nature. Traveling alone a hilltop, forest, or remote shore to participate in his initiation ceremony or vision quest, a young man contemplates and seeks the aid of a spirit guide who assists him in dealing with nature's spiritual life force. These ceremonies include fasting, thirsting, hardships while waiting for a vision or a hallucination of an honored animal with supernatural powers, teaching a song or providing special instructions to aid the young initiate's personal power for life. If these visions in nature are particularly intense, the young man may even be called upon to be a shaman—a spiritual leader—for his people.

During an the Apache girl's puberty ceremony, the creation of and the relationship of earth and humans are symbolically recreated. Extending over four days and four nights, this event honors the youth's entry into womanhood as she ritualistically represents Mother Earth or White Painted Woman.

NATURE, DANCE, AND CEREMONY

Likewise, human motion among the America Indians has served as a powerful medium in the American Indian celebration of nature. Through ritualized dance, the spiritual body transcends itself into a prayer for rain, a cure for one who has lost touch with the forces of nature, or a means to celebrate creation or to express gratitude for nature's gifts. Ritual dancers may also outwardly imitate entities of the natural world while inwardly endeavoring to transform themselves into these entities.

The Yaqui deer dancer does not simply represent the image of a deer in the Deer Dance but seeks to transform himself into the deer itself. By doing so, he honors his brother the deer while requesting that it willingly allow itself to be sacrificed by the hunter so that humankind might live. Because this Native American does not try to dominate nature, his relationship to the deer is one of intimacy and courtesy (Cordes, 1990). Similarly, when a buffalo was killed, Lame Deer and Erdoes (1972) explained,

> We apologized to his spirit, tried to make him understand why we did it, honoring with a prayer the bones of those who gave their flesh to keep us alive, praying for their return, praying for the life of our brothers, the buffalo nation, as well as our own people. (p. 111)

To encourage animals to return and regenerate as game, the Alaskan Eskimos of Nunivak Island hold a dance and feast in honor of the souls of game animals at an annual ceremony. During a hunt, some American Indians wear an animal fetish or carving over the heart, for example, which magically provides aid to the hunter through the charm's quality of instinctiveness. For the Zunis of the Southwest, such objects may represent mother, earth, rain, and all the life giving forces upon which humans depend. Likewise, any phenomenon of nature can be associated with an animal analogous to that phenomenon. Lightning, for example, is personified by the snake. Both strike instantly, may cause disastrous results, and are easily illustrated by a zigzag design. Since the snake is more closely aligned to lightning than is a human, but more closely related to humans than is lightning, the ritualized activity is directed and transmitted to the more mysterious and remote powers of nature through animals (Cushing, 1988). In fact, the serpent fetish or ritualized image has been observed in all quarters of the earth.

The Hopi Snake Dance is one of the most ancient snake ceremonies that is still performed. During the August ceremony on the Hopi mesas in Arizona, members of the Hopi snake clan collect snakes from the four cardinal directions: north, south, east, and west. After several days of private rituals and a dance in the plaza, the snakes are released to return to the four sacred directions of the earth accompanied by the Hopi prayer for rain (Fergusson, 1988; Fewkes, 1986).

Nature, Architecture, and the Cosmos

A culture's relationship with nature may also be evident in its sense of space. The ancient ancestors of the Pueblo people, who lived in Arizona, Colorado, Utah, and New Mexico, ritualized their relationship to the land, which represented the divine. This outlook is evident in their architecture, which manifests balance and harmony with the landscape. The *kiva* or ceremonial center of the Pueblo represents the sacred center of the world. In an Acoma account, trees are symbolized by the four pillars that support the kiva's roof. Each pillar points to one of the four sacred directions. The sky is represented by the walls, and the Milky Way is represented by the beams of the roof. Corresponding-

The largest known serpent-effigy mound in the world is found at Serpent Mound State Park in southern Ohio. The mound exemplifies American Indian ritual artifacts that express veneration of wild creatures.

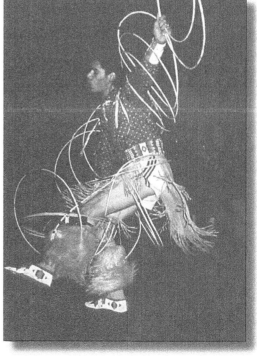

To many tribes, the hoop symbolizes the world or the universe. Time and even the seasons move in a circle.

ly, the door of the Navajo Hogan faces east toward the rising sun with centrally located fireplace, symbolizing the cosmic center of the earth (Hadingham, 1984; Highwater, 1982).

Observatories built by ancient peoples to record the movement of the solar system can be visited today in Hovenweep National Monument in Utah and Casa Grande Ruins National Monument in Arizona. Winter and summer solstices and fall and spring equinoxes were observed by sungazers through alignments with geological features such as mountain peaks, caves, and rock formations. Rock art such as that of the Chumash Indians of California appears to represent the sun, moon, stars, eclipses, and comets. Their priests held daily rituals to interpret the behavior of the sky when the entire community gathered for midwinter ceremonies. The high priest, impersonating the sun's rays, ceremoniously anchored a wooden shaft into the ground as an emblem of the axis of the world. Capped with a stone disc symbolizing the sun, it was positioned so only the shadow of the stone would appear on the ground during both solstices. Medicine wheel solar calendars made of rock are found in Mani-

toba, Saskatchewan, and Alberta as well as in the United States, including Medicine Wheel Park in North Dakota (Valley City State University, 2014).

THE WESTERN VIEW OF NATURE

When agriculture replaced hunting and gathering as the dominant form of subsistence, there was a radical change in the way people responded to their natural surroundings. As Westerners departed from wild nature, their view of nature revolved more around the belief that humans are superior to other life forms and that the universe exists to serve the needs of human beings. Value began to be placed on life forms that demonstrated usefulness to humans (Sessions, 1995). Ritual was relegated to an inferior position and was not incorporated intentionally into the predominant technological society. Even basic ritualistic symbols were considered too simple for the language-bound mentality of Western people. European America was cut off from rhythmic-natural expressiveness, and most of the population tended to neutralize, rather than ritualize, nature (Highwater, 1982). Thinking became more linear, with high value placed on logic, organization, critical thinking, and judicious planning (Gernes, 2000). Granted, there are many positives in the advancement of human society; nonetheless, many believe that the loss of the link between people and nature is a negative outcome (Garvey, 1990).

The Movement Away From Ritual and Nature

The movement away from ritual and nature started long ago in both East and West. By the time the cultures of Egypt and the Far East began to develop, ritual had become highly structured and visually formalized to

This five-story, 20-room cliff dwelling built by the Salado Indians around 1100 A.D. manifests balance and harmony with the land. The site in northern Arizona is protected by the Montezuma Castle National Monument.

influence an observer, not the participant. The concern was with the organization of a sociopolitical structure and hierarchy, not the power of nature (Highwater, 1985). The original impulse receded, and ritual came to express literal ideas. For instance, during the Hellenic Age, dance symbolically expressed the humanistic value system, and in the Middle Ages, it was transformed into a source of entertainment. By the time of the Renaissance, ballet had emerged as an art form. Early Western architecture also turned away from nature. For example, departing from early temple architecture, the Greek temple became a place to worship human-conceived divinity rather than nature's divinity (Highwater, 1982). Although balanced artistically, the temple was not viewed as a part of nature.

As pioneers settled in America, they generally had an antagonistic attitude toward the wilderness. For them the wilderness posed dangers, and they saw the major value of the forest as a source of wood for shelter and warmth. In contrast to the American Indians, the pioneers believed that civilization, not nature, conveyed the sacred lifestyle. In Europe and America, the ensuing Romantic period dissolved some of these antagonistic attitudes toward nature by recognizing nature's seductive splendor, mystery, and spiritual potential. During this period, life was more comfortable and nature less intimidating. Philosopher Jean-Jacques Rousseau (1712–1778) is credited with leading the return to the notion that primal peoples were rational in seeking harmony with nature. He was not convinced that the technological advancements of Western society were an improvement in the social condition. This transitional period opened the door to the Romantic movement and later to transcendentalism, a movement that established nature as the vehicle to life consciousness and greater spiritual wisdom.

A Return to Nature

In the 18th century, a few Europeans began to recognize the charm of the lakes and mountains of Switzerland. Mountains had been seen as obstacles or nuisances,

inhibiting travel and communication, and their recreational potential was not recognized. In fact, only a few European contacts with the mountains were recorded in history prior to this period. In 1340, the poet Petrarch climbed a mountain to see the view from the top. Leonardo da Vinci (1452–1519) wandered around the Alps to study botany and geology and developed and maintained a constant interaction in the study of nature throughout his career. The Flemish artist Peter Brueghel (1525–1569) painted the Alps in an inspired fashion ahead of his time (Clark, 1969; Marani, 2000).

Recorded, too, was Saint Francis of Assisi's (1181/82–1226) special relationship with nature and his belief in the equality of all creatures rather than human domination over creation (Sessions, 1995). Dutch philosopher Baruch Spinoza (1632–1677) drew upon ancient Jewish pantheistic roots of aligning God with nature, but few other instances are noted. Spinoza's beliefs that humans can only obtain happiness and dignity by identifying themselves with all of nature inspired future environmentalists as well as 18th century Romantics, including the English poet William Wordsworth (1770–1850), whose poems and essays expressed a new attitude toward nature (Sessions, 1995). Reflecting harmony with nature, the layout of English gardens began to evolve from rigid walkways to more natural, maze-like paths, and the practice of taking walks in the countryside became fashionable, in part inspired by Wordsworth, who took them frequently. Intellectuals, poets, and philosophers followed his lead (Clark, 1969).

Rousseau was moved by the lakes and alpine valleys of Switzerland. His total absorption in nature was a mystical experience that ultimately had a profound effect on the Western mind because it inspired him to set forth a new philosophy. In advocating for a return to nature to discover the ultimate source of reason, Rousseau opened his contemporaries to the beauty of nature. His original thinking, however, caused him to be persecuted, and eventually, he sought refuge on an island in Lake Bien around 1765. Listening and watching the rhythmic waves, he

Structures such as this one in Chaco Culture National Historical Park in New Mexico provide evidence of the celestial observations of pre-Columbian Pueblo civilization.

surrendered himself completely to nature; he became at one with the experience. In a mystical fashion, he lost all consciousness of an independent self and later realized that existence is nothing more than a succession of moments perceived through the senses. He said, "I feel, therefore I am." He believed the qualities of beauty and innocence he observed in nature were also present in human beings. He believed that "natural man" was virtuous. Rousseau's theories are propounded in his treatise, "A Discourse in the Origins of Inequality Among Men" (Clark, 1969; Marceau, 1998).

Twenty years after Rousseau wrote his landmark treatise, the islands of Tahiti were discovered, which seemed to confirm that the simple, natural existence of the natives was superior to the squalor that existed among the 18th century European communities. This attractive goodness of natural living, and the ability of a human being to completely surrender to nature, was a precursor to the reappearance of nature as a divinity. The common denominator was a

desire to probe the depths of the soul and return to nature, which was acclaimed as the ultimate source of reason (Janson & Janson, 1997; Marceau, 1998). The early proponents of this belief, Rousseau, Wordsworth, German poet and natural philosopher Johann Wolfgang von Goethe (1749–1832), and English lyrical poet Samuel Taylor Coleridge (1772–1834), sought to approximate nature with Truth. Later, during the Romantic era, a larger group of philosophers and artists embraced these concepts.

Other Significant Breakthroughs

Other significant breakthroughs in the nature movement occurred. In the United States during the early 1800s, at the time of the Industrial Revolution, a group of dedicated landscape painters, called the Hudson River School, hiked into what was then the wilderness of the Hudson River Valley. Recognizing that the natural environment was being undermined, they left their studios to sketch and later paint the unspoiled countryside, especially in the Catskill Mountains. In their own way, they became early environmental activists (Smith, 2006).

Meanwhile, their depictions of landscapes as the primary subject became a revolutionary and popular style. Struck by nature's elegance, they aspired to become one with nature to experience and share with others the sublime and supernatural powers of a landscape. To elevate the recipient on a personal, aesthetical, and spiritual level, one of the most effective techniques used was called Romanticism, which was a combination of realism and an embellished use of light that emphasized nature's splendor. As will not be seen, this celebration of nature was reinforced by the American literature of the era promoting nature's grand purpose (the transcendentalists are discussed below).

In turn, the unique qualities of the native landscape stirred the public's emotional responses and attention to the land (AskART, 2007). As artists such Albert Bierstadt (1830–1902) and Thomas Moran (1837–1926) of the Hudson River School began to capture the grandeur of the American West by creating epic-sized works on a scale with the landscapes they represented, including Bierstadt's 9.5 feet by 15 feet *Domes of the Yosemite* and Moran's 7 feet by 12 feet *Grand Canyon of the Yellowstone,* they helped to trigger a movement to preserve the West, establish national parks (discussed in Chapter 7), and create parks in urban areas (McIntosh, 2005).

The Hudson River School, credited with developing the first uniquely American approach to landscape painting, made landscape a legitimate subject of its own. After the Civil War, the romanticized landscapes were replaced by a more realistic style in which nature was to become a springboard for personal expression and experimentation. Impressionism, which started in France between 1859 and 1864, was a style used to explore new techniques, especially with light, mood, and brushwork (AskART, 2007). Because of the experimentation of the early Hudson School painters, not all of the style's elements were new to American art. The most humble subjects of nature, however, were now on an even scale with the loftiest forms. Entwined with leisure, impressionists celebrated the recreation of their contemporaries (Bruce Museum, 2005). Regattas and beach parties were painted along the New England coast. To capture the subject, they painted *en plein air* (in the open air), where the artist could become immersed in the outdoor experience. In an effort to depict the natural reflections in ripples of water, for instance, the impressionist strove to paint an impression of sunlight. This attempt at pure depiction of the impression, first captured by Claude Monet (1840–1926) and Pierre Renoir (1841–1919), was an innovation in painting. During the period of Post-Impressionism that followed in the late 19th century, Paul Gauguin (1848–1903) traveled to unspoiled Tahiti and other South Pacific islands to capture natural life. Although nature alone was no longer the subject matter, a return to the aesthetic primal art allowed for a more personal spiritual expression of a human connection with nature. In the United States, the impressionist style, which was developed in the late 19th century, led to the establishment of art colonies around the country from the Old Lyme Colony in Connecticut to those in Carmel and Laguna Beach in California. In general, these artists felt a responsibility to document the landscape for the joy and education of future generations (Sneed, Davick, & Braselle, 2005). In California, William Wendt (1865–1946), called the Dean of California painters, believed that nature was an indicator of a higher power and viewed himself as a faithful interpreter (Smith, 2006).

Nature, too, was the most important source of inspiration for Art Nouveau (The New Art) artists and designers in Europe and North America between 1890 and 1914. Motifs from the natural world such as flower stalks and buds, vine tendrils, and insect wings decorated buildings, furniture, glass, jewelry, ceramics, and textiles. In New York, Louis Comfort Tiffany (1848–1933), one of the greatest glass artists of his time, transformed colorful images of plants and insects into luminous glass creations that celebrated the natural world. Some designers conventionalized natural forms by creating abstract curvilinear patterns, whereas others copied nature in a realistic manner, often to convey a sense of spiritual affinity with the natural world. Even American modern dancer Loie Fuller (1862–1928), who used cloth veils in a dance to transform herself into a flower, inspired the artists who were exploring the metamorphosis and the idea that humankind was no longer above nature, but inextricably part of it (Greenhalgh & Griffith, 2000; Janson & Janson, 1997).

A 19th century movement of New England writers and philosophers was based in a belief in the essential unity of all creation. The transcendentalist movement, founded by Ralph Waldo Emerson (1803–1882) and Henry David Thoreau (1817–1862), viewed nature as a means to transcend everyday

> The outdoor experience can be more spiritual than physical as the beauty of nature inspires awe in the recreationist's soul and, at times, a sense of the deeper truths in life.

5. Natural man is virtuous and in general sympathizes with the humble and downtrodden.
6. Nature equals truth.
7. As a result of total absorption in nature, one can lose one's sense of identity and become enraptured. (Clark, 1969)

Modern authors such as Catherine Alabanese, Thomas Berry, Charles Cummings, Jamake Highwater, Jack Kornfield, Dolores LaChapelle, George Sessions, Gary Snyder, and Al Gore refer to the separation of humans from nature and the need for a renewed reverence for the earth. Thomas Berry (1990) believes that this reverence for nature is important to the planet's survival. He joins another environmentalist, Gary Synder (1995, pp. 459–460), in the belief that people can relearn this attitude from the American Indians, who are overwhelmingly in support of a full and sensitive acknowledgment of nature, in contrast to modern society's experiences in nature, which are usually brief and sandwiched between urban experiences.

LaChapelle (1995) explained that the Western European industrial culture developed a limited practicality. In rationalizing their world, they developed the left side of the brain. American Indians knew that their relationship with the natural world, however, called for a more holistic approach that would allow nonhumans to commune with humans. Rituals, ceremonies, and festivals present a sophisticated spiritual technology that allows humans to transcend the limitations imposed by the structure of language, normally associated with the left hemisphere of the brain. They allow the whole being—the rational and the spiritual—to connect with others and the nonhuman world through the use of the right and left hemispheres of the brain. By connecting with the world in various ways, people learn

life to encounter the divine (see Chapter 3). This philosophy influenced future naturalists (discussed in Chapter 3) to attempt to preserve the American wilderness (Clark, 1969). However, people caught up in the economic expansion in America persisted in using the natural resources to achieve a better life on earth. In general, Western society continued to view nature as a means to an end with little thought given to the potential repercussions. Several elements of a contemporary reverence for nature, sometimes referred to as "nature religion," can be traced to these 18th and 19th century artists and philosophers. These elements are as follows:

1. Value exists in the simple life.
2. Walking is both a spiritual and physical exercise.
3. Mountains are viewed as sacred places, and clouds are sources of divine inspiration.
4. There is a healing power in nature.

to respect the complexity that is inherent in the unity of the whole. Finding ballet too standardized, contemporary dancers such as Fuller (discussed earlier in this chapter) and Isadora Duncan (1877–1927) led the way to a natural movement form and ritualization. The new *modern dance* revived the oldest form of dance as a means to provide expression for that which cannot be externalized by rational means. Today, ballet and modern dance companies use indigenous themes involving nature as a basis for choreography (Heth, 1993). Like the Yacqui deer dancer, performers did not simply imitate but became the dance by transforming themselves into the idea, the feeling, or the emotion. Ritual can also be a tool for learning to think logically, analogically, and ecologically as people move toward a sustainable culture (LaChapelle, 1995).

Back to Nature

As seen in world literature, feelings of connectedness and/or relationship are nurtured through encounters with nature (Dustin, 1994). Although the spiritual life may initially be focused on self-transformation and wise human relationships, Kornfield (2000) believes that these relationships ultimately lead to a oneness with the mountains. This oneness comes from a sense of selflessness that means taking a hard look at habits, including consumerism, as they relate to a person's interconnection with the earth and all life on earth. Transformations of this magnitude are not automatic. To learn to lose that human-centeredness, outdoor educators encourage students to connect with something in nature. Along these lines, John Seed, an environmental leader, developed a group meditation, called Council of All Beings, that is practiced around the world. Participants spend time meditating and connecting with a particular part of the earth, such as waterfowl or rivers or mountains. Later, in a group session, individuals speak for the part of the earth they repre-

sent. A representative of waterfowl, perhaps Canada Geese, may speak of the flock's difficult seasonal migration because the places of rest and refreshment, the wetlands, are disappearing. A participant who personifies a river may tell of its sadness in carrying wastes and toxins. The representative of the mountains may talk about the steady peace it feels and offers to all who come to see it.

The goal is not to reenact American Indian rituals or return to a pioneer state of wilderness but to recognize that modern technological knowledge may neglect the natural experience that humans yearn to experience. Increased visitations to parks and wilderness areas may be in part attributable to this search for the natural. Albanese (1990) asserted that a call to the natural has grown out of an innate concern for the environment. Cummings (1991) referred to a phenomenon known as eco-spirituality, or the reverence for life in all its diversity, including balance with nonliving things. Gore (1992, 2006) challenged people to rethink their relationship with nature to save the earth's

A spontaneous celebration of nature.

Pioneers brought another view of nature. The wilderness was to be conquered and tamed. Today, the open spaces in land managed by the BLM in Wyoming are enjoyed by those traveling on the Oregon National Historic Trail. Reliving the experience of the past, modern travelers have a tendency to ritualize the camping experience with picnics, with evening songs, and by telling stories.

ecology and rallied them to make ethical decisions that they can act on personally and politically.

Although many believe that technology is impacting relationships with nature, over 370 organizations have united to encourage parents to "rewild" their children, and thousands of citizens in North America are participating more intimately with nature. Thousands of Americans belong to environmental organizations or maintain an interest. A reawakening of the celebration of nature in art has energized artists as it did over 100 years ago (Smith, 2006). There is also a growing public interest in outdoor-oriented travel (Honey, 1999). The U.S. Department of Commerce (2012) found that 3 out 4 people in the United States are participating in active outdoor recreation. Likewise, the country's outdoor recreation industry is boosting the economy. Growth in adventure travel has accelerated at a 65% yearly rate since 2009

(Adventure Travel Trade Association, 2014). Meanwhile, approximately 280 million people visit the national parks, with the units of the national park system representing one of the largest tourist destinations in the world (National Park Service, 2014).

Nature as a Spiritual Resource

In some cases, outdoor recreational activities provide more than the recreational and physical values of the activity—they provide a forum in which activities may become ritualized events allowing attainment of a spiritual level of oneness with nature year after year. These outdoor activities may become a person's own vision quest in nature, and the event is not necessarily planned or anticipated. It could occur after a tiring day of hiking on a backpack trip or while enjoying a quiet moment of reflection on the grassy banks of a small stream. One hiker (Monczunski, 1990) described his experience:

I was there under the blue sky. And I could only be there by being related to everything else that was there. Not only related, but really part of it, an extension of everything else. So I was not so significant, not so separate, not so egotistical, not so important, not so self-derived. I surrendered into it and was part of it. (p. 39)

Simply embarking on a journey may somehow signal newfound freedom, a liberation of spirit, an openness, and a willingness to experience (Leshner, 2001). Inspired and with deeper insight, one is more at peace. One backpacker expressed,

You walk, eat, sit, sleep. And when you've covered some miles, you realize you've learned as much about yourself as about the land you've crossed—and that what you've explored has been the geography of the soul. You may learn that Walt Whitman was right when he said, "Now I see the secret of making the best persons. It is to grow in the open air and to eat and sleep with the earth!" (Temple, 1990, p. 42)

Today's outdoor rituals may be anachronistic: relating hunting to American Indians, survival skills to mountain men, or horseback riding to cowboys. A participant in the midst of nature's beauty may develop an acute awareness of its sights, sounds, and smells. A surfer may admire the power of the ocean, a climber may prepare for a gathering storm, and a birder may recognize a species vanishing into extinction. An intimacy with nature, with the mysteries of life, and even with the past, can be achieved. Deeper experiences or spiritual occasions do not necessarily occur at formally planned times, but often unfold when the senses rise to unusual heights of perception (Meier & Mitchell, 1993). Experiences may come during periods of meditation focused on a single delicate flower in the wild, under a vast canopy of stars, or at the moment of reaching the summit of a mountain. These are times when awareness may reflect everything with total clarity and brightness, and when one's whole attitude toward life can be transformed (May, 1982).

The outdoors can bring people back to a natural order (Rolston, 1986). They return to basics and are in contact with *creation*, which is at the root of the word *recreation*. While testing their prowess in the outdoors, people may be participating in their own nature ritual. As activities in nature become ritualized, the meaning of the activity becomes more important than the activity itself. The outdoors becomes a cathedral to the sacredness of nature. One backpacker wrote, "I try to memorize the view, to lock this feeling inside my head" (Temple, 1990, pp. 44–45). The ego is lost in nature's magnificence as recreation merges with creation. "The happiest man," wrote Emerson, "is he who learns from Nature the lesson of worship" (Temple, 1990, p. 42).

Clearly more than amusement is found in outdoor activities. Family backpack trips and campouts held every year at the same time are referred to as yearly rituals and create deep family bonds. Through outdoor experiences, a common reality is shared. The participants assume various roles. Moreover, at many organized camps, daily activities are planned that highlight the spiritual experience.

A "wilderness cathedral" or "woodland chapel" located in a natural amphitheater, on a hilltop with a view of a valley, in a clearing surrounded by trees, or beside a gently flowing stream, can set the stage for inspired thought. The ceremonial campfire may also be a significant spiritual event to campers. Typically, these planned events start with a light mood, progress to a more serious tone, and are focused on beauty and serenity of the group's experience in nature. Some camps ceremonially mix partially burned wood and ashes from last year's campfire with the first fire of the year (Meier & Mitchell, 1993). Alternatives to the traditional fire include beams from flashlights, artificially colored lights, and slide presentations when laws or one's ethics prohibit building a fire.

Meditating in a giant redwood.

The very nature of camp draws campers out of themselves and encourages spiritual growth (Drovdahl, 1991). Stepping out of their routine, campers at a campfire or those on a quiet hike have the opportunity to reflect. They may be surrounded by trees, mountains, sky, and creatures, all elements in life not created by humans yet related in an internal way. This environment is a natural theater for spiritual reflection or for the life within, around, and beyond the individual (Brothers, 2000). Nature is a philosophical, psychological, scientific, economic, aesthetic, and recreational resource, and the great outdoors, as a spiritual resource, works on the recreationist's soul.

SUMMARY

In the past, Western civilization believed it had progressed beyond nature by outgrowing the experiences of primal peoples, leaving them behind and viewing their experience as less valuable than the focus and priorities of civilized society. The American Indian appears to symbolize harmony with nature. Authentic ceremonials on the reservations are religious observations, performed in the same spirit as religious ceremonies held anywhere in the world, and pervading all these ceremonies is the principle of living in harmony with nature. Today, many Westerners are seeking a more harmonious relationship with nature. The outdoor experience of the hiker, camper, or outdoor adventurer is often more than a fun adventure; it has the capacity to offer spiritual renewal and awakening to many and is even a life-altering, profound experience for some.

REFERENCES

Adventure Travel Trade Association. (2014). New adventure tourism report reveals $263B market, up 65% per annum since 2009. Retrieved from http://www.adventuretravelnews.com/new-adventure-tourism-report-reveals-263b-market-up-65-per-annum-since-2009

Albanese, C. (1990). *Nature religion in America*. Chicago, IL: The University of Chicago Press.

AskART. (2007). Hudson river school painters. Retrieved from http://www.askart.com/AskART/interest/hudson_river_school_painters_1.aspx?id=9

Beck, P., & Walters, A. (1988). *The sacred*. Tsaile, AZ: Navajo Community College Press.

Berry, T. (1990). *The dream of the earth*. San Francisco, CA: Sierra Club Books.

Berry, T. (2000). *The great work*. New York, NY: Random House.

Brothers, J. (2000, October). You can lead a more joyful life. *Parade Magazine, 2000*, 6–8.

Bruce Museum. (2005, August). American impressionism: The beauty of work [Press release]. Greenwich, CT: Author.

Clark, K. (Writer). (1969). The worship of nature [Television documentary series episode]. In M. Gill & P. Montagnon (Producers), *Civilisation*. United Kingdom: BBC Television Distributors.

Cordes, K. (1990). Values of another culture through dance and ceremonials. In *Proceeding of the International Conference on the Global Village*. Miami, FL: Barry University.

Cummings, C. (1991). *Eco-spirituality*. Mahwah, NJ: Paulist Press.

Cushing, F. (1988). *Zuni fetishes*. Las Vegas, NV: K. C. Publications.

Driver, B. L., Dustin, D., Baltic, T., Elsner, G., & Peterson, G. (Eds.). (1996). *Nature and the human spirit*. State College, PA: Venture.

Drovdahl, R. (1991, May). Touching the spirit. *Camping Magazine, 63*(7), 24–27.

Dustin, D. (1994). Managing public lands for the human spirit. *Parks & Recreation, 29*(9), 92–96.

Fergusson, E. (1988). *Dancing gods: Indian ceremonials of New Mexico and Arizona*. Albuquerque: University of New Mexico Press.

Fewkes, J. (1986). *Hopi snake ceremonies*. Albuquerque, NM: Avanyu.

Garvey, J. (1990). The stories we live. *Notre Dame Magazine, 19*(1), 40–45.

Gernes, S. (2000). Soul at play. *Notre Dame Magazine, 29*(2), 33.

Gore, A. (1992). *Earth in the balance: Ecology and the human spirit*. New York, NY: Houghton Mifflin.

Gore, A. (Writer). (2006). *An inconvenient truth* [Documentary]. United States: Lawrence Bender Productions and Participant Productions.

Greenhalgh, P., & Griffith, M. (2000). *Art Nouveau*. Washington, DC: National Gallery of Art.

Hadingham, E. (1984). *Early man and the cosmos*. Norman: University of Oklahoma Press.

Heth, C. (Ed.). (1993). *Native American dance: Ceremonies and social traditions*. Washington, DC: National Museum of the American Indian Smithsonian Institution with Starwood Publishing.

Highwater, J. (1982). *The primal mind*. New York, NY: Penguin.

Highwater, J. (1985). *Dance rituals of experience*. New York, NY: Alfred van der Marck Editions.

Imber-Black, E., & Roberts, J. (1997). *Rituals for our times*. New York, NY: HarperCollins.

Janson, H., & Janson, A. (1997). *The history of art*. New York, NY: Harry M. Abrams.

Kaplan, M. (1979). *Leisure: Lifestyle and lifespan*. Philadelphia, PA: W. B. Saunders.

Kornfield, J. (2000). *After the ecstasy, the laundry*. New York, NY: Bantam Books.

Kraus, R. (1984). *Recreation and modern society*. Glenview, IL: Scott, Foresman, and Company.

LaChapelle, D. (1995). Ritual: The pattern that connects. In G. Sessions (Ed.), *Deep ecology for the 21st century* (pp. 58–63). Boston, MA: Shambhala.

Lame Deer, J., & Erdoes, R. (1972). *Lame Deer: Seeker of visions*. New York, NY: Washington Square Press.

Leshner, M. (2001). Why travel? *Westways, 6*(4), 26–27.

McIntosh, P. (2005). Pictures worth a thousand acres. *National Parks, 79*(2), 30–35.

Mails, T. (1997). *The Hopi survival kit*. New York, NY: Media Holdings.

Marani, P. (2000). *Leonardo da Vinci*. New York, NY: Harry N. Abrams.

Marceau, J. (Ed.). (1998). *Art: A world history*. London, England: DK Publishing.

May, G. (1982). *Will and spirit: A contemplative psychology.* San Francisco, CA: Harper.

Meier, J., & Mitchell, A. V. (1993). *Camp counseling: Leadership and programming for organized camp.* Dubuque, IA: William C. Brown.

Monczunski, J. (1990). What the hermits know. *Notre Dame Magazine, 19*(1), 33–39.

National Park Service. (2014). Frequently asked questions. Retrieved from http://www.nps.gov/faqs.htm

Rolston, H. (1986). Beyond recreational value: The greater outdoors preservation-related and environmental benefits. In L. B. Szwak (Ed.), *Americans Outdoors: A Literature Review* (pp. 103–113). Washington DC: U.S. Government Printing Office.

Sessions, G. (1995). Ecocentrism and the anthropocentric detour. In G. Sessions (Ed.), *Deep ecology for the 21st century* (pp. 356–375). Boston, MA: Shambhala.

Smith, J. (2006). *Saving California's vanishing treasures.* Irvine, CA: The Irvine Museum.

Sneed, K., Davick, J., & Braselle, M. (2005). *Crystal Cove cottages.* San Francisco, CA: Chronicle Books.

Snyder, G. (1995). The rediscovery of Turtle Island. In G. Sessions (Ed.), *Deep ecology for the 21st century* (pp. 454–462). Boston, MA: Shambhala.

Stegner, W. (1990, April). *It all began with conservation.* Washington, DC: Smithsonian Associates.

Temple, K. (1990). Over the rise. *Notre Dame Magazine, 19*(1), 40–45.

U.S. Department of Commerce. (2012). U.S. outdoor recreation industry found to boost the economy. Retrieved from http://www.commerce.gov/blog/2012/06/20/us-outdoor-recreation-industry-found-boost-economy

Valley City State University. (2014). Medicine Wheel Park. Retrieved from http://medicinewheel.vcsu.edu/

Zuefle, C. (1999). The spirituality of recreation. *Parks & Recreation, 34*(5), 28–48.

Chapter 3

Visionaries and Pioneers

The early Americans, including the Puritans and pioneers, ordinarily had an antagonistic attitude toward nature and wilderness, believing that it was to be tamed and conquered. The major value of the forest was to cut it down to provide wood for homes and shelters. These early attitudes began to change through the efforts of a few leaders who recognized nature's mystery and spiritual potential. In Chapter 2, we noted that the Romantics moved toward greater harmony with nature. Also, life in the mid-19th century became more comfortable and nature less intimidating. Romanticism paved the way for transcendentalism, a philosophy in which nature is viewed as the vehicle to inspire intuitive thought that lifts the consciousness to greater spiritual wisdom. This mode of thought influenced future naturalists toward preserving the American wilderness.

THE TRANSCENDENTALISTS

As a mode of perception, transcendentalism became an indefinable movement of abstract American intellectual thought. It intrigued New Englanders during the mid-19th century, some of whom were turning to an inner world and exploring oneness with the universe. To them, natural objects commandeered significance, and if used properly, they reflected universal spiritual truths. Two of the leading transcendentalists, Emerson and Thoreau, will be presented here. Both believed that human beings have the potential to transcend materialism. Emerson defined transcendentalism simply as "belief in the Higher Law of God" (Wolf, 1974, p. 125). Henry David Thoreau expounded on Emerson's idea that when a person is close to nature something happens to his or her perceptions. Inspired by Emerson, Thoreau lived close to nature to experience and express his own heightened senses. He focused on nature in his writings, describing what he beheld and then generalized about overlying implications. Emerson, on the other hand, focused his perceptions on the human being using deductive logic and philosophical abstractions (Ronald, 1987). Many characteristics of Emerson's and Thoreau's transcendentalism, such as the trust in organic form, the correspondences between elements of the natural world, the concern with people's relationship to the environment, and the institution of being solitary, are echoed by naturalists today and continue to exert great influence on today's naturalism and wilderness preservation.

Ralph Waldo Emerson (1803–1882)

Born in Boston, Ralph Waldo Emerson became one of the most famous, original 19th century thinkers and one of the most quoted American writers. He endured the loss of his father and sister at an early age, which undoubtedly affected his writing. Drawn to nature, Emerson began to feel a profound affection for it and for the solitude it could provide him, which sustained him for the rest of his life. He proclaimed, "Nature is loved by what is best in us" (Atkinson, 1950, p. 411). At the age of 14, he received a grant from his father's church and entered Harvard College. Appointed "President's freshman," he was provided free board. Here he began writing his journals, which became his constant companion for some 50 years. These gave rise to literary material in lectures, essays, and books. Upon graduation, Emerson joined his brother William in teaching and operating a finishing school in his mother's home. It was an unhappy time for him; he filled his journals with discouragement and self-doubt. He wrote to a friend who was also teaching: "How my heart bleeds for you! Better tug at the oar, dig the mine, or saw wood; better sow hemp, or hang with it, than sow the seeds of instruction" (Gilbert, 1914, p. 124).

Descended from eight generations of ministers, Emerson enrolled in the Divinity School at Harvard, and once licensed, he stopped teaching. He married Ellen Tucker, whose health was delicate, and who died of tuberculosis after only 17 months of marriage. Afterward, Emerson resolved that he was not in sympathy with some of the doctrines of his church, and as a result, he resigned his post and sailed for Europe. The trip revived him, and upon his return, he met and married his second wife, Lydia. He soon suffered the death of two of his beloved brothers. Later, Emerson and his wife lost the eldest of their four children to scarlet fever.

After his return from Europe, Emerson spent an allotted portion of each day walking in the woods and along the rivers with his eyes open to the natural surroundings. He occasionally preached and lectured to enthusiastic audiences on the moral and psychological interaction between nature and the human spirit. In Concord, he became involved in local affairs and was a respected and valued member of the community. His presence made Concord a significant intellectual and cultural center.

Emerson helped to organize a discussion group whose members called themselves "transcendentalists." Serving as their first literary proponent, Emerson envisioned a unity of nature, humans, and God; he believed that through the use of intuition, a heightened awareness could be reached that would transcend one's thoughts to a grander level of ultimate (transcendental) understanding. Through natural phenomena he believed one could intuitively understand human relationships to the universe, its components, and to God (Ronald, 1987). Transcendentalist notions were expressed by others, but Emerson's literary style set him apart. In his first book, *Nature* (1836), he enumerated the values of nature:

> If a man would be alone, let him look at the stars. The rays that come from those heavenly worlds will separate between him and what he touches. One might think the atmosphere was made transparent with this design, to give man, in the heavenly bodies, the perpetual presence of the sublime. Seen in the streets of cities, how great they are! If the stars should appear one night in a thousand years, how would men believe and adore; and preserve for many generations the remembrance of the City of God which had been shown! But every night come out these envoys of beauty, and light the universe with their admonishing smile. (Atkinson, 1950, p. 5)

In 1840, he helped to found and later edited a magazine called *The Dial*. Surviving only until 1844, it proved to be an excellent way for younger members of the transcendentalist school, including Henry David Thoreau, to express their ideas. During the same productive period, Emerson's *Essays,* derived from his lecture series, was published in two volumes (1841, 1844), and his reputation grew. During the American Renaissance in literature (1835–1865), when Emerson was in his prime, he was recognized as a leading lecturer and author. His other publications included *Poems* (1846), *Representative Men* (1849), *The Conduct of Life* (1860), and *May Day* (1867).

In "Nature" in *Essays: Second Series* (Atkinson, 1950), Emerson wrote,

> It seems as if the day was not wholly profane in which we have given heed to some natural object. The fall of snowflakes in a still air, preserving to each crystal its perfect form; the blowing of sleet over a wide sheet of water, and over plains; the waving rye-field; the mimic waving of acres of houstonia, whose innumerable florets whiten and ripple before the eye; the reflections of trees and flowers in glassy lakes; the musical, steaming, odorous south wind, which converts all trees to wind-harps; the crackling and spurting of hemlock in the flames, or of pine logs, which yield glory to the walls and faces in the sitting-room—these are the music and pictures of the most ancient religion. (p. 408)

Inspiration and many ideas for his writings came to him on his long afternoon walks in the Concord hills. An observer of nature, he was not generally an active participant. On some occasions he hunted, but his friends implied that he never shot a living thing. Emerson enjoyed his excursions to the mountains with members of the Adirondack Club, and later in life he took a trip to California where he met John Muir (described later in this chapter). The two men drew close, but Muir believed that Emerson was by 1871 only a ghost of what he had once been (M.V.D., 1931).

Henry David Thoreau (1817–1862)

Henry David Thoreau, who was introduced to the transcendentalists by his longtime friend Ralph Waldo Emerson, is regarded a classic writer and cultural hero. He established the tradition of nature writing that was later developed by naturalists John Burroughs and John Muir. His pioneer studies of the human uses of nature deeply affected conservationists including Benton MacKaye, founder of the Appalachian Trail. In searching for a spiritual dimension in a commercially expanding society, Thoreau demonstrated "the value of leisure, contemplation, and a harmonious appreciation of and coexistence with nature" ("Henry David Thoreau," 1998). Although he oscillated between a transcendental and scientific examination of nature, it was this alliance between contemplative thoughtfulness and close observation and speculation that became the pattern for his prose and essays. Neither style was as notably sentimental or romantic as Audubon's or Muir's writings (to be discussed later in his chapter).

The third of four children, Thoreau was born and raised in a beautiful setting in Concord, Massachusetts. During his early years, he shared his mother's love of the out-of-doors and developed an affinity for hunting, fishing, and solitude in nature. He especially admired the pond called Walden. His family contributed to his education at Harvard, where he also received aid from a beneficiary fund for needy students. While in college, he was granted a leave to teach and to assist his father, a pencil manufacturer. Originally christened David Henry, he reversed his names at age 20, demonstrating an early act of independence. After graduation, he was unsure of his goals, and teaching appeared to be a means to support himself. He soon resigned after he was coerced into flogging students who lacked discipline. Thoreau returned to the family business of pencil making, which gave him leisure for his reading, studying, and walking. In 1837, after reading Emerson's *Nature,* he began to write about nature in his journal, which he kept throughout his life (Benet, 1966). Living simply, he found wealth in enjoyment rather than in possession. In later, more successful years, he wrote in his journal,

> Ah, how I have thriven on solitude and poverty! I cannot overstate this advantage. I do not see how I could have enjoyed it, if the public had been expecting as much of me as there is danger now that they will. If I go abroad lecturing, how shall I ever recover the lost Winter? (E. Teale, 1962, p. 73)

Thoreau opened a school with his brother John, and they introduced field trips for nature study, an innovation in American education, discussed in Chapter 14. In 1839, the two brothers took a 13-day vacation voyage on the Concord and Merrimack Rivers, a journey Thoreau later immortalized in his writings. By 1841, the school closed due to his brother's ill health. He met Emerson at one of his lectures, and Emerson invited him to his home and introduced Thoreau to other transcendentalists. They appreciated Thoreau's freedom of thought. An acquaintance, Nathaniel Hawthorne, believed that Thoreau retained a wild and original nature and observed that he led a life similar to the American Indians (Harding, 1954). Thoreau did study the wisdom of Indians and later described in *The Maine Woods* a camping trip with an Indian friend and what he had learned from him.

As Thoreau read widely—from the explorations of Audubon to Hindu philosophy—his appreciation of solitude, meditation, and contemplation deepened. In solitude, he acquired an observant intimacy with nature, but he was not a lone woodsman. For Thoreau, nature also provided a lavish setting for wilderness excursions, where relationships with others were developed (Schildgen, 2001). He enjoyed the company of others, and his contemporaries attested that he was gregarious. The bachelor, Thoreau, had proposed marriage in 1840, but the engagement was broken upon the insistence

of his fiancée's parents. For a time, he lived with the Emersons, working as a handyman. Upon the death of his brother, he shared his loss with Emerson, who had just lost his son, and in their sorrow, the friendship grew. Emerson and others encouraged Thoreau to lecture and write, and in 1845, Emerson gave him land on the northwest shore of Walden Pond. After building a cabin, Thoreau entertained many guests and welcomed children. He often took short walks into Concord for a meal with his family. Thoreau also practiced meditation and spent long hours observing, recording, and writing about nature. When strangers insisted on joining him on his nature walks, he complained, "They do not consider that the wood-path and the boat are my studio, where I maintain a sacred solitude and cannot admit promiscuous company" (Strong, 1988, p. 11).

During Thoreau's 2-year stay at Walden, he, the abolitionist who helped send enslaved Americans north on the Underground Railroad, was arrested for his past refusal to pay a poll tax in protest against slavery. After only one night in jail, a disgusted Thoreau was released after someone, probably his aunt, paid the tax. He argued that people should follow their own conscience, not the dictates of an immoral government. He retold the story in his essay "Resistance to Civil Government" (later called "Civil Disobedience" and "On the Duty of Civil Disobedience"), which appeared a few years later in an obscure magazine. Leaving Walden forever, he spent the summer of 1847 at Emerson's home while Emerson was away in Europe. Thoreau then returned to his father's home and the family atmosphere with the first complete draft of his book *A Week on the Concord and Merrimack Rivers*. This book about his trip into the wilderness with his now-deceased brother was released in 1849 at his own risk in an edition of 1,000 copies. When it sold poorly, he remarked, "I have now a library of nearly nine hundred volumes, over seven hundred of which I wrote myself" (Strong, 1988, p. 14). An unfavorable review, probably due to his unorthodoxy in religion, criticized Thoreau's assertion that the Sacred Books of the Brahmins were not inferior to the Bible.

In his book *Walden,* published in 1854, Thoreau strove to describe nature and demonstrate that civilized people could escape the evils of competition. *Walden* sold slowly but steadily and became a classic in later years. Four books published after his death and derived in part from journeys taken during the 5 years following his *Walden* experience were *Excursions* (1863), *The Maine Woods* (1864), *Cape Cod* (1865), and *A Yankee in Canada* (1866). Drawing on these same experiences, he wrote "Ktaadn" [*sic*] and the "Maine Woods," "Excursion to Canada," and "Cape Cod," which appeared in *The Union Magazine* (1848), *Putnam's Monthly* (1853), and *Putnam Monthly* (1855), respectively.

Adopting a more conventional life after *Walden,* Thoreau made a living as a self-taught surveyor and worked in the family business. He continued to enjoy his walks and lectured occasionally. In later years, Thoreau became more of a scientific observer of animal behavior, the life cycle of plants, and features of the changing seasons. His most important scientific observation and contribution was presented in a lecture and article entitled "The Succession of Forest Trees." Some speculated that his resolve to count tree rings one bitterly cold winter day may have precipitated his early death at age 44 (Strong, 1988), apparently from tuberculosis. His final words, "moose" and "Indian," indicate his final thoughts were about his beloved wilderness experiences (R.W.A. & H.S.C., 1936). Emerson delivered a long eulogy and described Thoreau as someone who was a pleasure to walk with; was physically fit; was a good swimmer, runner, skater, and boatman; and knew the country like a fox. According to Emerson, Thoreau's study of nature inspired his friends, who appreciated hearing of his adventures and seeing the world through his eyes. Reading, writing, and the study of wildlife were the only occupations that really suited him. Thoreau's statement, "In wildness is the preservation of the world," that first appeared in "Walking" (republished in *Excursions* in 1862) became the motto of the wilderness society years later (E. Teale, 1962, p. 59).

Thoreau spiritualized his experiences with wilderness and nature, and through his writings, he influenced future naturalists and the destiny of North America. Living at a time when trees were appraised in terms of board feet, and not as shelters for birds or animals, he feared that human naturalness and oneness with the ecosystems would vanish. Thoreau was a visionary in concluding that there was a need to preserve parcels of wilderness for the people, and he helped to lead the intellectual revolution that found nature and wilderness attractive as opposed to threatening and disagreeable (Bolton, 1954; Vickery, 1989). To many, Thoreau is considered the father of the environmental movement. The following selection is taken from *The Maine Woods* (Thoreau, 1965):

> It is difficult to conceive of a region uninhabited by man. We habitually presume his presence and influence everywhere. And yet we have not seen pure Nature, unless we have seen her thus vast and drear and inhuman, though in the midst of cities. Nature was here something savage and awful, though beautiful. I looked with awe at the ground I trod on, to see what the Powers had made there, the form and fashion and material of their work. This was the Earth of which we have heard, made out of Chaos and Old Night. Here was no man's garden, but the unhandselled globe. It was not lawn, nor pasture, nor mead, nor woodland, nor lea, nor arable, nor wasteland. It was fresh and natural surface of the planet Earth, as it was made forever and ever... (pp. 87–88)

In the same book, in his essay "The Moose Hunt," he described his feelings after observing a moose hunt:

> Strange that so few ever came to the woods to see how the pine lives and grows and spires, lifting its evergreen arms to the light—to see

its perfect success; but most are content to behold it in the shape of many broad boards brought to market, and deem that its true success! But the pine is no more lumber than man is, and to be made into boards and houses is no more its true and highest use than the truest use of a man is to be cut down and made into manure. There is a higher law affecting our relation to pines as well as to men. . . . I saw the tops of the pines waving and reflecting the light at a distance high over all the rest of the forest, I realized that the former were not the highest uses of the pine.

THE NATURALISTS

Although naturalism began with the French philosopher Jean-Jacques Rousseau, on this continent, two great men led the natural movement. One of them was John Audubon, the other John Muir. Rachel Carson, a great woman, distinguished scientist, and accomplished writer of the 20th century, was the first to alert the nation to the damage suffered by the environment as a result of chemical technology of the 1900s. Their devotion to understanding, depicting, preserving, and writing about nature led to a more intimate understanding of nature and the outdoors.

John James Audubon (1785–1851)

Early conservationist, artist, ornithologist, and perhaps the most popular naturalist of North America, John James Audubon explored the Ohio and Mississippi Rivers, the wilderness of Kentucky, the dunes and lagoons of the Texas coast, the palmetto groves of Florida, and the wild coast of Labrador. Writing in his journals, he personalized and revolutionized the study, illustration, and description of birds and mammals.

Born the illegitimate son of a French naval officer, merchant, and slave trader, the 4-year-old, originally named Jean Rabine, and his younger (also illegitimate) half sis-

ter were taken to France and adopted by Captain Audubon and his legal wife in 1794. Audubon's real mother, Jeanne Rabine, a Creole girl who had worked on his father's sugar plantation in Santa Domingo (Haiti), died shortly after his birth there. In France, his stepmother encouraged his early attraction to nature. He also learned to fence and dance and to play the violin and flute. Later in life, with his flute Audubon was capable of imitating the songs of birds he observed, and he began to sketch them. Not showing much interest in scholarly work, he was sent to Paris to study drawing. Although the ability to draw eluded him at the time, he developed a desire to illustrate birds as they appeared in the forest, not in profile as they generally appeared in books (Audubon, 1960; Elman, 1977). His attempts to do so always reminded him of his father's admonition that "all things possessing life and animation were difficult to imitate" (C. Fisher, 1949, p. 15).

Believing that Audubon could learn English and enter a profitable trade in the United States, his father suggested that Audubon tend their farm in the United States near Philadelphia. The move was also strategic to keep the young Audubon out of a bloody conflict during the French Revolution. He considered himself the master of the farm at age 18, despite his father's hired agent, and continued to develop his fascination with nature and birds. It was at this time that the son changed his baptized name Jean-Jacques Fougere to the anglicized John James.

Using a vivid personal narrative rather than dry impersonal experimental reports, Audubon explained his methods of observing wildlife in their natural surroundings. He began to conduct scientific investigations with the birds he sketched and skillfully mastered how to closely examine birds and mammals without alarming them. He handled nestlings without causing the adult birds to abandon them, developing a method used by 20th century field biologists. In one of his experiments, he tied threads as leg bands to phoebes for identification. In this manner, he discovered that many of them returned in the spring to their fledgling region after winter migration. Little did he know that

100 years later, a Bird Banding Society would be formed to repeat his test to gather exact data on migratory species in every part of the American continent (Elman, 1977). Later, in his *Ornithological Biography,* he described one of his experiences observing nature:

> . . . rambling along the rocky banks …observing the watchful King fisher perched on some projecting stone over the clear water of the stream. Nay, now and then, the Fish Hawk itself, followed by a White-headed Eagle, would make his appearance, and by his graceful aerial motion, raise my thought far above them into the heavens. . . There it was that I studied the habits of the Pewee; and there I was taught most forcibly, that to destroy the nest of a bird or to deprive it of its eggs or young, is an act of great cruelty. (Elman, 1977, pp. 85–86)

After a quarrel with his father's hired agent, Audubon borrowed money from his fiancée's uncle and in 1805 set sail for France, where he remained for a year visiting family, hunting, and drawing his first known bird sketches. He may have served in the French navy before returning to Pennsylvania with Ferdinand Rozier, who agreed to work as a partner on his family's Mill Grove estate. They invested in a lead mine, which proved to be a bust. Audubon spent time studying birds and taught himself to wire dead birds into lifelike positions for his sketches. In New York as an apprentice in business, he met Samuel L. Mitchell, future founder of the Lyceum of Natural History, now the New York Academy of Sciences. Together, they went on excursions to prepare bird and mammal specimens.

Disenchanted with life at Mill Grove, Audubon and Rozier opened a retail store in Louisville and eventually in Henderson, Kentucky. Audubon made a brief return to Pennsylvania to marry Lucy Bakewell and soon struck up a friendship with Daniel Boone. He later met ornithologist Alexander Wilson, who was known for his drawings of birds. Samuel Mitchell believed that Audubon's art was superior to Wilson's and urged him to consider his own professional potential, but Audubon continued to try his luck in business. After failed attempts, he traveled to Missouri still in the pursuit of business success. En route, the weather proved to be bitterly cold, with ice forming on the Mississippi River. On the trip, Audubon taught his dispirited partner how to winter camp and expressed his exhilaration in observing the great snow-white birds lying on the ice. This proved to be a turning point in his career. Audubon sold out to his partner and journeyed back to Kentucky on foot, writing of his adventures, which were published later in his *Ornithological Biography.* In his journal he wrote,

> Winter was just bursting into spring when I left the land of lead mines. Nature leaped with joy, as it were, at her own new-born marvels, the prairies began to be dotted with beauteous flowers, abounded with deer, and my own heart was filled with happiness at the sights before me. (Audubon, 1960, pp. 23–31)

In Kentucky, Audubon attempted several enterprises, his last being a steam grist and lumber mill with his wife's brother that proved too elaborate for Henderson. Jailed for debt, he was released on the plea of bankruptcy, but grew increasingly despondent after the death of his infant daughter Rose, poignantly felt after their first daughter Lucy's death only a few years earlier. To support his wife and two sons, Audubon created charcoal portraits on commission until he found work as a taxidermist in Cincinnati in the new Western Museum. His wife persuaded him to devote himself to his artistic talents, and thereafter, his life course took aim. In 1820, Audubon explored the lands along the Ohio and Mississippi Rivers for birds with a student, Joseph Mason. Settling in New Orleans, he supported the undertaking and raised money to send for his family by painting portraits and teaching archery, dance, and music. Accompanied by Mason and his own sons, he traveled the swamps and forests to Natchez, where he drew full time. Enhancing watercolor application by using various media to express textures, Audubon developed his signature style, and Mason drew many backgrounds.

Determined to have his work published, Audubon went to Philadelphia with a large portfolio of work. Finding the cost of publication prohibitive, he made plans to travel to Europe, where engraving cost far less. Before departing, he visited Mitchell, president of the Lyceum of Natural History, who introduced Audubon to this society. Audubon's drawings were highly praised, and he was elected to the Lyceum membership. His credibility grew after his reading of two papers to this prestigious society. Later, his fellow Americans nominated him a fellow of the American Academy of Arts and Sciences.

During Audubon's 1826 voyage to Europe, the ship's crew would sometimes lower him onto the water in a small boat so he could collect specimens. Once in Liverpool, Audubon was favorably received, and he acquired the initial subscriptions for his four-volume book *Birds in America*. These and later subscriptions made possible the long-delayed publication of his 435 prints. After an exhibition of his drawings at the Royal Institution of Liverpool, Audubon was declared an American genius. In Edinburgh, he received a regal reception and was elected to its Royal Society. Many other honors came to him during his stay in England, including his election to the Fellowship in the Linnean Society. Having garnered enough subscriptions, he began to publish *Birds of America* (1827–1838). The monumental achievement, done in double elephant folio—27 by 40 inches—would result in the largest set of books ever published. All of the engravings were life-size, were set in copper, and were in color. Set in their natural environment, more than a thousand birds were depicted, as well as thousands of American flowers, trees, shrubs, insects, and animals from Labrador to Florida and from Louisiana and Maine to the Great Plains.

After spending 3 years in England, Audubon was reunited with his family and continued to search for new species to augment his growing project. During a visit to Washington, DC, in 1830, President Andrew Jackson received him, and the House of Representatives became an early subscriber. Other original subscribers included Daniel Webster, Henry Clay, the kings of France and England, as well as many important libraries of the Western world. During this successful decade, Audubon teamed with Scottish naturalist William MacGillivray to write the five-volume text for *Birds of America,* called *Ornithological Biography* (1831–1839), and *A Synopsis of Birds of North America* (1839). In the content of the first, which included a description of the habits of the birds he drew, he gave an interspersed account about life in America during this turbulent period. Today, Audubon's writings are recognized as a literary treasure (National Audubon Society, 2001). With his reputation now established internationally as a naturalist and artist and the foremost naturalist in the United States, the Audubon family chose to settle in New York (Elman, 1977; C. Fisher, 1949).

Still not content, Audubon entered into two new projects. These included his seven-volume Octavo or miniature edition of *Birds of America* (1840–1844) and a new three-volume work, *Viviparous Quadruped of North America* (1845–1848), with an accompanying three-volume text (1846–1853). The critically and commercially successful "miniature," produced under the guidance of Audubon and his son John, was entrusted to J. Bowen, a Philadelphia lithographer. The later companion book on mammals was done in collaboration with scholar and friend John Bachman with the aid of his sons, whose first wives were Bachman's daughters. Audubon's son John did the artistic work for over half of the 155 plates, and his other son Victor contributed by managing the sales and designing many of the backgrounds (National Audubon Society, 2001). *Viviparous Quadruped of North America* was the first book of its kind in America and without rival in Europe. Naturalists immediately accepted it as a standard and authoritative work (C. Fisher, 1949).

Throughout 1843, Audubon traveled and discovered species for the *Quadrupeds*.

During an 8-month expedition to the upper Missouri River and the Yellowstone country, he chased the great buffalo herds, but never realized his dream of reaching the west coast. At a later date, his comprehensive notes from this trip were published by his granddaughter in *Audubon and His Journals*. At the age of 60, Audubon's eyesight began to fail and an eventual stroke disabled him further. By the time of his death at his estate Minnie's Land in Upper Manhattan, his family fortunes were diminishing.

Thirty-five years later, the National Audubon Society was formed in 1886 in Audubon's honor by George Bird Grinnell, editor of *Forest and Stream*. The society attracted the distinguished support of John Greenleaf Whittier, Oliver Wendell Holmes, and others, and some 50,000 members joined within 2 years (Fox, 1981). Audubon's enjoyment of the physical process of exploring the wilderness, tracking down each new species of bird, and observing, recording, and cataloging it marks him as one of the finest artist-naturalists of the Romantic era in America, earning him his nickname, "The American Woodsman." Renowned ornithologist Elliott Coues said, "Audubon and his work are one; he lived in his work, and his work will live forever" (C. Fisher, 1949, p. 76).

John Muir (1838–1914)

John Muir was born in Dunbar, Scotland, and immigrated with his father, brother, and sister to Wisconsin at the age of 11. The rest of his family followed later. His mother, kindly and compassionate, and his father, an unbending religious zealot, brought the family to the United States to seek a less discordant religious environment. The eldest of three sons and the third in a succession of eight siblings, Muir was expected to do heavy farm labor from dawn to nightfall. In his book *The Story of My Boyhood and Youth*, Muir (1913/1975) recounted his harsh experience while digging a 90-foot-deep well. After he struck sandstone at 10 feet, his father was advised to blast the rock. Lacking the skills or the money to do it, he decided to send his son down in a bucket equipped with mason's chisels to do the work. Relentlessly chipping from morning to night, day after day for months, in a space about 3 feet in diameter, Muir finally struck water at 80 feet. In the process, carbonic acid gas that had settled at the bottom nearly killed him.

Experiencing the awe of the neighboring wilderness provided young Muir with some retreat from the harsh living conditions; however, he acknowledged in later years that it was on the farm site at Fountain Lake that he first conceived the idea of wildlands to be set aside by governments for their scenic and educational value (Downing, 1992). Although Muir rejected the religious fanaticism of his father, his spiritual roots profoundly influenced his thinking and writing in later years. Taking issue with the Christian concept of dominion over natural resources, Muir saw the spirit in everything natural and became a pioneer of the idea that wilderness should exist for the value of its existence alone (Leshuk, 1988). Finding beauty intrinsic to his natural surroundings, he described the Wisconsin groves of oak as a summer paradise for songbirds, saying, "Nature's fine love touches, every note going straight home into one's heart" (Muir, 1913/1975, pp. 137–138).

Inventive and hungry for knowledge, Muir made an arrangement with his father that he could read early in the morning before it was time for his chores. He rose at 1 o'clock, and the 0-degree weather made a fire necessary. Fearing that his father might object to the cost of firewood, which took valuable work time to chop, he invented a self-setting sawmill. Neighbors encouraged him to take some of his inventions to the state fair in Madison. Muir had a successful showing that resulted in some local fame, a position in a machine shop, and the favorable notice of university authorities. As a student at the University of Wisconsin, he selected a practical course of studies and disregarded the regimen required for a degree. Between work and study, he had only 4 hours to sleep each night, so he invented a bed that set him on his feet every morning at the hour desired. At his desk, he arranged his books in order so they would automatically open themselves up on a rack and then close according to schedule. After closing, each book would reposition itself in the appropriate slot as the next would appear.

The day after commencement Muir and two of his college mates headed out on a long botanical and geological excursion down the Wisconsin River Valley through Minnesota and Iowa. These travels pulled at his heart as he waited for a response to his letter of application from the University of Michigan, where he hoped to continue his studies. Muir, a pacifist by nature, had also registered for the Civil War draft. His number was passed in the early drawings, and he decided that if his number was not drawn that fall while he worked for his brother-in-law that he would head to Canada for the "University of the Wilderness" (Wilkins,1945, p. 39). In Canada, Muir "entered at once into harmonious relations with Nature" (Wolfe, 1945, p. 91). Returning after 2 years in Canada, he took on odd jobs in factories, which led to quick promotions due to his ability and his inventions of labor-saving equipment. He became foreman-engineer at an Indianapolis carriage factory until an industrial injury nearly blinded him. Convalescing for weeks in a dark hospital room, he finally recovered his sight. This convinced Muir that he should be true to himself, and he decided to follow nature and the inventions of God (Muir, 1975).

On September 2, 1867, Muir began a thousand-mile walk to the Gulf of Mexico. He recorded his observations about the forests, flora, and geography in his journal. He also wrote of his experiences with the inhabitants and of his personal reflections on human responsiveness toward nature. Edited and published posthumously, these observations appear under the title A Thousand-Mile Walk to the Gulf (1916). Once he reached the Gulf, he sailed to Cuba and then to Panama, where he crossed the Isthmus and sailed up the west coast, landing in San Francisco in March 1868. Immediately, Muir sought directions into the wilderness of the Yosemite Valley, where he worked on a ranch and continued his explorations while studying botany and the geology of the new state park. Muir's reflections, written at the age of 31, appeared

four decades later in perhaps his best-loved book My First Summer in the Sierra (1911). In an earlier publication, The Mountains of California, Muir (1894/1977) shared his enthusiasm of the unknown, portraying his climb on Mount Ritter located in the middle portion of the High Sierra:

> Its height above sea level is about 13,300 feet, and it is fenced round by steeply inclined glaciers, and canyons of tremendous depth and ruggedness, which render it almost inaccessible. But difficulties of this kind only exhilarate the mountaineer. . . . In so wild and so beautiful a region was spent my first day, every sight and sound inspiring, leading one far out of himself, yet feeding and building up his individuality. Now came the solemn, silent evening. Long blue, spiky shadows crept out across the snow-fields, while a rosy glow, at first scarce discernible, gradually deepened and suffused every mountain-top, flushing the glaciers and the harsh crags above them. This was the alpenglow, to me one of the most impressive of all the terrestrial manifestations of God. At the touch of this divine light, the mountains seemed to kindle to a rapt, religious consciousness, and stood hushed and waiting like devout worshipers. Just before the alpenglow began to fade, two crimson clouds came streaming across the summit like wings of flame, rendering the sublime scene yet more impressive; then came darkness and the stars.

During this period, Muir, who had learned of Emerson and Thoreau at the University of Wisconsin, acted as interpreter of natural history when Emerson visited Yosemite in 1871. Muir would later name a mountain in the Yosemite region in Emerson's honor (F. Teale, 1954). By this time, he had already discovered living glaciers in the Sierra and, contrary to the popular belief of the times, theorized that Yosemite Valley was produced by glaciation rather than by a devastating earthquake. As Muir became known throughout the country for his scientific writing, other famous men made their way to his pine cabin. He became publicly known for his writings in 1874 when a series of magazine articles entitled *Studies in the Sierra* was launched. His enchantment with nature did not end in the Sierra, however. In 1879, Muir took his first of seven journeys to Alaska, where he became one of the first white men to discover the area now known as Glacier Bay. In Alaska, his adventures included discoveries and observations of plants, fish, animals, birds, rivers, mountains, and glaciers.

A new turn in his life occurred in 1880 when Muir married Louie (short for Louisiana) Wanda Strentzel and leased, and later bought, a part of the Strentzel fruit ranch. After 10 years of prudent farming in Martinez, California, he saved $100,000. With enough to support his wife and two daughters, he could devote himself to his true ambitions, his hikes and observations. Supportive of his fight for conservation and travel, his wife encouraged him to go to the mountains for his health. Muir had no feeling for haste and could sit for hours studying the flowers. He was known to have taken 10 hours to walk 10 miles because he stopped so frequently to study or ponder (W.F.B., 1934).

Returning to his work as an advocate for wilderness and forest preservation, Muir wrote many articles about the need to transfer Yosemite back to the federal government and rename it a national park. He also introduced bills to save the majestic sequoia trees. By 1890, Yosemite, Sequoia, and General Grant (now King's Canyon) were all national parks. The next year his book *Our National Parks* was released. In 1903, Muir, who had helped persuade President Benjamin Harrison to set aside 13 million acres of forest and President Grover Cleveland to set aside another 21 million acres, camped with President Theodore Roosevelt during his tour of the American West. Together, they laid the foundation of Roosevelt's innovative and notable conservation programs (Downing, 1992). Between Presidents Roosevelt, Wilson,

and Taft, Muir's influence could be gauged by the designation of over 50 national parks, 200 national monuments, and 140 million acres of national forest (White, 1996). Muir credited Robert Underwood Johnson, an editor of *The Century Magazine*, as the "originator of Yosemite," but Muir himself is credited with saving the Grand Canyon and the Petrified Forest and with assisting in establishing Sequoia, Yosemite, Mount Rainier, Crater Lake, Glacier, and Mesa Verde National Parks as well as 12 national monuments (Ford, 1989). Two of these, the Grand Canyon and Olympic Peninsula, later became national parks. Deservedly, Muir is often called the father of the national park system because his work toward preservation later became the mission of the National Park Service.

To protect the newly created Yosemite National Park, Johnson and others suggested to Muir that an association be formed. On May 22, 1892, Muir helped to found the Sierra Club in San Francisco and served as the club's first and singular president for 22 years. In his invitational letter, he expressed his hope that this club would be able to "do something for wilderness, and make the mountains glad" (Downing, 1992). Although the club gained national recognition for its efforts to reserve and preserve scenic and forest areas first in California and then across the nation, Muir lost his last major battle when Congress in 1913 authorized the Hetch Hetchy reservoir in the valley adjacent to Yosemite Valley. Both were part of the Yosemite National Park (see Chapter 7). To Muir, who felt that a journey into the Yosemite Valley itself was an inherently spiritual experience, the loss of this beautiful land was most certainly a heartbreak. Yet the resilient man pulled his attention to a long-deferred book on Alaska. Optimistically, Muir wrote to Johnson, the long-drawn-out battle-work for nature's gardens has not been thrown away. The conscience of the whole country has been aroused from sleep, and from outrageous evil compensating good in some form must surely come (Wilkins, 1995).

The public conscience was so thoroughly aroused that wilderness preservation grew in popularity, and Muir was "enshrined at its heart" (Wilkins, 1995, p. 243). His great contribution to wilderness preservation lay in his ability to promote successfully the revolutionary idea that wilderness had spiritual as well as economic value (Ryan, 1990). His own deepest insight was perhaps in finding the inner oneness in all of nature, pointing out that no particle of nature is ever wasted. In the wilderness, Muir believed, one could appreciate fellow creatures, realizing one's part in a harmonious whole. He said, "In God's wildness lies the hope of the world, the great fresh, unblighted, unredeemed wilderness" (Wolfe, 1979, p. 317). Other books written by John Muir were *Stickeen* (1909) and *The Yosemite* (1912). Published posthumously were *Travels in Alaska* (1915), *The Cruise of the Corwin* (1917), and *Steep Trails* (1918).

Rachel Carson (1907–1964)

Scientist and ecologist Rachel Carson was employed by the U.S. Fish and Wildlife Service from 1936 to 1952. As a talented writer, she was capable of transforming government research into poetic prose. Together, her books *Under the Sea-Wind* (1941), *The Sea Around Us* (1951), and *Edge of the Sea* (1955) constituted a biography of the ocean that made her famous as a naturalist and science writer. Her best seller, *The Silent Spring* (1962), touched off an international controversy over the long-range effects of pesticides. By shocking the world with her presentation of disasters brewing, she magnified environmental awareness and "changed the course of history" (Gore, 2006).

The youngest of three children, Rachel Louise Carson was born in industrial Springdale, Pennsylvania, where she came to love the natural environment on her family's farm. In large measure, she owed her love of nature to her mother, a graduate of Washington Female Seminary, who "taught her as a tiny child joy in the out-of-doors and the lore of birds, insects, and residents of the streams and ponds" (Rothe, 1952, p. 101). In later years, the study of birds became a hobby. She became an associate member of the American Ornithologist's Union and a director of the Audubon Society of the District of Columbia.

Carson's writing career began at an early age with her contributions to *St. Nicholas* magazine beginning in 1918. Her last article for the magazine, published in 1922, was her first publication about nature. "My Favorite Recreation—Going Bird's-Nesting" displays an impressive knowledge, adult style, and intuitive sense of expression (Holmes, 2004). Intent on becoming a writer, she entered the Pennsylvania College for Women (now Chatham College) in Pittsburgh with a scholarship after graduating first in her high school class. She participated in a wide range of activities, including field hockey and basketball, but her interest in writing was redirected to science. "Biology," she told a friend, "has given me something to write about" (Strong, 1988, p. 180).

Her first publication about the sea appeared in the college magazine. Graduating magna cum laude in 1929 with a degree in zoology, Carson connected with the sea in August at the Marine Biological Laboratory at Woods Hole on Cape Cod. Enamored with the mysteries of the sea, she returned here at least four other summers. That fall she became one of 13 women to enter Johns Hopkins University for postgraduate study in the combined department of zoology, botany, and plant physiology, receiving her MA degree in 1932. During her early career, she taught at the University of Maryland, but she never fulfilled her plans to obtain a doctorate due to family responsibilities (Matthiessen, 1999). With the death of her ailing father in 1935 and her sister the following year, Carson's family responsibilities grew when she resolved to raise her two orphaned nieces. She elected not to marry and continued her devotion to her family throughout her life. In later years, she cared for her elderly mother and adopted her 5-year-old great nephew after the death of a beloved niece.

To make ends meet, "Ray" Carson, as she was known to some of her friends, began writing articles on scientific and ecological topics for the *Baltimore Sunday Sun* and other newspapers. She also wrote science radio scripts for the U.S. Bureau of Fisheries (later the Fish and Wildlife Service) in Washington, DC. This part-time position led to a full-time appointment as junior aquatic biologist in 1936. Remaining in the employment of the U.S. government for 16 years, she was promoted to assistant aquatic biologist in 1942, associate in 1943, and aquatic biologist before the war ended.

Rather than doing laboratory research, she wrote bulletins, leaflets, and other informative literature. One submission seemed so outstanding that her editor encouraged her to submit it to the *Atlantic Monthly*. "Undersea" appeared in 1937 and captured the attention of an editor from Simon and Schuster, who asked her to write a full-length book concerning the sea. This article, along with one of her *Sun* features, served as a starting point for her first and favorite book, *Under the Sea-Wind*. The 1941 book, subtitled "a naturalist's picture of ocean life," was critically and scientifically praised, but only 1,400 copies were sold in its first year (De Bruhl, 1981). Debuting 1 month before Pearl Harbor was attacked, the book about the shore, open sea, and deep abyss, written from the perspective of a shore bird and other nonhumans, had to wait for its audience. Upon republication by Oxford University Press in 1952, 40,000 copies were bought in advance with a portion of it appearing in *Life* magazine (Holmes, 2004).

After the department's reorganization as seen in Chapter 7, Carson rose within the ranks of the newly created U.S. Fish and Wildlife Service to biologist, information specialist, and editor-in-chief in 1949 while continuing her freelance work. Her most substantial writing for the government included a series of booklets about national wildlife refuges published in the early postwar years. To carry out the research, writing, and editing of the series, she traveled to refuges in Oregon, Utah, Montana, North Carolina, Massachusetts, and Virginia, which comprised the more than 300 sites already in existence in the late 1940s (Holmes, 2004). Today, the Rachel Carson National Wildlife Refuge along the southern Maine coast near the beach resort of Wells is named in her honor.

In 1949, she was given a Eugene F. Saxton Memorial Fellowship and in 1950 the George Westinghouse Foundation award for outstanding magazine writing in the field of science. She hired a literary agent for her second book that was serialized as "A Profile of the Sea" in *The New Yorker* before it was released in 1951. Entitled *The Sea Around Us,* the blockbuster went into a ninth printing, was placed on nonfiction best-seller lists throughout the country, was translated into more than 30 languages, and won the National Book Award. Drexel, Oberlin, Smith, and the Pennsylvania College for Women awarded her with honorary doctoral degrees. Taking the reader through successive periods of geological times in the book, she warns of the dangers of polluting the oceans with atomic wastes. In her chapter "The Long Snowfall," Carson (1951) shared her scientific insight and emotional sensitivity:

> Every part of earth or air or sea has an atmosphere peculiarly its own, a quality or characteristic that sets it apart from all others. When I think of the floor of the deep sea, the single, overwhelming fact that possesses my imagination is the accumulation of sediments. I see always the steady, unremitting, downward drift of materials from above, flake upon flake, layer upon layer—a drift that has continued for hundreds of millions of years, that will go on as long as there are seas and continents. For the sediments are the materials of the most stupendous "snowfall" the earth has ever seen. . . (p. 74)

Research for the book entailed learning deep-sea diving at shallow depths and included a 10-day voyage on a research ship. With little time to do her own creative work, her book progressed slowly, taking 3 years. Everything changed after its success. A Guggenheim Fellowship awarded in June allowed her the opportunity for a year's sabbatical to begin work on a third book. Royalties from both books gave her the economic independence to resign her position at the Fish and Wildlife Service the next year. Following her dream, she continued to write and bought property on Southport Island in Maine, where she could be near the natural environment that she relished and wrote about.

Preparation for *The Edge of the Sea,* which explored the border zone where sea meets land, included wading in icy tidal pools for so long that she sometimes became numb with cold and had to be carried out. By studying minute sea creatures under her binocular microscope, she felt a spiritual closeness to the individual creatures about whom she wrote. She covered rocky shores, sandy beaches, and coastal reefs of the Atlantic coast in her third book of the sea trilogy, which also became a best seller, with *The New Yorker* printing a condensation of part of the book before the 1955 publication.

It was her fourth book, the landmark *Silent Spring,* that ushered in environmentalism, one of the great movements of the century (De Bruhl, 1981). Carson's grim warning was instrumental in bringing about awareness of the dangers of some pesticides and herbicides that could kill everyone and everything if humanity failed to check its use. Her text ended on the following note:

> The "control of nature" is a phrase conceived in arrogance, born of the Neanderthal age of biology and philosophy, when it was supposed that nature exists for the convenience of man. The concepts and practices of applied entomology for the most part date from that Stone Age of science. It is our alarming misfortune that so primitive a science has armed itself with the most modern and terrible weapons, and that in turning them against the insects it has also turned them against the earth. (Carson, 1962)

Before the book's release, *Silent Spring* was serialized in *The New Yorker,* which brought public attention to the book. By the time it reached the bookstores in 1962, it became an instantaneous best seller likened in historical significance to Charles Darwin's *The Origin of the Species* and Harriet Beecher Stowe's *Uncle Tom's Cabin* (Holmes, 2004). Opponents threatened lawsuits and called

Carson an alarmist. Monsanto Chemical Company responded with a report to advise the public of the horrors of a pesticide-free world (De Bruhl, 1981). Like brochures, disseminated to the press, gave credence to her warning about the danger of a growing liaison between science and industry. Speaking to the Women's Press, she stressed the need to recognize who was supporting the research, thereby indicating that unfavorable facts may not always be revealed (Holmes, 2004). Realizing the controversial nature of her topic, she was confident about her facts and knew that she could count on the support of leading scientists and conservation organizations (Matthiessen, 1999). "Who are we," Carson questioned, "to say that those who come after us may never see some of today's rare and endangered species?" (Carson, 1963, p. 262).

About the same time, newspapers reported the death of 5 million fish on the lower Mississippi River, the worst of a series of incidents (Strong, 1988). Public outcry could not be ignored. President John F. Kennedy read the best seller with its call to prove "our mastery, not of nature, but of ourselves" (Steinbauer, 1990, p. 18). This encounter eventually led to the setting up of the Environmental Protection Agency (EPA). In the meantime, he appointed a presidential advisory committee to study the issue. The committee called for more research into the potential health hazard of pesticides and warned against indiscriminate use. Despite failing health, Carson made specific recommendations at congressional hearings in 1963. Many pesticides, including DDT, were eventually banned, and others were brought under stricter controls. With the ban on DDT enacted in 1972, the recovery of several endangered species has been taking place, including the nesting population of the bald eagle and peregrine falcon, which had been reduced by 90% in the contiguous United States at that time ("DDT ban accelerated," 1997). "We spray our elms," she explained, "and the following springs are silent of robin song..." (Elliott, 2007, para. 3).

Even after Carson's death by cancer, her books continue to reach new audiences. No doubt, Carson would have preferred to be remembered for her books about the sea, where the grandeur of her style is visible (Graham, 1970). Her joy came from sharing the wonder and beauty of the living world with others. In her 1955 article "Help Your Child to Wonder," she even challenged her readers to do the same by encouraging children to keep alive their instinctive interests in what is "beautiful and awe-inspiring" (Strong, 1988, p. 184). In her posthumously published book, she laid down her philosophy, "The lasting pleasures of contact with the natural world are not reserved for scientists but are available to anyone who will place himself under the influence of earth, sea and sky and their amazing life" (Carson, 1965, p. 33).

Reluctantly, her focus changed, when her reverence for life called her to bring the message of modern crisis to public attention in *Silent Spring*. As she explained it, "What I discovered was that everything which meant most to me as a naturalist was being threatened, and that nothing I could do would be more important" (Brooks, 1972, p. 233). Embedded in all of Carson's writings was her belief that humans constituted only a portion of nature, and what differentiated them from the rest of nature was their ability to destroy it, in some cases irreversibly (Lear, 2000).

The various aspects of her life—zoologist, writer, policymaker, conservationist, birder, and government employee—were represented at her funeral at the National Cathedral in Washington, DC, by the pallbearers who carried her casket: Robert Cushman Murphy, internationally reknown ornithologist; Edwin Way Teale, nature writer; U.S. Senator Abraham Ribicoff; Stewart Udall, secretary of the interior; Charles Callison of the National Audubon Society; and Bob Hines, wildlife illustrator and colleague at the U.S. Fish and Wildlife Service (Holmes, 2004). Her numerous awards included her election to the American Academy of Arts and Science, and her unusual blend of science and art was acknowledged through the Burroughs Medal, an honor that associated her with immortals in nature such as Henry David Thoreau (Gartner, 1983). In 1973, she was elected to the Women's Hall of Fame, and at the end of the 20th century, she was listed by *Time* magazine as one of the 100 most important Americans of the century.

THE PRACTITIONER PIONEERS

The mere description of nature and the advocacy to preserve it would not have saved natural areas if it were not for the efforts of the practitioners, those who worked in the parks and wilderness areas and struggled to conserve and preserve their qualities and make areas available to others and future generations. Standouts among these leaders are Frederick Law Olmsted, Gifford Pinchot, Stephen Mather, and Aldo Leopold.

Frederick Law Olmsted (1822–1903)

In the early years of the 19th century, New York City had a number of pleasure gardens that gradually gave way to buildings. By 1855, there were no gardens left, and city residents began visiting cemeteries for their foliage, lawns, and park-like amenities (Olmsted & Kimball, 1970). Although other cities of America at that time may have had open space and/or small parks, it was the establishment of New York's Central Park under the watchful eye of its architect, Frederick Law Olmsted, that signaled the birth of city parks in the United States.

As complaints about insufficient open space in New York continued, the common council of the city acquired an 840-acre parcel of rocky swampland just north of the city's boundaries. In 1857, a nonpartisan board was appointed to develop the park. A design competition was conducted in which Olmsted and British-born architect Calvert Vaux participated. Their design, nicknamed "Greensward," was awarded top prize over more than 30 competitors in April 1858, a year after Olmsted was appointed superintendent of the yet-undesigned Central Park (Doell & Twardzik, 1979).

Born in Hartford, Connecticut, Frederick Law Olmsted was placed in the care of a congregational minister after his mother's death when he was 6. His enrollment in a succession of schools was interspersed with long vacations that were taken in New York, New England, and Canada with his father, a wealthy merchant. After nearly being blinded by sumac poisoning at age 15, he abandoned his plans for college. A favorite activity during his convalescence was drawing plans for hypothetical cities and towns. It may have been his upbringing and tendency to ramble in the New England countryside that contributed to his interest in extending the natural environment into urban lifestyle (Havard, 1989). Nevertheless, before embarking on a career as a landscape architect, the profession that he created, he shipped out for China as an apprentice seaman in 1843 and also tried his hand at farming, writing, and other occupations.

Settling on a farm financed by Olmsted's father in Staten Island in 1848, Olmsted practiced landscape gardening and improved the grounds to such an extent that his neighbors often sought his advice. He chose to interrupt rural life in 1850 to take an extensive trip to Europe, where the English landscape and city parks in Liverpool and London made a lasting impression on him. When he returned, he wrote *Walks and Talks of an American Farmer in England,* and he was soon embarking on a career as a writer. Almost immediately, Olmsted gained literary success (Strong, 1988). Among the most influential books that he produced were *Journey in the Backcountry* (1860) and *The Cotton Kingdom* (1861), both published by Mason brothers of New York. His writing was based on his dispatches as a *New York Times* correspondent in the pre–Civil War South. He also helped launch *The Nation,* the respected liberal journal still in circulation today. In 1855, he became partner in a New York publishing firm and for a time edited *Putnam's Monthly Magazine.* When his firm went bankrupt 2 years later, he needed capital, but in his absence the condition of the farm had become run down.

Olmsted's second career as environmental planner and designer began with his appointment in 1857, at the age of 35, as the superintendent of Central Park. He had to be politically astute to get such an appointment at a time when New York City was having many political battles over the potential park development. The state legislature passed an act for "the Regulation and Governance of Central Park in the City of New York." The act was a reaction to the lack of progress in developing the park coupled with the corruption and inefficiency of the politicians in charge (Jubenville, 1976). The idea for the park dated back to at least 1844 when poet William Cullen Bryant made the proposal.

Central Park, Olmsted's first and most famous work, is so natural today that it is hard to believe that it emerged as a direct result of two men's ingenuity. Their design suggested that the development of the park revolve around a number of concepts that are still used in the planning of outdoor recreational areas. The two planners felt that a park is a single, coordinated work of art that should be framed upon a single, noble motive. The park should allow for some relief from the confinement of urban life. Yet uses of the park are not necessarily compatible, and accordingly, different areas of the park should be spatially separated to reduce conflict and confusion. Moreover, the primary purpose of the park is to provide the best practicable means of healthful recreation for inhabitants of all classes. Olmsted wanted to provide the lower classes with "a specimen of God's handiwork that shall be to them, inexpensively, what a month or two in the White Mountains, or the Adirondacks is. . . to those in easier circumstances" (Olmsted & Kimball, 1970, p. 46).

When the Civil War broke out in 1861, the U.S. Sanitary Commission, which became the American Red Cross, asked Olmsted to serve as its general secretary. In that capacity he was charged with providing troops with medical and sanitary supplies. Two years later, he was offered the position of general manager of the Mariposa Company, a gold mining company near the Yosemite in California. The more lucrative position helped him pay his debt and support his wife and her three children; he had married his brother's widow. A year later Olmsted became commissioner of Yosemite and Mariposa Big Tree Grove. In a report, he set forth his justification and philosophic base for setting aside future parks—the first statement of its kind in the United States—and recommended that they be treated as museums of natural history. Although he listed reasons to establish Yosemite as a park, his report went unnoticed and even disappeared, perhaps because there was such competition for state funds (Strong, 1988). Nonetheless, his justification that government could justify the protection of a land as a means to protect the public's inalienable right to the pursuit of happiness would in time become a sacred text (Duncan & Burns, 2009). During his stay, he was asked to provide a plan for the campus of the new University of California at Berkeley and Golden Gate Park in San Francisco.

Olmsted returned to the East Coast in 1865, where he completed Central Park and undertook a number of landscaping projects, among which were Prospect Park in Brooklyn, Fairmont in Philadelphia, and Lincoln Park in Chicago. One of Olmsted's innovative concepts was the idea of a string of green spaces around a city to bring recreational areas close to every citizen. In 1888, Olmsted and Charles Eliot introduced this concept in Boston. The park was named the "Emerald Necklace." The idea was adopted by many cities.

The success of Central Park set off a mania for park building, and Olmsted's trademark sprouted up in the Midwest as well, in Belle Isle Park in Detroit, Cherokee Park in Louisville, and Lake Park in Milwaukee (Havard, 1989). His idea of a commuter village, a suburb of an urban center such as Riverside is to Chicago, is still regarded as a model for suburban design.

Among many of Olmsted's contributions aimed at underscoring the natural environment in the lives of those who live surrounded by buildings were landscape plans for numerous campuses and private estates. The Amherst, Trinity, West Point, George Washington, and Stanford campuses have his stamp. Biltmore, the estate of George Vanderbilt in Asheville, North Carolina, was designed by Olmsted and later proclaimed by the nation's first chief of the Forest Service, Gifford Pinchot, as the "nest egg for practical Forestry in the United States" (Stevenson,

1977, p. 404). He helped plan Boston's Arnold Arboretum, which served as a forest laboratory. In 1874, Olmsted improved the grounds of the Capitol in Washington, DC. He played a major role in petitioning the U.S. and Canadian governments to protect Niagara Falls from waterpower development and helped to establish the Adirondacks as a state forest preserve.

As an advocate of comprehensive city planning, Olmsted urged that a city plan "make provisions for physical and mental health, safety and transportation needs in commercial and residential districts, proper housing and recreation" (I. Fisher, 1986, p. 2). Although Olmsted recognized the importance of outdoor recreation and sightseeing for health, vigor, and social transformation, he had no patience with requests for organized recreation. "He saw his parks as places for walking, riding and relaxing in a naturalistic retreat from the harshness of the city" (Knudson, 1984, p. 164). This attitude may have caused the friction that led to the rise of the playground and recreation movement of Joseph Lee, Jane Addams, and Luther Gulick, which will be discussed later. Today, the park and recreation movements have come together to form a union, where the legacy of the nation's foremost park maker endures.

Following Olmsted's retirement in 1895, his son Frederick Law Olmsted Jr. led his father's firm along with his stepbrother John Charles. The Olmsted Brothers' firm continued to carry on the work of Frederick Law Olmsted, employing nearly 60 staff at its peak in the early 1930s. Olmsted Jr., who founded the first formal training program in landscape architecture at Harvard University in 1900, maintained a lifelong commitment to conservation, contributing the guiding language in legislation establishing the National Park Service in 1916. John Charles became the first president of the American Society of Landscape Architects in 1899 and led the office in comprehensive planning for metropolitan open spaces and park systems (National Park Service, 1998). From this office, the first full-scale professional office for the practice of landscape design, Olmsted and his successors designed thousands of public and private landscapes that forever changed the face of the nation. Today, the spirit of his work lives on at the same location at the Frederick Law Olmsted National Historic Site in Brookline, Massachusetts, now used as a center for the study and preservation of American landscapes.

Gifford Pinchot (1865–1946)

America's first professionally trained forester, Gifford Pinchot, could have lived a life of luxury and ease. Instead, he chose to travel wilderness trails and camp the wooded country, rising to national prominence as a conservationist and politician who fought for wiser use of natural resources. Pinchot, born to wealth and social prominence at his family's summer home in Simsbury, Connecticut, was raised in New York City and at his family's wooded estate in Pennsylvania. Aware of his father's concern for the dwindling state of the nation's forests, he was quick to notice the more impressive European management of forests when he vacationed abroad with his family. Because no American university offered a course of instruction in forestry, he arranged his course of study at Yale. After graduation, he studied European forests while doing postgraduate work at the French National Forestry School at Nancy.

Upon his return to the United States, he began to explore the nation, observing the relationship of people and forests. He noted that forests were facing a desperate and losing struggle to loggers. Trees were vanishing along the eastern seaboard; also the hardwood forests of the South and the pine forests of the Midwest had been decimated. Recognizing that it was only a matter of time before timberlands in the West would disappear, Pinchot advocated regulating the commercial use of public and private forests. This included selective cutting, planning for future growth, and establishing fire prevention measures. If properly managed, he was convinced that sustained yield was possible if it could be shown to be both practical and profitable. Pinchot expressed his sentiments at a later date:

When I came home [from France] not a single acre of Government, State, or private timberland was under systematic forest management anywhere on the most richly timbered of all continents. . . . When the Gay Nineties began, the common word for forests was "inexhaustible." To waste timber was a virtue and not a crime. There would always be plenty of timber. . . . The lumbermen… regarded forest devastation as normal and second growth as a delusion of fools. . . . And as for sustained yield, no such idea had ever entered their heads. The few friends of the forest were spoken of, when they were spoken of at all, as impractical theorists, fanatics, or "denudatics," more or less touched in the head. What talk there was about forest protection was no more to the average American than the buzzing of a mosquito, and just about as irritating. (Williams, 2000, pp. 14–15)

Pinchot applied principles of scientific forestry in the private North Carolina forest of George W. Vanderbilt. Here Pinchot initiated the principle of selective logging, where young trees are given the opportunity to mature, and some mature trees are protected so that they may seed. After achieving a reasonable amount of success, Pinchot prepared an exhibit for the Chicago World's Fair in 1893 with an accompanying pamphlet, *Biltmore Forest*, the first of his many publications. Shortly thereafter, he became a consultant forester in New York City, made surveys of the forestlands of New Jersey, and drew plans for two private tracts in the Adirondacks. Greatly impacting Pinchot's career was the congressional passage in 1891 of a bill providing that forest reserves could be set aside as government land through a presidential proclamation. Many of these reserved lands would eventually come under his supervision.

In 1896, Pinchot was appointed to the National Forest Commission of the National

Academy of Science, whose chairman supported U.S. Army protection to defend the reserves from poachers. Pinchot, the commission's secretary, voiced his objectives, which favored regulated use through a forest service whose members had received scientific training. Since he was the first American to make forestry a profession, Pinchot presumably saw himself in a leading position (Fox, 1981). In the end, the National Forest Commission's study helped bring about authorization for commercial use of these reserves through passage of the Forest Management Act of 1897 (see Chapter 7).

After serving as "special forest agent" for the secretary of the interior, Pinchot was named chief of the small Federal Division of Forestry with the Agriculture Department in 1898, a departmental shift that Pinchot had supported since the later department employed professional foresters. Establishing a decentralized organization with built-in flexibility, he immediately began to establish his concepts of scientific forestry. His loyal, dedicated, and competent employees offered advice to some of the nation's largest lumber companies. Gradually, they took on more responsibilities toward managing the forest reserves, which remained with the Interior Department in the General Land Office. By 1901, his division had become the Bureau of Forestry. With the firm support and backing of President Theodore Roosevelt, Pinchot campaigned for Congress to transfer the forest reserves to the Department of Agriculture. The transfer bill was backed by stockmen, lumbermen, and others who preferred the advantages of Pinchot's promise of long-term protection through controlled use to the potential prohibition of commercial use that might result from the formation of parks and game reserves with the Department of the Interior (Strong, 1988).

In 1905, passage of the Transfer Act gave the Bureau, which was renamed the Forest Service, control of the national forest reserves. During Pinchot's administration, the national forests increased from 60 "forest reserves" covering 56 million acres in 1905 to 150 "national forests" covering 172 million acres in 1910 (Williams, 2000). He controlled

their use, instituted a system of permits and fees, and regulated their harvest—it was not until after World War II that large-scale logging and other controversial procedures, such as clear-cutting took place (Strong, 1988). Pinchot also arranged for the creation of an official badge for the forest rangers, encouraged uniform standards, and encouraged a high level of competency. He composed the principles upon which the Forest Service was to administer its new responsibilities:

In the administration of the forest reserves it must be clearly borne in mind that all land is to be devoted to its most productive use for the permanent good of the whole people and not for the temporary benefit of individuals or companies. All the resources of the forest reserves are for use, and this use must be brought about in a thoroughly prompt and business-like manner, under such restrictions only as will insure the permanence of these resources. (Cameron, 1928, p. 239)

Pinchot believed in the public control of natural resources to ensure the rational, scientific use of the land to maximize its benefits for the greatest number of people. Opponents of the Pinchot-Roosevelt conservation program did not believe in the expansion of government control. Still, others wished to exploit the nation's resources. With President Theodore Roosevelt's help, Pinchot organized a White House Conference on the Conservation of Natural Resources to which all the nation's governors and other leading figures were invited. Additionally, the National Conservation Commission, chaired by Pinchot, was organized to make an inventory of the country's resources and their date of probable exhaustion. Once Roosevelt left office, however, the conservation movement declined. Pinchot's conservation policies went under the direct attack of the new secretary of the interior, Richard A. Ballinger. Ballinger's appointment, by President William H. Taft, ended the interdepartmental cooperative agreements that had taken place between the Forest Service and Interior when James R. Garfield (son of former President Garfield) served as secretary of the interior in the Roosevelt administration. The eventual struggle between Ballinger and Pinchot led to a split in the Taft administration. In 1910, Taft felt forced to dismiss Pinchot from government service after his public criticism of the President's decision to support Ballinger.

Application of Pinchot's *conservation* policy—using the land and its resources "for the benefit of many, and not merely for the profit of a few"—caused the loss of the support of the preservationist wing of the conservationists. With his policy in mind, Pinchot consistently chose the wise use of resources over proposals to use the land for parks (Strong, 1988). In the Hetch Hetchy debate, for example (see Chapter 7), John Muir and the preservationists supported protection of the Hetch Hetchy Valley in Yosemite National Park for its beauty, whereas Pinchot supported San Francisco's request to acquire the area as a reservoir. Pinchot's view was brought before congressional hearings in 1913. When asked if he knew of John Muir and his criticism of the bill, he replied,

> Yes, sir; I know him very well. He is an old and a very good friend of mine…. When I became Forester and denied the right to exclude sheep and cows from the Sierras, Mr. Muir thought I had made a great mistake, because I allowed the use by an acquired right of a large number of people to interfere with what would have been the utmost beauty of the forest. In this case, I think he has unduly given away to beauty as against use. (Nash, 1970, p. 88)

Still interested in national politics, Pinchot made his first of several unsuccessful attempts for the Senate in 1914, running as a Progressive. That same year he married Cornelia Bryce at age 49. They had a son, Gifford Bryce Pinchot. She used her boundless energy to help with the campaigning, ad-dressed housewives demanding the vote, and eventually sought election herself. In 1920, Pinchot was appointed commissioner of forestry by the governor of Pennsylvania, and in 1922, he was elected governor. Barred from succeeding himself, he tried again for the Senate as a Republican candidate before being elected to a second term as governor in 1930. During his last year in office, he gave one last try for the U.S. Senate, but failed to gain the assistance of Republicans due to his support of Democrat Franklin D. Roosevelt's economic recovery programs. At age 72, he made a bid for nomination for governor once again, but the Republican votes overwhelmingly defeated him. Pinchot suffered a major heart attack in 1939, but he filled his remaining years by writing a book about his life as a forester, giving advice to the president, and devising a fishing kit that was used in lifeboats during World War II (Pennsylvania Historical and Museum Commission, 2001). Pinchot died of leukemia at age 81.

Throughout his years, Pinchot was a leader in matters involving conservation. In 1909, he founded the National Conservation Association and directed it from 1910 until it dissolved in 1923. He was involved in the passage of the Weeks Act in 1911, which provided for the expansion of forest reserves by purchase. A founder of the Society of American Foresters, he served as its president from 1900–1908 and 1910–1911. He continued his interest in forestry by serving as a nonresident lecturer and professor at the Yale School of Forestry, established through a lectureship grant awarded by his father. He wrote *The Fight for Conservation* in 1910, and his autobiography, *Breaking New Ground*, was published posthumously in 1947 (Penick, 1974).

Gifford Pinchot, the utilitarian champion, viewed conservation as a demand for the welfare of the present generation first and future generations later. Eventually, this view gave way. Men of the Forest Service, such as Aldo Leopold, shifted from a dominance of nature, in the Pinchot tradition, to a more cooperative harmony with nature. As such, the foundation was laid for stronger recreational and wilderness values. Pinchot's legacy remained, however, molding Forest Service culture and values of conservation leadership, public service, responsiveness, integrity, a strong land ethic, and professionalism characterized by people who know their jobs and do them well. These values are the bedrock on which the Forest Service stands (see the Chapter 7 on federal resources).

Stephen Mather (1867–1930)

Stephen Mather was a staunch conservationist, and he was among the first to urge the U.S. Congress to set aside areas that are of scenic, historical, and scientific significance. Born in San Francisco, California, he developed at an early age a great affection for the natural beauty of the great Sierras. In 1887, Mather graduated from the University of California, Berkeley, and moved to the East Coast to work as a reporter for the *New York Sun* for 5 years. After he married Jane Floy he decided to pursue a career as his father had in the borax mining business, where he became an executive with a passion for advertising. In this capacity he helped to create the celebrated trade slogan "20 Mule Team Borax." A lucrative partnership developed with a friend followed in 1903. The 11-year association at the Thorkildsen-Mather Borax Company not only made Mather a millionaire, but also provided the committed conservationist with time to do volunteer work and enjoy hiking and mountaineering.

As a member of the Sierra Club, Mather took trips to the Sierra Nevada, where he met John Muir, who urged him to take a stand to protect the region against destructive activities such as logging and mining. While visiting the Yosemite and Sequoia National Parks, Mather became aware of private landholdings in scenic areas, cattle grazing in the national parks, and poor roads and trails (Strong, 1988). Concerned about the deteriorating condition of the national parks, Mather wrote to this effect to his acquaintance Frank Lane, the secretary of the interior. Lane simply invited him "to come to Washington and do something about it." Enticed out of retirement, Mather showed up in 1915 ready to go to work. Mather was made assistant to the secretary. Until his appointment, there had been no one person to take on the direction of the 13 national parks and 18 national monuments. In fact, their management, which came under the auspices of the Department of the Interior at the time of his arrival, was accomplished by a loose organizational coalition of the Departments of Interior, War, and Agriculture (Simpson, 1989). Moreover, the pool from which park superintendents were selected was political rather than professional in nature. Mather realized that the system needed a vast overhaul, which he set forth to accomplish. The plan was to tackle the problem on five fronts (Shankland, 1970):

1. Get Congress interested enough in the national parks (a) to make vast increases in their appropriations and (b) to authorize a bureau of national parks.
2. Authorize a bureau and start it functioning.
3. Get the public excited about the national parks.
4. Make park travel easier by promoting wholesale improvements in hotels, camps, and other concessions and in roads and transportation facilities both inside the national parks and outside.
5. Sell national park integrity to the point where Congress would
   (a) add to the system all appropriate sites possible,
   (b) keep out inappropriate sites,
   (c) keep the established sites safe from invasion, and
   (d) purge the established sites of private holdings.

The first task was not easy, as previous attempts to get the U.S. Congress to establish a federal bureau had failed, beginning with a bill drafted by J. Horace McFarland and Frederick Law Olmsted Jr. in 1910. Seeing the difficult road ahead, Lane helped by appointing a young lawyer from California, Horace Albright, to assist him. Mather contributed to the cause by reaching into his own pockets to create the position of publicity chief, which he offered to Robert Sterling Yard, a friend from the *New York Sun*. Yard served in this position, and then chief, from 1915 to 1919. During his first year, Yard prepared *The National Parks Portfolio* for distribution to 270,000 opinion makers throughout the country, helped to generate numerous articles about the national parks, and personally wrote pamphlets and articles designed to capture the attention of the public (Albright, 1990). To convince Congress to support a bureau of national parks, Mather invited influential persons, including newspaper publishers and editors, railroad executives, and influential Congressmen to tour Sequoia National Park at his expense. As could be expected, primary opposition came from the Forest Service. With many of the parks next to national forests, Forest Service administrators hoped that the national parks would be transferred to the Department of Agriculture. On the other hand, the 1913 loss of Hetch Hetchy caused many conservationists to support the development of a bureau that could provide protection for the parks.

Mather's public relations campaign was a success. Congress appropriated the majority of the money needed to purchase Giant Forest within Sequoia National Park and the National Geographic Society donated the remainder needed. Public awareness increased as articles in prestigious magazines such as *National Geographic* and *Saturday Evening Post* as well as in prominent newspapers exulted America's natural beauty and supported the need for its preservation. In the meantime, Mather, too, visited most of the parks, gathering information about basic visitor needs.

In August 1916, President Woodrow Wilson signed the bill to establish the National Park Service that became Public Law 64-235. For 15 years, Mather ran the National Park Service as its first director, and Albright, who succeeded him as director in 1929, became his assistant. Major achievements soon followed. In 1916, Lassen Volcanic National Park (in California) and Hawaii National Park (now called Haleakala) were added to the system. Mount McKinley (now Denali) National Park was added in 1917. Attendance at all of the parks increased at a rapid rate, as did the de-

mand for material about the parks. Nonetheless, Mather was always under constant pressure from critics. He suffered a breakdown. During an 18-month rest, Albright took over. Returning with new zeal, Mather worked to open the parks to recreational activities, joined Albright in his fight to ward off commercial pressures, and opposed proposals for waterpower development in Yellowstone National Park (Strong, 1988). In his director's report, Mather made the following plea:

> Is there not some place in this great nation of ours where lakes can be preserved in their natural state; where we and all generations to follow us can enjoy the beauty and charm of mountain waters in the midst of primeval forests? The country is large enough to spare a few such lakes and beauty spots. The nation has wisely set apart a few national parks where a state of nature is to be preserved. If the lakes and forest of these parks cannot be spared from the hand of commercialization, what hope can we entertain for the preservation of any scenic features of the mountains in the interest of posterity? (*Report of the Director of the National Park Service*, 1919, p. 963)

Once the National Park Service was on solid ground, Mather took a few months off after a friend died and to recuperate from his latest round of battles. His next goal was to increase the service's holdings to include "scenery of supreme and distinctive quality or some natural features so extraordinary or unique as to be of national interest and importance" (*Report of the Secretary of Interior*, 1918, pp. 112–113). After the number of national parks and monuments nearly doubled, Mather decided to concentrate on extending some of their boundaries. Since extensions often involved expanding into the national forests, the rivalry between the two agencies openly grew. Although the Forest Service responded by preserving some of their prized scenic areas, most were eventually lost to the National Park Service. Mather also set up a commission to study potential parks in the east, supported the Save-the-Redwoods League to save the coastal redwoods of California, and championed the development of state parks throughout the nation by organizing a convention on state parks at Des Moines, Iowa, in 1921 (Strong, 1988).

In an effort to make all of the national parks and monuments accessible to the majority of Americans, Mather continued to invite congressional representatives and their families to visit these outstanding lands. While there, they were also driven on the poor roads. When appropriations for roads more than doubled, Mather stressed the importance of building roads through a portion of the most representative sections of the parks, but maintained that the remainder of the parks should remain as natural as possible. To arrange for visitor needs, Mather recommended that one qualified operator hold a license for the concessions to eliminate potential for commercialization and waste. This would also enable the government to approve rates and standards of service (Strong, 1988). Although there were those who opposed this system of regulated monopoly, others protested any form of improvements in the parks. Mather's greatest clash, however, was with corrupt politicians who pushed for franchises for friends. Mather fought back and won.

Stephen Mather, who accepted the invitation to come to Washington, did do something about the conditions of the nation's fledgling national parks and monuments. During his administration, he publicized the value of preserving the nation's heritage, designed policies that guide the public's use of scenic and historical resources, cultivated an exceptional personnel organization, launched campfire programs with park rangers, promoted museums and other means of interpretation, improved public access and use, blocked private enterprise from actions that would destroy a park's scenic beauty, arranged for large donations, and won the cooperation of Congress and big business. The national park system thus became a model for other countries. Although he planned to

stay in his position longer, Mather left the service after he suffered a massive stroke. His life is summarized on bronze markers through many parks, which read,

> He laid the foundation of the National Park Service, defining and establishing the policies under which its areas shall be developed and conserved, unimpaired for future generations. There will never come an end to the good he has done. . .

Aldo Leopold (1887–1948)

Prominent wildlife ecologist, uncommon conservationist, and environmental philosopher Aldo Leopold was born the eldest of four children in Burlington, Iowa. This Mississippi River community afforded him the opportunity to become acquainted with wildlife at a young age. He recognized the steady decline of the wood duck population and the forestlands. His father, Carl Leopold, who owned a thriving desk factory, enjoyed the outdoors and nature. Setting an example of sportsmanship for the younger Leopold, he refused to hunt waterfowl during the nesting season long before such practices were enacted by federal law. While in high school, Leopold kept a journal of his observations of nature, the beginnings of his prolific writings. Expected to take over the family business, he instead entered Yale University's Sheffield's Scientific School, where he received his BS in 1908. The following year he entered the Yale School of Forestry, founded by a grant from James Pinchot, and received his master of forestry degree. After graduation he was employed as a forest assistant on the Apache National Forest in Arizona in the Arizona Territory, just 4 years after the Forest Service was established. By 1911, Leopold was promoted to deputy forest supervisor and a year later to supervisor of the Carson National Forest in the New Mexico Territory, where he became aware that the country was losing its wilderness (Strong,1988, p. 137). He married Estella Bergere from Santa Fe, with whom he had five children. Starker, Luna, Nina, Carl, and Estella all built their own careers as conservationists and scientists.

Leopold's career was placed on hold for almost 17 months when he suffered from a near-fatal attack of acute nephritis, probably as a result of overexposure while camping during an assignment. During his convalescence he read widely including, most likely, the writings of Thoreau (Rogers & Ford, 1989). Returning to the service in 1914, he was assigned to the Office of Grazing at district headquarters in Albuquerque, where he became interested in the new science of ecology and began his life's work on wildlife management issues, including game refuges, law enforcement, and predator control (Williams, 2000). While working on recreation, fish, and game, Leopold recommended that game refuges be established within the district, and he prepared the Forest Service's first game and fish handbook. He founded a number of big-game protective associations in New Mexico and Arizona, edited a quarterly newspaper of the New Mexico Game Protective Association called *The Pine Cone*, and received the W. T. Hornaday's Permanent Wildlife Protection Fund's Gold Medal for his work in the field. Although Leopold was once an advocate of eliminating predators, including wolves and mountain lions, to preserve game species such as deer, he changed his opinion, advocating ecological balance. Years later in his essay "Thinking Like a Mountain," he shared a story about his earlier encounter with a dying old wolf, explaining, "I thought that because fewer wolves meant more deer, that no wolves would mean hunters' paradise. But after seeing the green fire die, I sensed that neither the wolf nor the mountain agreed with such a view" (Gibbons, 1981, p. 690).

In 1918, Leopold took a leave of absence from the Forest Service to become secretary of the Albuquerque Chamber of Commerce. Leopold was supportive of congressional action, which allowed national forestlands to be used for recreational as well as commercial purposes. With the United States' entry into World War I, the Forest Service was obligated to shift priorities from recreational development to a more utilitarian management of forest resources. Upon his return the next year as assistant district forester for operations in the southwestern region, he became concerned about the rapid pace of road expansion after the war and began to call for the protection of wilderness lands within the national forests as places of preservation and human activity. In 1921, he wrote his most significant article, "The Wilderness and its Place in Forest Recreational Policy," which was published in the *Journal of Forestry*. Through his efforts, the 500,000-acre Gila Wilderness Area in New Mexico became the first administrative wilderness designated for recreation in 1924. Camping and backpacking were permissible activities in the wilderness area, but tourist campgrounds were not to be provided. This novel plan was articulated 40 years later at the national level in the Wilderness Act, thereby making Leopold a "Pioneer of Wilderness" (Rogers & Ford, 1989, pp. 187–188). Leopold believed that wilderness preservation symbolized self-restraint in the developing society, served as a reminder of the pioneer legacy, and provided an undisturbed ecosystem for environmental study (Nash, 1974).

In 1924, Leopold moved to Madison, Wisconsin, to become the assistant, then associate director of the Forest Products Laboratory of the Forest Service. Continuing his efforts toward wilderness preservation, he wrote a 1925 article entitled "Wilderness as a Form of Land Use," in which he developed the notion that Americans no longer needed to conquer the wilderness, but that they needed to set aside large portions of it for posterity. As a speaker at the second National Conference on Outdoor Recreation in 1926, he called wilderness a fundamental recreational resource and urged the development of national wilderness preservation policy. William B. Greeley, U.S. Forest Service chief, endorsed his idea, and an inventory of roadless land areas in the United States was conducted and reported at the Third National Conference on Outdoor Recreation in 1928. By 1929, the pathfinding L-20 Regulations directed the Forest Service districts to preserve undeveloped land; thus began the movement to establish "primitive areas" within national forests (Rogers & Ford, 1989, pp. 188–189).

Leopold resigned from the Forest Service in 1928 to design a new profession in game management, which he modeled on the profession of forestry. His game survey of nine Midwestern states was funded by the Sporting Arms and Ammunition Manufacturers' Institute. These surveys were summarized in his 1931 *Report on a Game Survey of the North Central States,* one of the first intensive studies of game population ever undertaken in the United States. He also helped develop the country's first game management policy for the American Game Protective Association and was appointed to President Franklin D. Roosevelt's Committee on Wildlife Restoration. As one of the country's finest authorities on native game, Leopold became known as the "Father of Game Management" and more recently the "Father of Wildlife Ecology." In his landmark book, *Game Management* (1933), he clarified the fundamental skills and techniques for managing and restoring wildlife populations. By weaving forestry, agriculture, biology, zoology, ecology, education, and communication, he had created a new science and defined the new profession (Aldo Leopold Nature Center, 2001). Soon after publication, Leopold accepted an appointment to a new chair in the Department of Agricultural Economics at the University of Wisconsin. When the university created the Department of Wildlife Management in 1939, Leopold became the first person in the nation to chair the new science, holding this position until his death. Although Leopold spent the next several decades with wildlife management issues, his interests expanded to the field of ecology, where he is most revered today (Williams, 2000).

Leopold's concepts, based on the emerging science of systems ecology, synthesized the most progressive knowledge of population dynamics, food chains, and habitat protection (Nash, 1974). He noted that "we stand guard over works of art, but species representing the work of aeons are stolen from under our noses" (Gibbons, 1981, pp. 690–691). Basic to his beliefs was the idea that the environment is not a commodity for humans to control but a community to which they belong. This innovative idea stimulated the development of Leopold's most important concept, "the land ethic," which he wrote of in his most widely read book, *A Sand County Almanac:*

> A land ethic, then, reflects the existence of an ecological conscience, and this in turn reflects a conviction of individual responsibility for the health of the land. Health is the capacity of the land for self-renewal. Conservation is our effort to understand and preserve this capacity. . . . It is inconceivable to me that an ethical relation to land can exist without love, respect, and admiration for land, and a high regard for its value. By value, I of course mean something far broader than mere economic value; I mean value in the philosophical sense. Perhaps the most serious obstacle impeding the evolution of a land ethic is the fact that our educational and economic system is headed away from, rather than toward, an intense consciousness of land. . . . In short, land is something he has "outgrown." (Leopold, 1966, p. 236)

Although he had no religious affiliation of his own, many consider Leopold's "land ethic" a spiritual act of consequence to the future of life on earth (Nash, 1974). He rationalized that people develop a revolutionary appreciation for land by entering it, for land brings the human race to it as a responsible member of that land community, not as its conqueror. Although published after his death, *A Sand County Almanac* (1949) contains ecological essays that Leopold began before World War II. It shares a lifetime of his observations of nature and the development of his ideas. His work, which has been compared to that of Henry David Thoreau and John Muir, is regarded as a classic in environmental literature and a bible for the environmental movement. Many of his observations and essays were written at his vacation home, fondly known as "The Shack." When the Leopold family purchased a worn-out farm on the Wisconsin River in an area known as the sand counties near Baraboo in 1935, they rebuilt the only standing structure on the property, an old chicken coop, turning it into a cabin. Today, it is still called The Shack, and he would be proud to see the forest and prairie that surround it. True to his creed, Leopold and his family participated in the land's restoration by planting prairie and thousands of trees on the property. They also revitalized a low area into a wetland that attracts waterfowl. According to Leopold, "We abuse land when we regard it as a commodity belonging to us. When we see land as a community to which we belong, we may begin to use it with love and respect" (Hirsh, 1971, p. 150).

During Leopold's last vacation at The Shack, smoke was spotted across the swamp on a neighbor's farm. Gathering his family, he handed out buckets and brooms, and went with them to put out the fire, but in the process he died of a heart attack at age 61. Before his death, Leopold had been active in a number of conservation endeavors, which included member of the council of the Society of American Foresters (1927–1931); elected fellow 1946; director of the National Audubon Society; vice president of the American Forestry Association; founder of the Wilderness Society in 1935 with Robert Marshall, Benton MacKaye (also mentioned in the section on Thoreau), Harvey Broome, Barnard Frank, Harold Anderson, Ernest Oberholtzer, and Sterling Yard; president of the Wilderness Society in 1939; president of the Ecological Society of America (1947); and member of the Wisconsin Conservation Commission from 1943 until his death (Nash, 1974). Additionally, Leopold traveled to Germany to study forestry and wildlife management in the fall of 1935 when he received the Carl Schurz fellowship, and he took the first of two pack trips along the Rio Gavilan in Chihuahua, Mexico, in 1936. *Round River: From the Journal of Aldo Leopold* (1953), like *A Sand County Almanac,* was edited by his daughter Luna B. Leopold and published posthumously. Today, the Aldo Leopold Foundation holds the rights to all of his unpublished material and those works published by nonextant publications at the University of Wisconsin Archives.

SUMMARY

This chapter dealt with visionaries and practitioner pioneers who foresaw the need for preserving areas, establishing programs, and developing concepts that enhance the pursuit of leisure in natural resources. Transcendentalists Ralph Waldo Emerson and Henry David Thoreau venerated nature and called on citizens of this country and the world to respect and preserve it. The depth of their commitment is only overshadowed by the depth of the meaning behind their words. Both men were among the literary giants of the 19th century.

Scientist-naturalists John Audubon, John Muir, and Rachel Carson observed nature and recorded their observations, which were eventually shared with millions of people. Wilderness to them was a place of awe and worship. Their life work spearheaded a preservation movement that gained momentum in the mid-1900s and is in the mainstream of society's activity today.

Pioneer practitioners Frederick Law Olmsted, Gifford Pinchot, Stephen Mather, and Aldo Leopold put into practice the concepts gained from the transcendentalists and scientist-naturalists. They laid the foundations for the nation's fledgling institutions that manage the recreational resources, and they helped to shape the roles of the park rangers and foresters who manage the natural resources for multiple use, limited use, and the betterment of the ecosystem. Frederick Law Olmsted is called the father of the American park, Gifford Pinchot was the pioneer of American forests, Stephen Mather was the first director of the National Park Service, and Aldo Leopold was a promoter of wilderness areas and a founder of the Wilderness Society.

REFERENCES

Albright, J. (1990). Yard, R. S. In W. Sontag (Ed.), *National Park Service: The first 75 years* (p. 63). Fort Washington, PA: Eastern National Park & Monument Association.

Aldo Leopold Nature Center. (2001). Who was Aldo Leopold? Retrieved from http://www.naturenet.com/alnc/aldo.html

Atkinson, B. (Ed.). (1950). *The selected writings of Ralph Waldo Emerson.* New York, NY: Modern.

Audubon, J. J. (1960). *Audubon and his journals* (Vol. I–II). New York, NY: Dover.

Benet, L. (1966). *Famous English and American essayists.* New York, NY: Dodd-Mead.

Bolton, S. (1954). *Famous American authors.* New York, NY: Thomas Y. Crowell.

Brooks, P. (1972). *The house of life: Rachel Carson at work.* Boston, MA: Houghton Mifflin.

Cameron, J. (1928). *The development of forest control in the United States.* Baltimore, MD: Johns Hopkins University Press.

Carson, R. L. (1951). *The sea around us.* New York, NY: Oxford University Press.

Carson, R. L. (1962). *Silent spring.* New York, NY: Houghton Mifflin.

Carson, R. (1963, September/October). Rachel Carson answers her critics. *Audubon, 1963,* 65–66, 262.

Carson, R. (1965). Rachel Carson answers her critics. *Audubon, 65,* 262–265, 313–315.

DDT ban accelerated. (1997). *Birders World, 1997.*

De Bruhl, M. (1981). Carson. In *Dictionary of American biography* (Suppl. 7, pp. 1961–1965). New York, NY: Charles Scribner's Sons.

Doell, C., & Twardzik, L. (1979). *Elements of park and recreation administration.* Minneapolis, MN: Burgess.

Downing, L. (1992). *John Muir and the United States national park system* [Speech]. Retrieved from http://vault.sierraclub.org/john_muir_exhibit/life/muir_and_nps_downing_1992.aspx

Duncan, D., & Burns, K. (2009). *The national parks: America's best idea.* New York, NY: Alfred A. Knopf.

Elliott, D. (2007, May 27). Carson's 'Silent Spring' still making noise [Transcript]. Retrieved from http://www.npr.org/templates/story/story.php:storyId=10486240.

Elman, R. (1977). *First in the field.* New York, NY: Mason/Chartu.

Fisher, C. (1949). *The life of Audubon.* New York, NY: Harper and Brothers.

Fisher, I. D. (1986). *Frederick Law Olmsted and the city planning movement in the United States.* Ann Arbor, MI: UMI Research Press.

Ford, P. (1989). John Muir. In H. Ibrahim (Ed.), *Pioneers in leisure* (pp. 35–46). Reston, VA: American Alliance for Health, Physical Education, Recreation, and Dance.

Fox, S. R. (1981). *John Muir and his legacy: The American conservation movement.* Boston, MA: Little, Brown.

Gartner, C. (1983). *Rachel Carson.* New York, NY: Frederick Ungar.

Gibbons, B. (1981, November). Aldo Leopold: A durable scale of values. *National Geographic, 160*(5), 682–708.

Gilbert, A. (1914). *More than conquerors.* New York, NY: Century.

Gore, A. (2006). Foreword. In R. Carson (narrated by Kaiulani Lee), *Silent spring* [Audio book]. New York, NY: Recorded Books.

Graham, F., Jr. (1970). *Since silent spring.* Boston, MA: Houghton Mifflin.

Grossman, A., & Beardwood, V. (1961). *Trails of his own.* New York, NY: Longmans, Green.

Harding, W. (1954). *Thoreau: A century of criticism.* Dallas, TX: Southern Methodist University Press.

Havard, R. (1989). Frederick Law Olmsted. In H. Ibrahim (Ed.), *Pioneers in leisure and recreation* (pp. 27–34). Reston, VA: American Alliance for Health, Physical Education, Recreation, and Dance.

Henry David Thoreau. (1998). In *Encyclopædia Britannica* (15th ed.) [CD-ROM]. Chicago, IL: Encyclopædia Britannica.

Hirsh, C. S. (1971). *Guardians of tomorrow.* New York, NY: Viking.

Holmes, M. (2004). *American women conservationists.* Jefferson, NC: McFarland.

Jubenville, A. (1976). *Outdoor recreation planning.* Philadelphia, PA: W. B. Saunders.

Knudson, D. (1984). *Outdoor recreation.* New York, NY: Macmillan.

Lear, L. (2000). Rachel Louise Carson. Retrieved from http://www.rachelcarson.org/index.cfm?fuseaction=bio

Leopold, A. (1966). *A Sand County almanac.* New York, NY: Oxford University Press.

Leshuk, D. (1988). John Muir's Wisconsin days. Retrieved from http://www.sierraclub.org/john_muir_exhibit/life/muir_wisconsin_dave_leshuk.html

Matthiessen, P. (1999, June 14). Environmentalist Rachel Carson. *Time.* Retrieved from www.time.com/time/time100/scientist/profile/carson.html

Muir, J. (1975). *The story of my boyhood and youth.* Dunwoody, GA: Norman S. Berg. (Original work published 1913)

Muir, J. (1977). *The mountains of California.* Berkeley, CA: Ten Speed Press. (Original work published 1984)

M.V.D. (1931). Emerson. In *Dictionary of American biography* (Vol. VI). New York, NY: Charles Scribner's Sons.

Nash, R. (1970). *The call of the wild* (1900–1916). New York, NY: George Braziller.

Nash, R. (1974). Aldo Leopold. In *Dictionary of American biography* (Suppl. 4, pp. 146–150). New York, NY: Charles Scribner's Sons.

National Audubon Society. (2001). John James Audubon 1785–1851. Retrieved from http//www.jjaudubon.com/bio/chronos.html

National Park Service. (1998). Olmsted and sons: The Olmsted office, 1–4. Retrieved from http://www.nps.gov/frla/background.htm

Olmsted, F., Jr., & Kimball, T. (Eds.). (1970). *Frederick Law Olmsted, landscape architect, 1822–1903.* New York, NY: Benjamin Blorn.

Penick, J., Jr. (1974). Gifford Pinchot. In *Dictionary of American biography* (Suppl. 4, p. 1946) New York, NY: Charles Scribner's Sons.

Pennsylvania Historical and Museum Commission. (2001). Gifford Pinchot. Retrieved from http://www.portal.state.pa.us/portal/server.pt/community/gifford_pinchot/13877

Report of the Director of the National Park Service, 66th Congress 2nd session, H.Doc. 409 (1919).

Report of the Secretary of Interior, 65th Congress, 3rd session, H.Doc.1455 (1918).

Rogers, S. E., & Ford, P. (1989). Aldo Leopold. In H. Ibrahim (Ed.), *Pioneers in leisure and recreation* (pp. 183–194). Reston, VA: American Alliance of Health, Physical Education, Recreation, and Dance.

Ronald, A. (1987). *Words from the wild.* San Francisco, CA: Sierra Club Books.

Rothe, A. (Ed.). (1952). *Current biography: Who's new and why, 1951.* New York, NY: H. W. Wilson.

R.W.A. & H.S.C. (1936). Thoreau. In *Dictionary of American biography* (Vol. XVIII). New York, NY: Charles Scribner's Sons.

Ryan, P. (1990). John Muir. In W. Sontag (Ed.), *National Park Service: The first 75 years.* Fort Washington, PA: Eastern National Park & Monument Association.

Schildgen, B. (2001). Deconstructing Thoreau. *Sierra, 86*(6), 74.

Shankland, R. (1970). *Steven Mather of the national parks* (3rd ed.). New York, NY: Alfred A. Knopf.

Simpson, R. (1989). Stephen T. Mather. In H. Ibrahim (Ed.), *Pioneers in leisure and recreation* (pp. 93–101). Reston, VA: American Alliance for Health, Physical Education, Recreation, and Dance.

Steinbauer, M. (Ed.). (1990). The life of 100 most important Americans of the 20th century [Special issue]. *Life, 13*(12).

Stevenson, E. (1977). *Park maker: A life of Frederick Law Olmsted.* New York, NY: Macmillan.

Strong, D. (1988). *Dreamers and defenders: American conservationists.* Lincoln: University of Nebraska Press.

Teale, E. (1962). *The thoughts of Thoreau.* New York, NY: Dodd, Mead.

Teale, F. (1954). *The wilderness world of John Muir.* Boston, MA: Houghton Mifflin.

Thoreau, H. (1965). *The Maine woods.* West Raven, CT: College and University Press. (Original work published 1864)

Vickery, J. (1989). Wilderness visions. *Backpacker, 17*(5), 45.

W.F.B. (1934). John Muir. In *Dictionary of American biography* (Vol. XIII). New York, NY: Charles Scribner's Sons.

White, G. (Ed.). (1996). *John Muir: The wilderness journeys.* Retrieved from http://www.sierraclub.org/john_muir_exhibit/life/wilderness_journeys_white.html

Wilkins, T. (1995). *John Muir: Apostle of nature.* Norman: University of Oklahoma Press.

Williams, G. (2000). *The USDA Forest Service–The first century* (FS-650). Washington, DC: USDA Forest Service.

Wolf, W. (1974). *Thoreau: Mystic, prophet, ecologist.* Philadelphia, PA: Pilgrim Press.

Wolfe, L. M. (1979). *John of the Mountains The unpublished journals of John Muir.* Madison: University of Wisconsin Press.

Wolfe, L. (1945). *Son of the wilderness: The life of John Muir.* Madison: The University of Wisconsin Press.

Chapter 4

Psychology and the Natural Environment

This chapter concerns the psychology of the outdoor experience. We will give a short presentation of the field of psychology, followed by a presentation of the different attempts to explain the outdoor experience in psychological terms. Attempts at analyzing leisure activities as a unit have not been fruitful in producing a unified psychology of leisure. Ingham (1986) suggested that these attempts can be classified into two approaches: the experiential approach, which emphasizes the subjective qualities of the leisure experience, relying extensively on self-reporting with little attempt at discovering the underlying physiological bases that accompany these experiences, and a second approach that includes the reported motivation, satisfaction, and attribute of the leisure experience. It seems that the two schools of thought do not see eye to eye as few mutual citations appear in the research, but they both tend to agree that perceived freedom (from obligation) and intrinsic motivation (an activity for its own sake) are two concepts to which they can subscribe.

LEISURE AS A STATE OF MIND

The difficulty in viewing leisure as a state of mind lies only in that leisure is a complex phenomenon. Its physiological, social, and psychological dimensions usually overlap. Analyzing the psychological side of the leisure experience is of interest to a small number of psychologists, who suggested a number of criteria for a bona fide leisure experience to occur.

Perceived Freedom

To John Neulinger (1974), at least early in his career, the primary psychological factor in a leisure experience is perceived freedom. This is "a state in which the person feels that what he is doing, he is doing by choice and because he wants to do it" (p. 15). What is relevant is that the person perceives the activity as being freely chosen. Neulinger later added two more criteria: motivation for the leisure activity and the quality of its outcome. According to Kelly (1987), these two criteria are attitudinal, criteria which "can be found in almost any context since there is no necessary condition for the perception outside the individual" (p. 26). A recent study showed that when adolescents engaged in activities because they wanted to, they reported lower levels of boredom and higher levels of intrinsic motivation (Caldwell, Darling, Payne, & Dowdy, 1999).

The concept of freedom in leisure research has been criticized in that it does not differentiate between freedom from (stress) and freedom to (choose an activity). Nonetheless, this concept is still in use in defining leisure behavior (Mannell & Kleiber, 1999).

Autotelic Activities

These are activities that are meaningful in, and by, themselves. "Does greater freedom always lead to greater leisure?" asked Mannell and Bradley (1986). In their study of freedom and leisure, they found that externally oriented subjects were less absorbed in their leisure experience than the internally oriented subjects. Their findings add support to the contention that it is perceived freedom that is critical in determining the experience of leisure.

Perception continues to be important in the work of Mihaly Csikszentmihalyi (1975). To him, the individual's perception of the activity is what matters, not the mere perception of freedom. If the participant perceives the activity as too difficult to handle, anxiety will occur. On the other hand, if the activity is perceived as too easy, boredom will result. He labeled the optimum condition for a meaningful experience of activity as "flow." More on this concept will be discussed later.

Beneficial Outcome

The work of Driver (1976) concentrated on studying the benefits derived from leisure experiences. Driver employed a series of scales to measure the outcomes of the recreational use of natural resources. Thirty-nine psychological benefits representing 19 domains were identified, and the Recreation Experience Preference (REP) scales were constructed to measure these benefits. According to Driver's model, a person will partake of a leisure activity because of his or her expectations for a positively valued benefit.

Driver and Brown (1978) later developed a system that would assist managers of leisure delivery systems to use the information gained from REP scales which they entitled the Recreation Opportunity Spectrum (ROS). The system presents the leisure environment as a spectrum of opportunity available to the individual. It identifies six levels of "naturalness": primitive, semi primitive non-motorized, semi primitive motorized, roaded natural, rural, and urban. For ROS, the more primitive the setting, the more one can experience solitude, tranquility, self-reliance, and closeness to nature.

There will be more discussion of the psychological benefits of outdoor experience later in this chapter. We will first examine whether certain traits in some individuals make them inclined to partake of leisure experience.

TRAITS AND THE LEISURE EXPERIENCE

Personality traits can be looked upon as continuous dimensions on which individual differences can be observed. Thus, different leisure preferences may be arranged quantitatively or qualitatively. Traits are dispositions that may determine leisure behavior. Perhaps the most intriguing trait pertaining to outdoor recreation is the type T personality, belonging to the thrill seekers, risk takers, and adventurers who seek excitement and stimulation, giving activity providers great worry and undue headaches.

Although personality may cause or direct leisure behavior and experience, that relationship is complex (Mannell & Kleiber, 1999). Nonetheless, it is important to look into the traits that may affect leisure choice.

Leisure and the Type T Personality

According to Farley (1986), the type T personality is on one end of a continuum. At the opposite end of that continuum is the type t personality (with a lowercase t), belonging to those who cling to certainty and predictability. Most people fall in between these two extremes. One with a type T personality has a low physiological arousability and therefore seeks excitement. Humans normally seek to adjust to some middle ground between high and low arousals. Some are born with unusually low arousability and are not very responsive to mental or physical stimuli, and these are big *T* persons who may seek highly stimulating experiences and environments. The precise biological bases for their low arousability is not yet known. Coupled with biological differences are personality traits that set big *T* persons apart from others: They tend to be more creative, more extroverted, and more experimental, and they tend to take more risks.

The Explorers Club, perhaps the most prestigious organization for adventurers in the world, which in the recent past was for males only, had 85 women among its 3,000 members in the 1990s. Among the risk activities women have partaken are crossing the Australian outback alone on a camel for 5 months covering 1,700 miles, ascending Ana Purna's 26,000 feet, and crossing Papua New Guinea alone on foot. Why did Jan Reynolds climb up to 25,000 feet to ski off peak Mustagata in western China? She answered, "The deep, smooth satisfaction I felt after I skied off Mustagata, under the golden, fading light of day was something that I will feel very seldom, if ever again, and that I will treasure like a precious jewel" (Mills, 1986, p. 27).

Leisure and Personality Traits

In studying personality, theorists describe it as comprising trait dimensions along a series of continua. These traits affect behavior, including leisure choices. Driver and Knopf (1977) used the Personality Research Form (PRF) to investigate the traits of 50 recreationists and arrived at the following conclusions:

1. Personality traits probably influence the choice of the recreational activity in which a person engages most frequently.
2. Selected personality variables are significantly related to the amount of participation in a preferred activity once the choice has been made.
3. Personality traits influence how important different desired consequences (or experiences) are to a recreationist when he or she decides to engage in preferred activities.

A criticism of the dependence on traits to try to understand leisure behavior is based on the exclusion of the role of the environment, both physical and social. A relatively

Personality traits seem to influence the choice of the recreational activity in which people engage most frequently. The Chesapeake and Ohio Canal National Historical Park follows the route of the 184-mile canal along the Potomac River. At Great Falls in Maryland, a number of activities are available to suit individual tastes from a peaceful day of fishing to an adventurous day of white-water kayaking in the falls. Other activities include hiking, bicycling, horseback riding, rock climbing, nature photography, ranger-led programs, and visitations to historic sites.

new interest in environmental psychology helps in discovering the role it plays in leisure behavior.

ENVIRONMENT AND THE LEISURE EXPERIENCE

What role does the environment, particularly the natural environment, play in the motivation for, attitudes toward, and satisfaction with a leisure experience? Stokols and Altman (1987), experts in environmental psychology, suggested that the emphasis in psychological research in the past concentrated on personal traits and interaction. Those who study traits look for universal laws, and those who study interaction focus on the relationships among the elements. Units of analysis are used to arrive at conclusions concerning the motivation for and the satisfaction with certain behaviors.

For our purposes, neither the trait nor the interactional approach produces a theoretical framework that is useful for the understanding of leisure behavior. We agree with the authors that if the transactional approach is examined, a better understanding of the role of the environment in human behavior will occur. Needless to say, such an approach is also relevant to the understanding of the leisure experience in a natural setting, which is the focus of this volume.

Attempts at finding answers to the question posed earlier on the role that the environment plays in the motivation for, attitudes toward, and the satisfaction with certain experiences, including leisure experiences, were made by a new type of psychologist. According to Williams (1986), a shift in the approach of social psychology from examining the person independent of his or her setting to examining the person within his or her setting occurred in the late 1960s. Research conducted on the relationship between the individual and the setting can be roughly divided into three perspectives. The first approach, called experimental aesthetics, is used to address the meaning of the setting in the person's experience. The second approach, environmental cognition,

is used to address the meaning of the setting in the experience, which is a reflection of one's perception of the setting. The third approach, called behavioral ecology, is focused on directly observable behavioral patterns in the natural setting. Williams summarized the findings of each approach as follows.

Experimental Aesthetics

Research in this area is focused on structural or organizational qualities of the natural environment, for example, how manicured is the park? An aesthetic experience occurs following an affective event that is based on a certain level of arousal. This level is dependent on the structural or organizational qualities mentioned. Physiological arousal is experienced as a euphoric feeling and is seen as a major source of intrinsic motivation (Ellis, 1973), yet arousal alone is not a sufficient condition for a leisure experience to take place—arousal could occur at work, for example. In fact, too much arousal, even in leisure activity, may end the perception of the activity as leisure. An activity that started as leisure may become too structured.

Environmental Cognition

According to Williams (1986), the emphasis here is on the perception of the environment, which is looked upon as a source of information rather than a source of stimulation. Interpreting the attributes of a natural setting could give clues as to the recreationally significant conditions and outcomes, for example, a fully packed slope will provide for an exhilarating skiing experience. Because human beings tend to categorize and label their experiences, accumulation of categories and labels could be useful, particularly to the manager of a leisure delivery system. Tversky and Hemenway (1983) applied this technique to natural environments; they identified their attributes and asked the subjects to identify the activities that were appropriate to each category, a process that could prove helpful to planners and managers, as will be presented under a subsequent section on the experience of nature.

Behavioral Ecology

This approach is concerned with how people experience and behave in everyday settings, including natural settings and not in research-contrived settings. Settings become the basic units that are used in analyzing behavior within a given space and for a specific time span; for example, studying behavior within a park at a particular season takes into consideration not only the physical attributes of the setting but also the psychological and social dimensions of behavior in the recreational place. This approach could prove helpful to managers and providers of leisure experiences including experiences in natural settings.

THE EXPERIENCE OF NATURE

Kaplan and Kaplan (1989) tried to answer a number of questions on the effect of the natural environment on human behavior:

1. Is the effect of nature on humans as powerful as it intuitively seems to be?
2. What lies behind the power of environments that not only attracts the appreciation of individuals but also makes many of them capable of restoring healthy and effective functioning?
3. Are some natural patterns, such as meadows, more effective than others, such as lakes?

In a more recent study on the nature experience, data were collected from a sample of wilderness visitors multiple times during a visit to the Okefenokee National Wildlife Refuge. Four modes of environmental experience (focus on self, others, task, and environment) and four aspects of wilderness experience (a combined oneness/primitiveness/humility variable, timelessness, solitude, and care) were measured. Univariate and multivariate repeated measures analyses demonstrated significant change from the entry, through immersion, to the exit phases of the wilderness experience. This ex-

periential change included greater focus on the environment and on self/introspection at the exit compared with the entry phase and less focus on others/social acceptance during the immersion phase. Scores on humility/primitiveness/oneness were higher at both the immersion and exit phases than during entry, and care for the wilderness was higher during the exit phase than during entry (Borrie & Roggenbuck, 2001).

Ongoing empirical work also highlights the power of emotions in predicting pro-environmental behaviors and intentions. Hinds and Sparks (2008) found that increased emotional environmental connection indicates a higher likelihood of engagement with environmental issues among 199 undergraduate students in the United Kingdom. Sia, Hungerford, and Tomera (1985/1986) and Vaske and Kobrin (2001) found that if people identify with places and/or have a high sensitivity toward places, they may be more likely to engage in day-to-day pro-environmental behaviors. Finally, Brehm, Eisenhauer, and Stedman (2013) found that place meanings (the emotional dimensions of person–place relations) are more predictive of environmental concern than place attachment (the strength of connection to a setting). In summary, emotions should be carefully considered in exploring the puzzle and potential of person–place relationships and the ability of those relationships to translate into environmental concern, intentions, and behaviors.

Earlier, Kaplan and Kaplan (1989) came to a number of conclusions on the experience of nature. To them, humans are very sensitive to the spatial property of the environment and tend to categorize environments on the basis of their perception. This process produces a number of coherent perceptual categories. For example, research shows that wide-open, undifferentiated vistas as well as dense, impenetrable forests fail to provide information about one's whereabouts. These two settings tend to fall within a distinct category. Scenes that convey a sense of orderliness, such as manicured settings, are a second category, and a third category includes forests that are transparent, allowing sunlight to filter down, providing information on both accessibility and direction. These last two categories are preferred, which means that to attract the most people, a natural setting must include informational patterns that are readily interpretable. These informational patterns are, in many instances, provided by nature itself, and not necessarily by humans, as seen in the case of the transparent forest.

Natural Settings and Information Rate

Mehrebian and Russell (1974) suggested that because an outdoor natural setting is characterized by having a smaller density and slower pace of change than an artificially created setting whether outdoor or indoors, a natural setting has a lower information rate, which many recreationists prefer. The concept of information rate can be explained by comparing two paintings, one containing two colors, the other eight colors, which means that the latter has four times as much "information" to deal with than the former. But the idea behind information rate is much more complicated and requires the use of mathematical formulas that are beyond the scope of this volume. Suffice it to say that the number of colors in the above examples is not the only variable to be considered in calculating the information rate. The space that each color covers and its location on the painting need to be considered as well.

According to aforementioned authors, the acceleration of information input triggers the general adaptation syndrome suggested by Selye in 1956. The syndrome begins with a burdensome physiological arousal and a concomitant feeling of displeasure. A high rate of information input takes place in crowded, condensed areas. As a result, "understandably, those residing in congested urban areas express unrelenting desires to visit simple and rural settings such as national parks" (Mehrebian & Russell, 1974, p. 205). Mehrebian and Russell (1974) concluded that the relationship between internal behavioral patterns and external rhythms suggests a mechanism that directly relates arousal to information rate from the environment. It is not surprising, therefore, that the tempo of work, and even recreation, in an urban setting far exceeds that in a natural setting.

Preference for Natural Settings

Kaplan and Kaplan (1989) suggested that in the context of natural settings, those with human intrusions are less preferred than those where nature dominates. In the meantime, in very open vistas as well as in blocked areas, where it is difficult to anticipate what might happen, preference tends to be very low. In other words, humans respond negatively to both a high rate and paucity of visual information. This suggests that preference for a setting is related to how effectively a person can perceive himself or herself functioning in it. Humans prefer a setting where they feel safe, comfortable, and competent. Nonetheless, a natural setting could post an enticing challenge to some persons or to others under their charge, who may have low arousability. A challenge of nature may help some people to achieve optimal arousability (see Leisure and the Type T Personality section).

Wilderness: A Threat or a Challenge

In the past, the wilderness posed a problem to human beings in their quest for survival. Although survival in the wilderness is rarely a concern in modern life, today human activities in the wilderness are basically recreational in nature. Some recreationists may encounter threats, yet others welcome the challenge presented by nature.

Programs in wilderness survival abound and are used to experience self-discovery and enhance self-concept. In the 1980s, there were over 300 wilderness programs in the world, many of which were directed toward special populations such as juvenile delinquents and those who live with a disability. These programs are conducted for young people, adults, and seniors (see Table 4.1). Outward Bound was established by Kurt Hahn and is considered a prototype wilderness challenge program (Ewert & Hahn, 1989). The first Outward Bound school was started in Wales in 1941 to train merchant marines to withstand the challenges they

Table 4.1
Outdoor Challenge Participants

Year	No. groups	Boys	Girls	Adults	Total	
1972	2	10			10	
1973	2	12	8		20	
1974	1	8			8	
1975	3	13	6	4	23	
1976	3	6	12	8	26	
1977	2	6	3	3	12	
1978	3	6	7	6	19	
1979	3	5	3	3	11	
1980	6	11	11	13	35	
1981	2		3	9	12	
Total	27	77	53	46	176	

Note. From *The Experience of Nature*, by R. Kaplan and S. Kaplan, 1989, Cambridge, United Kingdom: Cambridge University Press, p. 124. Reprinted with permission.

had to face during World War II. The school was later moved to the United States. Burton (1981) listed five features of Outward Bound and similar programs:

1. a contrasting or novel physical environment,
2. a challenging set of problem-solving tasks,
3. a duration of at least seven days,
4. a leader or instructor, and
5. a group of at least four participants.

In outdoor activities wilderness may include many threats to the recreationist. Coping with threats in the wilderness varies according to the setting and the situation. A study showed that solo hikers experience five types of fears: the fear of getting hurt by another individual, the fear of accidental injury/life-threatening emergency, the fear of getting lost, the fear of wild animals and dogs, and the fear of the theft of belongings left in one's vehicle. Accordingly, five strategies were employed by solo hikers to negotiate objective threats and perceived fears including avoiding perceived threats, modifying their participation in solo hiking, using aids or protective devices, expanding their knowledge or skills, and employing a psy-

chological approach. Results from the study suggest that the solo hiking experience can be diminished, maintained, or optimized depending on the capacity of the participant to negotiate these threats and fears (Coble, Selin, & Erickson, 2003).

In a previous study, the relationships between a number of encounters (i.e., crowding, solitude, and overall experience) among 185 backcountry visitors were measured, and it seems that most backpackers were negatively affected by encountering more groups, but the resultant effect was too small. That means that careful understanding of supply and demand for different recreational experiences should provide the basis to impose use limits (Stewart & Cole, 2001).

A number of pertinent questions were raised by Kaplan and Kaplan (1989): Does it require a wilderness setting to experience self-discovery and enhance self-concept? Does it take 2 weeks to achieve such gains? Are there shortcuts to achieve a sense of tranquility and a feeling of oneness with nature?

Kaplan and Kaplan (1989) stated that Thoreau wrote of nature as a source of spiritual renewal and inspiration. A surprising outcome of the wilderness research that they reviewed is the remarkable depth of spiritual impact wilderness experiences have on those who participate in them. Yet the participants spent much less time in the wilderness and were engaged in less overtly cerebral activities than those of Thoreau. Kaplan and Kaplan called his quest for tranquility, peace, and silence a quest for serenity. In addition, the researchers seem to have found two more quests occurring among the participants: oneness and integration. Kaplan and Kaplan concluded that they had not anticipated this research program would provide them with an education in the ways of human nature. They felt they had been introduced to human concerns that are bound to broaden the conception of human motivation and priorities.

What is intriguing about the aforementioned results is that they correspond with what Aristotle suggested in the remote past—that the greatest of leisure experience is contemplation, which he placed at the top of the hierarchy of leisure experiences (see Figure 1.1). Human life has become so complicated that contemplation is rarely a priority in human affairs. Understanding the nature of human motivation as it relates to human needs may shed more light on the nature of the leisure experience.

MOTIVATION, HUMAN NEEDS, AND LEISURE

Among the many attempts to understand human behavior, including leisure behavior in the natural setting, is the attempt to answer the question, what motivates a person to partake of a certain activity? The question of motivation has been a major part of research in psychology from the beginning. Researchers concentrated their efforts on finding a single factor that is responsible for human behavior. The terms *instinct* and *drive* were used to describe this single factor.

Early Motivational Theories

The term *instinct* was used to describe a variety of human behaviors in the pre–World War I era. In his classic textbook *The Principles of Psychology*, James (1890) defined instinct as the capability to act so as to bring about a certain event. Human beings possess many instincts, among which is the one (or ones) that motivate(s) them to play, recreate, and participate in leisure activity. The question became, which instinct? Although the scholars who attempted to answer this question at that time agreed that humans are instinctually motivated to play and recreate, they did not agree on the nature of the instinct. Accordingly, four theories were forwarded, which could lead to contradictory outcomes given the same circumstances (Levy, 1979). The surplus energy theory, which explains play as based on leftover energy, contradicts the relaxation theory and the teleological theory, which explain leisure behavior in terms of the future, and all three contradict the recapitulation theory, which explains leisure behavior in terms of the past. Although these theories have been, in general, discarded by leisure scholars, they served as precursors to some of the recent interpretations that there is a biological basis for play and recreation (Eisen, 1988; Marano, 1999).

The concept of drive was adopted by psychologists after World War I and was used to explain human behavior as attempts to reduce certain needs. An essential group of needs were termed primary needs, which were deemed necessary for survival. Human beings attempt to reduce the need for food, warmth, exertion, sex, and security and accordingly achieve homeostasis, a state of physiologic equilibrium. Another group of needs were called secondary needs, which stem from the circumstances that surround people's attempts to satisfy the primary needs. Among these needs are achievement, affiliation, creativity, curiosity, gregariousness, risk, self-abasement, and self-assertion. Later, the terms *basic needs* and *acquired needs* were used to describe primary and secondary needs, respectively (see Table 4.2). At a working session on needs and leisure held at the University of Illinois some years ago, the following list of 17 needs or groups of needs deemed important to leisure behavior were generated:

Table 4.2

Selected Goals and Philosophy of Science

	Unit of analysis	Time and change	Causation	Observations	Other
Trait	Persons, Psychological qualities of persons.	Usually assume stability; change infrequent in present operation: change often occurs according to preestablished teleological mechanisms and developmental stages.	Emphasizes *material causes* objective, and detached from phenomena: i.e., cause internal to phenomena.	Observers are separate, objective, and detached from phenomena; equivalent observations by different observers.	Focus on trait and seek universal laws of psychological functioning according to few principles associated with person qualities; study prediction and manifestation of trait in various psychological domains.
Interactional	Psychological qualities of person and social or physical environment underlying entities, between parts.	Change results from interaction of separate person and environment times occurs in accord with underlying regulatory mechanisms, e.g., homeostasis; time and not intrinsic to phenomena.	Emphasizes *efficient causes* from phenomena: i.e., antecedent consequent relations, causation.	Observers are separate, objective, and detached from phenomena; equivalent observations by different observers.	Focus on elements and relations between variables and parts of system: understand system by prediction and control and by cumulating additive information about relations between elements.
Organismic	Holistic entities composed of separate person and environment components, elements or parts whose relations and interactions yield qualities of the whole that are "more than the sum of the parts."	Change results from interaction of person and environment entities. Change usually occurs in accord with underlying regulatory mechanisms, e.g., homeostasis and long-range directional teleological mechanisms, i.e., ideal developmental states. Change irrelevant once ideal state is reached, assumes that system is goal.	Emphasizes *final causes*, i.e., teleology, "pull" toward ideal state.	Observers are separate, objective, and detached from phenomena; equivalent observations by different observers.	Focus on principles that govern the whole, emphasize unity of knowledge, principles of holistic systems and hierarchy of subsystems; identify principles and laws of whole system.
Transactional	Holistic entities composed of "aspects," not separate parts or psychological phenomena; aspects are mutually defining: temporal qualities are intrinsic wholes.	Stability/change are intrinsic and defining features of psychological phenomena; change occurs continuously; directions of change emergent and not preestablished.	Emphasizes *formal causes*, i.e., description and understanding of patterns, shapes, and form of phenomena.	Relative: Observers are aspects of phenomena; observers in different "locations" (physical and psychological) yield different information about phenomena.	Focus on event, i.e., confluence people, space, and time; describe and understand patterning and forms of events; openness in seeking general principles, but primary interest in accounting for event: pragmatic application of principles and laws as appropriate to situations; openness to emergent explanation principles; prediction acceptable if not necessary.

Note. From *Handbook of Environmental Psychology*, by D. Stokols and I. Altman, 1987, New York, NY: John Wiley and Sons, pp. 12–13. Reprinted with permission.

1. Enjoying nature, escaping civilization
2. Escape from routine and responsibility
3. Physical exercise
4. Creativity
5. Relaxation, self-improvement, ability
6. Social contact
7. Meeting new people
8. Contact with prospective mates
9. Family contact
10. Recognition status
11. Social power
12. Altruism (helping others)
13. Stimulus seeking
14. Self-actualization (feedback, self-improvement, ability utilization)
15. Challenge, achievement, competition
16. Killing time, avoiding boredom
17. Intellectual aestheticism

Crandall (1980) suggested that behavior, including leisure behavior, is caused by the interaction of the person and the situation. Levy (1979) advocated that behavior is a function of the interaction of needs (of persons) and pressure (from the environment). This interactive model was used to identify a number of environmental contexts. When it comes to leisure behavior, the person–environment interactive model could be used to explain the need for a leisure experience. Levy (1977) reported that the need for relaxation is a leading motive for engaging in leisure behavior, a position which supported Dumazedier's (1967) claim to the same.

A few years later Ruskin and Shamir (1984) identified relaxation as a key motivation in leisure behavior. No research has been conducted since then, and recently, an author lamented the fact that relaxation is neglected in leisure research (Kleiber, 2000). On the other hand, human needs are much more complicated than simple responses to primary and secondary drives, as shown in the following study.

London, Crandall, and Fitzgibbons (1977) found that the respondents in their study viewed leisure activities in terms of three need dimensions: liking, feedback, and positive interpersonal involvement (see Table 4.3). To develop a psychologically meaningful categorization of leisure activities, the authors considered three elements simultaneously: the activities, the needs they satisfy, and individual differences in perceiving the activity. Factor analyses were applied, and the findings seem to replicate activity dimensions found in previous studies. Leisure activity in a natural setting was not included among these activities, but the data show that leisure activities fulfill a multitude of needs such as feedback, liking, and positive interpersonal involvement. Tinsley and Kass (1978) found their results to be in substantial agreement with previous studies. Needs such as catharsis, independence, advancement, getting along with others, reward, understanding, activity, ability, utilization, and exhibition appear to be mostly leisure activity specific.

Need, as a concept, became central to the attempts to give psychological meaning to leisure behavior. But what is a leisure need? Most of the studies cited here treated it as being stable, whereas Iso-Ahola and Allen (1982) suggested that the need for leisure is not stable but is always changing. They referred to a leisure need as a perceived reason for participating in a variety of activities. One of the assumptions in their approach involves change across situations under which needs change from before to after participation. After testing this hypothesis, they concluded that leisure needs seem to be sensitive to the influence of the leisure experience itself. Does that mean that the need to participate in leisure activity is changing? Or is the way that it is fulfilled changing? For example, the need to survive motivates humans to eat. Varieties in foods have nothing to do with the need to survive, but food does. On that very basic level, survival is supreme, whether the person likes the food or not. Whether the food was stimulating or not, the person will have to eat to survive. Is (are) the leisure need(s) that powerful? The answer may lie in the hierarchy of needs. In lieu of need, other leisure scholars explored the term *expectation* on the assumption that the participant

Table 4.3
Core Matrix Bases on Rotated Factors

Individual factor	Activities factor	Feedback	Liking	Positive interpersonal involvement
I	Sports	60.1	45.5	9.9
	Cultural-Passive	−53.2	58.0	−16.4
	Productive-Intellectual	59.9	38.3	−34.5
II	Sports	−17.1	37.0	−35.4
	Cultural-Passive	−94.3	25.3	−66.1
	Productive-Intellectual	−8.1	8.9	−86.4
III	Sports	77.2	65.8	64.0
	Cultural-Passive	−47.7	40.6	−14.9
	Productive-Intellectual	61.3	29.4	−10.9

Note. From "The Psychological Structure of Leisure Activities, Needs, People," by M. London, R. Crandall, and D. Fitzgibbons, 1977, *Journal of Leisure Research*, p. 260. Reprinted with permission.

in a leisure pursuit is goal oriented, is knowledgeable, and selects the activity that suits him or her (Mannell & Kleiber, 1999). Nonetheless, a visit to Maslow's hierarchy of needs is appropriate at this point.

The Hierarchy of Human Needs

Although the idea of placing human needs in a hierarchy is credited to Maslow (1968), the concept was forwarded almost 5 centuries ago by a medieval Arab scholar. In a hierarchical model, Ibn Khaldun placed bodily appetite at the bottom level progressing to the desires for security, companionship, and superiority and on to the final desire for leisure (Ibrahim, 1988). It is interesting to note that the original conceptualization of Maslow also included a need (desire) for leisure, as shown in Figure 4.1.

Levy (1979) presented the hierarchical order of Maslow's modified five prepotent need sets in Figure 4.2. Although the historian Ibn Khaldun never indicated the outcome of fulfilling these desires, the psychologist Maslow (1968) promised self-actualization as the outcome of fulfilling the needs in his hierarchy.

To Maslow (1968), self-actualization is a positive ideal of mental health. Could leisure experience, particularly in a natural setting, help in achieving such an ideal? Scott (1974) and Young and Crandall (1984) tested such a claim by comparing wilderness users to nonusers in their self-actualization scores. Using Shostrom's (1974) Person Orientation Inventory, which is the most validated measure of self-actualization as defined by Maslow, the authors concluded that although wilderness activities may help some individuals self-actualize, the relationship between self-actualization and wilderness use is very weak. In 1991, Csikszentmihalyi and Kleiber reported that there seems to be a link between leisure pursuit, in general, and self-actualization.

SATISFACTION, ATTITUDES, AND THE LEISURE EXPERIENCE

If the need for a leisure experience is satisfactorily met, does satisfaction then become the causative factor in further participation in the same leisure experience? Does this lead to a positive attitude toward the leisure experience?

Satisfaction and Leisure

The National Academy of Science (1969) suggested that to understand recreation better, research should be directed at the analysis of satisfactions sought in it. Hawes (1979) sought to study satisfactions derived

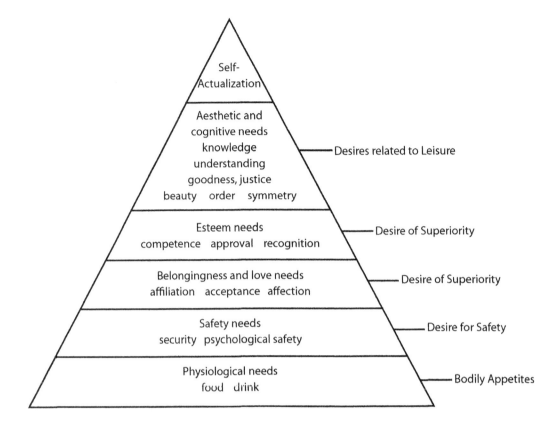

Figure 4.1. Representation of Ibn Khadun's list of human desires versus Maslow's hierarchy of needs.

from participation in leisure activity in an attempt to steer away from the traditional head count. In his nationwide exploratory study, he used 50 selected leisure pursuits along with 12 "satisfaction" statements. A sample of 603 females and 512 males was used for analysis. Of interest is Hawes's finding that individuals can relate their participation in outdoor, active, group-oriented pursuits more readily to satisfactions than they can participation in indoor, passive, primarily individual pursuits.

In a study among water-based recreationists, Burns, Graefe, and Absher (2003) used a battery of 19 individual attributes of satisfaction with their activity such as facilities, services, information, and recreational experience. Both the satisfaction-only item scores and gap scores (difference between importance and satisfaction level) were analyzed. The satisfaction-only measures were found to be better indicators than the gap scores of overall satisfaction.

Csikszentmihalyi's (1975) flow theory has been put to the test in outdoor experiences. Jones, Hollenhorst, and Perna (2000) examined its validation in an outdoor recreational experience. They adopted hypotheses that emphasized three concerns: (1) the relationship between a four-channel model of flow and specific levels of flow indicators, (2) differences in the explanatory power of the four-channel model and an original model of flow, and (3) the relationship between river difficulty and the frequencies of four channels (flow, anxiety, apathy, and boredom). On-site experiences of 52 white-water kayakers were assessed using apriori hypothesis testing, which was based on the results of statistical analyses supporting the validation of the flow theory. Results show that white-water kayakers may have positive experienc-

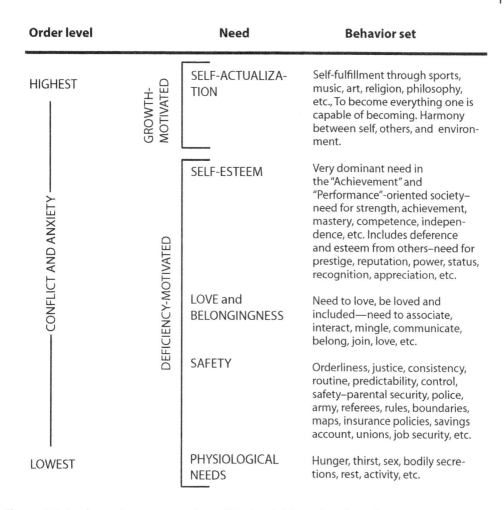

Order level		Need	Behavior set
HIGHEST	GROWTH-MOTIVATED	SELF-ACTUALIZA-TION	Self-fulfillment through sports, music, art, religion, philosophy, etc., To become everything one is capable of becoming. Harmony between self, others, and environment.
	DEFICIENCY-MOTIVATED	SELF-ESTEEM	Very dominant need in the "Achievement" and "Performance"-oriented society–need for strength, achievement, mastery, competence, independence, etc. Includes deference and esteem from others–need for prestige, reputation, power, status, recognition, appreciation, etc.
		LOVE and BELONGINGNESS	Need to love, be loved and included—need to associate, interact, mingle, communicate, belong, join, love, etc.
		SAFETY	Orderliness, justice, consistency, routine, predictability, control, safety–parental security, police, army, referees, rules, boundaries, maps, insurance policies, savings account, unions, job security, etc.
LOWEST		PHYSIOLOGICAL NEEDS	Hunger, thirst, sex, bodily secretions, rest, activity, etc.

(left vertical axis: CONFLICT AND ANXIETY)

Figure 4.2. A schematic representation of Maslow's hierarchy of needs.

es even when their abilities are exceeded by the difficulty of the river.

In a study of women climbers (Kiewa, 2001), it seems that self-determination, or a person's control over the structure of the activity, was an important element that determined satisfaction with nature experience. A precondition for the experience was identified as control over self, or competence, leading to a flow experience. Perceptions of control were developed through narratives that interpreted past actions, but also contributed to a desired identity that formed a motive for future behavior.

According to Ingham (1986), leisure satisfaction is very much linked to motivation. He quoted Calder and Shaw (1975) stating that "satisfaction derives from an activity which is perceived as intrinsically motivated because of a person's need to feel a sense of personal causation in his or her action" (p. 599). This brings back into focus the notion of perceived freedom as being crucial to a bona fide leisure experience. Graef, Csikszentmihalyi, and Gianimo (1983) found that intrinsically motivated activities, leisure activities or otherwise, lead to a state of happiness. Their study supports the notion that satisfaction with an activity depends on perceived intrinsic motivation, which relies on a freedom of choice.

Another study showed that satisfaction increases with better performance and familiarity with the setting (Hultsman, 1998). A study in the same year showed that leisure satisfaction has an inverse relationship with burnout (Stanton-Rich & Iso-Ahola, 1998). Still, a third study showed that satisfaction with life is influenced indirectly by satisfaction with leisure activities (Fernández-Ballesteros, Zamarrón, & Ruiz, 2001). Studies in leisure satisfaction continue despite the warning that the measurement of satisfaction in leisure pursuit is inadequate because satisfaction is relative, too broad, and a multidimensional concept (Mannell & Kleiber, 1999).

Attitudes Toward Leisure

A concept that is much related to, and to some extent dependent on, satisfaction is attitude, which is defined as a learned predisposition to respond in a constantly favorable or unfavorable manner to a given object (Crandall, 1979). Implicit in this definition is that attitudes can predict behavior. This requires that attitudes be measured. Attempts at measuring attitudes toward leisure activities are found in Burdge (1961), Neulinger (1974), and Crandall and Slivken (1979). Not only have applications of the scales constructed by these scholars been limited, but also the one constructed by Burdge has deteriorated considerably over time, as per the author himself (Yoesting & Burdge, 1976). Neulinger suggested that leisure attitudes manifest themselves clearly in cultural settings, a point that will be covered in a different section of this volume.

Studies in leisure attitudes could be useful for managers and providers of leisure programs, as shown by Wohlwill and Heft (1977). In comparing attitudes toward development and facilities in two contrasting natural recreational areas, the authors suggested that one-time study would not suffice in providing information on leisure preference. They suggested a feedback model, the basis of which is the interaction of three separable factors: objectives of the agency, attitude of visitors (to the natural areas), and the impact of visitations.

Another use of attitudinal studies is the effect of leisure participation on the attitude toward the environment. Jackson (1986) found that participants in "appreciative" activities (e.g., cross-country skiing and hiking) hold more pro-environmental attitudes than participants in "consumptive" activities (e.g., snowmobiling and trail biking). He also found that participation in outdoor pursuits is strongly related to attitudes toward those specific aspects of the environment necessary in pursuing the activities than to general issues of environmental concerns. In 1998, a study showed that participation in outdoor recreation is positively associated with pro-environmental behavior (Theodori, Luloff, & Wilitis, 1998).

On the other hand, Ewert, Place, and Sibthorp (2005) investigated the effects of early-life experiences on an individual's environmental beliefs. They analyzed data from a survey of 533 university undergraduate students from 20 areas of academic study using sequential regression to determine the degree to which current environmental beliefs could be explained by early childhood experiences. Four of the seven independent variables (appreciative outdoor activities, consumptive outdoor activities, media exposure, and witnessing negative environmental events) explained 14% of the variance in the ecocentric/anthropocentric beliefs. Three of the independent variables (early-life participation in mechanized outdoor activities, education, and involvement with organizations) were not significant predictors of ecocentric/anthropocentric beliefs.

PSYCHOLOGICAL BENEFITS OF LEISURE EXPERIENCE

Societies sanction activities that are deemed beneficial to the membership collectively and individually. Leisure activities provide many benefits. Some are economic, others are social, and many are psychological. Tinsley (1986) listed the psychological benefits derived from leisure experiences as measured by the Recreation Experience Preference scale:

- Achievement
- Leadership/autonomy
- Risk-taking
- Successful use of equipment
- Family togetherness

- Social contact
- Meeting/observing new people
- Learning/discovery
- Relationships with nature
- Reflection on personal values
- Creativity
- Nostalgia
- Exercise/physical fitness
- Physical rest
- Escape personal and social pressures
- Escape physical pressure
- Security
- Escape family
- Enjoyment of temperature

Much earlier, Tinsley, Barrett, and Kass (1977) identified 44 psychological benefits derived from leisure experiences. Using the Leisure Activities Questionnaire (LAQ), they produced the following lists from information from over 4,000 respondents participating in 82 activities.

Leisure Activity Specific Benefits

These are benefits that can be gained to a significantly greater degree through participation in some leisure activities than by participation in other leisure activities.

Ability	Cooperation	Security
Utilization	Creativity	Self-esteem
Achievement	Dominance	Sentience
Activity	Exhibition	Sex
Advancement	Independence	Social service
Affiliation	Nurturance	Social status
Aggression	Play	Supervision
Authority	Responsibility	Understanding
Catharsis	Reward	Variety
Compensation		

Leisure Activity General Benefits

These are benefits that are gained to approximately the same degree from leisure activities.

Abasement	Justice	Self-control
Autonomy	Moral value	Succorance
Counteraction	Order	Task
Deference	Recognition	Generalization
Harm	Rejection	Tolerance
Avoidance	Relaxation	

Tinsley et al. (1977) derived the following psychological benefit factors that can be used in distinguishing among leisure activities:

- Self-expression
- Companionship
- Compensation
- Security
- Service
- Intellectual aestheticism
- Solitude

Psychological Benefits of Outdoor Experience

So far, what has been listed refers to leisure experiences in general, be they active, passive, indoor, or outdoor. Does the leisure experience that takes place outdoors have its own characteristic benefits? Brown (1981) identified a number of highly valued experiences gained during outdoor recreational activities coming from many sources, and covering research conducted in many sections of the United States:

- Relationship with nature
- Escape from physical pressures
- Escape from social pressures
- Achievement/challenge
- Autonomy/independence/freedom
- Reflection on personal values
- Recollection/nostalgia
- Risk-taking/action/excitement
- Meeting/observing other people
- Use and care of equipment
- Exercise/physical fitness
- Being with one's recreational group
- Learning/exploration
- Family togetherness
- Privacy
- Security
- Physical rest

As can be clearly seen, relationship with nature was one of the most valued experiences in a natural setting, along with being with one's recreational group, a topic to be discussed in the next chapter.

Despite the tremendous desirability of an outdoor recreational experience, there are reasons why many individuals may not participate. Barriers to participation in outdoor experience can be psychological, for example, phobias. These exaggerated fears include fear of dogs, snakes, insects, and other animals, which could render an outing miserable. A social phobia triggered when one is exposed to possible scrutiny by others would render group camping difficult. Other barriers are cultural, which fall within the parameters of the next chapter.

SUMMARY

We discussed the psychological elements of an outdoor experience in this chapter. As defined, leisure is predicated as a state of mind, which by its nature impacts one's psychological orientation. Yet there are personal traits that may affect a person's involvement in a leisure experience. Additionally, the external environment plays a decisive role in the enjoyment of such an experience. For instance, humans prefer places where they feel safe and comfortable and where they believe they can function effectively.

When the leisure experience takes place in the out-of-doors, a new set of elements must be considered. In general, the average natural setting with a lower information rate, that is, with a low number of stimuli, has relatively limited appeal to humans. Sometimes a natural setting has too few stimuli, as in a barren area, which may lead to boredom. On the other hand, too many stimuli may lead to anxiety. Thus, humans seek natural areas with optimum stimuli.

What motivates a person to participate in an outdoor activity in the first place was discussed in relation to the prevailing theories of motivation. The psychological benefits from such participation as reported in the literature were presented. Fulfilling primary needs may serve to reduce physiological disequilibrium, yet secondary needs may include the need for achievement, affiliation, curiosity, self-assertion, and the like. Leisure pursuits provide opportunities to fulfill these needs.

REFERENCES

Borrie, W. T., & Roggenbuck J. W. (2001). The dynamic, emergent, and multiphasic nature of on-site wilderness experiences. *Journal of Leisure Research, 33*(2), 202–228.

Brehm, J. M., Eisenhauer, B. W., Stedman, R. C. (2013). Environmental concern: Examining the role of place meaning and place attachment. *Society and Natural Resources, 26*(5), 522–538.

Brown, P. (1981). Psychological benefits of outdoor recreation. In J. Kelly (Ed.), *Social benefits of outdoor recreation.* Champaign: University of Illinois.

Burdge, R. J. (1961). *The development of a leisure orientation scale* (Unpublished master's thesis). Ohio State University, Columbus, OH.

Burns, R. C., Graefe, A. R., & Absher, J. D. (2003). Alternate measurement approaches to recreational customer satisfaction: Satisfaction only versus gap scores. *Leisure Science, 25*(4), 363–380.

Burton, L. M. (1981). A critical analysis and review of the research on Outward Bound and related programs (Order No. 8122147). Available from ProQuest Dissertations and Theses Global. (303181743). Retrieved from http://search.proquest.com/docview/3031817 43?accountid=9744

Calder, B. J., & Shaw, B. M. (1975). Self-perception of extrinsic motivation. *Journal of Personality and Social Psychology, 31,* 599–605.

Caldwell, L. L., Darling, N., Payne, L. L., & Dowdy, B. (1999). "Why are you bored?": An examination of psychological and social control causes of boredom among adolescents. *Journal of Leisure Research, 31*(2), 103–121.

Coble, T. G., Selin, S. W., & Erickson, B. B. (2003). Hiking alone: Understanding fear, negotiation strategies, and leisure experience. *Journal of Leisure Research, 35*(1), 1–22.

Crandall, R. (1979). Attitudes toward leisure. In H. Ibrahim, & R. Crandall (Eds.), *Leisure: A psychological approach.* Los Alamitos, CA: Hwong.

Crandall, R. (1980). Motivations for leisure. *Journal of Leisure Research, 12,* 45–54.

Crandall, R., & Slivken, K. (1979). Leisure attitudes and their measurement. In S. Iso-Ahola (Ed.), *Social psychological perspectives on leisure and recreation.* Springfield, IL: C. Thomas.

Csikszentmihalyi, M. (1975). *Beyond boredom and anxiety.* San Francisco, CA: Jossey-Bass.

Csikszentmihalyi, M., & Kleiber, D. A. (1991). Leisure and self-actualization. In B. L. Driver (Ed.), *Benefits of leisure.* State College, PA: Venture.

Driver, B. L. (1976). Quantification of outdoor recreationists' preferences. In B. Vander Smissen (Ed.), *Research, camping, and environmental education* (pp. 165-187, Penn State Series II). University Park, PA: Penn State University.

Driver, B. L., & Brown, P. (1978). *The opportunity spectrum concept and behavioral information in outdoor recreation resource supply inventories.* Fort Collins, CO: Rocky Mountain Experiment Station of the United States Forest Service.

Driver, B. L., & Knopf, R. C. (1977). Personality: Outdoor recreation and expected consequences. *Environment and Behavior, 9,* 169.

Dumazedier, J. (1967). *Toward a society of leisure.* New York, NY: Free Press.

Eisen, G. (1988). Theories of play. In G. Gerson et al. (Ed.), *Understanding leisure.* Dubuque, IA: Kendall and Hunt.

Ellis, M. (1973). *Why people play.* Englewood Cliffs, NJ: Prentice Hall.

Ewert. A. (1991). Kurt Hahn 1886-1974. In H. Ibrahim (Ed.), *Pioneers in leisure and recreation* (pp. 161–181). Reston, VA: American Alliance for Health, Physical Education, Recreation, and Dance.

Ewert, A., Place, G., & Sibthorp, J. (2005). Early-life outdoor experiences and an indiviudal's environmental attitudes. *Leisure Sciences, 27*(3), 225–239.

Farley, F. (1986, May). The big Tin personality. *Psychology Today, 1986,* 44–50.

Fernández-Ballesteros, R., Zamarrón, M. D., & Ruiz, M. Á. (2001). The contribution of socio-demographic and psychological factors to life satisfaction. *Ageing and Society, 21,* 25–43.

Graef, R., Csikszentmihalyi, M., & Gianimo, S.J. (1983). Measuring intrinsic motivation in everyday life. *Leisure Studies, 2,* 155–168.

Hawes, D. K. (1979). Satisfaction derived from leisure pursuits: An exploratory nationwide survey. *Journal of Leisure Research, 10,* 247–264.

Hinds, J., & Sparks, P. (2008). Engaging with the natural environment: The role of affective connection and identity. *Journal of Environmental Psychology, 28*(2), 109–120.

Hultsman, W. (1998). The multiday, competitive leisure event: Examining satisfaction over time. *Journal of Leisure Research, 30,* 472–486.

Ibrahim, H. (1988). Leisure, idleness and Ibn Khaldun. *Leisure Studies, 7,* 51–58.

Ingham, R. (1986). Psychological contribution to the study of leisure. *Leisure Studies, 5,* 255–279.

Iso-Ahola, S. C., & Allen, J. (1982). The dynamics of leisure motivation: The effect outcome on leisure needs. *Research Quarterly for Exercise and Sport, 53,* 141–149.

Jackson, E. (1986). Outdoor recreation participation and attitudes toward the environment. *Leisure Studies, 5,* 1–23.

James, W. (1890). *The principles of psychology.* New York, NY: H. Holt.

Jones, C. D., Hollenhorst, F., & Perna, F. (2000). Validation of the flow theory in an on-site whitewater kayaking setting. *Journal of Leisure Research, 32*(2), 247–261.

Kaplan, R., & Kaplan, S. (1989). *The experience of nature: A psychological perspective.* Cambridge, United Kingdom: Cambridge University Press.

Kelly, J. (1987). *Freedom to be: A new sociology of leisure.* New York, NY: Macmillan.

Kiewa, J. (2001). Control over self and space in rockclimbing. *Journal of Leisure Research, 33*(4), 363–382.

Kleiber, D. A. (2000). The neglect of relaxation. *Journal of Leisure Research, 32*(1), 82–86.

Levy, J. (1977, October). *Leisure module: A multidimensional approach to the study of leisure behavior.* Paper presented at the Symposium on Leisure Research, Congress of the National Recreation and Park Association, Las Vegas, NV.

Levy, J. (1979). Motivation for leisure: An interactionist approach. In H. Ibrahim & R. Crandall (Eds.), *Leisure: A psychological approach.* Los Alamitos, CA: Hwong.

London, M., Crandall, R., & Fitzgibbons, D. (1977). The psychological structure of leisure activities, needs, people. *Journal of Leisure Research, 9,* 252–263.

Mannell, R., & Bradley, W. (1986). Does greater freedom always lead to a greater leisure? *Journal of Leisure Research, 12,* 215–230.

Mannell, R., & Kleiber, D. A. (1999). *A social psychology of leisure.* State College, PA: Venture.

Marano, H. E. (1999). The power of play. *Psychology Today, 32,* 36.

Maslow, A. (1968). *Toward a psychology of being.* Princeton, NJ: Van Nostrand.

Mehrebian, A., & Russell, J. (1974). *An approach to environmental psychology.* Cambridge, MA: MIT Press.

National Academy of Science. (1969). *A program for outdoor recreation research.* Washington, DC: National Academy of Science.

Neulinger, J. (1974). *The psychology of leisure.* Springfield, IL: C. C. Thomas.

Ruskin, H., & Shamir, B. (1984). Motivation as a factor affecting males' participation in physical activity during leisure time. *Society and Leisure, 7,* 141–161.

Scott, N. (1974). Toward a psychology of wilderness experience. *Natural Resource Journal, 14,* 231–237.

Selye, H. (1956). *The stress of life.* New York, NY: McGraw-Hill.

Shostrom, E. (1974). *Manual for the Personality Orientation Inventory.* San Diego, CA: Educational and Industrial Testing Service.

Sia, A., Hungerford, H., & Tomera, A. (1985/1986). Selected predictors of responsible environmental behavior: An analysis. *Journal of Environmental Education, 17*(2), 31–40.

Stanton-Rich, H. M., & Iso Ahola, S. E. (1998). Burnout and leisure. *Journal of Applied Social Psychology, 28*(21), 1–31.

Stewart, W. P., & Cole, D. N. (2001). Number of encounters and experience quality in Grand Canyon backcountry: Consistently negative and weak relationships. *Journal of Leisure Research, 33*(1), 106–120.

Stokols, D., & Altman, L. (1987). *Handbook of environmental psychology.* New York, NY: John Wiley and Sons.

Theodori, G. L., Luloff, A. E., & Wilitis, F. K. (1998). The association of outdoor recreation and environmental concern. *Sociology, 63*(1), 94.

Tinsley, H. (1986). Motivations to participate in recreation: Their identification and measurements. In The President's Commission on Americans Outdoors, *A literature review* (pp. 9–16). Washington, DC: U.S. Government Printing Office.

Tinsley, H., Barrett, T. C., & Kass, R. A. (1977). Leisure activities and need satisfaction. *Journal of Leisure Research, 9,* 110–120.

Tinsley, H., & Kass, R. A. (1978). Leisure activities and need satisfaction: A replication and extension. *Journal of Leisure Research, 10,* 191–202.

Tversky, B., & Hemenway, K. (1983). Categories of environmental scenes. *Cognitive Psychology, 15,* 23–42.

Vaske, J. J., & Kobrin, K. C. (2001). Place attachment and environmentally responsible behavior. *Journal of Environmental Education, 32*(4), 16–21.

Williams, D. (1986). Psychological perspectives on the environment. Experience relationship: Implications for recreation resources management. In The President's Commission on American Outdoors, *A literature review* (pp. 17–32). Washington, DC: U.S. Government Printing Office.

Wohlwill, J. F., & Heft, H. (1977). A comparative study of user attitudes towards development and facilities in two contrasting natural recreation areas. *Journal of Leisure Research, 9,* 264–280.

Yoesting, D. R., & Burdge, R. J. (1976). Utility of a leisure orientation scale. *Journal of Research, 50,* 345–356.

Young, R., & Crandall, R. (1984). Wilderness use and self-actualization. *Journal of Leisure Research, 16,* 149–160.

Chapter 5

The Social Aspects of Outdoor Recreation

In the last chapter, we concentrated on the individual as an individual, on his or her traits, needs, attitudes, and satisfactions as they relate to leisure pursuits, with an emphasis on outdoor experiences. We will look at the individual as a member of a society and as a member of its subgroups in this chapter. We will probe the roles of culture and subculture as they pertain to leisure behavior.

At the turn of the 20th century, the *Journal of Leisure Science* allocated a special issue to the sociological aspects of leisure research including an article by Donald Field (2000), who was involved in such research for a number of years. He stated that sociological scholarship on people in parks has matured over time, particularly in the 1970s and the 1980s. This chapter is devoted to the social aspects of outdoor experiences using past and recent research, but first a discussion of the elements that constitute a society.

THE NATURE OF HUMAN SOCIETY

As a system, human society comprises different structures and performs certain functions. Regardless of their historical time or geographical locations, all human societies are, to a great extent, similar when it comes to social structures and social functions. Following are the basic social institutions of society.

The Family

The family could be nuclear, referring to a male, a female, and their offspring, or extended to include blood and marriage relatives. The impact of the family on the life of both young and old cannot be denied, perhaps because the family is involved in many social, psychological, and economical functions as follows:

1. Sexual satisfaction
2. Reproduction
3. Socialization
4. Psychological sustenance
5. Economic support

The role of the family on leisure behavior in general, and on outdoor recreation in particular, along with the impact of leisure on the individual family members, will be elaborated on later.

Religion

Religion is the second most important major social institution in almost all societies. Durkheim (1915) suggested that religion is the outcome of the collectivity of ritual. As indicated, rituals played and still play an important role in the lives of individuals and societies. One view is that ritual was and is the cement that holds the society together. Such views were challenged by Turner (1982), who believes that in addition to its role in maintaining the social order, the ritual is the locus for rudimentary forms of leisure pursuits.

An important function of religion is that it determines that which is sacred and that which is profane. In other words, religion determines, to a great extent, what is acceptable and unacceptable human behavior. The role of religion, then, is important in leisure pursuits. An example comes from colonial America when the Puritans and Quakers not only frowned on horse racing and mixed dancing but suggested that the U.S. Constitution include a prohibition against such "extravaganza."

Political Institutions

The political structure of any society revolves around the source of power and its allocation. The organization of political power can produce, or may fail to produce, the following:

1. Internal calm and peace
2. External protection and expansion
3. National, regional, and local policies
4. Interest alignment
5. Distribution of wealth
6. Protection of the environment

Although leisure and recreation were not of governmental concern in the past, recently their role in the lives of citizens has prompted all levels of government—federal, state, and local—to become involved in not only regulating offerings through legislature, but also providing facilities and programs. These will be discussed in in Chapters 7, 8, and 9.

The Economic System

The economic system evolved from a simple system of barter to a complex system of the stock markets, long-term financing, and multinational corporations. One way of looking at the level of economic sophistication of a given society or region is through a tripartite classification based on the location of the bulk of the labor force, as follows:

1. Primary economy: agriculture and extractive business dominate
2. Secondary economy: industry and manufacturing dominate
3. Tertiary economy: most of the labor force in services and trade

American society and Canadian society have reached a tertiary economy in that most of their labor forces are in services and trade. In the leisure sector of the economy, this means an increasing number of workers and professionals are seen in the leisure delivery systems, be they public or private. Chapter 6 is devoted to the relationship between leisure pursuits in general, and outdoor recreational activities in particular, and the status of the American economy, nationally, regionally, and locally.

Technology

Technology is both a social and a material institution. It refers to the organization, dissipation, and utilization of knowledge in the service of societal goals. Social technology includes formal and informal education, the media, and voluntary education. Material technology, on the other hand, includes science and industry. Leisure scholars agree that the technological industrial advances of the last two centuries helped increase free time, an important ingredient for leisure pursuits. It is clear that some people who are living in this age of technology pay a heavy toll in that technology does not make their lives easier, just busier ("Breaking point," 1995). On the other hand, some scholars believe that a convergence is occurring between leisure and technology (Hill & McLean, 1999).

Besides the five social institutions of family, religion, government, the economy, and technology, secondary institutions such as play and work groups play important roles in people's lives. Accordingly, a number of social processes help the individual learn the roles he or she is supposed to play in these institutions. Foremost among these social processes is socialization.

SOCIALIZATION AND LEISURE BEHAVIOR

A human being is born socially neutral. Socialization is a process through which the culture of the community and/or society is instilled in the individual. This process, which begins at birth and continues throughout life, helps the individual to play his or her assigned roles in society correctly. Playing the role, as expected by the social groups with which the individual interacts, not only gives needed admission to these groups, but also serves as a threshold to self-esteem. Humans play many roles in their lifetime, among which are leisure roles. Leisure roles include, but are not limited to, being a player on a sports team, an actor in a school play, or a member of the church choir.

The Age of Socialization Into Leisure

As previously stated, socialization is a continual process, yet social scientists agree that there is a certain age when socialization is so powerful that the activity partaken could become a lifelong practice. There are a number of studies that are focused on the age of socialization into outdoor recreational activities. Bevins, Bond, Concorn, McIntosh, and McNeil (1968) found that childhood participation in hunting and fishing is highly correlated with adulthood participation in the same activities. Hendee (1969) found that 70% of the adult participants in wilderness camping had taken their first camping trip before the age of 15. Bradshaw and Jackson (1979) investigated socialization into leisure activities in general and concluded such socialization occurs before age 13. Yoesting and Burkhead (1973) found that individuals who are active in outdoor recreation continue to be active in outdoor life during their adult years and that the opposite is true: inactive children continue being inactive in these activities as adults. Their findings do not support Kelly's (1983) study that humans can be socialized into new activities in adulthood. Yet it is possible that the inactive persons were not exposed to outdoor recreational

pursuits. Had they been, they may have become active in them.

On the other hand, it seems that elementary and junior high school students pass through an "extracurricular career" that begins with recreational ambience, progressing from competitive to elite activities as they grow older. Their leisure pursuits become less spontaneous and more rationalized. This may be the means of socializing them into the corporate world of the American culture (Adler & Adler, 1999).

Agents of Socialization Into Leisure

The family seems to be the most influential agent of socialization into leisure generally and also into outdoor recreational activities. Kelly (1974) found that of the 744 activities reported in his study, 63% began with the family, most of which were either sports or outdoor recreational activities.

The school is considered by many as another socializing agent for leisure. Yet there is a paucity of studies on the role of the school as a socializing agent into outdoor recreational pursuits. As early as 1936, Neumeyer and Neumeyer suggested that in preparation for leisure, nature studies and activities for exploring the out-of-doors should be included in the school curriculum. In many of the school districts in the United States, some form of outdoor experience is provided, but the impact of these offerings has not been investigated. One of the early studies conducted in the United States showed that the less educated go more often to parks, but how much they appreciate nature is not known (White, 1955). Also, do the less educated go to the park because it is the only leisure outlet available, compared with the theatre, the movies, and the zoo, where the middle and upper classes tend to go more often because they can afford them?

Empirical studies have been conducted on the role of youth-serving agencies (YMCA, Boy Scouts, Campfire Girls, and the like) in experiences in the outdoors. Kleiber and Rickards (1981) suggested that the outdoor experiences these agencies provide serve as a theatre. Experiences in that theatre, according to Shepard (1977), enhance the process of gathering and consolidating a range of skills at the end of childhood in preparation for the emancipation from the parental home.

In places of worship, whether they are churches, synagogues, temples, or mosques, outdoor recreational activities have been provided for many years for both youth and adults, yet there is hardly any empirical study on their role in enhancing, or reducing, the leisure experience in natural settings. According to MacLean, Peterson, and Martin (1985), the sponsors value outdoor experiences so much that they assume part of the expense and provide volunteer counselors. This eventually led to the provision of organized family camping.

Private and publicly sponsored camps are also agencies for outdoor experiences. The private camp may be operated by a non-profit organization such as the YMCA or by an entrepreneur for profit. Public recreation and park agencies also conduct both day and resident camps for the young. The American Camp Association (ACA, 2013) highlighted the many benefits of camp for youth in a burgeoning program of research:

> Between 2001 and 2004 the American Camp Association conducted national research with over 5000 families from 80 ACA-Accredited camps to determine the outcomes of the camp experience as expressed by parents and children.
>
> Parents, camp staff, and children reported significant growth in:
>
> - Self-esteem
> - Peer relationships
> - Independence
> - Adventure and exploration
> - Leadership
> - Environmental awareness
> - Friendship skills
> - Values and decisions
> - Social comfort
> - Spirituality

> The findings from this national study indicated that camp is a unique educational institution and a positive force in youth development. The camp experience can benefit children by increasing:
>
> - confidence and self-esteem
> - social skills and making friends
> - independence and leadership qualities
> - willingness to try and adventurousness
> - spiritual growth, especially at camps focused on spirituality.
>
> No differences were found based on the camp type (day, resident) or session length. (para. 1–4, used with permission)

Visit www.ACAcamps.org/research for a full review of recent findings.

Leisure as a Socializing Agent

Csikszentmihalyi (1981) advocated that socialization into leisure, or more precisely into expressive activities, is important because these activities could serve as the criteria by which instrumental activities are evaluated. In general, an instrumental activity is one in which the end product is supreme (fishing commercially for the purpose of selling the fish) as opposed to an expressive activity in which the process is more important (fishing for sport). Although most leisure pursuits are to some extent expressive, Csikszentmihalyi's notion does not pertain solely to leisure activities. Work could be expressive to some. His point, though, is that expressive activities are used in the growing years as criteria by which other activities are evaluated.

Humans are socialized into a number of leisure roles in their lives. They might move from being young athletes to adult poker players to senior RV campers. In the process, they become acquainted with the requirements for playing any of these roles. In the evolution of societies, leisure roles were not crucial to the society's welfare or to its members' survival. These roles are becoming

Parents of the very youngest children are the most likely to report involvement in outdoor recreation as a family. These two dads expose their children to a fun day of activity at Kings Mountain National Military Park in South Carolina. Mom goes backpacking with her baby on the Appalachian Trail at Grafton Notch in Bethel, Maine.

increasingly important to the members of industrial/bureaucratic societies. According to Kelly (1983), leisure may be found to be central rather than residual in some phases of life, mainly in the growing years and in retirement. Two spheres that affect human behavior are leisure behavior in primary and secondary groups, as discussed in the following sections.

PRIMARY GROUPS AND LEISURE PURSUITS

Human dependency on others, which is witnessed from birth, tends to continue throughout life. Dependency is greater in the early years of life and remains at a high rate during childhood. Having the longest childhood among animals, including primates, humans are more dependent on others for a longer period than are other animals. Humans are by necessity social, and they enter a greater number of social circles of different sizes and importance in their life course. The smallest of these circles consists of only two persons, called a dyad. Other circles include primary face-to-face groups such as family and peers and secondary groups such as schoolmates, neighbors, and coworkers. Dyads, primary groups, and secondary groups are socializing agents as well as providers of outdoor recreational opportunities.

Dyads and Outdoor Pursuits

Perhaps the first dyadic relationships to occur are mother–infant, father–infant, and two-sibling dyads. It was Erikson (1977) who brought to attention the importance of the mother–infant dyad in the particular relationship of ritualization. Manning (1975) pioneered a theoretic study on backpacking and the basic needs of infants that included information on how to plan for toddlers and how to make hiking acceptable to children.

Another form of dyadic relationship, partnership, begins at the late teens and early adulthood and can lead to sexual intimacy, which could be enhanced through leisure pursuits. It is no wonder that commercial advertisements use outdoor and leisure scenes intimating closeness between lovers. Empirical studies on the role of outdoor pursuits in the lives of couples are lacking, yet studies of the role of organized sport in the lives of couples exist (Eitzen & Sage, 1989). In either case, the couples' participation in these pursuits is expected to increase marriage stability and reduce gender inequality (Fong & Zhang, 2001).

Other than sexual dyads, dyadic friendship also exists in the form of two-person long-term relationships. The role that leisure pursuits, including outdoor experiences, play in dyadic relationships is still under investigation. Although few studies have been conducted, a recent one showed that individual leisure satisfaction is not necessarily reflected on the dyadic relationship (Berg, Trost, Schneider, & Allison, 2000). These findings support the findings of Fink and Wild (1995).

The role of leisure pursuits in enhancing, or destroying, dyadic relationship, be they romantic or friendship, remains to be investigated. This does not mean that small primacy groups such as family or peers do not play a role in these relationships.

The Family and Outdoor Pursuits

Despite the changes that have taken place in the family structure, its main function as the dominant socializing agent in human societies remains the same—this, despite the encroachment of school, church, and peers on this particular function, let alone the most recent assault by the powerful medium of television. The family provides both the physical setting and the social setting for leisure activities. Glyptis and Chambers (1982) reported that not only is most free time spent at home, but the home is also a physical source for many leisure pursuits, providing space and equipment. The backyard as a space for outdoor pursuits has not been thoroughly studied, but it is evident that many pursuits take place there.

According to Orthner (1976), leisure, in general, contributes to marital cohesion. In an earlier study, West and Merriam (1970) found that outdoor recreational activities lead to family cohesiveness. According to Kelly (1981), the critical variable for the building of family cohesion is the nature of the integration. He suggested that the work of B. L. Driver indicates that the perceived benefits of outdoor experience include two elements for effective interaction: the strengthening of significant relationships and the enjoyment of companionship.

Where the family as a unit is concerned, leisure experience, including outdoor pursuits, supports key needs over the life cycle. These key needs include attachment, bonding, identification, interaction, stress management, and social support (Orthner, Barnett, & Ancinin, 1994).

The influence of challenge-based recreation on the collective efficacy of families with at-risk youth was seen in the increase of conflict resolution efficacy among 34 families who participated in a study to investigate such a relationship (Wells, Wiidmer, & McCoy, 2004).

Peers and Outdoor Pursuits

According to Cheek (1981), in leisure literature, both professional and investigatory, outdoor recreational activities have often been described as taking place in a group of around four persons. Although escaping urban pressure is an important motivational factor in participating in a wilderness experience, hardly anyone does it alone. The solitude sought is usually a communal, not a solo, solitude. Based on the findings of the research conducted in the 1960s and 1970s, Cheek concluded that it is either kinship or friendship that is the basis of the social group in an outdoor leisure pursuit. Earlier, Cheek and Burch (1976) reported that members of an outdoor leisure pursuit group tend to remain physically together and to share decision making, two elements that add to cohesion and intimacy.

Cheek (1981) also suggested that outdoor pursuits offer a unique opportunity for a human being to behave as a human being, a condition denied him or her in the too-rational industrial society. He asked,

> When may humans exalt their natures in addition or perhaps in contrast to their exactness? . . . Only under very limited conditions; for limited periods of time; and with very few others of their kind. Outdoor recreation activities appear to offer the unique combination of these conditions in modern industrial societies. (p. 51)

To Cheek (1981), the most important use of outdoor settings is an all too infrequently recognized function: to feel and exchange indications of special caring and liking. Recently, Edwards (2001) underscored that the need for more contact with peers can be provided in the recreational opportunities for middle school children and young adults.

LEISURE AND SECONDARY GROUPS

Other than the primary groups where frequent face-to-face interaction takes place, secondary groups play important roles as agents for leisure. Among secondary groups are schoolmates, youth groups, and adult groups.

Outdoor Pursuits With Schoolmates

It seems the first programs that provided outdoor experience through a school were made possible by the Kellogg Foundation of Battle Creek, Michigan, in the early 1930s (Smith, Carlson, Donaldson, & Masters, 1970). The Clear Lake Camp and its staff were made available to three Michigan schools. Students from Grades 4 to 12 went to the camp for 2 weeks. The program was enhanced when an act was passed by the Michigan legislature in 1945, which enabled school districts to acquire camps and operate them as a part of the regular educational and recreational programs of the schools.

According to Burrus-Bammel and Bammel (1990), there is sufficient evidence to conclude that outdoor/environmental education programs have the potential to produce benefits for the participants and society. Although results of specific program evaluation cannot be generalized, the results have a remarkable consistency of demonstrative positive change. Malsam and Nelson (1984) reported an increase in the trust and respect for teachers, leaders, and other students after a 4-day residential program for sixth graders. According to Burrus-Bammel and Bammel, programs do not have to be of long duration to promote lasting effects.

Outdoor Pursuits and Youth Groups

Youth groups include members of youth-serving organizations, young church members, and members of youth clubs. The idea of organizing activities for the young under the tutelage of adults is an old idea that most likely emanated from the need to socialize them in a manner acceptable to the elders. Neumeyer and Neumeyer (1936) wrote of Jünglingsverein, a club of young unmarried men in Bremen, Germany, in 1709. By 1863, when George Williams organized his first YMCA in London, England, many of these Jünglingsverein clubs still existed (Neumeyer & Neumeyer, 1949). The YMCA and YWCA were originally urban youth centers whose staff concentrated on serving youth.

According to Turner (1985), YMCA camping could date as far back as 1867, but actual records show that the Brooklyn's YMCA took 30 boys on a trip described as camping in 1881. In April 1884, the first encampment took place by Orange Lake, New Jersey, where YMCA boys went boating and fishing.

Bible study took 1 to 2 hours each day. A year later some YMCA boys went to an encampment by Lake Champlain, New York, under the leadership of Sumner Dudley, after whose death it was named Dudley Camp. In 1908, the camp was moved to Westport, New York. Today, the YMCA in the United States operates over 240 resident camps across the country (YMCA USA, 2013). In Canada, the YMCA operates 28 resident summer camps, which serve more than 18,000 campers each summer (YMCA Canada, 2013).

The youth group that conducted its activity in natural settings from its inception was the paramilitary Boy Scouts, initiated by Lord Robert Stephenson Smyth Baden-Powell in London in 1908 at the heel of the British defeat in the Boer War in South Africa. His idea was to use the outdoors in developing physical fitness, self-reliance, and patriotism. According to Rosenthal (1986), the notion of the Scout as a serviceable citizen trained to follow orders in wartime is at the heart of Scouting. Yet Baden-Powell tried from the beginning to define the movement as anti-militaristic (Rosenthal, 1986). In fact, Baden-Powell was much influenced by Ernest Thompson Seton, one of the great artist-naturalists of the 20th century. Seton founded the Woodcraft Movement after his immigration to America in the 1880s. Rosenthal stated,

> For Seton, the natural wisdom of the woods was the highest available to man: individuals had to learn to trust their instincts and open themselves to the prompting of nature in order to achieve their full realization as human beings. (p. 65)

Today, the Scout movement, for both boys and girls, has touched the lives of many young Americans. The impact that the Scouts have had on youth-based outdoor recreation is impressive. In total, the Scouts served 114,304,329 boys and girls in the United States between 1910 and 2010 (Boy Scouts of Amercia, 2013).

According to Butler (1961), Dr. Luther Gulick and his wife, who were instrumental in establishing the Boy Scout movement in America in 1910, became interested in a similar movement for girls. Moreover, the Gulicks were convinced that the Scouts' educational curriculum at the time was in need of something more. Camp Fire has long been known for its emphasis on inclusivity and encourages acceptance and celebration of difference. The following is Camp Fire's (2013) statement of inclusion:

> Camp Fire works to realize the dignity and worth of each individual and to eliminate human barriers based on all assumptions which prejudge individuals. Our program standards are designed and implemented to reduce sexual, racial, religious, and cultural stereotypes and to foster positive intercultural relationships. In Camp Fire, everyone is welcome. (para. 1)

The Gulicks encouraged William Chauncy Langdon, a poet and a consultant on pageantry, to organize an outing experience for a dozen girls from Thetford, Vermont. The girls were called Camp Fire Girls, and they were set up in three ranks of achievement—Wood Gatherers, Fire Makers, and Torch Bearers—ranks that are still in use today. The philosophy of Ernest Thompson Seton was more influential in this movement than in the Scout movement. The Woodcraft Ranger approach, teaching youngsters to use their hands as rangers do, with its strong American motif, Native American lore, is clear in the Camp Fire Girls. Now, after admitting boys, the organization is called simply Camp Fire.

Outdoor Pursuits With Adult Groups

For the lack of a better word, the term *adult group* is used to include the stable membership of voluntary associations, the makeshift groups that form around an outdoor experience, and workplace-centered groups. Voluntary associations include instrumental and expressive groups. The instrumental associations usually revolve around professions and occupations and are concerned with specific outcomes for their members, usually of extrinsic value, such as wage increases and fringe benefits. Sometimes, they also offer the membership leisure and expressive activities. On the other hand, expressive voluntary associations revolve around activities that are of intrinsic value. The following are expressive associations that deal with nature: American Camping Association, American Youth Hostels, National Audubon Society, Save-the-Redwood League, and the Sierra Club.

DEMOGRAPHIC CORRELATES OF OUTDOOR PURSUITS

The demographic factors that have an affect–effect relationship to leisure behavior include age, life course, gender, occupation, residence, and ethnicity. Although these factors only provide a moderate basis for participation in outdoor recreation (Manning, 1985), they should nonetheless be presented and discussed. In 2002, Cordell, Green, and Betz examined the differences in recreational behaviors and environmental attitudes in the United States and broadly explored the changing demands of outdoor recreation, environmental opinions, and demographics in the United States. Survey data in recreational behavior (participation) and environmental attitudes nationwide across six sociodemographic factors—race, country of birth, rural–urban residence, region of the country, age, and income—indicate that demographic differences, recreational activity choices, and people's environmental positions are linked.

On the local level, Payne, Mowen, and Orsega-Smith (2002) examined the relationship among age, race, and residential location with respect to the newly opened Ohio-Erie Canal Reservation in Cleveland, Ohio. They found that although all three variables contributed significantly to what was expected of the new park, age was the strongest/nonsupport for additional parkland. On the other hand, older adults and African Americans were more likely to prefer recreation over conservation.

These members of an outrigger club function together as a team and socialize during race events.

Leisure Pursuits and Age

Play is witnessed in the upper orders of the animal kingdom. Play activities of young humans seem to go through stages that are universal despite differences in race, ethnicity, or cultural background. These activities are usually simple and become increasingly complex as the society itself becomes more complex. Play seems to be natural, so learning to play seems unnecessary, but learning to play helps one appreciate the intrinsic values of instrumental activities (activities that may lack the element of play; Csikszentmihalyi, 1981).

Leisure education describes the acquisition of skills for the enjoyment of leisure activities both now and in the future. *Leisure counseling* is a term used to describe the process a professional uses to help a person choose and become involved in a leisure pursuit. A young age is ideal for acquiring a desire for lifelong leisure pursuit (Bevins et al., 1968; Bradshaw & Jackson, 1979; Hendee, 1969), but leisure counseling is useful to the adult who needs help in selecting a meaningful leisure pursuit. Recently, the Sierra Club initiated the program Building Bridges to the Outdoors, which works with established nature education programs and educates political bodies on the need to increase opportunities to play outdoors (Rauber, 2006).

Leisure Pursuits and Life Course

As life progresses, individuals assume new roles, including leisure roles. Also, they give up some roles, sometimes by choice and sometimes not by choice. Examples of the taking on and abandoning of leisure roles are provided by Snyder and Spreitzer (1978). Young men and women were found to assess their own competence as athletes, and if they believed that their competencies were below group expectations, they tended to withdraw from the leisure activity. Kelly (1983) suggested that participants in leisure pursuits evaluate not only their satisfaction with the activity but also its long-term benefits. Accordingly, they form attitudes, either negative or positive, toward the activity. This process of evaluation goes on throughout life.

As life progresses, individuals should take on new leisure roles and abandon old ones. Examples of leisure roles in different phases of life are given by Bammel and Burrus-Bammel (1981), Kelly (1983), and Gerson, Ibrahim, DeVries, and Eisen (1988) and are summarized and shown in Table 5.1. A study conducted some years ago showed that the level of leisure pursuits declines with age, but it is not clear if the decline is in all three levels—amusive, recreative, or contemplative (Gordon, Gaitz, & Scott, 1976).

Leisure Pursuits and Gender

Leisure pursuits and gender is an important topic. Society and societal values seem to play an important part in determining interests, at least when it comes to considering time free from familial and civic obligation, as shown in the next study. Jackson and Henderson (1995) suggested that constraints to leisure participation among women are functions of cultural interpretation and not merely a biological tendency. According to Bialeschki and Henderson (1986), women are often expected to balance career focus with family responsibilities. More recent reviews of the research on women and leisure constraints highlight that social role expectations and other social factors continue to be prominent factors that shape women's leisure (Henderson & Hickerson, 2007). In cross-cultural studies, men were found to have more time for leisure in Egypt (Ibrahim, 1981), Israel (Shamir & Ruskin, 1983), Russia (Moskoff, 1984), Norway (Fasting & Sisjord, 1985), and Canada (Shaw, 1985). How the imbalance of free time between genders is reflected in outdoor pursuits has not been empirically investigated.

A study of women with histories of participation in adventure recreation revealed that they experienced varying sources of constraint similar to findings in previous studies, but they could also successfully negotiate these constraints by restructuring their adventure experience or by reinforcing their commitment to adventure as a life priority (Little, 2002).

On the other hand, McDermott (2004) claimed that there is a relative dearth of scholarly examination within leisure studies of women experiencing their physical abilities through active outdoor recreation and the potentially empowering effects on them. McDermott sought to draw out the connections between these seemingly disparate observations through a qualitative examination of women's experiences of female-only wilderness canoeing. Women undertaking such an experience did not explicitly identify issues related to their physicalities. This in turn provides support for claims regarding the importance of the provision of all-female outdoor experiences.

Can outdoor recreation aid in the deconstruction of gender and gender stereotyping? Outcomes from recreational experiences can transfer into other realms of daily life, resulting in a heightened sense of empowerment and social change for women. In an examination of the connection between wilderness recreation and social change for women, data were collected from 24 qualitative interviews with women in a wilderness setting. Wilderness recreation can influence women's everyday lives in the forms of self-sufficiency, shift in perspective, connection to others, and mental clarity (Pohl, Borrie, & Patterson, 2000).

Issues such as gender and ethnicity are related to preferences for various park characteristics, visitation to urban parks and open spaces, and perception of park benefits were polled in a mail survey of residents in two metropolitan areas in the eastern United States. In total, 1,570 questionnaires were completed, and the overall response rate for the survey was approximately 27%. Women were no more likely than men to evaluate some park characteristics as *important*. Also, there were no significant gender differences in the types of visits or the perceived benefits of parks. There was a significant ethnic variation in preferred park attributes, frequency and type of visits, and perceptions of the positive and negative effects of parks. The effects of ethnicity were not found to be different for men and women (Ho, Sasidharan, & Elmendorf, 2005).

Leisure Pursuits and Occupation

Among the early studies conducted on the relationship between occupation and leisure is Clarke's (1956). He used five levels of occupational groupings: professional, managerial, clerical, skilled, and unskilled workers. Members of the top occupations tend to go to theaters, concerts, lectures, and art galleries and to read, study, and play bridge more often than do members of other occupations. Greater attendance at sports events and in commercial recreation is witnessed among members of the middle occupations. Members of the blue-collar occupations tend to attend bars and watch television more often than do the members of the higher occupations. Burdge (1969) used the same classification of occupations and concluded that members of higher occupations seem to participate in greater variety of leisure pursuits, including more participation in outdoor recreational pursuits. Bultena and Field (1978) found occupations to be significantly related to participation in outdoor activity, supporting Burdge's conclusion that persons occupying higher paying positions tend to participate in more leisure pursuits, including outdoor ones.

Roberts (1970) suggested that occupations affect leisure pursuits and are affected by them as follows:

1. Manual occupations demand a great deal of time and energy, sometimes leaving manual laborers without energy to cultivate active leisure pursuits.
2. Manual occupations are physically arduous and therefore may result in a need to spend leisure simply relaxing or recuperating.
3. Less financially stable persons may not have substantial incomes to invest in leisure interests outside the home and may not have discretionary money to spare for club subscriptions, recreational equipment, and the like.

Table 5.1

Leisure Pursuits and Age Groups

Kelly	Bammel and Burrus-Bammel	Gerson et al.
I. Preparation Period: (Birth to early 20s) Play in childhood varies with age and gender and is a means of interaction and a way of self-discovery.	*Teens:* Active participation in vigorous form of recreation activity both outdoors and indoors. *Twenties:* Active participation, especially in outdoor activities. Wilderness backpacking, canoeing, and so forth. *Thirties:* Less active and less frequent participation in outdoor recreation. Camping replaces backpacking.	*Birth–2:* Individual play, expanding horizon, becoming aware of environment. *2–3:* Beginning of imitative and creative play. *3–4:* Parallel and symbolic play, social play, begin aquatics. *5–7:* Large muscle development. Family activities important. *8–9:* Greater desire to participate and to succeed. *9–12:* Team sport. Sexual differences in play.
II. Establishment Period: (mid-1920s to mid-1940s) Leisure roles complement family and community roles. Investment in leisure pursuits increases after children are grown.	*Forties:* Less active participation, more spectating. Car or van camping replaces tent camping. *Fifties:* Greater emphasis on spectating for the great majority. For a minority, renewed attempt at physical conditioning. Bowling.	*13–18:* Group influence, instant gratification, need to accept socially acceptable activities. *19–22 (Identity):* Testing intimate relationships. Test self through high-risk activities. *23–30 (Intimacy):* Peak of physical prowess. Active in sports and high-risk activities. *30–38 (Establishment):* Activities of couples, social and community services. Children may be used as prestige symbols.
III. Culmination Period: (mid-1940s on) More choices in leisure pursuit are seen. Reestablishment of marital dyad occurs.	*Sixties:* Spectating and decrease in physical character of activities. Gardening. *Seventies:* Some new sport activities may begin with retirement. Golf, swimming, shuffleboard, etc.	*38–55 (Adjustments):* Less physical activity. Participation more spontaneous. Preference in smaller and family groups. *55–65 (Mellow):* Enjoyment of cultural and creative activities. Expansion to large groups for entertainment. *65+ (Seniors):* Physical fitness paramount. Preference for activity with same age group.

Note. Adapted from *Leisure Identities and Interaction*, by J. Kelly, 1983, London, England: George Allen and Unwin; *Human Behavior and Leisure*, by G. Bammel and L. Burrus-Bammel, 1981, Dubuque, IA: Wm. C. Brown; and *Understanding Leisure: An Interdisciplinary Approach*, by G. Gerson, H. M. Ibrahim, J. DeVries, and G. Eisen, 1988, Dubuque, IA: Kendall/Hunt.

4. White-collar families have a greater opportunity to travel abroad, and this exposure may stimulate other leisure interests. Certain leisure activities appear to trigger participation in others.
5. Education awakens white-collar people to leisure interests found outside the sphere of the manual worker.
6. A white-collar worker's job may create more opportunities for one to acquire skills that can be exploited during leisure time.
7. Leisure habits emerge as status attitudes generated at work spill over into and influence people's leisure lives.

Is income a factor in selecting outdoor pursuits? According to Burdge (1969), the more expensive outdoor activities seem to appeal to the person in the higher levels of occupation with higher incomes, and this certainly seems to remain true today. A quarter of a century after Burdge's work this assertion was supported by Walker and Kiecolt (1995), who found that wilderness use is dominated by highly educated professionals.

Leisure Pursuits and Residence

To what extent does the rural–urban dichotomy affect one's leisure pursuit? Knopp (1972) found that the urban male is more inclined to seek solitude and exercise than is his rural counterpart. Bammel and Burrus-Bammel (1981) stated that urban residents tend to watch TV, go to the movies, and enjoy swimming more often than do rural dwellers, who appreciate the amenities provided in a natural setting, such as solitude and sentience. Allen, Long, and Perdue (1987) surveyed rural households to determine their satisfaction with their leisure activities. Their neutral responses led the authors to conclude that rural residents may be seeking more leisure opportunities than the ones provided in nearby areas. Their conclusion confirms Foret's (1985) conclusions drawn when she investigated the relationship between life satisfaction and leisure activities

of rural and urban residents. She found that age and residence caused no significant differences in leisure satisfaction. However, urban dwellers were more recreationally active than were rural residents. In 1963, Sessoms reviewed most of the studies on age, residence, and occupation conducted up until 1963, which had to do with demographic characteristics and concluded the following:

1. Active participation in outdoor pursuits declines with age.
2. Greater participation is witnessed with higher income.
3. Varied participation increases with higher occupational prestige.
4. More participation is observed among urban residents.
5. Less participation is seen by families with small children.

According to Manning (1985), research conducted on the demographic correlates since 1963 has tended to corroborate Sessoms' findings. The studies cited by Manning show near uniformity in who uses outdoor recreational resources: younger persons of higher socioeconomic status. This does not mean persons from a particular social class. In fact, the whole concept of social class is being replaced by another concept: lifestyle.

Leisure and Ethnicity

Ethnicity refers to one's ancestral identity, which involves one's total heritage such as values and customs, taste and ritual, and some physical features. In the pluralistic American society, a number of ethnic groups—African Americans, Hispanics, Asians, and others—are important parts of the American mosaic. In the early 1960s, The Outdoor Recreation Resources Review Committee reported a significant difference in the outdoor pursuits between Whites and America's minority population. The Committee's assertion was confirmed by many other studies (Manning, 1985).

Ethnic groups should be encouraged to participate in outdoor pursuits but not necessarily to be assimilated into the main culture. Ethnic identity should be maintained, although assimilation in the main culture has its advantages as shown in these two studies. It seems that interethnic contacts increase similarity in leisure pursuits between Blacks and Whites (Floyd & Shinew, 1999). Also, bicultural Hispanic groups place greater importance on family-related recreation benefits compared with the least assimilated Hispanics (Shaull & Gramann, 2001). The number of persons with Asian heritage is increasing in the United Sates. Although this population practices many traditional activities depending on the country of origin, it seems that the assimilation of youth with these backgrounds into the main culture is meeting difficulties (Tirone & Pedlar, 1997).

Thapa, Graef, and Absher (2002) examined aspects of information use and search behaviors of ethnic groups in Angeles and San Bernardino National Forest in California. Consistent with previous studies, Whites generally reported using all available information sources to a greater extent than Hispanics or other minority groups. Hispanics were least likely to approach rangers or employees for information, and other minority groups were least likely to pay attention to bulletin boards. Flyers and brochures were among the most frequently used information sources for all ethnic groups. Whites were more likely to seek out information for orientation and educational purposes, and Hispanics attributed more importance to instrumental uses, such as seeking information about parking facilities, permits, and operating hours. Needless to say that these are important for both research and management of outdoor activities.

In another study (Gobster, 2002), the planning for Chicago's largest park provided an opportunity to examine use patterns and preferences in outdoor recreation among a racially and ethnically diverse clientele. Results from on-site surveys of 898 park users (217 Black, 210 Latino, 182 Asian, and 289 White) showed that park users shared a core set of interests, preferences, and concerns about the park. But there were also important differences among and within racial and ethnic groups with respect to park use patterns, participation, and reports of racial discrimination. Possibly other demographic factors come into play within the ethnic community.

OUTDOOR PURSUITS AND SPECIAL POPULATIONS

Kennedy, Austin, and Smith (1987) stated that there are many shortcomings in the labeling of the members of special populations, yet labels must be used to emphasize their special needs. Special populations are groups of individuals with special needs or exceptionalities who should be attended to by specially trained and qualified personnel. Select information is needed on the quality of life of each group so programs may be provided for them in the outdoors. Data on their quality of life are readily available, but data on the numbers of the members in each special population are sometimes difficult to locate.

Persons With Disabilities and Outdoor Experiences

It is estimated that over 6 million Americans have some limitation that could prevent them from participating in regular recreational programs (Pati et al., 1997). These cases include persons with orthopedic challenges; persons with cerebral palsy; the blind; the deaf; and persons suffering from muscular dystrophy, multiple sclerosis, and cardiac malfunction. Many of these people show interest in leisure pursuits, including outdoor ones. Depending on the case, the outdoor experience should be modified accordingly. Kennedy et al. (1987) suggested the following guidelines:

1. Change as little as necessary. For example, try to keep the structure of the activity as close as possible to the existing activity. It is better to undermodify so as to challenge the individual and to provide normalized experiences.
2. Where possible, involve the person in the selection and activity modification process. Many times the user is a good source of information. Trails

for persons with physical disabilities are based on this phenomenon. All of the modifications have historically needed the approval of the participants.

3. There may be elements of competition to consider when working with groups of children and adults. For instance, in ski competitions, past performance, age, and gender of the participant are usually considered when pairing individuals for competitive purposes.

4. Try to offer activities that are characteristic of individuals who are in mainstream society. Offer the same leisure opportunities that exist in society to persons with disabilities. The normalization principle should be emphasized, and the idea of inventing activities should be de-emphasized.

5. Where possible, activities should have common denominators, especially if they are modified. For example, in ski competitions everyone follows the same rules. The physical disability and the fact that everyone follows the same rules are the common denominators for equality in participation.

6. In many instances, the person with a disability is cast in a role of spectator. The authors of this volume strongly feel that individuals should be provided opportunities to participate in participant-based activities.

7. Although the authors do not devalue cooperative and other noncompetitive leisure experiences, the person with a disability should have ample opportunities to participate in equitable competitive situations.

8. Start at the level where the participants are currently functioning. This does not mean starting at the lowest level.

9. Individuals should be given opportunities for free choice. This may enhance the feeling of control.

When it comes to the availability of outdoor experiences for persons with disabilities, the Americans With Disabilities Act of 1990 reconciled itself with the Wilderness Act of 1964 by stating that those who use wheelchairs for everyday indoor activities shall not be barred from enjoying wilderness (Schultz, 2005).

The Socially Deviant and Outdoor Experiences

While sociologists look at deviancy as the outcome of cultural and environmental factors, psychologists tend to view it as the result of personality disorganization. Whatever the case, the individuals who are in the correctional system may benefit from recreational experiences in natural settings. In some instances, the experience is used as a form of rehabilitation, as is the case with the deep-sea diving program in the men's colony in Chino, California. If these men were type T personalities, risk-takers, such a program would provide the challenge they need. In other cases, the activity is deemed somewhat preventive, as with provisions of outdoor experiences in the Outward Bound program for youth at risk. The activity is thought to keep the person from deteriorating into further deviancy.

Older Adults and Outdoor Experiences

As shown earlier in the section on leisure pursuits and life course, the interests of older adults change due to a number of factors. According to Burdman (1986), the reduction in the number of muscular and nerve cells is accompanied by a loss of elasticity. Also, the person suffers from less efficiency in all body systems. The outcome is an increase in ailments such as cardiovascular, respiratory, and musculoskeletal problems; diabetes mellitus; and hypothermia. Moreover, older adults could suffer from psychological problems such as depression, dementia, and alcoholism. Recreational programs including outdoor experiences have proven beneficial. For instance, Owens (1982) found that satisfaction with leisure contributed significantly to life satisfaction of the 205 older adults he studied.

According to Leitner and Leitner (1985), the leisure patterns of older adults, although diverse, are dominated by television viewing and reading. A possible reason for this could be their physical limitations. This may add to the feeling of loneliness as shown by the study of Creecy, Wright, and Berg (1982). On the other hand, popular outdoor activities, including gardening and camping, may decrease loneliness through socialization (Leitner & Leitner, 1985; McAvoy, 1982).

Stress can have a negative influence on psychological and physical health, particularly among older adults. Orsega-Smith, Mowen, Payne, and Godbey (2004) examined the relationship between stress, park-based leisure, and physiological health among older adults (aged 50–86). There were significant interactive effects between (a) stress and length of park stay and (b) stress and desired health benefits in their relationship to the physiological health indicator body mass index (BMI). There were also direct relationships between park companionship and perceived physical health and between length of park stay and lower systolic blood pressure.

SUMMARY

In this chapter on the social aspects of outdoor experiences, we considered the roles played by the socializing agents. The family is one of the most important in that respect, as is religion. Both agents could determine what is acceptable and what is not as a recreational activity. Although there are enough empirical studies on the role that the family plays in this regard, there is a paucity of empirical evidence on the role of religion. Still, it is clear from the study of rituals that some elements of leisure pursuits may have evolved thereof. For example, Shrove Tuesday activities in Chester, England, were the starting point for soccer, which has evolved into the world's most popular sport.

Three other social institutions affect leisure behavior, namely, the political structure, the economic system, and the technological level of the society at hand. The political structure controls leisure offerings through legislation on the local, state, or federal level. We will give details on these three levels in Chapters 7, 8, and 9. In the next chapter, we present the relationship between the economic structure and leisure. We presented technology here as divided into two aspects: material and social technology. Material technology refers to scientific advances as well as industrialization. Their impact on outdoor pursuits is exemplified in the increasing number of snowmobiles in North America. Social technology refers to education and the mass media. The introduction of nature documentaries on television has helped to make people aware of the importance of conservation.

Other than primary and secondary groups, demographic factors such as age, gender, occupation, residence, and ethnicity have been studied by researchers. We presented the results of these studies in this chapter. For instance, early socialization into outdoor pursuits has been shown to be desirable. Also, it has been found that men seem to have more free time than women and that the higher paying one's occupation is, the greater the participation in outdoor pursuits. Rural dwellers seem to enjoy more nature activities than do urban dwellers.

We also presented the role that recreational activities play in the lives of special populations. It seems that outdoor recreational activities help self-awareness of persons with mental disabilities, the self-confidence of persons with physical disabilities, and the self-expression of social deviants.

REFERENCES

Adler, P. A., & Adler, A. (1999). Social reproduction and the corporate other: The institutionalization of after school activities. *The Sociological Quarterly, 35*(2), 309.

Allen, L., Long, P., & Perdue, R. (1987). The role of leisure: Satisfaction in rural communities. *Leisure Today, 1987,* 5–8.

American Camp Association. (2013). ACA REPORT- Directions: Youth development outcomes of the camp experience. Retrieved June 28, 2013, from http://www.acacamps.org/research/enhance/directions

Bammel, G., & Burrus-Bammel, L. (1981). *Human behavior and leisure.* Dubuque, IA: Wm. C. Brown.

Berg, E. C., Trost, M., Schneider, I. E., & Allison, M. T. (2000). Dyadic exploration of the relationship of leisure satisfaction, leisure time and gender to relationship satisfaction. *Leisure Sciences, 23,* 35–46.

Bevins, M., Bond, R., Concorn, T., McIntosh, K., & McNeil, R. (1968). *Characteristics of hunters and fishermen in six northeastern states* (Vermont Agriculture Experimental Station Bulletin 565). Burlington, VA: Vermont Agriculture Experimental Station.

Bialeschki, M., & Henderson, K. (1986). Leisure in the common world of women. *Leisure Studies, 53,* 299–308.

Boy Scouts of America (2013). 100 years in review 1910–2010. Retrieved June 28, 2013, from http://www.scouting.org/About/FactSheets/100_years.aspx

Bradshaw, R., & Jackson, J. (1979). Socialization for leisure. In H. Ibrahim & R. Crandall (Eds.), *Leisure: A psychological approach.* Los Alamitos, CA: Hwong.

Breaking point. (1995, March). *Newsweek, 6,* 56.

Bultena, G., & Field, D. (1978). Visitors to national parks: Test of the elitism argument. *Leisure Sciences, 1*(4), 395–409.

Burdge, R. J. (1969). Levels of occupational prestige and leisure activity. *Journal of Leisure Research, 1*(3), 202–224.

Burdman, G. M. (1986). *Healthful aging.* Englewood Cliffs, NJ: Prentice Hall.

Burrus-Bammel, L., & Bammel, G. (1990, April). Outdoor/environmental education: An overview for the wise use of leisure. *Leisure Today, 1990,* 17–22.

Butler, G. (1961). *Introduction to community recreation.* New York, NY: Macmillan.

Camp Fire. (2013). Camp fire recognizes dignity and worth. Retrieved June 28, 2013, from http://www.campfireusa.org/inclusionPolicy.aspx

Cheek, N. (1981). Social cohesion and outdoor recreation. In J. Kelly (Ed.), *Social benefits of outdoor recreation.* Champaign, IL: Leisure Behavior Laboratory, University of Illinois.

Cheek, N., & Burch, W. (1976). *The social organization of leisure in human society.* New York, NY: Harper and Row.

Clarke, A. C. (1956). The use of leisure and its relation to levels of occupational prestige. *American Sociological Review, 21,* 301–307.

Cordell, H. K., Green, G. T., & Betz, C. J. (2002). Recreation and environment as cultural dimensions in contemporary American society. *Leisure Sciences, 24*(1), 13–41.

Creecy, R. F., Wright, R., & Berg, W. E. (1982). Correlates of loneliness among the black elderly. *Activities Adaptation and Aging, 3*(2), 9–16.

Csikszentmihalyi, M. (1981, December). Leisure and socialization. *Social Forces, 60,* 2.

Csikszentmihalyi, M., & Larson, R. (1984). *Being adolescent.* New York, NY: Basic Books.

DiPietro, J. (1981). Rough and tumble play: A function of gender. *Developmental Psychology, 12,* 50–58.

Durkheim, E. (1915). *The elementary forms of religious life.* London, England: George Allen and Unwin.

Edwards, C. P. (2001). Worlds of experience after school. *Human Development, 44,* 59.

Eitzen, D. S., & Sage, G. (1989). *Sociology of North American sport.* Dubuque, IA: Wm. C. Brown.

Erikson, E. (1977). *Toys and reason: Stages in the ritualization of experience.* New York, NY: Norton.

Ewert. A. (1991). Luther Gulick 1865–1918. In H. Ibrahim (Ed.), *Pioneers in leisure and recreation* (pp. 79–92). Reston, VA: American Alliance for Health, Physical Education, Recreation, and Dance.

Fasting, K., & Sisjord, M. K. (1985). Gender roles and barriers to participation in sport. *Sociology of Sport Journal, 2*(4), 345–351.

Field, D. R. (2000). Social groups and parks: Leisure behavior in time and space. *Journal of Leisure Research, 32*(1), 27–31.

Fink, B., & Wild, K. (1995). Similarities in leisure interests: Effect of selection and socialization on friendships. *Journal of Social Psychology, 135*, 471–482.

Floyd, M. R., & Shinew, K. J. (1999). Convergence and divergence toward an interracial contact hypothesis. *Journal of Leisure Research, 3*(4), 359–384.

Fong, Y., & Zhang, J. (2001). The identification of unobservable independent and spousal leisure. *Journal of Political Economy, 109*, 19.

Foret, C. M. (1985). *Life satisfaction and leisure satisfaction among young-old and old-old adults with rural and urban residence* (Unpublished doctoral dissertation). Texas Women's University, Denton, TX.

Gerson, G., Ibrahim, H. M., DeVries, J., & Eisen, G. (1988). *Understanding leisure: An interdisciplinary approach.* Dubuque, IA: Kendall/Hunt.

Glyptis, S., & Chambers, D. (1982). No place like home. *Leisure Studies, 1,* 247–262.

Gobster, P. H. (2002). Managing urban parks for racially and ethnically diverse clientele. *Leisure Sciences, 24*(2), 143–159.

Gordon, C., Gaitz, C. M., & Scott, J. (1976). Leisure and life. In R. Binstock & E. Shamas (Eds.), *Handbook of aging and social science.* New York, NY: Van Nostrand Reinhold.

Hendee, J. (1969). Rural-urban differences reflected in outdoor recreation participation. *Journal of Leisure Research, 1,* 33–41.

Henderson, K. A., & Hickerson, B. (2007). Women and leisure: Premises and performances uncovered in an integrative review. *Journal of Leisure Research, 39*(4), 591–610.

Hill, J., & McLean, D. (1999). Introduction: Defining our perspective of the future. *JOPERD, 70,* 21.

Ho, C., Sasidharan, V., & Elmendorf, W. (2005). Gender and ethnic variations in urban park preferences, visitation and percieved benefits. *Journal of Leisure Research, 37*(3), 281–306.

Ibrahim, H. (1981). Leisure behavior among contemporary Egyptians. *Journal of Leisure Research, 13,* 89–104.

Jackson, E., & Henderson, K. (1995). Gender-based analysis of leisure constraints. *Leisure Sciences, 17,* 31.

Kelly, J. (1974). Socialization toward leisure: A developmental approach. *Journal of Leisure Research, 6,* 181-93.

Kelly, J. (1981). Family benefit from outdoor recreation. In J. Kelly (Ed.), *The social benefits of outdoor recreation.* Champaign, IL: Leisure Behavior Laboratory, University of Illinois.

Kelly, J. (1983). *Leisure identities and interaction.* London, England: George Allen and Unwin.

Kennedy, D., Austin, D., & Smith, R. (1987). *Special recreation: Opportunities for persons with disabilities.* Philadelphia, PA: Saunders.

Kleiber, D., & Rickards, W. (1981). Outdoor recreation and child development. In J. Kelly (Ed.), *Social benefits of outdoor recreation.* Champaign, IL: Leisure Behavior Laboratory, University of Illinois.

Knopp, T. (1972). Environmental determinants of recreation behavior. *Journal of Leisure Behavior, 4,* 129–138.

Leitner, M., & Leitner, S. (1985). *Leisure in later life.* New York, NY: Hawthorn Press.

Little, D. E. (2002). Women and adventure recreation: Reconstructing leisure constraints and adventure experiences to negotiate continuing participation. *Journal of Leisure Research, 34*(2), 157–177.

Maclean, J., Peterson, J., & Martin, W. D. (1985). *Recreation and leisure: The changing scene.* New York, NY: Macmillan.

Malsam, M., & Nelson, L. (1984). Integrating curriculum objectives. *JOPERD, 55*(7), 52–54.

Manning, H. (1975). *Backpacking: One step at a time.* New York, NY: Vintage Books.

Manning, R. (1985*). Studies in outdoor recreation: Search and research for satisfaction.* Corvallis: Oregon State University Press.

Martin, D. C. (2004). Apartheid in the Great Outdoors: American advertising and the reproduction of racialized outdoor leisure identity. *Journal of Leisure Research, 36*(4), 513–535.

McAvoy, L. H. (1982). The leisure preference problems and needs of the elderly. *Journal of Gerontology, 11*(1), 40–47.

McDermott, L. (2004). Exploring intersections of physicality and female-only canoeing experiences. *Leisure Studies, 23,* 283–301

Moskoff, W. (1984). *Labor and leisure in the Soviet Union.* New York, NY: St. Martin's Press.

Neumeyer, M., & Neumeyer, E. (1936). *Leisure and recreation.* New York, NY: A. S. Barnes.

Neumeyer, M., & Neumeyer, E. (1949). *Leisure and recreation* (Rev. ed.). New York, NY: A. S. Barnes.

Orsega-Smith, E., Mowen, A. J., Payne, L. L., & Godbey, G. (2004). The interaction of stress and park use on psycho-physiological health in older adults. *Journal of Leisure Research, 36*(2), 232–256.

Orthner, D. (1976). Patterns of leisure and marital interaction. *Journal of Leisure Research, 8,* 98–116.

Orthner, D., Barnett, L., & Ancinin, J. (1994). Leisure and family over the life cycle. In L. L'Abate (Ed.), *Handbook of developmental psychology and psychotherapy.* New York, NY: John Wiley.

Owens, D. J. (1982). The relationship of frequency and types of activity to life satisfaction in elderly deaf people. *Dissertation Abstracts International, 42,* 311A.

Pati, A.B., et al. (1997). Recreation/leisure interest of inpatient rehabilitation clients. *Physical Therapy, 79*(5), 78.

Payne, L. L., Mowen, A. J., & Orsega-Smith, E. (2002). An examination of park preference and behavior among urban residents: The role of residential location, race and age. *Leisure Science, 24*(2), 181–198.

Pohl, S., Borrie, W. T., & Patterson, M. E. (2000). Women, wilderness and everyday life: A documentation of the connection between wilderness recreation and women's everyday lives. *Journal of Leisure Research, 32*(4), 415–434.

Rauber, P. (2006). Building bridges to the outdoors. *Sierra, 91*(4), 55.

Roberts, K. (1970). *Leisure.* London, England: Longman.

Rosenthal, M. (1986). *The character factory: Baden-Powell's Boy Scouts and the imperative of the empire.* New York, NY: Pantheon Books.

Schultz, E. (2005). New paths in the wilderness. *Wilderness, 2005,* 39–60.

Sessoms, H. D. (1963, October). An analysis of selected variables affecting outdoor recreation patterns. *Social Forces, 42,* 112–115.

Shamir, B., & Ruskin, H. (1983). Sex differences in recreational sport behavior and attitudes: A study of married couples in Israel. *Leisure Studies, 2*(3), 253–268.

Shaull, S. L., & Gramann, J. H. (2001). The effect of cultural assimilation on the importance of family related and nature related recreation among Hispanic Americans. *Journal of Leisure Research, 30*(1), 47–63.

Shaw, S. (1985). Gender and leisure: Inequality in the distribution of leisure time. *Journal of Leisure Research, 17*(4), 266–282.

Shepard, P. (1977). Place and human development. In *Children, nature, and the urban environment* (Gen. Tech. Rep. NE 30, pp. 7–12). Washington, DC: U.S. Government Printing Office.

Smith, J., Carlson, R., Donaldson, G., & Masters, H. (1970). *Outdoor education.* Englewood Cliffs, NJ: Prentice Hall.

Snyder, E., & Spreitzer, E. (1978). *Social aspects of sport.* Englewood Cliffs, NJ: Prentice Hall.

Thapa, B., Graef, A. R., & Absher, J. D. (2002). Information needs and search behaviors: A comparative study of ethnic groups in the Angeles and San Bernadino national forests, California. *Leisure Sciences, 24*(2), 143–159.

Tirone, S., & Pedlar, A. (1997). Assimilation and conflict: Leisure experiences in the lives of South Asian adolescents in Canada. In National Recreation and Park Association, *Abstracts from the 1997 Symposium on Leisure Research* (p. 2). Ashburn, VA: National Recreation and Park Association.

Turner, V. (1985). *100 years of YMCA camping.* Chicago, IL: YMCA of the USA.

Walker, G. J., & Kiecolt, K. I. (1995). Social class and wilderness use. *Leisure Sciences, 17,* 295–308.

Wells, M. S., Wiidmer, M. A., & McCoy, J. K. (2004). Grubs and grasshoppers: Challenge-based recreation and the collective efficacy of families. *Family Relations, 53*(3), 326–333.

West, P., & Merriam, L. (1970). Outdoor recreation and family cohesiveness. *Journal of Leisure Research, 2,* 251–259.

White, C. (1955). Social class differences in the uses of leisure. *American Journal of Sociology, 61,* 145–150.

YMCA Canada. (2013). Day and resident camp. Retrieved June 28, 2013, from http://www.ymca.ca/en/programs-and-services/camps.aspx

YMCA USA. (2013). Discover: Find a camp. Retrieved June 28, 2013, from http://www.ymca.net/find-a-y-camp/

Yoesting, D., & Burkhead, D. (1973). Significance of childhood recreation experience on adult leisure behavior. *Journal of Leisure Research, 5,* 25–36.

Chapter 6
The Economics of Outdoor Pursuits

Why is it that in a society with such a capitalistic orientation, many American politicians and naturalists argue for the preservation of large chunks of government land for outdoor enjoyment? Why do they also fight for the provision of programs and activities on those lands? Perhaps because some of them feel that Americans should be rewarded for their hard work. Work is a necessity, but leisure can also be meaningful (Marano, 1999). Meaningful activities are those with which a person can easily identify. Some claim that leisure in a natural setting is more than pleasant, it is important to human welfare and can be therapeutic, if not euphoric (Esteve, Martín, & López, 1999).

Many believe the claim that leisure is beneficial to human welfare is exaggerated (Olson, 1961), yet the provisions for outdoor experiences continue to exist even though the number of those who participate in genuine outdoor pursuits may seem too small to some to warrant the expense of maintaining vast outdoor recreational opportunities. What these people do not realize is that outdoor recreational pursuits are integral to the total leisure scene in the countries of the Western world, particularly the United States and Canada. Likewise, natural areas and related programs are provided in many developing countries, although not necessarily for

their own citizens but for badly needed hard currency coming from foreign tourists (Ibrahim, 1991). In other words, leisure is a source of income for the producers of its goods and services as well as a source of pleasure and meaningfulness for the ones who consume these goods and services. How did this come about in a country such as the United States that was not so long ago straddled with a puritanical ideology? Even by the time of the writing of its Constitution, a proposal was forwarded to include in its articles a prohibition against horse racing, gambling, and all extravagance (Dulles, 1965). A presentation on the nature of the economic system and the changes that have occurred will shed light on this development.

THE NATURE OF THE ECONOMIC SYSTEM

In 1960, Rostow showed that certain requirements have to be met and certain steps have to be taken before leisure spending can become an important ingredient in society's economic system. In essence, the society should be at the stage of high consumption (i.e., when most of its citizens could become high consumers of goods and services including leisure goods and services). At an earlier stage of economic development, it is possible that only a few privileged citizens become high consumers. These were the members of the leisure class of past eras (Veblen, 1953). Today, many Americans are members of that leisure class; most of them are high consumers.

The American economy entered the high mass consumption phase, which includes leisure spending in the 1920s, when most of the American economic output consisted of goods and services for individuals, households, and groups to consume, a good share of which are included under leisure spending. See Figure 6.1 showing spending trends for leisure in the United States. In 1962, leisure spending was about $48 billion, and in a quarter of a century, the figure jumped to almost $320 billion. Today, it places $646 billion into the U.S. economy each year and creates 6.1 million jobs nationally (Hyatt, 2012). What makes leisure such a potent force in the American economy? Three important factors follow (MacLean, Peterson, & Martin, 1985):

1. **Productivity:** The gross national product (GNP), which is the total market value of goods and services, has increased at an average rate of 3% per year for many years. Increased productivity means that more goods and services are provided to be consumed. This requires a concomitant increase in income.

2. **Increased income:** A substantial increase in income above and beyond what is needed to purchase essential goods and services is necessary to consume "the nonessentials," that is, leisure services and equipment, whether provided by the private or public sector. This increase is called discretionary income. An increase in productivity and a viable discretionary income may not, in themselves, have led to the general increase in leisure pursuits that has been witnessed in the last few decades in the United States. Another Ingredient was at work, an increase in free time.

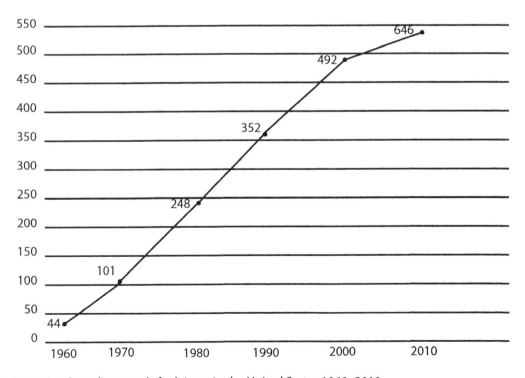

Figure 6.1. Spending trends for leisure in the United States 1960–2010.

3. **Increased free time:** For leisure to become an important facet of a society, it is crucial to have time free from familial, civil, and work obligations—time in which a person can partake in an activity for its own sake, for its intrinsic value. Societal values play important roles in how an individual perceives time as being free from obligations. The value system in the United States has changed drastically since the early settlement of the country. There were attempts to include in the U.S. Constitution provisions that prohibit gambling, horse racing, and the like. Today, some of these activities are sponsored by government agencies. Also, Americans have witnessed a change in their attitude toward work. The drop in work time from 50+ hours per week to 30+ hours per week from 1870 to 1970 allowed for an increase in free time to about 32 hours per week (Jensen, 1985; United Media Enterprises, 1983). Jensen's (1985) figures are based on a summary of previous time-budget studies, and the United Media Enterprises (1983) work is based on interviews of 1,024 persons from the general public, 101 newspaper editors, 105 cable television directors, and 116 network television news directors. Today, the average nonfarm private sector employee works 34.5 hours per week (U.S. Bureau of Labor Statistics, 2014).

In addition to increased productivity, increased income, and increased free time, the higher level of mobility of Americans played an important role in the phenomenal increase in leisure pursuits in the United States. The automobile, which facilitated business and trade, became an important element in leisure pursuits as well by providing access to recreational resources. More recently, people of all ages began using RVs to go into areas that had been inaccessible. There, they found another U.S. invention, the campground,

which has evolved in a short time into a convenient recreational facility with amenities such as flush toilets and hot showers. The convenience of the campground is surpassed only by the convenience of the RV, which has been described as the great indoors in the great outdoors.

These four variables, productivity, discretionary income, discretionary time, and mobility, are still affecting leisure behavior in the United States, Canada, and other industrial societies. For instance, a shift in work structure and the evolution of the workweek continues as technology allows employees to work from home and can save commuting time, but can also cause interruptions due to a less structured work time. A primary barrier to family leisure time is work. One study showed that those working full or part time spend the least amount of time with family each week, 28.1 hours and 27.9 hours, respectively (Mintel International Group, 2011). Nonetheless, spending on leisure goods such as pleasure boats, RVs, snowmobiles, athletic equipment, and sportswear has continued to climb in the last few years, as shown in Tables 6.1 and 6.2.

Active Outdoor Recreation Economy

The active outdoor recreation economy begins with the more than 3 out of 4 Americans who participate in active outdoor recreation each year (Outdoor Industry Association [OIA], 2006). By simply hiking, biking, camping, and participating in other outdoor activities, this diverse group of Americans from all income levels spends money, creates jobs, and supports local communities. The outdoor recreation economy depends on two forms of spending (OIA, 2012):

1. **Outdoor recreation product sales:** This vital, growing economic super sector is essential to the American economy and is responsible for contributing $120.7 billion per year. It is interesting to note that Americans spend nearly $53 billion on snow sports alone. That is almost as much as the $54 billion spent on Internet access.

Table 6.1

Economic Contributions to the National Economy of National Park Service Visitor Spending

Sector	Jobs	Labor income ($ millions)	Value added ($ millions)	Output ($ millions)
Direct Effects				
Hotels, motels, and B&Bs	38,707	1,363.1	2,577.2	4,454.6
Camping and other accomodations	3,970	148.7	197.7	358.8
Restaurants and bars	50,741	1,172.0	1,701.5	2,964.3
Grocery and convenience stores	5,200	162.8	220.3	306.3
Gas stations	2,740	99.8	150.8	200.5
Transit and ground transportation services	8,315	380.2	725.4	1,071.3
Other amusement and recreation industries	28,604	716.8	1,028.8	1,490.1
Retail establishments	7,051	201.6	330.6	410.9
Total Direct Effects	**145,328**	**4,245.0**	**6,932.3**	**11,256.8**
Secondary Effects	97,384	5,102.3	8,876.9	15,497.3
Total Effects	**242,712**	**9,347.0**	**15,809.0**	**26,754.0**

Table 6.2

Measures of Economic Significance of the U.S. National Park System

Analytic approach	Indicators	Geographic concern
Economic Benefits	Value derived from *direct use* such as recreation, or *passive use*, such as the value of knowing national treasures are protected and will be passed on to future generations	National
Economic Impact	Sales, jobs, personal income, and value added generated from visitor spending	Local
Economic Growth	Trends in population, per capita income, employment, wages, housing costs, and the distributional effects throughout the economy	Local and Regional

Note. From *U.S. National Park System: An Economic Asset at Risk*, prepared by J. Hardner and B. McKenney for the National Parks Conservation Association, 2006, http://www.npca.org/assets/pdf/NPCA_Economic_Significance_Report.pdf, p. 7.

2. **Dollars spent on trips and travel:** U.S. citizens and international visitors who travel to the nation's parks, forests, and waters produce immense economic capacity, drive the economy, and initiate a ripple effect that reaches out and motivates other economic sectors. For instance, more than a billion visits are made to state (720 million) and national (276 million) parks each year (America's State Parks, 2013). These visits create a wide range of spending including entry fees, lessons, tickets, souvenirs, groceries or restaurants, rental cars, and airfares. Trips and travel-related spending add up to $524.8 billion each year (OIA, 2012).

When these direct sales enter the economy, millions of Americans also go to work. The outdoor economy supports 6.1 million jobs across the nation. This includes those in manufacturing, innovators in technical apparel, entrepreneurs, outdoor professionals, and so on. The active outdoor recreation economy does the following (OIA, 2012):

1. Contributes $646 billion dollars annually to the U.S. economy
2. Supports 6.1 million jobs across the nation
3. Generates $39.9 billion in federal tax revenue
4. Generates $39.7 billion in state and local tax revenue

MacLean et al. (1985) classified leisure spending in five categories:

1. **Recreation supplies and equipment:** This category includes durable items such as recreational vehicles and motorcycles; televisions, radios, and tape recorders; camping and sports equipment; musical instruments and art supplies; and garden supplies.
2. **Travel and vacation businesses:** With the marked improvement in transportation, travel and vacationing have become large businesses in this country. It includes ownership of a second home (for vacations) accommodation. Many states, such as Florida, are becoming dependent on travel as their most important source of income. Also, many countries today are becoming dependent on tourism, for example, Greece and Mexico.
3. **Sport and outdoor recreation:** Next to travel and vacationing, outdoor recreation and sports are the largest expenditure on leisure activities. Sports have been an important part of the leisure scene in America for many years. In addition, the increased interest in wellness and fitness has added to the expenditure in this category. A quarter of a century ago, the Bureau of Outdoor Recreation predicted a 141% increase in outdoor pursuits from 1965 to 2000. It is estimated that 140 million Americans made outdoor recreation a priority in their daily lives (OIA, 2012).
4. **Cultural activities:** This category includes music, drama, dance, arts and crafts, books and other publications, and museums. Not only are televisions and digital devices and recordings selling in record numbers, but attendance at musical and outdoor dramatic plays has also increased. Expenditure on arts and crafts supplies has increased. The same is witnessed in books and other publications. Attendance at museums has increased significantly.
5. **Home expenditure:** As stated in a previous chapter, the home is the most important center for leisure activity. Not only are most homes equipped with a backyard, but some are also equipped with a recreation or exercise room, a hot tub, and a swimming pool. Other home expenditures on leisure include playground equipment, hobby shops, and entertainment equipment, including computerized games. In the

neighborhood, the family spending on leisure includes going to movies, amusement parks, and theme restaurants.

Not only does outdoor activity improve the health of the nation, but it also improves the American economy through expeditures on travel, vacationing, and outdoor recreation product sales. They are supplemented by government expenditures in the provision of outdoor recreational areas, as discussed next.

Government Expenditures

Since all three levels of government—local, state, and federal—are involved directly in outdoor recreation, the amount of monies spent by each are investigated. Their major contribution is in the provision of areas such as parks and forests as well as the programs that occur in many of these areas. Originally, it was difficult to find out the amount of government allocations on recreation because, in many instances, these expenditures were not listed under a separate category. In more recent years, the U.S. government has begun to publish how much is spent on maintaining the huge pieces of land under its jurisdiction. State and local governments have been doing so for many years by publishing their budgets, including spending on recreation. More on these two levels of government in Chapters 8 and 9.

Federal Government Expenditures

Two federal departments are directly involved in the outdoor pursuits of Americans as they take place on federal lands: the Department of Agriculture through the management of national forests and the Department of the Interior through the management of national parks. The U.S. Forest Service and the National Park Service spend large sums of money on maintaining the areas under their control. Other federal agencies, such as the Bureau of Land Management and the Corps of Engineers, provide recreation for millions of Americans on their lands.

The national park system, for instance, provides a positive economic influence to surrounding communities and to the entire national tourism economy. The distribution of National Park Service (NPS) spending is displayed in Figure 6.2, and NPS visitor spending contributions to the national economy are exhibited Table 6.1. Visitors to the NPS spent $14.7 billion in local gateway communities while visiting NPS lands. These expenditures directly supported over 145,000 jobs, $4.2 billion in labor income, $6.9 billion in value added, and $11.3 billion in output in the national economy. The secondary effects of visitor spending supported 97,000 jobs, $5.1 billion in labor income, $8.9 billion in value added, and $15.5 billion in output in the national economy. Combined NPS visitor spending supported 242,000 jobs, $9.3 billion in labor income, $15.8 billion in value added, and $26.8 billion in output in the national economy (Thomas, Huber, & Koontz, 2014). The distribution of NPS visitor spending by spending category is displayed in Figure 6.2, and economic contributions to the national economy of NPS visitor spending is shown in Table 6.1. Measures of economic significance of the NPS are indicated in Table 6.2.

Nonetheless, the nearly $3 billion overall budget for the NPS is about $400 million or 13% less than it was 10 years ago. There tends to be about a $500 million to $600 million shortfall each year, and maintenance and construction falls about $325 million short of the amount necessary to prevent maintenance backlog. When this happens over several years, there is an estimated need for over $3 billion to avoid fiscal crisis and another $4.5 billion to $9.7 billion to eliminate the maintenance backlog (Hardner & McKenney, 2006; National Parks Conservation Association, 2011).

Without appropriate funds, there is obviously less money to staff visitor centers or to teach visitors about natural and cultural resources, but a fiscal crisis can mean infrastructure decay. Ecosystems can be overrun by exotic species, wildlife is more vulnerable to poachers, historic treasures are inadequately preserved, and/or public safety

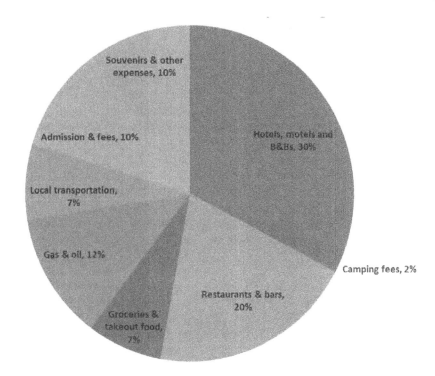

Figure 6.2. Distribution of NPS visitor spending. In 2012, visitors to NPS lands spent an estimated $14.7 billion in local gateway communities.

may be jeopardized. Projects such as road improvement can be delayed, but other park treasures could be lost forever.

Much, then, is dependent on the way the nation's parks, forests, and waters are managed. In 2013, national parks and surrounding communities lost an estimated $414 million in visitor spending during the 16-day government shutdown that resulted in nearly 8 million fewer visits to the parks, according to an interior department report (Associated Press, 2014). To help make ends meet, the NPS has turned to the following (National Parks Conservation Association, 2012):

1. Volunteers
2. Park friends groups and park philanthropies
3. Partnerships and collaborations
4. Private corporations
5. Charging recreational fees

State Expenditures

More than 720 million visits are made to over 7,000 of America's state parks with an economic impact of more than $20 billion in economic advantage to communities surrounding these parks nationwide (OIA, 2012).

Since 1965, the primary federal funding source for federal land acquisitions and grants to state government has been the Land and Water Conservation Fund (LWCF). Today, state grants are so low, however, that many states no longer apply for them. Other programs at the federal level now exist for funding land conservation activities, including habitat conservation and restoration, development of trails, urban parks, wetlands, forests, and farmland. These are managed by nine agencies (Walls, Darley, & Siikamäki, 2009).

Many states have also developed their own conservation funding programs and tax incentives. A few states provide a relatively new income tax credit for conservation land or easement donations. States with a sizable credit or those that make the credit transferrable have considerably impacted acreage preserved. Other funding and financing trends include the following (Walls et al., 2009):

1. Private conservation financing driven by wetlands and endangered species regulatory requirements
2. The use of voter referenda to raise funds for conservation, open space, and parks
3. Development of foundations, conservancies, and other nonprofit groups that benefit state parks

Beyond referenda, there appears to be a great deal of inconsistency among the states.

Local Government Expenditures

Sufficient funding for operations and maintenance, park programs, capital expenditures, and land acquisitions presents considerable challenges. Local governments contribute approximately $30 billion to parks and recreation, but in recent years, city parks rely more heavily on the nonprofit community and volunteers to fund often limited local government finances, launch new programs, and invest in park infrastructure (Walls et al., 2009). Local ballot initiatives are also a common means to procure money for open space and conservation programs. Some states also offer government funding programs.

In the United States and Canada, there are thousands of foundations that yearly fund parks and recreation. When local governments turn from lower tax supported funding to these foundations, it is meaningful for them to supply the community with the economic benefits of parks and to offer services that meet the demands of the community (Kirshman, 2012; Tharman & Gilbert, 2012). To help the community understand the economic value of parks and open spaces, it is important they understand the impacts of tourism. This is calculated by using local tourism spending and visitation data. Another example is providing statistics that show the property values of homes near these areas. Because people generally pay more for these homes, increased home values and sales lead to additional county property taxes (Kirshman, 2012). Finally, when community demands are met, more revenue and community support will likely be generated (Tharman & Gilbert, 2012).

Other Expenditures

Other than leisure pursuit expenditures by individuals, households, and governments, there are expenditures by public and private agencies that should be included in the estimates of the total expenditure picture. For instance, camps of youth service organizations are examples of nonprofit organizations spending on leisure pursuits and a school camp is an example of what a public agency spends on leisure pursuits.

Spending on, and for, leisure pursuits is only half of the total picture, the other half being the incomes accrued from these activities. These incomes have strong impact on the economy of the nation, state, region, and locality.

NATIONAL ECONOMIC IMPACT

It is estimated that the private recreation business provides nearly 7% of the total employment in the United States (Walsh, 1986). When the number of those employed in the leisure delivery system provided by the public sector is added to the above, the impact of leisure spending on the American economy becomes clearer. In addition, foreign tourists account for 4% of the total exports of American goods and services, which helps in addressing the problem of trade deficits in the U.S. economy.

Demand and Supply

The outdoor recreation system can be seen as a composition of four elements (Knudson, 1984):

Visitors and their characteristics	Demand
Recreational resources	Supply
Plans and policies	Pricing
Tools for implementation	Management

These four economic parallels affect outdoor pursuits. In the U.S. economic system, the concepts of demand and supply are used to determine economic policy. Demand is based on the ability and willingness of consumers to buy specific quantities of goods and services at a given time. To what extent is the American consumer able and willing to buy goods and services pertaining to outdoor pursuits? It is clear that the consumer has the purchasing power, as depicted in a discretionary income. This person is willing, as a consequence of value inculcation and lifestyle, to pursue leisure activities. What comes next is the matter of supply.

The supply mechanisms in the leisure business include direct supply and indirect supply (Kelly, 1985). Direct supply includes manufacturing, wholesaling, and retailing of equipment and apparel as well as the provision of services. In direct supply, the supplier deals directly with the consumer. In the second type of supply, some suppliers deal indirectly with the consumer, such as the writers who write the books that people read during free time or the actor in the movies that people watch.

In one study of demand in outdoor recreation in America, the researchers used a single exploratory variable, the average direct cost of auto operation times the distance, as a proxy for the price the consumer is willing to pay for an outdoor leisure experience (Clawson & Knetsch, 1966). Over the years, researchers have agreed that other nonprice variables are important determinants in the demand for recreational goods and leisure services (Walsh, 1986):

1. Socioeconomic characteristics of the consumer.
2. Attractiveness and quality of the recreational site.
3. Availability of substitute service.
4. Travel time.
5. Congestion or crowding.
6. Taste and preference of the consumer.

The supply side of the demand–supply continuum in outdoor recreation includes the recreational resources that are available to the consumer. A simple classification of these resources follows (Clawson & Knetsch, 1966):

1. **User-oriented areas:** The primary consideration is easy accessibility for the recreation consumer. Most local public and private facilities fall into this category.
2. **Intermediate areas:** The resource partially dictates the accessibility into these areas. Most regional and state-run facilities fall into this category.
3. **Resource-oriented areas:** The resource determines to a great extent the accessibility of the area to the consumer. National parks, forests, and wildlife refuges fall into this category.

PRICING AND MANAGING

It is hard to determine the price that a leisure consumer should pay for the use of a government-run recreational facility due to the absence of competitive markets. Running a proficient business such as a recreational program hinges upon management of an appropriate "least-cost price policy" (Walsh, 1986, p. 503). Accordingly, user fees should be set at the intersection of the demand curve with the marginal cost and average cost curve.

The demand curve shows how the quantity demanded of some recreational activity during a specific period will change as its price changes. Average cost includes the cost of investment plus the cost of operation. When and if the demand is equal to the supply, marginal cost will equal average cost. If the demand exceeds the supply, marginal cost will increase and profits will result. If the supply exceeds the demand, marginal cost will decrease and subsidy will be needed. It is clear how difficult it is to set user fees for a government-run recreational facility. Suffice it to say that one of the most difficult decisions to make concerning fees, as based on the above formula, is the cost of investment: What is the monetary value of a national park or a national forest? Adding to the difficulty is the inverse relationship between the demand for outdoor recreation and the supply of natural resources. The supply of these resources is abundant in areas that are located far from population concentration where the demand is great.

The problem of the inverse relationship between location of public lands and population centers was recognized in the report of the Outdoor Recreation Resources Review Commission (ORRRC) in 1962. It was recommended that the individual states develop comprehensive plans detailing their outdoor recreation supply and demand and providing recommendations for improving the situation. The plan was to be repeated every 5 years. A nationwide plan for outdoor recreation was prepared by the Bureau of Outdoor Recreation in 1973. Another plan was issued in 1979. Further details are provided in Chapters 7 and 8.

Management plays a key role in the economic aspects of an outdoor experience. Conceptual, biological, legal, and organizational skills are needed to manage these areas effectively and the programs provided in them (Knudson, 1984). Successful programs are an economic asset to their sponsoring agency. If success in management of outdoor recreational resources is to be attained, it must be preceded by an attempt to improve management constantly. It is also important for fiscal managers to consider the sensitivity of tourism and leisure consumers to price changes (Brayley & McLean, 2008). Price changes impact supply and demand, which affect revenue and profit.

The Economic Benefits of Outdoor Recreation

Outdoor recreation programs along with their facilities and lands, being a service to the public, appear to involve expenditures only. In fact, there are economic benefits to the general public, which is the actual owner of the lands involved. Economic benefits are generally defined relative to two basic

economic objectives. First, efficiency is seen when the monetary value of the benefits exceeds the monetary value of the costs. Second, equity is seen when the distribution of purchasing power among individual citizens is fair. There are many concerns related to efficiency and equity. Granted, the interest on the national level is in seeing that growth in national assets occurs and that the wealth of Americans improves, "however, our national concern in the international scene is not so much for efficiency at a world scale as it is for a favorable national balance of payment" (Peterson & Brown, 1986, p. V13). The same may be applied to state and local governments, where each jurisdiction tries to become internally efficient by maximizing internal net gain within their own boundaries.

Another important concern is, how much should governments spend on outdoor recreation projects? Will these projects contribute to National Economic Development (NED)? The NED objective is to increase the value of the output of goods and services. The contribution of outdoor recreation to NED is defined in terms of the net willingness of consumers to pay for the goods and services. Payments are done in the form of taxes to be approved by the citizens and in fees to be paid by recreationists. An estimate can be based on the direct consumption benefits of on-site leisure activities and the indirect consumption of the flow of information about these activities and sites and the preservation and protection of the sites (Walsh & Loomis, 1986).

REGIONAL AND LOCAL ECONOMIC IMPACTS

Economic activities are generated in a region or locality through the recreational use of natural resources within its boundaries. Many regions, states, and local communities establish their own economic development projects. The capitalization of parkland into the value of nearby property is termed *proximate principle*.

Researchers have suggested a positive impact of about 20% on property value abut-

Tourism has become a strong economic institution of global significance. An island resort on Cozumel Island in Mexico attracts scuba divers, who can take a break to visit ancient Mayan ruins.

ting or fronting a passive park (Curry, 2001). Nonetheless, abutting or fronting an active park may not be as desirable.

An outdoor recreation project may look economically beneficial, but planners must consider the loss of the natural resource to activities other than recreation, the increase in medical and other assistance to nonlocal tourists, and the increase in local prices due to the willingness of the tourists to overpay (Millard & Fischer, 1979).

The economic effects of investing in recreational development projects are divided into two categories. The first category includes the direct impact of transactions intimately related to the project or activities. The second category encompasses the chain of consequences that result from the direct effect (Alward, 1986). These secondary economic impacts go beyond the recreational site. Recreationists visit motels and restaurants on their way to and from recreational sites, and gas stations supply them with fuel to make the trip. Most, if not all, of the direct economic impacts will occur at or close to

the recreational site, yet the indirect impacts may be felt far from the site due to the predominance of interregional trade links.

Spatially, a hierarchical conceptualization of the impacted region can be seen in Figure 6.3 (Stevens & Rose, 1985). In the figure, the smallest spatial unit is the recreational site. Most of the direct economic impact of recreational activities occurs in the second unit, the support area. This area encompasses the retail outlets where the recreationists buy services and goods. A third area includes the travel corridors where there are impacts on transportation, food, and lodging services. The fourth area includes the residences of the recreationists along with the businesses that will provide them with the goods needed for the activities—the recreational clothing, equipment, and supplies. The fifth and final area extends beyond the fourth into the rest of the country and possibly the world where most, if not all, of the clothing, equipment, and supplies purchased in the fourth area may have been manufactured.

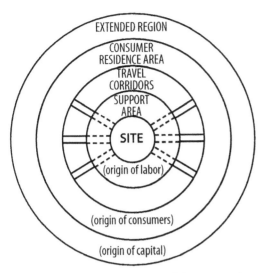

Figure 6.3. Regions impacted by recreation. From "Regional Input–Output Methods for Tourism Impact Analysis," by B. Stevens and A. Z. Rose, 1985, in *Assessing the Economic Impacts of Recreation and Tourism*, D. Propst, Ed., Asheville, NC: USDA Forest Service, Southeastern Forest Experiment Station, p. 17.

The economic impacts of outdoor recreation are difficult and difficult to assess. The task is easier when the recreational site is small, serving a small circle of recreationists. But when the recreational site is large, the analysis of its economic impact becomes more difficult. The situation becomes more complicated once the site becomes nationally and internationally renowned, as is true of some of the national parks. For example, tourists from abroad may have purchased their camping equipment from a country other than the one they are visiting.

Empirical Findings

The National Environmental Policy Act (NEPA) of 1969 requires under certain circumstances that project plans include information on social and economic effects. Environmental impact studies have yielded important information on the economic impact in the vicinity of a large recreational site. Large in this case means that the construction of the site would have an environmental impact. If there were no such impacts, infor-

mation on the economic and social impact would be lacking because the construction would have no significant effect on the quality of the environment. These studies include the estimated changes in direct and indirect output of each industry and business, income and employment, population shifts, and tax revenue and expenditure for social services in the region (Walsh, 1986). In addition, the effects on environmental quality are included such as air and water pollution. The studies also show the distribution of economic gains and losses of industry and businesses resulting from the construction of the recreational site.

Walsh (1986) stated that in studies of regional economic impacts, researchers have tended to emphasize gains and have failed to count losses, particularly of secondary nature. He reviewed Millard and Fischer (1979) and showed the following:

1. Development of a recreational site usually means that the natural resource cannot be used for other purposes.
2. An increase in local services occurs to provide for the influx of tourists and recreationists.
3. The site tends to be overused during the season and underused otherwise.
4. Higher prices may result as the influx of out-of-towners increases, who are willing to pay more for goods and services.
5. Congestion may result on roads and in the local businesses, which can alter the locals' lifestyle.
6. The average resident, who is not employed in an industry or business having to do with the recreational site, may be affected negatively by the change.

The Multiplier Effect

Positive or negative economic stimuli cause economic impacts that originate growth or cause reduction. When recreationists bring dollars into a local economy, they are making economic contributions.

Thus, these contributions are represented as jobs, income, retail sales (expenditures), and tax revenues (Southwick Associates, 2013). Whenever an injection of new demand is placed into the circular flow there is likely to be a multiplier effect that results when the extra income leads to additional spending and the creation of more income that ripples through the economy. The multiplier effect refers to this increase in final income that in turn arouses any new boost of additional spending (Economics Online, 2014). Table 6.3 shows direct total impacts by activities with the multiplier effect.

Table 6.3

The Outdoor Recreation Economy Direct and Total Impact by Activity Category[1]

	Gear, Accessories & Vehicles	Trip Related Sales	Total
Bicycling	$10,538,970,178	$70,781,975,693	$81,320,945,871
Camping	$18,613,995,403	$124,769,735,895	$143,383,731,298
Fishing[2]	$9,742,089,046	$25,725,732,919	$35,467,821,965
Hunting[3]	$8,525,723,987	$14,636,912,252	$23,162,636,239
Motorcycling	$10,024,945,513	$32,501,773,446	$42,526,718,959
Off-Roading	$13,160,580,559	$53,334,247,815	$66,494,828,375
Snow Sports	$7,718,490,380	$45,328,719,522	$53,047,209,901
Trail Sports	$12,251,578,246	$68,376,967,617	$80,628,545,863
Water Sports	$19,420,893,225	$66,776,605,002	$86,197,498,227
Wildlife Viewing[4]	$10,736,692,517	$22,585,482,854	$33,322,175,371
All Activities	$120,733,959,053	$524,818,153,015	$645,552,112,068

THE DIRECT IMPACTS BUSINESSES SERVING RECREATIONISTS ANNUALLY PROVIDE:

	Participants' Spending	Jobs Supported[5]	Income[6]	Federal Taxes	State & Local Taxes
Bicycling	$81,320,945,871	772,146	$38,648,426,853	$5,174,111,079	$5,574,649,290
Camping	$143,383,731,298	1,356,902	$68,478,337,142	$9,427,118,081	$7,129,695,106
Fishing[2]	$35,467,821,965	307,175	$12,665,085,157	$2,150,221,890	$2,424,626,040
Hunting[3]	$23,162,636,239	201,822	$9,016,303,488	$1,477,166,379	$1,545,494,202
Motorcycling	$42,526,718,959	410,972	$20,826,351,065	$2,793,477,670	$2,592,588,678
Off-Roading	$66,494,828,375	684,464	$33,589,472,749	$4,410,555,545	$4,056,094,360
Snow Sports	$53,047,209,901	504,342	$25,248,804,500	$3,187,138,690	$3,714,016,392
Trail Sports	$80,628,545,863	768,251	$38,431,908,045	$5,140,507,597	$5,555,850,984
Water Sports	$86,197,498,227	802,062	$40,325,800,635	$3,730,693,094	$4,853,254,404
Wildlife Viewing[4]	$33,322,175,371	289,168	$13,018,994,705	$2,378,112,717	$2,229,661,345
All Activities	$645,552,112,068	6,097,303	$300,249,484,338	$39,869,102,741	$39,675,930,802

THE RIPPLE EFFECT CREATED FROM THE DIRECT IMPACTS IS EVEN GREATER:

	Ripple Effect Spending[7]	Jobs Supported[5]	Income[6]	Federal Taxes	State & Local Taxes
Bicycling	$198,747,895,981	1,478,475	$101,437,240,467	$12,650,585,765	$13,636,495,368
Camping	$356,462,236,509	2,618,577	$180,781,845,610	$23,043,702,517	$17,416,053,882
Fishing[2]	$97,759,933,329	763,262	$34,168,207,715	$5,722,310,749	$6,499,863,763
Hunting[3]	$61,924,172,768	460,223	$23,711,273,356	$3,745,306,917	$3,953,276,857
Motorcycling	$102,072,982,246	767,363	$52,994,114,496	$6,717,463,094	$6,254,971,503
Off-Roading	$165,046,037,979	1,273,130	$86,679,309,235	$10,946,221,713	$10,061,337,739
Snow Sports	$129,617,935,438	964,884	$66,206,588,130	$7,799,705,749	$9,080,167,867
Trail Sports	$196,884,308,195	1,466,941	$100,659,948,859	$12,560,296,484	$13,582,923,165
Water Sports	$206,311,014,957	1,521,486	$104,811,013,503	$9,118,759,152	$11,689,789,939
Wildlife Viewing[4]	$100,808,196,738	722,398	$36,548,075,766	$6,655,021,673	$6,255,499,241
All Activities	$1,615,634,714,139	12,036,739	$787,997,617,135	$98,959,373,813	$98,430,379,325

Note. From *The Outdoor Recreation Economy,* by Outdoor Industry Association, 2012, https://outdoorindustry.org/pdf/OIA_OutdoorRecEconomyReport2012.pdf , p. 17.
[1]View technical report for full details at outdoorindustry.org. [2]American Sportfishing Association, Sportfishing in America: An Economic Engine and Conservation Powerhouse, 2007. [3]Association of Fish and Wildlife Agencies, Hunting in America: An Economic Engine and Conservation Powerhouse, 2007. [4]U.S. Fish and Wildlife Service, Wildlife Watching in the U.S.: The Economic Impacts on National and State Economies in 2006, 2008. [5]Jobs are full-time and part-time. [6]Income includes salaries, wages, business profits (proprietors profit and corporate dividends) and is comparable to Gross Domestic Production. [7]The total spending in the economy stimulated by businesses and their employees re-spending recreational dollars on business inputs and via paychecks.

Economic contributions and impacts branch into direct, indirect, and induced effects. When a recreationist buys a meal, for example, a portion of that purchase remains in the local economy, but some of that purchase will likely go outside the region as an indirect effect. In other words, the local restaurant directly receives the dollars and then pays a portion of those dollars to others, often outside the region, who have supplied the food, power, or building. The direct impact, then, ultimately has an indirect effect on other industries either within or without the local community. Induced effects result from wages and salaries that are paid by directly and indirectly impacted industries. Since employees of these industries will also spend their income, these induced effects generate a continual cycle (Southwick Associates, 2013).

The sum of the direct, indirect, and induced effects equates to the total economic impact or contribution. After going through round after round of indirect and induced effects, the original retail purchase or direct effect is multiplied, thereby bettering multiple industries and individuals. Outdoor recreation directly contributes $646 billion to the national economy, and many of those dollars indirectly ripple through the economy to create approximately $1.6 trillion in economic impact and as many as 12 million jobs (OIA, 2012). As they say, "That ain't hay!"

Just as it can be a benefit to the economy, though, any withdrawal of income from the circular flow will lead to a downward multiplier effect. Therefore, whenever there is an increased withdrawal, there is a potential downward multiplier effect on the rest of the economy. In this case, each unbroken round of spending grows smaller until it can no longer be counted.

OUTDOOR RESOURCES AND TAXATION

Land is a good source of income to the government if it is privately owned and taxed. Once private land is acquired by a government agency, taxes are lost. The reduction in government income in such cases is negligible when the piece of land is small and the acquisition is gradual (Knudson, 1984). Moreover, fees, licensing, and sales tax on the site, once developed, compensate for the lost property tax.

To encourage proper management of private land, certain tax laws have been created for individuals. In Wisconsin, forest tax laws encourage sustainable forest management by providing property incentives for an approved management plan that includes landowner objectives along with timber, wildlife, and environmental management, along with water quality plans. Landowners who meet requirements will then be able to pay forest tax law program rates as opposed to regular property taxes (Wisconsin Department of Natural Resources, 2013). Other incentives exist. For instance, federal and state tax deductions and credits may be available to landowners who offer open space and conservation easements.

COMMERCIAL, PRIVATE OUTDOOR RECREATION

Commercial, private outdoor recreation enterprises vary in size from a small pond opened for fishing on weekends to Disneyland and Disney World. The economic impact of these enterprises vary according to the size, type, and orientation of each. Overall, outdoor recreation accounts for 20% of U.S. manufacturing. Meanwhile, more than $120.7 billion is spent on outdoor products every year (OIA, 2012).

Fortunately, commercial, private outdoor recreation enterprises have formed a close working relationship with park agencies that provide mutual benefits for both. Examples include the following (Lankford, Lankford, & Wheeler, 2011):

1. Commercial firms can provide funding for agency documents, guides, brochures, or electronic media for which both will receive credit.
2. A commercial venture may include the development and operation of a campground, golf course, or ski area that follows agency rules and

regulations to make a profit and to provide a public service.

3. A utility easement across agency land can be granted to a private developer to establish a needed development.

4. Passage of an ordinance could allow the development of new subdivisions as long as they set aside park areas or provide money to generate lands and funds for an agency.

Problems can develop from commercialization. The economic impact of Disney World has included the construction of close to 20,000 hotel/motel rooms along the interstate highways leading to the site, displacing thousands of acres of orange groves. Commercial campgrounds are also located within easy driving distance. Along with positive economic impacts, negative impacts include water pollution, congested traffic, overcommercialization, and high prices for local residents.

The problem of overcommercialization is greater in the case of Niagara Falls, where commercial enterprises has grown on both sides of the river as soon as the area gained fame and tourists began to visit the falls in the early 1900s. Both the Province of Ontario and New York State tried certain controls that proved difficult to implement. Great Smoky Mountains National Park, Gettysburg National Military Park, and Rocky Mountain National Park have had similar problems with commercialization, although a positive multiplier effect has been working (Knudson, 1984).

CAREERS IN OUTDOOR RECREATION

It has only been in more recent times that most people work and play indoors. In the past, the majority of human endeavors took place outdoors. Today, many people long for an outdoor career, fresh air, and a natural setting.

Outdoor careers are found in many fields other than outdoor recreation, such as agriculture, anthropology, archeology, botany, conservation, and construction. Careers in engineering, geology, marine biology, meteorology, mining, seamanship, and surveying can also be outdoor careers. This section will be limited to presenting some of the career possibilities directly involved in outdoor recreation (Cordes, 2013).

Adventure/Risk Recreation

Employers look for people with outdoor leadership experience and technical training. In addition to college/university curricula, training is provided by private organizations such as the National Outdoor Leadership School, Outward Bound, and the Wilderness Education Association. Employers may require certification in advanced first aid, in CPR (cardiopulmonary resuscitation), as an EMT (emergency medical technician), or as a Wilderness First Responder.

College/University Teaching/ Campus Recreation

Teaching at the community college level requires at least a master's degree. Four-year universities and 4-year colleges generally prefer a doctorate or completion of the degree before tenure or promotion is granted.

Commercial/Private

Recreation is big business. Students who seek careers in this field benefit from courses in leisure behavior, recreation leadership, program management, facility design, marketing, business law, risk management, budgeting, and finance. Coursework in business or business management is often required. Supervisory and management positions are available in travel agencies, resorts, amusement and theme parks, campgrounds, and sales-related outdoor merchandise.

Community Recreation

In this field, professional careers are available in administration, public information, park management, planning and development, garden and grounds, golf course management, recreation supervision, aquatics, outdoor therapeutic recreation, and interpretive and outdoor program management. Certification is mandatory or preferred for many positions. Most support and paraprofessional positions require an associate's degree in recreation. An advanced degree in recreation is generally required for management and administrative positions.

Foresters

Foresters manage and protect forests. They also estimate the potential growth of areas under their jurisdiction. Jobs are available with the local, state, and federal government as well as in private companies. The duties of the forester vary significantly from wildlife protection to providing information to the public. A bachelor's degree in forestry is a minimum educational requirement for an entry-level job in forestry, with specialization in forestry, outdoor recreation, or landscape management.

Forestry Technicians

Foresters are supported in their work by forestry technicians, who usually have 1 or 2 years of college education. Forestry technicians may take part in maintaining recreational areas in forests, as well as inspecting trees for disease and engaging in fire fighting and flood control.

Game Wardens/Wildlife Managers

Game wardens are the professionals charged with protecting natural wildlife resources. State conservation departments as well as federal agencies employ most game wardens. A college degree plus some experience in outdoor life is required. Further study in the natural services is helpful.

Naturalists

Naturalists are the interpreters of nature in outdoor recreational sites. Skill in oral communication is needed as well as a college degree. Jobs are found with the federal and state governments and also with private companies that outfit recreationists for outdoor experiences into remote areas such as the Everglades. Knowledge and skill in the use of equipment needed for the outings are desirable.

Nature Photographers

Most nature photographers are freelancers who work in harsh and sometimes hazardous environments in pursuit of unique photographs of animals, plants, or nature scenes. Other than technical training, certain personal traits are required for success in this field, including dedication, patience, and perseverance.

Outdoor Recreation/Education

This field offers a variety of career opportunities: camp director, tour guide, nature leader, museum director, outdoor education instructor/administrator, park ranger, recreation specialist, resort owner/operator, ski lodge operator, radio/TV program naturalist, nature center programmer, and youth or adult programmer. To prepare for professional positions in this field, students need a bachelor's degree in recreation and leisure studies and to take a variety of courses related to people, natural resources, and outdoor activities.

Park Rangers

Park rangers, particularly the ones at small parks, are jacks- and jills-of-all-trades. Their work varies from recreation planning to park administration. A park ranger supervises aides, gives out information, serves as an interpreter of nature, and checks on public safety. He or she may act as a police officer in many instances. Positions are available through national, state, county, and municipal parks and generally require a bachelor's degree.

Range Managers

Range managers are professionals charged with the management and protection of range resources in determining the degree of their multiple use: grazing, lumber cutting, fishing, hunting, and other outdoor recreational activities. Most range managers are employed with federal and state government agencies.

This backcountry guide in Wyoming takes time out to check his GPS for directions.

Recreation Specialists

National parks and forests as well as state and local parks need the services of recreation specialists in planning and executing outdoor recreational activities, which may be of a general nature or highly specialized.

The following are highly specialized careers in outdoor recreation:

1. **Deep-sea sportfishing guide:** These guides organize excursions for sport fishing at offshore locations. Knowledge and experience in deep-sea sport fishing are needed in this job as well as the ability to operate a boat. A license from the U.S. Coast Guard is required. The license is obtained by taking a test.

2. **Hang glider instructor:** Needless to say, a special skill and lengthy prior experience are needed for this career. There generally are not that many career opportunities.

3. **Hunting and fishing guide:** Knowledge of the fish and game habitats and hunting and fishing techniques in the region is needed by a successful guide. This means that substantial experience in fishing and/or hunting in the particular territory is needed before embarking on this career.

4. **Scuba diving instructor:** The recent growth in recreational diving has led to the increased demand for scuba diving instructors. Certification is needed and offered through professional organizations.

5. **Ski instructor:** There is certification to become a ski instructor, and clinics are conducted in some ski areas for the purpose of preparing instructors.

6. **White-water rafting guide:** These guides take parties on large rubber rafts through rapids, over falls, and around boulders, through churning white water. Substantial experience and strength is required to row these.

7. **Backcountry adventure guide:** These individuals generally operate adventure tours through scenic

areas. An intimate knowledge of special sites ranging from American Indian petroglyphs to spectacular waterfalls is necessary. Frequently transportation via four-wheel drive vehicles, horses, or mules is provided, so training in these specialized areas may also be needed. Most guides are self-employed or work for a small outfitter, although there are outfitters that are growing rapidly into bigger organizations due to the popularity of the adventures.

Resource and Park Management

Positions in this field include management, development, and protection of wildland; wildlife, fishery, and soil conservation; and timber, watershed, and recreation management. Students interested in this field are encouraged to obtain a bachelor's degree in forestry or recreation management and to take courses in natural resource management, wildlife management, biology, environmental interpretation, and outdoor systems management. For more information, contact the Soil Conservation Service, the Department of the Interior, and the U.S. Forest Service (see also Park Ranger, Forester, and Game Warden/Wildlife Manager in this section).

Travel/Tourism

Tourism ranks as one of the top three industries in most states. Because tourism is one of the largest industries in the world, it has a range of employment opportunities: travel agencies, resorts, cruise ships, airline industry, amusement and theme parks, campgrounds, hotel or resort management, ecotourism, and public and private organizations that promote tourism. Many entry-level positions offer only modest remuneration but provide attractive fringe benefits such as free or discounted travel. Some institutions have curriculum tracks that concentrate on travel and tourism; coursework in geography, psychology, sociology, economics, technology/computer applications, and business administration is also useful. The state office of tourism can provide information on local statistics, trends, and career opportunities.

SUMMARY

This chapter dealt with the economics of outdoor pursuits and began with a question: Why does the national policy of a capitalistic-oriented society include the preservation of a large part of public lands for outdoor pursuits? Moreover, the policy calls for the provision of costly programs and facilities to be provided on these lands. Despite the appearance of these provisions and activities as being mere expenditures, outdoor pursuits represent an important part of national, regional, and state economies.

A delicate balance between consumption and production occurs as the economic system evolves. Personal expenditure on leisure pursuits is calculated in the total economic picture, which reached $48 billion in 1962. In a quarter of a century, the figure jumped to $320 billion. Today, it places $646 billion into the U.S. economy, making leisure a potent force in the American economy. Productivity, increased income, increased free time, and mobility were suggested as the reasons for making leisure play a leading role in the economy. Americans are spending good sums of money on recreational supplies and equipment, travel and vacations, sports and outdoor pursuits, cultural activities, and home entertainment.

It is hard to estimate the exact amounts of governmental expenditure on the provision of areas, facilities, and programs in recreation. It is also difficult to estimate the expenditure of nonprofit organizations on similar activities. But expenditure is only half of the picture of the relationship between leisure and the economy. The other half is the economic impact of such expenditures. The economy of the outdoor recreation system revolves around four elements: demands of the recreationists, supply of natural resources and programs, plans and policies concerning the use of these resources and programs, and the management and implementation of these plans and policies.

The economic impact of leisure is exemplified in the tourism business. Regional and local economic impacts are felt. If $1 is spent locally, its impact is felt regionally and even nationally. Yet there are some negative impacts from the use of an outdoor recreational site, including overuse during the season, higher prices for locals, and congestion on roads and in local businesses.

The expansion in the provision of outdoor recreational pursuits has helped create specialties, some of which require rigorous and professional training. Some of these career possibilities in outdoor recreation include foresters, forestry technicians, game wardens, naturalists, nature photographers, park rangers, range managers, and recreation specialists.

REFERENCES

Alward, G. (1986). *Local and regional economic impacts of outdoor recreation development.* In The President's Commission on Americans Outdoors, *A literature review* (pp. 47–57). Washington, DC: U.S. Government Printing Office.

America's State Parks. (2013). About America's state parks. Retrieved from http://www.americasstateparks.org/About

Associated Press. (2014, March 4). US national parks lost $414m in vistor spending during government shutdown. *The Guardian.* Retrieved from http://www.theguardian.com/world/2014/mar/04/national-parks-lost414m-vistor-spending-government-shutdown

Brayley, R., & McLean, D. (2008). *Financial resource management* (2nd ed.). Urbana, IL: Sagamore.

Clawson, M., & Knetsch, J. (1966). *Economics of outdoor recreation.* Baltimore, MD: Johns Hopkins University Press.

Cordell, H. K. (1999). *Outdoor recreation in American life: A national assessment of demand and supply trends.* Champaign, IL: Sagamore.

Cordes, K. (2013). *Applications in recreation and leisure.* Urbana, IL: Sagamore.

Curry, N. (2001). The impact of parks on property values: A review of empirical evidence. *Journal of Leisure Research, 33*(1), 1–31.

Dulles, F. R. (1965). *A history of recreation.* New York, NY: Appleton-Century-Croft.

Economics Online. (2014). The multiplier effect. Retrieved from http://economicsonline.co.uk/Managing_the_economy/The_multiplier_effect.html

Esteve, R., Martín, J. S., & López, A. E. (1999). Grasping the meaning of leisure: Developing a self-report measurement tool. *Leisure Studies, 18*(2), 79.

Hardner, J., & McKenney, B. (2006). *The U.S. national park system: An economic asset at risk.* Retrieved from National Parks Conservation Association website: http://www.npca.org/assets/pdf/NPCA_Economic_Significance_Report.pdf

Hyatt, K. E. (2012, June 20). U.S. outdoor recreation industry found to boost the economy [Blog post]. Retrieved from http://www.commerce.gov/blog/2012/06/20/us-outdoor-recreation-industry-found-boost-economy

Ibrahim, H. (1991). *Leisure and society: A comparative approach.* Dubuque, IA: Wm. C. Brown

Jensen, C. (1985). *Outdoor recreation in America.* Minneapolis, MN: Burgess.

Kelly, J. (1985). *Recreation business.* New York, NY: Macmillan.

Kirshman, M. (2012). How parklands provide real value. *Parks & Recreation, 2012,* 45.

Knudson, D. (1984). *Outdoor recreation.* New York, NY: Macmillan.

Lankford, S., Lankford, J., & Wheeler, D. (2011). *An introduction to park management.* Urbana, IL: Sagamore.

MacLean, J., Peterson, J., & Martin, D. (1985). *Leisure and recreation: The changing scene.* New York, NY: Macmillan.

Marano, H. E. (1999). The power of play. *Psychology Today, 32,* 36.

Millard, F., & Fischer, D. (1979). The local economic impact of outdoor recreation. In C. Van Doren et al. (Eds.), *Land and leisure: Concepts and methods in outdoor recreation.* Chicago, IL: Maaroufa Press.

Mintel International Group. (2011). *Family leisure trends—U.S.* Available from http://reports.mintel.com/display/542924/?__cc=1

National Environmental Policy Act, 42 U.S.C. § 4321 (1969).

National Parks Conservation Association. (2011). *Made in America: Investing in national parks for our heritage and our economy.* Retrieved from http://www.npca.org/news/reports/made-in-america.html

Olson, S. (1961). The spiritual aspects of wilderness. In D. Brower (Ed.), *Wilderness: America's living heritage.* San Francisco, CA: Sierra Club.

Outdoor Industry Association. (2006). *2006 active outdoor recreation economy.* Retrieved from http://outdoorindustry.org/research/economicimpact.php?action=detail&research_id=26

Outdoor Industry Association. (2012). *The outdoor economy 2012.* Retrieved from http://outdoorindustry.org/research/economicimpact.php?action=detail&research_id=167

Peterson, G., & Brown, T. (1986). The economic benefits of outdoor recreation. In The President's Commission on Americans Outdoors, *A literature review* (pp. 11–18). Washington, DC: U.S. Government Printing Office.

Rostow, E. (1960). *The stages of economic growth.* Cambridge, MA: Harvard University Press.

Southwick Associates. (2013). *The conservation economy in America: Direct investments and economic contributions.* Retrieved from http://www.avcrp.org/wp-content/uploads-2013/04NWF-conservation-economy

Stevens, B., & Rose, A. Z. (1985). Regional input–output methods for tourism impact analysis. In D. Propst (Ed.), *Assessing the economic impacts of recreation and tourism* (pp. 16–22). Asheville, NC: USDA Forest Service, Southeastern Forest Experiment Station.

Tharman, M., & Gilbert, P. (2012). Financial stability and the new norm. *Parks & Recreation, 2012,* 18.

Thomas, C. C., Huber, C., & Koontz, L. (2014). *2012 National Park Service: Economic contributions to local communities, states, and the nation* (Natural Resource Report NPS/NRSS/EQD/NRR-2014/765). Fort Collins, CO: National Park Service.

United Media Enterprises. (1983). *Where does the time go?* New York, NY: Newspaper Enterprises Association.

U.S. Bureau of Labor Statistics. (2014, July 3). The employment situation [News release]. Retrieved from http://www.bls.gov/news.release/archives/empsit_08012014.pdf

U.S. Fish and Wildlife Service. (2001). *National survey of fishing, hunting, and wildlife-associated recreation.* Retrieved from U.S. Census Bureau website: http://www.census.gov/prod/www/fishing.html#fhwaronline

Veblen, T. (1953). *The theory of leisure class.* New York, NY: New American Library.

Walls, M., Darley, S., & Siikamäki, J. (2009). *The state of the great outdoors: America's public lands and recreational resources.* Retrieved from Resources for the Future website: http://www.rff.org/RFF/Documents/RFF-RPT-ORRG-State-of-Outdoors.pdf

Walsh, R. (1986). *Recreation economic decision: Comparing benefits and costs.* State College, PA: Venture.

Walsh, R., & Loomis, J. (1986). The contribution of recreation to national economic development. In The President's Commission on Americans Outdoors, *A literature review* (pp. 35–46). Washington, DC: U.S. Government Printing Office.

Wisconsin Department of Natural Resources. (2013). Forest tax laws. Retrieved from http://dnr.wi.gov/topic/ForestLandowners/tax.html

Part Two

Outdoor Resources

This part consists of five chapters in which we examine the locations of outdoor recreational areas. Chapters 7, 8, and 9 cover the recreational areas and facilities owned and operated by federal, state, and local governments in the United States. Chapter 10 is devoted to looking into the contributions of commercial enterprises and private individuals to outdoor pursuits. In Chapter 11, we present the outdoor recreational opportunities in Canada.

Chapter 7

Federal Resources and Recreation

The United States, a global leader in conservation legislation, has assembled a world-class system of public lands for outdoor recreation, beginning with the protection of Yosemite Valley in the 1860s and Yellowstone, the first national park, in 1872. The system has been carved mostly from the old "public domain," the unregulated expanses of western open space acquired by the United States through treaty, purchase, and the forcible eviction of earlier inhabitants. By the late 19th century, private enterprises had come to regard the public domain as common property and spoils for the bold. They had profitably stripped its timber, mined its substrates for minerals, and diverted and dammed its rivers, often leaving behind a burned, scarred, and eroded landscape. Though the public owned the resources, the exploiters paid little or no fee for the booty. Prodded by some foresighted Americans, Congress acted, albeit in piecemeal fashion, to limit the abuse and future exploitation. Thus the first national park (1872), the first national wildlife refuge (1903), the first national monuments (1906), and the National Park System (1916) were born, all managed by the Department of the Interior. Congress "withdrew" these lands from the public domain and preserved them because they exhibited special values. Most of the remaining public domain, still vast, stayed with the Department of the Interior under what is now the Bureau of Land Management. The extent of federal public domain today is shown in Figure 7.1.

In addition, Congress created the Forest Service in 1905 and endowed it by transferring 85 million acres to the Department of Agriculture for forest management. The National Forest System embodies the Forest Service's tradition of regarding timber as a crop, to be harvested according to the principle of sustainability, that is, to cut and grow wood at a rate that can be sustained over the long term. This principle has evolved to include the sustainability of the ecosystem of the forest. At the federal level, the Forest Service and the National Park Service (NPS) represent two types of agencies. The latter agency practices preservation, and the former practices multiple use, wherein the primary challenge is to balance economic use and conservation. The diverse uses of forest and rangeland resources are illustrated in Figure 7.2.

Multiple-use management takes advantage of the resource's ability to provide a bundle of uses and benefits from the same land. The Forest Service, for example, has a special legislative mandate to implement multiple-use management on National Forest Systems by administering the national

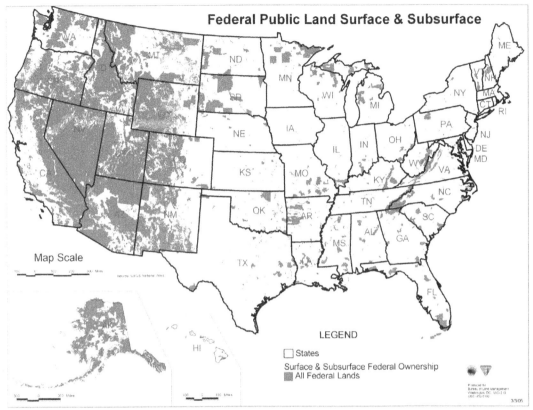

Figure 7.1. Federal lands in the United States. Prepared by U.S. Geological Survey.

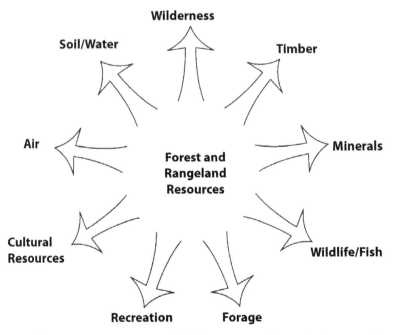

Figure 7.2. Multiple-use management provides the opportunity to simultaneously produce a number of resource benefits from the same parcel of land. Adapted from *Program for Forest and Rangeland Resources: A Long-Term Strategic Plan*, by U.S. Forest Service, 1990, Washington, DC: U.S. Government Printing Office, pp. 1–3.

forests for outdoor recreation, range, timber, watershed, and wildlife and fish. Other multiple-use agencies include the Bureau of Land Management, Bureau of Reclamation, U.S. Army Corps of Engineers, Tennessee Valley Authority, and National Marine Fisheries Service.

The NPS represents the single-use, or restricted use, concept. The 1916 Organic Act that established the agency (Mackintosh, 1990) directed the NPS, in managing the parks, to conserve the scenery, the natural and historic objects, and the wildlife therein to provide for the enjoyment of the same in such manner and by such means as will leave them unimpaired for the enjoyment of future generations. The resources do not exist to be exploited for profit by harvesting or milling. Recreation is permitted as long as the activity is not destructive to the unique values of the park unit. Another single-use agency is the U.S. Fish and Wildlife Service. Wild and scenic rivers and wilderness areas are also managed under the single-use philosophy. From the purist sense, any recreation use on wilderness lands is disruptive to the wild ecological system. Therefore, decisions involving recreational use on these lands are critical (Jensen, 1985).

The distinction between agencies' land management philosophies is narrowing. For instance, traditionally hunting has not been permitted in national parks, but is permitted on designated areas of the Bureau of Land Management lands and the national forests. Today, hunting occurs in the national reserves administered by the NPS. Despite the differences in land management philosophy, recreation usage is a major concern of each federal agency that has federal lands under management. The proportion of federal lands managed by the federal land management agencies is shown in Figure 7.3.

These two philosophies, single use and multiple use, led to a split between two early outdoor leaders, John Muir and Gifford Pinchot (refer to Chapter 3 for their biographies), who were once allies in the crusade to redeem the public domain from uncontrolled exploitation. Their differences surfaced over the Hetch Hetchy Valley controversy in which the proponents of multiple use won the right to create a water reservoir by inundating a spectacularly beautiful valley next to the Yosemite Valley, both contained within Yosemite National Park. This reservoir would serve the water needs of the growing city of San Francisco. Pinchot, the spokesperson for the emerging doctrine of conservation, argued for damming the Hetch Hetchy. He believed that the strict preservation creed of the park bureau supporters unnecessarily limited the use of the nation's resources. As such, he believed that preserving Yosemite Valley in its pristine state met the needs of the park and that a more practical use of the neighboring

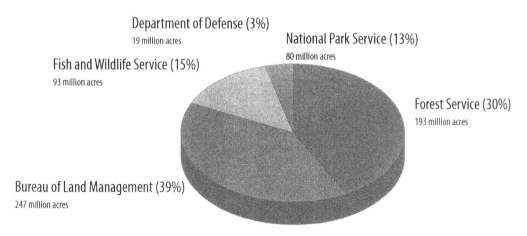

Figure 7.3. Who manages the federal lands?

valley allowed for multiple use of this land. To him, this arrangement permitted aesthetic and economic uses.

An outraged Muir, a major proponent of the preservationists, claimed that the argument of the dam builders was a device for destruction. He believed that the entire park should be preserved in its natural state, including both spectacular valleys. In his preservationist outlook, there was no room for compromise. This dispute was closely followed by the San Francisco media, and because of this, a schism between the conservationists and preservationists was in full view of the public. A closer look at the different philosophies is possible by profiling the agencies that practice them.

USDA FOREST SERVICE

The National Forest System, the oldest of the four national land management agencies, contains approximately 193 million acres of public land dispersed throughout 44 states,

Puerto Rico, and the Virgin Islands (see Figure 7.4). This expanse constitutes 8.5% of the total land area in the United States and about 30% of the federal land holdings (Hoover, 2014). See Figure 7.3 for land comparisons of the major federal landowners. Roughly 18% of the national forestland comprises 400 congressionally designated wilderness areas that span more than 35 million acres. These wilderness areas offer some of the country's most spectacular scenery and a more primitive recreational experience. The National Forest System includes 155 national forests and 20 national grasslands administered by more than 600 district ranger offices in nine regions. It is believed that more outdoor recreation takes place on these national forestlands, with 192 million visitors a year, than on any other public lands. National recreation areas, national scenic areas or national monuments, and national heritage sites are significant Forest Service attractions. To cross the lands, there are approximately 375,000 miles of roads and scenic byways and

Figure 7.4. Forest Service lands in the United States. From *The U.S. Forest Service - An Overview*, by U.S. Department of Agriculture, 2007, Washington, DC: Author, p. 36.

143,000 miles of trails including portions of national scenic trails, national historic trails, and more than 400 national recreation trails. More than 4,000 miles of rivers are managed as wild and scenic rivers. In cooperation with the private sector, the national forests have more than 40% of the nation's downhill skiing, as well as sites for 480 lodges or resorts, and more than 15,000 summer homes. There are at least 10,000 recreational sites including 4,300 campgrounds, 1,400 picnic grounds, and 50 major visitor centers (Forest Service, 2000; U.S. Department of Agriculture [USDA], 2012).

To manage these assets, the Forest Service has a dedicated workforce of approximately 34,000 permanent employees (Forest Service, 2000a), more than 59,000 volunteers, and a budget of $5.5 billion (USDA, 2012).

History of the National Forests

The Creative Act of March 3, 1891 authorized the president to establish forest reserves from forests and rangelands in the public domain. The impetus for establishing these reserves came from recreation and conservation groups who believed strongly that forested areas should be placed under official governmental protection (Tweed, 1980). By 1897, the Organic Administration Act was passed, which, however, provided for the right of entry to persons for prospecting, locating, and developing mineral resources and for the use of water and timber resources found on forest reserves. On February 1, 1905, President Theodore Roosevelt signed the Transfer Act, which transferred the nation's forest reserves from the Department of the Interior to the USDA. That same day, Secretary of Agriculture James Wilson endorsed Gifford Pinchot's conservation philosophy establishing that the forests were to be used and not merely reserved. The forest reserves, later renamed the national forests, were to be managed for the greatest good for the greatest number of people on a long-term basis. Local officials were to decide local questions, a philosophy that has made the Forest Service one of the most decentralized and responsive agencies in the federal government.

A national forest visit is
the entry of one person to a national forest to participate in recreation activities for an unspecified period of time. A national forest visit can be composed of multiple site visits.

A national forest site visit is
the entry of one person to a national forest site or area to participate in recreation activities for an unspecified period of time.

Forests cover about one third of the United States—about 751 million acres. The Forest Service has a stewardship role in about 80% of these forests. Trees, forests, and forest ecosystems provide habitat for wildlife; help to cleanse air and water; supply timber and fuel wood and other harvested products; and serve as wonderful places for hiking, camping, and fishing (USDA, 2012).

Recreational development. Recreational use of forestlands grew slowly at first and then more rapidly as automobiles became numerous and roads penetrated into previously remote and inaccessible areas. Increased prosperity and more free time encouraged recreational improvements. The first official report recognizing the prominence of recreational use in the national forests was made in the USDA's 1919 edition of the annual *Report of the Forester*. Tweed (1980) researched early recreation use in the national forests up to World War II and found that recreation was one of the major activities on the forests with the granting of temporary leases for summer cottages and campsites. Thousands of recreation permits were issued in 1913 for pleasure resorts and boathouses, and there were over 1 million day visitors; 231,000 campers, hunters, anglers, boaters, swimmers, and climbers; and 191,000 guests at houses, hotels, and sanitariums. Early budget limitations and priorities precluded recreation spending by the federal government, so to a large extent these visitors depended upon privately owned facilities for their basic needs. Forest rangers cleared inflammable material from around heavily used camp spots and built crude rock fireplaces, erected toilets, dug garbage pits, and developed sources of water supply.

According to Tweed (1980), the initial areas of concentration of summer visitors were in the Angeles National Forest of southern California, the Oregon (later renamed Mt. Hood) National Forest in northern Oregon, and the Pike and San Isabel National Forests of central Colorado, all in mountains areas near cities. Holders of summer-home permits often formed cooperative associations to provide common facilities and services. In 1915, forester Henry Graves recommended to the secretary of agriculture that the Columbia Gorge Park be developed in the Oregon National Forest. This became the first time that the Forest Service dedicated an extended area for purely recreational use, prohibiting timber sales and the distribution of permits for home sites. Soon the Eagle Creek Campground and Eagle Creek Trail were developed by the Forest Service, and by 1919, the North Pacific District had created a recreation office.

It may have been that a broader interest in recreation resulted from the constant creation of national parks out of national forests. Mt. Rainier National Park was created from part of the Mt. Rainier Forest Reserve in 1899, Crater Lake National Park from part of the Cascade Forest Reserve in 1902, Glacier National Park from part of the Blackfoot National Forest in 1910, Rocky Mountain National Park from parts of the Arapaho and Colorado National Forests in 1915, and Lassen Volcanic National Park from part of the Lassen National Forest in 1916. More transfers followed.

Pinchot and his division, the Bureau of Forestry (later renamed the Forest Service), campaigned to assume the administration of the national parks. But by 1910, another campaign was developed to create a separate Bureau of National Parks within the Department of the Interior. Supporters of the park bureau concept, such as John Muir and Robert Underwood Johnson, based their rejection of possible Forest Service management largely on fears of Pinchot's controversial support of the Hetch Hetchy reservoir project within Yosemite National Park. Pinchot and his successor, Henry Graves, viewed strict preservation by supporters of the park bureau to be unnecessarily limiting and wasteful of the nation's resources. It is probably safe to assume that at least a portion of the Forest Service's recreation interest in the second decade resulted from the Forest Service's hope of preventing the creation of (or limiting the growth of) a park bureau that would have as a major purpose the development of recreational facilities.

Because of the role of landscape architects in developing the nation's urban parks, landscape architects looked upon themselves as the logical people to develop professionally planned recreational facilities in the national forests and parks. As early as 1910, proposals for a park bureau included a role in the new agency for landscape architects. And by 1916, it became apparent to the Forest Service that if it were to compete successfully with the newly created NPS, it ultimately would have to develop professionally planned recreational facilities.

Frank A. Waugh. Early in 1917, the service employed Frank A. Waugh, professor of landscape architecture at Massachusetts Agricultural College in Amherst, to prepare a national study of recreation uses of the national forests. In his report, Waugh suggested that certain parts of the forest be developed as scenic reservations, allowing no use that would significantly detract from the inherent recreation values. He discussed briefly the recreation potential of the national monuments, then under Forest Service control, explaining their status as scenic or scientific preserves. Waugh argued that recreation must be considered one of the major uses of the national forests, equal in importance to timber harvesting, watershed protection, and grazing. It was his belief that nearly all national forestlands had potential for public recreational use. Under these circumstances, he felt that it would be impossible for one agency to manage all of the recreational development while another looked after other resource management problems. Either the Forest Service and the NPS would have to merge, or each would have to develop its own recreation program. To him, the latter was preferable. He concluded that there was a need for the Forest Service to hire professional personnel for its recreation program (Tweed, 1980).

World War I to the Great Depression. As soon as World War I ended, the Forest Service hired landscape engineer Arthur H. Carhart to work in the Rocky Mountain District. At the same time, the North Pacific District made forester Fred Cleator its recreation specialist. Carhart designed a foot trail for tourist use on Pikes Peak. Because Congress had appropriated no funds for recreation, the Commerce Club of Pueblo (Colorado) raised money and cooperated with the city to erect a few shelters, toilets, and fireplaces in Squirrel Creek Canyon, 30 miles from town. It was Carhart's belief that recreation planning for the national forests would inevitably have to pass beyond the construction of single campgrounds to comprehensive general planning. By late 1919, he began work on such a plan for the San Isabel National Forest (Carhart, 1959).

Financially backed by the San Isabel Public Recreation Association, Carhart's plans for an extensive system of campgrounds, picnic grounds, roads, and trails were implemented. This collaboration served as a model for other communities that continued until the Great Depression. Similar cooperation eventually produced a significant number of national forest recreation areas at a time when the Forest Service chose not to, or could not, expend much of its regular appropriation on such work. Carhart also helped to develop the idea of wilderness, or limited recreational development, in certain superb natural environments. One result was a landmark policy statement on wilderness from Secretary of Agriculture William M. Jardine in 1926, which pledged 1,000 square miles of wilderness in the Superior National Forest, the forerunner of the Boundary Waters Canoe Area.

Convinced that important progress had occurred, Carhart asked Chief Forester William B. Greeley to seek $50,000 for recreation work in the national forests for 1922. The request was made, but the money was not approved. Carhart made a similar request for funding for 1923. Again funding was de-

nied, and instead, Congress reluctantly provided $10,000 for simple facilities required by recreationists for fire and sanitary protection. Carhart responded with his resignation, which vacated the single position in the Forest Service dedicated wholly to recreation. The Forest Service generally held that the recreational role of the national forest was to provide space for recreation. Publicly financed recreational facilities in these forest areas remained limited in number and simple in nature.

For nearly a decade after Carhart's resignation, two groups, foresters and collaborators, handled Forest Service recreation problems. Most of the responsibility fell to the foresters, who assumed responsibility for the design, construction, and administration of recreational sites. In the meantime, H. R. Francis of New York State College of Forestry at Syracuse University developed a general course for forestry students in the basic concepts and requirements of forest recreation. Whether academically trained in recreation work or not, foresters carried out the Forest Service recreation program. It was these foresters who received the first congressional appropriations for recreational development beyond fire prevention and sanitary facilities. As campgrounds improved, recreational use rose by 38% in the mid-1920s. A few positions specializing in recreation work began to be developed as the Forest Service found itself year after year settling deeper into the recreation business (Tweed, 1980). But just as it became apparent that the hiring of technically trained personnel in recreation was necessary, the Great Depression forced Congress to cut rather than increase recreational spending.

The Great Depression through World War II. A policy statement in the 1930s reaffirmed that the responsibility for recreational planning still rested entirely on regional foresters and forest supervisors. A cautious, conservative site development policy continued that fit the budget and goals of the Hoover administration. This modest level of national forest recreation development escalated, however, with the election of President Franklin Delano Roosevelt in 1933. A decade of frenzied activity followed that was checked only by World War II. During the height of the New Deal, the Forest Service received recreation funds and support far beyond its wildest dreams. These changes in the magnitude and scope of the Forest Service recreation program resulted in major changes in its recreation policy. To cope with the severe national economic crisis, authorization and funds for public works in forest, water, and soil conservation were provided. With Executive Order 6101, Roosevelt created the Emergency Conservation Work program to carry out specified activities. The Civilian Conservation Corps (CCC) was viewed by FDR as primarily a forestry organization dedicated to fighting fires, planting trees, thinning timber stands, and stopping soil erosion and floods. But the field personnel of the state and federal agencies soon realized that CCC labor may also be directed toward the construction of forest improvements, particularly roads, trails, buildings, and recreational sites. Through its provisions for public works spending, the National Industrial Recovery Act of June 16, 1933, provided yet another opportunity for Forest Service recreational facilities to be built. Permanent recreation improvements were encouraged and erected from coast to coast. The level of development of some of the more popular national forest areas in the Northwest even surpassed that of the national parks of the region. Public Works Administration (PWA) funds were made available for the building of the beautiful Timberline Lodge on Mt. Hood, which became known as one of the wonders of the Northwest. By 1935, it became apparent that a central office for recreation was needed to oversee recreation planning and development in the National Forest System. Ernest E. Walker, a trained landscape architect, was hired for the Washington office.

Robert Marshall. In 1937, the Recreation and Lands Division received a chief, Robert Marshall. This forester wilderness enthusiast and visionary had previously served as the chief forester for the Indian Service, U.S. Department of the Interior. Marshall had a strong and long-lasting influence on Forest Service recreation policy and development,

despite that his career was cut short by an early death after only 30 months in office. He worked tirelessly to establish a secure position for recreation on an equal footing with other more dominant phases of national forest management such as timber and range use.

An ardent outdoorsman, indefatigable hiker, and persistent advocate of wilderness and primitive areas, Marshall was a strong advocate for adequate camping, outing, scenic, and other recreation areas. He wrote the recreation section of the *National Plan for American Forestry* in 1933. Independently wealthy, he helped to found and endow the Wilderness Society. Under his direction, the Forest Service built a number of camps, along with substantial facilities designed primarily for the use of low-income adults, 4-H clubs, and similar youth groups (Glover, 1986).

Soon downhill skiing areas began to appear as interest increased. Expansion of facilities had become impressive, and by 1939, the Forest Service's first book on recreation, *Forest Outings*, had appeared. Recreation had been established as a major priority (Tweed, 1980).

The 1940s. The 1940s brought a decline of the CCC recreation projects and employment of technical personnel. Entry of the United States into World War II in December 1941 caused national defense to take priority. Later rebuilding of a recreational staff would take many years, although work continued on individual family camping and picnic units. Never again, however, did the Forest Service look at recreation as a mere designation of a few roadside camping areas with tables and privies. National forest recreation had become a valued part of life for millions of Americans.

Post–World War II: The 1950s and 1960s. In 1954, the agency became responsible for nearly 4 million acres of Land Utilization Project holdings. These grazing lands were relinquished or were abandoned farms the federal government acquired during the Depression years of the 1930s. In the 1960s, these would become the first of the national grasslands. By 1957, Operation Outdoors commenced to improve and replace the aging CCC-built Forest Service structures and to expand the recreational facilities to meet the increased demand for recreation. As this 5-year program drew to a close, the Accelerated Public Works program of 1963 and 1964 employed more that 9,000 men to make improvements including picnic grounds, trails, lookout towers, and other facilities on more than 100 forests. Another new work program, Job Corps, began in 1964 and used unemployed youth in Forest Service work including recreation activities (Williams, 2000).

In the meantime, the Multiple-Use Sustained-Yield Act of 1960 supplemented the purpose for which the national forests were established to include outdoor recreation, watershed, range, timber, and wildlife and fish purposes. Meeting increased demands for recreational opportunities became a major aim of forestland managers. Because each acre of the National Forest System has recreation potential, it was routinely mandated that recreation be considered when planning or executing resources management programs (Collins, 2004). Containing some of the nation's greatest assets, almost all National Forest System lands became available for outdoor recreation.

The culmination of decades of work on the part of several Forest Service employees and other leaders resulted in the establishment of the National Wilderness Preservation System in 1964. Overnight, the Forest Service wilderness became a part of the new system, as did the wild and scenic rivers in 1968 when that legislation passed. Both will be discussed in this chapter.

Closing decades of the 20th century. In 1974, Congress enacted the Forest and Rangeland Renewable Resources Planning Act (RPA), which directed the secretary of agriculture to periodically assess the nation's forest and rangeland resources and to regularly recommend long-range Forest Service programs. For the first program, an increase in the supply of outdoor recreational opportunities and services was recommended. The new programs would emphasize dispersed recreation, that is, forest- and rangeland-oriented recreation that makes use of sites other than ones already designed for concentrated recreational use.

In 1987, a new plan, the National Recreation Strategy Project, was developed. The plan called for a strategy to manage recreation on national forestlands within the context of multiple-use management and for the development of several marketing plans that would be focused on customer satisfaction (Forest Service, 1988). The importance of meeting the needs of urban populations through recreational opportunities in nearby national forests began to be emphasized. The strategy allowed the Forest Service the flexibility to reach its outdoor recreation potential without dictating policy. It encouraged creative and imaginative thinking, increased opportunities for professionals in recreation, built on cost-sharing programs, and promoted interpretation and environmental education as an important part of outdoor recreation.

Partly as a result of the National Recreation Strategy Project, the Forest Service in the 1990s developed partnerships with local, county, state, and federal governments; private interest groups; senior citizen groups; groups of youth with disabilities; correction facility inmates; high schools; colleges and universities; utility companies, recreation industry corporations; timber operators; interpretive associations; and private businesses. These projects provided barrier-free access to recreational facilities, improved hiking trails, rehabilitated and modernized campgrounds, interpretive signing, summer youth employment in recreational site operation and maintenance, vegetation management for scenic resources, development of the 1988 Forest Service Scenic Byways program for vehicular recreation, renovation of historic buildings for interpretation, and initiatives promoting river safety. Innovations included partnerships with private cruise lines in Alaska that paid Forest Service interpreters. In the eastern United States, a partnership among the Forest Service, the NPS, the Appalachian Trail Conference, and others helped make the Appalachian National Scenic Trail world renowned. The National Trails System will be discussed later in this chapter.

Trends. The Forest Service (2000a) indicated an important shift in focus when the central mission in managing the national forests and grasslands moved away from producing timber, range, and other outputs to restoring and maintaining healthy, resilient ecosystems. Although sustainability has been the essence of Forest Service land and natural resource management from the beginnings of the National Forest System, sustainability has come to mean sustaining ecosystem health as well as multiple products and uses. Strategic plans are now focused on outcomes or long-term results, such as the following:

1. Restore, sustain, and enhance the nation's forests and grasslands.
2. Provide and sustain benefits to the American people.
3. Conserve open space.
4. Sustain and enhance outdoor recreational opportunities.
5. Maintain basic management capabilities of the Forest Service.

Aspen, balsam, birch, maple, oak, and pine present a profusion of fall color along the Ice Age National Scenic Trail in the Chequamegon National Forest in Wisconsin.

6. Engage urban America with Forest Service programs.
7. Provide science-based applications and tools for sustainable natural resources management.

These strategic goals are responsive to their mission: to sustain the health, diversity, and productivity of the nation's forests and grasslands to meet the needs of present and future generations. Goals collectively provide purpose and context for future management actions and investments as well as a set of milestones for evaluating progress toward the goals.

The recreational use of forests and grasslands has been increasing for decades and is expected to continue to increase. One of every 7 Americans lives within a 2-hour drive of a national forest. The most popular outdoor recreational activities (measured in number of days) are walking, nonconsumptive wildlife activities, biking, sightseeing, nonpool swimming, fishing, family gathering, and picnicking. The five fastest growing outdoor recreational activities (measured in number of days) through the year 2050 are projected to be visiting historic places, downhill skiing, snowmobiling, sightseeing, and participating in nonconsumptive wildlife activity (Forest Service, 2000a).

The Forest Service contains the greatest diversity of wildlife, fish, and plant species of any single land ownership in the country. With goals to maintain ecosystem diversity, the Forest Service responds to recreational and commercial uses of fish and wildlife. Fish and wildlife resources of the Forest Service provide recreation for anglers, hunters, and nonconsumptive fish and wildlife users, representing about 17% of recreation in national forests (Forest Service, 2000a). Forestland recreational development has continued to expand in scope and significance, showing no sign of diminishing at this time.

NATIONAL PARK SERVICE

NPS holdings constitute about 13% of the federal land holdings, or 84 million acres of land, in 49 states, the District of Columbia, American Samoa, Guam, Puerto Rico, Saipan, and the Virgin Islands (as shown in Figures 7.5 and 7.6), and are referred to as the National Park System. A national park is of such national significance as to justify special recognition and protection, and it takes an act of Congress to create it. Additionally, the president has authority, under the Antiquities Act of 1906, to proclaim national monuments on lands already under federal jurisdiction. This distinction has been given to great natural reservations, historic military fortifications, prehistoric ruins, fossil sites, and the Statue of Liberty. Most but not all national monuments are managed by the NPS. The secretary of the interior is usually asked by Congress for recommendations on proposed additions to the system. The Secretary is counseled by the National Park System Advisory Board, which comprises private citizens who offer advice on possible additions to the system and policies for its management.

Areas added to the National Park System may be of exceptional historical, cultural, or natural value. Areas set aside due to their natural values are expanses or features of land or water of great scenic and scientific quality and are usually designated as national parks, monuments, preserves, seashores, lakeshores, riverways, or trails. Such areas contain one or more distinctive attributes such as forest, grassland, tundra, desert, estuary, or river systems, or they may contain "windows" on the past for a view of geological history, or they may have imposing landforms such as mountains, mesas, thermal areas, and caverns. They may also be habitats of abundant or rare wildlife and plant life. Components, individually known as units, of the National Park System are listed in Table 7.1.

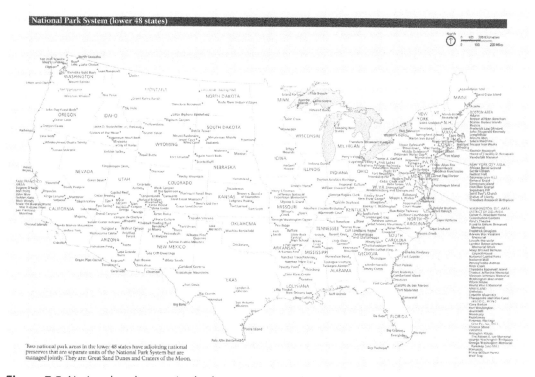

National Park System (lower 48 states)

Two national park areas in the lower 48 states have adjoining national preserves that are separate units of the National Park System but are managed jointly. They are: Great Sand Dunes and Craters of the Moon.

Figure 7.5. National park areas in the lower 48 states. From *The National Parks: Index 2009–2011*, by U.S. Department of the Interior, 2009, http://www.nps.gov/parkhistory/online_books/nps/nps/contents.htm, pp. 10–11

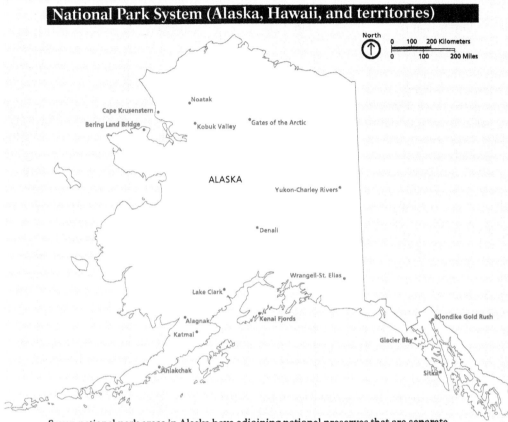

Seven national park areas in Alaska have adjoining national preserves that are separate units of the National Park System but are managed jointly. They are: Aniakchak, Denali, Gates of the Arctic, Glacier Bay, Katmai, Lake Clark, and Wrangell-St. Elias.

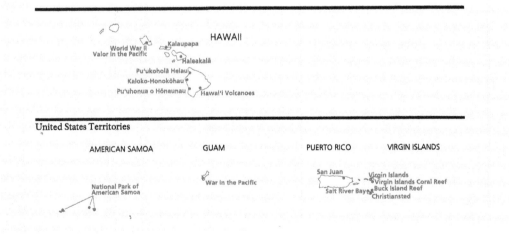

Figure 7.6. National park areas of Alaska, Hawaii, and U.S. territories. From *The National Parks: Index, 2009–2011,* by U.S. Department of the Interior, 2009, http://www.nps.gov/history/history/online_books/nps/index2009_11.pdf, p. 12.

Table 7.1
*Statistical Summary of the
National Park System*

Classification	Number
National Battlefields	24
National Historic Parks	123
National Lakeshores	4
National Memorials	27
National Monuments	74
National Parks	58
National Parkways	4
National Preserves	20
National Recreation Areas	18
National Rivers	15
National Scenic Trails	3
National Seashores	10
Units Without Designation	11
Total	**391**

National Park History

After America won its independence from Britain, the country had few unique sites of natural beauty that had been recognized as recreation areas, the most prominent of which, Niagara Falls, had been exploited commercially to its detriment. During the western expansion, the giant sierra redwood trees of California were rediscovered in Yosemite Valley. The magnificence of the Yosemite Valley displaced all claims that the European countryside was more scenic. America finally had a claim to antiquity; the huge trees had been growing before the time of Christ, and they certainly made up for America's lack of old European castles in the countryside. By 1864, the nation moved to preserve and showcase their greatness, and the nation's greatness, too, when the U.S. government ceded lands in Yosemite Valley to the state of California to protect the magnificent sequoia trees. Specifically, in the conditions of acceptance, the federal government stated the retention of the land was for "public use, resort, and recreation" and the lands were to be held "inalienable for all time" (Runte, 1987, pp. 29–30).

Later, in 1872, Yellowstone National Park was established. For these lands, no state government existed to which the parklands could be entrusted; therefore, Yellowstone remained in the custody of the Department of the Interior as a national park (Mackintosh, 1990). This was the first time the term *national park* appeared, although the earlier Yosemite protection had embodied the concept. Even earlier, the artist George Catlin is credited with articulating the need for a wildland park for the nation. In 1832, after traveling through Sioux Indian lands and foreseeing their eventual destruction, he proposed that a park be established to preserve the Sioux culture and the bison on which they were dependent (Wellman, 1987). Catlin's vision never fully materialized, though, and even after Yellowstone was created, it was almost two decades later before another national park was set aside. At the urging of John Muir and Robert Underwood Johnson, Congress passed bills in 1890 providing for the protection of additional lands that would become Sequoia, General Grant, and Yosemite National Parks. Soon after, Mount Rainier National Park and Crater Lake National Park were added.

During these early years, a policy had evolved in Congress that only "worthless" lands could be set aside as national parks. This meant that it was necessary to first demonstrate there was no possibility of economic viability before Congress would act to set land aside. Therefore, repeatedly in congressional hearings, exhaustive lists of the unsuitability of the land for development and profit, save for scenic beauty, were presented (Runte, 1987).

In 1891, the passage of the Forest Reserve Act gave the president unilateral authority to proclaim forest reservations, which provided a means to avoid the lengthy congressional "worthlessness" debates. Within 2 years, President Benjamin Harrison proclaimed 13 million acres in the West as forest reserves. These holdings were increased to 46 million acres by Presidents Grover Cleveland and William McKinley. During the administration of President Theodore Roosevelt, the naturalist and conservationist more than tripled the forestlands to nearly 130 million acres, and many of the subsequently named national parks were carved from these holdings. Roosevelt also made expansive use of the Antiquities Act of 1906, which empowers the president to preserve "objects of historic or scientific interest" as national monuments if the land is already under the jurisdiction of the federal government. Until then, national parks had only been established to preserve scenic wonders; Roosevelt interpreted "scientific" to mean of geological significance as well, and as such, he designated Devil's Tower, a basalt monolith rising 865 feet in the air in Wyoming, the first scientific national monument. Petrified Forest, Montezuma Castle, El Morro, other Indian cliff dwellings, and Lassen Peak soon followed as national monuments. All of the monuments were relatively modest in size until 800,000 acres were set aside around the Grand Canyon and 600,000 acres around Mount Olympus as national monuments (Runte, 1987). Before Roosevelt left office, he used the Antiquities Act to proclaim 18 national monuments (Mackintosh, 1990).

During this period, it was still important that the lands be considered useless or worthless for economic gain to be set aside, and they needed to meet the criterion that the lands be of unique scenic beauty for designation as a national park. Many believe a dismal failure of conservation was a result of this narrow policy. Next to Yosemite Valley lay Hetch Hetchy Valley, which to some was just as beautiful and magnificent as Yosemite. However, since there were two valleys right next to each other, Hetch Hetchy was not deemed unique, and it was this absence of singularity that permitted its demise. Together with the establishment of its economic worth as a water reservoir, its park status was stripped. At the close of the long and bitter struggle by preservationists to save the area, San Francisco won the right to flood the valley to create a reservoir for the city. Even today, the debate continues, especially because a study indicated that it would be "technically feasible" to restore Hecth Hetchy (Good, 2006). The original loss of Hetch Hetchy Valley in 1913 was blamed in part on the dispersed nature of federal land management. With the spotlight on the need to unify the management and protection of the parks, the Organic Act of 1916 was passed, creating the NPS. No longer would the management of the parks, monuments, and forests be distributed among numerous government agencies with no one agency clearly the protector of the parks.

Stephen Mather, a skilled promoter and eventually the first director of the NPS (see Chapter 3), appealed to the utilitarian conservatives in Congress in his cause to establish a bureau to protect the parks. He demonstrated that the parks, too, had economic worth measured in tourism dollars when he vigorously promoted the See America First campaign, designed to keep tourists in the United States rather than going abroad. Economic mandates were heard in Congress again, and the valuable asset of the national parks was recognized and protected by the 1916 act (Runte, 1987). More than 120 nations have followed the United States' lead in creating the world's first NPS (Craig, 1991).

The preservationists' idea of protecting and preserving parklands through annexation of areas within the park ecosystem did not take hold for years. The authorization of Everglades National Park in 1934 was a clear public pledge in this direction of preservation. For the first time, flora and fauna in a fragile ecosystem were protected, although sadly, the boundaries of the park were not large enough to protect against the damage from residues of farming and urban populations. The increasingly high cost of setting aside land for national parks was evident, too, as private holdings were allowed to stand and dot the otherwise public parklands. In that same year, Great Smoky Mountains National Park was authorized, and Shenandoah National Park had joined the system a year earlier, both largely possible due to donations from private citizens, including $3 million from John D. Rockefeller Jr.

Earlier, Rockefeller had also acquired approximately 35,000 acres near Jackson Hole, Wyoming, to supplement the expansion of Yellowstone National Park and to thwart the blight of gas stations and tourist traps in the area. Although the purchase was completed by 1929, Congress did not expand the park status for another 20 years. Instead, in 1929, they authorized Grand Teton National Park, which comprised only mountaintops that were clearly economically insignificant. Congress viewed the Jackson Hole Valley area connecting Grand Teton to Yellowstone as too valuable to be set aside despite that the land would be donated. In essence, Congress continued to ignore the preservation of wildlife that wintered in this lower elevation area and were therefore open game during hunting season. Once again, the need to protect the entire ecosystem was overlooked. Finally, in 1950, Congress annexed a large segment of the valley to Grand Teton National Park, after appeasing hunters with a proposal to omit from the park a strip of forestland between Grand Teton and Yellowstone.

Throughout the 1930s, the Depression-era Civilian Conservation Corps completed conservation, rehabilitation, and construction projects in federal and state parklands that continue to provide value today. At the program's peak in 1935, there were 600 Civilian Conservation Corps camps with 118 in federal parklands and 482 in state parks. The NPS oversaw the program that had 6,000 professional supervisors and 120,000 enrollees that came from the ranks of the unemployed (Mackintosh, 1990). Other labor-intensive projects that were added to the National Park System in the 1930s were the Blue Ridge Parkway, the Natchez Trace Parkway, and the recreational resources surrounding the Hoover Dam reservoir, later named Lake Mead.

World War II brought park development to a halt and decreased park use. Afterward, visitation catapulted from 6 million in 1942, to 33 million in 1950, to 72 million in 1960. This rapid increase demanded the rehabilitation of existing infrastructure and the construction of more. By 1960, the NPS had developed 56 visitor centers with interpretive exhibits and audiovisual programs, with many more to follow. The National Historic Preservation Act of 1966 expanded the historical interpretation role of the NPS with the maintenance of the National Register of Historic Places. Listed properties were afforded assistance to encourage historical preservation (Mackintosh, 1990).

Independence Hall was constructed between 1732 and 1756 and is part of Independence Hall National Historical Park in Philadelphia.

Ecosystem management was prominent in NPS activities in the 1960s. In 1963, a team of distinguished scientists chaired by Aldo Starker Leopold wrote in *Wildlife Management in the National Parks*, "The major policy change that we would recommend to the National Park Service, is that it recognize the enormous complexity of ecologic communities...." (Runte, 1987, p. 198). Although the Save the Redwoods movement had begun as early as 1892 and major groves had been set aside as state parks and Muir Woods National Monument, the movement's goal to protect the redwoods' coastal ecosystem from the lumberman's ax was not achieved until the late 1960s. Finally, the Redwood National Park was designated, and three state parks were adjoined through the federal purchase of contiguous private lands. A painful catalyst for designation was the neighbor-

Visitors climb a ladder to one of the well-preserved cliff dwellings at Mesa Verde National Park in southwestern Colorado.

ing lumbering activity that toppled more than 300 huge redwoods (Runte, 1987). The Land and Water Conservation Fund of 1965 (see Chapter 12) provided the majority of funds to acquire additional parklands from revenues from offshore drilling leases for oil and gas, admissions and user fees at federal recreational sites, surplus-land sales, and excise taxes on motorboat fuel (Jensen, 1985; Knudson, 1984).

With Alaska achieving statehood in 1959, it offered the last frontier in which complete ecological preserves could be set aside as national parks, wilderness areas, and wildlife refuges. This fertile setting created a long controversial debate that culminated in President Jimmy Carter and Secretary of the Interior Cecil D. Andrus taking action to force Congress to finally protect more than 100 million acres, or 28% of the state. The Alaska National Interests Lands Conservation Act of 1980 more than doubled the acreage of national parklands, by setting aside 43.6 million acres for new national parklands, 53.8 million acres for wildlife refuges, and 1.2 million acres for the National Wild and Scenic Rivers System. Even with the vast amount of land protected, preservationists gradually learned that ecosystems had been severed by economic interests. For instance, significant expanses of land were protected as "preserves" that permitted hunting, fishing, and mining. These designations were a compromise struck to accommodate the economic interests of tourism and mining (Runte, 1987).

The 1980s were a time of reassessment and expansion of urban parklands. In a 1988 study, The National Park System Plan, it was concluded that 69% of all national parks needed their boundaries expanded for the National Park System to preserve them for future generations (Craig, 1991). Much of this expansion is necessary because ecosystems were not well understood at the time the parks were established. Boundaries are being considered for other reasons, too. For instance, the boundaries of the Petrified Forest National Park in Arizona were based primarily on survey lines rather than resource boundaries. When George W. Bush signed a bill that authorized expanded boundaries,

the park nearly doubled in size to incorporate, for protection, preservation, and study, fragile resources that are as significant as those that were already protected (NPS, 2006). Boundary changes do not come easily; the movement to increase the park took 12 years (Kirkwood, 2005).

Not Only Parks and Monuments

The NPS's role in historical interpretation was greatly expanded in the 1930s with the transfer of the War Department's historic parks, monuments, and battlefield sites and the transfer of the national capital parks, including the Jefferson Memorial and the Washington Monument. Together, more than 50 historic areas in the East rounded out the park system that had previously been heavily weighted in the western states, rendering the system national in scope (Mackintosh, 1990). Many other nontraditional national areas were established in the 1960s and 1970s, including Cape Cod National Seashore, Indiana Dunes National Lakeshore, and Gateway National Recreation Area on the outskirts of New York. Many of these acquisitions were funded by the Land and Water Conservation Fund. The Wild and Scenic Rivers System was established with 1968 legislation, and passage of the National Trails System Act of 1968 created the National Trails System. The passage of the National Parks and Recreation Act of 1978 provided for a host of even more new and expanded park areas, including Santa Monica Mountains National Recreation Area near Los Angeles and New River Gorge National River in western Virginia. In all, 15 units were added to the National Park System by the 1978 act.

Recreational Opportunities and Park Nomenclature

The NPS offers some of the world's greatest camping areas, backcountry camping, camping modifications for persons with disabilities, especially those who use wheelchairs or those who have difficulty walking, and concessions for tourists. Park diversity impacts the recreational opportunities available, and a range of special activities from horseback riding to canoeing to studying wildlife is available for visitors. Park rangers conduct interpretive programs and evening programs around the campfire. In more recent years, Congress and the NPS have attempted to simplify the nomenclature and to establish basic criteria for use of the different official titles. Brief definitions of various titles as described by the NPS (2009) follow.

National park. Generally, a national park contains a variety of resources and encompasses large land or water areas to help provide adequate protection of the resources. For example, Hawaii's Haleakala National Park preserves the outstanding features of Haleakala Crater on that island of Maui and protects the unique and fragile ecosystems of the Kipahulu Valley.

National monument. A national monument is intended to preserve at least one nationally significant resource. It is usually smaller than a national park and lacks its diversity of attractions. For example, New York's Fort Stanwix National Monument is a complete reconstruction of the fort where the Americans withstood British invasion and the site of the treaty with the Iroquois. National monuments are also managed by other federal agencies such as the Bureau of Land Management.

National preserves. The category of national preserve was established primarily for the protection of certain resources. Activities such as hunting and fishing or extracting minerals and fuels may be permitted if they do not jeopardize the natural values of a site. In 1974, Big Cypress and Big Thicket were authorized as the first national preserves. Big Cypress National Preserves (Florida) adjoins Everglades National Park, providing a fresh water supply crucial to the park's development. Big Thicket National Preserve (Texas) offers an excellent opportunity to study and research a great number of plant and animal species in this "biological crossroad of North America" (NPS, 2000, p. 82). National reserves are similar, but management may be transferred to local or state authorities. City of Rocks was the first reserve in 1988.

National lakeshores and national seashores. Designated to preserve shoreline areas and offshore islands, national lakeshores

and national seashores are focused on preserving natural values and providing water-oriented recreation. Although national lakeshores can be established on the shore of any natural freshwater lake, the existing four are located on the shores of the Great Lakes. Sleeping Bear Dunes National Lakeshore and Indiana Dunes are on Lake Michigan, and Pictured Rocks and Apostle Islands are on Lake Superior. The 10 national seashores are on the Atlantic, Gulf, and Pacific coasts. They include Assateague Island (Maryland and Virginia), Canaveral (Florida), Cape Cod (Massachusetts), Cape Lookout and Cape Hatteras (North Carolina), Cumberland Island (Georgia), Fire Island (New York), Gulf Islands (Mississippi), Padre Island (Texas), and Point Reyes (California).

National rivers and wild and scenic riverways. These designations preserve ribbons of land bordering free-flowing streams that have not been dammed, channelized, or otherwise altered by humans. Besides preserving rivers in their natural state, these areas provide opportunities for outdoor activities such as hiking, canoeing, and hunting. The Merced River (California), Alatna Wild River (Alaska), and Delaware National Scenic River (Pennsylvania) are examples of rivers preserved in these categories.

National scenic trails. These trails are generally long-distance footpaths winding through extended corridors of natural beauty. The Appalachian National Scenic Trail, for example, follows the Appalachian Mountains from Mount Katahdin in Maine to Springer Mountain in Georgia for approximately 2,000 miles. The Pacific Crest National Scenic Trail stretches along the mountain crests from the Canadian border in Washington state to the Mexican border in California. The National Trails System (described later in this chapter), of which the national scenic trails are a part, is administered by the NPS. The NPS coordinates with the Forest Service, who manages several of the individual national scenic trails and encourages other public and private agencies to develop, maintain, and protect trails; expand and designate trails; and where feasible, cooperate with and support the efforts of the trails community nationwide. The

Historic reenactments occur at many of the national battlefield and military parks, such as Antietam National Battlefield in Maryland and Vicksburg National Military Park in Mississippi.

Petrified Forest National Park in Arizona was first protected as a national monument in 1906.

Pecos National Historical Park in New Mexico protects two Spanish missions and the ruins of the ancient pueblo of Pecos, a landmark along the Santa Fe Trail.

Continental Divide, Florida, Ice Age, Natchez Trace, North Country, and Potomac Heritage are additional national scenic trails (Cordes, 2001).

National historic trails. These trails recognize past routes of exploration and migration and of freedom-seeking and military actions. They preserve stories of the United State's past. Not necessarily continuous, they identify historic routes (often paralleled by marked driving routes), remains, and artifacts that together tell the story of past adventures and conflicts. They invite today's adventurer back into time and into an environment that was experienced by earlier inhabitants, explorers, pioneers, entrepreneurs, and freedom fighters. Trails such as the Lewis and Clark expeditions; the Overmountain Revolutionary War campaign; the Trail of Tears; the flight of the Nez Perce; the Iditarod race for gold; and the Selma-to-Montgomery voting rights march have captured the American spirit. The NPS oversees the national trails, and the Bureau of Land Management has more miles of national historic trails on its lands (Cordes & Lammers, 1999).

National historic sites. These sites preserve places and commemorate persons, events, and activities important in the nation's history. They range from archeological sites associated with prehistoric Indian civilizations to sites related to the lives of modern Americans. Historic areas are customarily preserved or restored to reflect their appearance during the period of their greatest historical significance. A variety of titles—national military park, national battlefield park, national battlefield site, and national battlefield—have been used for areas associated with American military history. But other areas such as national monuments and national historic parks may include features associated with military history. National historic parks are commonly areas of greater physical extent and complexity than national historic sites. The lone international historic site, International Peace Garden (North Dakota and Manitoba), is a site relevant to U.S. and Canadian history.

National memorials. The title national memorial is most often used for areas that are primarily commemorative. But they need not be sites or structures historically associated with their subjects. For example, the home of Abraham Lincoln (Illinois) is a national historic site, but the Lincoln Memorial (Washington, DC) is a national memorial. Several other areas administered by the National Capital Region whose titles do not include the words national memorial, such as the Washington Monument (Washington, DC), are nevertheless classified as national memorials.

National recreation areas. Originally, national recreation areas such as Coulee Dam National Recreation Area (Washington) were units surrounding reservoirs impounded by dams built by other federal agencies. The NPS manages many of these areas under cooperative agreements. The concept of recreational areas has grown to encompass other lands and waters set aside for recreational use by acts of Congress and now includes major areas in urban centers such as Gateway National Recreation Area (New York) and Santa Monica Mountains National Recreation Area (California). There are also national recreation areas outside the National Park System that are administered by the Forest Service. For example, the latter two units of the Whiskeytown–Shasta–Trinity National Recreation Area are administered by the Forest Service.

National parkways. National parkways encompass ribbons of land flanking roadways and offer an opportunity for leisurely driving through areas of scenic interest. They are not designed for high-speed travel. Besides the areas set aside as parkways, other units of the National Park System include parkways within their boundaries. The Blue Ridge Parkway (North Carolina and Virginia), for example, is a 470-mile parkway that follows the crest of the Blue Ridge Mountains. A portion of the Blue Ridge Parkway and all of the Natchez Trace Parkway have been designated All-American Roads by the National Scenic Byway Program of the Department of Transportation (Cordes, 2001).

Ruins of a large pueblo of the Salado Indians who flourished in the Verde Valley between A.D. 1100 and 1450 can be seen at Tuzigoot National Monument near Clarksdale, Arizona.

The dome-shaped white-cap rock along the Freemont River accounts for the name of Capitol Reef National Park in Utah.

National wilderness areas. Congress designated national wilderness areas (discussed later in this chapter) in 47 units of the National Park System as well as within units managed by other federal agencies. This designation does not remove wilderness lands from the parks, but it ensures that they will be managed to retain the "primeval character and influence, without permanent improvements or human habitation..." (Wilderness Act, 1964).

Performing arts. Areas of the National Park System that have been set aside primarily as sites for the performing arts include Wolf Trap Farm Park for the Performing Arts (Virginia)—America's first such national park—and the John F. Kennedy Center for the Performing Arts (Washington, DC). Two historic areas, Ford's Theater National Historic Site (Washington, D.C.) and Chamizal National Memorial (Texas), also provide facilities for the performing arts.

National capital parks. Parks in the nation's capital are administered by the NPS under the Reorganization Act of 1933, which was the first major expansion of the NPS's holdings. Most parklands in the capital are included in the federal holdings, although the District of Columbia also operates parks, playgrounds, and recreational facilities. The NPS also administers several units in Maryland, Virginia, and West Virginia.

Related areas. Besides the National Park System, the Wild and Scenic Rivers System, and the National Trails System, there are areas known as affiliated areas and national heritage areas. These are areas that are neither federally owned nor directly administered by the NPS but that use NPS assistance. They comprise a variety of locations in the United States and Canada where significant properties outside the National Park System are preserved, such as the Iñupiat Heritage Center in Alaska that is affiliated with New Bedford Whaling National Historical Park. Some affiliated areas have been recognized by acts of Congress, and others have been designated national historic sites by the secretary of the interior under authority of the Historic Sites

Act of 1935. All draw on technical or financial aid from the NPS.

National heritage areas. National heritage areas expand on traditional approaches to resource stewardship by supporting large-scale community-centered initiatives that connect local citizens to the preservation, conservation, and planning processes. Through the facilitation of a local coordinating entity, such as a private nonprofit corporation or a public commission, residents of a region come together to improve regional quality of life by protecting their shared cultural and natural resources.

In national heritage areas, businesses, governments, nonprofit organizations, and private individuals collaborate to promote sustainable economic development and community revitalization projects. Designated by Congress, each national heritage area is governed by separate authorizing legislation and operates under provisions unique to its resources and desired goals. The NPS provides technical planning and limited financial assistance. Serving as a partner and advisor, the NPS leaves decision-making authority in the hands of local people and organizations.

First inaugurated in 1984, national heritage areas encompass 40 regions, ranging from factory towns and city neighborhoods to farmland and battlefields. As part of a living, working, evolving landscape, national heritage areas reflect the diverse and evolving histories and cultures of the people who call the region home. For instance, visitors who explore West Virginia National Coal Heritage Area will gain insight into a rich cultural geography that has been influenced for more than 125 years by the role of coal extraction. The Coal Heritage National Scenic Byway is a convenient route for exploring this national heritage area that impacted America's development (NPS, 2009).

The National Park Service in the 21st century. The National Park System Advisory Board (2001) recommended that the NPS address these challenges throughout the 21st century:

- Embrace its mission, as educator, to become a more significant part of America's educational system for students and learners of all ages.
- Encourage the study of the American past.
- Adopt the conservation of biodiversity as a core principle in efforts to protect marine as well as terrestrial resources.
- Advance the principles of sustainability while first practicing preservation.
- Actively acknowledge the connections between cultures and the parks and ensure that no relevant chapter in the American heritage experience remains unopened.
- Encourage collaboration among park and recreation systems at every level to help build a network of outdoor recreation accessible to all Americans.
- Develop new organizational talents and abilities and a workforce that reflects America's diversity.

The 10 most visited units of the National Park System are identified in Table 7.2.

U.S. Fish and Wildlife Service

The U.S. Fish and Wildlife Service (FWS) is the principal agency through which the federal government carries out its responsibilities to conserve, protect, and enhance the nation's fish and wildlife and their habitats for the continuing benefit of people. Its major responsibilities are for migratory birds, endangered species, certain marine mammals, and freshwater and anadromous fisheries.

> Wild beasts and birds are by right not the property merely of the people who are alive today, but the property of unknown generations, whose belongings we have no right to squander.
>
> Theodore Roosevelt

Table 7.2
Ten Most Visited Units of the National Park System

Park unit	Recreational visits
1. Blue Ridge Parkway (NC, VA)	15,205,059
2. Golden Gate National Recreation Area (CA)	14,540,338
3. Great Smoky Mountains National Park (TN, NC)	9,685,829
4. George Washington Memorial Parkway (MD, VA, DC)	7,425,577
5. Lake Mead National Recreation Area (NV, AZ)	6,285,439
6. Lincoln Memorial (DC)	6,191,361
7. Natchez Trace Parkway (MS, AL, TN)	5,560,668
8. Gateway National Recreation Area (NY, NJ)	5,043,863
9. Gulf Islands National Seashore (FL, MS)	4,973,462
10. Delaware Water Gap National Recreation Area (PA, NJ)	4,970,802

Note. From "Top 10 Visited Sites in National Park System Revealed," by National Park Service, 2013, http://www.nps.gov/news/release.htm?id=1457.

The service's origins date back to 1871 when Congress established the U.S. Fish Commission to study the decrease of the nation's food fishes and recommend ways to reverse the decline. Created as an independent agency, it was placed under the Department of Commerce in 1903 and renamed the Bureau of Fisheries. Meanwhile, in 1885, Congress created an Office of Economic Ornithology in the U.S. Department of Agriculture. The staff of this office studied the food habits and migratory patterns of birds, especially the ones that have an effect on agriculture. This office gradually grew in responsibilities and was renamed the Bureau of Biological Survey in 1905. In addition to studying the abundance, distribution, and habitats of birds and mammals, the survey managed the nation's first wildlife refuges, controlled predators, enforced wildlife laws, and conserved dwindling populations of heron, egrets, and other waterfowl and migratory birds.

The Bureau of Fisheries and Bureau of Biological Survey were transferred to the Department of the Interior in 1939. One year later, in 1940, they were combined and named the Fish and Wildlife Service. Further reorganization came in 1956 when the Fish and Wildlife Act created the U.S. Fish and Wildlife Service and established within the agency two bureaus: (a) Commercial Fisheries and (b) Sport Fisheries and Wildlife. The Bureau of Commercial Fisheries was transferred to the Department of Commerce in 1970 and is now known as the National Marine Fisheries Service (described later in this chapter). The Bureau of Sport Fisheries and Wildlife remained in the Department of the Interior. In 1974, *Bureau* was dropped and the agency was called simply the U.S. Fish and Wildlife Service. Today, the service employs approximately 7,500 people at facilities across the country, including a headquarters office in Washington, DC, seven regional offices including one for research, and over 700 field units. Among these are national wildlife refuges and fish hatcheries, research laboratories, field offices, and law enforcement agencies.

The Fish and Wildlife Service leads the federal effort to protect and restore animals and plants that are in danger of extinction in the United States and worldwide. It maintains major research laboratories and field stations as well as cooperative research units at universities across the country. It provides biological advice to other agencies and members of the public concerning the conservation of habitat that may be affected by development activities. For instance, service biologists developed many of the captive breeding techniques that have benefited rare species such as whooping cranes, California condors, and black-footed ferrets. Rachel Carson (see Chapter 3), once a service employee, awakened the American public in her book *Silent Spring* to threats to fish and wildlife from highly toxic and long-lasting pesticides such as DDT. The service is making major efforts to restore nationally significant fisheries depleted by overfishing, pollution, or other habitat damage. The service is responsible for the conservation of over 800 species of migratory birds, regulates hunting of bird populations, and acquires and manages many national wildlife refuges to provide secure habitats for migratory birds.

The National Wildlife Refuge System

The National Wildlife Refuge System is a network of federal lands and waters managed specifically for wildlife. Vitally important, refuges provide habitat for approximately 60 endangered species and hundreds of species of birds, mammals, reptiles, amphibians, fish, and plants. More than 561 refuges, 209 waterfowl production areas, and 50 coordination areas are located on 15% of all federal lands (U.S. Fish and Wildlife Service, 2014b). The national wildlife refuges are located in all 50 states. Waterfowl production areas are small, natural wetland and associated grassland acquired primarily under the authority of the Migratory Bird Hunting and Conservation Stamp Act. Coordination areas account for federal land that states manage as wildlife habitat under cooperative agreements.

As seen in Figure 7.7, units of the National Wildlife Refuge System stretch across the continent from the north shore of Alaska to the Florida Keys and range in size from Minnesota's small Lake Mille Lacs to Alaska's 20 million–acre Arctic National Wildlife Refuge, the crown jewel of wild America. Over 70 refuges are located within 5 miles of an urban population center. These support the Fish and Wildlife Service urban initiative to "connect people with nature." Urban refuges offer unique environmental education and recreation opportunities in highly populated areas. They promote their mission to protect wildlife and their habitats for present and future generations, but also fulfill their goal to work with community partners to establish a 21st century conservation ethic by reconnecting people—especially youth—to the natural world (U.S. Fish and Wildlife Service, 2014b).

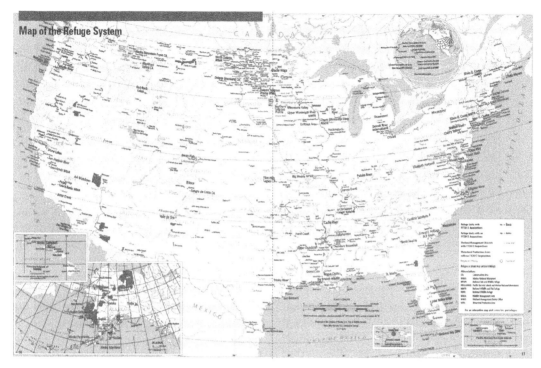

Figure 7.7. The National Wildlife Refuge System. From *Annual Report of Lands Under Control of U.S. Fish and Wildlife Service as of September 2013*, by U.S. Fish and Wildlife Service, 2014, http://www. fws.gov/refuges/land/PDF/2013_Annual_Report_of_Lands-June-2014.pdf, pp. 16–17.

At the turn of the century, ladies' fashions contributed to the need for establishing the first refuges. Herons and egrets were being killed in large numbers for their plumes, used for hats. Other human and natural calamities also contributed to the need to establish refuges. In 1903, President Theodore Roosevelt signed an executive order protecting the herons, egrets, and other birds on Florida's Pelican Island, making it the first national wildlife refuge. During his tenure as president, Roosevelt designated 66 other properties as national wildlife reservations, laying the foundation of the present-day refuge system. The first refuges established for big-game animals are Oklahoma's Wichita Mountains Wildlife Refuge in 1905, the National Bison Range in Montana in 1908, and Wyoming's National Elk Refuge in 1912.

Initial passage of the Migratory Bird Treaty Act of 1918 was a landmark in wildlife conservation legislation and provides for the regulation of migratory bird hunting. Later, as the wheat fields of North America dried up and blew away in the 1930s, so did many of the wetlands necessary for the breeding of migratory waterfowl. In response, President Franklin Roosevelt appointed a special committee to discover a means to conserve migratory waterfowl. Headed by Thomas Beck, editor of *Collier's* magazine, the committee eventually included Aldo Leopold (Chapter 3) and Jay Norwood "Ding" Darling. With surprising swiftness in March 1934, Roosevelt signed the Migratory Bird Hunting Stamp Act of 1934, and the first duck stamps, designed by Darling (see Figure 7.8), were sold for $1. Meanwhile, thousands of Depression-era workers from the Civilian Conservation Corps and Works Progress Administration improved habitat and built the infrastructure of over 50 national wildlife refuges and fish hatcheries (Madison, 2001).

Figure 7.8. The first duck stamp, 1934. Brush-and-ink drawing of mallards by Jay N. "Ding" Darling.

The passage of numerous laws have had a powerful influence on the development and management of the system. Significant legislation includes the Federal Aid in Wildlife Restoration Act of 1937 (commonly referred to as the Pittman–Robertson Act), the Fish and Wildlife Coordination Act of 1946, Federal Aid in Sport Fish Restoration Act of 1950 (commonly referred to as the Dingell–Johnson Act), the Fish and Wildlife Act of 1956, the Duck Stamp Act of 1958, the Refuge Recreation Act of 1962, the National Wildlife Refuge System Administration Act of 1964, the Land and Water Conservation Fund Act of 1965, the Wilderness Act of 1964, the National Wildlife Refuge System Act of 1966, the Endangered Species Act of 1967 and 1973, the Alaska National Interest Lands Conservation Act of 1980, the National Wildlife Refuge System Improvement Act of 1997, and the National Wildlife Refuge System Centennial Act of 2000 (U.S. Fish and Wildlife Service, 2000).

Today, the refuge system is a unique collection of diverse areas administered by the U.S. Fish and Wildlife Service. Many refuges are located along the major north–south flyways, providing feeding and resting areas for the great semiannual migrations of ducks, geese, and other birds. Other areas serve as sanctuaries for endangered or unusual species. For example, the Aransas Refuge in Texas is the winter home of the whooping crane, and the Hawaiian Islands Refuge provides the only habitat for a number of endangered species including the Hawaiian monk seal and green sea turtle.

Archeological artifacts and areas of historical significance located on refuge lands are preserved along with wildlife habitat. DeSoto Refuge in Iowa, for instance, maintains an exhibit and collection of items reclaimed from the historic steamship Bertrand, which sank in the Missouri River in 1865.

Recreation

National wildlife refuges offer a variety of recreational opportunities. An estimated 47 million people visit these lands annually, contributing $4.87 in economic output for every $1 appropriated (U.S. Fish and Wildlife Service, 2014). Although public uses are regulated so they do not interfere with the wildlife purposes of the refuge, many activities are available. Recreational uses may include wildlife observation, photography, nature study, hiking, boating, hunting, and fishing. Some refuges provide visitor centers, special study areas, environmental education programs, interpretive trails and drives, wildlife observation towers, photographic blinds, and other public facilities. Activities vary with each refuge and may depend on the season of the year. Visitors are advised to check with refuge personnel prior to a visit to determine which activities are allowed and what regulations apply toward the consideration of the wildlife. Every visit to a refuge is different, and each person has an individual experience.

The prevailing refuge management philosophy for many years was a commitment to anonymity, the belief being that the fewer who knew about refuges, the better. People have discovered that refuges are natural treasures (see Chapter 15), and the U.S. Fish and Wildlife Service is meeting the challenge of tourists by providing extensive outdoor experiences while protecting the wildlife for which the refuges were created. The Center for Wildlife Information (2012) suggests etiquette for viewing and photographing wildlife to avoid stressing the animals or birds. Their guidelines include observing from a distance through binoculars, spotting scopes, and telephoto lenses; allowing wildlife to keep the visitor in view; not following or chasing wildlife; and viewing wildlife for a limited time. Viewing early or late in the day provides optimum viewing opportunities.

THE BUREAU OF LAND MANAGEMENT

The Bureau of Land Management (BLM) is responsible for managing 247 million acres of the nation's public lands, more than any other federal agency. These lands, heavily concentrated (99.8%) in 11 western states, are massed in a combination of ways that best serves the needs of the American people (see Table 7.3). These are lands that remain of the nation's once vast land holdings—the public domain had once included nearly 2 billion acres of land. In the course of the country's national expansion and development, public lands were sold or deeded by the federal government to the states and their counties and municipalities, to educational institutions, to private citizens, and to industries. Other lands were set aside as national parks and monuments, forests, wildlife refuges, and military installations. Today, the BLM manages about 37% of federal land holdings. The public lands are a vast storehouse of fossil fuels, other important minerals, and timber. Livestock forage on millions of acres, and the lands support hundreds of thousands of pronghorn antelope, deer, elk, and caribou; millions of smaller creatures; and about 37,000 wild horses and burros (BLM, 2012). They offer endless recreational opportunities and settings including mountain ranges, alpine tundra, evergreen forests, expanses of sage bush, and rock canyons that were once called "the land nobody wanted."

Mission of the Bureau of Land Management

It is the mission of the Bureau of Land Management to sustain the health, diversity, and productivity of the public lands for the use and enjoyment of present and future organizations.

Management is based on the principles of multiple use and sustained yield, combining uses and balancing needs of future generations for renewable and nonrenewable resources. These resources include recreation, range, timber, minerals, watershed, fish and wildlife, and wilderness. Most of the BLM's 10,000 employees and 170,000 volunteers work in field offices in the western United States, although the headquarters is in Washington, DC (BLM, 2012). There are 12 state offices, 58 district offices, and 140 resource area offices. Diverse skills and talents are required for positions such as recreation specialists, foresters, range conservationists, wildlife biologists, archeologists, surveyors, and engineers. Two threats facing the land holdings are widespread noxious weeds that have taken hold and the prevalence of abandoned land mine shafts that are hazardous to visitors.

History of the BLM

The BLM's roots go back to the Land Ordinance of 1785 and the Northwest Ordinance of 1787. These laws provided for the survey and settlement of the lands that the original 13 colonies ceded to the federal government after the War of Independence. As additional lands were acquired by the United States from Spain, France, and other countries, Congress directed that they be explored, surveyed, and made available for settlement. In 1812, Congress established the General Land Office in the Department of the Treasury to oversee the disposition of these federal lands. As the 19th century progressed and the nation's land base expanded further west, Congress encouraged the settlement of the land by enacting a variety of laws, including the Homesteading Laws and the Mining Law of 1872. These statutes served one of the major policy goals of the young country: settlement of the western territories. With the exception of the Mining Law of 1872 and the Desert Land Act of 1877, all have since been repealed or superseded by other statutes (BLM, 2001).

The late 19th century marked a shift in federal land management priorities with the creation of the first national parks, forests,

Table 7.3

National Landscape Conservation System: Number and Size of Designated Areas

NLCS area	Type of designation	Number	Total BLM acres	Total BLM miles
National Monuments	Presidential or Congressional	16	4,828,240	0
National Conservation Areas		16	3,663,725	0
Steens Mountain Cooperative Management and Protection Area	Congressional	1	428,242	0
Yaquina Head Outstanding Natural Area	Congressional	1	95	0
Piedras Blancas Historic Light Station Outstanding Natural Area[b]	Congressional	1	18	0
Jupiter Inlet Lighthouse Outstanding Natural Area[c]	Congressional	1	63	0
Wilderness Areas[d]	Congressional	221	8,700,956	0
Wilderness Study Areas	Administrative	545	12,835,035	0
National Wild and Scenic Rivers	Congressional	69	1,002,016	2,425[e]
National Historic Trails	Congressional	13	0	5,078
National Scenic Trails	Congressional	5	0	683
Headwaters Forest Reserve	Congressional	1	7,542	0
Total		890[f]	31,465,932	8,186

Note. From *Public Land Statistics: 2012* (Vol. 197), by Bureau of Land Management, 2013, http://www.blm.gov/public_land_statistics/pls12/pls2012.pdf, pp. 201–202.

[a]The total acres figure includes double-counted acres. The Geographic Information System (GIS) analysis has shown that when double-counted acres are considered (i.e., wilderness areas within a national monument or national conservation area), the National Landscape Conservation System (NLCS) provides for special management prescriptions on approximately 25 million acres of public land. [b]Area established by Congress in 2008 in Public Law 110-226. [c]Area established by Congress in 2008 in Public Law 110-226. One hundred and twenty-six acres are owned by six federal and nonfederal entities. [d]The Tabeguache Area in Colorado is, by act of Congress, to be managed like wilderness but is not shown here because it has not been officially designated as wilderness. [e]The total may appear incorrect because the number was rounded after addition. [f]The White Mountains National Recreation Area is no longer a part of the NLCS per Public Law 111-11, the Omnibus Public Land Management Act of 2009.

and wildlife refuges. By withdrawing these lands from settlement, Congress signaled a shift in the policy goals served by the public lands. Instead of using them to promote settlement, Congress recognized that they should be held in public ownership because of their other resource values. In the early 20th century, Congress took additional steps toward recognizing the value of the assets on public lands and directed the Executive Branch to manage activities on the remaining public lands. The Mineral Leasing Act of 1920 allowed leasing, exploration, and production of selected commodities such as coal, oil, gas, and sodium to take place on public lands. The Taylor Grazing Act of 1934 established the U.S. Grazing Service to manage the public rangelands. And the Oregon and California Act of August 28, 1937, required sustained yield management of the timberlands in western Oregon. In 1946, the Grazing Service was merged with the General Land Office to form the BLM within the Department of the Interior. When the BLM was initially created, there were over 2,000 unrelated and often conflicting laws for managing the public lands (BLM, 2001).

The BLM had no unified legislative mandate until Congress enacted the Federal Land Policy Management Act of 1976. In it, Congress recognized the value of the remaining public lands by declaring that these lands would remain in public ownership, and it established a coherent legislative mandate for managing the public lands, making the BLM a true multiple-use agency (Ibrahim & Cordes, 2003). With more land to manage with a smaller budget and fewer personnel than the USDA Forest Service or NPS, it establishes partnerships with private enterprises. Its more recent move toward ecosystem management has produced clashes with some ranchers whose single-use needs do not agree with monitored procedures.

Recreation

The BLM has taken on an increasingly dynamic role in outdoor recreation. As the new millennium unfolded, the BLM took a bold step to raise the profile of recreation on its lands by establishing the National Landscape Conservation System (NLCS). The system holds some of the nation's most remarkable and rugged landscapes including the agency's national monuments including the impressive Grand Staircase Escalante in Utah and the Grand Canyon Parashant in Arizona. Included, too, are the 16 congressionally designated national conservation areas including California's vast 9.5 million–acre California Desert and Nevada's 1.2 million–acre Black Rock Desert–High Rock Canyon Emigrant Trails. The latter, established in 2000, protects wagon ruts, historic inscriptions, and a wilderness landscape that is largely unchanged from when pioneers moved westward in the 1800s. Other lands of the NLCS include the Headwaters Forest Reserve in California, a stand of old-growth redwoods and surrounding lands totaling 7,400 acres, 221 wilderness areas, 545 wilderness study

areas, 2,425 miles of 69 wild and scenic rivers, 5,078 miles of 13 national historic trails, 683 miles of national scenic trails, and other areas designated for important scientific and ecological characteristics.

Offering a greater diversity of outdoor recreational opportunities than national parks and national forests, the BLM accommodates over 61 million fee-related recreation visits each year (BLM, 2014). For estimated fee-related activities, see Table 7.4. Overall, visitors engage in many recreational activities, including camping, hiking, hunting, fishing, boating, skiing, hang gliding, mountain biking, off-road travel, cave exploration, rock-hounding, watching wildlife, birding, visiting natural and cultural heritage sites, and enjoying solitude. The BLM administers developed recreational sites that offer fishable streams with trout, salmon, and other sport fish. They also have lakes and reservoirs, floatable rivers, boating access points, national backcountry byways, and watchable wildlife sites as well as thousands of miles of multiple-use trails used by motorcyclists, hikers, equestrians, and mountain bikers. BLM also offers wilderness areas, national wild and scenic rivers, and national historic and scenic trails. Estimated recreational use of BLM land is shown in Table 7.4.

OTHER FEDERAL AGENCIES

Other federal agencies, because of the vast resources they manage, have a significant impact on outdoor recreation. These include the Bureau of Indian Affairs, the U.S. Army Corps of Engineers, the Bureau of Reclamation, the Tennessee Valley Authority, and the National Oceanic and Atmospheric Administration.

The Bureau of Indian Affairs

The mission of the Bureau of Indian Affairs (BIA) is to enhance the quality of life, to promote economic opportunity, and to carry out the responsibility to protect and improve the trust assets of American Indians, Indian tribes, and Alaskan natives. BIA accomplishes this through the delivery of quality services, maintaining   government-to-government

Table 7.4

Estimated Recreational Use of BLM-Administered Public Lands for Recreation Activities Under Various Fee Authorizations

Recreation activities	Fee sites and areas[b]		Visitor days[a]				Total public lands	
			Special recreation permitted activities[c]		Areas without permits or fees[d]			
	Thousands	Percent	Thousands	Percent	Thousands	Percent	Thousands	Percent for activity group
Land-Based Activities								
Camping and Picnicking	2,681	3.69	410	0.56	24,100	33.17	27,191	37.43
Nonmotorized Travel	624	0.86	149	0.21	7,849	10.80	8,622	11.87
Off-Highway Travel	299	0.41	75	0.10	7,494	10.32	7,868	10.83
Driving for Pleasure	84	0.12	3	0.00	3,039	4.18	3,126	4.30
Viewing Public Land Resources	325	0.45	37	0.05	4,237	5.83	4,599	6.33
Interpretation and Education	113	0.16	225	0.31	1,970	2.71	2,308	3.18
Hunting	33	0.05	19	0.03	6,399	8.81	6,451	8.88
Specialized Sports, Events, and Activities	305	0.42	346	0.48	3,892	5.36	4,543	6.25
Water-Based Activities								
Boating/Motorized	366	0.50	42	0.06	1,138	1.57	1,546	2.13
Boating/ Row/ Float/Paddle	122	0.17	190	0.26	2,472	3.40	2,784	3.83
Fishing	423	0.58	17	0.02	1,842	2.54	2,282	3.14
Swimming and Other Water Activities	113	0.16	1	0.00	486	0.67	600	0.83
Snow- and Ice-Based Activities								
Snowmobile and Motorized Travel	6	0.01	2	0.00	216	0.30	224	0.31
Other Winter Activities	12	0.02	2	0.00	492	0.68	506	0.70
Total	5,506	7.58	1,518	2.09	65,626	90.33	72,650	100.00

Note. This table shows participation levels for various activity groupings. Recreation activity type and duration (visitor days) are recorded at fee and nonfee sites and areas, as well as for special recreation permits. Visitor days, grouped into Activity Groups (summarized from a list of 99 recreational activities), are based on registrations, permit records, observations, postseason permittee reports, and the professional judgment of the field staffs. Some totals may not appear correct because of rounding. From *Public Land Statistics: 2012* (Vol. 197), by Bureau of Land Management, 2013, http://www.blm.gov/public_land_statistics/pls12/pls2012.pdf, pp. 191–192.

[a] A visitor day is a common unit of measure of recreation use among federal agencies. One visitor day represents an aggregate of 12 visitor hours at a site or area. [b] Visitor days occurring at designated fee sites and areas with entrance permits, recreational use permits, and special area permits, usually with fee collection at the site. [c] Visitor days occurring on public lands that are subject to authorization under the Special Recreation Permit regulations, including the activities of private parties, commercial outfitters and guides, competitive events, organized groups, and other events. [d] Visitor days occurring at nonfee sites and dispersed areas when neither permits nor fees are required.

relationships within the spirit of Indian self-determination. The BIA, established in 1824, is the principal agent of the United States in carrying on the government-to-government relationship that exists between the United States and federally recognized Indian tribes.

One of the principal programs of the BIA is administering and managing some 56 million acres of land held in trust by the United States. The program is designed to assist tribes with the protection and development of forest, water, mineral, and energy resources. Although the BIA is headquartered in Washington, DC, most of its employees work in area offices, agencies, and 180 schools throughout the country. Most of the employees are American Indian. Their land provides a cultural, religious, and economic subsistence base.

Recreation. The substantial land and water resource base is used by Indians and non-Indians for outdoor recreation. These areas constitute an additional wilderness resource for the country and contain habitat that is critical to the recovery of a number of species that are listed as threatened or endangered, from fish and birds to big game. Not so many years ago, remote reservations were generally inaccessible to the public, but today they are open to visitors and offer numerous recreational facilities. Because of their economic potential, the BIA has supported commercial recreational developments with financial and administrative assistance. Tourism efforts have promoted job opportunities on reservations with Indians operating facilities, supervising campgrounds, and working as rangers similar to rangers in the national parks and forests. Navajo Tribal Park in Monument Valley of Arizona and Utah abounds with ancient ruins and spectacular vistas. Navajo rangers run the park and offer interpretive services.

Many reservations have spectacular scenery, and most offer hiking opportunities and hunting and fishing facilities. Others offer horseback riding, boating, and skiing. Major reservations conduct tours to archeological sites and areas of scenic interest. Powwows, dance ceremonials, crafts sales, casinos, and museums also attract many visitors.

Developments include those of the White Mountain Apaches of Arizona, the Mescalero Apaches of New Mexico, and the Confederated Warm Springs Tribes of Oregon. According to the U.S. Commission on Civil Rights (1973), a state cannot enforce its game and fish laws within the boundaries of an Indian reservation; therefore, permission to hunt or fish on reservations must be received from the tribe. When visiting reservations, visitors are guests in a place where cultural attitudes, social customs, and often language can be distinctive. Entry fees may be required for parks, and permits are required for backcountry travel. A fee or permit may also be required for photography, and permission to photograph individuals and ceremonies is required. Photography of restricted events is generally not allowed.

National Reservoir Areas

With approximately 75,000 dams in the United States, the water-related recreational opportunities are abundant (American Rivers, 2014). In general, reservoirs are popular recreational sites for fishing, boating, waterskiing, swimming, camping, picnicking, hiking, sightseeing, and other activities. Large dams built under the direction of the U.S. Army Corps of Engineers, the Bureau of Reclamation, and the Tennessee Valley Authority offer recreational attractions. These agencies, however, had few official responsibilities for recreational planning and management before 1962, when President John F. Kennedy approved Senate Document 97, which specified the need for outdoor recreation and fish and wildlife enhancement in planning for water projects. With the passage of the Federal Water Projects Recreation Act of 1965, procedures for developing multipurpose water resource projects were established, and plans for recreational use were required. The act provided the following:

- Recreation, fish, and wildlife enhancement be considered a purpose of federal water resource projects, though not to exceed 50% of the benefits or costs of such multipurpose projects.

- Recreational possibilities be considered for existent and planned federal, state, and local public developments.
- Recreation, fish, and wildlife enhancement features be administered by nonfederal administration.

The benefits of recreation bolstered the justification of new projects, but a provision requiring state and local cooperation gave veto power to these groups, which on occasion stopped projects. Implementation of the act, however, clearly made the federal government the nation's largest provider of inland water-related opportunities. Conversely, although these projects created new water-related recreational opportunities, previous recreational opportunities were impaired due to the destruction of excellent trout streams, scenic canyons, and archeological remains. Public concern for natural diversity has caused public resistance to many new dam projects and the dismantling of existing dams where feasible. Nonetheless, large flood control projects attract a multitude of recreationists.

U.S. Army Corps of Engineers

The U.S. Army Corps of Engineers (US-ACE), the largest federal provider of water-based recreation, accommodates some 370 million visitors at its lake and river projects each year (USACE, 2014). Housed in the Department of Defense, the Corps traces its origins to the American Revolution. On June 16, 1775, when the Continental Congress established the army, it provided for a chief engineer to direct fortifications for the Battle of Bunker Hill. By 1802, the Corps of Engineers was made permanent, and the U.S. Military Academy was established at West Point, New York, under the chief of army engineers as the only engineering college in the nation. The Corps has maintained a tradition of responding to the nation's military and civil engineering needs. In earlier times, those needs included coastal fortifications and lighthouses, surveying and pathfinding on the frontier, construction of public buildings, clearing of

river channels, and operation of early national parks such as Yellowstone and Yosemite.

The Corps (USACE, 2001) is engaged in complex military facilities, flood control, comprehensive water resources management, fish and wildlife conservation, recreational resources, environmental restoration, management of toxic wastes, energy resources, and the space program. They maintain inland waterways and operate locks. These waterways—a system of rivers, lakes, and coastal bays improved for commercial and recreational transportation—carry intercity freight. USACE also maintains smaller harbors and commercial harbors.

The Corps employs military civilian members, architect engineer and construction firms, and 53,000 volunteers (USACE, 2014). It has a network of nine divisions and subordinate districts, major laboratories and research centers, and hundreds of offices at projects throughout the country. Legislation passed in 1990 established environmental protection as one of the primary missions of water resources projects, along with navigation and flood control. The Corps and the NPS are cooperating on restoring the hydrologic regime for the Everglades in Florida.

Recreational development. The army engineers, as explorers and cartographers for pioneers, were among the first to advocate protection of natural resources according to Turhollow (n.d.). Among the first to explore the Yellowstone area, they urged that it be set aside and protected. Eventually, the roads they designed, built, and maintained opened the spectacular area to the public. Army engineers, along with the U.S. Geological Survey, also explored and mapped the Yosemite Valley. After John Muir and other conservationists persuaded Congress in 1890 to declare it a national park under joint control of California and the federal government, the Army was asked by the Department of the Interior to take administrative charge of the park until 1911. Besides policing the park, army engineers also laid out trails, produced a map for tourists, and preserved the fauna and flora from destruction by tourists and private owners of land in the park. Army en-

A corps of Navajo rangers offer interpretive services at Monument Valley National Tribal Park.

gineer Hiram M. Chitenden, who had helped preserve Yellowstone and published the first book-length study of that area, *Yellowstone National Park,* was selected to oversee the new park. Based on recommendations from Chitenden's commission, the park boundary was established to include 1,200 square miles that became the Yosemite National Park.

In 1876, Congress assigned the Corps the task of reengineering the Washington Monument—originally the work of a privately funded organization to honor the memory of the first president—after technical problems and bankruptcy caused a half-finished eyesore to stand for almost 30 years. The Corps, after 12 years of construction, completed the monument with a lightning rod placed on top made of a strange new metal for that time called aluminum. The monument, as part of the National Park System, is the tallest load-bearing masonry structure in the world.

The Federal Water Project Recreation Act of 1965 requires that the planning of all projects by the Corps give consideration to the inclusion of facilities for swimming, boating, fishing, camping, and sightseeing where appropriate. In developing plans for recreational facilities, the Corps seeks the cooperation of all federal and state agencies concerned. In addition, the Corps bears responsibility for the environmental protection of the sources for various recreational activities. It manages recreational sites at 422 lakes and reservoirs and leases additional sites to state, local, and private recreational groups (USACE, 2014). Corps-operated visitor centers, campgrounds, picnic areas, boat ramps, and hiking facilities are available at most projects, and cooperative arrangements exist with many state parks. Fishing, hunting, summer vacation activities, snorkeling, windsurfing, white-water rafting, moutain biking, geocaching, and winter sport activities such as cross-country skiing are popular. Seven of the top 10 migratory bird flyways in the United States cross over USACE-managed waters.

Because the vast majority of the recreational areas are located next to water, the Corps, in partnership with other agencies, is active in the National Water Safety Program that provides materials to teach and pro-

mote water safety. Of the 12 million acres of public lands and water that USACE manages, more than 90% of their recreational areas are located within 50 miles of a major metropolitan center (USACE, 2014). Eau Galle Reservoir, just 50 miles east of the Twin Cities and 40 miles west of Eau Claire, Wisconsin, is a 150-acre impoundment surrounded by two day use areas, a beach, two boat launches, one campground, several miles of hiking and equestrian trails, and year-round fishing from shore or a boat.

Bureau of Reclamation

The Bureau of Reclamation (BR) is housed in the Department of the Interior and is best known for the 476 dams, 8,116 miles of canals, and 53 power plants constructed in the western states (BR, 2014). The two most notable projects are the Grand Coulee Dam on the Columbia River and Hoover Dam on the Colorado River. These huge projects and their forerunners made a significant impact on settlement in the West. The BR was chartered in 1902, and its name comes from its original mission to reclaim the arid lands of the western United States for farming by providing a secure year-round supply of water for irrigation. Impetus for the great dams came from farmers and townspeople who repaid the costs of construction many times over through production of food, fiber, jobs, energy, and other investments that contributed to America's prosperity.

As the West grew and water resource needs increased, the BR's mission expanded as well. In addition to irrigation, its responsibilities include hydroelectric power generation, management of municipal and industrial water supplies, river regulation and flood control, development and management of outdoor recreation, enhancement of fish and wildlife habitats, and research. It has seven regional offices located throughout the United States, with 5,344 employees and more than 2,000 volunteers (BR, 2014).

Recreational development. The BR (2014) provides more than 90 million visitors a year with exciting water-based recreation at more than 300 reservoirs in the 17 western states. Nearly 300 of these recreational areas are managed with nonfederal governmental partners, such as state and county parks. Many are managed with other federal agencies, such as the NPS and the USDA Forest Service. There are 11 national recreational areas including Lake Mead in Nevada and Chickasaw in Oklahoma.

Partnerships have also been developed with organizations such as the Bass Anglers Sportsman's Society, Trout Unlimited, and America Outdoors to sponsor fishing and outdoor events in cooperation with local businesses and community groups. In addition, there are concession operations that offer facilities and services such as marinas, campgrounds, swimming beaches, equestrian centers, and golf courses. Fishing and boating are the most popular activities.

The BR offers guided tours at some of its major structures, such as Hoover Dam near Las Vegas, Nevada, and Grand Coulee Dam near Spokane, Washington. The visitor center at Hoover Dam accommodates 1 million visitors for visits of the dam and the power plant.

The Tennessee Valley Authority

The Tennessee Valley Authority (TVA) is a government-owned corporation created by an act passed May 18, 1933. In the depths of the Great Depression, President Franklin Roosevelt asked Congress to create "a corporation clothed with the power of government but possessed of the flexibility and initiative of a private enterprise." Today, the TVA is America's largest public power company with 11 fossil plants, 29 hydroelectric dams, three nuclear plants, and six combustion-turbine plants (TVA, 2007). A system of dams built by the TVA on the Tennessee River and its larger tributaries provides flood regulation and maintains a continuous 9-foot draft channel for navigation for the length of the mainstream of the 650-mile Tennessee River. The dams harness the power of the rivers to produce electricity and provide other benefits, including potential for outdoor recreation (Henderson, 1991).

The TVA conducts a unified program of resource development for growth in the Tennessee Valley region. Technical assistance is available in industrial development, regional waste management, trail management, tourism promotion, community preparedness, and vanpool organization. In cooperation with other agencies, the TVA conducts research and development programs in forestry, fish and game, watershed protection, health services related to the operation, and economic development of Tennessee Valley communities.

Recreational development. From its beginning, the TVA has worked to encourage development of a variety of outdoor recreational facilities in the valley, particularly on TVA lakes and shorelines. To secure the involvement of those most affected, their recreation policy is structured to stimulate, support, and complement the actions of concerned agencies and individuals. This policy includes identification of recreational resources for development by other public agencies and private investors, technical assistance to achieve this development, and the provision of basic facilities to ensure safe access to the lakes and to protect the shoreline.

Since 1969, the TVA has provided basic recreational improvements, including picnic facilities, boat ramps, access roads, and sanitary facilities along many of its reservoir shorelines. By 1978, use of these facilities grew to such an extent that a new policy for facility management was needed. The new policy maintained TVA's long-standing recreational goals: to provide a quality outdoor experience, to encourage state and local government agencies to develop parks and other recreational facilities where feasible, and to assist in the growth and development of quality private recreational opportunities in the valley. Implementation of specific plans for facilities on reservoir properties began in 1979. The TVA designated certain areas for day use or overnight camping and began employing on-site resident caretakers.

One of the most effective ways the TVA supports its recreational commitment is to make suitable portions of its shoreline lands available to others for development. Land and land rights are transferred or conveyed for a nominal consideration to federal, state, and local governmental agencies for the development of public parks and access areas. Lands have been leased, licensed, and sold to quasi-public groups and organizations for group camps. Today, millions enjoy recreational activities on TVA reservoirs and the 290 acres of land surrounding them each year. They participate in swimming, waterskiing, windsurfing, sailing, kayaking, canoeing, boating, fishing, hiking, biking, bird-watching, nature photography, camping, and picnicking (TVA, 2014). The TVA is working with various groups to promote protection of streams as well as providing for their use and addressing environmental concerns. In addition to activities on reservoir lands, the TVA has provided a range of technical assistance to others to help them improve their own recreational programs.

Large tracts of reservoir shoreline have been set aside for wildlife management, hunting areas, wildlife refuges, and duck and geese feeding areas that are managed by state fish and game agencies and the U.S. Fish and Wildlife Service. Also, over 100,000 acres of reservoir lands have been transferred to the NPS and the USDA Forest Service, which administer them as natural forestlands.

National Oceanic and Atmospheric Administration

Title III of the Marine Protection, Research, and Sanctuaries Act of 1972 authorized the secretary of commerce to designate discrete marine areas of special national significance as national marine sanctuaries to provide comprehensive, protective management of their conservation and recreational, ecological, historical, research, educational, or aesthetic value. The marine sanctuary program is administered by the National Oceanic and Atmospheric Administration (NOAA), an agency of the U.S. Department of Commerce, through the Sanctuaries and Reserves Division of the Office of Ocean and Coastal Resource Management. Two years after the act was passed, the nation's first marine sanctuary was designated to preserve the wreckage of the USS Monitor, a Civil War

ironclad, resting in 240 feet of water, 16 miles off the coast of North Carolina.

Twelve additional marine sanctuaries and one national marine monument (as shown in Figure 7.9) have been added since then that encompass deep ocean gardens, nearshore coral reefs, whale migration corridors, deep sea canyons, and even underwater archeological sites. They range in size from one-quarter square mile in Fagatele Bay, American Samoa, to over 5,300 square miles in Monterey Bay, California, one of the largest marine protected areas in the world. Together, these sanctuaries protect nearly 18,000 square miles of ocean waters and habitats, an area nearly the size of Vermont and New Hampshire combined. Although some activities are regulated or prohibited in sanctuaries to protect resources, multiple uses such as recreation, commercial fishing, and shipping are encouraged in certain areas. Research, educational, and outreach activities are other major components (NOAA, 2001).

In the Atlantic Ocean, Gray's Reef, Stellwagen Bank, and the Florida Keys National Marine Sanctuaries protect delicate coral reefs and rich fishing grounds, loggerhead turtles, and right whales. The Flower Garden Banks is a coral oasis in a sea of oil rigs in the Gulf of Mexico. Thunder Bay, in Michigan, is the first named in the Great Lakes region and offers a wealth of historic shipwrecks preserved in the cold waters of Lake Huron. On the Pacific Ocean, Cordell Bank, Monterey Bay, Gulf of the Farallones, Olympic Coast, and Washington State National Marine Sanctuaries contribute a rich diversity of marine ecosystems to the system. In the Hawaiian Islands, the Humpback Whale National Marine Sanctuary protects important breeding grounds of these vulnerable cetaceans. The marine sanctuary farthest from the U.S. mainland is Fagatele Bay, American Samoa, in a fringing coral reef nestled within an eroded volcanic crater (NOAA, 2014). Papahanaumokuakea Marine National Monument, the world's largest marine conservation area located off the coast of the northern Hawai-

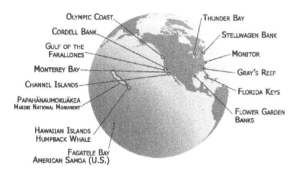

Figure 7.9. The National Marine Sanctuary System. From National Oceanic and Atmospheric Administration website, 2014, http://sanctuaries.noaa.gov/about/welcome.html

ian Islands, was designated by President George W. Bush in 2006 to protect coral reefs and marine species including the endangered Hawaiian monk seal and threatened green sea turtle.

These national sanctuaries are the aquatic counterpart of national parks and are managed for the long-term benefit and enjoyment of the public. Specifically, resources are to be protected, although some traditional commercial activities are allowed as long as they do not undermine the fundamental health and integrity of the area. For Instance, integrity of the ecosystem was of major concern when the Florida Keys National Marine Sanctuary was designated. Encompassing approximately 2,600 square nautical miles, it extends 220 miles in a northeast to southwest arc between the southern tip of Key Biscayne, to beyond, but not including the Dry Tortugas Islands. This immense sanctuary was established to stem mounting threats to the health and ecological future of the coral reef ecosystem. Major issues facing the sanctuary include declines in healthy corals brought on by an increase in coral disease and coral bleaching, invasion of algae in seagrass beds and coral reefs, overfishing, reduced freshwater inflow from Florida Bay, and damage to coral from careless boaters, snorkelers, divers, and occasional large ship groundings (NOAA, 2001). Threats to the coral reef are discussed in Chapter 16.

The National Marine Fisheries Service

The National Marine Fisheries Service (NMFS; Figure 7.9) is the federal service that manages the sea's living resources between 3 and 200 miles off the U.S. coast. Organized in 1970, the NMFS is composed of headquarters offices, six regional offices, and five regional fisheries. It administers federal regulations designed to ensure that fishing practices remain within sound biological and economic limitations and that U.S. commercial and recreational anglers have the opportunity to harvest resources within these limitations. The NMFS regulates foreign fishing in the U.S. exclusive economic zone (EEZ). It also protects marine habitats and marine animals such as the great whales, porpoises, and sea turtles. The NMFS shares with the U.S. Fish and Wildlife Service the administration of the Marine Mammal Protection Act, which protects marine mammals. In addition, the NMFS collects data on commercial and recreational catch. In the Marine Recreational Fisheries Statistics—Executive Order 12962—President Clinton required federal agencies, in cooperation with states and tribes, to work to improve the quantity, function, sustainable productivity, and distribution of U.S. aquatic resources for increased recreational fishing opportunities.

Recreational development. The NMFS (2000) Office of Intergovernmental and

Recreational Fisheries is committed to the promotion of increased opportunities for marine recreational fishing. It also provides a forum at the national level for interaction with the marine recreational fishing community and other agencies involved in marine recreational fisheries issues, working to provide for increased marine recreational fishing opportunities. Recognizing that fishery resources and aquatic ecosystems are integral components of the country's heritage and play an important role in the nation's social, cultural, and economic well-being, NMFS is increasingly engaged in the rebuilding and conservation of marine fishery resources and habitats.

Since 1979, NMFS has conducted the annual Marine Recreational Fisheries Statistics Survey to provide a reliable database for estimating the impact of recreational fishing on marine resources. This impact can be large for many recreationally fished species. Some of these fisheries have a high sport harvest including bluefish, red drum, striped bass, Spanish mackerel, spotted seatrout, summer flounder, and winter flounder. The research center reviews, evaluates, and upgrades its stock assessment capabilities as needed to ensure that assessments for species of recreational importance, and for forage species upon which these fish depend, are provided. Developed in cooperation with constituent groups, NMFS's (2000) Code of Angling Ethics was published in *The Federal Register*. The development of the angling code represents just one of the steps the NMFS has taken to foster sound resource management attitudes and actions among recreationists. In the section on nomenclature in this chapter, wilderness areas, wild and scenic rivers, and national trails were briefly discussed. More on these important assets are provided in this section on the National Wilderness Preservation System, Wild and Scenic Rivers System, and the National Trails System.

NATIONAL WILDERNESS PRESERVATION SYSTEM

Wilderness is a place where the imprint of humans is substantially unnoticed and where natural processes are the primary influences and human activity is limited to primitive recreation and minimum tools. Change will occur primarily through natural disturbance and minimum human influence. And those who experience wild places go there without intention to disturb or destroy natural processes. The passage of the Wilderness Act in 1964 formalized the nation's desire to protect its wilderness resource, restricting grazing, mining, timber cutting, and mechanized vehicles in these areas. These lands are protected and valued for their ecological, historical, scientific, and experiential resources (see Figure 7.10). The law protects these values for future generations (Wilderness, 2001). Wilderness areas are defined by the act as follows:

- Are affected primarily by the forces of nature, where humans are visitors.
- Possess outstanding opportunities for solitude or primitive and unconfined recreation.
- Are undeveloped, federally owned, and generally over 5,000 acres in size.
- Are protected and managed to allow natural ecological processes to operate freely.
- May contain ecological, geological, scenic, or historical value.

Wilderness History

The early national parks were intended to provide an outdoor experience in relative comfort. Visitors enjoyed transportation by train or carriage, and plush resorts awaited them after a day's sojourn in the spectacular scenery. But there was a growing issue between recreationists who wanted comfort and facilities and those who wished to rough it in a wilderness environment. The current federal concept of wilderness—land left essentially wild and free from human impact—originated with the Forest Service. In the 1920s, the Forest Service's Aldo Leopold, Arthur Carhart, and others advocated the preservation of large areas in an undisturbed state. In 1921, Leopold (see Chapter 3) defined wilderness as "a continuous stretch of

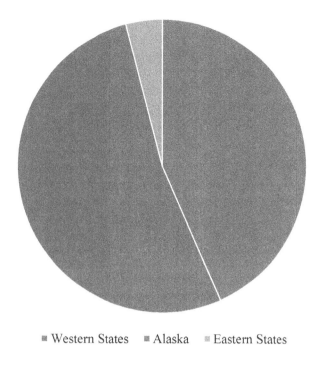

■ Western States   ■ Alaska   ▧ Eastern States

Figure 7.10. Regional distribution of wilderness designations. From *Wilderness Overview and Statistics*, by K. Hoover, 2014, http://nationalaglawcenter.org/wp-content/uploads/assets/crs/RL31447.pdf, p. 10.

country preserved in its natural state, open to lawful hunting and fishing, big enough to absorb a two-week's pack trip, and kept devoid of roads, artificial trails, cottages, or other works of man" (Wellman, 1987, p. 132).

Leopold advocated that for a minority of people, preserving wilderness would be the greatest priority and that these views should be represented when possible. His proposal in 1921 for a wilderness area in New Mexico's Gila National Forest, backed by local hunters, won support the following year, and in 1924, the area was designated the Gila Roadless Area. The nation's first wilderness preserve consisted of approximately 500,000 acres. Soon five other roadless areas were established within the National Forest System, and several more were under consideration. In the meantime, Arthur Carhart was also making progress toward establishing a roadless area in the Superior National Forest in Minnesota. His proposal for a lakeland wilderness area was approved by the secretary of agri-

culture in 1923. Supported by later legislation, his plan provided the foundation for the million-acre Boundary Waters Canoe Area Wilderness (Wellman, 1987). Soon, the NPS had to respond to the pressures of preservationists. Scientific research parks were established, one of the earliest being a 4,480-acre "primitive" area in Yosemite National Park.

Responding to this NPS challenge and to Leopold and others within the Forest Service, the Forest Service developed the L-20 Regulation of 1929, which directed national forest staffs to protect primitive undeveloped lands. This represented one of the first attempts to establish wilderness as a general classification of land use with specific management guidelines. Under these regulations, some 63 primitive areas encompassing nearly 8.5 million acres were established. But protection was tenuous, boundaries could be changed by administrative order, and many wilderness areas contained state or private lands that were subject to development. Wilderness advocates, especially Robert Marshall, then chief of the Forest Service's Recreation and Lands Division, pressed for far stronger measures. The result was the "U-Regulations" of 1939, which established three land categories: U-I "wilderness" (areas of more than 100,000 acres to be left undeveloped), U-2 "wild" (5,000–100,000 acres to be managed as wilderness), and U-3 "recreation" (roadless areas where timber harvest and some other development were permitted; Cordell, Bergstrom, Hartmenn, & English, 1990).

Following World War II, wilderness proponents, led by Howard Zahniser of the Wilderness Society, pressed for congressional action to provide greater protection. With impetus provided by the Outdoor Recreation Resources Review Commission (ORRRC), the Wilderness Act became law in 1964 (P. L. 8-577; see Chapter 15). Passage of the act created the National Wilderness Preservation System (NWPS), which required affirmative action by Congress on each addition to the wilderness system. As such, the process of wilderness designation was shifted from the Forest Service to Congress.

Marshall's 1939 definition became the basis for the legislative definition of wilderness, and his equal emphasis on human use and preservation of the primitive environment carried through to current wilderness management guidelines. The Wilderness Act applied to the national forests, national parks, and national wildlife refuges. Its early effects were felt mainly by the Forest Service, which already possessed large areas of protected wilderness (Cordell et al., 1990). The NPS had used a zoning system to protect wilderness values in undeveloped areas more than a half-mile from roads. The Fish and Wildlife Service had not managed any area specifically for wilderness purposes (although today they manage significant portions of the wilderness expanse) because manipulation of habitat to enhance wildlife values often resulted in substantial modification of areas, thereby conflicting with wilderness values. Nevertheless, once charged with wilderness responsibilities, Congress designated Great Swamp Wildlife Refuge in New Jersey as the first refuge to be admitted to the National Wilderness Preservation System (Hendee, Stankey, & Lucas, 1978). Lands managed by the Bureau of Land Management were not subject to the Wilderness Act until passage of the Federal Land Policy and Management Act of 1976.

The Wilderness Act accorded statutory protection specifically to lands that met the wilderness definition: an area where the earth and its community of life are untrammeled by humans, where humans themselves are visitors who do not remain. It was the Wilderness Act that did much to alter the concept of wilderness from that of a residual land resource or even useless land to that of a primary resource central to national recreation policy. Prior to the act's passage, the first wilderness bill was introduced in Congress by Senator Hubert H. Humphrey in 1956. Subsequently, 64 additional wilderness bills were introduced and considered by Congress before passage (Browning, Hendee, & Roggenbuck, 1988). After President Lyndon B. Johnson signed the Wilderness Act of 1964, 9 million acres were immediately designated as national wilderness, but it was not until 1970 and then 1976 and 1978 that other significant lands were set aside.

The nearly 720-unit National Wilderness Preservation System spans more than 107 million acres and is considered by many the best of America's public land heritage. In fact, by its 40th birthday, the network was 12 times as large as it was in 1964 and had spread from the original 13 states to 44 (Downey, 2004). The lands are managed by the NPS (43.5 million acres), the Forest Service (35.4 million acres), the Fish and Wildlife Service (20.7 million acres), and the Bureau of Land Management (7.8 million acres; Wilderness, 2006). These wilderness areas stand as living testimony to the wisdom and foresight of Congress and the American people to preserve the lands in their natural state for the enjoyment of future generations. Accordingly, wilderness areas are protected from development—the construction of roads, dams, or other permanent structures; timber cutting; the operation of motorized vehicles and equipment; and, since 1984, new mining claims and mineral leasing. The following are purposes of wilderness areas (Wilderness Society, 2014):

- Provide habitat for wildlife and havens for threatened species.
- Filter and clean the air.
- Protect watershed and provide clean drinking water to communities.
- Boost nearby economies with tourism and recreation dollars.
- Provide outstanding places to recreate and to escape the modern world.

Congress considers additional proposals every year, recommended by federal agencies and conservation and other organizations. For more information about wilderness management see Chapters 12 and 13.

Wild and Scenic Rivers System

The Wild and Scenic Rivers Act of 1968 provided for the establishment of a system of rivers to be preserved as free-flowing streams accessible for public use and enjoyment. According to the NPS (2000), components of the system, or portions of component rivers, may be designated as wild, scenic, or recreational rivers. Rivers are classified according to the natural qualities they possess and the evidence as viewed from the river of human presence in the area. Rivers have been classified as wild, scenic, or recreational on the basis of the following traits:

- *Wild rivers* display little evidence of human presence in the area. These rivers are free of impoundments (dams) and are generally inaccessible except by trail.
- *Scenic rivers* have relatively primitive shorelines and are largely undeveloped, but they are accessible in places by road.
- *Recreational rivers* have more development, are accessible by road or railroad, and may have been dammed.

Federally managed components of the system are designated by an act of Congress. Usually Congress first requires, by law, a detailed study to determine the qualification of a river area for the system and then makes the decision. Rivers administered by federal land managers are units of their respective systems as well. For instance, rivers administered by the NPS are units of the National Park System and those administered by the U.S. Fish and Wildlife Service are components of the National Wildlife Refuge System. State rivers and streams may become units of the Wild and Scenic Rivers System when established under state laws and developed with river management plans acceptable to the secretary of the interior. Once a river area is designated a component of the Wild and Scenic Rivers System, the objective of the managing agency—local, state, or federal—is to preserve or enhance those qualities that qualified the river for inclusion within the system. Recreational use must be compatible with preservation. Wild and scenic river designation provides the following important protections (Hendee et al., 1978):

- It provides protection against dam construction and other water development projects.
- It prohibits construction of power transmission lines.
- It permits administering agencies to condemn private land if less than 50% of the entire river area is owned by federal, state, or local government. However, land within a city, village, or borough cannot be condemned if valid zoning ordinances protecting the river areas are in effect.
- It calls for withdrawal from mineral entry of lands within a quarter of a mile of the bank of any river designated for management under the "wild" category.

Passage of the Wild and Scenic Rivers Act established an important milestone in the conservation of America's great natural resources. It recognized the value of rivers and their environments as an outstanding natural feature that must be preserved for future generations to enjoy.

The National Trails System

The National Trail System Act of 1968 calls for establishing trails in urban and rural settings for persons of all ages, interests, skills, and physical abilities. The act established four classes of trails: congressionally designated long-distance national scenic trails (NST), national historic trails (NHT), national recreation trails (NRT), and side or connecting trails (Cordes, 2001). To date, 11 NSTs and 19 NHTs have been designated with the Appalachian and the Pacific Crest national scenic trails being the first long-distance trails (NPS, 2014; see Table 7.5). The NSTs wind through some of the most striking natural beauty in the country, and the NHTs retrace history on trails and motorized routes marked with distinctive signs and interpretive centers along the way. These trails are administered by the NPS, USDA Forest Service, or the Bureau of Land Management, although land along the corridor comes under public or private ownership. Trail associations, state agencies, local communities, historical societies, and other organizations play a critical role in establishing and maintaining these trails. The other two trail categories are designated by the secretary of interior or the secretary of agriculture upon application.

NRTs are managed by public or private agencies at local, state, and national levels and include nature trails, river routes, and historical tours. Unlike the congressionally designated trails, an NRT must be fully developed and ready to be used at the time of designation. The administering agency must also certify that the trail will be open for public use for at least 10 years. These may include a variety of trail types, uses, lengths, topography, and physical challenges. Located primarily on federal lands throughout the country and Puerto Rico, the more than 1,000 NRTs are jointly administered by the NPS and USDA Forest Service with support from the Bureau of Land Management, U.S.

Fish and Wildlife Service, U.S. Army Corps of Engineers, Federal Highway Administration, American Recreation Coalition, Rails-to-Trails Conservancy, American Trails, American Hiking Society, and the National Association of State Administrators (Cordes & Lammers, 1999).

Side and connecting trails are intended to encourage travel between major trails and from trails to town and cities; they will also link parks, forests, and historic sites. For instance, the *Trails for All Americans* report, created by a task force of 15 trails leaders led by the American Hiking Society, calls for a vast interconnecting network of trails across the country (American Trails & the U.S. Department of Interior, National Park Service, 1990). Secretary of Transportation Rodney Slater and Senator (then First Lady) Hillary Rodham Clinton designated a set of spectacular millennium trails to celebrate the millennium and to spark the further development of this vision of a national network of trails accessible by all Americans (Cordes & Lammers, 2002). The successful establishment of new trails has resulted in the designation of old aqueducts, abandoned railroad corridors, canal towpaths, and old logging trails for public use. Numerous trail users benefit from the designations including hikers, backpackers, horseback riders, bicyclists, motorcyclists, ski tourers, snowshoers, snowmobilers, all-terrain vehicle riders, joggers, and mountain bikers. Because trails are used by diverse groups, the potential for conflict exists. Managers have attempted to designate trails for specific use to minimize conflicts, including designations that separate motorized users from hikers.

Trail use is on the increase, and resources are attempting to catch up with the demand (see Chapter 15). The task of building national trails is difficult, as they typically cross private and government land, with the latter managed by federal and state agencies. Many trails are severely threatened by forces such as urban sprawl, air pollution, or conflicts with other trail users. In a massive volunteer effort, hundreds of dynamic trail clubs and organizations comprising dedicated volunteers work hard to address these threats

Table 7.5

National Trails System

Trail name	Year est'd	Authorized length (miles)	Adm. agency
Appalachian NST	1968	2,158	NPS
Pacific Crest NST	1968	2,638	USDA-FS
Continental Divide NST	1978	3,100	USDA-FS
Oregon NHT	1978	2,170	NPS
Mormon Pioneer NHT	1978	1,300	NPS
Lewis and Clark NHT	1978	3,700	NPS
Iditarod NHT	1978	2,350	BLM
North Country NST	1980	3,200	NPS
Overmountain Victory NHT	1980	275	NPS
Ice Age NST	1980	1,000	NPS
Florida NST	1983	1,300	USDA-FS
Potomac Heritage NST	1983	700	NPS
Natchez Trace NST	1983	95	NPS
Nez Perce (Nee-me-poo) NHT	1986	1,170	USDA-FS
Santa Fe NHT	1987	1,203	NPS
Trail of Tears NHT	1987	5,045[a]	NPS
Juan Bautista de Anza NHT	1990	1,200	NPS
California NHT	1992	5,665	NPS
Pony Express NHT	1992	1,966	NPS
Selma to Montgomery NHT	1996	54	NPS
El Camino Real de Tierra Adentro NHT	2000	404	NPS & BLM
Ala Kahakai NHT	2000	175	NPS
Old Spanish NHT	2002	2,700	NPS & BLM
El Camino Real de los Tejas NHT	2004	2,580	NPS
Captain John Smith Chesapeake NHT	2006	3,000	NPS
Star-Spangled Banner NHT	2008	290	NPS
Arizona NST	2009	761	USDA-FS
New England NST	2009	190	NPS
Washington–Rochambeau Revolutionary Route NHT	2009	2,020	NPS
Pacific Northwest NST	2009	1,200	USDA-FS

Note. NST = national scenic trail; NPS = National Park Service; USDA-FS = U.S. Department of Agriculture - Forest Service; NHT = national historic trail; BLM = Bureau of Land Management. From "Frequently Asked Questions," by National Trails System, 2014, http://www.nps.gov/nts/nts_faq.html

[a]Includes both overland and water routes between Tennessee and Oklahoma.

and to build and maintain trails. American Trails, Rails-to-Trails Conservancy, and American Hiking Society are leading the way. The latter's national Web directory lists 1-week to 1-year volunteer positions. The most successful individual trail organization to date is the Appalachian Trail Conference (ATC) comprising 31 volunteer trail clubs. Through a public–private partnership, the ATC manages the day-to-day operations of the Appalachian National Scenic Trail known throughout the world.

Public–Private Federal Programs

Two public–private partnership arrangements, Scenic Byways and Watchable Wild-

Passing through Yosemite National Park, the Tioga Road/Big Oak Flat Road, designated an All-American Road by the secretary of transportation, offers one of the most spectacular passages over the Sierra Nevada.

life, provide major outdoor recreational opportunities. Although driving for pleasure and watching wildlife have long traditions in America, these two formal federal programs began designating national-level opportunities in the 1990s.

National Scenic Byways Program. The U.S. Department of Transportation (2013) Federal Highway Administration manages the 150-unit National Scenic Byways Program. This program is the result of the Intermodal Surface Transportation Efficiency Act of 1991, referred to as ISTEA. The legislation charged the secretary of transportation with developing criteria for designations of roads that have outstanding scenic, historical, recreational, cultural, natural, and/or archaeological qualities as either National Scenic Byways or All-American Roads. To be designated a National Scenic Byway, a road must meet the criteria for at least one of the six intrinsic qualities. Examples of National Scenic Byways are the Merritt Parkway in Connecticut, the Coal Heritage Trail in West Virginia, the Gold Belt Tour in Colorado, and the Outback Scenic Byway in Oregon. All-American Roads must meet the criteria for multiple intrinsic qualities, and these routes are destinations unto themselves that attract national and international visitors. Examples of All-American Roads are the Big Sur in California and the Acadia Byway in Maine.

The Department of Transportation nomination process allows state designated byways and federal agency byways to be nominated for the National Scenic Byways Program, and participation in the program is voluntary. As a result, several of the National Scenic Byways and All-American Roads are also roads that have been designated by the

Federal Aid and International Programs

Two laws administered by the Fish and Wildlife Service—the Federal Aid in Wildlife Restoration Act of 1937 and the Federal Aid in Sport Fisheries Restoration Act of 1950—have created some of the most successful programs in the history of fish and wildlife conservation. Known as Pittman–Robertson (wildlife) and Dingell–Johnson (fish) after their congressional sponsors, these programs provide hundreds of millions in federal grant money to support specific projects carried out by state fish and wildlife agencies. The money comes from federal excise taxes on sporting arms and ammunition, archery equipment, and sport fishing tackle. In 1984, the sport fisheries restoration legislation was supplemented by new provisions known as the Wallop-Breaux amendments. These provisions increased revenue for sport fish restoration by extending the excise tax to previously untaxed items of sporting equipment and by channeling into fisheries restoration a portion of the existing federal tax on motorboat fuels and import duties on fishing tackle and pleasure boats. Funds are used to acquire land for wildlife habitat and for fishing and recreation, for research to provide access to hunting, to develop fishing and boating areas, to manage and maintain fish and wildlife habitats, and to carry out hunter safety training and aquatic education.

Cooperating with other countries on wildlife research and management programs, the Fish and Wildlife Service also has international responsibilities under some 40 treaties, statutes, and agreements. When requested, it offers technical assistance to foreign countries. Additionally, it seeks to stem the global loss of wetlands and establish guidelines for wise use of wetlands through the international wetlands convention.

USDA Forest Service's National Forest Scenic Byways Program that began in 1988. South Dakota's Peter Norbeck Scenic Byway and Colorado's Grand Mesa Scenic and Historic Byway have this dual designation as National Scenic Byways and Forest Service Scenic Byways. The Forest Service emphasis is on showcasing roads with outstanding scenic vistas. National Scenic Byways may also be a part of the Bureau of Land Management's Back Country Byways Program that started in 1989. The goal of this program is to provide visitors with the opportunity to explore some of the Bureau of Land Management's less accessible unique and scenic lands. Most of the National Scenic Byways and All-American Roads hold dual status as a State Scenic Byway (Cordes, 2001). There are 46 states plus the District of Columbia that have scenic byway programs (Tannen, 1999).

Watchable Wildlife. The Watchable Wildlife program provides a framework for federal, state, and private conservation groups to coordinate their numerous wildlife-viewing programs. In 1990, a formal memorandum of understanding (MOU) was signed by the federal participants at the time, including the Bureau of Land Management, the Fish and Wildlife Service, and the USDA Forest Service. A variety of facilities and activities fall under the umbrella of the program: observing wildlife including fish, birds, and animals; viewing insects and flowers; general nature study; butterfly gardens; visitor center interpretive displays; aquariums; and fish hatcheries (Anderson, 1999).

The Forest Service started its own wildlife-watching program in 1988 and has been the driving force behind the development of the national collaborative effort. Current federal participants include the Bureau of Land Management, Bureau of Reclamation, Department of the Air Force, Department of the Navy, NPS, Forest Service, and the Fish and Wildlife Service. Conservation groups include the American Birding Association, Defender of Wildlife, Ducks Unlimited, Humane Society, International Association of Fish and Wildlife Agencies, National Fish and Wildlife Foundation, Izaak Walton League of America, and Wildlife Forever. They work together as a coalition to meet the high level of keen interest in wildlife-associated recreation. There is now a network of viewing sites, a uniform viewing site signing system, a series of more than 30 (Anderson, 1999) viewing guidebooks, and a public awareness and support program. The binocular logo designates nearby wildlife viewing areas on federal highway signs across the country.

SUMMARY

The U.S. government plays a crucial role in outdoor recreation in America, and four of the federal agencies, the U.S. Forest Service, the NPS, the U.S. Fish and Wildlife Service, and the Bureau of Land Management, were presented in detail. Numerous federal agencies are involved in the offerings of outdoor pursuits. Among these are the Bureau of Indian Affairs, the U.S. Army Corps of Engineers, the Bureau of Land Reclamation, the Tennessee Valley Authority, the National Oceanic and Atmospheric Administration with its National Marine Sanctuary Program, and the National Marine Fisheries Service. We covered the historical development of these agencies and the extent of their offerings. We gave attention to the provision of wilderness areas on federal land. The idea of preserving areas in their pristine condition has been gaining support, and a number of federal acts have been passed underscoring the importance of these areas to the American people. Accordingly, a number of systems are now provided for the enjoyment of the recreationist, for example, the Wild and Scenic Rivers System and the National Trails System. We presented two public–private partnerships: the Department of Transportation–administered National Scenic Byways Program and the Forest Service–led Watchable Wildlife program.

REFERENCES

American Rivers. (2014). Frequently asked questions. Retrieved from http://www.americanrivers.org/initiatives/dams/faqs/

American Trails & the U.S. Department of Interior, National Park Service. (1990). *Trails for all Americans report.* Retrieved from http://www.nps.gov/ncrc/programs/rtca/helpfultools/trailsforall.pdf

Anderson, K. (1999). Watchable wildlife. In H. K. Cordell (Ed.), *Outdoor recreation in American life: A national assessment of demand and supply trends.* Champaign, IL: Sagamore.

Browning, J., Hendee, J., & Roggenbuck, J. (1988). *Wilderness laws: Milestones and management direction in wilderness legislation, 1964–1987* (Bulletin No. 5). Moscow: University of Idaho.

Bureau of Land Management. (2001). Facts and history of the BLM. Retrieved from http://www.blm.gov/nhp/facts

Bureau of Land Management. (2012). About the BLM. Retrieved from http://www.blm.gov/wo/st/en/info/About_BLM.html

Bureau of Land Management. (2013). *Public land activities 2012* (Vol. 97). Washington, DC: U.S. Department of the Interior.

Bureau of Land Management. (2014). *Public land statistics 2013.* Retrieved http://www.blm.gov/public_land_statistics/p/513/pls2013pdf

Bureau of Reclamation. (2014). Bureau of Reclamation quickfacts. Retrieved from http://www.usbr.gov/facts.html

Carhart, A. (1959). *The national forest.* New York, NY: Alfred A. Knopf.

Center for Wildlife Information. (2012). Photographing and viewing wildlife. Retrieved from http://centerforwildlifeinformation.org/WildlifeStewardship/Photographing-ViewingWS/photographing-viewingws.html

Collins, C. (2004). A century of service. In U.S. Forest Service, *Forest Service centennial* (pp. 22–37). Tampa, FL: Faircount.

Cordell, H., Bergstrom, J., Hartmenn, L., & English, D. (1990). *An analysis of the outdoor recreation and wilderness situation in the United States: 1989–2040* (Gen. Tech. Report RM-189). Fort Collins, CO: U.S. Department of Agriculture, Forest Service, Rocky Mountain Forest and Range Experiment Station.

Cordes, K. (2001). Millennium trails and scenic byways. *Journal of Physical Education, Recreation, and Dance, 72*(1), pp. 21–22.

Cordes, K., & Lammers, J. (Photographer). (1999). *America's national historic trails.* Norman: University of Oklahoma Press.

Cordes, K., & Lammers, J. (Photographer). (2001). *America's national scenic trails.* Norman: University of Oklahoma Press.

Cordes, K., & Lammers, J. (Photographer). (2002). *America's millennium trails pathways for the 21st century.* Reston, VA: American Assocation for Leisure and Recreation.

Craig, B. (1991, May/June). Diamonds and rust. *National Parks, 65*(6), p. 3.

Downey, D. (2004, August 22). Wilderness grows more vibrant with age. *North County Times,* E-1.

Glover, J. (1986). *A wilderness original.* Seattle, WA: The Mountaineers.

Good, R. (2006). *Restore Hetch Hetchy.* Sonora, CA: Restore Hetch Hetchy.

Hendee, J., Stankey, G., & Lucas, R. (1978). *Wilderness management.* Washington, DC: U.S. Government Printing Office.

Henderson, G. (Ed.). (1991). TVA. In *United States government manual: 1990–1991.* Tanham, MD: Bernan Press.

Hoover, K. (2014). *Wilderness overview and statistics* (CRS Report 7-5700/ RL31447). Retrieved from The National Agricultural Law Center website: http:// nationalaglawcenter.org/wp-content/ uploads/assets/crs/RL31447.pdf

Ibrahim, H., & Cordes, K. (2003). *Parks, recreation and leisure service management.* Peostra, IA: Eddie Bowers.

Jensen, C. (1985). *Outdoor recreation in America.* Minneapolis, MN: Burgess.

Kirkwood, S. (2005). Western expansion. *National Parks, 79*(1), 8–9.

Knudson, D. (1984). *Outdoor recreation.* New York, NY: Macmillan.

Mackintosh, B. (1990). Parks and people: Preserving our past for the future. In B. Sontag (Ed.), *National Park Service the first 75 years.* Fort Washington, PA: Eastern National Park and Monument Association. Retrieved from http://www. nps.gov/parkhistory/online_books/ sontag/sontag1.htm

Madison, M. (2001). *At the forefront of conservation: A history of the U.S. Fish and Wildlife Service in conserving our nations resources.* Retrieved from U.S. Fish and Wildlife Service website: http://training. fws.gov/history

National Marine Fisheries Service. (2000). Recreational fisheries. Retrieved from http://www.nmfs.noaa.gov/irf/ethics. html,www.st.nmfs.gov/st1/recreational/ executive_order.html

National Oceanic and Atmospheric Administration. (2001). The national marine sanctuaries. Retrieved from http://www.sanctuaries.nos.noaa.gov/

National Oceanic and Atmospheric Administration. (2014). National marine sanctuaries. Retrieved from http:// sanctuaries.noaa.gov/about/welcome. html

National Park Service (2000). *The national parks: Index 1999.* Washington, DC: U.S. Government Printing Office.

National Park Service. (2006). *Park boundary expansion.* Washington, DC: Author.

National Park Service. (2009). *The national parks: Index 2009–2011.* Washington, DC: U.S. Department of the Interior.

National Park Service. (2013). Top 10 visited sites in National Park System revealed. Retrieved from http://www.nps.gov/ news/release.htm?id=1457

National Park Service. (2014). National Trails System. Retrieved from http://www.nps. gov/nts/nts_faq.html

National Park System Advisory Board. (2001). *Rethinking the national parks for the 21st century.* Retrieved from http://www.nps. gov /policy/report.htm.

Runte, A. (1987). *National parks: The American experience.* Lincoln: University of Nebraska Press.

Tennessee Valley Authority. (n.d.). Recreation. Retrieved from http://www.tva.com/ river/recreation

Tennessee Valley Authority. (2007a). Our bottom line is the public good. Retrieved from http://tva.gov/power/index

Tilden, F. (1959). *The national parks: What they mean to me.* New York, NY: Alfred A. Knopf.

Turhollow, A. (n.d.). *Do you know?* Los Angeles: U.S. Army Corp of Engineers.

Tweed, W. (1980). *Recreation site planning and improvement in national forests 1891–1942.* Washington, DC: U.S. Government Printing Office.

U.S. Army Corps of Engineers. (2001). Services for the public. Retrieved from http://www.usace.army.mil/public.html#Civil

U.S. Army Corps of Engineers. (2014). National initiatives. Retrieved from http://www.usace.army.mil/Missions/CivilWorks/Recreation.aspx

U.S. Commission on Civil Rights. (1973, March). *Staff memorandum: Constitutional States of American Indians.* Washington, DC: Author.

U.S. Department of Agriculture. (2012). *The U.S. Forest Service - An overview.* Retrieved from http://www.fs.fed.us/documents/USFS_An_Overview_0106MJS.pdf

U.S. Department of Transportation. (2013). America's byways. Retrieved from http://www.fhwa.dot.gov/byways/

U.S. Fish and Wildlife Service. (2000). *America's national wildlife refuge system: A century of conservation.* Washington, DC: U.S. Department of the Interior.

U.S. Fish and Wildlife Service. (2014). *Annual report of lands under control of the U.S. Fish and Wildlife Service as of September 30, 2013.* Retrieved from http://www.fws.gov/refuges/land/PDF/2013_Annual_Report_of_Lands-June-2014.pdf

U.S. Forest Service. (1988). *The national forests: America's great outdoors national recreation strategy.* Washington, DC: U.S. Government Printing Office.

U.S. Forest Service. (1990). *Report of the Forest Service fiscal year 1989.* Washington, DC: U.S. Government Printing Office.

U.S. Forest Service. (2000a). *Draft USDA Forest Service strategic plan.* Washington, DC: U.S. Government Printing Office.

U.S. Forest Service. (2000b). *The recreation agenda* (FS-691). Washington, DC: U.S. Government Printing Office.

Wellman, J. (1987). *Midland recreation policy.* New York, NY: John Wiley and Sons.

Wilderness. (2001). Land management agencies. Retrieved from http://www.wilderness.net

Wilderness. (2006). The wilderness preservation system. Retrieved from http://www.wilderness.net

Wilderness Act, 16 U.S.C. §§ 1131-1136 (1964).

Wilderness Society. (2014). Wilderness Act. Retrieved from http://wilderness.org/article/wilderness-act

Williams, G. (2000). *The USDA Forest Service-The first century* (FS-650) Washington, DC: Author.

Chapter 8

State Resources and Recreation

Prior to the establishment of the United States of America, the Massachusetts Bay Colony set aside 90,000 acres for fishing and fowling. The Great Ponds Act of 1641 protected about 2,000 sites of freshwater bodies, each 10 acres or more in size. The hunting and fishing that took place at these ponds were for survival, not recreational, purposes. Nonetheless, the Great Ponds Act could be looked upon as the genesis of state involvement in preserving natural resources (Foss, 1968).

After independence and the establishment of the United States, the federal government in 1832 granted the territorial governor of the Arkansas Territory the right to hold the Arkansas Hot Springs and Washita River Salt Springs from private ownership. The governor had the right to lease these areas, which were considered valuable because of their healing power (Fazio, 1979). Arkansas Hot Springs was taken back by the federal government and made into a national park in 1921 in a manner similar to what happened to the Yosemite Valley, which was granted to California in 1864 but was taken back to eventually become the nation's second national park in 1875. These actions by the states and the federal government were not intended to enhance recreational opportunities, but rather to preserve some of the nation's natural resources.

Fazio (1979) credits the state of New York with the earliest significant, lasting contributions to state action concerning recreational resources. Its action came as a response to the deplorable conditions and uncontrollable commercial development of the areas surrounding Niagara Falls, which led Frederick Olmsted to decry the loss of beauty around the falls. In 1885, the U.S. Congress placed these areas under the care of the state of New York as the New York State Reservation of Niagara. Conditions at Niagara may have improved slightly after that. According to Knudson (1984), "It was difficult to see the falls because of all the hucksters and makeshift commercial shops that lined the sides of the scenic wonder" (p. 86).

At the time Niagara was put under its care, New York was considering the creation of another open-space area, the Adirondack Wilderness. A total of 715,000 acres of lakes and mountains were dedicated as the state's "Forest Preserve." Although it was the fear of water shortage that prompted the action initially, Nash (1967) argued that recreational rationale had finally achieved legal recognition when the Adirondack and Catskill regions became "forever wild" as stipulated in the New York state constitution.

State park legislation increased at the turn of the century. Minnesota developed Itasca State Park when it received a federal grant to protect the headwaters of the Mississippi River. Illinois initiated the nation's first state agency for state parks in 1903. Its first park was Fort Massac, which led to the establishment of the state's park system.

Stephen Mather, director of the National Park Service since 1916, became interested in helping states develop their own systems of parks. He organized the first National Conference on State Parks in Des Moines, Iowa, in 1921. At that time, only 19 states had state park systems or similar arrangements, such as state forests and preserves. The National Conference on State Parks became a permanent organization known today as the National Society for Park Resources, an affiliate of the National Recreation and Park Association.

The Depression years brought about greater cooperation between the states and the federal government. The Park, Parkway, and Recreational Area Study Act of 1936 produced numerous inventories, which were developed by National Park Service personnel on states' situations. The states became aware of their needs for natural resources. Two more acts helped the states acquire more natural resources: the Surplus Property Act of 1944 and the Recreation and Public Purposes Act of 1954. And with the passage of the Land and Water Conservation Act of 1965, the states were able not only to acquire lands but also to receive technical assistance in expanding their natural resources.

In general, state-run recreational areas have become important features in outdoor recreation. Studies that were conducted over the past three decades show that these areas make significant contributions to the local economies. This despite that visitor days are much fewer than the ones at national areas (Donnelly, Vaske, DeRuiter, & Loomis, 1998).

THE STATE AND OUTDOOR RECREATION

The Tenth Amendment to the Constitution of the United States (also known as "the states' rights"), which passed in 1923, clarified the role of the state vis-à-vis the role of the federal government in providing services to its residents. The amendment specifies that "the powers not delegated to the United States by the Constitution, not prohibited by it to the states, are reserved to the states respectively, or to the people." The Tenth Amendment became the authority by which state governments began to provide services that had been provided by private agencies. The earlier services included education, health, and welfare. Eventually, recreation became a recognized function of state government.

In the Third Nationwide Outdoor Recreation Plan (Heritage Conservation and Recreation Service, 1979), the state is described as having several unique powers that give it a dominant role in providing recreational service:

1. The state has a repository of police powers for land-use control, which is the basic tool for land preservation or designation for recreation.
2. The state can finance recreation through bond issues, special taxes, and fees. It is also responsible for the administration of the monies allocated to local authorities for recreation through the Land and Water Conservation Fund. The enactment of these funds requires a statewide comprehensive outdoor recreation plan (SCORP), which makes it clear that the state could play an important role in outdoor recreation.

According to the plan (Heritage Conservation and Recreation Service, 1979), public visitations to outdoor recreational areas managed by the state increased drastically from the 1960s to the 1970s. From the inception of the Land and Water Conservation Fund in 1965 until 1978, close to $2 billion were given, on a matching basis, to state and local governments. This means that close to $3.9 billion were spent in 14 years to enhance outdoor recreational opportunities on state and local natural resources. About 1.77 million acres of new recreational land were acquired nationwide during this time.

From 1965 to 1978, approximately 22,000 recreation units were assisted through the Land and Water Conservation Fund. The units ranged from small neighborhood parks to large regional or state recreational areas. Local projects used 58% of funding and accounted for 16,779 projects and 312,000 acres. The states used the remaining 42% of funding and accounted for 5,272 projects and 1.46 million acres. The states provided guidance and technical assistance to the local authorities in their quest for enhancing recreational services.

Today, the states own millions of acres of land and water that are used, or have the potential to be used, for outdoor recreation. The classification of state lands is shown in Table 8.1.

Table 8.1
State Land Classification

Classification	Acreage
Parks	9,036,345
Recreation Areas	1,360,447
Natural Areas	3,991,181
Historical Areas	126,505
Environmental Education Areas	18,365
Scientific Areas	19,499
Forests	1,593,198
Fish and Wildlife Areas	1,163,382
Misc.	898,396
Total	18,207,318

Note. From *Statistical Report of State Park Operations: 2013-2014,* by Y-F. Leung, J. Smith, & A. Miller, 2015, Raleigh, NC: National Association of State Park Directors.

In 1979, the Heritage Conservation and Recreation Service suggested that the 13 western states have the most state-owned acreage and the 12 southern states the least. Alaska and California have the most acreage in state parks, Washington and Minnesota in state forests, and Mississippi and Pennsylvania in state fish and wildlife areas. It seems that this is true today. According to Cordell (2004), outdoor recreational areas managed by the state range in size from less than 10,000 acres to over 3.2 million acres. These areas fill the gap between the much larger federal areas and the much smaller mostly developed areas of local government. Table 8.1 shows the number of open space/parkland by each of the 50 states, and Table 8.2 shows the total number of areas, acreage, and trails within state parks for each state.

Many states conduct a statewide comprehensive outdoor recreation plan (SCORP) as a requirement to participate in the Federal Land and Water Conservation Fund program. Usually the plan covers state responsibilities when it comes to outdoor recreation. But the role of the state is much wider when it comes to recreation as shown in the following section.

State Functions and Recreation

Today, most of the 50 states see recreation as an important service to be provided for their residents. Although there is no universal agreement as to what constitutes a good package in leisure and recreational services to be offered, facilitated, or enhanced by the state government, the following functions are considered sufficient by MacLean, Peterson, and Martin (1985):

1. **Enactment of permissive legislation:** Permissive legislation refers to state laws that allow local public bodies to finance and operate services. Certain qualification of personnel involved in the service may be required. Education, health, and welfare, as well as recreation, are enacted by local authorities according to permissive legislation. The first enabling act in recreation was passed in 1919 in New Jersey. Today, all states have such acts.

2. **Service to local recreation authorities:** Many states have established offices or departments of recreation, one function of which is to assist the local authority in providing adequate service to the local residents. Assistance could come in many ways, among which are studying needs, providing information, conducting programs, conducting in-service training, developing stan-

Table 8.2

Total Number of Areas, Acreage, and Trails Within State Parks for Each State

State	Total areas Number	Number operating	Acreage	Total trails Number	Number operating	Miles
Alabama	22	22	48,164	119	119	194
Alaska	139	139	3,386,702	102	102	550
Arizona	31	30	64,090 81	81	124	
Arkansas	52	52	54,466	143	143	409
California	280	280	1,624,216	2,323	2,323	4,755
Colorado	613	588	1,238,488	466	466	728
Connecticut	138	138	206,988	6	6	95
Delaware	34	26	26,071	64	64	161
Florida	171	171	758,031	549	549	2,294
Georgia	64	64	92,880	303	303	543
Hawaii	68	68	33,780	44	44	92
Idaho	32	29	58,922	3	3	108
Illinois	322	322	480,818	6	6	262
Indiana	35	36	172,180	-	-	-
Iowa	188	177	71,234	1	1	6
Kansas	25	47	163,975	2	2	82
Kentucky	51	51	45,180	178	178	333
Louisiana	61	37	43,851	26	26	132
Maine	139	115	98,298	14	14	331
Maryland	66	66	134,539	27	27	789
Massachusetts	339	317	353,889	35	35	2,145
Michigan	315	310	293,703	24	24	644
Minnesota	1,719	1,719	287,029	25	25	1,323
Mississippi	25	25	24,591	38	38	115
Missouri	87	85	207,219	242	242	980
Montana	66	66	46,035	-	-	-
Nebraska	77	77	135,464	2	2	324
Nevada	25	23	146,225	114	114	290
New Hampshire	91	90	231,164	131	131	3,864
New Jersey	118	112	444,170	378	378	990
New Mexico	39	39	196,677	60	60	140
New York	3,220	3,220	4,264,102	292	292	5,438
North Carolina	70	41	221,843	4	-	806
North Dakota	37	40	34,792	36	36	3,252
Ohio	74	74	173,887	498	498	1,498
Oklahoma	35	35	70,031	36	36	402
Oregon	256	220	108,499	6	6	154
Pennsylvania	120	120	297,170	963	963	1,470
Rhode Island	79	67	9,630	16	16	112
South Carolina	56	56	90,167	153	153	370
South Dakota	131	131	101,987	129	129	1,922
Tennessee	55	55	168,617	220	220	998
Texas	97	94	629,339	3	3	97
Utah	50	50	150,758	105	105	302
Vermont	103	86	70,570	47	47	249
Virginia	43	37	71,704	298	298	508
Washington	208	177	121,983	5	5	467
West Virginia	47	47	177,133	2	2	149
Wisconsin	80	78	156,508	42	39	2,021
Wyoming	41	41	119,559	286	286	129
Total	10,234	9,990	18,207,318	8,647	8,640	43,146

Note. From *Statistical Report of State Park Operations: 2013–2014,* by Y-F. Leung, J. Smith, & A. Miller, 2015, Raleigh, NC: National Association of State Park Directors, p. 9.

dards, allocating grants-in-aid, and coordinating and monitoring federally funded programs.

3. **Provision of areas, facilities, and programs:** Although the acreage of the lands provided for recreation by the state is dwarfed by the acreage of the lands provided by the federal government, the proximity of state lands to population centers makes them more accessible. The total acreage of state lands available for recreation is approximately 6% of the amount of federal lands available for the same purpose. On state lands the states have developed roads, trails, swimming pools, beaches, picnic grounds, playgrounds, and campgrounds. In addition, recreation is offered in state-run institutions such as hospitals, prisons, colleges, and universities.

4. **Management of plants and wildlife:** The propagation, distribution, and protection of living plant or animal fall under the joint concern of the state and federal governments. The latter is concerned with wildlife that crosses state and international boundaries, such as migratory birds. Within its boundaries, each state manages plants and wildlife through activities such as reforestation; protection of rare trees, plants, flowers, and endangered species; setting aside of reserves; improvement of wildlife habitat; and regulation of hunting and fishing.

5. **Research and education:** Most of the above functions require the backing of research. In many instances, research units are established within the concerned department. Social research is conducted in relationship to the use and the need for areas, facilities, and programs. Scientific research is conducted in relationship to the management of plants and wildlife. Recreation education is provided by the state in a number of ways: Education that prepares a recreation professional is offered through state colleges and universities; recreation education for the layperson is offered through publications, films, videos, exhibits, and lectures and in media education that could be provided by the state department of parks and recreation directly or through assistance given by the state to local recreation authorities.

6. **Promotion of tourism:** Tourism has become a leading business for some states, which, along with many other states, are waging campaigns to attract tourists. Special efforts are exerted to provide the tourist with the necessary conveniences in improved roads, adequate accommodations, and necessary services.

7. **Standards and regulations:** The state endeavors to protect both the recreationist and the resource through standards and regulations. The recreationist is protected through safety and health standards and regulations that are observed in beaches, camps, resorts, restaurants, and swimming pools. The resource is protected through inspection, licenses, and permits.

8. **Cooperation with federal agencies:** As previously stated, a number of federal laws pertain to recreation in the natural environment that have some bearing on state and local offerings either directly or indirectly. Cooperation with federal agencies, as has been shown, enables all 50 states to expand their recreational resources, facilities, and programs. Moreover, because most states have counterparts to federal agencies, it makes sense that agencies of the same orientation should cooperate and coordinate their efforts in achieving what seem to be similar goals. For instance, the National Park Service and the state park department, also the U.S. Forest Service and the state forestry service, should enhance their offerings through cooperation and coordination.

Baxter State Park in Maine presents a tranquil view of Katahdin from the banks of Daicey Pond. The mountain, named by the Penobscot Indian Tribe, is the crown jewel of the park and the northern terminus of the Appalachian Trail.

State Recreation Commissions and Boards

Thirty-four of the 50 United States have commissions or boards to monitor and promote the recreational offerings by the state.

State Department of Parks and Recreation

Not all states will have a department entitled as such, but all have an agency that serves as a liaison for recreation. This service is required in the administration of the Land and Water Conservation Act funds provided by the 1965 act, which led to the next service.

State Outdoor Recreation Plan

To become eligible for federal money from the Land and Water Conservation Act, the state is required to designate an agency to handle the funds, to prepare an outdoor recreation plan, and to develop a procedure for raising matching funds required of the local community. This requirement led to an increase in the number of park and recreation commissions and boards on local and state levels. It also made each state take a serious look at its natural resources.

State Recreational Resources

Most of state recreational lands, whether they are forests or parks, were originally acquired as gifts, tax-delinquent lands, original holdings since colonial time, or federal land turned over to the states. As the demand for recreation increased after World War II, states began to purchase lands using bonds or earmarked taxes. Bonds were the main sources for acquiring lands, but special taxes on cigarettes and gasoline were also used for that purpose.

Some federal laws made acquisition of recreational lands easier on most states by applying the concept of matching funds. The first of these laws was the Pittman–Robertson Act of 1937, which allowed federal funds to be used in wildlife management. In 1950, the Dingell–Johnson Act was used to improve fisheries. But it was the Land and Water Conservation Act of 1965 that allowed for matching funds to be used for the acquisition of lands for recreation and as open space.

Today, state resources that can be used for outdoor recreation are classified into categories such as parks, recreational areas, forests, natural areas, fish and wildlife areas, historic sites, educational areas, and scientific areas. The acreage of state lands, including lands that are used for recreation, is shown in Table 8.2.

STATE PARKS

The impetus for establishing state parks that resulted in the First National Conference in Des Moines, Iowa, in 1921 was provided by the desire of members of the federal government to get the states to develop their own systems. The two criteria for park site selection suggested then by Richard Leiber, a leader in that movement, were scenic value and/or historical significance. Yet the state park was, in fact, dedicated to the public for the intelligent use of its leisure time (Knudson, 1984).

Today, all 50 states have state parks, although the parks vary in number, size, and administrative affiliation. They range in type from highly developed, with lodges and marinas, to completely primitive, without roads or signs. The numbers and sizes of parks are so disproportionately distributed that 53% of state park lands are in only three states: Alaska, California, and New York. New York's Adirondack State Park is the largest state park in the United States with its 6 million acres. Most state parks are of medium size and are close enough to population centers for the citizens' enjoyment of outdoor activities such as boating, camping, and hiking, along with the organized activities of golf and tennis. New York may have the largest acreage of state parks, located mainly in the Adirondacks, but California has over 1 million acres of state park land and Alaska has a little less than 1 million acres.

The organizational structures under which these parks are administered vary according to each state's administrative setup. The State Park Department oversees the state parks in Arizona, Georgia, Idaho, and Kentucky, whereas the Department of Conservation oversees them in Alabama, Illinois, Iowa, and New York. The Department of Natural Resources manages the state parks in Alaska, California, Hawaii, Indiana, Michigan, and Utah. In Arkansas and South Carolina, state parks are charged to the Tourism Division. In some states, the highway department administers the state parks.

STATE FORESTS

Of the 50 states, only four do not have state forests: Kansas, Nebraska, Oklahoma, and Texas (Knudson, 1984). According to Jensen (1985), state forests are better developed in the Eastern, Southern, and Midwestern states where the forests are of high quality. The forests in the Plains states and the Western states are of poorer quality and are less developed.

When state forests were acquired, the major thrust was to protect the land from erosion, to develop areas for timber, and to provide experimental and demonstration areas. Recreation as such was not considered until after World War II. Today, outdoor recreation is an acceptable activity in most state forests. Although many specific areas have been designated for recreation, attempts have been made to keep these areas as primitive as possible and still provide comfortable accommodations and, in many instances, interpretive service.

The activities that occur in state forests typically include boating, camping, fishing, horseback riding, hunting, nature study, and picnicking. Campsites, with or without modern conveniences, are provided in many of the nation's state forests.

Table 8.3

Parks' Share of State Expenditures

State	State operating budget	State park operating budget	% of state budget
		Share of budget	
Alabama	24,520,000,000	34,139,906	0.139%
Alaska	11,838,000,000	14,129,600	0.119%
Arizona	28,297,000,000	22,459,200	0.079%
Arkansas	21,445,000,000	68,226,506	0.318%
California	211,432,000,000	443,891,000	0.210%
Colorado	29,035,000,000	54,761,622	0.189%
Connecticut	27,852,000,000	17,490,844	0.063%
Delaware	9,162,000,000	20,407,800	0.223%
Florida	63,971,000,000	82,307,152	0.129%
Georgia	42,444,000,000	46,939,650	0.111%
Hawaii	11,584,000,000	12,970,055	0.112%
Idaho	6,691,000,000	15,717,900	0.235%
Illinois	65,287,000,000	65,000,000	0.100%
Indiana	28,171,000,000	58,602,383	0.208%
Iowa	19,531,000,000	16,882,874	0.086%
Kansas	13,969,000,000	11,413,403	0.082%
Kentucky	25,673,000,000	81,358,200	0.317%
Louisiana	27,317,000,000	30,409,086	0.111%
Maine	7,679,000,000	8,176,448	0.106%
Maryland	36,255,000,000	39,886,587	0.110%
Massachusetts	57,541,000,000	70,169,366	0.122%
Michigan	47,398,000,000	62,070,400	0.131%
Minnesota	33,074,000,000	72,278,000	0.219%
Mississippi	18,512,000,000	17,746,059	0.096%
Missouri	22,943,000,000	57,772,035	0.252%
Montana	6,040,000,000	8,865,354	0.147%
Nebraska	10,162,000,000	23,166,067	0.228%
Nevada	8,897,000,000	12,115,210	0.136%
New Hampshire	5,017,000,000	19,458,038	0.388%
New Jersey	50,811,000,000	36,237,858	0.071%
New Mexico	14,696,000,000	21,657,500	0.147%
New York	133,097,000,000	224,338,500	0.169%
North Carolina	43,105,000,000	36,922,555	0.086%
North Dakota	5,712,000,000	4,296,588	0.075%
Ohio	58,268,000,000	62,859,580	0.108%
Oklahoma	21,430,000,000	22,365,821	0.104%
Oregon	25,803,000,000	64,119,560	0.248%
Pennsylvania	85,378,000,000	90,075,000	0.106%
Rhode Island	7,866,000,000	9,740,813	0.124%
South Carolina	22,208,000,000	28,077,411	0.126%
South Dakota	4,098,000,000	19,710,556	0.481%
Tennessee	30,491,000,000	82,154,300	0.269%
Texas	93,244,000,000	90,870,000	0.097%
Utah	12,679,000,000	26,622,905	0.210%
Vermont	4,965,000,000	9,513,021	0.192%
Virginia	45,737,000,000	35,724,517	0.078%
Washington	33,996,000,000	63,646,000	0.187%
West Virginia	22,320,000,000	43,235,926	0.194%
Wisconsin	42,769,000,000	23,512,000	0.055%
Wyoming	9,132,000,000	9,293,459	0.102%
Total	1,689,542,000,000	2,493,784,615	
Average			0.160%

Note. From *Statistical Report of State Park Operations: 2013–2014,* by Y-F. Leung, J. Smith, & A. Miller, 2015, Raleigh, NC: National Association of State Park Directors, p. 31.

NATURE PRESERVES

Among the many nonprofit organizations that promote the enjoyment of the aesthetic aspects of outdoor recreation (e.g., the National Wildlife Federation, the National Park and Conservation Association, the Izaak Walton League, the Audubon Society, and the Sierra Club), The Nature Conservancy is unique in that it directs its efforts to acquiring and preserving land. The conservancy buys endangered natural areas and turns them over to other agencies for protection and management. Its Heritage Program is conducted in cooperation with state governments in identifying, locating, and inventorying natural areas, endangered species, and unusual physical phenomena, which could become the basis for acquisition.

Many states have followed the concept of preserving lands that have outstanding natural significance. According to Knudson (1984), Illinois' efforts in this direction started as early as 1858. Cook County, Illinois, has more dedicated natural areas—areas to be preserved for posterity—than any other county in the state. They are not all administered by one agency; some are still held privately or run by industry.

FISH AND WILDLIFE AREAS

Each of the 50 states has a department charged with managing fish and wildlife or a division in an agency for the same purpose. The responsibilities of such a department or agency are to propagate fish and wildlife; to distribute game animals, game birds, and game fish; and to manage fisheries and refuges. In the areas administered by such a department or agency, fishing, hunting, and trapping take place according to state laws and regulations and with the licensing obtained from the department or agency.

According to Knudson (1984), wildlife management by regulation began during the colonial period. In fact, bounty was imposed on some wildlife. By the mid-1800s, the concept of seasons was used to protect big game as land clearing and wetland drainage were threatening many habitats. Still, human population expansion continued to threaten many wildlife species. It was not until the opening years of the 20th century that recreational hunters and fishermen set aside refuges and preserves for exotic and threatened species.

Despite, or maybe because of, the primitive nature of wildlife and fish areas, recreation has become popular there. Fishing and hunting are on top of the list of activities that occur in wildlife and fish areas, yet other outdoor recreational activities are also observed there; in fact, camping, hiking, nature study, and picnicking are more popular because their seasons are longer compared with the fishing and hunting seasons. Interpretive services are also provided in many of these areas along with facilities for observing wildlife.

REGIONAL DIFFERENCES

The National Association of State Park Directors publishes an *Annual Information Exchange*, the latest of which was published in May 2015. The data collected by the association detailing the total number of areas, acreage, and trails in each of the 50 states are shown in Table 8.2. According to Chubb and Chubb (1981), there are regional differences not only in the number of units but also in their characteristics.

The degree of development varies from state to state and park to park, as do the activities that occur in each park. Some parks adhere to the original concept of a state park as suggested by Richard Leiber, a leading authority on state parks, in 1928:

> A typical portion of the state's original domain; tract of adequate size, preserved in primeval, unspoilt, "unimproved," or "beautified" condition. It is a physical expression of life, liberty, and the pursuit of happiness. A state park must have either scenic or historical value or both, and is dedicated to the public for the intelligent use of its leisure time. (Michaud, 1966, p. 561)

The early state parks were oriented toward providing for contemplative leisure. The features that were commonly protected or displayed were waterfalls, river gorges, picturesque coastlines, beautiful lakes, cave systems, mountain peaks, mature forests, undisturbed swamps, paleontological sites, geologic phenomena, and important historic sites (Chubb & Chubb, 1981). As the demand for recreative leisure increased, so did the types of facilities to accommodate their users: picnickers, beach users, horseback riders, and winter sport enthusiasts. Lodges were provided in the early era when there was a lack of commercial accommodations outside parks and when reaching many parks required a long trek by automobile traveling slowly on undeveloped roads.

Recently, attempts have been made to classify state parks according to use. The idea is to limit the use of the term *state park* to rustic areas as the original concept indicated and to give names such as *state recreation area* to spots where there is more active participation in outdoor activities than in actual contemplation of rustic nature. Today, there are over 4,500 recreational areas run by the 50 states and over 9,950 operating areas managed as part of a state park system as shown in Table 8.2.

Spending on state parks varies from state to state, as shown in Table 8.3, which shows that South Dakota spends the highest percentage of its budget on state parks at just over .48% of the state budget.

CALIFORNIA AND OUTDOOR RECREATION: A CASE STUDY

Article I, Declaration of Rights, Section I of the California State Constitution (1849) reads as follows:

All men are by nature free and independent, and have certain inalienable rights, among which are those of enjoying and defending life and liberty; acquiring, possessing, and protecting property and pursuing and obtaining safety and happiness.

Pursuit of happiness through leisure and recreation started with the first settlers in California and became part of the state and local government beginning at the turn of the 20th century. Although the federal government gave Yosemite to California in 1864, it was eventually taken back to become the second national park after Yellowstone, so the California state park system actually began with the creation of Redwood Park at Big Basin in 1902. In 1909, California passed the Park and Playground Act, the purpose of which was to enable local authorities to establish such facilities. But it was not until 1939 that the state park system was formalized with the establishment of the State Park Commission (State of California Recreation Commission, 1950).

In 1961, Edmund G. Brown, governor of California, adopted a recreation policy for the state of California. At the time of the adoption of the policy, the California Department of Natural Resources had four divisions, one of which was called the Division of Beaches and Parks. The division was to be administered by a chief, appointed by the director (of the Department of Natural Resources) upon nomination by the State Park Commission.

The State Park Commission was established in 1947 and consisted of five members appointed by the governor with the advice and consent of the state senate. Members are selected because of their interest in park and conservation matters and serve for terms of 4 years.

The Department of Natural Resources, through the State Park Commission, has control of the California Park System. The commission is to administer, protect, and develop the system for the use and enjoyment of the public. In its annual report to the governor, it should gather, digest, and summarize information concerning the state park system, including suggesting means for conserving, developing, and using the scenic and recreational resources of the state. The commission is authorized to receive and accept in the name of the people of California any gift to be added or used in connection with the state park system. The commission, whenever in its judgment it is practicable to do so, shall collect fees, rentals, and other return for the use of parks. The state of California created in its treasury a state park fund to be used for improvement and maintenance of the state parks.

California Recreation Policy

The California Public Resources Code (art. I, § 540) states that the commission (now called the California Park and Recreation Commission)

> shall formulate, in cooperation with other agencies, interested organizations and citizens, and shall recommend to the director [of the Department of Parks and Recreation], for adoption by him, a comprehensive recreational policy for the State of California.

The policy statement of 1974 was reviewed and another statement was approved by the commission and issued on July 15, 1981, which indicated the general scope and direction for all recreation and recreation-related programs and actions undertaken or funded by the state. It gives clear indication of the objectives desired for federal and local agencies as well as for private sector activities in the recreation field. This policy has been put into effect through a planning process, as indicated in the following section.

California Recreation Planning Program

California's statewide recreation planning program calls for a continuous process of identifying, analyzing, and solving the problems of providing recreational opportunities for the state's citizens and visitors. Under direction of the California Department of Parks and Recreation, the planning program provides leadership, policy guidance, program direction, and information to public and private recreation suppliers. This effort helps suppliers offer the facilities and programs best suited to the needs and desires of recreationists.

The major objectives of this program are as follows:

- To identify, on a statewide basis, the recreational needs of Californians.
- To examine critical problems related to providing needed recreational opportunities.
- To provide a policy and program framework in which the public and private recreation suppliers can work together to meet the public's recreational needs.
- To have government agencies and the private sector work together to devise solutions, mobilize resources, and resolve conflicts related to recreational matters.
- To maintain California's eligibility to receive money from the federal Land and Water Conservation Fund.

In both its concept and execution, this approach to statewide recreation planning is new in California and the nation. This program is innovative in its orientation toward future trends, its emphasis on process and continuity, its variety of activities and products, its overall unity, and its process of making state agencies accountable for following the plan.

The state of California, to receive federal grants, must publish a recreation plan every 5 years. The purposes of this document are to examine the current recreational environment in California periodically, to evaluate existing programs and planning materials, to rethink current state recreation policy and objectives, and to recommend or direct relevant public and private recreation involvement in the subsequent 5-year planning period.

At any given time, the California Outdoor Recreation Plan is the summary of all current materials and efforts. The Outdoor Recreation Plan does not specify programs as such. The California Recreation Action Program Reports, when approved by the governor, direct recreation efforts of all state agencies and regulate their relationships with other suppliers of recreational opportunities from the private sector.

Today, the California Parks and Recreation Department is in charge of the following:

Park Units 266
Acres .... 1.4 million
Visitors .... 80 million
Employees 2,500
Picnic Sites 11,000
Campsites 15,000
Miles of Coastline 280
Miles of Lake and River Frontage 630
Miles of Trails 3,000
Historic, Archaeological,
	and Archival Artifacts .... 2.8 million
Historic Buildings 1,500

Leisure Pursuits of Californians

Over a decade ago, the Department of Parks and Recreation conducted a survey of 2,140 randomly selected California residents. The survey shows that Californians devote more than a billion participation days per year to the pursuit of outdoor recreation. A participation day reflects the engagement of one person in a recreational activity for any amount of time on any one day. The average household in California for purposes of statistics consists of 2.4 persons. The survey contained 38 recreational pursuits.

The California Department of Parks and Recreation interpretation is that the activities in which the highest percentages of California's population participate are among the simplest and least expensive. Examples are walking, picnicking, and beach activities. These same activities have also been consistently identified as most popular since such research began in the early 1960s.

Water activities seem to play an important role in California. More than two thirds of all Californians engage in beach activities, and more than half go swimming each year. More than 20% of all household activities are directly related to water and beaches. The less popular activities among Californians tend to require expensive and specialized equipment, a high degree of skill or proficiency, or physical prowess. These activities involve smaller numbers of people who participate more frequently in them. For example, soccer players constitute only about 7.4% of the population, with a high degree of participation.

At the turn of the century, the Department of Parks and Recreation revealed that over 80 million day visits took place between July 2000 and June 2001 in the following percentages (Planning Division, 2001):

- Free Day Use
  - In Vehicle 35.20%
  - Non-Vehicle 28.80%
  - In Groups 1.90%
- Pay Day Use
  - In Vehicle 22.60%
  - Non-Vehicle 2.20%
  - In Groups 0.38%
- Overnight Camping
  - In Sites 7.70%
  - Other Areas 0.26%
  - In Groups 0.53%

- Boat Launched 0.40%
  _____
  99.97%

These statistics show that the highest use is free day areas followed by pay day use, overnight camping, and boat launching.

The latest California Outdoor Recreation Plan (CORP) includes a section in which the percentage of adult residents who reported no leisure pursuit including physical activities, which was conducted in the year 2000. The results reveal that 24% of males and 29% of females do not engage in such activities. When it comes to ethnicity, 17.6% of Whites, 24.9% of African Americans, 30.4% of Asians, and 41.4% of Hispanics do not engage in vigorous activities.

In 2005, California State Parks published a booklet on park and recreation trends in the state suggesting the following:

- Californians are avid and active outdoor recreation enthusiasts.

- Californians look to their outdoor recreational pursuits for relaxation and natural values.
- Californians are different in their participation patterns and styles of outdoor recreation.
- Californians are using advances in technology and transportation to expand their outdoor recreational opportunities.
- Californians will continue their love affair with the great outdoors into the foreseeable future.

California State Parks considered that California's population is becoming more culturally and racially diverse. Although California constitutes only 12% of the entire U.S. population, it is the home to varying percentages of racial and ethnic groups:

- 36.1% of the U.S. Asian American population.
- 31.1% of the U.S. Hispanic or Latino population.
- 29.3% of U.S. Native Hawaiians/Pacific Islanders.
- 23.6% of all persons choosing "Two or More" races in the 2000 census.
- 13.5% of the U.S. American Indian/Alaska Native population.
- 9.5% of the U.S. White population.
- 6.5% of the U.S. Black population.

When it comes to the Hispanic/Latino population, 10 years of study in Southern California wildlands managed by the Forest Service and the Bureau of Land Management confirmed the following features of their interest in outdoor recreation (Chavez, 2001):

- They prefer to recreate in larger groups and prefer forested sites with water features and amenities to support a daylong, extended family social outing with extensive on-site meal preparation.
- They are interested in an outdoor experience with a strong social recreation component, such as facilities and programs that involve families, programs for children and youth, and family-oriented entertainment events and festivals.
- They identify stress relief and having a good family experience as the most important features of a satisfying outdoor recreational excursion.
- They enjoy picnicking, day hiking, camping, and large family gatherings in outdoor settings.

Providers of State Recreation

A number of state agencies play one or more roles in the provision of outdoor recreational opportunities, as described in the following paragraphs.

Department of Parks and Recreation

As shown previously, the California state park system includes 266 units totaling 1,412,825 acres. Recreational facilities provided at these units include over 12,000 campsites and almost 11,000 picnic sites as well as 57 boat ramps, over 2,300 boat slips, and over 3,000 miles of trails. Many of the units offer interpretive programs and facilities including visitor centers, museums, and interpretive panels and displays. There are more than 1,500 historic structures within the units of the state park system. A series of subunits within the system offers increased protection to designated areas. Currently, there are 10 cultural preserves, 33 natural preserves, and seven state wildernesses.

Over 80 million visits are made to the state park system each year. Day-use visitation to the system has continued to increase. The number of visitors seems to increase as the population increases around the state's major population centers. The problem with expanding facilities to serve the increased number of visitors is that it not only costs more to buy near-urban land, but it is also more expensive to operate recreational facilities near such areas.

An important factor in the state's growing and changing population is the large increases in Hispanic and Asian people immigrating to California. These groups have different recreational preferences and habits than those of the Anglo clientele of the past. Both groups tend to prefer family-oriented facilities, activities, and programs. These demographic changes are forcing the state park system to reevaluate its program and rethink its role as a recreation provider.

The Off-Highway Motor Vehicle Recreation (OHMVR) Program has been established by law as a separate program entity within the Department of Parks and Recreation. A seven-member OHMVR Commission, with three members appointed by the governor and two members each appointed by the Senate Rules Committee and the Speaker of the Assembly, oversees the program. A deputy director manages the program with a staff of about 70 full-time and 40 part-time employees. The program includes two major components:

- The state OHMVR system.
- Assistance to other agencies for OHMVR facilities.

The law establishing the state's OHMVR program expired January 1, 1988. New legislation passed in the 1987 session of the legislature that extended the program again. The legislation mandates that 33% of the program's budget be allocated to pay for conservation and law enforcement measures. This provision is designed to ensure a solid resource management program that includes law enforcement and wildlife enhancement. The OHMVR system includes seven state vehicular recreation areas (SVRAs) covering approximately 40,000 acres serving about 1.5 million visitors each year. There is a growing demand due to the strong attraction of back-country off-roading for people who feel constrained by their urban existence and due to the limitations being placed on this type of recreational use in many open-space areas in the state. In addition to the visitors to the state areas, over 4.5 million off-highway visitor-days of use are estimated to take place at federal and local off-road facilities each year.

The Historic Preservation Program helps to ensure that examples of California's diverse cultural heritage are preserved. The program's scope includes preserving historic buildings, archeological sites, artifacts, records, and traditions. Many of these historical materials are integral to outdoor recreation, offering scenery for many urban residents and providing backdrops for outdoor recreation such as picnicking, playing ball, sunbathing, photography, painting, and nature study. Visiting museums and historic sites are popular outdoor recreational activities for which there is a great deal of public support.

The program has two major components: federal historical preservation in California and state financial assistance for historical preservation. Under the federal program, the department identifies historic properties, places outstanding examples on the National Register, and takes further action to help preserve many of them. This may include granting of federal monies for restoration or rehabilitation. State financial assistance has been provided by the 1984 State Park Bond Act, which included $10 million for this purpose. Also, $4 million was appropriated in 1987 to assist major historical preservation projects. Park bond issues that passed later provided $20 million for historical preservation projects.

Financial assistance to local park and recreation agencies as well as a limited amount of technical advice and consultation have been available through the Department of Parks and Recreation. Most of the money has come from state general obligation bonds approved at periodic intervals by California voters. Also, a small amount of money is made available from the federal Land and Water Conservation Fund. This money is administered by the department under the supervision of the National Park Service, which dictates firm guidelines on how these funds can be distributed and used. The money is used for acquiring park properties and developing new facilities, but not for park operation and maintenance. In recent years, the lack of such money has served to restrain enthusiasm for grants acquisition and development. This factor could become critical in the coming years. In addition to the Land and Water Conservation Fund money, which has been reduced to only $2.5 million in 1986–1987, most local grant funds come from the following state bond acts:

a. The California Park and Recreational Facilities Act of 1984.
b. The Community Parklands Act of 1986.

The Department of Boating and Waterways

This department has the responsibility for developing and improving boating facilities throughout the state. This is accomplished through loans to agencies and jurisdictions for small-craft harbors and marinas as well as by providing launching-facility grants and capital outlay investment in boating facilities at state park system units and facilities.

The department's annual financial assistance for boating facilities amounts to more than $25 million. The department also promotes boating safety and conducts beach erosion control efforts in cooperation with federal and local agencies.

The department is concerned that the demand for additional boating facilities is outstripping the supply. This problem is aggravated by a growing inability or unwillingness of many client agencies to assume responsibility for operating more facilities. Many existing facilities are not being kept in proper condition for the intensive use they receive.

The Department of Fish and Game

This department manages the state's game and nongame species for scientific, economic, and recreational purposes. It owns about 350,000 acres of land and water, most of which offer opportunities for wildlife-associated recreational activities such as hunting and fishing. Recently, the numbers of hunters and anglers have declined, with a significant increase in more nonconsumptive wildlife recreation such as bird-watching, nature photography, sketching, and painting. To offset the drop in hunting and fishing license fees and to help cover the cost of maintaining the facilities needed for the nonhunting and nonfishing activities, the department is charging a fee at some of its wildlife areas for these activities.

Department of Water Resources

This agency manages California's vast complex of dams, aqueducts, pumping plants, and other appurtenant structures that store and transport water. Although these facilities are designed primarily to generate power and deliver water to contracting agricultural, industrial, and residential users, they have great recreational potential. Unfortunately, the department is experiencing a problem of meeting public expectations for recreation and an inability of other public agencies to supply funds for this purpose. Also, the department is having problems with water quality at some reservoirs as a result of the poor hygienic practices of recreationists. Growing liability problems are reflected in an increasing number of lawsuits brought by people who claim they have been injured while recreating at water project facilities. Large awards have been made to claimants in many cases, which forced the department to close some of its sites to recreationists.

Department of Forestry and Fire Protection

This department's primary responsibility is to provide fire protection and watershed management services for private and state-owned forests, deserts, and grasslands. The department is finding that operating its recreational offerings is a growing problem because of drug and alcohol abuse, vandalism, theft, and the presence of an increasing number of homeless people. Also, off-highway vehicle operators tear up the terrain, contributing to higher patrol and training costs. In addition, the department finds that many recreationists fail to understand that their behavior leads to a less than pristine appearance of the forests. Accordingly, the department is experiencing increasing costs in operating its recreational sites.

Coastal Commission

This regulatory agency for California's coastal resources is concerned with providing access to recreational opportunities, protecting the marine environment, promoting land-use policies, and regulating development. The commission does not operate recreational lands or facilities; it depends entirely on other agencies to assume this responsibility. Tighter operating budgets for those agencies, stricter staffing limitations, expenditure ceilings, and liability concerns are hampering the commission's mission.

State Coastal Conservancy

Under its Public Access Program, the conservancy grants awards to public agencies or nonprofit organizations to provide coastal accessways, acquire land for public access to significant coastline resources, and accept dedication of lands to provide public access to recreational and resource areas.

The conservancy is authorized to receive sites for parks, recreation, fish and wildlife habitat, historical preservation, or scientific study. It can acquire excess lands, open-space lands, and areas needed to undertake enhancement. The conservancy does not manage or operate lands on a long-term basis. It turns over its properties to cities, counties, state or federal agencies, or nonprofit organizations for operational responsibility.

The conservancy has a role in urban waterfront restoration and in providing funding for parks, open space, coastal access, and other public areas and facilities. It plans and coordinates federal surplus land sales in the coastal zone.

Wildlife Conservation Board

The Wildlife Conservation Board acquires property to preserve or restore wildlife habitat, and it develops or improves facilities for wildlife-associated recreation on land owned by itself and local government agencies. These facilities may include fishing piers and floats, boat ramps, jetty access walkways, lake or reservoir improvements, boardwalks, nature trails, and interpretive areas. These projects are generally undertaken in coordination with local agencies, which operate and maintain the facilities for public use.

The board has acquired or developed 467 state and local units. Each unit offers wildlife-associated recreation. The lands acquired or dedicated to this purpose by the board comprise most of the 350,000 acres owned by the Department of Fish and Game. These lands are managed by the department, either directly or by agreement with local agencies.

As project operators, local agencies are being allowed to impose user fees or to develop revenue-generating-related facilities, such as campgrounds, at their cost, to help offset operation and maintenance costs. The board is aware of the public pressure for more urban and suburban recreational opportunities as well as the emerging interest in barrier-free design for accessibility wherever possible.

Tahoe Conservancy

The conservancy was established to implement the $85 million Lake Tahoe Acquisition Bond Act through land acquisition, land management, resource protection, and public access and recreation. At present, the conservancy is managing 2,900 acres at Lake Tahoe, focusing on erosion control in the lake basin. Grants are provided to local jurisdictions to provide lake access and recreational opportunities and to state and federal agencies for wildlife management. The overriding concern for the conservancy is the deterioration in the quality of Lake Tahoe's water.

Santa Monica Mountains Conservancy

This agency implements the Santa Monica Mountains Comprehensive Plan by acquiring, restoring, and consolidating land in the Santa Monica Mountains Zone for park, recreational, or conservation purposes. To accomplish this, the conservancy acquires property to protect the natural environment, manages the lands on an interim basis, and works with established land management agencies to take over these lands. Its acquisition program is focused on the most critical open space and recreational land in the area.

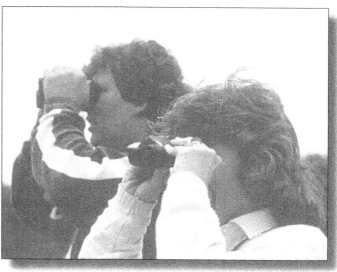

Although the number of hunters and anglers have declined, bird-watching, wildlife viewing, and other nonconsumptive wildlife recreation have increased.

In addition, the conservancy is providing grants to local agencies for acquisition and development of their own parks and recreational lands.

The conservancy has identified a number of concerns. Primary among them is the need to link existing park units through development of a trail system. The state department of parks and recreation owns 35,000 acres, the National Park Service owns about 15,000 acres, and the conservancy itself owns 10,000 acres. These lands need to be tied together. Other concerns include the increasing use of trails, the need for additional camping facilities, and the need to improve public access to the land already in public ownership.

SUMMARY

We discussed the development and role of state governments in outdoor recreational areas and offerings in this chapter. Although the initial involvement was through the development of parks, other functions such as coastal conservation and desert preserva-

tion were added over the years. In addition, state structures dealing with recreation directly were established in many states. As the recreational services increased, areas that are owned and run by the state came into being. Today, few states do not have a state park, a state forest, or a historical monument.

A number of federal acts that were passed during the last four decades increased the pressure on the states to develop comprehensive outdoor recreation plans. A plan is required if the state is to receive federal funds. Typically, the plan covers the state policy on recreation and describes the issues the state faces concerning recreation is concerned.

There are regional differences in what the states offer in the way of outdoor recreation. We gave an example of state offerings with a case study of California, along with an examination of the state's role in regional and local recreational offerings. The study of what Californians like to do plays an important role in developing comprehensive plans for the state.

REFERENCES

Cal. Const. art. I, § 1.

Cal. Pub. Res. Code art. I, § 540(b).

California State Parks. (2005). *Park and recreation trends in California.* Sacramento, CA: Author.

Chavez, D. J. (2001). *Managing outdoor recreation in California: Visitor contact studies, 1989–1998* (Gen. Tech. Rep. PSW-GTR-180). Albany, CA: Pacific Southwest Research Station, USDA Forest Service.

Chubb, M., & Chubb, C. (1981). *One third of our time? An introduction to recreation behavior and resources.* New York, NY: John Wiley and Sons.

Cordell, H. K. (2004). *Outdoor recreation for 21st century America: A report to the nation—The national survey on recreation and the environment.* State College, PA: Venture.

Donnelly, M. P., Vaske, J. J., DeRuiter, D. S., & Loomis, J. B. (1998). Economic impacts of state parks: Effect of park visitation, park facilities, and county economic diversity. *Journal of Park and Recreation Administration, 18*(3), 57–72.

Fazio, J. (1979). Parks and other recreational resources. In H. Ibrahim & J. Shivers (Eds.), *Leisure: Emergence and expansion* (pp. 197–231). Los Alamitos, CA: Hwong.

Foss, P. (1968). *Recreation: Conservation in the United States—A documentary history.* New York, NY: Chelsea House.

Jensen, C. (1985). *Outdoor recreation in America.* Minneapolis, MN: Burgess Press.

Heritage Conservation and Recreation Service. (1979). *The third nationwide outdoor recreation plan.* Washington, DC: U.S. Government Printing Office.

Knudson, D. (1984). *Outdoor recreation.* New York, NY: Macmillan.

Leung, Y-F., Smith, J., & Miller, A. (2015). *Statistical report of state park operations: 2013–2014.* Raleigh, NC: National Association of State Park Directors.

MacLean, J., Peterson, J., & Martin, W. (1985). *Recreation and leisure: The changing scene.* New York, NY: MacMillan.

Michaud, H. (1966). State parks. In A. Lindsey (Ed.), *Natural features of Indiana.* Indianapolis, IN: Indiana Academy of Science.

Nash, R. (1967). *Wilderness and the American mind.* New Haven, CT: Yale University Press.

Planning Division. (2001). *Planning milestones: California state park system.* Sacramento, CA: Department of Parks and Recreation.

State of California Recreation Commission. (1950). *Recreation in California.* Sacramento, CA: Author.

U.S. Const. amend. X.

Chapter 9

Local Resources and Recreation

In colonial America, the dominance of puritan values kept recreational activities from being a local concern. Localities were settlements built on land that was granted to homogeneous groups who agreed to participate in their community affairs, which were handled in town meetings. As communities increased in size, a committee was selected to run the affairs of each community. Recreation was not a concern then, but open space was.

The town common played an important role in providing public open space. The earliest common was established in Boston in 1634. William Penn decreed a 10-acre common in the center of Philadelphia in 1682. Another common comparable in size to the one in Philadelphia was provided in Savannah, Georgia, in 1733. Earlier, in the area settled by Spain in the New World, it was required that the new cities include a plaza or a city square, as was the case in Saint Augustine, Florida.

It is questionable whether recreational activity motivated the establishment of these open spaces. According to Fazio (1979), most of the commons then were meant to be meeting lots, used as an equivalent to a church, except in open air. And according to Knudson (1984), a common served many other purposes, including being a cow pas-

ture, a military training field, and a public hanging post where pirates, witches, and Quakers met their earthly ends. Also, the commons served as America's version of Hyde Park, London, for public speakers and their hecklers. The commons later became the open space for parades and celebrations, the place for music and sport, and the spot for strolling and picnicking.

The Boston Public Garden was founded in 1832 across the street from Boston Commons; it included the first botanical garden in America. Arnold Arboretum was established there in 1876. Boston also saw the first children's sand garden, which was promoted by Dr. Maria Zakrzewska. A large sand pile was placed in the yard of the Children's Mission on Parmenter Street, where 15 children spent 3 days a week for 6 weeks during July and August 1883. In 1887, paid matrons were hired to observe the children; a supervisor was hired in 1893, and organized play was introduced. Funds for operating the playground were provided by the Massachusetts Emergency and Hygiene Association. In 1899, the City Council allocated $3,000 toward meeting the playground operating costs.

The concept of urban parks was promoted by Charles Eliot and Frederick Law Olmsted. The first planned park, New York's Cen-

The Boston Common, originally established in 1634 for common use as a cow pasture and training field, is the oldest public park in the country.

tral Park, was authorized in 1833 by the city of New York, and it took many years to complete. The park set the standard for municipal parks in the United States. In 1888, Boston set aside a string of green spaces on the city outskirts, which were nicknamed the "Emerald Necklace." According to Haines (1977), William Cullen Bryan began to emphasize the need for a park in New York City in 1836. In fact, there was an earlier complaint by a citizen to the city's mayor in 1783 about the lack of a "proper spot where the inhabitants [of New York] could enjoy the benefits of exercise necessary for health and amusement" (Foss, 1968, p. 304). The city acquired 740 acres of swamps and brambles for open spaces. But Frederick Law Olmsted advocated that human existence would be more bearable if parks rather than swamps and brambles were provided. He believed that parks are facsimiles of rural landscapes, which provide tranquility and rest to the mind (Gans, 1974). His adoption of the natural style in this urban park served as the model for America's city parks in the future. According to Fazio (1979), parkland development follows certain steps, as shown in Figure 9.1.

Many city parks were built in the second half of the 19th century, except during the Civil War years. The first three decades of the 20th century saw some growth in state and national natural resources, and the Depression years led to a phenomenal growth in urban parks. Many of the anti-Depression public works programs provided by the federal government proved to be beneficial to city parks.

According to Caro (1974), in 1932, New York City had about 13,000 acres of parkland and 119 playgrounds. By 1939, 20,000 acres were added to the city parks, along with 233 new playgrounds and 10 new swimming pools. Despite this growth, many of the city's poorer areas did not benefit from it.

After World War II, a number of federal acts helped in the development of urban open space and recreational resources. Notably, the Land and Water Conservation Fund Act of 1965 led to considerable growth in urban and suburban parks. Many states added developed land at a rate of 10% or more during the 1982 to 1992 decade. The President's Commission on Americans Outdoors estimated in 1987 that 60% of recreational areas nationwide were provided by local government, most of which are highly developed and managed for intensive use. This has been the traditional emphasis of local government since the origins of the "recreation movement" in crowded urban areas in the late 19th century.

According to Cordell (2004), in most of the assessment of outdoor recreational facilities and areas, the recurring theme is the need for recreational opportunities close to where most people live, particularly as America is becoming an increasingly urban nation. Much of what local governments provide is geared toward indoor, rather than outdoor, recreation. Recently, green spaces and railroad trails have been adopted in many localities.

Figure 9.1. Stages of park development.

Typically, the nation's counties provide recreational facilities such as parks, picnic areas, campgrounds, cabins, lodges, beaches, horseback riding, hiking trails, and athletic facilities. Some 18,000 municipal governments provide parks, playgrounds, and playing fields and offer programs that include aquatics, outdoor and nature-oriented classes and activities, outdoor arts and performance, social opportunities, festivals, and hobby and activity groups. Local recreation and parks departments may team up with other community agencies to offer youth a broader variety of outdoor opportunities. Facilities may also be available for self-directed activities such as cycling, cross-country skiing, and garden walks. Some areas are designated wildlife and waterfowl sanctuaries and others have facilities for fishing and water activities (Cordes, 2013).

LOCAL GOVERNMENT STRUCTURE

All states empower their local governments to provide services to their citizens. The states do so through enabling legislation or by allowing the local governments to use their charters and special laws. An enabling law is an act by the state legislature that allows the local government to do the following:

1. Authorization for local government to exercise certain powers.
2. Authorization for local government to establish a board or agency to administer the powers granted.
3. Authorization of powers given under specific limits or under certain conditions.
4. Provision for joint exercise of power by two or more local political juris-

dictions to establish and deliver park and recreational services.
5. Provision for financing the powers granted, usually including authorization to appropriate money from the general fund to operate a park and recreation agency, to accept monetary gifts or other donations, and to establish a user fee system.

MacLean, Peterson, and Martin (1985) suggested that state enabling acts include the following:

1. A method of establishing the managing authority and board.
2. A listing of powers of the administrative authority and executive.
3. A description of fiscal procedures to be followed, including how money can be obtained, accounted for, and spent.
4. Cooperative agreements among existing government agencies.
5. Guidelines for qualification and selection of personnel.

Enabling acts allow the local government to provide services to its constituency. Structurally, the types of local governments in the United States are county, city, and district. County and city government follow; special district is presented later.

County Government

There are 3,069 counties in the United States, varying in size from 26 square miles in Arlington County, Virginia, to 87,860 square miles in North Slope Borough, Alaska. Populations vary from 71 residents in Loving, Texas, to 9.2 million people in Los Angeles, California. Forty-eight of the 50 states have operational county governments. Connecticut and Rhode Island are divided into geographic regions, called counties, but do not have functioning governments (National Association of Counties, 2014). Technically, there are no counties in Louisiana, where the term *parish* is used instead, or in Alaska, where the term *borough* is used. There are three basic forms of county government:

1. The commission form of government began in Pennsylvania in 1724 and spread widely. The elected governing body fulfills executive and legislative functions in county government. The commissioners (called supervisors in some states, including California and Iowa) serve in a commission that is usually composed of three to seven members.
2. The supervisor form, another type of county government, evolved in New York and is different from the commission in that the governing body is made up of persons who were first elected as township supervisors. The typical size of the governing body is about 20 supervisors.
3. The executive form in county government revolves around a county manager who reports to a county board, which serves as the policy-making body.

Most American county governments superimpose a number of special boards or commissions for special purposes, among which are park, recreation, and leisure services.

City Government

It is estimated that there are over 19,000 municipalities in the United States, varying in the number of residents from less than a hundred to several million. The vast majority in the United States have populations under 25,000 (National League of Cities, 2013). There are basically three types of government in American cities:

1. The mayor–council type of government is the oldest and most common. Usually, voters at large vote for the mayor and voters by wards vote for the council.
2. The commission form of government allows the commissioners to perform legislative and executive functions. Each commissioner will oversee at least a department. Voters at large vote for the board of commissioners.
3. The council–manager type of government gives legislative power to the council and executive power to the manager.
4. The town meeting is found in fewer than 1% of cities. Primarily in New England municipalities, voters select a large number to represent them after the meeting has been announced with a warrant that provides date, time, location, and discussion items. For the form of government in the 30 most populous cities, see Table 9.1.

FUNCTIONS OF LOCAL BOARDS AND COMMISSIONS

A local board or commission typically performs the following functions:

1. **Approves the acts of the department under its jurisdiction:** As the governing board responsible for the results of the work of the department, the board or commission receives work reports through the superintendent and records its approval of them.
2. **Acts as a court of final appeal:** Any disagreement arising among employees or between the public and employees, if not satisfactorily resolved by the superintendent, may be considered by the commission, whose decisions are final.
3. **Advises the superintendent on problems of administration:** All superintendents need advice in the performance of their managerial duties and in carrying out the policies set by the commission. The advice of

Table 9.1

Form of Government in the 30 Most Populous Cities

Rank	City name	State	Form of government
1	New York	NY	Mayo–Council
2	Los Angeles	CA	Mayo–Council
3	Chicago	IL	Mayor–Council
4	Houston	TX	Mayor–Council
5	Philadelphia	PA	Mayor–Council
6	Phoenix	AZ	**Council–Manager**
7	San Antonio	TX	**Council–Manager**
8	San Diego	CA	Mayor–Council
9	Dallas	TX	**Council–Manager**
10	San Jose	CA	**Council–Manager**
11	Indianapolis	IN	Mayor–Council
12	Jacksonville	FL	Mayor–Council
13	San Francisco	CA	Mayor–Council
14	Austin	TX	**Council–Manager**
15	Columbus	OH	Mayor–Council
16	Fort Worth	TX	**Council–Manager**
17	Louisville-Jefferson County	KY	Mayor–Council
18	Charlotte	NC	**Council–Manager**
19	Detroit	MI	Mayor–Council
20	El Paso	TX	**Council–Manager**
21	Memphis	TN	Mayo–Council
22	Nashville-Davidson	TN	Mayor–Council
23	Baltimore	MD	Mayor–Council
24	Boston	MA	Mayor–Council
25	Seattle	WA	Mayor–Council
26	Washington	DC	Mayor–Council
27	Denver	CO	Mayor–Council
28	Milwaukee	WI	Mayor–Council
29	Portland	OR	Commission
30	Las Vegas	NV	**Council–Manager**

Note. The form of government for the 30 most populous cities in the United States is listed based on 2010 U.S. Census figures. The forms of government are informed by the member database at the National League of Cities. From "Number of Municipal Governments and Populations Distribution," by National League of Cities, 2013, http://www.nlc.org/build-skills-and-networks/resources/cities-101/city-structures/number-of-municipal-governments-and-population-distribution

the commission should not be interpreted as instructions or regulations unless given such force by action of the commission as a whole.

4. **Interprets the department and the general operation of the system to the public:** The commission fulfills this responsibility by published actions, by public discussion and address, and by planned use of available means of public communication. The members of the commission often symbolize the aims and objectives of the department, for the character of the department is reflected in the members, who are appointed commissioners, no less than by the employees.

5. **Represents the general public:** Commissioners should conduct

meetings that are open to the public and permit individuals or delegations to address them on pertinent subjects. Most frequently, the matter brought before a commission in this way is such that an immediate answer is not always possible or expedient. Often, the petitioner is not in agreement with the commission. The prerogative of the petitioner is only to state views and not to participate in the action. The responsibility for the action, if any is taken, rests with the commission, which after giving a respectful hearing to the petitioner, makes its own decision based on the facts involved. The decision need not be made at the time the matter is brought before the commission; the subject may be taken under advisement and a decision announced in due course.

6. **Represents the department at official occasions:** Commissioners often act as spokespersons for the department at public ceremonies, public hearings on problems concerning the department, and conferences on recreational programs, policies, or other relevant issues.

7. **Negotiates advantages for the department:** Because of their individual and collective prestige, commissioners are often in a better position than the superintendent or others to negotiate advantages for the department with the local governing authority, other public officials, and the general public. Among these advantages may be an adequate budget for departmental operations. The layperson who does not derive pecuniary gain from the appropriation for the department is usually more effective than a salaried employee in such negotiations.

8. **Appoints standing and ad hoc committees:** When the work of the department becomes extensive, the commission may appoint a special committee, usually consisting of only one person. A standing committee can be conveniently assigned to a commissioner for further investigation and consideration. Committees will not have administrative powers in the matters referred to them. No committee or individual member has any authority except by referral to and through the entire body.

9. **Separates managerial from policy-making activities:** Execution of policy is delegated to the superintendent and the employed staff. Although there is no lack of interest in all phases of departmental operations by commission members, creation of an administrative department to handle such matters provides for a sharp delineation between formulation and administration of policy.

LOCAL GOVERNMENT AND LEISURE SERVICES

Leisure services, which include the provisions for outdoor recreational opportunities, were not among the services provided by local governments initially. The dominant puritanical outlook of colonial America was that play was sinful. The puritans adopted a harsh work ethic emphasizing the virtue of simplicity of living and industry in working. To create God's kingdom on earth, they believed recreation was to be negated. The councils or commissions that were set up to run local affairs had nothing to do with the establishment of facilities or the provision of programs in recreation. Eventually, the local government became involved in the provision of open space and the building of parks, but it was voluntary associations that became concerned with the provision of recreation, particularly for the young.

Some years after the Boston experiment of the Sand Garden of 1883, Chicago Hull House became involved in the creation of a children's playground in 1892. Hull House, which began as a center for improvement of the conditions of slum dwellers, became involved in recreation. More playgrounds sprang up in the East and Midwest. The Playground Association of America was formed by concerned citizens such as Jane Addams, Henry Curtis, and Luther Gulick. In the association's magazine, *Playground*, the association voiced its concern over the lack of recreational opportunities for the young. With the change of its name, the Playground and Recreation Association of America in 1911 voiced concern over recreation for everyone. This voluntary association was named the National Recreation Association in 1926. In 1963, the name was changed to the National Recreation and Park Association. The word *park* signaled an emphasis on the role that the outdoors played in American recreation as well as in the work of this voluntary association.

It was not until the early 1900s that local governments began to show interest in providing local leisure services. Butler (1940) suggested that municipal recreation started in large metropolitan areas with the provision of children's playgrounds. This occurred before local governments were empowered by the states to do so through enabling legislation. General welfare laws and/or police powers in state constitutions or local charters were used as bases for the provision of these early recreational services.

As suggested by Rainwater (1922), the playground movement, which started as a philanthropic deed, went through the following distinct transitions from its inception in the 1880s until the end of World War I:

1. The limited provisions of activities to little children expanded to all ages.
2. The summer-only programs expanded to yearlong programs.
3. The offerings expanded to include indoor activities, instead of outdoor activities only.
4. The program expanded to rural areas, rather than existing merely in congested urban centers.
5. The support shifted from philanthropic groups to total community support.
6. Play became organized instead of being free, with schedules provided for activities.

7. The projects became complex and varied.
8. The philosophy shifted to include varied activities, not just the provision of facilities.
9. Community and group activities were considered before individual interests.

These transitions are witnessed in seven distinct stages through which the playground movement evolved, accompanied by the expansion in the number of local parks (Rainwater, 1922):

1. The sand garden, 1883–1895.
2. The model playground, 1895–1900.
3. The small park, 1900–1905.
4. The recreation center, 1905–1912.
5. Civic art and welfare, 1912–1915.
6. Neighborhood organization, 1915–1918.
7. Community service, 1918–1922.

Hjelte (1940) suggested that between 1922 and 1940 five additional transitions took place:

1. The play movement became a recreation movement.
2. The movement became more than just municipal; it became a state and national movement.
3. The program became integrated with public education curriculum and systems.
4. The organization expanded into rural as well as urban areas.
5. The organization eventually came under the public sector in place of the previously subsidized quasi-public control.

The new social conscience of the 1930s helped to increase understanding of the need for the provision of municipal recreation assisted by the much welcomed role of the federal government in alleviating the scourge of the Depression. To combat the rampaging unemployment at that time, federal projects were organized, among which were the building of many local parks under the auspices of the Work Projects Administration.

Originally, these local parks were organized under a department, which became responsible for acquiring, developing, and maintaining parks and outdoor resources. Eventually, another function, that is, recreation, evolved to provide various activities initially for children and later for adults. In many instances, a separate department for recreation was established; otherwise, parks and recreation went hand in hand. Today, more than two thirds of local governments have a combined department of parks and recreation. Samples of structures for small, medium, and large cities are found in Figures 9.2, 9.3, and 9.4. Parks and recreational services have grown to the extent that small towns and cities offer some financial support for these services. In 2005, 145 cities offered full-time park and recreational services (Vick, 2007).

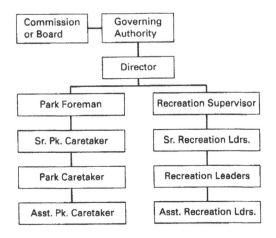

Figure 9.2. Small city park and recreation structure.

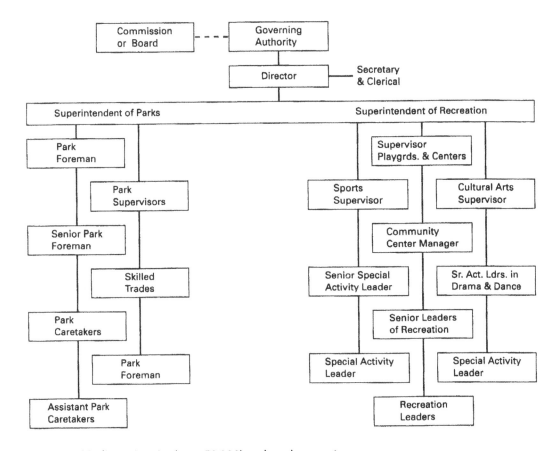

Figure 9.3. Medium-size city (over 50,000) park and recreation structure.

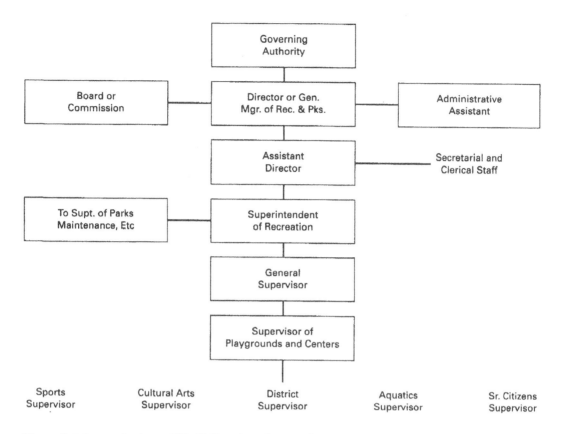

Figure 9.4. Large city (over 100 ,000) park and recreation structure.

Park and recreation agencies at the local level serve broadest needs and the largest clientele. As a level of government that is the closest to the citizens, they are also better able to meet their needs (Russell, 2009). They may also team up with other community agencies to offer activities. Facilities are sometimes available for self-directed activities such as hiking and picnicking. Some areas are designated as wildlife and waterfowl sanctuaries and offer facilities for water or winter activities. Large cities may have aquatic centers, zoos, aquariums, gardens, golf courses, museums, galleries, and facilities for the performing arts (Cordes, 2013).

Counties typically provide recreational facilities such as parks, picnic areas, horseback riding, hiking trails, athletic fields, campgrounds, beaches, lodges, and cabins. Some 18,000 municipal governments provide parks, playgrounds, and playing fields and offer programs that typically include games and sports, aquatics, outdoor and nature-oriented classes and activities, arts and crafts instruction, performing arts, social opportunities, festivals, and hobby groups (Cordes, 2013).

Special Districts

In some states, enabling laws allow for the formation of a special district that allows two or more municipalities to establish a joint park and recreational service. There are numerous metropolitan districts of this sort, and there are rural ones as well. The board controlling some of these park and recreation districts is elected directly by the constituents.

Recreation Through School Districts

In many instances, local recreational offerings are provided through the education board. This is neither the major administrative organization for park and recreational services nor the most desirable one because it may exclude, by design, the adult population (Hjelte & Shivers, 1972).

Recreation Through a Single Local Agency

Ibrahim, Banes, and Gerson (1987) listed the advantages and disadvantages of combined and separate parks and recreation:

I. Combined park and recreation department

Advantages:

1. Consolidation of all related activities under one municipal department.
2. Development of a comprehensive and diversified program of passive and leadership-oriented activities.
3. Reduction of dual development of facilities and areas.
4. Central control.
5. Flexibility of budget.
6. Even distribution of workload.
7. Improved communication.
8. Better understanding by public.
9. Elimination of duplication of efforts.
10. Scope of leisure philosophy not splintered within a personal framework.

Disadvantages:

1. Park or recreational developments may be seriously subordinated to opposite ideology depending on interest or background of administrator.
2. School facilities are not automatically utilized.

II. Separate recreation department

Advantages:

1. Selection of recreation specialists as staff members.

2. Orientation toward activity, planning of facilities accordingly.
3. Assurance that a recreation board can coordinate efforts on recreation.
4. Recreation budgets specifically set aside for that purpose and not sacrificed for other services.
5. Broad perspective for providing programs and services.
6. Easier placement of responsibility for success or failure of recreation administration.
7. Emphasis on studying recreational needs and interests of a community.
8. Effective recreational service rendered.

Disadvantages:

1. Overlapping and duplication of effort.
2. Public confusion over responsibility.
3. Duplication impedes planning.
4. Overlapping with schools.
5. Additional administrative machinery needs.
6. Difficulty in defining recreation role and jurisdiction.
7. Recreation cannot work in a vacuum, cuts across the work of other departments.
8. Facilities used are under control of a second agency.
9. Lack of coordination between parks and programs.

III. Separate parks department

Advantages:

1. Development and maintenance of park facilities under own auspices.
2. Experience in dealing with large numbers of patrons.
3. Large budgets usually allocated.
4. Park board is less likely to be politically influenced.
5. Parks lend prestige to recreation.
6. Trained staff in horticulture, construction, and maintenance of parks.

Disadvantages:

1. Major attention on physical properties and natural resources.
2. Buildings needed for recreation are in the jurisdiction of park departments, which means that the parks department may refuse to allow certain activities in the park.
3. Boards burdened with property problems.
4. Attitude of park authorities toward recreation is conservative and hesitant.
5. Recreation is of secondary importance.
6. Lack of motivation to insist on high-quality recreation leadership.
7. Great difficulty in securing school buildings.
8. Budget cuts affect recreation more than park services.

FINANCING LOCAL RECREATION

The principal sources of funds for the co-operation of local services, which are different from capital development funds, are as follows:

1. **Appropriation from general fund:** The monies collected for local services are to be appropriated as needed by the government body, be it the city council or the county board of supervisors. These are usually tax monies collected for services such as police, fire, and public works. In most cases, the park and recreation board or commission reviews the needs, as presented by the head or heads of the departments concerned. The request for funds is then sent to the city council or board of supervisors for approval.
2. **Special recreation tax:** Some states authorize the levying of a tax for a special purpose such as recreation.

In this case, the money is, by law, allocated for that very purpose and only that purpose. This provides stability from year to year, and the advisory body does not have to sell its program to the city council or board of supervisors year after year. It also provides the local park and recreation boards with some independence. This special tax is usually expressed in so many cents of the valuation of the local community to be served. For instance, if the amount needed to administer a program is $200,000 and fees and charges will bring in $80,000, the amount to be levied would be $200,000 − $80,000 = $120,000. And if the total valuation of the community equals $60,000,000, the special tax rate would be $120,000 ÷ $60,000,000 = $0.20 per $100 assessed valuation. This means that the owner of a property worth $100,000 in that community will pay $200 a year to support the local recreational program.

3. **Fees and charges:** Park and recreation departments used to attempt to provide their programs at either low cost or no cost. The budget crisis has altered the situation recently, and more and more departments are increasing their fees and charges. An alternative would be that fees and charges be a percentage of total expenses. Fees and charges for use of recreational areas, including outdoor recreational facilities, fall in one of six categories: entrance fees for large areas such as zoos and botanical gardens, admission fees for entry into a building having a program or event, rental fees for the exclusive use of a facility, user fees for participation in an activity, permit fees for the privilege of participation, and special service fees for specific uses. Higher fees could be charged to nonresidents. Fees and charges must be approved by the local legislative authority.

Boardwalks over marshy wetlands are creating parks out of previously inaccessible areas and are within easy access of many large cities.

4. **Other sources:** Beginning in the mid-1960s, many municipal recreation and parks departments began calling on major companies for more significant help. Among the types of help are outright gifts, sponsorship of programs and events, adoption of a facility or area, and provision of technical assistance. To stimulate giving this assistance, some park and recreation departments have developed gift catalogs in which the specific needs of the department are itemized and illustrated. Among the plans that enhance outdoor recreation is the adopt a park idea. The adoption is often for a specified period, such as 3 years. Friends of the park is another idea that revolves around forming a tax-exempt organization for the purpose of maintaining and improving the facility.

SOURCES FOR CAPITAL DEVELOPMENT

The adding of facilities and areas may come from funds raised for this particular purpose and could include the following:

1. **Bond issues:** The money accrued from a bond, which is to be paid along with interest in the future, is to be used for building costly projects that could otherwise not be afforded with the current budget. Although a bond is a liability, it is a reasonable means for expanding areas and facilities. General obligation bonds are paid off with additional assessments on property. Revenue bonds are paid off with the revenues accrued from the use of a facility or area built with bond monies.

2. **Federal funds:** Federal acts in the 1960s and 1970s such as the Land

Miramar Lake, a reservoir for the city of San Diego, is frequented by nearby city dwellers and has a 5-mile path around its perimeter.

and Water Conservation Fund assisted many localities in acquiring and developing open space and outdoor recreational areas. Community development block grants were used in some local recreational facilities and programs. General revenue sharing (GRS) grants provided millions of dollars to local recreation, which ranked fifth among all local government expenditures of GRS funds.

3. **Donations and gifts:** Decreasing federal funding led local park and recreation agencies to seek donations and gifts as means of capital development. For instance, Catalina Island Company donated a 41,000-acre open space to Los Angeles County.

4. **Special assessment:** This is the least used, and least recommended, method in financing capital development for park and recreational services. The assessment is to be paid by those who use the facility or area among the property owners in the community. If the facility or area is needed in a well-to-do neighborhood, the residents may be persuaded to vote for the special assessment. In a poorer area, however, a special assessment is likely to present a hardship for many of them.

EXAMPLES OF LOCAL OFFERINGS

Recreational offerings in Los Angeles County, California, and Tacoma, Washington, are examined as examples of what a county or city can provide.

Los Angeles County

Los Angeles has long been the largest county in the United States and in 2013 became the first in the nation to reach 10 million people (NeoGAF, 2013). There are 88 cities in the county. Its largest city, Los Angeles, is the most populous city in the country. A board of five supervisors serves legislative and executive functions. It is the governing body for the benefit of the citizens of the unincorporated county area. It enacts ordinances and establishes rules for the administration of the county's departments and special districts. The board is assisted by the chief administrative officer, who is responsible for making recommendations concerning procedures and actions. A subdivision of the state of California, Los Angeles County is charged with the responsibility of providing services to all its citizens if such services are not provided by the municipalities in which they live.

The Los Angeles County Department of Parks and Recreation (LADPR, 2014) seeks to meet the needs of the people who live in the county. The prime responsibility of the department is to serve the residents of unincorporated areas. To do so, it operates a network of major regional parks to provide specialized outdoor recreation for county residents. Regional parks include lakes, boating, fishing, hiking, swimming, hiking, bicycling, and horseback riding. Community regional parks provide facilities with playing fields and walking clubs. The county provides several nature centers and wildlife sanctuaries as well to provide education of nature, flora, and fauna. The LADPR also has four arboreta and botanical gardens. The county parks are designed to provide individuals with formal and informal spaces where they can make connections with the natural world, be physically active, build community, socialize, and relax. They are also to make urban spaces more inviting and provide environmental benefits and wildlife habitats. The Planning and Development Agency works to maximize the benefits that the parks, recreational facilities, open spaces, and trails bring to people and the natural environment. They see to it that parks and trails are well planned, designed, constructed, and preserved. They must also be socially and culturally relevant, equitably located, physically accessible, and safe.

Created by ordinance in 1944, the LADPR has an even longer history. Before that time, it was charged to the Parks Division and to Parks and Recreation, Camps, and Playgrounds. Today, the LADPR (2014) owns 177 parks. Among many operations and cultural venues are the outdoor John Anson Ford Amphitheater and the Hollywood Bowl. Outdoor activities include hiking, bicycling, horseback riding, bird walks, swimming, and boating. There are after-school programs, day camps, and camping. Placerita Canyon Natural Area in the San Gabriel Mountains, for example, has camping, outdoor activities, and a nature center surrounded by the Angeles National Forest. Frank Bonelli Regional Park provides camping and a 250-acre lake with multiuse trails for hiking, cycling, and horseback riding.

LADPR preparations for even greener communities in the county are to be funded through a grant program to improve air and water quality and to protect natural resources and reduce greenhouse gas emission. Additional new parks, trails, and urban forestry plans will further promote exercise and activity outdoors (LADPR, 2014).

Tacoma, Washington

Tacoma has a population of 795,225. It is located in Pierce County, which has a population of about 812,000. Three local government agencies are responsible for the majority of public park and recreational offerings (Suburbanstats, 2015):

1. **Metropolitan Park District:** The park and recreational facilities and programs for the city are primarily the responsibility of the Metropolitan Park District. The five board members are elected directly by the voters of the district. The board appoints the director, who is responsible for developing and maintaining the district's parks and recreational facilities and programs. As a separate governmental agency, the Metropolitan Park District has taxing authority for special levies and bonds.

2. **City of Tacoma:** Since 1953, Tacoma has had a council manager government. The council is directly elected by the voters of the city electoral districts with three at-large posi-

tions. These positions, as well as that of mayor, are part-time positions. The Tacoma City Council has the responsibility for establishing city policy, formulating annual budgets, appointing the city manager and director of public utilities, and appointing citizens to citizens' boards and commissions. At least four major city departments are actively engaged in planning, maintaining, and implementing recreational opportunities. City departments outside the public utilities department are the responsibility of the city manager.

3. **Tacoma School District:** The Tacoma School District board members are elected by the district at large. The superintendent of schools, appointed by the board, is responsible for implementing policies established by the board and for fulfilling criteria mandated by state education requirements. The Tacoma School District makes gymnasiums, athletic fields, and playgrounds available for public recreational purposes. District recreational facilities are the responsibility of the assistant superintendent for school facilities. The Tacoma Recreation System comprises three agencies of the public sector that, individually and collectively, provide recreational opportunities to the people of Tacoma. Although the Metropolitan Park District is charged with the primary responsibility of providing parks and recreational opportunities to the city's residents, the Tacoma School District, as well as the City of Tacoma, through several departments, also contributes to the overall recreation system. In addition to the formal governmental structure, advisory committees such as the City/Metropolitan Park Board and the Joint Municipal Action Committee (composed of members of the Tacoma School Board and the Tacoma City Council) meet on matters of mutual interest.

Recreation and open space planning is a function of the Tacoma City Planning Department under the direction of the Tacoma Planning Commission and in close coordination with the Metropolitan Park District and the Tacoma School District. Implementation is primarily the responsibility of the Metropolitan Park District. Metro Parks Tacoma (2014), created in 1907, has 70 parks and facilities and offers a wide spectrum on 3,000 acres of park and open space resources. Adventure camps offer hiking, swimming, fishing, canoeing, kayaking, fishing, and rock climbing. Northwest Trek Wildlife Park has family camps with opportunities to see animals at night on self-guided walking tours or narrated tram tours. Tacoma Nature Center Camp offers deep ocean discoveries, wetlands, tide pools, and birding. Sleeping under the stars is available at Owen Beach in Point Defiance Park and Brown's Point Lighthouse.

Staffs of the Metropolitan Park District, the Tacoma School District, and the City of Tacoma work closely in planning programs and services to provide recreational opportunities to the people of Tacoma. This cooperative planning aims at providing efficient service and using public dollars effectively. The city of Tacoma published data concerning the finances of its metro parks, as shown in Figures 9.5 and 9.6.

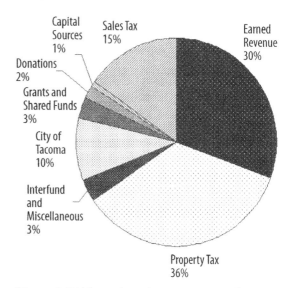

Figure 9.5. Where does the money come from?

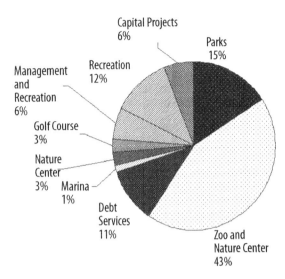

Figure 9.6. Where does the money go?

PROBLEMS IN LOCAL OFFERINGS

In studying the recreational resources, behaviors, and evaluations of people in the Detroit region, Marans and Fly (1999) compared those living in the inner city to those in its suburbs. Low levels of participation in leisure pursuits characterized residents of the city of Detroit, where only 1 in 10 children played in the public park. Instead, most of the children were playing in backyards or on sidewalks.

Too often, recreational resources are unevenly distributed, favoring the suburban resident over the inner-city resident. For instance, local parks may be available to the city dweller, but their use is limited due to the same problems found in other inner cities: gangs, vandalism, alcoholism, stray dogs, and other unsafe conditions. Marans and Fly (1999) suggested that the municipal department of recreation consider the qualitative and quantitative dimensions of recreational resources under its jurisdiction.

The commissioners and the Department of Parks and Recreation are examining their policies, often finding it necessary to allocate more resources. Personnel are trained to reduce the gap between inner-city recreation-

al offerings and those found in the suburbs. Departments involve the local community when organizing advisory councils to help plan strategies to meet local needs (Lawrence, 1984). Problems are compounded as these parks are located in densely populated sections (Ibrahim, 1999).

SUMMARY

The evolution of offerings in outdoor recreation at the local level, be it municipal or county, is traced from the mere provision of open space to the establishment of highly complex recreational organizations. The leaders in this respect, Frederick Law Olmsted and Charles Eliot, were presented first along with the philosophy that guided them in designing parks that represented the American way of life.

Local government structures as they relate to the establishment of natural resources and the provision of outdoor programs were investigated, as was the role of citizens in overseeing the services provided to local citizens. Sources for the financing of areas, facilities, and programs were enumerated. Sources for operations include appropriations for the general fund, special recreation taxes, fees and charges, and gifts and development including bond issues, federal funds, donations, and special assessment.

We cited two examples of local offerings in outdoor recreation: the county of Los Angeles, California, and the city of Tacoma, Washington. Some of the problems facing local authorities wherein public recreation is concerned include low level of participation, uneven distribution of resources, and unsafe conditions in the recreational place. We gave suggestions for improvement of leisure services offerings.

REFERENCES

Butler, G. (1940). *Introduction to community recreation.* New York, NY: McGraw Hill.

Caro, R. (1974). *The power broker.* New York, NY: Vintage Press.

City of Tacoma. (1982). *Five-year recovery action plan.* Tacoma, WA: Author.

Cordell, H. K. (2004). *Outdoor recreation for 21st century America: A report to the nation: The national survey on recreation and the environment.* State College, PA: Venture.

Cordes, K. (2013). *Applications in recreation and leisure.* Urbana, IL: Sagamore.

County of Los Angeles (1990). *Los Angeles County almanac: A guide to government.* Los Angeles, CA: Author.

Fazio, J. (1979). Parks and other recreation resources. In H. Ibrahim & J. Shivers (Eds.), *Leisure: Emergence and expansion.* Los Alamitos, CA: Hwong.

Foss, P. (1968). *Recreation: Conservation in the United States—A documentary history.* New York, NY: Chelsea House.

Gans, H. (1974). Outdoor recreation and mental health. In D. Fischer, T. Lewis, & G. Priddle (Eds.), *Land and leisure: Concepts and methods in outdoor recreation.* Chicago, IL: Maaroufa Press.

Haines, A. (1977). *The Yellowstone story.* Yellowstone, WY: Yellowstone Library and Museum Association.

Hjelte, G. (1940). *The administration of public recreation.* New York, NY: Macmillan.

Hjelte, G., & Shivers, J. (1972). *Public administration of recreational services.* Philadelphia, PA: Lea and Febiger.

Ibrahim, H. (1999). *Environmental justice: The Whittier College study of parkland and open space.* Santa Clara, CA: CPRS Research Session.

Ibrahim, H., Banes, R., & Gerson, G. (1987). *Effective park and recreation boards and commissions.* Reston, VA: American Association of Health, Physical Education, Recreation, and Dance.

Knudson, D. (1984). *Outdoor recreation.* New York, NY: Macmillan.

Lawrence, D. (1984). *The recreation gap.* Los Angeles: University of Southern California.

Los Angeles County Department of Parks and Recreation. (2014). About us. Retrieved from http://parks.lacounty.gov/wps/portal/dpr/AboutUs/

MacLean, J., Peterson, P., & Martin, W. (1985). *Recreation and leisure: The changing scene.* New York, NY: Macmillan.

Marans, R., & Fly, J. (1999). *Recreation and the quality of urban life.* Ann Arbor, MI: Institute of Urban Research, University of Michigan.

Metro Parks Tacoma. (2014). About Metro Parks. Retrieved from http://www.metroparkstacoma.org/about/

National Association of Counties. (2014). Overview of county government. Retrieved from http://www.naco.org/Counties/learn/Pages/Overview.aspx

National League of Cities. (2013). Number of municipal governments and population distribution. Retrieved from http://www.nlc.org/build-skills-and-networks/resources/cities-101/city-structures/number-of-municipal-governments-and-population-distribution

NeoGAF. (2013, December 13). Los Angeles County first in nation to reach 10 million people. Retrieved from http://www.neogaf.com/forum/showthread.php?t+73428

President's Commission on Americans Outdoors. (1987). *Americans outdoors: The legacy, the challenge.* Washington, DC: Island Press.

Rainwater, C. (1922). *The play movement in the United States.* Chicago, IL: University of Chicago.

Russell, R. (2009). *Pastimes.* Champaign, IL: Sagamore.

Suburban Stats. (2015). List of counties and cities in Washington. Retrieved from http://suburbanstats.org/population/washington/list-of-counties-and-cities-in-washington.

Vick, C. G. (2007). Parks and recreation. In *County and municipal government in North Carolina.* Retrieved from http://www.sogpubs.unc.edu/cmg/cmg48.pdf

Chapter 10

Other Outdoor Recreational Resources

The natural resources that we discussed in the previous three chapters are owned by governmental agencies. In this chapter, we discuss the nongovernmental lands and resources available for outdoor recreation. Private rural lands make up over 60% of the land base of the 48 contiguous states (Patterson, 2013). In the East, private land is an extremely important potential resource. Unlike public lands, there is less information known about the availability of these lands for use by recreationists.

Private resources are classified in this chapter into five categories:

1. Personal resources including second homes, cottages, RVs and trailers, time-share facilities, houseboats, and hunting facilities.
2. Private organization resources such as social and athletic clubs, hiking and mountaineering groups, and travel associations.
3. Semipublic organization resources such as youth organizations and preservation associations.
4. Industrial and business resources available to employees or communities.
5. Commercial recreational resources such as amusement parks, campgrounds, marinas, farms, ranches, and resorts.

PERSONAL RESOURCES

Personal resources that allow for outdoor recreational opportunities include one's primary residence as well as other facilities such as vacation homes, campers, houseboats, and land.

Primary Residence Resources

American residences are equipped for the most part with backyards or balconies that provide facilities for outdoor recreational activities, including wildlife watching, outdoor games, and family barbecues on summer evenings. Many children have their first outdoor recreational experience in their backyard, and approximately 71.8 million wildlife watchers participate in at least one type of wildlife-watching activity including observing, feeding, or photographing at their home or within a mile of it (U.S. Fish and Wildlife Service, 2014). The material in Table 10.1 provides additional information about

Table 10.1

2001–2011 Wildlife-Watching Participants, Days, and Expenditures

	2001		2011		2001–2011 percent change
	Number	Percent	Number	Percent	
Wildlife-watching participants, total	66,105	100	71,776	100	9
Around the home	62,928	95	68,598	96	9
Observers	42,111	64	45,046	63	7
Photographers	13,937	21	25,370	35	82
Feeders	53,988	82	52,817	74	NS–2
Visitors of parks or natural areas	10,981	17	12,311	17	12
Maintainers of plantings or natural areas	13,072	20	13,399	19	NS3
Away from home	21,823	33	22,496	31	NS3
Observers	20,080	30	19,808	28	NS–1
Photographers	9,427	14	12,354	17	31
Feeders	7,077	11	5,399	8	–24
Days, away from home	372,006	100	335,625	100	NS–10
Observing	295,345	79	268,798	80	NS–9
Photographing	76,324	21	110,459	33	45
Feeding	103,307	28	59,255	18	–43
Wildlife-watching expenditures, total (2011 dollars)	$48,791,172	100	$54,890,272	100	NS13
Trip-related	10,367,312	21	17,274,675	31	67
Equipment, total	29,898,207	61	27,150,921	49	NS–9
Wildlife-watching equipment	9,340,464	19	11,323,179	21	21
Auxiliary equipment	910,552	2	1,555,374	3	71
Special equipment	19,647,191	40	14,272,368	26	NS–27
Other	8,525,654	17	10,464,677	19	NS23

Note. U.S. population 16 years old and older. Numbers in thousands. From *2011 National Survey of Fishing, Hunting, and Wildlife Association Recreation*, by U.S. Fish and Wildlife Service and U.S. Census Bureau, 2011, http://www.census.gov/prod/2012pubs/fhw11-nat.pdf, p. 52.

NSNot different from zero at the 5% level of significance.

wildlife watching. More than ever families are looking to their backyard "nests" to entertain and live well and are creating outdoor living spaces with heaters, fireplaces, furniture, artwork, kitchens, and grills. Eighty percent of U.S. households already own an outdoor grill or smoker, and another 30% are considering improving their outdoor living area (Hearth, Patio, and Barbecue Association, 2014).

In residences that lack backyards, many have balconies and flat roofs that function as resources for outdoor recreational activities, including wildlife watching, stargazing, gardening, and eating outside. Another important home facility for outdoor recreation is the family swimming pool and/or spa. Entirely new resort and retirement communities have primary residences that are used year-round as a base for outdoor recreational activities.

Second Home Resources

The idea of having a vacation home, which was limited to the very rich in earlier times, gained popularity in Great Britain during the Victorian era (Ibrahim, 1991). In the United States, the Forest Service began as early as 1915 to lease summer home sites. Although this practice is now de-emphasized, it became a big business in the 1960s when real estate companies offered millions of acres of forestland and/or waterfront land, most by mail or telephone to customers who sometimes acquired the land without even seeing it. Beginning in the late 1960s, many ski resorts developed new mountain villages adjacent to ski areas that are visited year-round and offer second homes and time-share arrangements. Resort real estate development is integral to most ski area businesses.

About 8 million American families own a second home for seasonal or occasional use (National Association of Realtors, 2014). Some are cottages or cabins that are not suitable for year-round use, and others are co-operatives or condominiums. Still others are second homes used by the owners as rentals (U.S. Census Bureau, 2000). Locations of these second homes vary greatly. Originally, when the British middle class began to imitate the wealthy stratum, second homes were places in the country away from the crowded English industrial cities of the late 1800s. These were retreats for the well-off to enjoy open space, socialize with friends, or work on a hobby. In the United States, more than half of the owners reported that the area surrounding their second home is open space, park, woods, farm, or ranch (U.S. Census Bureau, 2000). Forty-one percent of vacation homes are in the South, followed by the West (28%), the Northeast (18%), and the Midwest (14%; National Association of Realtors, 2014).

Mountain second homes are often located at all-season ski resorts or are cabins that are used primarily during the hunting season and are located away from lakes or rivers. Fishing, hiking, biking, snowmobiling, and ski-oriented activities could occur while vacationing at a mountain second home. Water-oriented second homes are prevalent, with nearly 40% located very close to a body of water and with 21% actually waterfront property (U.S. Census Bureau, 2000). Many of these homes are more modest structures that are extensively used in summer months along the Atlantic, Pacific, and Great Lakes shorelines. Naturally, aquatic recreational activities are dominant along these shorelines. Desert second homes are used in the winter months by owners whose primary homes are in areas with cold climates. These homes are located in the Southwestern United States.

The alternative to individual or family ownership of a second home involves property sharing. This is an arrangement that allows individuals and families to enjoy the benefits of a personal second home without having to carry the whole financial burden. When a second home is owned by two or more individuals or families, a shared whole ownership is in practice. Time-sharing is another concept for second homes, which is generally practiced in two ways. In the membership plan, the developers continue to own the property and give the person and/or the family the right to use it for a specific time. In the interval ownership plan, the buyer receives the title to the property for a particular period.

Other Personal Resources

Some people in North America use boats and yachts as second homes. Houseboats, for instance, are generally less expensive than many traditional second homes. In addition, they can be moved from one location to another. Scarcity of berths and high docking and berthing fees are making this alternative increasingly difficult, with more people choosing to rent houseboats at the lake visited. Recreational vehicles (RVs) and recreational trailers, referred to as *fifth-wheels,* are also used as second homes. Also, 1 in 10 Americans owns a sport utility vehicle (SUV) that offers advantages when camping and exploring the outdoors. Although they are also used for routine transportation, more than one third of SUV owners cite recreational use as very important in their decision to buy their SUV (Roper Starch, 2001).

Privately Owned Lands

Another resource that is used for outdoor pursuits is private land. Farms, ranches, woodlands, ponds, and laneways can be used for hunting, fishing, swimming, boating, horseback riding, snowmobiling, cross-country skiing, observing wildlife, or simply walking.

In 1962, the Outdoor Recreation Resources Review Commission projected that by the year 2000 recreational demand would triple, but that mark was surpassed in 1983 resulting in "overuse and degradation of public land."

Many recreational activities are pursued on private land such as hunting, fishing, hiking, and camping. Activities less pursued are swimming, nature study, and target shooting. Landowners allow access to the land for recreation to maintain goodwill with their neighbors and others and to help pay taxes and provide income. Teasley, Bergstrom, Cordell, Zarnoch, and Gentle estimated that there are 9.9 million owners of 393.5 million acres of privately owned forest. They found that many recreational activities occur on private land, with hunting, fishing, hiking, and camping among the most popular. Seventy percent of landowners across the United States said they engaged in recreational activities on their own land, and only 50% said they allowed access to others outside their own family. One third of the rural landowners said portions of their lands were completely closed to others, and only 15% allowed access to outside people, with the largest percentage of owners allowing access to only family, friends, and other people they knew personally. The "completely closed" category showed a significant decrease from 10 years earlier when 25% of respondents allowed access to outside people. This decrease may have been due to the concern with liability that is always an issue with landowners.

Providing a slightly different view, Betz, English, and Cordell (1999) estimated that of the 1.3 billion acres of nonfederal forests and agricultural lands in the United States (excluding Alaska), approximately 181 million acres are nonindustrial private lands available for others to recreate on, with most, or 72%, open to the general public. The remainder are leased to either individuals or groups. The South, with about 64.2 million acres either open or leased, has over one third of the U.S. private land that is available to others for recreation, with the Rocky Mountain Region at 56.3 million acres being the second most available.

Private lands are used for hunting by the majority of the nation's 13.7 million hunters, and a substantial number of the 33.1 million anglers also use or lease private land. People also purchase or lease land primarily for wildlife watching. These outdoor recreational activities are considered to have the best potential for future use of private land as well. Table 10.2 indicates day of hunting on public and private land. Outdoor recreational opportunities on private land complement the inability of public land to provide a comprehensive program for the growing population of the United States.

The provision of outdoor recreational opportunities on privately owned land is subject to the tendencies of the landowners. Wright, Kaiser, and Fltecher (1988) divided owners into the following groups depending on the strictness of access rules: Prohibitive landowners allow no access at all, exclusionists limit the access to themselves and family members, restrictionists allow friends as well, and open landowners allow for public access.

The question of access brings about the question of liability. Although the laws governing liability vary from state to state, the trend is to reduce the landowner's liability by creating a category of entrance on private land. For instance, the law makes a distinction between an individual having "a permission" to enter private land and "an agreement" with the landowner to enter.

PRIVATE ORGANIZATION RESOURCES

Humans tend to organize themselves into groups to fulfill specific functions. Pri-

Table 10.2

Hunters and Days of Hunting on Public and Private Land by Type of Hunting

Hunters and days of hunting	Total, all hunting		Big game		Small game		Migratory birds		Other animals	
	Number	Percent	Number	Percent	Number	Percent	Number	Percent	Number	Percent
HUNTERS										
Total, all land	13,674	100	11,570	100	4,506	100	2,583	100	2,168	100
Public land, total	4,918	36	3,767	33	1,410	31	923	36	523	24
Public land only	1,733	13	1,578	14	606	13	526	20	250	12
Public and private land	3,185	23	2,189	19	805	18	397	15	273	13
Private land, total	11,537	84	9,696	84	3,756	83	1,999	77	1,886	87
Private land only	8,352	61	7,507	65	2,951	65	1,602	62	1,614	74
Private and public land	3,185	23	2,189	19	805	18	397	15	273	13
DAYS OF HUNTING										
Total, all land	281,884	100	212,116	100	50,884	100	23,263	100	34,434	100
Public land[1]	61,486	22	39,149	18	13,915	27	8,467	36	5,452	16
Private land[2]	218,839	78	167,271	79	36,951	73	13,292	57	27,161	79

Note. Population 16 years old and older. Numbers in thousands. Detail does not add to total because of multiple responses and nonresponse. From *2011 National Survey of Fishing, Hunting, and Wildlife Association Recreation*, by U.S. Fish and Wildlife Service and U.S. Census Bureau, 2011, http://www.census.gov/prod/2012pubs/fhw11-nat.pdf, p. 80.

[1]Days of hunting on public land include both days spent solely on public land and those spent on public and private land. [2]Days of hunting on private land include both days spent solely on private land and those spent on private and public land.

vate organizations are witnessed in almost all societies and should be distinguished from semipublic organizations. Membership in private organizations is usually more restricted than is membership in semipublic organizations. Private organizations can generally be divided into two groups. The first—*instrumental organizations*—emphasize the achievement of certain goals. Examples of instrumental associations are professional organizations and labor unions. In contrast, the emphasis of the second group—*expressive organizations*—is associational and interactional. Examples are social, sport, and hobby clubs. The concept may have started with Saint Andrew's Golf Club in Scotland in the 1500s, but the idea did not reach North America until 1888 when Brookline Country Club was established near Boston (Dulles, 1965).

Sport and Athletic Clubs

Like social clubs that cater to all kinds of expressive activities, sport and athletic clubs vary in size from small, loosely organized teams that do not own facilities to powerful, sometimes elitist country clubs with expansive grounds and facilities. The most frequently found types of sport and athletic clubs in Canada and the United States cater mostly to those who play golf, tennis, and racquetball. In the United States, some golf courses and country clubs are exempt from federal income taxes. Other golf courses and country clubs that are in the United States are considered commercial enterprises. The annual revenues and receipts of these clubs are more than $5.6 billion and $7.9 billion, respectively (U.S. Census Bureau, 2001). Although a current study is not available, some private ski clubs not only own the slopes and the lifts, but are also equipped with a clubhouse and all the needed amenities. Skating and curling clubs are found particularly in Canada, and tennis and soccer clubs are also popular.

Sportspersons Clubs

In the United States, there are approximately 46.8 million sportspersons (U.S. Fish and Wildlife Service, 2014). Many of these participants belong to sportspersons clubs, usually oriented around fishing, hunting, and shooting. The size and structure of these clubs vary significantly. Some clubs are formed by middle-income individuals who acquire a few acres of land with a potential for outdoor activities. The more affluent outdoor aficionados purchase or lease prime areas and sometimes employ a warden to manage the fish or game. Among all hunters, for instance, 82% use private land compared with 40% who use public land (Aiken, 2004). Also, a number of private rifle and skeet shooting clubs hold demonstrations and competitions. It was estimated in the National Private Forest Land Study that 7.76 million acres of forestland are owned by recreation/sport clubs or associations.

Boat and Yacht Clubs

Boat and yacht clubs purchase or lease waterfront property, the development of which varies according to the financial resources of the club members. The basic service provided is the mooring and/or storing of vessels. Services may expand to include a clubhouse, an extensive marina, and a restaurant. There are 4,300 commercial marinas in the United States with annual receipts of $3 billion (Guest5c6461, 2009; U.S. Census Bureau, 2011). It is unclear how many of these marinas have facilities associated with clubs, or how many of the more than 20 million boat owners belong to boating clubs (Recreational Boating and Fishing Foundation & The Outdoor Foundation, 2013), but their sheer numbers provide an idea of the impact this activity has on society.

Hiking and Mountaineering Clubs

Although most hiking occurs on publicly owned land in the United States and Canada, shelters and lodges are provided on leased and owned land by hiking and mountaineering clubs. Thirty-one such clubs, organized into the Appalachian Trail Conference, provide shelters along the 2,100-mile Appalachian Trail from Georgia to Maine. The Appalachian Mountain Club (AMC) of Boston, the biggest and oldest affiliate of the Appalachian Trail Conference, offers to the public eight huts and a lodge that are situated about a day's hike apart in the White Mountains region of New Hampshire. AMC's Pinkham Notch Lodge has an impressive visitor center tailored for hikers and also manages the historic Bascom Lodge along the Appalachian Trail in Massachusetts (Cordes & Lammers, 2001). Similarly, the Adirondack Mountain Club owns and operates two lodges in the Adirondack Mountains, and the Alpine Club of Canada owns and operates similar facilities in Alberta and British Columbia.

The Sierra Club operates several rustic alpine lodges and huts in California. These facilities give members and potential members the opportunity to explore and enjoy wild areas and encourage a commitment to wilderness preservation. For instance, at the Clair Tappaan Lodge, constructed in 1934 and located at Donner Pass, there is no membership requirement and activities include hiking, swimming, fishing, road/mountain biking, rock climbing, cross-country skiing, and photography. There are regional and local clubs around the country that have facilities for members and, in some cases, the public. In the shadow of Mount Washington and the Presidential Range in New Hampshire is the Jackson Ski Touring Foundation, a nonprofit membership organization chartered to maintain trails in and about the village of Jackson. The foundation provides a lodge from which to base activities and rentals for winter recreation and educational opportunities such as cross-country skiing and snowshoeing. The foundation also maintains more than 100 miles of the area's trail system.

SEMIPUBLIC ORGANIZATION RESOURCES

Semipublic organizations depend on public donations and/or government grants. Although the line of demarcation is blurred between purely private organizations and semipublic ones, the latter are open to public scrutiny more than are the former because they receive and accept public funds. Today in the United States, numerous entities are exempt from federal income tax that pro-

vides recreational resources to the public. For instance, exempt nature parks and other similar institutions, such as museums and historic sites, by their nature have land resources available to the public. Exempt zoos and aquariums, for instance, earn 79 cents from revenue and donations, with 21 cents coming from public funding. Although they receive $278 million in public funding, they earn over $1.3 billion in operations that benefit visitors and wildlife (Association of Zoos and Aquariums, n.d.). Also, some fitness and recreational sports centers and museums are exempt. In this section, two types of semipublic organizations are presented: youth-serving organizations and preservation organizations.

Youth-Serving Organizations

Some youth-serving organizations own or lease outdoor recreational resources; others are not owners but are involved in outdoor recreational activities. Many of the organizations do not own the land on which the camps reside. Instead, they have long-term contracts to build and operate facilities on Forest Service or other public lands. Nonprofits including youth agencies and religious organizations have some 9,500 camps, and 2,500 are privately owned, independent, for-profit operations. Of the estimated 12,000 camps in the United States, approximately 7,000 are resident camps and 5,000 are day camps (American Camping Association [ACA], 2014).

Not all of these camps are for children; adults, families, and seniors attend as well, and some are specialized programs such as for youth at risk, persons with disabilities, and campers with cancer. These camps have a major impact; the $2.8 billion industry serves 11 million children and adults and employs 300,000 adults as counselors, leaders, and program directors and many others for support services (ACA, 2014). Where feasible, many camp facilities are undergoing conversions to all-season use to accommodate year-round schools. Some camp facilities are available for rent by other groups that wish to hold a group camp experience, a conference, or a retreat. The ACA publishes *A Guide to ACA-Accredited Camps* with a list of programs for potential campers and for those seeking summer employment opportunities. Of the ACA-accredited camps, approximately 22% offer wilderness trips, 48% offer horseback riding, and over 50% offer ropes courses, climbing walls, zip lines, backpacking, mountain biking, and cave exploration (ACA, 2007). Several of the youth organizations are discussed in more detail in this section.

Boy Scouts of America. The Boy Scouts began in England in 1901 by Lord Baden-Powell who, during the Boer War, had seen the English soldiers in need of outdoor survival skills. He set about to help boys secure this essential training. William D. Boyce, a Chicago publisher, and other enthusiastic supporters organized the Boy Scouts of America (BSA) in 1910. The movement has spread to become the largest voluntary youth movement in the world, with an international structure representing over 200 countries with its world headquarters in Switzerland. The BSA (2014) has more than 2 million youth members. Since its inception, the BSA's membership has included more than 110 million persons (U.S. Census Bureau, 2006).

Scouting is open to boys of all religions and races, and troops are sponsored by religious, educational, civic, fraternal, business, and labor organizations; governmental bodies; corporations; professional associations; and citizens' groups. The purpose of the overall BSA is to provide an educational program for boys and young adults to build character, to train in the responsibilities of participating citizenship, and to develop personal fitness. Various Scouting programs are available depending on age, such as the Cub Scouts and the Boy Scouts. Boy Scouting uses a vigorous outdoor program and peer group leadership with the counsel of an adult Scoutmaster and is designed to take place outdoors. It is in the outdoor setting where Scouts share responsibilities and learn to live with one another. And it is in the outdoors where the skills and activities practiced at troop meetings come alive with purpose. Being close to nature helps Boy Scouts gain an appreciation for the beauty of the world. The outdoors is the laboratory in which Boy Scouts learn ecology and practice conservation of nature's resources.

Most of the Scout troops in the United States have access to one or more of the hundreds of Scout camps operated by the local Scout councils, and the national office has four national high adventure areas. The Northern Tier National High Adventure Program offers wilderness canoe expeditions, fishing, and cold-weather camping in Minnesota and Canada; the Florida National High Adventure Sea Base offers aquatics programs in the Florida Keys; and Philmont Scout Ranch offers backpacking treks, rock climbing, and horseback riding in the rugged high country of northern New Mexico. The Philmont Scout Ranch is on 137,000 acres and is well equipped for outdoor pursuits in hiking, camping, and wilderness survival. Volunteer leaders may attend the Philmont Training Center each summer for a weeklong training conference. Paul R. Christen National High Adventure Base, located at Summit Bechtel National Scout Reserve, offers white-water rafting on the New River Gorge in West Virginia, as well as rock climbing, rappelling, hiking, mountain hiking, geocaching, and orienteering.

Girl Scout/Girl Guide. The Girl Scout/Girl Guide movement started in Great Britain by Lord Robert Baden-Powell and his sister, Lady Agnes Baden-Powell, in 1909. The organization has 2.3 million youth members, and through its membership in the World Association of Girl Guides and Girl Scouts (WAGGGS), Girl Scouts of the USA (GSUSA, 2014) is part of a family of 10 million girls and adults in 145 countries. The WAGGGS maintains world centers in Switzerland, England, Mexico, and India. The centers offer Girl Scouts and Girl Guides opportunities to meet members of Scouting movements in other countries. In the United States, the first Girl Scout troop was formed in 1912 in Savannah, Georgia, by Juliette Gordon Low, who organized the troop in her hometown. She had been active in the Girl Guide movement in England and Scotland, and she patterned the American troops accordingly. Today, more than 59 million women in the United States have belonged to Girl Scouts in their childhood (GSUSA, 2014).

The Girl Scout movement provides girls with opportunities to develop their potential to make new friends, to take active leadership roles in their communities, and to learn outdoor survival skills at the many camp facilities. Day camp and resident camp properties are shared by troops for their outdoor programs and by leaders for training sessions. Larger national centers are found in Wyoming, New York, Maryland, and Georgia. The Girl Scout National Center West in Wyoming provides a variety of outdoor living opportunities for older Scouts, including backpacking and saddle treks for a week or more. The Rockwood Girl Scout camp in Potomac, Maryland, offers camping and hiking, and University of the Woods, near New York City, offers training.

YMCA (the Y). The Young Men's Christian Association (YMCA) began with George Williams in London, England, in 1844 for the purpose of instilling Christian morals among youth. The first American YMCA was formed in Boston in 1851. Today, the National Council of the Young Men's Christian Association of the United States is headquartered in Chicago and has about 2,400 member associations serving more than 22 million men, women, and children of all faiths, races, ages and incomes, in 10,000 communities (YMCA, 2014). After World War II, women and girls were admitted as members and today comprise half of the membership of the nation's largest for-profit community service organization. YMCAs operate low-cost rooms to encourage less affluent travelers to visit the United States. Worldwide, there are 45 million members in more than 119 countries with facilities that include thousands of swimming pools, gymnasia, hostels, and cafeterias (YMCA, 2015).

American YMCAs operate resident camps and day camps. Their day and overnight resident camps provide the opportunity to have fun and learn how to make new friends, build new skills, and grow in self-reliance. Many Y camps use a natural setting to teach youth about the wonders of the world around them

and how they can take good care of it. In the Y-Adventure Guides and Explorers Program, curriculum is based on nature. Tribes get together for tribal meetings and participate in fun and educational outside activities. The Y is well known for its swimming facilities and a staff that offers instruction in swimming and SCUBA. In fact, the history of national diving training in the United States began with the development of the YMCA SCUBA Program based on the principles of the YMCA triangle: the Spirit, the Mind, and the Body. Camp Surf in San Diego Imperial Beach offers overnight and day camps, outdoor education, and retreats that specialize in beach, wetland, and intertidal community activities and discoveries.

YWCA. The Young Women's Christian Association (YWCA) began in London, England, in 1855 to meet the needs of working women. By 1894, a worldwide YWCA was in the making, with 83 nations represented in its membership. The YWCA now operates facilities, many including lodging, in more than 100 countries, reaching 3 million members worldwide (World YWCA, 2011). In the United States, the YWCA is one of the oldest and largest organizations in the nation, reaching over 2 million women, girls, and their families. In the United States, Boston was the first association to use YWCA in its name in 1859, although the YWCA of New York City formed its association a year earlier, in 1858. The YWCA pioneered in the task of working against racial discrimination toward full integration, fighting obvious segregation practices and exposing hidden patterns of discrimination in legislation, institutions, and systems. Although there has been emphasis on outdoor pursuits and camps for children, the YWCAs programs revolve around providing health programs, day care services, and affordable housing, including lodging when traveling abroad.

4-H. The Smith–Lever Act of 1914 provided for cooperative extension work in agriculture and home economics, and it included boys' and girls' 4-H Clubs. The 4-H still stands for Head, Heart, Hands, and Health and is symbolized by the four-leaf clover. The 4-H idea has spread to 7 million people in more than 50 countries (4-H, 2015a). Through the International Four-H Youth Exchange, young Americans visit other countries and young foreigners may live and work with American families for months at a time. In the United States, some 6 million young people are empowered through the Cooperative Extension, comprising 110 land-grant universities, the National Institute of Food and Agriculture of the U.S. Department of Agriculture, and county governments. The nation's largest youth development organization is also supported by 611,800 volunteers, 3,500 professionals, and more than 60 million alumni. Together they reach these elementary through high school children and adolescents in urban, suburban, and rural communities from every county of the nation through various programs (4-H, 2015b). Their science program, for instance, offers studies in robotics, aerospace, alternative energy, engineering, environmental science, agri-science, and veterinary science. The 4-H organization also offers camping opportunities.

Camp Fire USA. Although the name may indicate an exclusively outdoor orientation, the Camp Fire organization serves youth in a variety of ways including camp facilities. The organization was started as the Camp Fire Girls by Luther and Charlotte Gulick in 1910. In 1975, admission of boys to this once all-girls organization led to a change in the name to Camp Fire and then to Camp Fire, Inc. in 1984. In the late 1980s, they became known as Camp Fire Boys and Girls, a name selected for the 21st century. Today, Camp Fire USA (2013) is a national organization with 300,000 youth. Its purpose is to provide a program of informal education and opportunities for youth to realize their potential to function effectively as caring, self-directed individuals and leaders for tomorrow. The organization also seeks to improve conditions in society that affect youth. This nonprofit agency for youth is open to all without regard to race, creed, ethnic origin, sex, or income level. The entire family is engaged in many of the organization's activities, and scholarships are given to send low-income members to camp. Three broad program areas include Environmental and Camp, Out-of-School-Time, and Teen Service and Leadership programs involving outdoor learning and skills.

Boys & Girls Clubs of America. The Boys & Girls Clubs of America (2014) has more than 4,000 neighborhood-based facilities that serve some 4 million young people annually, primarily from disadvantaged circumstances. Known as "The Positive Place for Kids," clubs provide guidance-oriented programs daily for children 6 to 18 years old, conducted by full-time professional staff. Key programs emphasize character and leadership development, the environment, educational enhancement, career preparation, health and life skills, the arts, sports, fitness, and recreation, and they offer day and overnight camping experiences. National headquarters are located in Atlanta. The Boys & Girls Clubs movement originated in 1860 when three women in Hartford, Connecticut, invited a group of street boys into their home for tea and cake, and from this, the movement took off. In 1931, the Boys Federation of America became the Boys Club of America. Taking its present name in 1990, its mission is to enable youth to reach full potential and was established for boys and girls alike.

Preservation Organizations

Although the main objective of preservation organizations is the preservation of natural areas and historic sites, numerous outdoor pursuits can take place on the premises. Not all organizations concerned with preservation own the property to be preserved; many of these organizations work to encourage other organizations, agencies, and individuals to preserve property for future generations. Some land and conservation easements donated by companies, corporations, or individuals can be used as tax deductions. Following are just a few of the nonprofit organizations that deal with preservation and outdoor pursuits.

The Nature Conservancy. The Nature Conservancy (NC, 2014), the largest preservation organization in the United States, has about 1 million members. Its mission is to preserve the plants, animals, and natural communities that represent the diversity of life on earth by protecting the lands and waters they need to survive. Since 1951, the NC has protected more than 119 million acres of land and thousands of miles of river in 50 states and 35 countries. It owns more than 1,400 preserves in the United States—the largest private system of nature sanctuaries in the world—and other tracts of land referred to as managed areas with about half open to the public. The land is purchased, donated, or acquired because it is ecologically significant, and many times the land acquired by the NC is turned over to governmental agencies to manage. The Virginia Coast Reserve, a popular recreational area, consists of 14 barrier islands with their tidal pools to establish the Eastern Seaboard's longest coastal wilderness. In Canada, the NC joined the Lutsel K'e Dene First Nation to establish a protected homeland in the Northwest Territories. Thaidene Nene National Park Reserve is now the second largest protected area in Canada. A growing number of Nature Conservancy programs and projects offer overnight accommodations, and their international ecotourism program strives to enhance biodiversity conservation and sustainable community development through partnerships in countries such as Ecuador and Belize. More than 100 preservation deals are currently in process.

National Audubon Society. Founded in 1905 throughout the Americas, the National Audubon Society (2014) conserves and restores natural ecosystems for the benefit of humanity and the earth's biological diversity. The organization is supported by more than 500 chapters that seek the protection of wildlife populations, particularly birds. Their more than 100 wildlife sanctuaries and wildlife centers vary in size from 12 to 26,800 acres and may be open to the public or require permission well in advance of a visit. For instance, the 5,400-acre Francis Beidler Forest Sanctuary northwest of Charleston, South Carolina, with a visitor center and on-site manager, is the largest known tract of virgin tupelo/bald cypress left in the world. This sanctuary is dwarfed by the special-arrangement-only, 26,800-acre Rainey Wildlife Sanctuary that is a coastal marsh in Louisiana. This is the oldest and largest refuge, where

a restoration project was expanded to reestablish marsh along the coastline after storm damage (Louisiana Department of Natural Resources, 2005). Audubon has six national outdoor education centers and the 192-acre Aullwood Audubon Center and Farm outside of Dayton, Ohio. Their three summer ecology camps in Maine, Connecticut, and Wyoming offer intense natural history sessions for adults, and the Audubon Expedition Institute offers travel–study programs. The permanent staff at some of the sanctuaries serve as interpreters of wildlife and conduct hikes through the refuges (see also Chapter 14). The more than 2,500 Audubon-designated important bird areas identify and protect vital bird habitat in partnership with Birdlife International.

The Sierra Club. The Sierra Club (2014), founded in 1892 by John Muir (also Chapter 3), strives to preserve irreplaceable wildlands, save endangered and threatened wildlife, and protect the fragile environment through congressional lobbying and grassroots action on environmental issues. They own several lodges as mentioned earlier, but their focus on preservation activities does not emphasize ownership of lands. According to the Property Right Foundation (Sierra Club, 2014), their nearly 750,000 national member organization's mission statement is to

- Explore, enjoy, and protect the wild places of the earth.
- Practice and promote the responsible use of the earth's ecosystems and resources.
- Educate and enlist humanity to protect and restore the quality of the natural and human environment.
- Use all lawful means to carry out these objectives.

Most Sierra Club chapter-sponsored outings across the nation have no membership requirement and may be day hikes, peak scrambles, bird-watching trips, or conservation-oriented walks into the remaining natural areas of a major urban region. Sierra Club is one of the older, larger, and most influential environmental organizations.

National Trust for Historic Preservation. The National Trust for Historic Preservation (NTHP, 2014), with more than 150,000 members, encourages and assists agencies, organizations, and individuals to undertake historical preservation. The NTHP owns and operates 28 historic sites that serve more than 800,000 visitors annually and has an Associate Sites Program that is a national network of historic places grouped by theme and region. Working with the National Park Service, the NTHP serves as the principal partner for planning and implementing Save America's Treasures, a national effort to protect America's threatened cultural treasures, including significant documents, works of art, maps, journals, and historic structures that document and illuminate the history and culture of the United States. New Mexico's Acoma Sky Cliffs, the oldest continuing inhabited community in North America, became a National Trust Historic Site in 2007.

Rails-to-Trails Conservancy. Rails-to-Trails Conservancy (RTC, 2013) is involved in developing and protecting greenways in the United States. Founded in 1986, their mission is to protect America's railroad corridors, which are being abandoned at the rate of about 2,000 miles per year. The creation of rail-trails is primarily a result of the efforts of local trail enthusiasts, including citizens, politicians, and business leaders who see the potential to convert a rail corridor and seize the opportunity. The RTC strengthens this process by providing technical, legal, and policy assistance to local trail development groups. Forty-one states have rail-trails. More than 10,000 miles of rail corridor has been converted to rail-trails so far, and this trend shows no signs of slowing down with more rail-trail projects underway. The RTC does not own any of the rail-trails. Missouri Katy Railroad Trail, 223 miles long, is the longest, and Virginia Wedd Railroad Trail is the most heavily used with its 3,000,000 yearly users (Rails, 2006).

RARE. RARE Center for Tropical Conservation (2014) is an international nonprofit organization based in Arlington, Virginia, that has been active in 56 countries in Latin America, the Caribbean, and the Pacific since 1973. RARE Center's mission is to protect wildlands of globally significant biological diversity by empowering local people to benefit from their preservation. Just north of Guatemala on the southern Pacific coast of Mexico, alliance members provide funds and technical assistance to create a nature trail for bird-watching. The trail contains breaks in the thick vegetation where birds can be seen, and a bird-watching tower allows visitors a view above the forest canopy.

Land Trust Alliance. Based in Washington, DC, and founded in 1982, the Land Trust Alliance (LTA, 2014) is the leader of local and regional land trusts. Together, the 1,700 trusts protect a variety of land types including wetlands, river corridors, watersheds/water quality, farmland, and ranchland that conserve more than 37 million acres of open space. The LTA provides resources and training at the grassroots level to help trusts protect important open spaces. California, Massachusetts, Connecticut, Pennsylvania, New York, and Maine lead the nation in the highest number of trusts.

The Trust for Public Lands. Since 1972, The Trust for Public Lands (TPL, 2007) has helped protect more than 2 million acres in 46 states in 3,000 park and open space projects. The areas range from expansive recreational areas to historic homesteads and small city parks. TPL's Conservation Finance Program works with community groups, elected officials, and public agencies to help design and pass conservation funding measures. Since 1994, the TPL has helped states and communities craft and pass measures generating $25 billion to protect parks and open space. The TPL and the U.S. Forest Service teamed to protect over 1,000 acres of important wildlife habitat in the Wasatch Mountain Range to be added to the Unita–Wasatch–Cache National Forest.

Other Organizations

There are numerous other organizations that are involved in nature preservation including American Land Conservation, The Conservation Fund, Brooks Bird Club, Bass Anglers Society, Sport Fishing Institute, and the Garden Club of America.

INDUSTRIAL AND BUSINESS RESOURCES

In this section, the provision of recreational resources by industry and business will be discussed.

Employee Recreation

Provision of recreational opportunities by industry and business for employees began in the mid-1800s. Peacedale Manufacturing Company of Rhode Island is credited with providing library resources and singing classes as early as 1854. Other companies followed suit when the Pullman Company, the National Cash Register Company, and the Metropolitan Life Insurance Company provided recreation centers and golf courses and organized picnics and outings for their employees.

In a 1913 survey, the U.S. Bureau of Labor Statistics found that more than 50% of the 51 companies surveyed offered some form of employee recreation. In 1918, San Francisco established the first citywide industrial recreation association. A significant increase in this sort of offering was witnessed in the late 1930s, when the international recreation department was established by the United Auto Workers. In 1941, the National Industrial Recreation Association was created.

Cummins Engine Company of Columbus, Indiana, has received national recognition for their employee recreation program started more than 40 years ago. The 345-acre Ceraland Park, owned and operated by the Cummins Employees Recreation Association, a nonprofit association, has wooded parkland with several large picnic shelters, lakefront log cabins, a large group campground with 56 stoned campsites, 265 individual campsites, a camp store, and an archery and rifle range. Groups, guests of employees, and Good Sam RV Club and FMCA members

Today, thousands of companies sponsor recreational activities for their employees from modest walking clubs to large on-site facilities.

are also welcome to rent the campsites for a limited number of days. The boat dock and aquatic center on 11-acre Lake Lucille has paddle boats, canoes, and rowboats available for rent at nominal fees.

Industrial Land and Outdoor Recreation

Industrial land provided a significant portion of outdoor recreational opportunities in the United States in the past, when 72% of corporate land was open for some form of recreation. Forty-four percent of the land was open to the general public for recreational use without permission. Most of the 68 million acres used for that purpose were in the southern states (Cordell, Legg, & McLellan, 1979). There are motivating factors behind the involvement of profit-oriented corporations in sponsoring outdoor pursuits, but profit does not seem to be the dominant factor, although there are indications that this may be on the rise.

Some companies open their lands to recreationists because the land was already open to the public. The company may feel that the best public relations can occur if the land is left open for recreational use. On the other hand, the opening of private land to public use may lead to difficulties, one of which is the cost of operation. To provide adequate service, the operating company may find it necessary to provide facilities, collect trash, control fire hazards, and build roads, among other things.

Another problem the company may face is legal liability. Innovative legal agreements have been drafted that ease this concern, as in the Hatfield–McCoy trails network in West Virginia (more in this section). States wanting private land to be open to public use in some form have passed legislation that shields landowners from liability in certain situations. All 50 states have recreation user statutes to limit the liability of landowners for injuries occurring to recreation visitors while on their land. Although the degree of immunity varies, the statutes are consistent in helping to shield the landowner who does not charge entry fees. Charging an entry fee typically negates the protection (Douglass, 1999).

Four types of industries—wood leasing companies, utility companies, manufacturing companies, and landholding companies—offer significant lands that are either used in outdoor pursuits or have potential for such use (Knudson, 1984). Several examples follow:

1. **Wood-using industries:** Weyerhaeuser Corporation was the first of the large wood-using companies to start a tree farm in 1941. Since 1975, portions of its lands have been open to the public as recreational resources. In Canada, Weyerhaeuser operates primarily on public land. In Oregon, for instance, the corporation allows access to company forestlands for recreation. Weyerhaeuser hires professional staff to protect and manage wildlife and to supervise and conduct activities on its natural resources.

2. **Utility companies:** Electric power derived from hydroelectric plants is monitored by the Federal Energy Regulatory Commission. Among the commission's requirements is the development of recreational opportunities and utilization of each plant's reservoir as a recreational site. In California, the Pacific Gas and Electric Company (PGE) derives its electric power from hydroelectric plants in the California mountains and owns acres of prime watershed land in the Sierra Nevada, Cascade and Coast ranges. Systems of dams built by PGE store this water in reservoirs, resulting in lakes operated by PGE that help sustain river flows during dry summer months. These lakes also store large volumes of water during heavy spring runoffs, thus diminishing the threat of floods. Large lakes such as Almanor, Spaulding, Silver, and Britton are man-made lakes used for hydroelectric power and recreation. Most of the lakes offer fishing, swimming, and boating. Additionally, because power company profits are limited by California laws,

excess income goes to recreation and park projects.

3. **Other manufacturing companies:** Included among these companies are steel and mining companies. In southern West Virginia, private companies in the coal mining region teamed with federal trail experts to develop the innovative Hatfield–McCoy Recreation Area with miles of multiple-use trails. The innovative Hatfield–McCoy, selected as one of the 16 National Millennium Trails, will eventually consist of more than 2,000 miles of trail in West Virginia and Kentucky.

4. **Land-holding companies:** Many companies have donated land as public preserves managed by non-profit preservation organizations such as The Nature Conservancy. Others open their own recreational resources to the public.

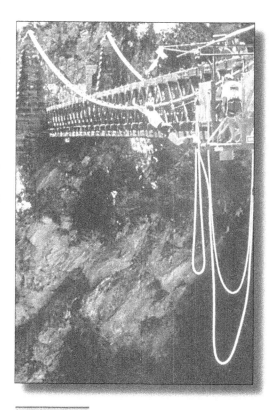

Private operators provide opportunities for thrill-seekers to bungee jump in many parts of the United States.

COMMERCIAL ENTERPRISES

In the past 20 years, the number of commercial facilities and leisure service providers offering recreational opportunities has burgeoned, with many of these enterprises combining private resources and operations with public land and water resources. Overall, the U.S. Census Bureau (2011) reports that there are nearly 21,000 commercial fitness and recreational sports centers and other commercial enterprises including marinas, golf courses, and ski facilities. Lodging operators have still more resources used for outdoor recreation.

Commercial enterprises having to do with outdoor pursuits come in many types, sizes, and orientations. There are small outfitters that have boathouses, rafts, vehicles, and even planes and lodges available for outdoor recreational adventures. Sky Trekking Alaska, for example, with a lodge and several small planes, offers custom small group adventures in the Alaskan outback to ice-fish, mush, snowshoe, hike, watch wildlife, fish for salmon, and photograph. Some larger companies such as Mountain Travel Sobek, Backroads, Backcountry, and GORP provide substantial resources that enable thousands to bike, hike, paddle, climb, snorkel, fish, hunt, cave, camp, watch wildlife, ski, snowboard, and drive outdoors. Many outfitters, lodges, and other commercial enterprises link together along national scenic byways to provide world-class outdoor adventures that combine private and public resources. Others, such as ARAMARK Sports and Entertainment, operate resorts at several national and state parks. One of ARAMARK's locations, Lake Powell Resorts and Marinas in Glen Canyon National Recreation Area, has marinas; several lodges; RV hookups; tour boats; and rental houseboats, powerboats, kayaks, and canoes.

The following section provides a closer look at commercial enterprises that offer camping facilities, ski areas, resorts, amusement parks, and guest ranches.

Camp Facilities and Commercial Campgrounds

Privately owned campgrounds have been in existence since the early 1930s; many private landowners started operating small campgrounds in the 1950s. Additional campgrounds were developed along interstate highways to serve the traveling campers. Today's luxurious RV parks offer manicured sites, full-service bathrooms, and numerous recreational amenities. The National Association of RV Parks and Campgrounds recognizes luxury RV parks as being distinct from campgrounds where visitors stay for shorter periods and receive fewer amenities (Cordell, 2004). Nationally, the number of private campgrounds began to shrink between 1977 and 1996. Most reports from private and public campsites support that private and public camping is on the rise in the United States: 14.9% of the population over age 6 went camping in 2011 (The Outdoor Foundation, The Coleman Company, & Kampgrounds of America, 2012). Lack of time is the most cited reason to reduce the number of camping trips in the future. Figure 10.1 shows where camping reservations are made.

The ACA (2014) is the accrediting body for the camp profession and accredits non-profit and for-profit resident and day camp facilities. Traditionally, campers are enrolled in these facilities during the summer months for a period that ranges from several days to a week, a month, or even the entire summer. As presented earlier in this chapter, of the estimated 12,000 American camps, 4,000 are privately owned by independent for-profit operators that either own or lease their camp facilities. Private camp operations may be found in rural, suburban, or urban communities and operate on several thousand backcountry acres or in city parks. Year-round use of private camp facilities is growing.

Another type of camp facility is the commercial campground that offers campsites for rent, lease, or sale. Directories published by Woodall's and Trailer Life list thousands of campgrounds nationwide, including public campgrounds (Betz et al., 1999). The majority of campgrounds are operated by commercial enterprises. Many commercial campgrounds have elaborate facilities such as swimming pools, tennis courts, and cable TV/phone hookups. A small number of campgrounds are rustic and provide traditional outdoor pursuits such as hiking and nature walks. A smaller number provide only roadside overnight camping with hardly any promise for outdoor pursuits. Horseshoes continues to be the most popular recreational facility at private campgrounds (McEwen, 1999).

Campground associations have been formed in many states and provinces to promote business, affect governmental decisions, and provide the needed information and education for members and others. On the national level, the Association of RV Parks

---

Behind Every Outdoor Recreation Experience There Is Generally a Person or Company With Heart

Lindblad Expeditions provides an alternative way to explore the outdoors via adventure travel cruises that carry Zodiac landing craft and kayaks to allow passengers and on-board naturalists to get off the ship almost anywhere to explore, take a hike, bird-watch, snorkel, or walk the shoreline. The company leaves the places visited as they found them and works with local governments and individuals to preserve them for others. Their owner, Sven-Olof Lindblad of the United States, has been honored by the United Nations Environment Programme (UNEP) for his contributions to the protection of the environment. Lindblad initiated the Galapagos Conservation Fund and in collaboration with the U.S. Tour Operators Association, established a Traveler's Conservation Foundation (TCF) made up of a range of companies associated with the tourism industry—a few of them without any previous involvement in conservation.

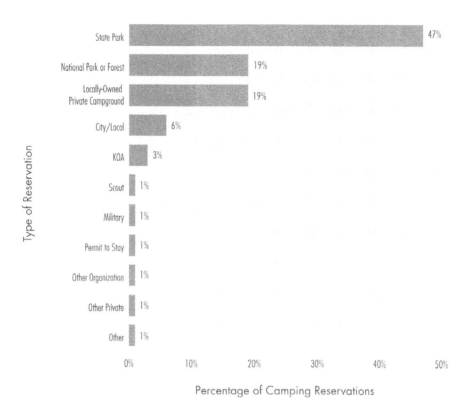

Figure 10.1. Type of camping reservation. Campers age 18+. The most popular place to make a camping reservation is at one of America's more than 7,000 state parks. Of those that made camping reservations during their last camping trip, almost half made the reservation at a state park. From *2012 American Camper Report*, by The Outdoor Foundation, The Coleman Company, and Kampgrounds of America, 2012, http://www.outdoorfoundation.org/pdf/research.camping.2012.pdf, p. 23.

& Campgrounds (2014), a trade association with over 3,000 members, represents the commercial RV park and campground industry throughout the United States and has certification programs for operators.

Campgrounds operate as businesses open for use by the general public as condominium-style campgrounds or as membership campgrounds. The condominium-style campground entails one of two approaches. The individual camper owns a specific lot located in the campground. This site can be rented out when the owner chooses or the person can own an undivided interest in the entire property. Examples of condominium-

style campgrounds are Bryn Mawr Camp Resorts and Yogi Bear Jellystone Parks Camp Resorts. Membership campgrounds require a membership to use sites at a network of campgrounds and sometimes offer a time-sharing arrangement at other campgrounds. Such an arrangement allows members to use other sites at affiliated campgrounds across the United States and Canada. For example, Camp Coast to Coast Resorts coordinates visits among hundreds of campgrounds in North America. Good Sam Parks offers another type of campground arrangement. The sites are not owned by the Good Sam Club, but rather are independently owned camp-

The first KOA Kampground was founded in Billings, Montana, in 1962 to serve travelers headed to and from Seattle World's Fair. Travelers could rent a space for the night or other short-term period to park their trailer or pitch their tent. As the franchise grew, the potential franchise owner of a KOA Kampground purchased the use of the KOA name and its services and received a guarantee of a certain territory in which there would be no other KOAs.

grounds that receive a stamp of approval from the oldest, largest 1.5 million–member RV club.

The development of KOA-type franchises, condominium-style campgrounds, and membership-style campgrounds expanded in the 1980s along with other full-hookup campgrounds. Kampgrounds of America (2014) offers 400 campsite and RV park camping locations, including basic tent sites, cabins, cottages, and luxury lodging.

Although public campgrounds tripled their capacity of improved sites over the past two decades and some offer advanced reservations, many travelers find commercial campgrounds more desirable because of the following features (Chubb & Chubb, 1981; McEwen, 1999):

- Acceptance of advance reservations, thus making it possible to plan an itinerary that includes a series of popular destinations without a concern about campsite availability.
- Availability of more amenities, such as electric, water, and sewer hookups; paved camping spaces; bathhouse and laundromat facilities; recreation halls; and well-lit, patrolled campsite areas.
- A policy of remaining open in the off-season, thus making it possible for people to camp while enjoying activities such as snowmobiling, ice fishing, hunting, and cross-country skiing.

- Provision by some campsites of fully equipped tents or RVs so campers traveling by air and others not wishing to bring their own equipment may still enjoy the advantages of camping; this also allows noncampers to try camping to see how they enjoy the experience before investing in equipment of their own.

Ski Areas

Lift-served skiing originated over 50 years ago in North America, and the number of facilities grew slowly until the 1960s when skiing exploded in popularity. According to the National Ski Association (2015), there are 470 ski areas in operation. The number is down some in recent years, but statistics have also been impacted by weather delaying openings. Most ski areas are owned by large corporations, a trend that began in 1990s. Two enterprises, the American Ski Company and the former owners of Vail Associates, purchased numerous ski resorts (Gardner, 1999).

About 50 to 60 million skier visits are recorded at American resorts each year (Statista, 2014) with snowboarders accounting for 30% of the total skiers (Solomon, 2013). The mix of activities and the concentration of visitors at destination resorts continue to shift. These areas have a variety of snow activities where people use their snowboards, fat skis, snowbikes, skwals, luge, and traditional skis. At least 50 of the ski areas in the United States and Canada are regarded as world-renowned resorts, including Aspen in Colorado, Snowbird in Utah, and Whistler in British Columbia. The Forest Service guides the establishment of new areas, as well as the development and operation of the areas located within its jurisdiction. For example, the number of skiers on a slope on a given day is controlled. Construction of ski trails is also controlled to reduce land disturbance. Material in Table 10.3 and the boxes provide additional information about ski areas in the United States.

Table 10.3
Characteristics of U.S. Ski Regions

Characteristics	The East	The Midwest	The Rocky Mountains	The Far West
Range	Northern Georgia and western North Carolina to Maine.	Michigan, Wisconsin, Minnesota, parts of Illinois, Ohio, and Indiana.	Mountain areas of New Mexico, Colorado, Utah, Idaho, and Montana.	Pacific coast mountain areas of California, Oregon, Washington, and Alaska.
Elevation (above sea level)	Modest: 460–1400 m (1500–4500 ft).	Minor: glacier-produced hills, 490 m (1600 ft) at most.	High; between 1500–3300 m (5000–11,000 ft); some resorts at 2400 m (8000 ft).	Similar to Rocky Mountains region.
Skiing opportunities	Enormous variety; some of the most interesting and stimulating skiing; most trails are carved through forests and are narrower than elsewhere; good cross-country skiing opportunities.	Less variety; ideal learner and intermediate slopes; runs are often cut through woods; lacks rugged terrain; drops 80–180 m (200–600 ft) at most; excellent slalom course and ski jump facilities; competitions numerous; exceptional cross-country skiing.	Best skiing for expert skiers; some runs are through forest; many open slopes are 300 ft or more in width; satisfying long runs; greatest vertical drop in United States; status-skiing opportunities; some gentle slopes permit use by less-than-expert skiers.	Exceptional bowl and panoramic skiing; excellent opportunities for learners as well as experts; sheer scale of High Sierra skiing unsurpassed; some ski areas are close to urban centers in Northwest.
Major resort areas	Intensive development along mountainous spine of Vermont; most challenging areas are in New Hampshire; one big mountain (Whiteface) is in New York along with 100 smaller areas; Sugarloaf area in Maine is well known and impressive; several popular resorts in Pennsylvania.	Clusters of centers ideal for learners around Detroit, Chicago, Milwaukee, Minneapolis–St. Paul metropolitan area; chain of resorts bordering Great Lakes from Lusten, Minnesota, across Wisconsin to Boyne City, Michigan; Boyne Country ski development is leader in Midwest—first in world to install a quadruple chairlift.	Contains nation's most prestigious resorts, match largest resorts elsewhere in skiable area but not necessarily in facilities; subregional differences not substantial, but southern resorts have drier powder snow, whereas northern areas have greater snow depths.	Two concentrations in southern California: areas within 160 km (100 miles) of Los Angeles and the High Sierra resorts of Lake Tahoe regions; prime ski area in northern California is in northern California is on flanks of Mt. Shasta; three areas on flanks of Mt. Hood near Portland, Oregon; three areas in Snoqualmie Pass near Seattle, WA; more than 30 areas in Oregon and Washington designed primarily as day areas.

Table 10.3 (cont.)

Characteristics	The East	The Midwest	The Rocky Mountains	The Far West
Advantages or disadvantages	Closest to heaviest concentrations of potential skiers; most areas readily accessible by car; best areas seriously overcrowded at times; many areas have distinctive atmospheres and many loyal users.	Many resorts within a 1- or 2-hour drive of large urban centers; Midwestern skiers known for their enthusiasm and dedication; excellent ski services and instruction opportunities.	Many resorts not readily accessible; cost and altitude problems for non-Westerners; some of the most beautiful settings in the world; great diversity of winter sports and après-ski opportunities.	Access often difficult in Sierra Nevadas; evening and weekend opportunities excellent in some areas; best areas are away from usual vacation routes; some cost and altitude problems for skiers from the East; exotic settings available on highest slopes.
Length of season	Usually 3 or 4 months; extended and made more reliable by heavy use of snow-making equipment; occasional mild winter can be disastrous, especially in the South.	Similar to the East, but colder temperatures an asset; adequate skiing almost a certainty throughout season where snow-making equipment is used.	Longer season than East or Midwest; depends on latitude and elevation.	Longest season; year-round skiing possible in some high northern locations.
Skiing conditions	Winds occasionally strong.	Often extremely cold temperatures, sometimes accompanied by strong winds.	Most comfortable climatic conditions; mostly skiing below timberline, which provides wind-protected trails; more sunny days than other regions.	Longest season; year-round skiing possible in some high northern locations.
Snow and trail conditions	Unpredictable; extreme cold periods alternate with devastating thaws; snow on trails often packed hard because of heavy use.	Heavy snowfalls supplemented by use of snow-making equipment; has most uniform conditions of all regions.	Large quantities of snow in average season; dry-air conditions produce snow that rarely packs into hard snow or ice; best consistency in world—better even than European Alps; danger of avalanches; problems with whiteouts and flat light.	Heavy snowfalls—often too much; reaches depths of 5 m (15 ft) in Sierra Nevadas in average snow season; snow very persistent—comes early and stays late; unfortunately often damp, sometimes wet conditions.
			Threat of storms; risk of being snowed in.	
Examples of major resort developments	Stowe, VT, considered to be the ski capital of the East; steep, narrow trails provide challenge; 660 m (2150 ft) vertical drop; 58 lodge facilities.	Boyne Country, MI, largest privately owned ski development in U.S.; foremost complex in Midwest; best racing slopes in region; 190-m vertical drop; can accommodate 1500 people in deluxe lodge, inn, and villa facilities.	Aspen, CO, considered by many to be the ski capital of the world; includes four huge mountain slopes; one just for beginners; 1160-m vertical drop; 95 places to stay, providing 1608 rooms and 1469 condominium facilities.	Heavenly Valley, CA–NV border, largest ski area in the world; 5200 hectares (20 sq miles) of lift-served terrain; 1100–1200-m (3600–4000 ft) vertical drop; 24 places to stay.

A Few of the World-Class Ski Resort Areas in the United States

Alta, Utah. Alta is famous for deep powder, spectacular runs, serious skiers, steep ungroomed chutes, on and off the trail map, and classic ski lodges. There are good beginner slopes, too, but over the years Alta has attracted and produced elite skiers. Alta is in the same canyon as Snowbird and about 35 miles from Salt Lake City.

Aspen, Colorado. Aspen has four mountains—Ajax, Buttermilk, Highlands, and Snowmass—that offer diverse good skiing, with few rivals in the Rockies. Outdoor activities of all kinds abound year-round. Denver is the major city nearby.

Breckenridge, Colorado. Breckenridge is about 100 miles from Denver. Its four mountains are quite different and offer terrain for all grades of skiers and outdoor enthusiasts. Imperial Bowl is the highest in-bounds skiing in the USA at slightly less than 13,000 ft.

Crested Butte, Colorado. Crested Butte is a paradox: It is small yet marketed internationally and has some of the gentlest and most challenging skiing in the Rockies. Its fame comes from its extreme skiing and for offering one of the biggest programs for skiers with disabilities in the country.

Heavenly, California. Heavenly is intersected by the California–Nevada border, where the views from the top are startlingly different: Lake Tahoe on the California side and the Nevada Desert on the other. With good intermediate skiing and hiking and biking trails, two thirds of the area's 150 miles of trails have snow-making.

Jackson Hole, Wyoming. Jackson Hole ski resort at Teton Village is mainly for intermediates and experts. It has a reputation as one of the best ski areas in the United States. It is not only the dynamic skiing or the vertical drop—the biggest in the U.S.—but the mix of slopes and scenery including the Teton mountain range, wildlife, Wild West atmosphere, and the wilderness of Yellowstone National Park.

Mammoth, California. Mammoth is 300 miles from Los Angeles and one of the biggest ski resorts stretching 7 miles from end to end. Located on an ancient volcano, it is in a remote and wild part of the Eastern Sierras not far from Yosemite National Park. Mammoth has dramatic scenery of its own, especially the jagged, toothy Minarets.

Park City, Utah. Park City, open since 1963, is known for world-renowned skiing and legendary for dry powder. There are three large ski resorts with areas for snowboarding, cross-country, and the full gamut of winter and summer sports. Park City hosted the Olympics in 2002.

Snowbird, Utah. Snowbird has excellent snow; challenging bowls; one of the widest intermediate trails in the country; a large, fast cablecar; and scenery. Snowbird's most challenging in-bounds skiing is in its steep-sided bowls where chutes serve as launching pads for those who like the "free-fall" dimension of skiing. It is 30 miles from Salt Lake City.

Squaw Valley, California. Squaw Valley is the most challenging of the 15 ski areas scattered around the shores of Lake Tahoe. Squaw's six mountains encompass every type of terrain: from moguls on a steep face to beginner slopes. Squaw has "radical" skiing off the Palisades and 33 lifts.

Sun Valley, Idaho. Sun Valley was built in 1936 by Averell Harriman, president of the Union Pacific Railway, but only after a long search to find a resort that would attract passengers during the lean winter months. Mount Baldy is a mountain with steep pitch and more than half a dozen bowls and 78 ski runs, many for intermediate cruising runs. Summertime has biking, hiking, skating, walking, horseback riding, and llama treks.

Taos, New Mexico. Taos ski area is known for light, dry powder and steep, deep, and high-adventure ungroomed runs with some still requiring an initial hike of an hour. Ernie Blake, a German-born Swiss who worked

A Few of the World-Class Ski Resort Areas in the United States (cont.)

as an interrogator for Allied Intelligence, invented this ski area in New Mexico's Sangre de Cristo mountains that has an exotic mixture of cultural influence from European to Pueblo Indian.

Telluride, Colorado. Telluride, with year-round sports, is famous for steep places and located in a box canyon in a remote corner of southwest Colorado, amidst the San Juan Mountains. The sophisticated cult ski resort is right next to a National Historic District, the 19th century silver mining town that has an old main street dominated by the New Sheridan Hotel. There are black diamond trails, cruising, and some easy skiing.

Vail/Beaver Creek, Colorado. Vail has some of the best back bowls in North America with more than two thirds of the 110 runs graded beginner or intermediate. Built in the early 1960s in the image of a Tyrolean–Bavarian hybrid, the resort has a cosmopolitan atmosphere, cross-country ski trails, and off-season activities such as rafting and mountain biking.

Note. Adapted from "Ski the World: The Best Resorts in the World," by Media Odyssey, Inc., 2001, http://www.wuwien.ac.at/usr/h94/h9450102/skiing.html.

Commercial ski resorts supply a variety of services, programs, and facilities for ski-related activities and for hikers, mountain bikers, and less active guests (BBC Research, 1999; Chubb & Chubb, 1981). Some of the facilities include the following:

- Lighted slopes and trails (especially at resorts close to metropolitan areas) to extend the skiing day and accommodate all-season visitors.

- Reasonably priced equipment rentals and ski, snowboarder, and climbing schools with ample beginners' facilities to attract new participants.

- Rope tows, chairlifts, gondolas, and trams to transport skiers, snowboarders, climbers, hikers, and other outdoor enthusiasts rapidly and effortlessly to the skiing and recreation areas.

- Snow-cat or helicopter transportation and guide services to make backcountry areas accessible.

- Ice-skating rinks, snow tubes, toboggan runs, sleigh rides, heated swimming pools, and multiuse trails to provide other outdoor activities and to attract nonskiers.

- Indoor swimming pools and tennis courts to attract nonskiers and skiers, most of whom swim and about 65% of whom play tennis.

- Après-ski programs, including movies, live entertainment, and parties involving the use of resort-provided lounges, game rooms, restaurants, bars, and nightclubs.

Other Resorts

Ski-oriented, multiseason resorts are resort facilities that have become elaborate, with most open year-round. They double as ski resorts in the winter season and destinations for outdoor recreation enthusiasts of all types during other seasons offering hiking, mountain biking, climbing, horseback riding, canoeing, kayaking, rafting, bird-watching, wildlife viewing, and fishing. For instance, the ski resort of Alta, Utah, has world-class fly-fishing and wildflower viewing and is a popular family reunion destination; Telluride is a skiing, snowboarding, and mountain-biking mecca; and Park City and most other mountain resorts have year-round outdoor adventures. Some double as spa and health resorts, but many health resorts do not have anything to do with winter ski activities. There are also strictly warm-weather resorts with water-oriented outdoor facilities that range from simple to luxurious, and sport resorts with a focus on instruction and practice facilities. Lodging facilities and resorts at national and state parks are frequently operated by commercial enterprises such as Xanterra Parks and Resorts and are usually oriented around use of the park and participation in outdoor activities.

Health and beauty resorts are more prevalent in Europe, but they are growing in popularity in North America. In Europe, they are found around the Czech Republic's Karlsbad, France's Vichy, and Germany's Bad Pyrmont. There the emphasis is on mineral water therapy that probably dates back to the Romans. Mineral hot springs have been meccas in the United States, too, with Hot Springs, Arkansas, developing facilities for tourists and benefiting from federal protection as early as 1832. During the roaring 1920s, ornate spas were built there along Bathhouse Row. Not all health spas are oriented around mineral springs, though. Rancho La Puerta, founded in 1940 in a broad valley just across from the United States border in Tecate, Baja California, Mexico, is considered one of the original North American health spas to emphasize mind, body, and spirit. At their facility, they have created a 3,000-acre nature preserve that extends to the foot of 3,885-foot Mt. Kuchumaa. They have hiking and fitness programs, lectures, healthy meals, as well as traditional spa activities such as facials, massages, and manicures. This model, with its outdoor activity, is followed by many of the health spas across the country.

Warm-weather active resorts exploded onto the scene in the 1950s with Club Mediterranean. War-weary Europeans needed a vacation, and an Olympic water polo champion from Belgium named Gerard Blitz organized a beach holiday for a few hundred of his friends in Majorca, Spain. The program was simple: sun and fun on the shores of the Mediterranean, activities, sports, and relaxation in a setting of natural beauty. The club operates resort villages in every continent from North America to Asia. Most of these resorts are beach oriented, and some are ski-oriented villages in the mountains. Couples, families, older individuals, and singles use these resorts. Many other sun resorts followed suit with active vacation facilities in relaxing locations, mostly near beaches.

With a private mile-long fishing pond, Tim Pond Camps in Maine is the oldest set of sporting camps in New England, hosting guests since the mid-1800s. At most sport resorts, water sports are by far the most popular activities, with fishing, boating, rafting, and waterskiing taking place. Many resorts provide outdoor pursuits such as horseback riding, hiking, birding, and wildlife viewing. In the past century, sport resorts have expanded rapidly, particularly those that emphasize tennis and golf, many with additional outdoor activities included. Besides golf, North Carolina's Pinehurst Club has features such as a health spa, a lake for boating, pools for swimming, lawn sports, walking and biking, and a fitness center. In a much more rustic approach, the privately run San Juan Hut Systems operates hut tours along a mountain bike route from Telluride, Colorado, to Moab, Utah, that crosses four national forests including alpine tundra of the San Juan Mountains to the desert canyon country of Utah. The Seaway Trail along New York's St. Lawrence Seaway and the Oregon Coast National Scenic Byways have networks of resorts and outfitters located along their respective shorelines that work with public officials to link substantial private resources for the benefit of outdoor recreationists. Sailors, water skiers, hang gliders, sailboarders, kayakers, and beachcombers all benefit, as do persons embarking on fishing, scuba, rafting, and hiking expeditions.

Theme and Amusement Parks

A small, private park, Jones Wood, provided entertainment on Manhattan Island as early as 1850. But it was the building of Coney Island on the southwestern end of Long Island, New York, that may have signaled the birth of amusement parks in America. The idea was copied from the world-famous

Luna Park in Paris. Today, more than 400 amusement theme parks and attractions in the United States are visited by approximately 290 million people. They generate $12 billion annually (International Association of Amusement Parks and Attractions, 2012). Besides theme parks, some water theme parks, zoos, historic sites, and nature parks are considered commercial enterprises in the United States. Parks vary from small in size, where rides, games, and shows are all together, to medium in size. Designated by the UNESCO as an international biosphere reserve, Grandfather Mountain is a medium-sized private park with nature exhibits and alpine trails on the highest peak in the Blue Ridge near Boone, North Carolina. Huge theme parks such as Seaworld and Disneyland's California Adventure Park draw millions of visitors annually. Some major theme parks are developed on large parcels of land with enough open space and natural features to contribute to a genuine outdoor experience.

Guest Ranches and Vacation Farms

Guest ranches, known to some as dude ranches, are working ranches and farms that acquire additional income by opening them to guests. Accommodating guests often becomes the main source of income, with livestock and the production of crops as secondary interests. Most of these ranches are 1,000 acres or more, but some are small. In Cedaredge, Colorado, along the Grand Mesa National Scenic Byway, the 10-acre Cedars' Edge Llama Bed and Breakfast has interactions with llamas, llama care, and llama breeding. At most guest ranches, such as Arizona's 2,000-acre Flying E Ranch in Wickenburg, horseback riding is the main outdoor activity. Because most of these ranches are in the West, the lifestyle is Western. In the Midwest, many small farmers have opened their farms for outdoor pursuits, particularly for fishing, as a means of augmenting their income. Hunting is also allowed for a seasonal or daily fee on farms with pastures and woodlands. Some farms provide swimming pools and golf courses.

SUMMARY

Private outdoor recreational resources could come from personal, nonprofit, semipublic, industrial, and business resources. Their offerings not only supplement public offerings, but also serve as models in a number of cases. Personal resources include residences, second homes, boats, RVs, and the like, and private organizations include social, sport, and hiking clubs; boat and yacht clubs; and nature clubs. Semipublic organizations such as the YMCA and the Girl Scouts and preservation organizations such as The Nature Conservancy and Audubon Society offer members many outdoor pursuits. In the meantime, a number of industries are seeking to provide their employees and local communities with these opportunities. Commercial enterprises have been in the business of providing outdoor recreational facilities and activities for many years. Campgrounds, ski areas, and resorts accommodate many recreationists. Other resorts, theme parks, and guest ranches have played important roles in providing outdoor opportunities for the young and mature alike.

REFERENCES

4-H. (2015a). 4-H around the world. Retrieved from http://www.4-h.org/about/gloval-network

4-H. (2015b). Youth development and mentoring programs. Retrieved from http://www.4-h.org/about/

Aiken, R. (2004). Private and public land use by hunters: Addendum to the 2001 national survey of fishing, hunting, and wildlife-associated recreation (Report 2001-8). Arlington, VA: U.S. Fish and Wildlife Service.

American Camping Association. (2007). Trend fact sheet. Martinsville, IN: Author.

American Camping Association. (2014). ACA facts and trends. Retrieved from http://www.acacamps.org/media/aca-facts-trends

Association of Zoos and Aquariums. (n.d.). The collective impact of America's zoos and aquariums. Retrieved from Pittsburg Zoo and PPG Aquarium website: http://pittsburghzoo.com/PressRoom/PressKit/ImpactOfZoos

Audubon. (2014). About us. Retrieved from http://www.audubon.org/about

BBC Research. (1999, August 20). New England winter recreation industry and market analysis final report prepared for the U.S. Department of Agriculture Forest Service.

Betz, C., English, D., & Cordell, H. K. (Eds.). (1999). Outdoor recreation resources. In *Outdoor recreation in American life: A national assessment of demand and supply trends* (pp. 39–182). Champaign, IL: Sagamore.

Boys & Girls Clubs of America. (2014). What we do. Retrieved from http://bgca.org/whatwedo/Pages/WhatWeDo.aspx

Boys Scouts of America. (2014). About. Retrieved from http://www.scouting.org/

Camp Fire USA. (2013). Frequently asked questions. Retrieved from http://www.campfireusa.org

Chubb, M., & Chubb, H. (1981). *One third of our time: An introduction to recreation behavior and resources.* New York, NY: Wiley and Sons.

Cordell, H. K. (2004). *Outdoor recreation for 21st century America: A report to the nation: The national survey on recreation and the environment.* State College, PA: Venture.

Cordell, H. K., Legg, H., & McLellan, R. (1979). *The private outdoor estate: The third nationwide outdoor recreation plan.* Washington, DC: U.S. Government Printing Office.

Cordes, K., & Lammers, J. (photographer). (2001). *America's national scenic trails.* Norman: University of Oklahoma Press.

Douglass, R. W. (1999). History of outdoor recreation and nature-based tourism in the United States. In H. K. Cordell (Ed.), *Outdoor recreation in American life: A national assessment of demand and supply trends* (pp. 15–24). Champaign, IL: Sagamore.

Dulles, F. (1965). *A history of recreation* (second ed.). New York: Appleton-Century-Crofts.

Gardner, S. (1999). Downhill ski area trends in the United States. In H. K. Cordell (Ed.), *Outdoor recreation in American life: A national assessment of demand and supply trends* (pp. 158–159). Champaign, IL: Sagamore.

Girl Scouts of the United States of America. (2014). Facts about scouting. Retrieved from http://www.girlscouts.org/who_we_are/facts/

Guest5c6461. (2009, May 3). The marina business [Slide show]. Retrieved from http://www.slideshare.net/guest5c6461/the-marina-business-1379264

Hearth, Patio, and Barbecue Association. (2014). Grilling facts and figures. Retrieved from http://www.hpba.org/consumers/barbecue/grilling-facts-and-figures/?searchterm=grilling%20facts

Ibrahim, H. (1991). *Leisure and society: A comparative approach.* Dubuque, IA: Wm. C. Brown.

International Association of Amusement Parks and Attractions. (2012). Amusement park and attractions industry statistics. Retrieved from http://www.iaapa.org/resources/by-park-type/amusement-parks-and-attractions/industry-statistics

Kampgrounds of America. (2014). Retrieved from http://koa.com/

Knudson, D. (1984). *Outdoor recreation.* New York, NY: Macmillan.

Land Trust Alliance. (2014). Land trusts. Retrieved from http://www.landtrustalliance.org/land-trusts

Louisiana Department of Natural Resources. (2005, April 22). Coastal restoration project celebrates Earth Day and Audubon Centennial. Retrieved from http://dnr.louisiana.gov/index.cfm?md=newsroom&tmp=detail&aid=597

McEwen, D. (1999). Campgrounds. In H.K. Cordell (Ed.), *Outdoor recreation in American life: A national assessment of demand and supply trends* (pp. 151–154). Champaign, IL: Sagamore.

Media Odyssey, Inc. (2001). Ski the world: The best resorts in the world. Retrieved from http://www.wuwien.ac.at/usr/h94/h9450102/skiing.html

National 4-H Headquarters. (2005). National 4-H headquarters fact sheet. Washington, DC: Author.

National Association of Realtors. (2014, April). Vacation home sales surge in 2013, investment properties decline [News release]. Retrieved from http://www.realtor.org/news-releases/2014/04/vacation-home-sales-surge-in-2013-investment-property-declines

National Association of RV Parks. (2014). RV parks and campground owners. Retrieved from http://www.arvc.org/membership/rv_park_and_campground_owners.aspx

National Ski Areas Association. (2015) *U.S. ski resorts in operation during 2013–14 season.* Retrieved from www.nsaa.org/media/214725/Number_of_Ski_Areas_by_Season_1314.pdf

The Nature Conservancy. (2014). About us. Retrieved from http://www.nature.org/about-us/index.htm

The Outdoor Foundation, The Coleman Company, & Kampgrounds of America. (2012). *2012 American camper report.* Retrieved from http://www.outdoorfoundation.org/pdf/research.camping.2012.pdf

Outdoor Recreation Resources Review Commission. (1962). *A report to the President and to Congress by the Outdoor Recreation Resources Review Commission.* Washington, DC: U.S. Department of Commerce, NOAA.

Patterson, S. (2013). Public and private land percentages. Retrieved from http://www.summitpost.org/public-and-private-land-percentages-by-us-states/186111

Rails. (2006). *Rail-trail statistics.* Washington DC: Rails-to-Trails Conservancy.

Rails-to-Trails. (2013). *America's rails-with-trails report.* Retrieved from http://www.railstotrails.org/ourwork/reports/railswithtrails/report.html

Rare. (2014). Rare inspires change so people and nature thrive. Retrieved from http://www.rare.org/

Recreational Boating and Fishing Foundation & The Outdoor Foundation. (2013). *Special report on fishing Alexandria: 2013.* Retrieved from http://takemefishing.org/uploadedFiles/Content/General/About_RBFF/Research_and_Evaluations/2013SpecialReportFinalWEB.2013-06-26.pdf

Roper Starch. (2001). *Outdoor recreation in America 1999: The family and the environment.* A report prepared for the Recreation Roundtable, Washington, DC.

Sierra Club. (2014). About us. Retrieved from http://texas2.sierraclub.org/

Solomon, C. (2013, January 20). Has snowboarding lost its edge? *The New York Times.* Retrieved from http://www.nytimes.com/

Statista. (2014). Estimated number of skier visits in the U.S. from 2000 to 2014. Retrieved from http://www.statista.com/statistics/206544/estimated-number-of-skier-visits-in-the-us-since-2000/

Teasley, R., Bergstrom, J., Cordell, H. K., Zarnoch, S., & Gentle, G. (1999). Private lands and outdoor recreation in the United States. In H. K. Cordell (Ed.), *Outdoor recreation in American life: A national assessment of demand and supply trends* (pp. 185–218). Champaign, IL: Sagamore.

The Trust for Public Land. (2007). About TPL. Annapolis, MD: The Trust for Public Land.

U.S. Census Bureau. (2000). *Statistical abstracts of the United States: 2000* (120th ed.). Washington, DC: U.S. Government Printing Office.

U.S. Census Bureau. (2001). *1997 Economic census arts, entertainment, and recreation subject series.* Washington, DC: U.S. Department of Commerce.

U.S. Census Bureau. (2006). U.S. Census 2000 Photius Coutsoukis and Information Technology Assoc. Retrieved from www.Allcountries.org/uscensus/parks_recreation_and travel.html

U.S. Census Bureau. (2011). *Statistical abstract of the United States: 2012.* Retrieved from http://www.census.gov/prod/2011pubs/12statab/arts.pdf

U.S.Fish and Wildlife Service. (2014). *National survey – 2011 survey.* Retrieved from http://wsfrprograms.fws.gov/Subpages/NationalSurvey/2011_survey.htm

U.S. Fish and Wildlife Service & U.S. Census Bureau. (2011). *2011 national survey of fishing, hunting, and wildlife-associated recreation* (FHW/11 Nat(RV)). Retrieved from http://www.fws.gov/verobeach/Home/fhw11-nat.pdf

YMCA. (2015). Organizational profile. Retrieved from http://www.ymca.net/organziational-profile

Chapter 11

Outdoor Recreation in Canada

"It is wonderful to feel the grandness of Canada in the raw, not because she is Canada but because she's something sublime that you were born into, some great rugged power that you are a part of" (Carr, 2006, p. 383). ~ **Emily Carr**

The purpose of this chapter is to provide an overview of outdoor recreation in Canada. Although there are many similarities between the United States' and Canada's approaches to and histories of outdoor recreation, there are many important differences and distinctions. Part of the purpose of this chapter is to highlight the Canadian outdoor recreation identity, which has been shaped by Canada's landscapes and weather patterns, rich cultural history, the emergence of federal and provincial parks, and the mystique and wild nature of "the North." First, we provide a background and overview of the country of Canada with a focus on Aboriginal peoples and early outdoor recreational practices. This section is followed by the history of the canoe and how it has shaped ways of traveling, hunting, and exploring Canadian wilderness. In the next section, we present more in-depth information about the settlement of Canada by the French and English and about the ways outdoor recreation continued to evolve. Finally, in the last sections, we highlight Canadian park development, history, and management from federal, provincial, and territorial perspectives.

BACKGROUND AND OVERVIEW OF CANADA

Canada is a vast country that extends from the Atlantic Ocean to the Pacific Ocean and from the Arctic to the northern border of the United States (see Figure 11.1 for a map of Canada). Located so far north, Canada has harsh winters in addition to its diverse topographic features, which include the Maritime provinces of Newfoundland, Prince Edward Island, New Brunswick, and Nova Scotia, followed by the densely forested regions of Quebec and Ontario that eventually turn into fertile lowlands. Continuing westward, there is an industrial region, followed by the Canadian Shield—a central depression of hard, old igneous rocks. The vast prairie region of southern Manitoba, Saskatchewan, and Alberta is followed by the mountains and forests of British Columbia. North of this expansive land are the three Canadian territories (Yukon, Northwest Territories, and Nunavut). Other diverse Aboriginal peoples of Canada (including First Nations, Métis, and Inuit) live across the entire country. The two European communities that settled in Canada—pri-

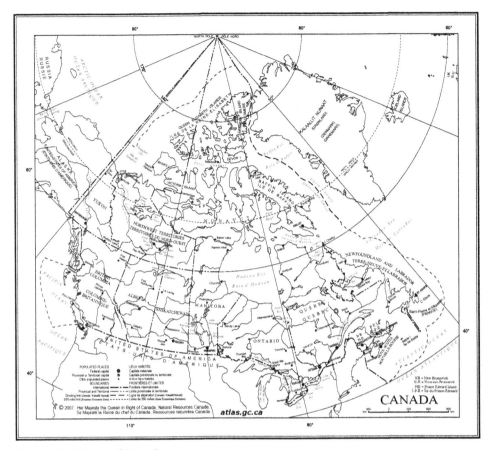

Figure 11.1. Map of Canada.

marily the French and the English—live in a variety of areas across the country as well. The greatest numbers of French-Canadians live in the province of Quebec.

It is assumed that the ancestors of the Inuit and First Nations of Canada came by the northwestern route across the Bering Strait between the present-day Russian Federation to Alaska, the United States, and eventually Canada. Despite the hazards of life in the Arctic region, the Inuit subsisted on whatever they were able to extract from their surroundings. Eventually, they established a lifestyle that some considered to be somewhat "playful" (Blanchard & Cheska, 1985). And most of these playful activities were related to survival techniques. According to Johnson (1979), "Most, if not all [Inuit] activities that might have had an impact on leisure in general, and outdoor recreation in

particular, disappeared with the advent of white people" (p. 338).

But this was not necessarily the case with many other Aboriginal peoples across Canada. Although many aboriginal activities that had some bearing on outdoor recreation disappeared, many other activities were adopted by the Europeans. An example is Baggataway, which was practiced by the Iroquois and Algonquins. Baggataway was a military scrimmage, infused with a religious ceremony designed to obtain the blessings of the gods, who would bestow health and fertility on the victorious team. Baggataway's new name, lacrosse, was given to it by the later-to-come French settlers, because the implement used in the activity had a curved, netted neck that resembles a bishop's crosier (a crooked staff). But the aboriginal implement that was adopted by European settlers that had the most profound impact on outdoor recreation in Canada (and elsewhere) in later years was the canoe.

"The canoe….. carries the vision, the values, and the beliefs of the old ones." ~ **Author unknown**

THE CANOE

There is no greater icon for Canadian outdoor recreation than the canoe. Canoes were first used by indigenous peoples in the Caribbean, but today's modern version of the canoe was inspired by the birch bark canoes developed by many early Aboriginal peoples across Canada. In the subarctic regions of Canada, spruce bark was used as a substitute for birch bark. Canoes enabled Aboriginal peoples to travel and hunt efficiently in Canada's vast and challenging landscapes where other modes of travel were simply unthinkable. European settlers used the canoe for similar reasons, which widely helped early settlers facilitate the fur trade, and eventually, the world's first canoe factory was built in Trois-Rivières, Quebec, around 1750 (Kent, 1999). *Voyageurs* (a French word meaning traveler) became a common way that those who used canoes and traveled for long distances during the fur trade were identified. However, another group called the Voyageurs also shaped more modern wilderness canoe exploration beginning in the 1950s.

Aboriginal peoples and the early French settlers helped to position the canoe as part of Canada's identity. Yet a group in the 1950s who also became known as the Voyageurs provided the foundation for wilderness canoeing as outdoor recreation to become distinctly Canadian. The group began with Eric Morse, Omond Solandt, and Blair Fraser taking three diplomats they had met at an Ottawa dinner event on a 10-day wilderness canoe trip to show them the "real" beauty of Canada in 1951. The success and joy gained from the initial trip spiraled forward and the group expanded to include other notable explorers including the famous American wilderness writer Sigurd Olson, as well as Elliot Rodger, Tony Lovink, Denis Coolican, and

Canoeing is a Canadian outdoor recreation favorite. Courtesy of Ryan Howard.

Tyler Thompson. Some of their notable trips between 1950 and 1960 included exploration of the Quetico–Superior region, the challenging Grand Portage to Fort Francis route, and the Camsell and Great Bear Rivers in the Northwest Territories. These pioneers for wilderness canoe exploration redefined the role of the canoe within Canada's culture as a purposeful method to experience the Canadian wilderness (Peake, 1993).

Another Canadian canoeing legend is Bill Mason (1929–1988). Mason was an artist, conservationist, canoeing instructor, explorer, and filmmaker whose passion for paddling canoes has inspired (and continues to inspire) generations of Canadians. Mason paddled extensively all over the United States and Canada, and he helped to refine and develop canoeing strokes and whitewater canoeing techniques throughout his life. His books *Path of the Paddle, Song of the Paddle,* and *Canoescapes* (Mason, 1980, 1988, 1995) and films *Song of the Paddle* and *Waterwalker* (Mason, 1978, 1984) remain popular today. Furthermore, the way Mason's life paints a picture of a modern Canadian explorer who practiced and cherished primitive outdoor recreation defines an important part of the foundation of Canadian wilderness values (Raffan, 1996). Overall, Mason's life and adventures shaped Canadian environmental ethics in a positive light by combining a passion for outdoor recreation, play, and conservation (Heintzman, 2007).

To highlight the intermingling of these concepts, Raffan (1996) noted,

> One of my favourite images of him [Bill Mason]… are those of a solitary, far from adulation, alone in his red canoe in a wilderness like Algoma or Algonquin Park. There he is oblivious to man or machine, paddling, watching, listening, suspended in a reverie piqued by a regard for nature and fixed by faith that there is a lesson to be learned from immersion in the Canadian wild. (p. 25)

White-water canoeing provides fun and challenge for Canadians to enjoy a primitive form of wilderness travel. Courtesy of Ryan Howard.

In summary, the canoe symbolizes the traditions and heritage of Aboriginal peoples, the adventures of the fur trade era, a contemporary emphasis on and reverence for primitive wilderness travel, and emergence of the Canadian outdoor recreation identity. The canoe continues to be a powerful symbol in Canada and permeates many aspects of modern Canadian life, which was also deeply shaped by the broader European settlement of Canada beginning in the mid-1500s.

EUROPEAN SETTLEMENT OF CANADA

The first Europeans to settle in Canada around the mid-1500s were French explorers who landed on the shores of Nova Scotia and Newfoundland. Some settlers followed the St. Lawrence River to the location of today's Montréal and on today's site of Quebec. The settlers sold knives and hatchets to the First Nations and began the fur trade. The country of New France was founded in 1627, and it became engaged in a war with the Iroquois tribe a decade later. A quarter of a century later, New France was at war with England. Although there were periods of peace between New France and England, the struggle continued. By 1763, most of Canada had become a British dominion. Nonetheless, there are still two distinct European communities in Canada: English and French.

French Canada

According to Johnson (1979), the Catholic Church played a decisive role in the lives of early French Canadians. Strict puritanical behavior was expected of every French Canadian, with gambling and dancing prohibited. Another important factor that affected recreational activities was the climate of Canada. Long winters required that settlers be physically fit to survive. Accordingly, the French Canadians developed proficiencies in outdoor activities, which served as the nucleus of recreational activities to follow. They became skillful at canoeing, hunting, and snowshoeing. During the severe Canadian winter, they participated in races on the snow and on frozen rivers. One of their favorite races was in the horse-drawn *cariole* (sleigh). Summer, on the other hand, was a time for hard work on the land.

After a few French settlements were built in New France, three distinct lifestyles evolved. The affluent, earlier settlers lived in a large population center and imitated the French aristocracy. Douville and Casanova (1967) suggested that during their lavish ceremonies and elaborate banquets, one could easily have imagined breathing the atmosphere of Versailles, France, rather than the air of Quebec, Canada.

The more typical French Canadians lived in the outlying settlements and depended on family and neighbors for their livelihoods. Life in the linear villages along the St. Lawrence had none of the pomp of life in the larger settlements. These inhabitants lived according to what the church and seigneur (the person in charge of land held by a grant from France) allowed or disallowed. Recreational activities revolved around and evolved from these close-knit communities.

A third type of French Canadian was the coureurs de bois, or "runners of the woods," who imitated the ways of the First Nations. These people not only abandoned European values, but they also adopted the habits, customs, and recreational activities of the First Nations. They lived in the wilderness and removed themselves from the moral dictates of the settled French and their authority. They traded furs often without a license and were labeled as troublemakers in the eyes of French authorities who were attempting to regulate the fur trade (Colpitts, 2002). The coureurs de bois used outdoor technical skills, in part, to live independently of these regulations.

English Canada

The English Canadians faced the same hard conditions, and settlers had to rely on communal activities to accomplish certain tasks. This cooperative spirit led to the rise of the *bee* (a group that worked together to harvest crops, raise a barn, and the like). Eventually, the bee included a social element in which the host supplied food, drink, and amusement. The drink was usually whiskey, and the amusement often included a hoedown and contests. The bee as a way of accomplishing a communal task eventually died out when the play element dominated the work element.

English villages of Canada began to provide for recreational outlets through inns and taverns, often patterned after the English pub. Travelers and residents alike began to participate in "bloodsports", which were also observed in Great Britain, such as bear and bull baiting and dog and chicken fighting.

Imitation of the British extended to the upper-class English in Canada. In their attempts to emulate the English aristocracy of the old country, the wealthy in the New World filled their lives with organized and informal outdoor activities. They became "fond of horse racing, and field sports, fishing and sailing in the summer, and skating and caroling in the winter…" (Guillet, 1933).

According to Baker (1982), curling was introduced to Canada by Scottish immigrants as early as 1807. An annual festivity was held called bonspiels, which involved sliding around flattened stones on a frozen lake. In the meantime, ice hockey was being practiced by the English troops stationed in Kingston in 1855. A few years earlier, in 1842, some of the English settlers began to compete with natives in their Baggataway. A set of rules and standards for fields and equipment was soon drawn, and the Europeans renamed the game lacrosse.

Settlement of western and northern Canada by Europeans was slow. Once it started, a true mix of people came to live in compact communities, each having its own traditions, amusements, and recreational activities. Communities were particularly far apart in the North.

At the end of the Seven Years War in Europe in the 1750s, most of Canada was ceded to Great Britain. Quebec was to retain a French civil law to protect the position of the Catholic Church. One hundred years later, the Dominion of Canada came into being on July 1, 1867. At that time, the early dominance of garrison towns came to an end and the strong class distinction in French and English Canada began to break down. Canada was turning into a modern industrial society. Canadians began to seek other forms of recreational activities, especially the mechanized forms of bicycling and motoring. The negative reaction of the conservative to such activities was swift, and the federal government's Lord's Day Act of 1906 was meant to keep the purity of the Sabbath. But in contrast, some civic-minded organizations were aware of the need for, and the value of, leisure pursuits, particularly among the young.

Canadians had at that time a reasonable acreage of dedicated open space, some of which was designated for recreation and leisure. In fact, as early as 1859, the Toronto City Council had described some parks as "breathing spaces where citizens might stroll, drive or sit to enjoy the open air" (McFarland, 1970, p. 14). Other Canadian cities had their designated open spaces. In a manner not dissimilar to what occurred in its neighboring country to the south, the United States, various levels of government (primarily federal and provincial) became involved in outdoor recreational resource management in Canada, as described in the following sections.

ROLE OF THE FEDERAL GOVERNMENT IN CREATING AND PROTECTING NATIONAL PARKS

Prior to the 1900s, the role of the federal government within the context of Canadian outdoor recreation was limited to the provision of open space. Federal agencies have had direct impacts on the outdoor recreational resources of Canada. One federal agency, which impacts the outdoor recreational pursuits and perceptions of Canadians from a national level, more so than any other, is Parks Canada. The creation of a national parks system in Canada evolved from the creation of Banff National Park in the province of Alberta (Canada's first national park). See Figure 11.2 for a map of Canada's national parks. The seed for Canada's first national park started to grow when Canadian Pacific Railway workers discovered hot

springs in 1883 near Banff National Park's present location. Soon after, a small area around the springs was reserved because it was thought the area would make a popular tourist attraction within the expanding western Canadian frontier. The area surrounding the hot springs became Canada's first national park (Banff) in 1885 (Boyd & Butler, 2000).

In 1887, parliament passed the Rocky Mountains Park Act, defining parks as a "pleasure ground for the benefit, advantage and enjoyment of the people of Canada," and the act greatly enlarged the boundary area for where Banff National Park currently existed. It is noteworthy that the original emphasis within the Rocky Mountains Park Act was more on economic growth than on the preservation or conservation of natural environments. This economic impetus for park creation mirrored the way Yellowstone National Park was developed in the United States 15 years prior, also along hot springs. Overall, the idea of reserving natural environments for use by people would eventually evolve to a more environmental focus, but remained central to the creation and vision of national parks in Canada for an additional 50 years (Campbell, 2011).

Greater emphasis on conservation and preservation of the natural environments inside national parks started to take hold with the passing of the Dominion Forest Reserves and Park Act of 1911. Although the act reduced national park borders, it created the Dominion Parks Branch to manage national parks (previously Canada's national parks were managed by the Dominion Forestry Branch) with Commissioner James B. Harkin in charge of the new agency. Under Harkin's leadership, the Dominion Parks Branch gave shape to a new vision for Canadian national parks—a vision of conservation and preservation of wild places alongside use-based park and land management approaches (Campbell, 2011). At this point in time (the early 1900s), Canada's national parks expanded

eastward into Saskatchewan, Manitoba, and Ontario—this last, in particular, to provide park space closer

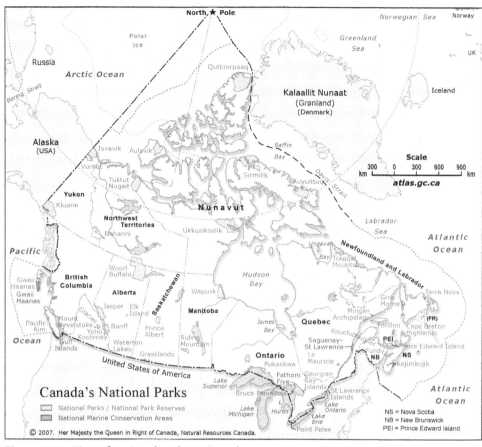

Figure 11.2. Map of national parks in Canada.

to where most Canadians lived—and created wildlife preserves for antelope, elk, and buffalo in Alberta and Saskatchewan. By twinning use and protection, the Branch was laying the foundations of an approach to national park management that would remain in place throughout the twentieth century. (Campbell, 2011, p. 5)

Modern Canadian national park management approaches continue to balance use and protection. To reiterate a point of historical significance, it is noteworthy that these approaches began to take form in Canada for the first time with the creation of the Dominion Parks Branch in 1911.

The National Parks Act of 1930 additionally put forth a stronger preservationist man-

date, which further combined the purposes of national parks as places to provide education and recreational opportunities while maintaining them in a way that would leave them "unimpaired" for others to enjoy. While the United States Wilderness Act of 1964 propelled preservation to the forefront of the U.S. national park and land management system, similar movements were taking place in Canada. For example, in 1963, the creation of the Canadian Parks and Wilderness Society, a national charity, began successfully championing for long-term park and land protection, highlighting preservationist and ecologically based momentum within the Canadian national park context (Canadian Parks and Wilderness Society, 2012).

Ecological integrity and preservation continue to be the central focus for Parks Canada today and recent policy and priority areas reflect this position (Parks Canada, 2012a). Various ecological initiatives and monitoring programs have been put into place to achieve this goal and to better understand the balance between use and preservation of Canada's natural heritage. Parks Canada's current successes and challenges are the result of its complex history (Plummer, 2009), and the contemporary challenge is to continue to find ways to serve people and the natural environment, which are sustainable from ecological and social perspectives.

Today, there are 42 national parks in Canada in 39 natural regions, representing one of the largest and most diverse national park systems in the world. Canadian national parks are located on the Atlantic and Pacific coasts, in Canada's interior prairies and mountain ranges, and in the farthest northern and southern reaches of the country (Parks Canada, 2012b). The park system is expansive, consisting today of 2.5% of all federal lands in Canada (Plummer, 2009). At 45,000 square kilometers (approximately 27,961 square miles), Wood Buffalo National Park is Canada's largest national park, and at 9 square kilometers (approximately 5.6 square miles), St. Lawrence Islands National Park is the smallest (Parks Canada, 2012b). With Wood Buffalo, other huge national parks in Canada include Kluane, Jasper, Glacier, and Banff, totaling over 26 million acres. Overall, as a federal entity, the evolution of Parks Canada symbolizes a significant aspect of Canada's national identity, which is tied to nature and pride in its natural and cultural heritage. This pride is also reflected in the ways outdoor recreational resources are managed at the provincial level.

ROLE OF PROVINCIAL GOVERNMENT IN CREATING AND PROTECTING PROVINCIAL PARKS

There are 10 provinces in Canada, and each has its own government. Canada's population exceeds 33 million people. Of those 33 million people, census figures indicate that 6.9% live in the Atlantic provinces of Newfoundland, Prince Edward Island, Nova

Scotia, and New Brunswick. Moving west, 23.6% live in Quebec and 38.4% live in Ontario. Finally, 30.7% live in the prairie and western provinces of Manitoba, Saskatchewan, Alberta, and British Columbia. The remaining population lives in the northern territories (Yukon, Northwest Territories, and Nunavut; Statistics Canada, 2012). This means that most of Canada's national parks and large open spaces are in the least populated areas. This makes the role of the provincial government, particularly in eastern parts of Canada, important when it comes to outdoor recreational resource offerings.

Unlike the situation in each state in the United States, provincial governments are less dependent on the federal government where public land and/or open space are concerned. Unsettled public lands in Canada, known as the Crown lands, are generally under the control of the provinces. Individual U.S. states generally do not control public lands, and their involvement in outdoor recreation on those lands is sometimes challenged by this factor. In Canada, the provinces have found that it is relatively easy, politically and financially, to allocate large pieces of land as parks and forests. What follows are brief histories and highlights of provincial outdoor recreational resources and some of the common management strategies for outdoor recreation used in each of Canada's 10 provinces.

Newfoundland and Labrador

Newfoundland and Labrador is Canada's easternmost province and the newest province to join the Confederation in 1949 (Government of Newfoundland and Labrador, 2013a). The Parks and Natural Areas Division of the Department of Environment and Conservation manages Newfoundland and Labrador's provincial parks. The mission of the Department is

> to protect and preserve in an unimpaired condition representative and rare examples of the Province's natural heritage as Provincial Parks and Wilderness and Ecological Reserves, and to provide a diverse range of outdoor recreational opportunities,

province-wide, which will encourage visitors to celebrate, discover, explore, understand and appreciate our natural heritage. (Government of Newfoundland and Labrador, 2013c)

Sir Richards Squire Memorial Park was the first provincial park in Newfoundland and Labrador created in 1954. There are now 13 provincial parks in Newfoundland and Labrador that allow overnight camping and seven natural and scenic attraction parks primarily designed for day use (Government of Newfoundland and Labrador, 2013e).

Additionally, Newfoundland and Labrador is known for its wilderness and ecological reserves made possible through the passing of the Wilderness and Ecological Reserves Act in 1980. The act was designed to set aside large natural areas with boundaries put in place through habitat needs of wildlife such as caribou. Wilderness reserves allow for traditional outdoor recreational activities such as hiking, canoeing, and fishing. One of the wilderness reserves in Newfoundland is the Avalon Wilderness Reserve located about 50 kilometers south of St. John's. Before Avalon was a protected area, the woodland caribou herd fell to only a few dozen in the 1960s. With the protection of the habitat, the herd's numbers have risen to the thousands, and these are the most southerly caribou in the nation (Government of Newfoundland and Labrador, 2013b). The Avalon is a prime example of a conservation success story made possible, in part, because of the passing of the Wilderness and Ecological Reserves Act at the provincial level.

Furthermore, ecological reserves are typically smaller and are managed in a more preservationist style to give greater protection to ecosystems and their species. Ecological reserves will generally only allow activities such as hiking and educational tours. These protected areas are classified by type and include botanical, fossil, seabird, and ecosystem reserves. They also include rare and endangered species as well as globally significant landscapes, rock types, and fossils (Government of Newfoundland and Labrador, 2013d).

Nova Scotia

The Nova Scotia provincial park system took form in 1959 with the enactment of the Provincial Parks Act. In the 1970s and 1980s, a greater emphasis was placed on developing inland outdoor recreational resources and on increasing coastal beach access. There are now over 300 provincial parks across the province. The provincial parks system operates on a five-pronged mandate based on offering protection of natural and cultural heritage, recreation, education, a land base for future recreation and education, and promotion of provincial tourism. Nova Scotia provincial parks receive 1.5 million visitors annually and host over 80,000 campers per year (Nova Scotia Canada, 2013).

One point of interest is Five Islands and Blomidon provincial parks, which border some of the world's highest tides in the Bay of Fundy. The Bay of Fundy is bordered by towering sea cliffs, which contain 300 million-year-old fossils (Discover Nova Scotia, 2013). The tidal change is so great that certain rivers that empty into the bay temporarily flow backwards, called a tidal bore, during the high tide. First Nations Mi'kmaq legend attributes the change in the tide as the result of a whale who became impatient with a native god, Glooscap, and broke a beaver dam to restore the flow of water to the area, creating the massive ebb and flow of water that exists today (Glooscap Heritage Centre, 2013).

Prince Edward Island

Prince Edward Island (or PEI as it is commonly referred) on the eastern coast is Canada's smallest province. PEI is an island province in the Gulf of St. Lawrence with an estimated 145,855 residents. It has also been suggested that PEI is Canada's greenest province surrounded by beautiful ocean waters with an island landscape dominated by red soil, forests, pristine coastline, and rolling hills. This landscape served as inspiration for Canadian author Lucy Maud Montgomery in her writing of the literary classic *Anne of Green Gables* in 1908 (Montgomery, 2000). PEI is joined to the province of New Brunswick by the Confederation Bridge, which at 12.9 kilometers (9 miles) is the longest bridge over ice-covered waters in the world. PEI is also home to the "tip-to-tip" Confederation Trail, which spans the entire island and is in itself a park for cycling, hiking, and snowmobiling (Government of Prince Edward Island, 2013a). The Confederation Trail was completed in 2000 and is the first segment of completion of the Trans Canada Trail—PEI being the first province to do so (Island Trails, 2013). Overall, PEI contains 11 provincial parks for camping and 15 for day use as well as 17 wildlife management areas (Government of Prince Edward Island, 2013b; Tourism Prince Edward Island, 2013).

New Brunswick

New Brunswick is the largest of the three Maritime provinces and sits beside the U.S. state of Maine. The people of New Brunswick have had a long-lasting historical relationship with forests. In fact, during the Napoleonic wars in the early 1800s, Great Britain was forced to import wood from North America, including New Brunswick. From this point forward, especially with its extensive river system that provides easy access to pine, spruce, and hemlock trees, New Brunswick forests became highly valued for their timber harvests. Forestry continues to be the largest industry in New Brunswick today. The 1982 Crown Lands and Forests Act helped to ensure sustainable approaches to forest use continue in New Brunswick's future (New Brunswick Department of Natural Resources, 2012).

New Brunswick parks are managed at two levels provincially. The Department of Tourism, Heritage, and Culture (formally the Department of Tourism and Parks) manages provincial parks, and the Department of Natural Resources manages smaller parks on Crown lands. Outdoor recreational opportunities are rich and varied. Sugarloaf Provincial Park provides Atlantic Canada's only lift-served mountain biking and excellent snow skiing. Parlee Beach Provincial Park celebrates some of the warmest salt waters north of the U.S. state of Virginia with beautiful beachside camping. Mount Carleton Provincial Park contains over 42,000 acres (17,000 hectares) of rugged wilderness, the highest peak in the Maritimes (Mt. Carleton), and is a dark sky preserve (Tourism New Brunswick, 2012).

Quebec

Quebec's provincial parks are called "national" parks across the province. The national park system in Quebec began with the establishment of Parc de la Montagne-Tremblante in 1895. Similar to other provincial parks across the country, this park was originally developed with the purpose to ensure the sustainable use of wildlife and forests. In 1896, Parc des Laurentides was created. It was not until 41 years later that Quebec's third national park (Parc de la Gaspésie) was established. In 1977, Quebec's government created the Parcs Act, which protected areas for the primary purposes of conservation and recreation. In 1999, the Quebec government appointed Sépaq (Society of Outdoor Recreation Establishments of Quebec) to manage outdoor recreational resources south of the 50th parallel. Since this point, Quebec's entire park network has fallen underneath the Parcs Act mandate (Parcs Québec, 2012). In 2001, the Parcs Act was amended to place greater emphasis on the concept of a "national" park with management guidelines congruent with the International Union for Conservation of Nature (IUCN). The main purpose of the IUCN national park designation is to protect natural areas for the purpose of recreation. More specifically,

> the IUCN defines a national park as a natural area designated to:
> a) protect the ecological integrity in one or more ecosystems for present and future generations
> b) exclude exploitation or occupation inimical to the purposes of the area
> c) provide foundation for spiritual, scientific, educational, recreational, and visitor opportunities, all of which must be environmentally and culturally compatible. (Parcs Quebec, 2012, Did You Know? section)

Niagara Falls ranks as a natural wonder of the world. On March 30, 1885, the Ontario legislature passed the Niagara Falls Park Act establishing Ontario's first provincial parkland. The Queen Victoria Niagara Falls Park Act in 1887 officially established the Niagara Parks Commission, and in May 1888, the park was officially opened to the public.

Like many national parks across the world, Quebec's national park system seeks to maintain balance among conservation, recreation, educational opportunities, and protection of the natural environment.

Ontario

Niagara Falls, which defines part of the border between the United States and Canada, is one of the natural wonders of the world. On March 30, 1885, the Ontario legislature passed the Niagara Falls Park Act establishing Ontario's first provincial parkland. The Queen Victoria Falls Park Act in 1887 officially established the Niagara Parks Commission, and in May 1888, the park was officially opened to the public. Today, the Niagara Parks System extends for 35 miles between Lake Erie and Lake Ontario. This is a chain of parks along the Niagara River with views of Niagara Falls and adjacent natural vistas.

Outdoor recreational and park resources in the chain include picnic areas, playing fields, a golf course, horticulture displays, a butterfly conservatory, nature areas, bike paths, and amphitheaters. It is also noteworthy that bouldering (a form of rock climbing) has become increasingly popular at the Niagara Glen Nature Reserve along the parkway and is currently the most extensive bouldering area in the province (Niagara Parks Commission, 2012).

The Ontario park system officially originated with a single park in 1893: Algonquin Provincial Park. Other parks were added during the next half-century, until the Provincial Parks Act of 1934 officially made the Ontario system the largest provincial park system in Canada at the time. The system totals nearly 8 million hectares with an annual attendance of over 9 million visitors. Of these visitors, about 1% use the parks for overnight camp-

The Niagara Glen Nature Reserve, near Niagara Falls, Ontario, is the largest bouldering area in the province and is managed by the Niagara Parks Commission. Courtesy of Garrett Hutson.

ing. The system consists of 329 parks with over 19,400 campsites (Statistics Canada, 2012). Ontario parks, which constitute 5% of the province's land, are administered by the Ontario Ministry of Natural Resources and Forestry. Most of Ontario's parks are either surrounded by or adjacent to Crown lands (federally and provincially controlled land), which makes it generally easy to expand the system.

The Ontario Ministry of Natural Resources and Forestry uses a classification system of parks, as follows:

1. Recreational parks typically have an abundance of outdoor recreational resources. Most recreational parks provide services including recreational facilities, hiking trails, and picnic tables. An example of a recreational park in Ontario is Bonnechere Provincial Park located in Renfrew County (Ontario Parks, 2014a).

2. Cultural heritage class parks protect Ontario's cultural heritage within open spaces and generally support (through these areas) education and research. An example of a cultural heritage park in Ontario is Inverhuron Provincial Park near the town of Tiverton (Ontario Parks, 2014b).

3. Natural environment class parks protect the landscapes and special features of the natural region in which they are located and provide a variety of recreational opportunities. An example of a natural environment park is Shorthills Provincial Park near St. Catharines, Ontario (Ontario Parks, 2014f).

4. Nature reserve class parks are established to represent and protect distinct and fragile habitats and landforms. These areas are protected for educational and research purposes. Due to the fragility of many of these natural features, only a few nature reserves are accessible to the public. An example of an Ontario nature reserve is Pushkin Hills near Cochrane, Ontario (Ontario Parks, 2014d).

5. Waterway class parks are river corridors that provide recreationists with high-quality river scenery and travel. An example of a waterway class park is Noganosh Lake Provincial Park near Port Loring (Ontario Parks, 2014e).

6. Wilderness class parks are large areas left to nature where visitors may travel on foot or by canoe. Offering few facilities for visitors, these areas provide the solitude and challenge of an undisturbed, natural setting. An example of a wilderness class park is Killarney Provincial Park in Killarney, Ontario (Ontario Parks, 2014c).

*Descriptions of park classifications were obtained and adapted from the *State of Ontario's Protected Areas Report* (2011).

Manitoba

Like many of the other provincial park systems, Manitoba's provincial park system began to take form in the early 1900s as more tracts of land were set aside by the federal government for the purpose of forestry. As the forestry industry expanded, so did roads into those forests, increasing opportunities for public access. In 1930, the federal government transferred control of natural and outdoor recreational resources to the province. In 1931, the Whiteshell Provincial Forest Reserve was created, which many consider to be Manitoba's most significant park area. In 1960, the Manitoba Provincial Park Act was passed with an emphasis on protecting recreational opportunities, yet it still allowed for extractive uses of parklands as long as those uses did not interfere with recreation. In 1972, the Provincial Parklands Act was passed to replace the original act with a stronger mandate on conservation and preservation alongside recreational and extractive land use. Atikaki, Manitoba's first wilderness park, was created in 1985 to fill a gap within Manitoba's park system in the spirit of land set aside for preservation. In 1993, another Provincial Parks Act was passed and outlined overall park classifications (Wilderness, Natural, Recreation, Heritage, and Reserve) and other land-use categories. These park classifications are currently in use today (Manitoba Government, 2012).

Saskatchewan

Saskatchewan has 34 provincial parks designated as wilderness, recreational, natural environment, or historic parks. The Saskatchewan Parks Service enacts its conservation philosophy through ecosystem management. The following statement highlights this approach:

> We know that it is possible to emulate the way nature works in our approaches to the management of parks. This challenge is being met with renewed vigor as the Saskatchewan Parks Service embarks on a program of working with nature to safeguard the forests, prairies, wa-

ters, and species across the system. Meeting this challenge will require resources, innovative thinking, communication, education and cooperation. These necessary factors for the conservation of parks are second nature to Saskatchewan people giving us an excellent opportunity to accomplish the long-term maintenance of ecosystems, species, and beauty in our parks. Without healthy and attractive parks, we would be a poorer province. Now, more than ever, we must work hard and long to conserve and protect what matters most in our parks. (Government of Saskatchewan, 2012b, Ecosystem Management section, para. 3)

Saskatchewan has a variety of notable parks and park features. The popular Cypress Hills in the southern part of the province is Canada's first interprovincial park, sharing its boundary with the province of Alberta. Additionally, Cypress Hills is Canada's first dark sky preserve and is further defined by an aboriginal history of spiritual ceremony. Danielson Provincial Park in the south central part of the province contains Canada's largest earth-filled dam, which also happens to be one of the largest of its kind in the world. One will likely hear the mystical call of the Loon at Angin Lake Provincial Park in the central part of the province, which contains one of the highest nesting Loon populations on the continent. Finally, the Athabasca Sand Dunes Provincial Park in the northern reaches of the province contains one of the most northern sand dunes in the world. One of the only ways to access the Athabasca sand dunes is by float plane (Government of Saskatchewan, 2012a).

Alberta

Many have attributed the beginnings of the Alberta provincial park system to Premier J. E. Brownlee. In the late 1920s, Brownlee began initiating conversations and meetings with an aim to develop a provincial park network in Alberta. In 1930, the Provincial Parks and Protected Areas Act was passed. Aspen

Beach Provincial Park was established in 1932 and became Alberta's first provincial park. Gooseberry Lake, Park Lake, Sylvan Lake, and Saskatoon Island followed shortly after the establishment of Aspen Beach. Alberta experienced tremendous growth in its provincial park system during the 1950s and 1960s with the passing of a new Parks Act in 1951and the establishment of 46 new provincial parks by 1971. During this time, management approaches began to expand from recreation to include a stronger preservationist lens. In 1964, the Alberta Parks Act was amended to include wilderness and natural areas. In 1971, Alberta passed the Wilderness Areas Act and amended it in 1980 to include natural areas and to establish and protect ecological reserves (Alberta Tourism, Parks, and Recreation, 2012a).

In 1995, the Alberta government expanded its park system further through an initiative called Special Places to better represent Alberta's diverse land regions, and by 2001, this resulted in 81 new protected areas. In 2009, Alberta released its Plan for Parks as a 10-year park plan to ensure the sustainability of Alberta's parks for the future. The plan is based on four principles: (1) involve Albertans; (2) offer modern facilities, policies, and programs; (3) provide recreation opportunities; and (4) improve quality of life for Albertans (Alberta Tourism, Parks, and Recreation, 2012b).

British Columbia

Situated west of Alberta, British Columbia (BC) is Canada's westernmost province and shares a southern border with Washington, Montana, and Idaho of the United States. The Yukon and Northwest Territories of Canada and the U.S. state of Alaska form British Columbia's border to the north and northwest. British Columbia's western shoreline borders the Pacific Ocean (British Columbia Parks, 2012b). On July 29, 1910, Price Ellison led a BC government expedition to the peak of Crown Mountain (1,504 meters, 4,934 feet) on Vancouver Island. The purpose of the expedition was to explore possibilities for BC's first provincial park. Soon thereafter, the BC park system began with the estab-

lishment of Strathcona Provincial Park on Vancouver Island in 1911 (BC Parks, 2012a). Today, the park system is administered by BC Parks:

> BC Parks is responsible for the designation, management and conservation of a system of ecological reserves, provincial parks and recreation areas located throughout the province. British Columbia's parks and protected areas contain nationally and internationally significant natural and cultural features and outdoor experiences. (BC Parks, 2012a, para. 1)

BC has the second largest park system in Canada, second only to the national park system. BC provincial parks protect more than 1,000 sites including parks, conservation areas, ecological reserves, and recreational areas totaling 13.16 million hectares of land and water, and they are classified as follows (BC Parks, 2012c):

1. **Class A park:**
   - Class A parks are dedicated to the preservation of their natural environments for the inspiration, use, and enjoyment of the public. A Class A park is Crown land designated under the Park Act or by the Protected Areas of British Columbia Act whose management and development are constrained by the Park Act. Sections 8 and 9 of the Park Act are the most pertinent in this regard and direct that a park use permit must not be issued respecting an interest in land or natural resources "unless, in the opinion of the minister, to do so is necessary to preserve or maintain the recreational values of the park involved."
   - Class A parks can be established by two means: by order in council under the Park Act or by inclusion in a schedule to the Pro-

tected Areas of British Columbia Act.

2. **Class B park:**
   - A Class B park is Crown land designated under the Park Act whose management and development are constrained by the act. They are different from Class A parks only with respect to the "test" that must be met to issue a park use permit. Sections 8 and 9 of the Park Act are the most pertinent in this regard and direct that a park use permit must not be issued respecting an interest in land or natural resources "unless, in the opinion of the minister, to do so is not detrimental to the recreational values of the park concerned." Accordingly, Class B parks may permit a broader range of activities and uses provided that such uses are not detrimental to the recreational values of the park.
   - Class B parks are established by order in council.

3. **Class C park:**
   - A Class C park is Crown land designated under the Park Act whose management and development are constrained by the Park Act. The requirements for the management of Class C parks with respect to restricting the alienation of interests and protecting natural resources are identical to those for Class A parks.
   - Class C parks are established by order in council.
   - A Class C park must be managed by a local board appointed by the minister.

4. **Conservancy:**
   - A conservancy is Crown land designated under the Park Act or by the Protected Areas of Brit-

ish Columbia Act whose management and development are constrained by the Park Act.
   - The conservancy designation explicitly recognizes the importance of these areas to First Nations for social, ceremonial, and cultural uses.
   - Commercial logging, mining, and hydroelectric power generation, other than local run-of-the-river projects, are prohibited in a conservancy.
   - Conservancies provide for a wider range of low impact, compatible economic opportunities than a Class A park. These economic opportunities must still not restrict, prevent, or hinder the conservancy from meeting its intended purpose with respect to maintaining biological diversity; natural environments; First Nations social, ceremonial, and cultural uses; and recreational values.
   - Conservancies can be designated by two means: by order in council under the Park Act or by inclusion in a schedule to the Protected Areas of British Columbia Act. Presently, all conservancies are established by inclusion in schedules to the Protected Areas of British Columbia Act.

5. **Recreation area:**
   - A recreation area is defined as Crown land reserved or set aside for public recreational use.
   - Recreation areas are different from parks in that the minister has greater discretion in issuing park use permits.
   - The recreation area designation has evolved over time. In the past, prior to consideration for designation as Class A parks, lands had to be open for a minimum interim period of 10

years to permit mineral resource evaluation. During this time, primacy was given to conservation and recreation values as no other industrial activities were permitted. With the introduction of the Protected Areas Strategy and strategic land-use planning processes, all recreation areas are being evaluated from both a protected area value perspective and an economic opportunity perspective to determine whether the area should be "upgraded" to full protected area status (i.e., Class A park) or returned to integrated resource management lands.

- Recreation areas are established by order in council.

6. **Ecological reserves:**
- The purpose of the Ecological Reserve Act is to reserve Crown land for ecological purposes, including the following areas:

  o Areas suitable for scientific research and educational purposes associated with studies in productivity and other aspects of the natural environment
  o Areas that are representative examples of natural ecosystems in British Columbia
  o Areas that serve as examples of ecosystems that have been modified by human beings and offer an opportunity to study the recovery of the natural ecosystem from modification
  o Areas where rare or endangered native plants and animals in their natural habitat may be preserved
  o Areas that contain unique and rare examples of botanical, zoological, or geological phenomena

- The legislation guiding the program is restrictive, and all extractive activities are prohibited. As such, ecological reserves are considered to be the areas most highly protected and least subject to human influence.
- Ecological reserves can be established by two means: by order in council under the Ecological Reserve Act or by inclusion in schedules to the Protected Areas of British Columbia Act.

7. **Designations under the Environment and Land Use Act:**
- The Environment and Land Use Act is a broad piece of legislation that empowers a Land Use Committee of Cabinet to ensure that all aspects of the preservation and maintenance of the natural environment are fully considered In the administration of land use and resource development. Orders can be made respecting the environment or land use.
- Protected area designations under the Environment and Land Use Act are by order in council.
- Management direction for protected areas is provided by any special conditions included in the establishing order in council and specified provisions of the Park Act and Park, Conservancy, and Recreation Area Regulation as identified in the order in council.

*Park designations have been reprinted with permission from British Columbia Parks. Further information related to park classifications can be found at http://www.env.gov.bc.ca/bcparks/aboutBCParks/prk_desig.html

OUTDOOR RECREATIONAL RESOURCES IN CANADA'S TERRITORIES

Outdoor recreational opportunities and resources in Canada's three territories (Yukon, Northwest Territories, and Nunavut) are vast and diverse. Territories are different from Canadian provinces in that they receive their mandates directly from the federal government, whereas provinces are self-governing. The territories represent some of the least populated parts of the country, yet they contain wilderness expanses that eclipse many other nations' largest wilderness areas. Northern Canada, often referred to simply as "the North," is an icon for the people of Canada, and for the purposes of this chapter, it represents the final piece of Canada's outdoor recreation identity. Although only a small percentage of Canadians live or venture to the North, many strongly identify with the wide-ranging wilderness in the territories, which has helped to further fuse a reverence for nature into Canada's identity.

For example, the Yukon (derived from the Locheux native word *Yuk-un-ah*, meaning great river in reference to the Yukon river) Territory is perhaps most well known for the adventures of the gold rush that began in 1896. These adventures helped to put the Yukon on the map as a Canadian territory in 1898 (Historica Canada, 2014). The Yukon Territory also contains remarkable wilderness expanses such as Kluane National Park. Kluane connects with three other magnificent wilderness areas: Wrangell–St. Elias and Glacier Bay National Park inside of USA's Alaska and Tatshenshini–Alsek Park in British Columbia. Kluane contains the highest mountains in Canada, including Mt. Logan at nearly 6,000 meters and the most continuous glacial ice fields in the country. Kluane attracts a variety of outdoor recreationists due to its diverse landscape. As a destination for outdoor recreation, Kluane is best known for its trail and backcountry hiking, mountaineering, and white-water rafting (Parks Canada, 2014a).

Situated between the Yukon Territory and Nunavut, the Northwest Territories contain many noteworthy outdoor recreational resources including sharing part of the mighty Wood Buffalo National Park with Alberta, one of the largest national parks in the world. Another noteworthy park in the Northwest Territories is Nahanni National Park Reserve. The South Nahanni River begins as a small stream in the Mackenzie Mountains and travels 580 kilometers through mountain valleys and deep canyons, with one waterfall (Virginia Falls) that has twice the vertical drop of Niagara Falls. Many consider the South Nahanni to be one of the most spectacular wilderness rivers in the world. Because of its unique ecological and geographical features, the South Nahanni was named as a UNESCO (United Nations Educational, Scientific, Cultural, and Cultural Organization) World Heritage Site in 1978 and as a Canadian Heritage River in 1987 in part due to its recreational significance (Parks Canada, 2014b).

Nunavut, from the *Inuktitut* (an Inuit language) word meaning our land, is Canada's largest and eastern-most territory. Parks Nunavut (2014) provides an excellent description of this diverse territory:

> For 4,000 years, Inuit and their ancestors have survived in a place that others perceive to be one of the world's harshest and most desolate environments—the treeless Arctic. In reality, at more than two million square kilometres, Nunavut's landscape is stunningly varied—vast tundra, wide seas, wild rivers and small, friendly communities. (para. 1)

As the preceding quotation attests, Nunavut is perhaps most well known for its Arctic character, but includes great diversity within its landscapes and outdoor recreational offerings. One of the most prominent of these is Baffin Island, which is an extension of the Canadian Shield and contains Nunavut's capital, Iqaluit, which has also been described as an important access point to Greenland. It is thought that one of the major ice sheets that covered most of Canada originated on or near Baffin Island 18,000 years ago—and much of the island is still covered by ice today. Baffin is the largest island in Canada and is the fifth largest island in the world. Baffin

Island's Auyuittuq National Park is Canada's first national park north of the Arctic Circle. *Sirmilik* (meaning place of glaciers) National Park is situated on the northwest part of the island and, as its name implies, is mostly glacier covered and shaped. Due to its northern position, Baffin Island also helps produce valuable data related to understanding human-induced climate change ("Baffin Island," 2014).

SUMMARY

Canada's vast landscapes and weather patterns, rich cultural history, the emergence of provincial and national parks, and the mystique of the North have shaped the Canadian outdoor recreation identity in many ways. Canadian landscapes have shaped that identity in their diversity and hard-to-travel features such as the Canadian Shield, which forced early peoples to develop tenacity and foresight reflected by the Aboriginal, English, and French use of the iconic canoe to hunt, travel, and explore the country. Cold winters shaped the Canadian outdoor recreation identity in the development and ensuing popularity of outdoor recreational pursuits and activities such as curling, snowshoeing, skiing, and other winter activities. The Canadian outdoor recreation identity originally shaped by Aboriginal peoples, English, and French has evolved into a rich multicultural mosaic as Canada is proud to be one of the most diverse countries in the world. Many of Canada's vast open spaces were transformed into parks at the federal level, beginning with Banff National Park in 1885, with many more following shortly thereafter. The provincial park systems have unique histories in each of the 10 provinces but share many similarities in their focus on improving quality of life for lands, wildlife, and people. Finally, Canadian territories and a sense of the North have shaped the Canadian outdoor recreation identity by their sheer size, cultural significance, vast wilderness character, and mystery. Overall, the Canadian outdoor recreation identity is fueled by a richness of natural and cultural resources and recreational opportunities. Canadians will continue to revere and celebrate outdoor recreation as part of their national identity.

REFERENCES

Alberta Tourism, Parks, and Recreation. (2012). Our history. Retrieved December 6, 2012, from http://albertaparks.ca/albertaparksca/about-us/our-history.aspx#Birth

Alberta Tourism, Parks, and Recreation. (2012). Plan for parks. Retrieved December 6, 2012, from http://albertaparks.ca/albertaparksca/about-us/plan-for-parks.aspx

Boyd, S. W., & Butler, R. W. (2000). Tourism and national parks: The origin of the concept. In R. W. Butler & S. W. Boyd (Eds.), *Tourism and national parks: Issues and implications* (pp. 13–27). New York, NY: John Wiley & Sons.

British Columbia Parks. (2012a). About BC parks. Retrieved June 20, 2012, from http://www.env.gov.bc.ca/bcparks/aboutBCParks.html

British Columbia Parks. (2012b). B.C. quick facts: Gateway to the Pacific. Retrieved August 13, 2014, from http://www.gov.bc.ca/bcfacts/index.html

Campbell, C. E. (2011). Governing a kingdom: Parks Canada, 1911–2011. In C. E. Campbell (Ed.), *A century of Parks Canada 1911–2011* (pp. 1–19). Calgary, Canada: University of Calgary Press.

Carr, E. (2006). *Hundreds and thousands: The journals of Emily Carr*. Vancouver, Canada: Douglas and McIntyre.

Baffin Island. (2014). In *The Canadian Encyclopedia.* Retrieved August 25, 2014, from http://www.thecanadianencyclopedia.ca/en/article/baffin-island/

Baker, W. (1982). *Sports in the western world*. Totowa, NJ: Rowan and Littlefield.

Blanchard, K., & Cheska, A. (1985). *The anthropology of sport: An introduction*. South Hadley, MA: Bergin and Garvey.

Canadian Parks and Wilderness Society. (2012). About the Canadian Parks and Wilderness Society. Retrieved June 5, 2012, from http://cpaws.org/about

Colpitts, G. (2002). 'Animated like us by commercial interests': Commercial ethnology and fur trade descriptions in New France 1660–1760. *Canadian Historical Review, 83*(3), 305–337.

Discover Nova Scotia. (2013). Nova Scotia's parks. Retrieved July 9, 2013, from http://www.novascotia.com/en/home/discovernovascotia/outdooradventure/provincialparks/default.aspx

Douville, R., & Casanova, J. (1967). *Daily life in early Canada.* New York, NY: MacMillan.

Glooscap Heritage Centre. (2013). Legend of Glooscap. Retrieved July 9, 2013, from http://www.glooscapheritagecentre.com/who-is-glooscap.html

Government of Newfoundland and Labrador. (2013a). About Newfoundland and Labrador. Retrieved July 9, 2013, from http://www.gov.nl.ca/aboutnl/location.html

Government of Newfoundland and Labrador. (2013b). Avalon wilderness reserve. Retrieved July 9, 2013, from http://www.env.gov.nl.ca/env/parks/wer/r_aw/index.html

Government of Newfoundland and Labrador. (2013c). Department of Environment and Conservation. Retrieved July 9, 2013, from http://www.env.gov.nl.ca/env/department/branches/divisions/parks.html

Government of Newfoundland and Labrador. (2013d). Ecological reserves. Retrieved July 9, 2013, from http://www.env.gov.nl.ca/env/parks/wer/eres.html

Government of Newfoundland and Labrador. (2013e). Experience adventure, interpretation, hiking, camping, nature. Retrieved July 9, 2013, from http://www.env.gov.nl.ca/env/publications/parks/parks_web.pdf

Government of Prince Edward Island. (2013a). About Prince Edward Island. Retrieved January 9, 2013, from http://www.gov.pe.ca/infopei/index.php3?number=13033&lang=E

Government of Prince Edward Island. (2013b). Wildlife management areas. Retrieved January 9, 2013, from http://www.gov.pe.ca/infopei/index.php3?number=67794&lang=E

Government of Saskatchewan. (2012a). Athabasca Sand Dunes Provincial Park. Retrieved August 15, 2012, from http://www.saskparks.net/Default.aspx?DN=468f5b70-ab8c-4f28-95b2-bd178dcd2f2b

Government of Saskatchewan. (2012b). Conservation. Retrieved August 15, 2012, from http://www.saskparks.net/conservation

Guillet, E. (1933). *Early life in upper Canada.* Toronto, Canada: University of Toronto Press.

Heintzman, P. (2007). The environmental ethics of Bill Mason: A model for environmental education. *Canadian Journal of Environmental Education, 12,* 160–174.

Historica Canada. (2014). Klondike Gold Rush. Retrieved, August 22, 2014, from http://www.thecanadianencyclopedia.ca/en/article/klondike-gold-rush/

Island Trails. (2013). The Confederation Trail. Retrieved, January 13, 2013, from http://www.islandtrails.ca/en/confederation-trail.php

Johnson, R. (1979). Leisure in Canada. In H. Ibrahim & J. Shivers (Eds.), *Leisure: Emergence and expansion.* Los Alamitos, CA: Hwong.

Kent, T. (1999). Manufacture of birchbark canoes for the fur trade in the St. Lawrence. In B. Hodgins, J. Jennings, & D. Small (Eds.), *The canoe in Canadian cultures* (pp. 100–143). Toronto, Canada: The Dundurn Group.

Mason, B. (Director). (1978). *Song of the paddle* [Documentary]. Montreal, QC: National Film Board of Canada.

Mason, B. (1980). *Path of the paddle.* Toronto, Canada: Van Nostrand Reinhold.

Mason, B. (Producer & Director). (1984). *Waterwalker* [Motion picture]. Ottawa, Canada: National Film Board of Canada and Imago.

Mason, B. (1988). *Song of the paddle.* Toronto, Canada: Key Porter Books.

Mason, B. (1995). *Canoescapes.* North York, Canada: Stoddart.

Manitoba Government. (2012). *Park planning: A system plan for Manitoba's parks*. Retrieved December 5, 2012, from http://www.gov.mb.ca/conservation/parks/pdf/planning/manitoba_parks_system_plan.pdf

McFarland, E. (1970). *The development of public recreation in Canada*. Ottawa, Canada: Canadian Parks and Recreation Association.

Montgomery, L. M. (2000). *Anne of Green Gables*. Northamptonshire, United Kingdom: Oxford University Press.

New Brunswick Department of Natural Resources. (2012). Our history. Retrieved from http://www2.gnb.ca/content/gnb/en/departments/natural_resources/ForestsCrownLands/content/OurHistory.html

Niagara Parks Commission. (2012). History. Retrieved June 20, 2012, from http://corporate.niagaraparks.com/about-the-commission/history/

Nova Scotia Canada. (2013). History of the Nova Scotia provincial park system. Retrieved July 9, 2013, from http://novascotia.ca/natr/strategy/parks/history.asp

Ontario Parks. (2014a). Bonnechere. Retrieved August 13, 2014, from http://www.ontarioparks.com/park/bonnechere

Ontario Parks. (2014b). Inverhuron. Retrieved August 13, 2014, from, http://www.ontarioparks.com/park/inverhuron

Ontario Parks. (2014c). Killarney. Retrieved August 13, 2014, from http://www.ontarioparks.com/park/killarney

Ontario Parks. (2014d). Pushkin Hills. Retrieved August 13, 2014, from http://www.ontarioparks.com/nonoperating/pushkinhills

Ontario Parks. (2014e). Noganosh Lake. Retrieved August 13, 2014, from http://www.ontarioparks.com/nonoperating/noganoshlake

Ontario Parks. (2014f). Shorthills. Retrieved August 13, 2014, from, http://www.ontarioparks.com/nonoperating/shorthills

Parks Canada. (2012a). National parks of Canada: Ecological integrity. Retrieved June 5, 2012, from http://www.pc.gc.ca/eng/progs/np-pn/ie-ei.aspx

Parks Canada. (2012b). National parks of Canada: National parks list. Retrieved June 5, 2012, from http://www.pc.gc.ca/progs/np-pn/recherche-search_e.asp?p=1

Parks Canada. (2014a). Kluane National Park and Reserve. Retrieved August 22, 2014, from http://www.pc.gc.ca/eng/pn-np/yt/kluane/natcul/info-fact.aspx

Parks Canada. (2014b). Nahanni National Park Reserve of Canada. Retrieved August 22, 2014, from http://www.pc.gc.ca/eng/pn-np/nt/nahanni/natcul/natcul1.aspx#sig

Parks Nunavut. (2014). People and places. Retrieved August 25, 2014, from http://nunavutparks.ca/english/park-planning/people-places.html

Parcs Québec. (2012). Mission. Retrieved December 4, 2012, from http://www.sepaq.com/pq/mission.dot

Peake, M. (1993). Meet the Voyageurs. *Che-Mun: The Journal of Canadian Wilderness Canoeing,* Outfit 69.

Plummer, R. (2009). *Outdoor recreation: An introduction*. New York, NY: Routledge.

Raffan, J. (1996). *Fire in the bones: Bill Mason and the Canadian canoeing tradition*. New York, NY: Harper-Collins E-Books.

State of Ontario's protected areas report. (2011). Retrieved June 5, 2012, from http://www.mnr.gov.on.ca/stdprodconsume/groups/lr/@mnr/@sorr/documents/document/stdprod_085564.pdf

Statistics Canada. (2012). Population and dwelling counts, for Canada, provinces and territories, 2011 and 2006 censuses. Retrieved June 3, 2012, from http://www12.statcan.gc.ca/census-recensement/2011/dp-pd/hlt-fst/pd-pl/Table-Tableau.cfm?LANG=Eng&T=101&S=50&O=A

Tourism Prince Edward Island. (2013). Provincial parks. Retrieved, January 9, 2013, from http://www.tourismpei.com/pei-provincial-parks

Tourism New Brunswick. Mount Carleton Provincial Park. Retrieved from http://www.tourismnewbrunswick.ca/Products/M/Mount-Carleton-Provincial-Park.aspx

Part Three

Management, Education, and Participation

The chapters in the last section of this volume deal with the policies, procedures, and problems in the management of outdoor recreational resources. Chapter 12 includes the policies in the management of these resources. We discuss management procedures such as charging fees, carrying capacity, and visitor management in Chapter 13. We discuss education of the participants and the training of outdoor recreation personnel in Chapter 14. Chapter 15 includes some of the activities that could be pursued out-of-doors which, without prudent use, may lead to problems. To reduce overuse and/or abuse of the limited natural resources where outdoor recreational activities occur, we include potential problems and solutions in Chapter 16.

Chapter 12

Management Policies in Outdoor Recreation

Can Americans continue to pursue their outdoor recreational activities without destroying America's natural resources? Recreation impact increases as one moves from the urban and developed end of the recreational opportunity spectrum toward its primitive and wild end. Vegetation and soil impacts are a problem in wilderness areas. A discussion on the policies toward American natural resources will provide the needed background for understanding current strategies that are intended to keep natural resources available for recreational use for many years to come.

There are two management policies used to govern the natural areas used for recreation in this country. The first policy is based on the preservation principle, which is followed in most of America's federal parks and is followed somewhat in state and local parks. The second policy, which is based on the multiple-use principle, is followed in federal, state, and private forests.

PRESERVATION POLICY

Only about 3% of the world's land area is now devoted to the preservation of nature. The United States has set aside approximate-ly 8% of its land under this policy, for single or restricted use (Ibrahim & Cordes, 2003).

The legislation that established the first national park, Yellowstone, is important in that it provided the basis for the concept that federal land would be dedicated and set apart as a public park or pleasuring ground for the benefit and enjoyment of the people (Frakt & Rankin, 1982). The park was established by an act of Congress in 1872. By the turn of the century, four more national parks had been established. The executive branch of the federal government had the authority to reserve land from the public domain and preserve it in its current status. Prior to 1910, this authority was exercised repeatedly for purposes including the establishment of wildlife reserves. Other purposes include the establishment of Indian and military reservations, reservation of timberland, and withdrawal of land from its current use pending classification. In 1906, the Antiquities Act was passed, which authorized the president of the United States to reserve lands with scenic beauty and scientific importance. In 1916, Congress established the National Park Service. The act creating this agency specified its purpose as follows:

To conserve the scenery and the natural and historic objects and the wildlife therein and to provide for the enjoyment of the same in such manner and by such means as will leave them unimpaired for the enjoyment of future generations. (Everhart, 1972)

According to Nash (1990), the passage of the National Park Service Act did not change the original concept of public enjoyment. It is clear in hindsight that pleasure-seeking people could (and did) impair nature despite the legislative stipulation that the scenery and wildlife at parks should be left "unimpaired." Nash wrote of how Stephen Mather, the first director of the National Park Service, was instructed by his boss, the secretary of the interior, in a letter dated May 13, 1918, to let the public enjoy the parks in the manner that best satisfied individual taste. In other words, no attempts were made then to define what kind of enjoyment was appropriate in a natural setting.

Nash (1990) believes that the concept of preservation of natural conditions was set aside for a time, and efforts appear to have been directed toward having the National Park Service stand on its own feet in its early years. A circus image of parks was generated, with drive-through sequoias, soap-sudded geysers, bear feedings, and caged wildlife as the techniques used to attract visitors. The firefall replaced the chicken fall in Yosemite where a giant wood fire on top of Glacier Point, 3,000 feet above the valley floor, was pushed over the cliff as music was played. This activity was not questioned until the late 1960s.

The results of these activities were on the minds of those who legislated for Everglades National Park in 1934. Their bill specified that no development of the project or plan for the entertainment of visitors should be undertaken that would interfere with preservation of natural conditions (Nash, 1990). George Wright and Lowell Sumner of the National Park Service helped to bring to the agency's attention the need for preservation by urging the establishment of a recreation

saturation point or a carrying capacity. This was defined as the maximum degree of the highest type of recreational use that a wilderness can receive consistent with its long-term preservation (Nash, 1990).

The Division of Forestry of the Department of Agriculture became the U.S. Forest Service in the early years of the 20th century. Soon thereafter, recreation was added as one of the multiple uses of the national forests. Preservation was not a priority, and roads and structures grew all over national forests. Two foresters, Arthur Carhart and Aldo Leopold, were instrumental in setting aside large blocks of acreage, which became the United States', and perhaps the world's, first designated wilderness (see Chapter 7). Preservation of these wilderness areas revolved around limiting the modes of travel permitted in them, but not the number of visitors to them. Later preservation was underscored with the establishment of research reserves, which included virgin forests of scientific importance. Today, these are called experimental stations.

Another pioneer in the preservation of wilderness areas was Robert Marshall who, as director of the Forestry Division of the U.S. Office of Indian Affairs, crusaded the curtailment of road building in primitive areas. Both he and Aldo Leopold were instrumental in forming The Wilderness Society. The Wilderness Society intervenes directly with government officials to halt projects that may threaten wilderness. The society has found it necessary to sue in court for this very purpose.

Preservation through management became the focus of attention of the Sierra Club in the late 1930s. Proposals were numerous, including the curtailing of buildings and use of trails, certification of outdoorsmen, and limits on overnight camping. The Sierra Club sponsored the High Sierra Wilderness Conference in 1949, which grew to today's Biennial Wilderness Conference. The idea of a National Wilderness Preservation System did not materialize until 1964 with the passage of the Wilderness Act. But this took hard work on the part of the preservationists fighting those who wanted to dam wild rivers and exploit the wilderness.

Absolute preservation dictates no human use, but even then there is no way to preserve a landscape as natural processes bring about change. In Bryce Canyon National Park, erosion has formed the innumerable highly colored pinnacles, walls, and spires that visitors come to see. Essentially, managers identify aspects of the biophysical and social environments that are important and can be monitored for change as recreational use proceeds.

The Wilderness Act of 1964 directed the secretaries of agriculture and the interior to review lands within their jurisdictions and recommend their suitability as wilderness areas. The earlier legislation emphasized pleasuring and enjoyment, but this time the law specified that the protected land was to be enjoyed as *wilderness* (Nash, 1990). Wilderness was defined as an area where the earth and its community of life are untrammeled (uninterrupted) by humans and where each person is considered a visitor only. If wilderness is not managed according to this definition, the alternatives are either to prohibit all use of wilderness areas or to permit an open door policy that will eventually lead to the destruction of wilderness areas.

In 1975, the Eastern Wilderness Act allowed select Forest Service areas east of the 100th meridian to be included as wilderness areas although they did not meet the criteri-

on of being free from human influence. They were to be allowed to revert to their natural condition. A few years later, a large section in Alaska was added to the system. By the mid-1980s, the National Wilderness Preservation System consisted of 445 areas totaling about 89 million acres, most of which were in Alaska. This led to an additional 700 units covering more than 1 million acres as stipulated in the Federal Land Policy and Management Act of 1976, under which the Bureau of Land Management set aside 8% of its land. These lands will help in sustaining natural sources and biological diversity. This larger system is more complete now because it includes representation of many of the country's ecosystems. In addition, many are located near urban centers. At the same time, developments in science and scholarship have evolved, making this highest level of preservation management more challenging.

WILDERNESS PRESERVATION, PRINCIPLES, AND STEWARDSHIP

The four managing agencies, under the Department of Agriculture and the Department of the Interior, are assigned the enormous task of overseeing the diverse National Wilderness Preservation System. Despite that the USDA Forest Service and Bureau of Land Management adhere to the multiple-use principle and that the National Park Service and U.S. Fish and Wildlife Service hold to the concept of preservation or single-use principle, the Wilderness Act bonds them together in planning, implementing, and monitoring the wilderness system for the use and enjoyment of people today and in the future (Wilderness.net, 2006). Each agency allows fishing in the wilderness, for instance, but their policies as to how it is to be conducted and managed may vary significantly. To guide wilderness activities, an understanding of wilderness values is necessary. The basics of the program as set out in the Wilderness Act are direct and follow ("Wilderness Act," 2007):

1. The wilderness lands that are protected are areas of public lands.
2. Congress designates selected portions of national forests, parks, wildlife refuges, and other public lands.
3. Human influences are restrained in wilderness units so nature can change as it wills.
4. Wilderness areas serve multiple uses consistent with the Wilderness Act mandate to preserve the character of the area, including watershed, agriculture, and endangered species.
5. They are a resource for diverse types of outdoor recreational activities so long as they are not motorized or do not make use of mechanical vehicles or equipment.

Over the past three-plus decades, much has been learned about wilderness management. It involves facilitating human use, car-

ing for and restoring wilderness resources, developing sound plans based on clearly articulated objectives, monitoring, funding, managing public and business relations, and promoting continued understanding through research. The question for the future is, should this be done in the generally understood manner that would call for acts of directing, guiding, controlling, and improving the natural outcomes? Because wilderness by definition is to be "untrammeled by man," many scholars and managers regard "stewardship" as the most appropriate perspective for safeguarding this unique resource in the future. An obstacle to this way of thinking is that federal agency cultures rarely reward those within its ranks who have shown the courage of their best professional judgment to do nothing or to manage in an uncontrolled manner (Pinchot Institute, 2001). To regulate human use and to preserve the quality, character, and integrity of those protected lands so the wilderness remains undisturbed for centuries, the Pinchot Institute (2001), comprising leaders in the field, recommends the following guidelines to improve wilderness stewardship in the new century:

1. Adhering to the Wilderness Act is a fundamental principle for wilderness stewardship in the United States.
2. U.S. wilderness is to be treated as a system of wildernesses.
3. Wildernesses are special places and are to be treated as special.
4. Stewardship should be science informed, logically planned, and publicly transparent.
5. Nondegradation of wilderness fundamentally should guide stewardship activities.
6. Preservation of wilderness character is a guiding idea of the Wilderness Act.
7. Recognizing the wild in wilderness distinguishes wilderness from other land classes.
8. Accountability is basic to sound stewardship.

To meet the challenges of wilderness stewardship and the preceding principles, the four wilderness agencies should or must do the following (Pinchot Institute, 2001):

1. Make a strong commitment to wilderness stewardship before the wilderness system is lost.
2. Organize to maximize stewardship effectiveness and develop a fully integrated stewardship system across the wilderness system.
3. Accelerate wilderness planning and prepare plans for the guidance of stewardship activities, enhance opportunities for evaluation and accountability, and increase the probability that the wilderness system will be sustained.
4. Enhance science, education, and training programs to provide information, professional expertise, and public support for wilderness stewardship.
5. Create wilderness stewardship positions and career opportunities from top to bottom and deploy financial resources for the explicit stewardship and support of wilderness. The people hired for such positions must be committed to sustaining the wilderness system.
6. Embrace the maintenance and sustainability of the wilderness system.

To manage wilderness as a system means that each area is part of a whole, no matter who administers it. When the future is shaped for success, the result will lead to enhanced opportunities that encourage preservation of some of the world's most beautiful natural areas. To help the four wilderness stewardship agencies to steward it and bring the pieces together, the secretaries should do the following (Pinchot Institute, 2001):

1. Issue joint policies and regulations specifying common interpretations of law and thus provide broad guidelines for the stewardship of wilderness.
2. Devise an organizational structure to make stewardship happen across the agencies so that a high-quality wilderness system continues in perpetuity.
3. Devise monitoring and evaluation systems to ensure that it is known how well wildernesses are being stewarded, especially in the context of a system of wildernesses, and they should regularly report on the state system.
4. Develop a means for informing the American people about the National Wilderness Preservation System and about their wilderness heritage.

On a global basis, the World Wilderness Congress has encouraged the designation and best management of wilderness areas by government agencies. The goal of the eighth world congress was to enhance wilderness stewardship globally.

MULTIPLE-USE POLICY

The multiple-use policy is applicable in most national forests, the lands administered by the Bureau of Land Management, and most state forests. Many activities are allowed under this concept, including grazing, timber cutting, and of course, recreation. The concept was reaffirmed in the Multiple-Use Sustained-Yield Act of 1960. Congress emphasized that the national forests are established and shall be administered for outdoor recreational, range, timber, watershed, and wildlife purposes.

Multiple use means that the management of all renewable surface resources are directed to meet the multiple needs of the American people. *Sustained yield* means the achievement and maintenance in perpetuity of a high-level output of these renewable resources. According to Knudson (1984), the concept of multiple use is slippery, and it is difficult to define to the satisfaction of each group that uses the land. The concept applies to the two largest land management agencies in the United States: the Bureau of Land Management and the USDA Forest Service. In application, certain areas of these two agencies may be administered under a single-use concept, but they should fit within the broad concept of multiple use within the agency. For example, a campground would be restricted to recreational use and a watershed to wildlife protection, and both would fit under the multiple-use concept.

The lands under the jurisdiction of the Bureau of Land Management (BLM) are managed under multiple use as described in the Federal Land Policy and Management Act. The act was passed in 1976, 16 years after the Multiple-Use Sustained-Yield Act of 1960, which regulated the use of national forests. The language of the 1976 act is similar to the language of the 1960 act in that it is stipulated that the lands under the jurisdiction of the BLM should be managed according to the multiple-use and sustained-yield principles. The 1976 act requires that certain areas of BLM lands that are qualified as wilderness areas be included under the National Wilderness Preservation System. The BLM was given 15 years (until 1991) to review its potential wilderness candidates. Although multiple use seems to be a sound policy, its application is met with difficulties. At the core of these difficulties is that different groups view America's natural resources differently. For instance, Knudson (1984) gave the following five views of the American forest.

Native Americans (19th Century and Before)

The forest was home, and nature was a force that could be used but not dominated. Small areas could be used up, but there was always more.

Pilgrims and Pioneers

The forest was a wilderness and the home of a hostile enemy, but it produced food, shelter, and export capital. Though the forest was a necessity, it was believed that the forest must be reduced by a substantial amount.

Lumbermen (at the Turn of the 19th Century)

The forest was a timber mine, a resource. (The forest was not yet treated as a renewable source.)

Foresters

The forest is a renewable resource. It must be protected and nurtured; the timber harvest must be rationalized.

Recreationists

The forest is a service environment. Romantic and aesthetic aspects predominate. Yet interests are in many instances incompatible. Philosophically and legally, the multiple-use concept centers on the greatest total benefit over a long period of time. This makes the task of the contemporary multiple-use manager difficult indeed, particularly because the demand for visitations on federal land increased dramatically, particularly during the second half of the 20th century. Since 1985, demand for recreation has continued to increase 65% on BLM lands and 80% on national wildlife refuges. The Bureau of Reclamation estimates an increase of 10 million recreation visits for a total of 90 million visits to their lakes, and the Forest Service estimates 211 million annual visits at the national forests each year ("Frequently asked questions," 2005).

CLASSIFICATION OF RECREATIONAL RESOURCES

The total area of the United States is 3.62 million square miles, 98% of which is land and 2% inland water. These are the two basic recreational resources.

Land Resources

Of the 2.2 billion acres of land in the United States, 58% is privately owned, 34% is owned by the federal government, 5% by the states, 2% by Native Americans (reservations), and 1% by local governments. There are many ways of classifying recreational sources on these lands. Each system has its own advantages, and various methods will be explained. The Clawson and Knetsch (1966) classification follows.

User-oriented areas are located and designed with the access and use by the visitor as the principal but not only consideration. This classification includes most city and county recreational areas and many commercial areas.

Intermediate areas are located and planned to meet the needs of users, but in areas dictated partially by the resource. These areas are managed with resource maintenance and used as balancing considerations; they include most state parks, forests, and reservoir projects; many fish and wildlife areas; and some commercial recreational areas.

Resource-oriented areas are located and planned with the resource base as the key criterion, with recreational use coming as a result of the resource. The large areas of national forests, most national wildlife refuges, national parks, national resource lands, and some large state properties fall into this category, as do forest industry lands.

Another method of classification is based on identifying the source of the recreational resource. For instance, ownership or jurisdiction is one method to describe the recreational opportunity that will be available. These may include private, industrial, city, county, state, and federal with each word sending a message. This method of classification also follows (Knudson, 1984):

1. **Ownership or jurisdiction classes:** This system does much to describe in a few words the goals and policies affecting the property.
2. **Designation classes:** Within each ownership there are various properties including parks, forests, wildlife areas, nature preserves, memorials, recreational areas, parkways, trails, scenic rivers, lakes, or reservoirs. There are also specific facility designations, such as wilderness, golf course, country club, arboretum, ski area, and camp that help define the character and features of the area. The commonly understood combinations of the jurisdiction and facility designation then quickly describe the recreational resource to people who are familiar with the resource system.

3. **Service area classification:** For people concerned primarily with planning, the classification approach defines the parks and open spaces by size and service areas of public facilities, regardless of the agency managing them. This system is used to define the character of a recreational resource or supply and to point out the resources most needed. A number of states and cities have adopted categories referring to facilities in terms of whether they serve a neighborhood, community, or region (see Chapter 9).

4. **Orientation classification:** This classification defines management and policy purposes in rough groupings as to whether they are user oriented, intermediate, or resource oriented. This merely identifies management emphasis. It is most valuable in explaining the policies of an agency to interested visitors or in interagency discussions of proper roles for resources.

5. **Resource classification:** Within a property, the land base can be classified into resources related to its purpose and intensity of development.

Six classes of resources were proposed by the Outdoor Recreation Resources Review Commission (ORRRC, 1962). This commission was established by the president of the United States in 1958. Its report in 1962 suggested the following classes of outdoor recreational resources:

I. **High-density recreational areas:** Intensively developed and managed for mass use.
   - *Facilities:* Heavy investment concentrated in relatively small areas, many facilities usually present.

- *Use:* Exclusively for recreating: heavy peak load pressures (e.g., weekends).
- *Land use:* Often competes with residential construction and commercial uses due to location near urban centers.
- *Examples:* Beaches, boardwalks, swimming pools, highly developed trailer camps, some mass-use picnic/game areas.

II. **General outdoor recreational areas:** Areas subject to substantial development for specific recreational uses.
- *Facilities:* Many, but usually fewer than in high-density recreational areas—always some human-built facilities.
- *Use:* Accommodates the major share of all outdoor recreation day, weekend, and vacation use. Use is concentrated, but not as much as in Category I. Zoning may be needed.
- *Land use:* Competes with a wide variety of uses due to locations in both urban and rural settings.
- *Examples:* Campsites, picnic areas, ski areas, resorts, coastal areas, hunting preserves.

III. **Natural environment areas:** Areas suitable for recreation in natural environments, intermediate between Categories II and IV.
- *Facilities:* Few and simple; user enjoys resources as is in an environment where humans fend largely for themselves; management emphasis is on the natural rather than the human made. Access roads, trails, primitive camping areas, and safety and fire provisions are present.
- *Use:* Generally dispersed, not concentrated; hunting, birding, fishing, canoeing, rustic camping, sightseeing, snowmobiling, or ORV use (family style).
- *Land use:* Often multiple-use lands; largest class in acreage.

- *Examples:* Most national forest and BLM lands, buffers in national parks. Most of state and county forests, most fish and wildlife areas, most reservoirs.

IV. **Unique natural areas:** Areas of outstanding scenic splendor, natural wonder, or scientific importance.
- *Facilities:* Few—acceptable only if they enhance protection of the natural feature.
- *Use:* Limited to observation and study in many cases. Management is focused on preserving feature, not public demand.
- *Land use:* Areas often small, special; incompatible uses excluded.
- *Examples:* Old Faithful geyser in Wyoming, Old Man of the Mountain in New Hampshire, Bristlecone Pine area of Inyo National Forest in California, nature preserves.

V. **Primitive areas:** Undisturbed roadless areas in a natural wild condition.
- *Facilities:* None except trails, no structures, no machines.
- *Use:* Goal is to provide solitude from evidence of civilization; commercial uses prohibited except guide service. Use may be restricted in order to
  a. provide opportunity for solitude by user and
  b. preserve primitive conditions.
- *Land use:* Competes with several other wildland uses: timber production, grazing, power dam construction, and mining. These uses and roads are generally excluded from primitive areas. (For reasons found acceptable by Congress, mining and grazing have been allowed to continue temporarily in some areas.)
- *Examples:* Gila Wilderness Area in Arizona; most of Rocky Mountain National Park in Colorado; portions of Porcupine Mountain

Different groups have different views regarding America's natural resources. Sometimes these interests are incompatible.

State Park in Michigan; Quetico–Superior Boundary Waters Canoe Area in Minnesota–Ontario; Wood Buffalo National Park in Alberta.

VI. **Historic and cultural sites:** Sites of major historic or cultural significance—local, regional, or national.

- *Facilities:* Emphasis is on restoring and preserving the historic features; facilities usually relate to protection of features during visitor use and interpretation of the historical significance, providing suitable access.
- *Use:* Varies considerably depending upon type and fragility of features; always appropriate to the historic feature. Overuse is prevented, not accommodated.

- *Land use:* Exclusively for appreciation of history and culture and associated recreational values of the site.
- *Examples:* Mt. Vernon in Virginia, Russell Cave in Alabama, Tippecanoe Battlefield in Indiana.

Land Mass

Land mass in the United States can be classified into four categories: forestlands, grasslands, deserts, and tundra. The features and resources of each are varied and are described in greater detail in Chapter 16 (Jensen, 1985).

Forestlands. America was covered with forests initially, but consumptive use of timber over the past two centuries has reduced the area of forest to only about one third of the nation. Forests vary in terrain, elevation, and type of trees that they support. They are an excellent source for many outdoor recreational activities.

Grasslands. The grasslands that supported grazing animals in the past have become America's food basket in the last two centuries. Attempts are now being made to recover as much of America's grasslands as possible for scenic, scientific, and recreational purposes. Heavy vegetation around water resources have high recreational potential. A Great Plains Grasslands National Park has been proposed.

Deserts. Lands receiving less than 10 inches of annual precipitation are generally classified as desert. These range from sand dunes and dry lake beds to plateaus, mountains, and canyons. Despite a concept that deserts may be inhospitable, they are a significant source for outdoor recreation. Traditional outdoor pursuits such as hiking have been augmented with newer ones such as sand sailing. The Bureau of Land Management controls most of the U.S. desert lands that have recreational value.

Tundra. This natural ecosystem around the arctic and alpine zones stretches across the northern section of the continent, with Alaska accounting for most of it. Smaller regions of tundra are found in the Rocky Mountains, the Sierra Nevada, and the Cascades. Tundra lacks trees but contains grasses, hedges, herbs, and shrubs. Its harsh winter makes recreational pursuits limited. In addition, its vegetation is too delicate to allow for mass leisure pursuits. The Bureau of Land Management and the National Park Service own most of the lands that are classified as tundra in the United States.

Water Resources

Water resources that are used for recreation can be classified into rivers, wetlands, shorelines, lakes, and reservoirs (see also Chapter 16).

Rivers. Although most American rivers are found in segments of 25 miles (40 kilometers) or less, these rivers serve as transportation routes with adjacent trails. There is approximately over 3.25 million miles (5.24 million kilometers) of rivers in the United States, some of which are free flow-

ing through natural settings (Delaware Ricer Basin Commission, 2006). Accordingly, rivers provide unique opportunities for leisure pursuits. Among these are swimming, boating, and fishing as well as rafting, kayaking, and canoeing (see Chapter 15).

Wetlands. This term describes marshes, swamps, bogs, wet meadows, and shallow ponds. It is estimated that there are about 100 million acres of wetlands in the lower United States (Environmental Protection Agency, 2006). Examples of wetlands are the Everglades in Florida, Hackensack Meadowlands in New Jersey, and the Great Dismal Swamp in Virginia. The recreational opportunities provided in wetlands include fishing, hunting, trapping, bird-watching, hiking, canoeing, and photography.

Shorelines. The coastlines around and within the United States total around 100,000 miles, or 161,000 kilometers. Most of the American coastline is developed; 70% of the continental U.S. coastline is privately owned. The federal government controls 11% of the coastline; state and local governments control 19%. This does not mean that the 30% of coastline controlled by government is available for public recreation. Topographically, only 10% of American coastline, or only 10,000 miles, is available for public recreation, including aquatic activities such as swimming, boating, sailing, fishing, and diving. Camping, hiking, and picnicking also take place along the coast.

Lakes. There are close to 100,000 natural lakes in the United States, varying in size from a prairie pond to the expansive Great Lakes (Environmental Protection Agency, 2006). The leisure pursuits on these lakes vary from swimming and fishing to sailing, boating, and waterskiing. At the lakeshores, recreationists camp, hike, picnic, jog, walk, and watch birds. The surface acreage of fresh water available for recreation is about 22 million acres, comprising natural lakes and human-made reservoirs.

Reservoirs. There are close to 50,000 reservoirs in this country, which have been constructed by government agencies and private individuals for the purpose of flood control, generating electricity, or providing water for irrigation. Most of these reservoirs are small, some are medium size, and a few are large. The medium ones were built with the help of the Soil Conservation Service or the Fish and Wildlife Service. The larger ones were built under the direction of the Bureau of Land Management, the U.S. Army Corps of Engineers, or the Tennessee Valley Authority, as can be seen in Chapter 7.

PLANNING FOR OUTDOOR RECREATION

Planning considers the general purpose related to the service being offered or suggested. In the case of outdoor recreation, the objective is to provide constructive leisure pursuits in a safe, natural environment. The work of the scholars who were concerned with leisure in the early years of the 20th century set the tone for such an objective. The formation of the Playground Association of America was in conjunction with advocacy for the children's welfare. Local, state, and federal agencies as well as private organizations began programs to fulfill this objective. As industrialization, automation, and urbanization increased, so did the demand for organized leisure pursuits, including outdoor recreational experiences.

By the middle of the 20th century, public interest in recreation was heightened when the demand for expanded facilities led to a crisis in outdoor recreation. The crisis was responded to with massive state and federal reinvestment in the public estate of outdoor recreation. This response included numerous state bond issues, the Forest Service's Operation Outdoor, and the National Park Service's Mission 66 (La Page, 1988). Most important was President Eisenhower's decision to appoint the ORRRC. It became clear from analyzing past offerings and considering present programs that planning is important for the future of outdoor recreation.

Planning Procedures

Planning is based on the policies, regulations, and goals of the agency or agencies involved. In addition, the public is involved in the planning procedure. Following are six methods of public involvement (Jensen, 1985):

1. Public meetings where people have a chance to hear proposals and voice their support or resistance.
2. Coverage in the news media. This exposes ideas and alternatives to the public and stimulates involvement.
3. The appointment of advisory committees to represent the public.
4. Public surveys or polls to provide information for the planning process.
5. Agency sensitivity to views of members of the public.
6. Presentations at the meetings of service clubs, political groups, and auxiliary organizations and through written strategic plans.

Stages in the planning procedure: After forming an advisory board, the following steps are taken:

1. The city council and/or the board should determine the guiding principles for designing the facility (i.e., the relation to the master plan, current and future needs, and realistic cost).
2. Services of a consultant may be beneficial. Qualifications of the consultant are important.
3. Data on enrollment trends, demographic changes, and new standards should be included.
4. Survey existing facilities as to size, features, conditions, and current standards. These figures are compared with currently acceptable standards.
5. Calculate the cost of the facility. The input by a consultant is useful at this point or a visit to a nearby facility may help this endeavor.
6. Prepare a document that describes the steps taken and includes the data collected. The document should be widely distributed and feedback required.

There are four levels of recreation plans in the United States that need to be considered. These are national plans, state comprehensive plans, local plans (city, district, or county), and project plans.

Regardless of the level of the plan, the following 12 principles are considered (Jensen, 1985):

1. Park and recreational areas provide opportunities for all persons regardless of race, creed, age, gender, or economic status.
2. To meet the needs in a particular geographic area, consideration is made of all the resources available, including lakes and streams, woodlands, marshes, mountains, historic and archeological sites, areas of scenic value, and areas of special interest.
3. Multiple use can often add to the total use of an area; therefore, it is considered even though it is not always accepted.
4. Early acquisition of land based on a comprehensive recreation plan is essential. Unless sites are acquired well in advance of demand, land costs often become prohibitive.
5. Timely evaluation is made of present recreational needs and future trends to project accurately for the future.
6. Insofar as possible, recreational areas and facilities are properly distributed in accordance with the population so all of the people have approximately equal availability of recreational opportunities.
7. The design of individual park and recreational sites is as flexible as possible to accommodate changing patterns of recreation in the given area.
8. Barriers are avoided whenever possible to provide for easy access to recreational areas by older adults, persons with disabilities, and others with mobility restrictions.
9. There should be citizen involvement in planning whenever possible because this results in good ideas and added enthusiasm toward using the areas once they are developed.
10. Responsibilities should be defined and agreed upon by governmental and private agencies so the duplication of areas, facilities, and services will be avoided and so the public will receive the best return possible on the dollars spent.
11. Park and recreational lands are protected in perpetuity against encroachment and nonrecreational purposes. These areas should not be considered the path of least resistance for highways, public utilities, and buildings.
12. The plan for a particular recreational area or the plan for a system of areas and facilities is carefully integrated with the total master plan for the particular agency or area. Park and recreation planning is not an isolated function. It is integrated with the total plan.

NATIONAL OUTDOOR RECREATION PLANS

There were unsuccessful attempts to develop some comprehensive national plans for outdoor recreation after World War I. President Calvin Coolidge called a National Conference on Outdoor Recreation in 1924, where 128 public and private agencies were represented. In the final report, which appeared in the Senate Document No. 158 of May 1928, recommendations were made for future outdoor recreational pursuits. But the recommendations were set aside with the coming of the Great Depression. With the establishment of the Works Progress Administration to ward off unemployment at that time, many facilities and programs were built on federal, state, and local lands. Perhaps due to a lack of planning, roads were built in wild places in national parks and forests by thousands of job-hungry men (Nash, 1990). Federal care threatened to divide and conquer the last really large wilderness areas in the country.

After World War II, federal agencies responded to the increasing demands for outdoor recreational pursuits by developing their own plans such as Mission 66 of the National Park Service and Operation Outdoor of the U.S. Forest Service. The first comprehensive planning effort on a national level was done by the ORRRC in the 1960s.

Outdoor Recreation Resources Review Commission

Upon the suggestion of President Eisenhower, Congress established the ORRRC in 1958. Eight members of Congress and seven private citizens were appointed by the president of the United States to serve on the commission, chaired by Laurance Rockefeller. The commission was charged to survey the outdoor recreational needs of the American people for the following four decades and to recommend a plan of action to meet those needs.

The commission surveyed America's stock of outdoor recreational areas, both actual and potential, and conducted interviews, giving questionnaires to a cross section of the American public in an attempt to discern recreational needs and demands on the natural resources. ORRRC's recommendations were included in its final report to Congress in 1961; the report included 27 volumes, each written on a separate topic.

The ORRRC report defined a policy framework, which divided the responsibilities for outdoor recreation in the United States along the following lines:

1. Local and state governments are to take the basic responsibility for supplying recreational opportunities.
2. The federal government is to preserve areas of national significance.
3. The federal government is to offer financial and technical assistance, provide leadership in getting states to supply increased opportunities, and manage existing federal lands for broad recreational benefits.
4. Individual and private efforts are expected to continue providing places

and activities, equipment, services, and other products and to lead preservation of land through nonprofit groups.

Unless certain actions were taken immediately, the commission recognized that demand would exceed supply in outdoor recreational opportunities in the following years. The problem was compounded by the extant facilities for outdoor recreation being not only overtaxed, but also antiquated. ORRRC's recommendations have been implemented to a remarkable degree. Most important was the establishment of the Bureau of Outdoor Recreation, which provided a federal focus on national planning for outdoor recreation, including the 1973 and 1979 nationwide outdoor recreation plans (Knudson, 1984). The bureau changed its name to the Heritage Conservation and Recreation Service in 1978 and was discontinued in 1981.

Other outcomes of the commission's recommendations include the following:

1. Expansion of the National Park System.
2. Establishment of the National Wilderness System.
3. Inauguration of the Land and Conservation Fund Program.
4. Establishment of the Wild and Scenic Rivers System.
5. Establishment of the National Trail System.
6. Authorization of state and local land acquisition programs.

Public Land Law Review Commission Report (1970)

Congress decided in 1964 that a bipartisan commission was needed to review the nation's land use, laws, and policies. The Public Land Law Review Commission (PLLRC) was to report to Congress the status of land use, the problems associated with such use, and the changes needed for more effective use. Its report of 1970 contained 452 recommendations based on the input of hundreds of economists, planners, and managers. The recommendations related to the recreational use of land were commensurate with the ORRRC's recommendations as follows:

- **Role of the federal government:** The federal government should be responsible for preserving scenic areas, natural wonders, primitive areas, and historic sites of national significance; for cooperating with states through technical and financial assistance; for promoting interstate arrangements; and for managing federal lands for the broadest recreational benefit consistent with other essential uses.
- **Role of state governments:** The states should play a pivotal role in making outdoor recreational opportunities available by effecting the acquisition of land; by developing sites; by providing and maintaining facilities of state or regional significance; by providing assistance to local governments; and by providing leadership and planning.
- **Role of local governments:** Local governments should expand their efforts to provide outdoor recreational opportunities, with particular emphasis on securing open space and developing recreational areas in and around metropolitan and other urban areas.
- **Role of the private sector:** Individual initiative and private enterprise should continue to be the most important force in outdoor recreation, providing many opportunities for a vast number of people, as well as the goods and services used by people in their recreational activities. Government should encourage the work of nonprofit groups wherever possible. It should also stimulate desirable commercial development, which can be particularly effective in providing facilities and services where demand is sufficient to return a profit.

Other recommendations of the PLLRC included the following:

1. Emphasis on the preservation concept for the public land under the jurisdiction of the National Park Service.
2. Continuation of the multiple-use policy of the public lands under the jurisdiction of the Forest Service and the Bureau of Land Management with recreation as a primary use.
3. Purchase of private lands that could provide for right-of-way corridors or access to otherwise inaccessible recreational areas.
4. Expansion of the National Park System, wilderness areas, seashores, and the Wild and Scenic Rivers System.
5. Improvement in the land classification and acquisition program as related to recreation with the use of advanced methods of financing acquisition and allocating funds for development.

Despite its significance to outdoor recreation, the report of the PLLRC has not received much attention because the commission chair, Wayne Aspinell, was not reelected and because there was no single program for implementation (Knudson, 1984). Nonetheless, the report raised a number of national and regional issues pertaining to recreation policy and planning in the United States.

Nationwide Outdoor Recreation Plan of 1973

Public Law 88-29, known as the Organic Act, requires that the secretary of the interior should

> … formulate and maintain a comprehensive nationwide outdoor recreation plan, taking into consideration the plans of the various Federal agencies, States, and their political subdivisions. The plan shall set forth the needs and demands of the public for outdoor recreation and the

current and foreseeable availability in the future of outdoor recreation resources to meet those needs. The plan shall identify critical outdoor recreation problems, recommend solutions, and recommend desirable actions to be taken at each level of government and by private interest. (Jensen & Thorstenson,1977, p. 247)

In 1973, the Bureau of Outdoor Recreation of the Department of the Interior published a national plan entitled *Outdoor Recreation: A Legacy for America*. It was a policy document on the roles of the three levels of government. A draft of the plan was presented to President Richard Nixon earlier with a strong urban emphasis and a multibillion-dollar price tag. The plan was printed for the record by the Senate Interior Committee under the title "The Recreation Imperative." The bureau recommended that 30% of the Land and Water Conservation Fund go to urban centers and that grants should be allowed for operational expenses such as implementing recreational programs (Knudson, 1984). This nationwide recreation plan was based on surveys of over 4,000 persons across the country. The data showed that participation in leisure pursuits had increased sharply since the previous ORRRC study. In the meantime, recreational resources did not increase at the same rate. The bureau called for quick action on part of all three levels of government and the private sector to aid in increasing resources. It also pointed to the increasing problem of pollution of America's natural resources that provide for recreational outlets. Carrying capacity determinants were suggested as an important managerial tool to reduce abuse.

The 1973 plan specified the following functions for the federal government (Jensen, 1985):

1. Complete a program of identification, selection, and planning for acquiring superlative areas needed to round out the federal recreation estate.
2. Continue to use the Land and Water Conservation Fund to acquire needed federal recreational lands and assist the states in doing the same.
3. Open to the public directly or through state and local entities underused portions of federal properties or facilities having public recreational values when such lands are not available for transfer.
4. Accelerate evaluations of proposed trails, wild and scenic rivers, wilderness areas, wetlands, and historic properties to ensure that those unique lands are preserved by federal, state, or local governments or private interests for the benefit of the public, and accelerate the evaluation of federal land holdings to determine if beaches, shorelines, islands, and natural areas can be made available for increased public recreational use.

Furthermore, it was stated in the plan that to improve the management and administration of recreational resources and programs, the federal government will need to do the following:

1. Accelerate the identification and no cost transfer of surplus and underused real property to state and local governments for parks and other recreational sites.
2. When the land is not available for transfer, and direct federal management is not necessary or desirable, take necessary steps to transfer management responsibility for existing recreational units to state and local governments.
3. Promote recreational developments on or near federal lands on the basis of regional land-use plans. Whenever possible, private investment should be used to provide these services.
4. Undertake preparation of recreation land-use plans for all management units and coordinate such planning with all interested federal, state, and local government agencies and private entities.

Nationwide Outdoor Recreation Plan of 1979

The Nationwide Outdoor Recreation Plan of 1979 was different from the plan of 1973 in that it was developed from a series of task force reports on specific issues, which were reviewed by the public and revised accordingly. It also included surveys on recreation preference and participation. The report followed two major themes: an assessment of outdoor recreation and a suggested action program (Jensen, 1985).

Assessment of Outdoor Recreation

The assessment provides a summary of trends, needs, and opportunities, along with benefits accrued from participation in recreational activities. Included were the demographic variables affecting participation and agencies providing facilities and programs, along with a description of problems facing recreation.

Action Program

A program of action was suggested to revolve around nine issues of national significance:

1. **Federal land acquisition:**
   a. A new and more effective planning and decision-making process will be instituted to identify and select lands eligible for the federal portion of the Land and Water Conservation Fund.
   b. A policy will be developed defining the federal role in protecting and acquiring land for conserving natural, cultural, and recreational resources. This policy will encourage alternatives to outright acquisition.
2. **Wild, scenic, and recreational rivers:**
   a. New guidelines will be developed to shorten the time required to study potential wild, scenic, and recreational rivers.
   b. Federal agencies will develop guidelines to avoid adverse effects on potential wild and scenic rivers identified in the nationwide rivers inventory.
   c. Federal land-managing agencies will assess the potential of rivers identified in the nationwide inventory located in their lands and take steps to designate or manage these rivers as components of the National Wild and Scenic Rivers System.
   d. Administration of the Clean Water Act and the Wild and Scenic Rivers Act will be better coordinated to ensure that investments made to clean up rivers and waterways provide maximum public recreational benefits.
3. **National trails and trail systems:**
   a. The Forest Service will establish 145 additional national recreation trails in the National Forest System.
   b. Federal land-managing agencies will establish goals for creating additional national recreation trails on public lands other than national forests.
   c. The Department of the Interior will accelerate its efforts to encourage state, local, and private land managers to submit applications for new national recreation trails.
   d. A grassroots effort will be undertaken across the country to assess national trail needs. This assessment will be made by representatives of state, local, and private trail interests in cooperation with federal agencies.
   e. States, localities, and private landholders will be more actively encouraged to develop trails on their lands and to participate with federal agencies and trail users in creating a national trails system to meet public needs.
   f. The accomplishments of the rail-to-trails program of the Railroad

Revitalization and Regulatory Reform Act will be evaluated and further recommendations made to eliminate outstanding problems.

g. State and local governments will be encouraged to develop appropriate bike ways using existing federal programs.

4. **Water resources:**
   a. Federal water quality grants will be more closely examined to determine the degree to which they include recreational considerations.
   b. Nonstructural alternatives to flood control, including preserving open space for recreation, will be evaluated for their applicability in flood-prone communities.
   c. Actions will be taken to ensure that urban waterfront revitalization projects include considerations for recreation and public access.

5. **Energy conservation:**
   A program of energy conservation will be developed for all recreational lands, facilities, and programs, and guidelines will be issued for all federal recreation grant programs to state and local governments.

6. **Environmental education:**
   Guidelines will be prepared for all Department of the Interior agencies and coordinated with other federal agencies.

7. **Access:**
   a. The Department of the Interior will provide improved access to recreational facilities.
   b. The Department of the Interior will establish procedures to involve citizens with disabilities in developing recreation policies and programs.

8. **The private sector:**
   The feasibility of cooperative agreements between the private sector and public recreation agencies will

be explored as an alternative method of improving public recreation opportunities, and appropriate demonstrations will be undertaken.

9. **Research:**
   A comprehensive national recreation research agenda will be prepared.

To ensure continuous planning, a division for this purpose was established in the National Park Service. Its mission is as follows:

1. To define and monitor the annual action programs.
2. To update the 5-year assessment.
3. To conduct nationwide recreation surveys and coordinate more specialized federal surveys.
4. To compile and update a national research agenda for recreation.
5. To promote long-range planning for the future of recreation in America.

The National Park Service initiated an intensive review of its responsibilities and future plans and presented the findings in a symposium entitled Our National Parks: Challenges and Strategies for the 21st Century. The symposium ended with the creation of a vision composed of six strategic objectives as listed in Table 12.1.

State Outdoor Recreation Plans

The role of the state in outdoor recreational activities was detailed in Chapter 8. In this chapter, the discussion is limited to the states' plans for outdoor recreational pursuits. Prior to the passage of the Land and Water Conservation Fund Act in 1965, individual states had no incentive to prepare a plan for . With the passage of the Land and Water Conservation Fund Act, an incentive was provided. For a state to receive financial assistance from the fund, it must have a current plan that spells out the ways in which it, the state, will help satisfy the recreational needs of its residents. A new plan must be prepared every 5 years. From 1965 to 1980, every state in the union prepared a compre-

Table 12.1
Six Strategic National Park Service Objectives

1. **Resource stewardship and protection.** The primary responsibility of the National Park Service must be the protection of park resources.

2. **Access and enjoyment.** Each park unit should be managed to provide the nation's diverse public with access to and recreational and educational enjoyment of the lessons contained in that unit while maintaining unimpaired those unique attributes that are its contribution to the National Park System.

3. **Education and interpretation.** It should be the responsibility of the National Park Service to interpret and convey each park unit's and the park system's contributions to the nation's values, character, and experience.

4. **Proactive leadership.** The National Park Service must be a leader in local, national, and international park affairs, actively pursuing the mission of the National Park System and assisting others in managing their park resources and values.

5. **Science and research.** The National Park Service must engage in a sustained and integrated program of natural, cultural, and social science resource management and research aimed at acquiring and using the information needed to manage and protect park resources.

6. **Professional.** The National Park Service must create and maintain a highly professional organization and workforce.

Note. From *The Vail Agenda*, by National Park Service, 1991, Washington, DC: U.S. Government Printing Office, p. 33, 123–124.

hensive outdoor recreation plan that was renewed every 5 years as required. Many states stopped the practice of developing a new plan every 5 years when the Bureau of Outdoor Recreation (Heritage Conservation and Recreation Service) was eliminated.

The state is empowered through the U.S. Constitution to assume the responsibility for services that are not specified as federal government responsibility. Recreation is one of these responsibilities, and the planning for it was encouraged by the Land and Water Conservation Fund Act. The typical state outdoor recreation plan revolves around three areas: demand, supply, and future projection. Problems and issues are addressed in some plans. The department charged with overseeing state park and recreational offerings is usually

the department responsible for developing the state's outdoor recreation plan and coordinating its implementation with the agencies of the federal government and within the state's political subdivisions such as counties and cities.

The guidelines require that, in preparing the plan, citizen input be considered. The state must seek the views of public officials and interested citizens. Public meetings are encouraged. The following information is required:

1. A brief description of factors such as climate, topography, wildlife, history, populations, and urbanization that influence outdoor recreation in the state.

2. A list of the federal and state agencies that are responsible for creating, administering, and financially assisting publicly owned recreational areas.
3. An inventory of recreational areas that are publicly or privately owned, summarized by region or county, and a list of historic sites.
4. An estimate of the number of people who participate in each of several recreational activities, now and in the future, and an estimate of the frequency with which they participate.
5. A statement of recreational needs that will be met by the state, county, and local governments.
6. A statement of recreational needs of special populations, such as older adults, persons with disabilities, and the poor.
7. A description of actions proposed for the next 5 years to provide more outdoor recreational opportunities, such as proposals for acquisition and development, legislation, financial and technical assistance, and research.

The special case of the state of California and its planning milestone for parks in the 21st century is provided in Chapter 8.

LOCAL OUTDOOR RECREATION PLAN

Chapter 9 is devoted to local recreation. In this section, the local outdoor recreation plan that addresses the demand and supply of local recreational opportunities and a prediction of future demands is presented. The same information that is to be included in a state plan should be included in a local plan, except that it would be limited to the locality. Most local governments, whether county, city, or township, have planning departments that can provide some of the needed information. Sometimes, the planning department prepares the whole document if the department charged with parks

and recreation would prefer not to prepare it because of lack of staff. In other instances, consultants are hired to prepare the local outdoor recreation plan.

Although there is no single best method of developing a plan, planners generally agree that the procedure can be divided into three major phases (Jensen, 1985):

1. Collection of data about history and present status.
2. Projection of future park and recreational needs.
3. Formulation of realistic proposals for the near and long-term future.

To implement the plan, cooperation of public agencies and private citizens must be secured. Input of all concerned must be sought during the different phases of preparing the document. Also, adequate financial support needed for implementation must be secured in advance. To be effective, the implementation of the plan needs to proceed according to an approved timetable. Time frames of 5 to 20 years are commonly used in preparing local outdoor recreation plans (Knudson, 1984). Five years is adequate, but 20 years seems to be a long time. Many changes, both demographic and spatial, take place in a span of 20 years. Not only would young adults become middle-aged persons in two decades, but also many new residents could move into the community, altering it considerably in less than 20 years. The altering of open space must be considered.

SITE OR PROJECT PLANS

On the macro level, nationwide plans for outdoor recreation have been discussed, and on the intermediate level, statewide and local plans are presented in this chapter. On the micro level, plans involving the development of a single site or project, whether public or private campground, waterfront, or ski resort, require that certain steps be observed.

First, a master plan is prepared that includes a description of the need for developing the site based on demographics and predicted participatory figures. An inventory of existing (even if limited) resources would support the need for the proposed site. Also, data on the physical characteristics of the site are needed. How the site will be managed, in general terms, should be included. An important part of the master plan of a site is the preparation and submission of an environmental impact statement. This statement is submitted in conjunction with requirements of the Land and Water Conservation Fund Act to the liaison office in each state.

It is imperative that the public become involved, not only because it is required in the case of public projects, but also because the public is, after all, the consumers to be served by the project. Market researchers for private enterprises conduct surveys to discover consumers' interests and preferences. A process of this nature lacks interactive debate, however, which is explicitly required in public projects.

Each public agency dealing with projects for outdoor recreation may have its own way of developing a project, but the approach the Forest Service uses might serve as a model. This approach entails four major steps (Jensen,1985; Knudson, 1984):

1. *Drafting of a detailed site map,* including the following:
   - Land lines and boundaries as well as ownership.
   - A permanently established baseline and reference points.
   - The map scale (usually no smaller than 1:600).
   - Contour lines with an interval of 1 or 2 feet (0.3 to 0.6 meters).
2. *A narrative report,* consisting of three main parts:
   - Analysis and discussion of the physical characteristics of the site as they may influence design and construction.
   - Analysis and discussion of the physical and aesthetic requirements of the use or uses and the desired level of experience of users.
   - Statement of design objectives—that which you intend to do with design to accommodate the desired uses within the capability of the site to withstand the use.
3. *A general development plan,* usually made by tracing the detailed site map and adding proposed improvements. It would contain the following:
   - An overall design scheme.
   - The type and placement of all facilities but not layout details.
   - Road plan.
   - Survey control baseline and description.
   - Map showing the site and surrounding area.
   - Orientation.
   - Legend.
   - Aerial photo coverage.
4. *A final construction plan,* which conveys instructions to the contractor and includes the following:
   - Road design.
   - Water and sewage system designs.
   - Grading plans, including all contour modifications.
   - Family unit layout and construction details.
   - Construction drawings of all facilities and structures.
   - Layout information for the location of all site improvements.
   - All necessary specifications.

SUMMARY

For the managers of outdoor recreational areas and programs to be able to provide adequate opportunities to their recreationists not only equitably, but also wisely, certain management policies must be followed. We detailed the two basic policies of preservation and multiple use in this chapter.

The preservation policy, which seeks to set apart certain lands for the benefit of all, is especially important to wilderness areas. We discussed this policy in light of some 12 principles. The multiple-use policy that allows for certain exploitation of natural resources is applicable to the national forests and is met with difficulties, at the core of which is that different users view American natural resources differently.

Outdoor recreational resources are classified into two basic categories, land and water, which are classified into smaller units such as forests, grasslands, deserts, and tundra as well as rivers, wetlands, shorelines, lakes, and reservoirs. We presented the policies to be followed in the utilization of each along with the process of planning.

National outdoor recreation plans are required by law, and we discussed them in this chapter. We also presented state comprehensive plans, which were prompted by the passage of a number of federal acts. State plans for outdoor recreation were conducted every 5 years. Local outdoor recreation plans address the demand and supply of local offerings. On a micro level, the plan for a single local project is detailed from the master plan to the environmental impact report.

REFERENCES

Clawson, M., & Knetsch, J. (1966). *Economics of outdoor recreation.* Baltimore, MD: Johns Hopkins University Press.

Delaware Ricer Basin Commission. (2006). *National wild and scenic rivers.* West Trenton, NJ: Author.

Environmental Protection Agency. (2006). *Status and trends.* Washington, DC: Author.

Everhart, W. (1972). *The National Park Service.* New York, NY: Praeger.

Frakt, A., & Rankin, J. (1982). *The law of parks, recreation resources, and leisure services.* Salt Lake City, UT: Brighton.

Frequently asked questions: Federal Land Recreation Enhancement Act (FLREA). (2005). Retrieved from http://www.doi.gov/initiatives/ImplementationFAQ.pdf

Ibrahim, H., & Cordes, K. (2003). *Parks, recreation, and leisure service management.* Peosta, IA: Eddie Bowers.

Jensen, C. (1985). *Outdoor recreation in America.* Minneapolis, MN: Burgess.

Jensen, C., & Thorstenson, C. (1977). *Issues in outdoor recreation.* Minneapolis, MN: Burgess.

Knudson, D. (1984). *Outdoor recreation.* New York, NY: Macmillan.

La Page, W. (1988). Recreation management: Physical resources and environment. In S. H. Smith (Ed.), *Leisure today: Selected readings* (Vol. IV). Reston, VA: American Alliance of Health, Physical Education, Recreation, and Dance.

Nash, R. (1990). Historical roots of wilderness management. In J. Hendee, G. Stankey, & C. Lucas (Eds.), *Wilderness management* (pp. 29–42). Golden, CO: North American Press.

National Park Service. (1991). *The Vail agenda.* Washington, DC: U.S. Government Printing Office.

Outdoor Recreation Resources Review Commission. (1962). *Outdoor recreation for America.* Washington, DC: U.S. Government Printing Office.

Pinchot Institute. (2001). *Enduring the stewardship of the national wilderness preservation system.* Milford, PA: Author.

Wilderness Act. (2007). In *Wikipedia.* Retrieved from http://en.wikipedia.org/wiki/wildernessact

Wilderness.net. (2006). The national preservation system. Retrieved from http://www.Wilderness.net/index.cfm.fuse=NWPS&sec=manage/issues overview

Chapter 13

Management Procedures in Outdoor Recreation

Management is both a science and an art. It has become increasingly important in recent years as social organizations have become more complex. Managers need experience to help an organization achieve its goals and run smoothly. The accumulation of ideas from early managers led to a body of knowledge that is supported by theories borrowed, sometimes, from other fields including sociology, psychology, economics, and business administration. A growing number of managers are depending on scientific knowledge to make decisions, but these decisions should be tempered by personal judgment, intuition, and inspiration, making management an art and a science.

The information in this chapter is drawn from past experiences and accumulated knowledge of the best possible procedures to follow in managing outdoor recreational resources and activities, but needless to say, managers must depend on their own best judgment to arrive at sound conclusions.

BASIC CONCEPTS OF MANAGEMENT

A number of fundamental concepts should be kept in mind in managing outdoor recreational resources and activities. The science and art of management were born out of the business and industrial sectors of society and not from its service sector. Although useful ideas emanate from business and industry, most outdoor recreational opportunities, nonetheless, are offered as a service to the individual citizen, and they should be kept this way. Accordingly, not all basic concepts in business and industrial management are applicable to the outdoor recreation sphere.

- **Benefit-based management:** This approach has potential in outdoor recreation in that managers may use it to measure and facilitate participation.
- **Management by objectives:** Requires that managers and their staff become involved in the establishment and/or the crystallization of the agency's objectives.
- **Strategy management:** This approach entails following a continual process to relate the agency's objectives and resources effectively to the available opportunities.
- **The planning, program, budgeting system (PPBS):** Calls for the careful development of goals, evaluation of the program or programs intended to reach these goals, and the

establishment of a budget for that very purpose.

- **The program evaluation review technique (PERT):** Mathematical formulas and computer simulations are used to identify key activities designed to achieve the stated goals of the agency. A flow sequence showing time, resources, and performance for each task.
- **Conflict resolution:** Is no longer viewed as always harmful or counterproductive. Conflict, in fact, may be an important vehicle for change. It is its resolution that should be handled with utmost care.
- **Decision making:** Is probably the central activity of management because its effectiveness is measured by the quality of decisions.

CARRYING CAPACITY

The manager must make a number of decisions, regardless of management style, such as carrying capacity. The concept of carrying capacity is simple: It is the resource capacity to sustain outdoor recreational activities without deterioration. The concept emerged in the 1950s when the demand for outdoor recreation reached new levels (Ibrahim & Cordes, 2005), but the interest in it peaked in the 1960s and 1970s, when the demand on the outdoor recreational resources in the United States increased dramatically. Now that it has become a global problem, carrying capacity has become an important element in tourism worldwide (Mak, 2004).

One of the most important decisions to be made about the management of an outdoor recreational resource is its carrying capacity. When the resource encounters heavy use, its capacity to sustain recreation without deterioration should be determined. The design load of a resource is dependent on several factors, which should take carrying capacity into consideration. These factors include the following:

1. The general attractiveness of the area.
2. The site in relation to population distribution.
3. The economic level of the tributary population.
4. The degree of urbanization of the tributary population.
5. The influence of an area of similar characteristics.

Carrying capacities are not necessarily permanent, but fluctuate according to the mix of relevant factors. Also, there are various approaches to mitigate the impact of visitors on the site. Two acceptable principles are used in dealing with carrying capacity: the direct technique, in which rationing is applied, and the indirect technique, such as the use of entry fees. More on fees will be discussed later (Ibrahim & Cordes, 2005). Many studies have been conducted on carrying capacity and its application in outdoor recreational areas (Stankey & Manning, 1986). Some studies show that there are difficulties in adopting the concept, and other studies show difficulties in implementing it. Washburne and Cole (1983) found that managers of two thirds of national wilderness areas believe that their use exceeds their capacity by far, and only one half of these managers reported progress in establishing carrying capacities.

According to Hendee, Stankey, and Lucas (1978), many people use recreation resources, seeking many different, and sometimes conflicting, experiences. Carrying capacity is designed to maintain the resources for as long as possible, and research has shown that capacity is a function of more than simple number of users: Intensity of use, habitat type, seasonality, and location play decisive roles in carrying capacity. Some researchers have criticized the term as inappropriate, inadequate, and misleading for recreation resource management. Hendee et al. suggested that the emphasis should be on the intent behind the concept of carrying capacity. They suggested the following criteria for carrying capacity:

1. The determination of carrying capacity is ultimately a judgmental decision.
2. Carrying capacity decisions depend on clearly defined objectives.
3. The range of available alternative opportunities must be considered.
4. Carrying capacity is a probabilistic concept and not an absolute measure.

Knudson (1984) discussed the factors that affect carrying capacity and grouped them into three major types:

1. **Characteristics of the resource base:** The geology and soil of the resource are important factors in determining carrying capacity. Good soil has high carrying capacity, which in turn is dependent on its drainage and depth. If the resource is dry enough to allow for reasonable use during the season, this will add to its capacity. Too dry or too muddy soil reduces the capacity. Texture of the soil, its depth, and the type of underlying rocks play important roles in determining these factors. Topography is an important factor in determining carrying capacity. Although rough topography does not allow for many campsites, smooth topography does. Slopes facing north hold snow longer, providing longer skiing seasons but shorter seasons for picnicking and swimming. Different types of vegetation are different in their ability to withstand use. Also, vegetation can be used to provide special benefits such as windbreaking along beaches, which may increase carrying capacity by extending the season. Climate is an important factor in determining the length of the season. Rainfall patterns, fog, and storms determine to a great extent the length of the season and the type of activities. The existence of water, or lack thereof, determines the type of use, thus the carrying capacity of the resource, for both people and wildlife.

2. **Characteristics of management:** The philosophy and laws that govern the agency in charge determine to a great extent the elements of the carrying capacity of the source. Examples of the philosophy and laws are seen in the number of campsites per acre and in the size of the campsite itself, which translates into a certain carrying capacity. The design of the resource determines its carrying capacity. Paved roads encourage more traffic in comparison to gravel roads. The addition of a beach to a lake would possibly increase use.

3. **Characteristics of users:** Some users visit an outdoor recreational area for the enjoyment of nature, and others may visit to be with a group. For the first type of users, crowding would be more of a problem than for the second type. Some recreationists use large equipment such as boats in their outings, and others are content with smaller equipment. Also, the type of activity practiced while in an outdoor recreational setting is very much related to carrying capacity. For instance, still hunting allows more hunters in an area than stalk hunting.

Knudson (1984) concluded that increased use or congestion may lead to sociologic impairment of the recreation experience and/or ecologic deterioration of the recreation resource. He suggested the use of the limiting factor approach, creating a ceiling of carrying capacity, not necessarily permanently. The ceiling can be raised to the next limiting factor as needed. On the other hand, Graefe, Kuss, and Vaske (1987) suggested that carrying capacity can be used within the framework of the Recreational Opportunity Spectrum (ROS). In the ROS, spatial allocations are combined with activities for the purpose of providing for a range of recreational opportunities. Carrying capacity is determined through the interaction of the physical, social, and managerial settings. Following are the factors affecting carrying capacity:

1. Land type:
   a. Height
   b. Density
   c. Resiliency
   d. Productivity
   e. Geologic size
   f. Resistance to compaction
2. Vegetation:
   a. Height
   b. Density
   c. Resiliency
   d. Reproducibility
3. Social:
   a. Number of contacts with others
   b. Types of encounters
   c. Types of activities
4. Other:
   a. Access
   b. Length of season
   c. Patterns of use
   d. Occupancy length
   e. Attractiveness of site for specific activities

Must carrying capacity be described in terms of standards for acceptable conditions? Washburne (1982) compared two standard-based approaches to carrying capacity. The traditional approach uses numerical capacity as being necessary to keep the desired conditions. This approach fails to recognize type and distribution as well as the setting of the activities. He suggested an alternative approach by rearranging the sequencing and priorities and by focusing greater attention on a monitoring program. Numerical capacities are still used but are placed in perspective. In essence, his suggestion is similar to Graefe et al.'s (1987). He proposed visitor impact management, in which five major areas are considered when dealing with carrying capacity and visitor impacts:

1. Impact interrelationships.
2. Use–impact relationships.
3. Varying tolerance to impacts.
4. Activity-specific influences.
5. Site-specific influences.

Research Findings

Stanley and Manning (1986) summarized research findings on carrying capacity according to the following sets of factors.

Natural resource factors. A curvilinear relationship exists between recreational use and the impact of such use. Most recreational use leads to impact, but additional use causes little additional impact. Also, secondary effects must be considered. It is difficult to determine the most appropriate indicator of the impact on a natural resource because many ecological impacts are subject to some degree of management control. In the meantime, most of the research done has been focused on vegetation and soil. Studies on water, air quality, and wildlife should be encouraged.

Social factors. Managers should make a distinction between crowding and overuse. Presence of others may be a motivational factor in recreation participation. The central factor seems to be that when others are seen to be sharing the same experience, perception of crowding declines. Satisfaction with an outdoor recreational experience is a complex, multifaceted concept.

Managerial factors. Managers can use the following basic strategies to handle carrying capacity:

1. Reduce use through restrictions.
2. Accommodate more use by providing more opportunities.
3. Modify the character of use to reduce impact.
4. Harden the resource base to increase its resilience.

Direct management techniques to control carrying capacity are focused on visitor behavior, and choice is limited through use of permits and regulations. Indirect techniques are used to attempt to influence visitor behavior.

Stanley and Manning (1986) indicated that several important gaps exist in understanding how carrying capacity works. They suggested that there is a need for better understanding of the interrelationships between ecological and social factors in setting carrying capacities. Also needed is an understanding of the consequences, social and ecological, when such capacities are exceeded. An understanding of how effective, or ineffective, certain management action is for addressing carrying capacity would be useful. Finally, more knowledge is needed on what constitutes compatibility among different groups, a concept that could be useful in minimizing crowding and conflict.

Several frameworks for determining and applying carrying capacity to outdoor recreation were presented in the literature. These frameworks provide a rational, structured process for making carrying capacity decisions.

In a comparative analysis of carrying capacity frameworks, similarity of their underlying structures was affirmed and a number of related themes shared among these frameworks were suggested (Nilsen & Tayler, 1997):

1. Encouragement of interdisciplinary planning teams.
2. A primary focus on management of recreation-related impacts.
3. A need for sound natural and social science information.
4. Establishment of clear, measurable management objectives.
5. Definition of recreation opportunities as comprising natural, social, and managerial conditions.
6. A linkage among recreation activities, settings, experiences, and benefits.
7. Recognition that relationships between recreation use and resulting environmental and social impacts can be complex.

ESTIMATING USE RATES

Data on the use rates of outdoor recreational resources are useful in many ways. They are useful in planning; facts are needed for the adequate preparation for future use of a park, a forest, or any outdoor recreational resource. Another reason for keeping data on the use rate of the resource is to trace the changes that are occurring in using the resource. The data could also be used, when needed, in public relations endeavors, whether directed to laypersons or to officials. Accurate data are also used in conjunction with obtaining federal and state grants and subsidies. Such data undoubtedly have budgetary implications on the local level.

Units of Measurement

The 1973 Nationwide Outdoor Recreation Plan required that each federal land-managing agency report annually to the Bureau of Outdoor Recreation, in accordance with the Land and Water Conservation Fund Act of 1965, as amended, on recreational use at each management unit, using the recreation visitor-hour as the standard unit of measure. When available and appropriate, agencies should also include recreation visit and activity-hour data. The definitions of these terms are as follows:

- A *recreation visitor-hour* is the presence for recreational purposes of one or more persons for continuous, intermittent, or simultaneous periods of time aggregating 60 minutes.
- A *recreation activity-hour* is a recreation visitor-hour attributable to a specific recreational activity.
- A *recreation visit* is the entry of any person into a site or area of land or water for recreational purposes.

States and localities have begun to use the same terms in preparing their reports on recreational management units.

Another unit of measurement that has come into use is *activity day* or *recreation day*, which gives the average number of hours of participation per day in a given activity.

Other than by making an actual count, which is not feasible in many instances, and pure guess, which is not accurate, Jensen (1985) suggested the following methods for keeping track of the use of a natural resource:

1. **Estimates based on observation:** This method involves no counting or sampling. It is simply a manager's best judgment of the number of visits to a particular area during a specified time. Obviously, with this method there is much room for error, and the errors tend to be on the high side.
2. **The sampling method:** This involves either direct counts of people or counts of a related element, such as number of cars. Generally, the larger the sample the more reliable the data. There is the problem of whether the sample is representative of the total population.
3. **The pure count method:** This is the most cumbersome yet most accurate method of counting either individuals or a related phenomenon such as cars, entry fees, user fees, number of boats, campsite occupancy, or one of a number of other related elements.

Over the next 50 years, the Forest Service expects demands to increase from 800 million to 1.2 billion visits to the national forests per year (U.S. Forest Service, 1989). Estimate rates depict current trends, and current trends help managers to project future use of resources. Nonconsumptive and wildlife activities are expected to increase 61% nationally by 2050, and hunting will decline by 11% (Cordell, Bergstrom, Hartmann, & English, 1990). Technological innovations may lead to jet-pack backcountry camping, jet snow skis, and night activity with special hovercraft. Cellular phones and geographic positioning systems (GPS) may improve safety and communications, but may add a sense of security leading to complications, such as overconfidence and increased risk-taking.

Characteristics of Uses

The characteristics of those using natural resource areas were described in Chapter 5. When, how, and with whom the participant uses the resource will be described in this section. According to Hendee et al. (1978), most visits to natural resource areas

are short. Day use seems to prevail in small and medium-sized areas. Day use in national park backcountry and national forest wilderness and primitive areas was 41% of total use. Length of stay for overnight campers in these natural resources varied from 1.6 to 5.9 days. The authors believe that length of stay has been the same for a number of years and that increased travel costs could lead to fewer trips in the future.

The parties of wilderness visitors are generally small, from two to four persons (Hendee et al., 1978). Parties of over 10 persons account for 5% of all groups in most areas. This may be due in part to managerial regulation to reduce the impact of large groups on the environment and on other visitors.

Summer seems to be the preferred season for engaging in recreational activities in natural settings. Hunting continues into the fall in many areas, and skiing is enjoyed in the winter. Only in the southern and southwestern United States, particularly in low elevation areas, would outdoor recreational activities continue in the winter and spring. Weekenders attend these activities more so than do day participants, even in the summer.

Most natural settings in the United States draw visitors from all over the nation. Nonetheless, it seems that close-by residents seem to dominate the scene. For instance, 92% of the Yosemite visits are made by Californians, and residents of the state of Washington account for 78% of visits to the national parks in that state (Hendee et al., 1978).

Carrying Capacity Is an Evolving Concept

It is noteworthy that the concept of carrying capacity is evolving. Some have suggested that the term is outdated, but others have argued that carrying capacity remains a valid point of reference from which managers and patrons can benefit. Some feel the term is outdated due to its original connection to range and wildlife research. The main argument extends from the notion that the term *capacity* should not always be associated with the maximum number of people that a resource can tolerate. More modern approaches to carrying capacity highlight the need to focus on managing impacts, which includes managing people. It is noteworthy that recreation impacts can also be thought of as indicators of success. For example, if a hiking trail is negatively impacted because of high use, this also suggests a high number of people are benefiting from the resource through enjoying physical activity in nature. This is not to suggest that impacts to an outdoor recreation resource should be minimized. It is, however, important to remember that managers can potentially use impacts to educate visitors about sustainability and carrying capacity. It is also important to remember that impacts, in some cases, indicate resource and activity popularity (Moore & Driver, 2005).

FINANCING OUTDOOR RECREATION

Although both public and private sectors deal with outdoor recreational opportunities, the former has much more to do with it than the latter. In turn, the public sector should be treated as comprising three subsectors when the subject is outdoor recreational resources and activities: municipal (city/county), state, and federal. How do these sectors finance outdoor recreation?

1. **Taxes:** General taxes are the most common form of revenue for a local program. There is usually a property tax in which an assessment is provided for a given fiscal year. The monies collected are used to provide municipal services such as education, sanitation, police, streets, health, recreation, and other local services by either a city, a township, or a county government. Sometimes more than one public body are joined to provide a service. In that case, one, two, or more public bodies are empowered to establish special districts, for example, a park and recreation district, with special taxes collected for such a purpose. Sometimes, a small

part of the general tax, expressed in mills, is collected. A mill is one thousandth of a dollar ($0.001). Millage taxes are allocated in some localities for a certain program, for example, a park and recreation program. In other instances, special assessment taxes are collected from those who stand to benefit from the activity and not from others.

2. **Bonds:** Bonds are used to finance major capital developments such as acquiring land and building facilities. There are many forms of bonds. A term bond is paid in its entirety at the end of a given period, usually 10 to 30 years. A callable bond allows the agency to pay it off before the end of the term. A serial bond allows for a specific portion to be paid yearly. A general obligation bond is paid from general tax revenue. An assessment bond is derived from special assessment on those who would benefit from the project. A revenue bond is paid off from the income derived from the facility that has been built.

3. **Fees and charges:** In public recreation, in general, there are seven common fees and charges (Warren, 1986). These are applicable to areas used for outdoor recreation, be they local, state, or federal.
   a. *Entrance fees:* These are charges for the entrance into large facilities such as zoos, botanical gardens, or game reserves.
   b. *Admission fees:* These charges are collected for performances, exhibitions, museums, and the like.
   c. *Rental fees:* These are charges for the use of a property that is not consumed and is to be returned, such as boats or motorcycles.
   d. *User fees:* These charges are for participation in an activity usually done with others, such as skiing, swimming, or playing golf.

e. *License and permit fees:* Certain activities are allowed upon the payment of these fees, for example, hunting, fishing, and camping.

f. *Special-service fees:* These charges cover special and atypical events, such as workshops, summer camp, and class instruction.

g. *Sales revenue:* These monies are obtained from the operation of concessions, restaurants, and stores.

The philosophic basis for, or against, charging for public recreation will be discussed later in this chapter.

4. **Government grants:** Grants through the federal government and other governments have brought billions of dollars to public recreation agencies. Although these have been drastically reduced in recent years, these funds allowed for an unprecedented expansion in outdoor recreational opportunities in the recent past.

   a. *Land and Water Conservation Fund:* Administered by the National Park Service, this fund assists municipalities and states in acquiring and developing open space. Each state must prepare a state comprehensive outdoor recreation plan (SCORP) listing existing resources and identifying its future needs.

   b. *Community development block grants:* In the 1970s, substantial sums were used from these grants to enhance outdoor recreational facilities, particularly within urban settings.

   c. *Revenue-sharing grants:* With no strings attached, expenditure of monies from revenue-sharing grants on recreation ranked fifth among all local government expenditure, after police, fire, transportation, and general expenditures. Most of the expenditure went to operating expenses rather than capital development in recreation.

   d. *Labor assistance programs:* Foremost among these programs is CETA, the Comprehensive Employment and Training Act, which was designed to provide short-term employment and training for unskilled workers. Grant monies were used instead to support operations and maintenance in recreation as well as other municipal services. The Job Training Partnership Act (JTPA) has replaced CETA.

   e. *Urban Park and Recreation Recovery Program.* This relatively small program was designed to help distressed communities rehabilitate rundown recreation systems. Indoor and outdoor facilities were included in the rehabilitation program.

There are grants, both federal and state, that can be used in outdoor recreation for capital development and operating expenses locally. In Canada, the federal government provides considerable assistance to provinces and municipalities.

5. **Foundation grants:** Due to a shortage of public monies from federal and state sources, many local park and recreation departments are approaching foundations and private citizens for grants and gifts. According to Kraus and Curtis (1982), there are several types of foundations:

   a. Special-purpose foundations are created to meet a special need. Recreation and sport are sometimes listed among those needs.

   b. Company-sponsored foundations are created for the purpose of corporate giving. Although a separate entity, this type of foundation is controlled by the mother company.

c. Community foundations are established to serve a particular community, be it spiritual or residential.

d. Family foundations are established by a person or a family for the purpose of reducing taxes.

Kraus and Curtis (1982) suggested the following strategy in approaching foundations for gifts or grants:

a. Establish a foundations committee comprising capable, willing individuals.

b. Prepare a list of foundations that may be interested in recreation, particularly outdoor recreation.

c. Develop a proposal concept that may be used to sound out the foundation before beginning the next step.

d. Prepare a formal grant proposal, which should be brief and convincing.

e. Present the proposal to the foundation in a timely fashion according to their published schedule.

f. Follow up by requesting a meeting within 2 to 3 weeks.

Grantsmanship is a relatively new term that shows how important it is to skillfully present a case to donors.

Kraus and Curtis (1982) suggested that to achieve maximum results in obtaining a grant, the following points should be observed:

1. Beat the crowd, develop contacts, know about new grants before they are fully announced.

2. Visit grant headquarters, meet the key people, and personalize your approach. Remember, they are bored by the mountains of paper that flood them.

3. Invite "them" to your city, and make the visit memorable; have "them" visit all sites.

4. Contact local political leaders for assistance; seek industry and business people with high contacts.

5. In your presentations, use films, displays, large sketches, and graphics.

6. At first refusal or resistance, question why and follow up; persist until successful.

7. If a grant is awarded, get full newspaper coverage.

FEES FOR OUTDOOR RECREATION

The fees charged for the use of outdoor resources were presented earlier. This section deals with the philosophy for or against charging for outdoor recreation. The use of fees and charges for outdoor recreational activities goes back to 1908, when Mount Rainier National Park instituted an automobile fee. Charges were levied in Central Park by its concessionaire. Fees were charged in Connecticut state parks in 1933. Yet the practice was not widespread. With the decline of governmental support, the need for new sources of financing became evident. In 1996, the federal land management agencies were allowed to conduct recreational fee demonstration programs, the purpose of which was to test new or increased fees. The U.S. General Accounting Office (1998) reviewed the result of this experiment and concluded that increased or new fees had no major adverse effect on visitation to the fee demonstration sites. This does not mean that the other methods of financing described earlier are to be abandoned or even reduced in importance. Taxes, bonds, and grants are, and will always be, important sources of financing public recreation.

Arguments for and Against Fees

There are numerous arguments against the collection of fees in public recreation if it is to continue to be public recreation. The bases for capital outlay and operational allocation should be taxes. The support for the stand against fee collection for recreation comes from the case of public education, where fees are not collected and everyone is admitted. The proponents argue that the same should be observed in recreation and at all levels of public enterprise: local, regional, state, and federal. Another objection to charging fees revolves around that those who need recreation the most are generally the least able to pay. Recreation is a service that should be provided not only on the same basis as education, but also on the same basis as sanitation and police protection (Kraus & Curtis, 1982). To charge for recreation means double taxation, which is not acceptable.

On the other hand, those who advocate the collection of fees in recreation argue that the public tends to appreciate more those services for which it pays. Moreover, charging fees can be a useful guide in that it points out the desired program and/or facility, which could be helpful in further planning.

Additional arguments for charging fees in outdoor recreation are (a) fees help control access to the natural setting and (b) fees help to expand and improve current offerings. In 1979, the Heritage Conservation and Recreation Service (1979), the successor to the Bureau of Outdoor Recreation (BOR), supported the collection of fees, suggesting that the American consumer is both willing and able to pay.

As early as the 1960s, Rodney (1964) suggested a series of useful guides in establishing and maintaining fees in public recreation:

1. All fees and charges for recreational services should be in conformity with the long-term program policy of the recreation system and should be consistent with the legal authorization governing such practices.
2. Fees and charges should be viewed as a supplemental source of recreation and park funds and not as the primary source. Therefore, the value of any proposed activity or facility should be judged with respect to its meeting public needs rather than its income-producing potential.
3. All services entailing fees or charges should be periodically reviewed by the department, and those facilities or programs meeting general and basic community recreation needs should not have fees imposed on them.
4. Sound business procedures and administrative controls should be used in the collection and disbursement of special revenues.
5. Policies regarding concession operations or the lease of departmental facilities should be determined as part of the general administrative responsibility with respect to fees and charges.
6. In general, recreational facilities, when not being used for departmental programs, should be made available free or at minimal cost to nonprofit and nonrestricted community organizations, particularly character-building organizations serving school-aged children.

Kraus and Curtis (1982) suggested a number of techniques in minimizing the impact of increased fees:

1. **Public relations:** Park and recreational facility users should be provided the courtesy of advance notice of fee changes as well as an explanation of the need for the revenues collected and the basis for them.
2. **Gradual increases:** Gradual increases clearly tied to rising costs may be more acceptable to the constituency than sudden or drastic fee increases.
3. **Fee-by-fee consideration:** Each activity or facility should be separately examined and an appropriate fee set according to the level of demand, cost of the activity, types of fees asked at competing opportunities, possible cosponsorship of the activity, or similar factors. In some cases, activities or facilities that tend to yield a profit may be used to subsidize or partially subsidize the cost of others.

A ranger at Fredericksburg and Spotsylvania National Military Park in Virginia identifies the four major battlefields and three historic structures where, during a 2-year period, at least 100,000 soldiers were either killed or wounded.

3. **Annual passes:** Agencies may also provide frequent visitors to parks with the opportunity to purchase annual passes or other special privileges. The method may be used to increase visitation volume and user identification with the recreation and park system; it is typically used for community swimming pools.

According to Manning (1985), the influence of fees on recreation use is dependent on several factors:

1. **"Elasticity of demand" for a park or recreation area:** Elasticity is the slope of the demand curve that defines the relationship between price and quality consumed.

2. **Significance of the recreation area:** Parks of national significance are likely to have a relatively inelastic demand, suggesting that fees are not likely to be effective in limiting use.

3. **Percentage of total cost represented by the fee:** In cases where the fee charged represents a relatively high percentage of the total cost of visiting a recreation area, pricing is likely to be a more effective use-limiting approach.

4. **Type of fee instituted:** Pricing structure can be a potentially important element in determining the effectiveness of fees as management practice.

The acceptability of fees depends on several factors, including the following:

1. If revenue derived from fee programs is reinvested in facilities and services, fees are often judged to be more acceptable by park visitors.
2. Public acceptance of new fees where none were charged before tends to be relatively low compared with increasing an existing fee.
3. Local visitors tend to be more resistant to new fees or increased fees than nonlocal visitors.
4. Visitors acceptance of fees is likely to be greater when information is provided on the cost of competing or substitute recreation opportunities.

One issue is that differential pricing may influence recreation use patterns. Another issue concerns the potential for pricing to discriminate against certain groups in society, particularly those with low incomes, as shown in Figure 13.1.

VISITOR MANAGEMENT

When a visitor arrives at an outdoor recreational site or area, a number of methods should be used to make his or her visit as pleasant as possible while maintaining and preserving the natural setting on which the activity is taking place. According to Moore and Driver (2005), management in outdoor recreation is different from other forms of management because the "product" of a natural experience is unique.

Physical Aspects of Visitor Management

In addition to providing roads and trails, the agency should place signs wherever necessary. Signs are a major form of communication in outdoor recreation. Douglass (1975) suggested that they give directions, identify areas, give warnings, supply information, and provide posting of agency regulations. He classified signs into the following categories:

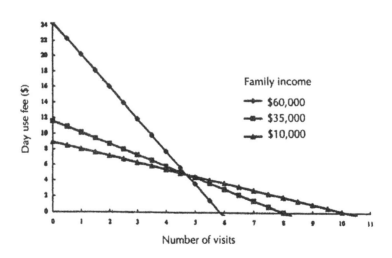

Figure 13.1. Demand curves for day-use recreation areas by income level. From Potential equity effects of a new day-use fee, by S. Reiling, H. Cheng, C. Robinson, R. McCarville, and C. White, 1996, *Proceedings of the 1995 Northeastern Recreation Research Symposium*, Newtown Square, PA: USDA Forest Service, Northeastern Experiment Station, p. 30.

1. **Administrative signs:** These signs are used to identify boundaries, offices, and areas.
2. **Directional signs:** The internal direction sign is meant to inform pedestrians, and the external direction sign is for motorists.
3. **Interpretive signs:** These are designed to highlight the attraction, tell a brief history, or give an interpretation of the area.
4. **Restrictive signs:** These signs post regulations, control visitor movement, and remind visitors of their responsibilities.

Other important physical aspects of visitor management are pedestrian and vehicular circulation. Both should be studied and developed according to the needs of the visitors as well as crowd control principles.

Information and Education

Roggenbuck and Ham (1986) conducted a review of literature on information education programs in natural recreational settings and found them to be important components of management by users and managers. These elements can be effective for solving certain management problems. They suggested that managers should endeavor to achieve the following:

- Develop an understanding of recreationists' characteristics, behaviors, and informational needs so programs can be designed to provide information that is important to managers.
- Develop cost-effective media presentations, both personal and nonpersonal, that are targeted at user groups whose wants are not being met or whose behavior is potentially problematic.
- Develop means to provide accurate information to recreationists early in the trip-planning process (computerized information systems seem to have potential).
- Assist in the benefit–cost analysis of information-education programs,

especially with regard to reducing physical impacts on recreational lands.

Hendee et al. (1978) noted that management actions are either direct or indirect. Direct action is authoritarian and allows little freedom of choice. Indirect action, which uses information and education, is more subtle and could be effective in modifying behavior. Ham (1984) found that campers' compliance with a park's efforts was related to the quality and clarity of instruction.

Instruction can be given via signs, in leaflets, or through personnel. The personnel-based technique can be costly (Martin & Taylor, 1981), and as a result, some managers resort to using volunteers. Some of the direct and indirect management techniques used in wilderness areas are shown in Table 13.1.

Interpretive Service

According to Knudson (1984), there are three visitor-oriented objectives of interpretive service:

1. Tell the story of the recreational place.
2. Shape the visitor's experience.
3. Involve the participant in the activities of the place.

According to Jensen (1985), the application of the environment is another goal of interpretive service. The scope of the interpretation program includes nature hikes and tours led by trained interpreters. Self-guided activities are sometimes used on trails and in nature centers and demonstration areas.

Tilden (1962) suggested the following principles as the guidelines of nature interpretation:

1. Interpretation is revelation based upon information. Build a story into your presentation and incorporate the visitors into your stories. True interpretation deals not with parts but with the historical and spiritual whole.

Table 13.1

Direct and Indirect Techniques for Managing the Character and Intensity of Wilderness Use

Type of management	Method	Specific techniques
Indirect		
(Emphasis on influencing or modifying behavior. Individual retains freedom to choose. Control less complete; more variation in use possible.)	Physical Alterations.....................	Improve, maintain, or neglect access roads. Improve, maintain, or neglect campsites. Make trails more or less difficult. Build trails or leave areas trailless. Improve fish or wildlife population or take no action (stock or allow depletion or elimination)
	Information Dispersed...............	Advertise specific attributes of the wilderness. Identify range of recreation opportunities in surrounding area. Educate users to basic concepts of ecology and care of ecosystems. Advertise underused areas and general patterns of use.
	Eligibility Requirements............	Charge constant entrance fee. Charge differential fees by trail zones, season, etc. Require proof of camping and ecological knowledge and/or skills.
Direct		
(Emphasis on regulation of behavior. Individual choice restricted. High degree of control.)	Increased Enforcement............	Impose fines. Increase surveillance of area.
	Zoning	Separate incompatible uses (hiker-only zones in areas with horse use). Prohibit use at times of high damage potential (no horse use in high meadows until soil moisture declines, say July 1) Limit camping in some campsites to one night, or some other limit.
	Rationing Use Intensity.............	Rotate use (open or close access points, trails, campsites). Require reservations. Assign campsites and/or travel routes to each camper group. Limit usage via access point. Limit size of groups, number of horses. Limit camping to designated campsites only. Limit length of stay in area (max/min).
	Restriction on Activities	Restrict building campfires. Restrict horse use, hunting, or fishing.

Note. From "Toward a Model of Travel Behavior in the Boundary Waters Canoe Area," by C. Gilbert, G. L. Peterson, and D. W. Lime, 1972, *Environment and Behavior, 4*(2), 131–157. Reprinted with permission.

2. Interpretation is art and can be taught. The story is art, not science. All people are poets and artists to some degree; images are adventures of the imagination. The interpreter must possess the skills of speaking and writing.

3. The chief aim is provocation, not instruction—to stimulate in readers or hearers a hunger to widen their horizon of interests and knowledge. The national park or monument, the preserved battlefield, the historic restoration, and the nature center in a public recreation spot are places where interpretation blooms and flourishes. First stimulate visitors' interest, and then stimulate them to see and understand.

4. Interpretation should aim to present the whole to the whole person. Toward a perfect whole, the interpreter works for a complete experience using all five senses. The visitor should leave with one or more pictures in mind.

5. A different approach should be used in interpretation programs for children than those for adults. Children enjoy using superlatives, such as the largest this, the smallest that. They love to touch objects with their fingers and hands. Challenge their senses. The interpreter can help children relate to phenomena in terms they understand without talking down to them.

Control of Undesirable Actions

Hendee et al. (1978) suggested that there are five undesirable actions, to which they suggested certain responses. The authors listed the following as categories of undesirable visitor behavior:

1. **Illegal actions with adverse impacts:** Examples are the illegal use of chain saws or motorbikes in wilderness. The manager should enforce the law in cases of illegal actions.

2. **Careless or thoughtless violations of regulation with adverse impacts:** Littering is an example, as are shortcutting a trail instead of walking on switchbacks, camping in closed areas, and building wood fires where they are not permitted. Informal education sessions could be useful in reducing careless and thoughtless behavior.

3. **Unskilled actions with adverse impacts:** Digging a drainage ditch around a tent is an example of an impact resulting from a lack of wilderness skills or knowledge. Perhaps a preactivity session that is designed to go over basic skills for the activity would be in order. Also, signs could be posted, both pictorial and with text, on how to pitch a tent.

4. **Uninformed behavior that intensifies use impacts:** This is illustrated by large numbers of visitors who enter a wilderness at a few well-known access points during peak use periods when they might have dispersed themselves over a number of access points if they had been more informed about alternative places. Some form of educational session would be useful to combat this behavior. Another way to control access entries would be closing off that entry point with a physical barrier, posting signs (pictorial), and indicating the next entry point.

5. **Unavoidable minimum impacts:** Examples are when visitors step on plants, when vegetation under a tent is damaged, and so on. The manager may have to revert to reduction in the use of the facility or area.

Litter Control

Research shows that litter detracts seriously from the wilderness experience (Lee, 1975; Stankey, 1973). The amount of litter that could be left by visitors might reach between 100 and 200 pounds for each visitor (Hendee et al., 1978). Fortunately, litter control incentives have proven successful (Clark, Hendee, & Burgess, 1972). This is the system in which the rangers contact families to solicit their children's help in keeping the natural area clean in return for rewards such as badges and presents. In the backcountry, where there are few children, an "appeal system" seems to be working in which the adult users are reminded to do their own litter pack-out.

The Permit System

The use of mandatory permits to use special areas such as trails has the important benefit of providing communication between the user and the manager (see Figure 13.2). Information is provided that could improve the user's experience and reduce his or her impact on the area. According to Hendee et al. (1978), a self-issued permit could be used where the impacts are not high enough to require rationing.

In a recent article, Pfister (1990) blamed the restrictive permit system on the sharp decline in the number of backcountry users of 19 California wilderness areas. Rationing of permits, suggested Pfister, could be the reason for the attitudinal change that has taken place among the enthusiastic backcountry backpackers who have adopted the concept of substitutability (Hendee & Burdge, 1974). They now freely shift among choices in outdoor activities, as shown in some market surveys. Pfister suggested that management policies should attempt to do the following:

1. Remove rationing techniques in areas of low participation.
2. Remove control over most areas except for those witnessing growth.
3. Devise new approaches to control use.

AREA MANAGEMENT: SPECIAL CASES

Outdoor recreation takes place in many locations, some of which have special characteristics that require special attention. Special management attention should be given to wilderness areas, rivers, and trails.

Wilderness Management

Wilderness in the United States is defined by the Wilderness Act of 1964. Wilderness is an area where human interference is kept at a minimum, yet recreation is practiced in it to a high degree. The act created the National Wilderness System, which contains 445 areas totaling close to 90 million acres, most of which are in Alaska and the West.

Patterns of use of these wilderness areas vary greatly, although day use seems to be the dominant pattern (Lucas & Krumpe, 1986). Hiking seems to be the most prevalent form of travel, followed by horseback riding and canoeing/boating. Hiking, fishing, photography, and nature study are also practiced in wilderness areas.

Visitors to these areas seem to be young, well educated, and mostly males. Most come in pairs or small groups. Wilderness areas are visited mainly in the summer, although visits in the spring take place in the desert wilderness of the southwestern United States. Intensity of use varies significantly.

According to Lucas and Krumpe (1986), research has been conducted on the management of wilderness areas, yet a large gap in knowledge still exists. Further research is needed. Nonetheless, they proposed the following recommendations, which are consistent with the recommendations suggested in another study (Frome, 1985):

1. Reaffirm the goal of keeping wilderness distinctive. Preservation of natural processes and conditions should be the overriding goal along with provision of opportunities for a unique visitor experience dependent on natural conditions.
2. Complement wilderness with provision of high-quality semiprimitive recreation opportunities on undeveloped public lands outside wilderness areas. This will meet diverse public recreation needs and desires and reduce pressures on wilderness areas for types of recreational use that would diminish their distinctive and special character.

WILDERNESS PERMIT
U.S. Department of Agriculture Forest Service

_____ Wilderness or Primitive Area

	1 — 2
	(Code)

When signed below, this Permit authorizes

_____
(Name)

_____
(Address)

	3 – 7
	(Zip Code)

_____
(City)   (State)

to visit this Wilderness or Primitive Area
and to build campfires in accordance with
applicable regulations.

from | 8 – 9 | 10 – 11 | to | 12 – 13 | 14 – 15 |
(Mo)   (Day)   (Mo)   (Day)

The number of people in the group will be . . . . | 16 – 17 |

The number of pack or saddle stock used will be . . . . | 18 – 19 |
(Enter "0" if no stock will be used)

The place of entry will be _____ | 20 – 21 |
(Location)

The trip will end _____ | 22 – 23 |
(Location)

I agree to abide by all laws, rules, and regulations which apply to this area, and to
follow the rules of behavior listed on, or attached to this permit. I will do my best
to see that everyone in my group does likewise.

_____   _____
(Date)   (Visitor's Signature)

_____   _____
(Date)   (Issuing Officer's Signature)

The visitor must have this permit in his
possession during his visit to the Wilderness

This section for optional use of issuing officer.
Planned travel route, duration, and location of camps.

Travel Zone (see map)	24 – 25	26 – 27	28 – 29	30 – 31	32 – 33	34 – 35	36 – 37	38 – 39	40 – 41	42 – 43
Nights of use by zone	44 – 45	46 – 47	48 – 49	50 – 51	52 – 53	54 – 55	56 – 57	58 – 59	60 – 61	62 – 63

Visitor receives white copy.
Send yellow copy to the Forest Service Regional Office in San Francisco.
Send pink copy to the Ranger District where the trip starts.

GPO 191 406   R5-2300-32 Rev. 3/72

Figure 13.2. Standard wilderness permit used in all national forest wilderness and national park
backcountry areas.

The Forest Service checks for permits in popular areas that are easily impacted by too many visitors.

3. Further apply and test the limits of an acceptable charge system as the most promising way of managing wilderness carrying capacity. (This idea was discussed in the section on carrying capacity.)
4. Emphasize the monitoring of wilderness use and conditions to provide a foundation for management.
5. Stress educational/informational approaches as a means of visitor management and as a means for minimizing regulations that tightly control visitor movement and behavior.
6. Increase trail maintenance to control environmental damage and meet visitor needs.
7. Relocate and redesign trail systems to reduce damage and provide better experiences for visitors.

8. Measure wilderness recreational use in comparable ways for all wildernesses administered by the National Park Service, Forest Service, Fish and Wildlife Service, and Bureau of Land Management to provide comparisons and to identify trends.

River Recreation

River recreation has grown steadily over the past few years. There are close to 3.5 million linear miles of rivers and streams in the United States. Some of these miles are fit for recreational settings, many of which have been protected as part of the Wild and Scenic Rivers System. According to Lime (1986), recreation associated with that system has become one of the fastest expanding segments in Forest Service management. Lime painted a picture of the river recreationists as follows:

1. River recreationists vary widely in their activities, use patterns, motivation, and attitudes.
2. Socialization seems to be the most mentioned motivational factor behind choosing rivers as the loci for recreation.
3. Risk-taking seems to be a characteristic common to river recreationists.
4. River recreation seems to be a novice experience for many of those participating in it.
5. Group size of river recreationists seems to be considerably larger than for most other outdoor recreational activities in natural settings.
6. Most river recreationists are young, many below the age of 30.
7. River recreationists begin their activities at a later age than do most other recreationists, with the exception of tubers.
8. Participants in river recreation are predominantly white-collar workers with above average incomes.

Lime (1986) expects that the demand for river recreation in the future will produce a number of challenges that should be met. Not only will there be an increase in the demand for access to urban water resources, but there will also be an increase in recreational use of existing river riders. As the number of river recreation increases, so will the need for expansion in service, equipment, and related industries. Organizations and clubs are being formed to promote water-based recreation and to increase demand for these opportunities by minority women and senior citizens. The manager of water-based resources should expect longer participation, demand for high-quality trips, and requests for inclusive access. Instruction in safety, good public relations, and high-tech equipment will be in demand on water-based sources. Demand will continue for outfitters, boat liveries, and other commercial establishments along river corridors.

Recreation Trails

Hiking on trails in a natural setting gained popularity as recreation in the early 1960s. In addition to hiking, trails provide other forms of recreation such as opportunities for nature study, photography, drawing and painting, and solitude. Trails can also serve as access to hunting, fishing, and camping. The passage of the National Trails System Act of 1968 provided the needed boost for these forms of recreation. The use of trails by recreationists more than doubled from 1969 to 1983.

Hiking, which takes place on the trail, is more or less a day use, and not much associated with overnight camping. The distances covered are modest. Hikers in wilderness areas desire solitude, low-level encounters, and an unmodified natural setting. Other trail users desire other amenities, which create conflicts. For example, cross-country skiers' interests clash with those of snowmobilers. Krumpe and Lucas (1986) suggested separating trail users whenever possible.

The impact on trail use is seen in littering, horse manure, and deterioration of trails generally. Most of the trails in the United States were built well over 50 years ago for administrative purposes. Time and inadequate finances have contributed to the problem of trail deterioration. Rationing of users

of trails has been suggested as a possible remedy. Other suggestions include a lottery system, a merit system, and trail fees. Limiting the number in a group entering a trail is another means of control.

According to Krumpe and Lucas (1986), researchers have concentrated on remote backcountry settings and little has been done to investigate the use of trails located near metropolitan areas. The relationship between trail systems and the broader spectrum of recreation opportunities should also be explored. For instance, trail use has grown recently with the increased interest in wellness and fitness.

BEHAVIOR MANAGEMENT: SPECIAL CASES

Problem Behavior

Research has helped in understanding why people sometimes behave irresponsibly in an outdoor setting. Two terms are now being used to distinguish between two basic categories of problem behavior (Moore & Driver, 2005):

1. *Depreciative behavior,* which distracts from the enjoyment of the environment.
2. *Vandalism,* which describes the act of damage to the setting and its environment.

Another way of looking at the irresponsible behaviors is to distinguish between unintentional and intentional problem behavior. Unintentional behavior occurs because the visitor is either uninformed or unskilled or the negative outcome is unavoidable. Intentional behavior could occur as a result of carelessness, as a result of protestation, or for material gain.

Accidents and Injuries

According to Hudson, Thompson, and Mack (1996), each year over 200,000 children are injured on America's playgrounds, with the bulk of these accidents involving falls. Earlier, the National Park System had 190 visitor fatalities and 2,483 visitor injuries as well as 1,505 injured employees in 1 year (Kraus & Curtis, 1982).

The following guidelines can be used in accident reduction and risk management:

1. **Systematic reporting and record keeping:** The agency should maintain an accurate picture of trends for possible future control.
2. **Facilities inspection and hazard abatement:** Regular inspection should be made of all areas imposing special risks such as rockslide areas, sharp curves, thin-iced places, and similar hazards. Also, all equipment should be regularly checked.
3. **Participant safety procedure:** All visitors should be made aware of the possible risk taken in some outdoor recreational activities. Unsafe conduct and hazardous areas should be pointed out through bulletins, signs, and oral warnings.
4. **Staff training:** Safety awareness and precautions should be made an important part of staff orientation and training. Members of the staff should take it upon themselves to make visitors aware of risky behavior and to apply rules and regulations related to such behavior firmly. Moreover, the staff should be licensed in first aid.
5. **Emergency procedures:** Emergency procedures should not only be established but also made known to all members of the staff. Regular patrols should be organized along with a speedy and effective means of communication with remote areas. Transportation should be available, and evacuation and escape routes should be delineated.

The process of law enforcement in a natural setting includes the following steps, according to Harmon (1979):

1. To recruit and train competent personnel experienced in and responsible for specialized duties.
2. To provide organization and training of personnel to deal with varied emergencies and challenges as they may occur, including ongoing in-service training in methods of law enforcement, first aid, and similar functions.
3. To promote safe design and construction of facilities; although law enforcement personnel are not usually involved in this process, they can contribute helpful information at the planning stage to prevent problems that may occur later.
4. To provide a sound public relations and interpretive program, to give the visitor a high-quality experience in the natural environment, improve the public image of the park system, and familiarize visitors with the rationale underlying park regulations and ecologically sound use of the park setting.
5. To carry out fair and thorough enforcement of the rules, with emphasis on a positive and pleasant approach to the public, stressing education and helping to build positive attitudes, rather than a punitive or threatening approach.

Risk Management

High-risk recreational activities, including many that are done outdoors, are growing in popularity. Thrill seekers are skiing unpatrolled backcountry and BASE jumping from publicly owned sites. Other risk activities include ice climbing, paragliding, and acrobatic snowboarding (Society of Park and Recreation Educators, 1998). According to American Sports Data, in the last decade of the 20th century, snowboarding has gone up 113% with 5.5 million participants, and their injuries resulting from their activities rose at an alarming rate (Greenfield, 1999). It is important that the possibility of a risk activity be identified, an evaluation of the risks in terms of severity follow, and a plan to mitigate such a possibility is implemented (Ibrahim & Cordes, 2005).

LAW AND OUTDOOR RECREATION

The following legal terms are useful in this discussion of law and outdoor recreation:

- **Act of God:** An unavoidable incident due to forces of nature that could not have been foreseen or prevented.
- **Assumption of risk:** Participation or involvement in an activity or situation where an element of risk is inherent. Voluntary participation can be interpreted as an acceptance of risk. In outdoor recreation, there is an element of reasonable risk that the participant assumes through his or her decision to participate.
- **Attractive nuisance:** A facility, area, or situation that attracts participation and is hazardous. Examples are a footbridge in poor repair, a designated swimming area that is unsupervised or improperly regulated, and children's play equipment in poor repair. Whether a situation would be legally declared an attractive nuisance would be influenced by the laws of the particular state, the age and competence of the injured person, and the circumstances surrounding the incident.
- **Civil law:** Civil action implies a noncriminal infringement upon the rights of a person, agency, or corporation. Tort and contract disputes are examples of civil suits. Civil law is different from criminal law in that it regulates private, ordinary matters.
- **Common law:** That body of governing principles and rules of action derived from past practices, customs, and traditions.
- **Contributory negligence:** Where an individual's action was not the primary cause of negligence, but it was a contributing factor to the negligent act.
- **Equal protection of the law:** The right of equal treatment by the law and the law enforcement agencies for all persons under similar circumstances.
- **Foreseeability:** The degree to which danger may have been expected or an accident foreseen.
- **Immunity:** Freedom or protection from legal action. Sovereign immunity is the protection of the government or the ruling body against possible suit or blame. It is based on the concept that "the king can do no wrong."
- **Injunction:** A prohibitive ruling issued by a court directing a person or agency to refrain from performing a specific act.
- **Liability:** Being responsible for a negligent act or other tort; having legal responsibility, which was not fulfilled and resulted in injury.
- **Liability insurance:** Insurance policies that provide protection against financial loss from liability claims.
- **Mandatory legislation:** Enacted legislation that must be observed. Its opposite is permissive legislation.
- **Negligent:** Not exercising the proper care or following the procedures that a person of ordinary prudence would do under similar circumstances. It can take the form of either commission or omission of an act.
- **Permissive legislation:** Legislation that legalizes an action but does not require or mandate it. Its opposite is mandatory legislation.
- **Proximate cause:** The situation or factor that was the main cause of an injury or incident.
- **Prudent person:** One who acts in a careful, discreet, and judicious manner in view of the particular circumstances.
- **Statutory law:** Law that is made through legislative acts.
- **Tort:** A civil wrong or injustice, independent of a contract, which produces an injury or damage to another person or to property.

Liability and Recreation Agencies

Not long ago liability was hardly a problem with which a recreation agency, public or private, had to contend. Today, the recreation provider and the equipment manufacturer are subject to the threats of a lawsuit. The tradition of sovereign immunity had previously protected public agencies, a right of government inherited from the British legal system where the king cannot be wrong. Today, the government and its agents are not immune, and neither are the provider and the manufacturer. Recreation agencies of all kinds must pay strict attention that all equipment is safe and all reasonable precautions are taken to prevent injury and subsequent lawsuits.

Tort Laws and Negligence

Civil wrongs that are not criminal in nature, such as trespassing, nuisance, defamation, and negligence, fall under tort laws. Most cases related to outdoor recreation come under negligence, which means that the person in charge failed to perform his or her responsibilities at the expected level of a prudent person under the same circumstances. Even if the acts of the person are not intentional, good intentions are not safeguards against prosecution. In the case of negligence, prosecution is done by the injured person and not by a law enforcement person. The prosecution must show by a preponderance of evidence (over 50%) that the defendant was negligent.

According to Jensen (1985), for a person to be declared negligent, the following elements must exist:

1. The defendant must have a *duty toward the plaintiff*. Employees of recreation-sponsoring agencies clearly have certain duties toward participants. In most states, a person does not have a legal duty toward a stranger even when the stranger is in dire need of help. To encourage aid when needed, some states have passed *Good Samaritan laws,* which provide legal protection for a person who tries to assist another person.

2. The plaintiff must have been harmed by the tort or wrong committed by the defendant. This could be in the form of property damage, personal injury, or damage to one's character or reputation.

3. The individual having *duty* must have breached that duty by an act of omission (*nonfeasance*). This means that a person who does nothing when something should have been done is often as liable as one who responds incorrectly.

4. The breach of duty mentioned in the previous item must have been directly related to the damage done to the plaintiff. In other words, the breach of duty was the proximate cause of the damage.

The situations that could lead to possible negligence include the following:

1. **Impudence:** (This is known as the reasonable-man test.) A duty of care is decided upon in court, which involves what a prudent individual should do to safeguard the persons under his or her care.

2. **Attractive nuisance:** This concept revolves around whether the facility or equipment therein are attractive yet hazardous, unsecured, and/or unsupervised.

3. **Faulty equipment:** The malfunction of equipment or an instrument may lead to the injuring of a participant.

Visitors to outdoor recreational areas are subject to protection under tort law according to their status, which is decided upon by the courts. Knudson (1984) classified these visitors into three categories:

- **Trespassers:** A trespasser is a person who enters the property of another without permission and not for the benefit of the property owner. The landowner has only minimal responsibility for protecting the trespasser, taking due care to avoid injuring the person if the trespasser's presence is known. The trespasser should be notified of dangers. Traps set for the trespasser or intentional shooting at the trespasser would make the landowner liable.

- **Licensees:** A licensee is a person who enters a property with the consent, implied or stated, of the owner but not for the benefit of the owner. Examples of licensees are cross-country skiers who receive permission (no fee paid) to use company land or a farm, a person who asks permission to hunt pheasants in a cornfield, or a fisherman who is allowed to cross private land to reach a stream. The landowner is required to warn the licensee of hidden hazards (deep hole, snow-covered stumps, a violent bull) known to the owner, and the landowner is required to prevent willful harm to the licensee. Other than fulfilling those requirements, the owner has few responsibilities for injury to visitors. The landowner is not obligated to inspect the premises for unknown dangers. The licensee cannot receive damages for injury to himself or herself, his or her vehicle, or equipment.

- **Invitees:** The invitee class includes any visitor to a public park, forest, lake, refuge, or other recreation area, or a business visitor to a commercial recreation area, or any visitor to industrial or other land for the benefit of the landowner. If both the visitor and the landowner receive mutual benefit, the visitor is usually classified as an invitee. The owner has an obligation to keep the premises (that portion that is designated for recreation use) safe and to prevent injury to the visitor. This requires the following:
  1. Warnings of danger to the visitor.
  2. Regular inspection of the premises and facilities.
  3. Removal of dangerous conditions or installation of safety measures where practicable.

Despite the vulnerable position of recreation agencies, recent lawsuits are showing that the courts are increasingly ruling in favor of the defendant agencies. According to Rankin (1990), there are two fundamental explanations for this. First, managers of outdoor recreational resources are upgrading equipment and facilities to meet accepted safety standards. Second, agency defense in court revolves around a statutory scheme that relieves the agency of duty to protect the participant. The Federal Tort Claims Act of 1946 and similar state statutes in the United States, which allowed public agencies and their employees to be sued, left several exceptions in the law, for example, policy-level immunity. Accordingly, when a lawsuit results from a questionable policy, the court will reinstate some immunity to insulate the agent from liability.

Although the implied immunity applies mainly to public agencies, another method of defense is used by private, as well as public, recreation providers. A model statute was initiated in 1965 by the Council of State Governments entitled Public Recreation on Private Lands: Limitations on Liability. It became the basis for many state laws on this subject. If the owner allows for the recreational use of her or his land or facilities without charge, she or he owes no duty to keep the property safe or warn of dangerous conditions. But if fees are charged, or if the owner were to willfully and maliciously fail to warn against danger, she or he is subject to a lawsuit.

Waivers/Release Agreements

There have been instances in which damage waivers were not upheld in court, but development in the closing years of the 20th century indicated differently (Rankin, 1990). As a general rule, the court holds up waivers unless there is a statute to the contrary (e.g., if the negligent act falls below the standard established by law or if the case involves public interest). The decision as to what is of public interest is left up to the court. Also, the court examines the language of the waiver to see that it is written in simple, clear, and unambiguous language understandable to laypersons.

Rankin (1990) reviewed a number of cases in risk recreation and suggested that although liability should be a concern of risk recreation providers, fear of unjust and excessive judgments by the courts is not justified. This claim is supported by the case of *Rubenstein v. United States* (Kaiser, 1986), wherein the court ruled in favor of the defendant (United States). Burrell Rubenstein brought action against the United States under the Federal Torts Claims Act to recover for injuries from a bear attack while camping at Yellowstone National Park. The plaintiff was warned through a brochure and signs that bears were dangerous animals. It was difficult to envisage what additional measures park authorities could have taken to ward off a possible bear attack. The plaintiff knew or should have known of the risk of an unprovoked attack.

But in another case, *Niddangh v. United States* (Kaiser, 1986), action was brought under the wrongful death statutes of the state of Wyoming. The plaintiff was acting on behalf of the estate of Stephan Athan, who was killed by a falling tree at a campsite at Yellowstone National Park. Stephan Athan was an invitee to whom the United States owed the duty to keep the premise safe and to warn him of any danger. He was encouraged to enter the campground with a sense of assurance and did not assume the risk of camping. The United States was found negligent.

Lee (1995) pointed out that almost all states have developed recreational-use statutes intended to immunize property owners from liability when people enter their land for activities such as hunting or fishing and are injured or killed, or when their property is damaged or destroyed. Nonetheless, private landowners have no guarantee of safety from lawsuits in this regard.

Kozlowski (1982) pointed out that property owners or facility managers are not held liable for the criminal acts of others in such settings as multiuse trails or open playing field; however, they may have a duty to provide security. Similarly, they are likely to be held liable in the case of rapes or other criminal acts against youthful participants on field trips or outings.

SUMMARY

In this chapter, we provided an idea of how some management procedures can be used in outdoor recreational resources. The basic concepts in management such as management by objectives, strategy management, PPBS, and PERT can be used in managing outdoor recreational resources.

The management techniques that can be used in managing outdoor resources include the process to determine the carrying capacity of a facility and the process to estimate user rates. Units to measure use were discussed as well.

Sources for financing outdoor recreation such as taxes, bonds, fees, and charges as well as grants were presented as possible avenues of financing outdoor recreation. We also presented arguments for and against charging fees for outdoor recreational pursuits on public lands. Those who oppose fees use public education as their model, whereas proponents of fees argue that charging of fees will help control access to natural resources. Also, improvements could result from the use of fees for such a purpose.

Visitor management is a problem for the manager of outdoor areas. We discussed procedures for visitor control, which has some bearing on carrying capacity, along with the need for management of special areas such as wilderness, rivers, and trails. Among the many techniques to be used in visitor management are improvement of the physical appearance of the natural resource, provision of adequate information and education systems, control of undesirable activities, litter control, and the permit system.

Because some outdoor pursuits present risk for many recreationists, we included a section on risk management along with the basic laws that govern liability. We described two court cases on agency liability.

REFERENCES

Clark, R., Hendee, J., & Burgess, R. (1972). The experimental control of littering. *Journal of Environmental Education, 4*(2), 22–28.

Cordell, H. K., Bergstrom, J. C., Hartmann, L. A., & English, B. K. (1990). *An analysis of the outdoor recreation and wilderness situation in the United States: 1989–2040.* (Forest Service RM-189). Washington, DC: U.S. Government Printing Office.

Douglass, R. (1975). *Forest recreation.* New York, NY: Pergamon Press.

Frome, M. (1985). *Issues in wilderness management.* Boulder, CO: Westview Press.

Gilbert, C., Peterson, G. L., & Lime, D. W. (1972). Toward a model of travel in the boundary water canoe area. *Environment and Behavior, 4*(2), 131–157.

Graefe, A., Kuss, F., & Vaske, J. (1987). *Recreation impacts and carrying capacity: A visitor impact management framework.* Washington, DC: National Parks and Conservation Association.

Greenfield, K. T. (1999). Life on the edge. *Time, 154.*

Ham, S. (1984). Communication and recycling in park campgrounds. *Journal of Environmental Education, 15*(2), 17–20.

Harmon, L. (1979, December). How to make park law enforcement work for you. *Parks and Recreation, 1979,* 20.

Hendee, J. C., & Burdge, R. J. (1974). The substitutability concept: Implication for recreation research and management. *Journal of Leisure Research, 7,* 157–163.

Hendee, J. C., Stankey, G. H., & Lucas, R. C. (1978). *Wilderness management.* Washington, DC: U.S. Government Printing Office.

Heritage Conservation and Recreation Service. (1979). *Fees and charges handbook.* Washington, DC: U.S. Government Printing Office.

Hudson, S., Thompson, D., & Mack, M. (1996, April). America's playgrounds: Make them safe. *Parks and Recreation, 1996,* 69.

Ibrahim, H., & Cordes, K. (2005). *Parks, recreation, and leisure service management.* Peosta, IA: Eddie Bowers.

Jensen, C. (1985). *Outdoor recreation in America.* Minneapolis, MN: Burgess.

Kaiser, R. (1986). *Liability and law in recreation, parks, and sports.* Englewood Cliffs, NJ: Prentice Hall.

Knudson, D. (1984). *Outdoor recreation.* New York, NY: Macmillan.

Kozlowski, J. (1982, March). Validity of nonresident and other discriminatory regulations in municipal recreations. *Parks and Recreation, 1982,* 28–34.

Kraus, R., & Curtis, J. (1982). *Creative management in recreation and parks.* St. Louis, MO: Mosby.

Krumpe, E., & Lucas, R. (1986). Research on recreation trails and trail users. In The President's Commission on Americans Outdoors, *A literature review* (pp. 151–163). Washington, DC: U.S. Government Printing Office.

Lee, R. (1975). *The management of human component in the Yosemite National Park ecosystem.* Yosemite, CA: The Yosemite Institute.

Lee, R. (1995). Recreational use statutes and private property in the 1900s. *Journal of Park and Recreation Administration, 13,* 71–83.

Lime, D. (1986). River recreation and natural resources management: A focus on river running and boating. In The President's Commission on Americans Outdoors, *A literature review* (pp. 137–150). Washington, DC: U.S. Government Printing Office.

Lucas, R., & Krumpe, E. (1986). Wilderness management. In The President's Commission on Americans Outdoors, *A literature review* (pp. 121–135). Washington, DC: U.S. Government Printing Office.

Mak, J. (2004). *Tourism and the economy: Understanding the economy of tourism.* Honolulu: University of Hawaii Press.

Manning, R. (1985). *Studies in outdoor recreation: Search and research for satisfaction.* Corvallis: Oregon University Press.

Martin, B. H., & Taylor, D. T. (1981). *Informing backcountry visitors: A catalog of techniques.* Gorham, NH: Appalachian Mountain Club.

Moore, R., & Driver, B. L. (2005). *Introduction to outdoor recreation: Providing and managing natural resource based opportunities.* State College, PA: Venture.

Nilsen, P., & Tayler, G. (1997). A comparative analysis of protected area planning and management frameworks. *Proceedings— Limits of acceptable change and related planning processes: Progress and future directions* (USDA Forest Service General Technical Report INT-371, pp. 49–57). Ogden, UT: U.S. Department of Agriculture, Forest Service, Rocky Mountain Research Station.

Pfister, R. (1990). Participation and management policy: Backcountry recreationists' new preferences. *Leisure Today, 1990,* 60–63.

Rankin, J. (1990). The risk of risks: Program liability for injuries in high adventure activities. *Leisure Today, 1990,* 7–10.

Reiling, S., Cheng, H., Robinson, C., McCarville, R., & White, C. (1996). Potential equity effects of a new day-use fee. In C. P. Dawson (Compiler), *Proceedings of the 1995 Northeastern Recreation Research Symposium* (pp. 27–31). Newtown Square, PA: USDA Forest Service, Northeastern Experiment Station.

Rodney, L. (1964). *Administration of public recreation.* New York, NY: Ronald Press.

Roggenbuck, J., & Ham, S. (1986). Use of information and education in recreation management. In The President's Commission on Americans Outdoors, *A literature review* (pp. 59–71). Washington, DC: U.S. Government Printing Office.

Society of Park and Recreation Educators. (1998, July). Research into action: Meeting the challenges of high risk recreation. *Park and Recreation, 33,* N7.

Stankey, G. (1973). *Visitor perception of wilderness recreation carrying capacity* (INT-142). Ogden, UT: Ranger Experimental Station, U.S. Forest Service.

Stankey, G., & Manning, R. (1986). Carrying capacity of recreational settings. In The President's Commission on Americans Outdoors, *A literature review* (pp. 47–56). Washington, DC: U.S. Government Printing Office.

Tilden, F. (1962). *Interpreting our heritage.* Chapel Hill: University of North Carolina Press.

U.S. Forest Service. (1988). *Use of national forest trails, National Wilderness Preservation System.* Washington, DC: U.S. Government Printing Office.

U.S. Forest Service. (1989). *Report on Forest Service fiscal year 1988.* Washington, DC: U.S. Government Printing Office.

U.S. General Accounting Office. (1998). *Recreation fees: Demonstrated fee program successful in raising revenues but could be improved.* Washington, DC: Author.

Warren, R. (1986). Fees and charges. In The President's Commission on Americans Outdoors, *A literature review* (pp. 5–14). Washington, DC: U.S. Government Printing Office.

Washburne, R. (1982). Wilderness recreational carrying capacity: Are numbers necessary? *Journal of Forestry, 80*(1), 726–728.

Washburne, R., & Cole, D. (1983). *Problems and practices in wilderness management: A survey of managers* (Research paper, INTD-304). Washington, DC: U.S. Forest Service.

Chapter 14

Education in the Outdoors

In some countries, including Canada, Australia, England, and Scotland, outdoor education means recreational activities such as hiking, camping, and canoeing. Many Americans also interpret it the same way, but outdoor education is also a technique to encourage direct learning experiences that enrich the curriculum. Lloyd Burgess Sharp, an early leader in outdoor education, said, "In simple terms, outdoor education means all of that learning included in the curriculum in any subject matter area and at any grade level which can best be learned outside the classroom" (Rillo, 1985, p. 7).

This statement suggests that outdoor education is not exclusionary. Rather, outdoor education is inclusive of many subject areas that deal directly with the natural environment and life situations outside of the classroom. Among the curricular areas often associated with outdoor education are language arts, social studies, physical education, mathematics, science, nature study, and music (Lappin, 2000). Outdoor education can take place in the schoolyard, on the playground, at a park, on a farm, at camping facilities, on a trail, or in the woods. School teachers, for example, can reorganize their classrooms so they become places to organize, analyze, synthesize, and evaluate data that students have gathered from outside the school

(Brown, 1998). An outdoor education experience can take place in minutes, overnight, or for a week or more. Programs are sponsored through educational institutions, camps, recreation departments, or private entrepreneurs, and they may be directed toward curriculum, behavior, recreation, ecology, or wilderness survival. Instructors and leaders have a variety of professional backgrounds, ranging from recreation to biology. They tend to enjoy nature, outdoor recreational pursuits, or high-risk outdoor adventure activities. They often include those who enjoy teaching in a holistic manner, including the mental, physical, and social aspects of learning; those who incorporate the subject and the medium of the outdoors into their programs; those who teach elementary school camping; and physical educators interested in lifelong fitness activities (Ford, 1989). As one outdoor physical education teacher put it, "If we want to keep our kids from staying inside and playing video games all year, we have to teach them how to play outside" (Rose, 2001, p. 17).

The most common definition of outdoor education is "education *in, about,* and *for* the out-of-doors" (Coles, 2000, p. 27). This simple definition, first coined by George Donaldson in 1950, uses three inseparable words to express the place, topic, and purpose of outdoor education. *In* suggests that outdoor education can take place in any outdoor setting that is conducive to direct experiences, allows contact with the topic, and permits participant interaction and socialization. *About* indicates that the topic includes the outdoors and all aspects related to the natural environment. Although any subject may be taught, direct learning must take place through the outdoor experience. And although soil, water, animals, and plants make up the basic areas of study, the student may also learn and practice outdoor activities pursued during leisure time. *For* shows that the purpose of outdoor education is related to developing knowledge, skills, and attitudes about the outdoor environment that will encourage protection and preservation. Programs that teach skills such as canoeing or rock climbing in the outdoors, for instance, have a responsibility to teach students about the setting that is being used so they will learn to appreciate it, care for it, and protect themselves from it (Council on Outdoor Education, 1989; Ford, 1987, 1989). The subject matter of outdoor education, then, represents a holistic approach to the study of the interrelationships of nature, humans, attitudes for caring about the environment, and skill development in using natural resources for survival, as well as leisure pursuits. In the broadest terms, outdoor education is "the interrelationship of the human being and the natural resources upon which societies depend, with the goal of stewardship in mind" (Ford, 1989, p. 7).

TERMINOLOGY

Another early leader in outdoor education, Julian Smith (1974a), explained the desire of many who were involved in outdoor education to keep terminology simple. The definition of outdoor education becomes more difficult when it is associated with or used interchangeably with environmental education, conservation education, camping education, outdoor recreation, adventure education, experiential education, environmental interpretation, resource-use educa-

tion, nature education and recreation, and others. Smith (1974a) said,

> Whatever label is given to the outdoor "thing" there seems to be some common agreement that the vitalization of learning and the guarantee of a healthful, beautiful and permanent natural environment for today's and tomorrow's generations are goals which should be and can be realized. To achieve such high purposes, there is a great need for better communication, but with fewer words and more cooperative action by those who would be educational leaders in these times.

Definitions are necessary when learning about continuing programs in outdoor education. Several definitions follow (Council on Outdoor Education, 1989):

- *Environmental education* refers to education about the total environment, including population growth, pollution, resource use and misuse, urban and rural planning, and modern technology with its demands on natural resources. Environmental education is all-encompassing, and outdoor education is seen by some to relate to natural resources and not to include the wide sense of the world environment. Many people, however, think of outdoor education in its broadest sense and prefer the term *outdoor/environmental education*.
- *Conservation education* is the study of the wise use of natural resources. It tends to be focused on animals, soil, water, and air as single topics in relation to their use for timber, agriculture, hunting, fishing, and human consumption. It is not usually concerned with preservation, recreation, or human relations and as such is more narrow than outdoor education. The use of this term has decreased since the 1960s.

Environmental interpretation is a term often associated with visitor centers administered by national park or forest service centers.

- *Resident outdoor school* is the process of taking children to a residential camp during school time usually for 3 to 5 days to extend the curriculum through learning in the outdoors. This process was originally called camping education. It was later referred to as school camping, but these phrases were discontinued when parents and taxpayers believed they meant the same thing as summer camp, which seemed to be more recreational than educational.

- *Outdoor recreation* refers to a broad spectrum of outdoor activities in which people participate during leisure time purely for pleasure or some other intrinsic value. Included are hiking, swimming, boating, winter activities, cycling, and camping. In many countries, and to some extent in the United States, these activities are called outdoor education, particularly if they are taught in the school as part of the curriculum.

- *Outdoor pursuits* are generally non-mechanized outdoor recreational activities done in areas remote from amenities, urban comforts, and sometimes emergency help. To many people, the terms *outdoor recreation* and *outdoor pursuits* are similar.

- *Adventure education* refers to activities into which are purposely built elements the participants perceive as being dangerous. The activities are not inherently dangerous as taught (under qualified instruction), but they appear to be so to the participant, and thus they generate a sense of adventure. Adventure activities include rope courses, white-water rafting, mountaineering, and rock climbing. Adventure is used to help people grow through adventure experiences (Martin, Cashel, Wagstaff, & Breunig, 2006).

White-water rafting is an exhilarating form of outdoor recreation, which brings people into close contact with elements of nature. White-water rafting may also be considered an outdoor pursuit or may be used to facilitate adventure education. Courtesy of Ryan Howard.

- *Experiential education* refers to learning by doing or by experience followed by focused reflection (Association for Experiential Education, 2013). Many experiential education activities are synonymous with adventure activities and outdoor pursuits; however, experiential education can also mean any pragmatic educational experience. In many ways, outdoor education may be viewed as experiential, especially when learning takes place through outdoor experiences.
- *Environmental interpretation* is a term usually associated with visitor centers administered, for instance, by national park or forest service centers. The term refers to a technique used to help visitors understand the meanings of the phenomena on display and to arouse curiosity for more information.
- *Nature education* and *nature recreation* are learning or leisure activities related to natural resources. The terms were used from the 1920s to the 1950s, and the activities were not usually interrelated, nor did they focus on the overriding concerns of ecology and stewardship of the land. They were usually isolated, individual activities during which participants used natural resources for equipment and facilities, and they involved knowledge of nature.
- *Organized camping* consists of education/recreation activities led by trained leaders in an outdoor setting with emphasis on individual

Environmental interpretation also happens through signs that explain the meaning of a natural area. Courtesy of Garrett Hutson.

development and group living. The camp is a residential or day-use site operated by private individuals, youth agencies such as the Scouts, churches, or governmental agencies. Regardless of the programs offered, the age of the participants, or the duration of the program, the focus is on education, recreation, group activities, and individual adjustment in the out-of-doors. When the program is sponsored by an educational agency, the program is usually referred to as an outdoor school or a school camp.

HISTORY

The origin of outdoor education is difficult to trace. Some believe its beginnings go back as far as Socrates and Plato or to the dawn of humanity. Others attribute the beginnings to the "outing trips" of private schools in the 1800s such as those taken by students of the Round Hill School of Northampton, Massachusetts. Several trace outdoor education to British tented schools, founded prior to World War I, and to German school country homes of the 1920s and early 1930s. Still others turn to the out-of-classroom activities in the Atlanta Public Schools of the 1920s and to summer recreation programs in California. But it is clear that industrialization of the early 1900s brought children from farms to crowded cities, and time and again participants in physical activities became spectators with physical health problems. An era in which tuberculosis frequently claimed the lives of citizens was upon the nation, and as a remedy, the enrichments of outdoor life were rediscovered. Like many other ideas, the notion of outdoor education did not bloom from a single advocate but grew from several movements and dedicated individuals. A closer look at two early programs in the United States and the thinking of several early leaders follows.

Round Hill School

Round Hill School of Northampton, Massachusetts, was a school for boys that operated from 1823 to 1834. The curriculum was unique in offering 2 hours a day of physical education and outdoor activities. Sharing an interest in nature, the outdoors, and hiking, the school's founders, Joseph Cogswell and George Bancroft, located their school on a round hill overlooking the scenic Connecticut River valley within view of the beautiful Berkshire Mountains. Joseph Cogswell is credited as the originator of school camping and outdoor education in the United States. (Bennett, 1974).

Bennett's research uncovered the following proposal in the school prospectus:

> . . . and certainly in the pleasant days of Spring and Autumn, so far from compelling them to remain at home, we would encourage them [the students] to go abroad and learn to feel the beauty of creation and the benevolence of its Author. Short journeys, whether on foot or by other means of conveyance, might quicken their powers of observation, and by refreshing and strengthening their bodies, prepare their minds for more profitable application. (Cogswell & Bancroft, 1823, p. 8–9)

Early after the school opened in 1823, outdoor activities were made available. Cogswell took six of the students on a 100-mile round-trip journey to Hartford. Changing off the entire way, they either walked or rode horses. Student letters refer to Cogswell leading other excursions to strawberry fields and gardens, on fishing and hunting trips, and on camping expeditions. Students participated extensively in outdoor activities such as skat-ing, coasting, swimming, and horseback riding. Art lessons were sometimes taught at the bank of the river. Crony Village was constructed by the boys by burrowing into the hill and adding a chimney and door. Many evenings were spent around the fire cooking and telling stories. Reports indicate the pupils enjoyed excellent health (Bennett, 1974).

Offering a fine education in which camping and outdoor education played an essential part, Round Hill School was described by a student in later years:

> When I left it in 1828 to enter my uncles' Boston office, I was strong, healthy, and self-reliant, though not remarkable in any degree; a fair swimmer, a good shot, and best of all a good rider; and I never can be grateful enough for the advantages which Mr. Cogswell conferred. (Bennett, 1974, p. 37)

Ernest Thompson Seton

The Boy Scout movement (see Chapter 10) took off immediately in the United States and quickly became the nation's largest nonschool youth organization. Other outdoor youth organizations of the early 1900s such as Woodcraft Indians, Sons of Daniel Boone, and Boy Pioneers set the stage for acceptance of the movement. Ernest Thompson Seton, who established Woodcraft Indians, had the background and interest in youth to establish him as the logical choice for the position of first Chief Scout of the Boy Scouts of America in 1910. His many volumes on Scout-craft became integral to Scouting, and his intelligence and enthusiasm helped turn an idea into reality. The handbook *Boy Scouts of America: A Handbook of Woodcraft, Scouting, and Life-Craft* first appeared in 1910, and within the first 30 years of publication an estimated 7 million copies were sold (Nash, 1970). In it, Seton listed nine pertinent principles necessary for achieving the joys of outdoor life. These principles were as follows:

1. This movement is essentially for recreation.

2. Camping is the simple life reduced to actual practice, as well as the culmination of the outdoor life.
3. Camps should be self-governing.
4. The campfire is the focal center of all primitive brotherhood. We shall not fail to use its magic powers.
5. Fine character and physique can be developed through the knowledge of *woodcraft pursuits*—riding, hunting, camper-craft, scouting, mountaineering, Indian-craft, Star-craft, signaling, boating, and all good outdoor athletics and sports including sailing, motoring, nature-study, wild animal photography and above all heroism.
6. Try not to "down the others, but to raise ourselves."
7. Personal achievements will receive decoration.
8. A heroic ideal leads to higher things.
9. The effect of the picturesque is magical. The charm of titles, costumes, ceremony, phrase, dance and song are utilized in all ways. (Nash, 1970, pp. 21–22)

The Boy Scout movement continues. Current programs are discussed later in this chapter. Seton, who immigrated to America from Scotland in the 1880s, wrote,

> Sport is the great incentive to Outdoor Life; nature study is the intellectual side of sport. I should like to lead this whole nation into the way of living outdoors for at least a month each year, reviving and expanding a custom that as far back as Moses was deemed essential to the national well-being . . . it is not enough to take men out-of-doors. We must also teach them to enjoy it.... (Nash, 1970, p. 21)

Other Leaders

In 1903, Liberty Hyde Bailey, another man of insight, wrote of the child's need to study nature. Borrowing ideas from American philosopher, psychologist, and educator John Dewey's progressive education, Bailey wrote,

> Nature-study is not science. It is not knowledge. It is not facts. It is spirit. It is concerned with the child's outlook on the world . . . nature-study is studying things and the reason of things, not about things. It is not reading from nature books. A child was asked if she had ever seen the great dipper. "Oh, yes," she replied, "I saw it in my geography." (Nash, 1970, pp. 65–66)

It is perhaps due to the influence of innovative thinkers and educational philosophers that outdoor education evolved. Two people, Lloyd B. Sharp and Julian W. Smith, are especially significant to the development of outdoor education in the United States.

Lloyd Burgess Sharp, known as "L.B." or as "The Chief," was born in Kansas in 1894. He was first called "Chief" by campers, but he eventually earned the title from others because he was an innovator, promoter, and chief in his field. Educated at Columbia University, Sharp received his BS, MA, and PhD degrees at a time when Columbia was noted for its progressiveness. For several years, he was with the National Recreation Association and taught at Columbia. In 1925, he was named executive director of Life Camps, Inc., and by 1926, he led the organization away from the traditional camping program of centralized camping to decentralized camping with each group responsible for its own program. During the 1930s, he continued pioneering in "camping education" at Life Camps. In 1940, Sharp established National Camp for the training of leaders, and by 1944, National Camp and Life Camps, Inc. had published *Extending Education.* Sharp's vision received national exposure in this publication and others, and his books and publications influenced many in the field of outdoor education (Vinal, 1974).

Numerous methods and practices that were proven successful in outdoor educational instruction were evolved by Sharp and his associates. Sharp made the original proposition that subjects, topics, and courses that could best be learned outdoors be carried out in their own optimum sphere. This concept was the basis of his writing and teaching (Conrad, 1974). Sharp explained, "That which ought and can best be taught inside the schoolroom should there be taught, and that which can best be learned through experience, dealing directly with native materials and life situation outside the school, should there be learned" (Rillo, 1985, p. 1).

Julian W. Smith has been referred to as the Dean of American outdoor education. He served as professor of education at Michigan State University and director of the Outdoor Education Project of the American Association for Health, Physical Education, and Recreation (AAHPERD, now SHAPE America, discussed later in this chapter). Smith's involvement with outdoor education began in 1940. As principal of Lakeview High School (Michigan), Smith arranged for the school to participate in one of the W. K. Kellogg Foundation school camping programs. In 1946, he became the head of a cooperative project between the Michigan Department of Conservation and the Department of Public Instruction to promote outdoor education. The Kellogg Foundation provided partial financial support. From 1946 to 1953, Michigan was known for its innovations in the field of outdoor education and became the nation's primary leader (Donaldson, 1974).

Smith joined the faculty of what was then called Michigan State College in 1953. By 1955, his ambition of the 1940s was realized when his strongly felt need for an umbrella organization to encompass the many fields involved in outdoor education came into being. He became the director of the far-reaching Outdoor Education Project at that time. Many activities were arranged through the project, including three national conferences and a newsletter, *A Newsletter for the Exchange of Ideas on Outdoor Education*. Smith's contributions made the newsletter preeminent among several such publications, and there was evidence that the project impacted and broadened the nation's concept of outdoor education. Eventually, the Council on Outdoor Education and Camping

was developed under the General Division of AAHPERD after more than 10 years of project status. Because of Smith's efforts, thousands of American youth are better off. Smith proclaimed,

> Outdoor education and camping are not frills to be scalloped around the curriculum. In the woods, fields, and streams children can see, feel, hear; they can even smell and taste. Here reality, with all its vividness, becomes both motivation and method for learning. (Donaldson, 1974, p. 59).

Developments

Julian Smith (1974a) described the significant developments of outdoor education in the United States. Early development prior to 1940 began with labels such as field and camping trips, outings, recreation, and camping education. Organized camping, combined with the educational philosophies of Dewey, Kilpatrick, and others whose leadership gave rise to "progressive" education, influenced outdoor education. From 1940 to 1950, resident outdoor schools grew in number, including those in the Battle Creek, Michigan, area conducted at the Clear Lake Camp; San Diego (California) City-County Camp Commission with a program at Cuyamaca; Tyler, Texas; Cleveland Heights, Ohio; and others. What occurred at resident outdoor schools was generally referred to by the term *outdoor education* during this period. An event of particular significance was the first state legislation passed in Michigan that allowed school districts to acquire and operate camps as a segment of a school program. To a great degree, outdoor education was strongly influenced by organized camping at this time, but developments in curriculum, professional training, and programs were strong forces. Near the end of this period, there was a surge of interest in all forms of outdoor pursuits.

The 1950s brought rapid growth in resident outdoor schools and greater emphasis on other out-of-classroom experiences. The Outdoor Education Project broadened the concept of outdoor education and further developed teaching of skills, attitudes, and appreciation for satisfying outdoor pursuits. The National Conference on Teacher Education for Outdoor Education was held at the Clear Lake Camp in Michigan in 1953, and the interdisciplinary approach to outdoor education was emphasized. During this period, the Taft Field Campus was established by Northern Illinois University with its excellent faculty in outdoor education.

The 1960s brought about growth in a wide variety of outdoor education activities, particularly the use of outdoor settings by elementary schools, teaching of outdoor skills, and the increase in the in-service and pre-service preparation of teachers and leaders. Institutions that developed graduate study in the field included Indiana University, Pennsylvania State University, State University of New York, Northern Colorado University at Greeley, and New York University. Expansion of programs was the result of the influence of organizations such as the Outdoor Recreation Resources Review Commission and the Bureau of Outdoor Recreation and was assisted by federal legislation and a number of federal programs in education. By the late 1960s, terminology began to expand, and an increased concern toward environmental education took root.

Since the 1970s, educators have recognized the need to provide environmental education programs throughout all academic levels and to integrate the subject with other subject matters. In 1970, a public outcry led to passage of the Environmental Education Act, which specified state and federal partnerships in the areas of teacher training, curriculum development, and community education programs. More than 50% of the funding never materialized, however, and in 1982, Congress decided not to extend the act. After coming to a virtual standstill during the Reagan administration, new proposals were forwarded by environmentalists for future consideration. These are contained in the Blueprint for the Environment. The formation of the President's Commission on Americans Outdoors also made an impact on outdoor education in the 1980s and 1990s.

This bipartisan commission was appointed by President Ronald Reagan in 1985 to look ahead to determine what Americans would want to do outdoors and to provide outdoor places where such activities could take place. Since the late 1990s, outdoor education appears to have been underrepresented in the school setting despite its potential (Crawford, 1998). Blame has been placed on time constraints, lack of funding, and liability. Creative solutions have resulted. These include staying on campus more often and forming partnerships with other core disciplines to make better use of time and to avoid liability problems connected with field trips. Partnerships with local, city, county, and state parks; federal agencies; sporting goods stores; university recreation departments or outdoor clubs; graduate programs; and nonprofit organizations have resulted in transportation, instructors, equipment, and liability advice. Liability waivers are completed for activities as needed by the school (Rose, 2001).

Philosophy and Teaching Methodology

The practice of teaching outdoor education evolved as a result of years of experience of devoted individuals, outdoor centers, laboratories, and community agencies. Ahead of its time in teaching interrelationships of areas of the curriculum with the outdoors and the environment, the movement offered another means to teach and reach children. Through outdoor education, urban children may learn about the earth by experiencing it. Observation is the theme, and the earth is the teacher. For example, students see erosion in process. They learn to problem solve and to cooperate with others. Students and teachers interact. With the focus off the individual, some students blossom in ways they never could in the classroom.

The primary goal, legal justification, and unique contribution of outdoor schools are found in the nurturing of understanding outdoor science and conservation. Other goals include social adjustments, work experience, and healthful living. Finally, students learn that life is more than mere existence. It is hoped that they discover things in the world that are beautiful. Whatever the outdoor program, the philosophy for outdoor education may be based on the following premises (Council on Outdoor Education, 1989):

1. A prime goal of outdoor education is to teach a commitment to human responsibility for stewardship or care of the land. The development of a land ethic that commands people to treat the land and all its resources with respect at all times and on all occasions is the first value for any outdoor education program. It is action oriented and attitude developing. It recognizes that whatever is taught in outdoor education must be translated into ethical ecological action.

2. Related to the goal of a land ethic or commitment to stewardship must be the belief in the importance of knowing certain facts or concepts. The cognitive purpose of outdoor education must be that of the interrelationship of all facets of the ecosystem. The interrelationship of natural resources with each other, and with humans and their societal customs, is the underlying curricular objective. The understanding of basic ecological, sociological, and cultural principles is prerequisite to the commitment to an ethic of land stewardship. Concurrently, outdoor education does not mandate specific choices in ecological ethics. It prepares people to choose carefully after weighing the impact of the action on the environment, culture, and humanity.

3. People not only need to know the natural environment for the survival of the species, but they need to know it as a medium through which they spend many hours of leisure. Just teaching people about the interrelationships of the resources will not enhance their leisure hours, nor save

them from the miseries encountered in harsh environmental situations. Because humans seek the outdoors for leisure pursuits, it is incumbent to teach the recreationist how to live comfortably in the outdoors and how to recreate with a minimum impact on the environment. The quality of the outdoor recreational experience is directly related to the quantity of the knowledge about the out-of-doors.

4. A fourth philosophical belief is that the outdoor educational experience extends beyond one field trip, 1 week at outdoor school, or even a once-a-year event. It should be taught at all levels and pursued throughout life.

Unfortunately, many young people, no matter where they are from, are at risk of never developing positive attitudes and feelings toward the natural environment because so much of their time is spent indoors with their computers or watching television, riding in cars, and in the classroom. As one professor noted,

> Education, for the most part, occurs in buildings with lots of squareness and straight lines. They tell no story, offer no clue about how they are maintained and at what ecological cost. . . . Students begin to suspect that the unraveling of the fabric of life on Earth is unreal, unsolvable, or occurring somewhere else. (Sierra Club, 1997, p. 2)

Contributions of outdoor education have included the following (Pullias, 1974):

1. A healing and growth-producing relationship with the natural world.

2. A promotion of sensitivity.

3. An assistance in the development of habits of withdrawal and renewal that are fundamental to physical, mental, and spiritual health in modern life.

4. A dealing with abstractions with simple direct experience.
5. A nurturing of the spirit and a bringing forth of communication with the earth.

To be an effective tool in the educational process, outdoor education must be planned, organized, and administered to take advantage of the outdoor situation. The land itself provides the information and, with the assistance of a qualified teacher, the land does the teaching. Because children come to the out-of-doors to learn, they spend as much time as possible learning in the outdoors by focusing their attention on nature. When inside, the instructor expects the attention of the students.

Sharp helped to mold many of the methods and practices that have been proven successful in outdoor teaching. These methods include discovery, inquiry, deliberation, and integration. Learning out-of-doors is a natural process with student and teacher developing a partnership. They observe objects together. Teachers serve as facilitators of the learning process. They must not attempt to be controlling, nor can they expect to have all of the answers. By learning together, students and teachers develop trust and confidence, both of which can often be carried back into the indoor environment. The methodology is simple and direct; it is learning by using the senses.

Discovery learning is the most appropriate method used to teach in outdoor education. Natural curiosity can be aroused in the out-of-doors. More important than knowing answers is the ability to ask questions. Children may be able to provide the answers, and answers can be provided through use of the five senses and through availability of reference materials at the outdoor site and in the classroom. Various curriculum approaches to outdoor education are used (Rillo, 1985):

1. **Vertical articulation:** This approach encompasses the use of a broad theme or basic understanding that is introduced at the kindergarten level. Students at each grade level study the theme but in a more refined and sophisticated manner.
2. **Horizontal articulation:** In this approach, outdoor activities are selected that correlate with basic concepts of each discipline in the curriculum. The study of art, for example, can be offered through opportunities to sketch in the natural environment.
3. **Modular approach:** In this approach, packaged instructional modules or planned units of study are used. Modular programs are particularly popular with recreation departments and park systems that organize programs for visiting groups of students. The modular approach is less time-consuming than the other approaches, but it does not allow for the careful curriculum correlation of the other approaches.

As with all programs in a curriculum, the outdoor education program is evaluated by every participant. It is important that the scope is broad to include not only the cognitive but also the other outcomes of the program, for example, social development, interpersonal skills, environmental awareness, and responsibility.

OUTDOOR EDUCATION IN SCHOOLS

Implementing the practice of studying in the out-of-doors varies by grade level. To date, outdoor education has had its largest impact upon the elementary school curriculum. Lower grade instructors tend to offer classroom-related field experiences and projects at parks, ponds, school sites, and the like. Teachers in the upper elementary levels and beyond may use camp settings. Students in higher grade levels tend to study the out-of-doors through activity and adventure programs. Some high schools arrange programs through outside agencies (see Nonschool Agency Contributions to Outdoor Education). Outdoor education programs are also seen in higher education in interesting ways, for example, in interdisciplinary programs.

Objectives specifically related to school camping programs were approved as early as 1949 by the then American Association of Health, Physical Education, and Recreation at their Boston Convention (Los Angeles City Schools, 1961). These include the following:

1. Consider the development of the whole child.
2. Ensure children's participation in the total program—planning, executing, evaluation.
3. Seek to integrate all of the educational activities around problems inherent in living together outdoors.
4. Make the setting the out-of-doors, and center all of the activities on outdoor traditions.
5. Make complete use of the country's natural resources and outdoor heritage.
6. Base methodology upon discovery, adventure, and direct experience.
7. Stress principles rather than detailed facts.
8. Emphasize the social process of cooperation rather than competition.
9. Make the education experience essentially a group process.
10. Make education essentially an experiential process.

Research done on outdoor education programs for behavior disordered students resulted in a number of positive findings such as improvement in self-concept, social adjustment, academic achievement, and group cohesion. Relationships with peers, parents, teachers, and counselors were improved in some of the programs. Teachers noticed an improved ability to learn specific skills and academic behaviors, and they reported that disruptive behavior decreased when they taught in the outdoor environment. Likewise, residential and nonresidential programs where wilderness camping was used were also reported to be a success. Success was escalated when they participated in high-adventure programming that presented a challenge (Lappin, 2000).

Outdoor Education in Preschool

A day camp program for preschoolers aged 3 to 5 was developed at a university in Ohio and implemented at a local, private day school. The program, offered one weekend of each season of the school year, was designed to give children a chance to grow as total individuals through outdoor skills and shared experiences. A second aim was to provide a social interaction between children and adults during leisure time, and a third aim was to train education and recreation leaders from nearby colleges to work with preschoolers and their families in a nontraditional outdoor setting. To foster the development of a natural, curious, creative childhood, children were given activities to encourage outdoor exploration and use of the senses without pressures. Organizers not only discovered that the preschool children "were developmentally ready for sensory learning, but that they wanted to feel and listen" (Shepard & Caruso, 1988, pp. 28–29). The children also participated in games that were focused on cooperation and sharpened movement skills and coordination.

On camp day, they assemble items in a day pack for their upcoming hike. Staff leaders pack the first aid kit, but each child must carry an item important to the group as a whole. The hike includes a group trip of 15 to 20 feet into the woods, where opportunities to use the senses abound. Here children begin to develop an environmental vocabulary. A color-coded frame tent is put together, and children learn about campfire safety. They mix their own instant drink, wash their dishes when done, and put them away. The children are also encouraged to read a map and a color-coded compass to aid in basic skill development and outdoor vocabulary.

Outdoor Education in Public Schools

Outdoor education programs are not mandated in California, but residential centers throughout the state influence thousands of students a year. Educators and interested citizens of San Diego city and county conducted an experimental community school camp at Cuyamaca State Park in 1946 to test the theory that camping could become integral to the educational program. Aims were twofold: first, to make democracy real and understandable through outdoor living, and second, to give every child of appropriate age a camp experience. The sixth grade level was selected for the experimental program, and 1,201 campers plus some 300 parents, teachers, volunteers, and visitors participated in the experience (Pumula, 1973; San Diego County Office of Education, 1999). Afterward, San Diego's elementary school principals met to evaluate the project, voting unanimously to continue and to expand the program.

San Diego's Outdoor Education Program, the oldest in California, now operates on two sites. Hundreds of sixth grade girls and boys go with their classroom teachers to the outdoor education schools in the mountains near San Diego. Living together in an attractive outdoor setting, children can participate in a 4- or 5-day residential program where they explore the environment with trained outdoor personnel. Students also take an active part in planning their week, setting standards of behavior, and accepting the responsibilities that are necessary for group outdoor living. The San Diego County Office of Education is responsible for administering the Outdoor Education Program, for providing and maintaining facilities, and for hiring the director of outdoor education, staff, and other support personnel.

As part of the regular school instructional program, classroom teachers are responsible for correlating indoor classroom learning with outdoor school instruction. The outdoor school curriculum is one of action: exploring, discovering, investigating, evaluating, working, creating, conserving, and sharing. Outdoor classroom activities include studies in life science, astronomy, biology, meteorology, outdoor skills, Native American lore, recreational activities, and crafts. The outdoor environment includes hills, valleys, rivers, skies, plants, and animals. Campers learn to use maps, compasses, telescopes, binoculars, microscopes, and magnets while using scientific methods of research: exploring, dis-

covering, collecting, recognizing problems, planning, cooperating, proposing, testing, investigating, and evaluating. In conjunction with work projects, students develop an appreciation for, and an understanding of, the complexity of the environment. They also learn the need to use natural resources wisely to ensure that they are available to provide a good quality of life in the future.

The American Institute for Research in their groundbreaking research, administered by the California Department of Education and published by the Sierra Club (2006), measured the behavioral and scholastic benefits of outdoor environmental education among underserved populations. The following was found in this 2003 study:

1. Children who attended an outdoor environmental education program raised their science scores 27%.
2. Children who participated in outdoor education programs showed gains in self-esteem, problem solving, and motivation to learn.

After-School Programs

More than 28 million school-aged children have parents who work outside the home, with possibly as many as 15 million "latchkey children" returning to empty homes after school (Chung, 2004). After-school programs can provide an array of benefits by helping children succeed, thereby strengthening communities. When properly designed, they provide children with a safe environment while shaping attitudes, values, skills, and academic performance. They will only be successful, however, if they have appeal for all stakeholders, including children, parents, teachers, and politicians (Witt, 2001).

Although children generally require some relief from formal learning, many schools are trying to find programs that enrich recreation activities by using them as tools for purposive learning. Outdoor education programs provide rich learning experiences in fun, informal environments and are great ways for park and recreation departments to become critical players in after-

Nontraditional outdoor settings provide a stimulating environment.

University outdoor education program participants enjoy canoeing in Algonquin Provincial Park in Ontario, Canada. Courtesy of Garrett Hutson.

school programs. In California, home to hundreds of high-quality outdoor environmental programs, Governor Arnold Schwarzenegger proclaimed that "every California Child deserves access to a proven quality life-changing school program" (Ruiz-Kohn, 2004, p. 1).

Higher Education Programs

A private college in the Southwest stresses experiential learning and self-direction within an interdisciplinary curriculum. The college expects its graduates to learn to adapt to a changing world. The process begins upon arrival through the college's Wilderness Orientation Program, which is a blend of recreation, social interaction, and inspired learning. Joining highly qualified student instructors, the novices are divided into groups of 10 and led on a 3-week outdoor backpacking expedition. Three days are reserved for supervised solitude and contemplation. Groups travel with the uppermost regard for safety and are taught outdoor techniques, campcraft skills, and low-impact camping. As students become acclimated to the southwestern environment, they are introduced to physical, social, and cultural conditions in which they learn the process of adaptation. Curiosity, wonder, and appreciation become major stimulants for learning. Personal attributes such as self-reliance, cooperation, self-motivation, and perseverance are encouraged. Working together, students evaluate environmental ethics, reverence for nature, and responsibility to the planet. All group members contribute by teaching basic ecological concepts of local flora, fauna, landscapes, and past and present inhabitants of the area. After returning to campus, academic orientation begins.

One liberal arts college used an interdisciplinary approach to teach the interconnections between recreation, language, culture, and the environment. It is a goal of the paired courses, Outdoor Recreation and Spanish, to contrast as well as explore the continuities between Latin American values and those of the United States with respect to recreation and leisure. In doing so, the Outdoor Recreation class emphasizes cultures and recreational opportunities of the Southwest and Mexico. An innovative technique, called Total Physical Response (TPR), is used in the activity-oriented Spanish class to teach language. The movement and actions taught are associated with the outdoor recreation class to provide the setting for learning the language while studying the culture and learning about the environment. Laboratory classes and field trips include outdoor activities conducted in Spanish.

A community college near the west coast takes advantage of the many touring companies, outdoor equipment businesses, rental supply stores, and federal agencies as resources when offering Outdoor Recreation/Education. For the cost of transportation, and in some rare instances, a minimal group fee, the instructor arranges for the class of 20 to have specialized instructors, equipment, and the opportunity to try kayaking at the bay, SCUBA diving in a pool, deep sea fishing off the coast, freshwater casting at a lake, surfing at the beach, ice skating and broomball on an indoor rink, rock climbing at an indoor facility, orienteering in a national forest, tidepooling at a national park, birding at the wetlands in a national wildlife refuge, and petroglyph hunting and desert hiking at a state park. Learning about the habitats and the environment becomes a firsthand experience. On campus, other representatives visit the class to share experiences, equipment, safety, and environmental material in other activities, including llama trekking, ballooning, hunting, stargazing, rockhounding, cross-country and downhill skiing, and backpacking. Local trails are used for plant identification. After drawing a specific outdoor location from a hat, each student plans and presents an imaginary trip for four students for their spring break, accounting for transportation, reasonable financing, outdoor ac-

tivities, environmental awareness, and tours planned en route. Students who might never have been exposed to these outdoor experiences refer to the class as one of their best college experiences, one that they carry with them for the rest of their lives.

A 2,400-acre Outdoor Leadership Center at a Midwestern university serves as a satellite campus. The learning resource has over 1,800 acres of woods and hills for study, a beach and boating facilities for camp programs, experiential and professional development programs, and a rustic retreat and conference facilities for year-round accommodations. Opportunities exist for persons to gain academic credit and practical experience in outdoor education, outdoor recreation, camping administration and leadership, resource management, therapeutic recreation, special education, and other areas. Major programs include outdoor and environmental education for elementary children and children in special education, adventure and challenge education programs, a full residential summer camping season for children and adults with disabilities, leadership conferences, seminars, professional development workshops, and weekend retreats. Training opportunities and internships are also available for students from universities throughout the United States.

Graduate Programs

Educational Directories Unlimited (2001) lists graduate programs that specialize in outdoor education. Some lead to the Master of Arts or Master of Science degree in Education. One of these programs is designed for teachers who hold certification in any subject area or grade level. When an experiential approach to education is used, the goals are to enhance existing curriculums, expand environmental awareness, and use resources beyond the school building. A graduate program in Outdoor Teacher Education is designed to help classroom teachers, outdoor professionals, such as summer camp and nature center personnel, and youth workers to use nature more effectively in their teaching and outdoor programs by helping them assume leadership roles in outdoor, nature, camping, and environmental education. A private college teamed with the Wilderness Learning Center to provide a Master of Arts in Educational Ministries with an emphasis in Leadership, Camp Ministry, and Adventure Education. At one state university, the oldest graduate program in experiential education in the United States grew out of a strong affiliation with Outward Bound and other adventure-based outdoor education programs to offer a Master of Science in Experiential Education.

The Master of Education degree within health and physical education at one state university prepares students as scholars, leaders, and educators. Graduate education provides the opportunity to acquire an advanced theoretical and research base for planning and providing education that is culturally sensitive and learner centered. Value for the health of individuals and communities is a focus of this educational preparation. Students acquire an education specialist option or use it for doctoral study.

Other graduate degrees are offered in Outdoor Education, Outdoor Adventure, Wilderness Leadership, Integrated Ecology, and Environmental Education. One private institute that offers a graduate program leading to an MS in Environmental Education or Ecological Teaching and Learning encourages students to travel in and study different bioregions of the United States, Canada, Mexico, and Bahamas. Research areas include Systematic Investigation of Local Flora and Fauna; Cultural Perspectives of Human Communities; Learning Communities: Group Dynamics, Ethics, and Decision Making; Philosophy of Education; Outdoor Skills and Leadership; Natural History and Ecology; Life Systems and Their Communication; Water Systems: Effects, Interrelationships, and Problems; Culture, Spirit, and Ethic: A Relationship to the Living Earth; Environmental Psychology; Science and Technology and Their Effects on Nature; Environmental Education and Its Applications; Special Topics in Ecology; Ethics of Water and Land Use; Sustainable Human Ecology; Learning Communities: Communication, Leadership, and Advocacy; Methods in Environmental Educa-

tion; Approaches to Research in Environmental Education; Independent Study in Writing; Independent Study; Practicum in Environmental Education.

Extracurricular Activities

The Outdoor Program at a university in the Northwest has been active for more than 30 years and serves as a model for other programs across the country. Embracing all aspects of outdoor pursuits and wilderness activities, it brings people from the campus and community together in a wide range of pursuits and environments. Unlike traditional outing clubs, there are no administrative obligations or mandatory meetings. Serving as a cooperative, the program offers those interested in pursuing an outdoor activity a chance to find others with similar plans. Wilderness goals range from learning new skills to extended expeditions all over the world. Several hundred trips are arranged each year, with a wide range of activities at various skill levels. Most are fairly spontaneous and are arranged by volunteers. All responsibilities, chores, and decisions are borne equally among trip participants who share cooperative costs of gas, food, and equipment rental if necessary. With a variety of resources available, the Outdoor Program can launch just about any trip. Vehicles of all sizes are available through the state motor pool, and a variety of outdoor gear for trips is also available. Resource staff help in any aspect of trip preparation. Trips are open to students, staff, and community. The objectives are cooperative learning and fun. The Outdoor Program provides the community with an outdoor resource center, with libraries and files teeming with valuable resource material.

Typical program activities include backpacking, day hikes, canoeing, kayaking, rafting, bike touring, photography, mountaineering, sailboarding, ski touring, telemark skiing, winter camping, ocean kayaking, and other self-propelled wilderness activities. On-campus events include films, slide shows, speakers, equipment swaps, equipment sessions, instructional sessions, kayak pool sessions, environmental action projects, and environmental symposiums and conferences.

NONSCHOOL AGENCY CONTRIBUTIONS TO OUTDOOR EDUCATION

Many nonschool agencies, including nonprofit organizations, federal and state agencies, local park and recreation departments, and special interest groups participate in outdoor education programs that complement the school setting. In some cases, these programs become part of a school curriculum, or they may serve in the capacity of extracurricular activity. Examples of such offerings are included next (see Chapter 10).

Boy Scouts of America

The Boy Scouts of America (BSA) teaches boys skills for outdoor adventures, with camping playing a vital role in this process. The Family Camping Program, launched in 1984, is designed to give family members ample opportunity to share the outdoor experience. The Boy Scout Conservation Program incorporates educational activities throughout the Scout program, which builds an awareness and understanding of wise and intelligent management of natural resources. The Conservation award, initiated as early as 1914, continues to inspire Scouts to work constructively for conservation by participating in community decision-making groups, research, individual skill development, the planning process, and the action needed. Follow-up includes unit evaluation of the project: what was learned, what else could have been done, and so forth.

Passport to High Adventure (BSA, 2001) is a complete package of everything needed to help older Scouts plan and safely guide council and unit high-adventure treks with the counsel of adult leaders. Ultimate goals include the development of teamwork, critical thinking and decision-making skills, and sound judgment. Some Explorer posts specialize in outdoor activities and conservation. Fields of study include camping, hiking, canoeing, ecology, mountaineering, field sports, fishing, conservation education, safety, survival, and proper outdoor living.

Girl Scouts of the USA

Outdoor activities have always been integral to Girl Scouting. Founder Juliette Low rebuffed the notion of the day that women do nothing strenuous. She believed that girls would be attracted to the out-of-doors for sports, camping, and nature study. Outdoor education experiences take place from preschool to adult training weekends. Camping experiences and facilities are important to the Girl Scouts' outdoor education experience. In Junior Scouting, for example, outdoor education may be divided into camping and campcraft skills, Scout ceremonies on outdoor themes in local parks, and nature, safety, and outdoor education activities. For a number of years, the Girl Scouts have worked with the Environmental Protection Agency (EPA) on environmental issues and projects to promote environmental stewardship. For example, Girl Scouts learn about wetlands management when earning the Water Drop Patch (Christie, 2001). With the EPA's counsel, the new Girl Scout Environmental Health badge will give thousands of girls the opportunity to learn about ways that the environment affects their health.

Young Men's Christian Association

Outdoor education programs are offered at a number of YMCA (Young Men's Christian Association or the Y) units. An example is Camp Cosby, a branch of the Birmingham, Alabama, YMCA, which is located 1 hour from the city on the wooded shores of a lake formed behind Logan Martin Dam on the Coosa River. Although its original site was in a different location, Camp Cosby was set up as a complete outdoor recreation center as early as 1922. In 1981, it opened its small outdoor environmental education program. Starting as an overnight program, it offered canoeing, fishing, and forestry. Growth and interest were phenomenal. Today, Camp Cosby Outdoor Environmental Education Program serves more than 80 schools with most students staying for 3 days and 2 nights, although some stay for a week (YMCA, 2000, 2007).

Girl Scouts gather for a traditional camp meeting at the conclusion of the weekend's activities, where they summarize what has been learned.

A dramatic part of the outdoor experience is the Living History Program. Held one morning or evening, Y camp staff reenact Alabama's past. One program takes students back to 1810, a time when Alabama was part of the Mississippi Territory and Birmingham was a sparsely populated wilderness. In this manner, the students learn history, geography, and basic survival skills. They are taught Native American sign language and how to use silence and the five senses to enjoy nature. The Underground Railroad is the topic of a more intense program that deals with racism and prejudice by presenting the enslaved Americans' quest for freedom.

Staff are young, energetic teachers and recent graduates from college. Besides participating in living history, the staff instruct parents, haul canoes, lead song and prayer, and teach students. Teachers from participating schools and some volunteer parents also teach classes, which include water ecology, orienteering, and outdoor skills, among others. A nominal fee that is charged includes food and lodging. The Y offers a number of

scholarships, called camperships, and many schools raise money to help send children to camp. The aim is to enable everyone to participate. The success of the outdoor environmental education program at Cosby has also renewed local interest in summer camp.

National Audubon Society

The National Audubon Society Ecology Camps for children, teenagers, families, adults, and teachers are guided by experts, who plan active programs designed to motivate participants so they will take a closer look at the natural world. Audubon Camp in Maine on Hog Island on Muscongus Bay was established in 1936 as a pioneering experiment in nature education for adult leaders and teachers. Today, the original homestead buildings are still on-site. Rustic dormitory accommodations house visitors on the 330-acre Todd Wildlife Sanctuary (Maine Audubon Society, 2007). Children aged 10 to 14 learn about nature and how they relate to it. Day and evening explorations instill respect and stewardship for the natural environ-

Desert environments require backpackers to master specialized skills while learning about the nature and wildlife.

ment. Maine youth camps offer marine biology, oceanography, geology, forest ecology, ornithology, and pond life. Adults attend summer camps, too, with subject specialties including field ornithology, nature photography, bird migration and conservation, natural history of the Maine Coast, kayaking, and other courses.

Sierra Club

More than 100 years ago, John Muir and his fledgling Sierra Club espoused to bring others to the wilderness. Sierra Club Inspiring Connections Outdoors (ICO) provides low-income inner-city youth with adventure trips into the wilderness with certified volunteers who are trained in recreation, outdoor, and safety skills, as well as environmental education. Community agencies such as schools, churches, rehabilitation centers, and outdoor clubs provide most of the outings at no cost to the students, and ICO contributes the needed equipment for a safe trip. First started in 1971 by the San Francisco Bay Chapter, the ICO now has some 50 groups of

volunteers located in cities across the country and Canada conducting as many as 900 outings a year that impact roughly 1,500 at-risk youth (Sierra Club, 2001). Their greatest challenge today is keeping up with demand.

ICO students leave the ghetto, barrio, and borough to explore places where forest trails replace sidewalks and concrete, sounds of waterfalls and brooks are swapped for ambulance and police car sirens, and a vast constellation of stars has been exchanged for traffic and headlights. For some, the everyday existence of hopelessness, poverty, and drugs are left behind, at least for a short time, and it is hoped that the mountains can bring a mind-set that will help them to aim high and to become stewards of nature. Meanwhile, Sierra's Youth in Wilderness project seeks to expand opportunities for low-income youth to experience nature by providing grant money for experiential learning in outdoor settings and by looking for barriers that keep schools from participating in outdoor education programs.

Rock climbing can be learned in outdoor adventure programs that stress safety and environmental awareness.

In addition, Sierra Club's Environmental Education Committee has developed a curriculum that is focused on historical and social studies issues for young people. For instance, on John Muir's birthday, the Sierra Club in California encourages all schools to study his impact on the environment, offers a John Muir Day Study Guide to help teachers, and offers the John Muir Youth Award Program to reward children who take action to protect wild places. The Sierra Club Outings program offers wilderness treks to adventurers of all levels. Each trip, planned by a volunteer with fees charged to just cover the costs, incorporates lessons about natural history and environmental issues via hiking, backpacking, rafting, sailing, and so forth. In Muir's words, "If people in general could be got into the woods, even for once, to hear the trees speak for themselves, all difficulties in the way of forest preservation would vanish" (McManus, 2001, p. 40).

Outward Bound

Outward Bound is an adventure-based educational program whose objective is leadership training and self-discovery through challenging activities in a wilderness setting. The concept was born in 1941 when German U-boats were sinking British merchant ships. It was discovered that the older seamen, who awaited rescue in the frigid waters, were more likely to survive than the younger, probably more fit sailors. In his research regarding the reasons for this, Outward Bound founder Kurt Hahn concluded that it was lack of confidence rather than lack of skill that made the difference. Realizing that confidence comes from experience, the Outward Bound "learn through doing" experience met with success (Neill, 2004). Now Outward Bound has a worldwide presence.

Centering on a specific activity, each Outward Bound program offers extensive technical training. Activities include mountaineering, canoeing, sailing, backpacking, sea kayaking, canyoneering, white-water rafting, dog sledding, horse training, coastal trekking, skiing, rock climbing, bicycling, or some combination. Instructors teach the technical skills needed for the particular environment and activities of choice and gradually turn the responsibility over to the participants. Each course offers opportunities to become proficient in basic campcraft, emergency care, wilderness navigation, food planning and preparation, and expedition planning. Care and protection of the environment are emphasized in all courses. During coursework, personal skills in leadership, problem solving, decision making, and communication may be augmented. Although Outward Bound does not consider itself to be a survival school, time alone or a solo experience is an important part of the program. This time is spent in a natural setting with minimum equipment.

Each course has regular on-site safety inspection, and external review teams audit each school's programs. Although students do not have to be athletic or experienced outdoor persons to join in the wilderness challenges, they should be in reasonably

Preparing for this outdoor education adventure in the tropics demands appropriate dress and the right safety equipment.

good physical condition because the courses are mentally, physically, and emotionally demanding. Recognizing that the period between adolescence and adulthood is characterized by rapid change, Outward Bound offers programs especially for young men and women aged 16 to 24. Some high school and college programs have formed partnerships with Outward Bound to offer outdoor experiences for their students. College credit is an option if available through individual institutions. Courses are also accessible to youth, families, adults, and professionals through corporate training programs. Some programs are found in urban centers. Applications are available for financial assistance.

U.S. Forest Service

The Forest Service's natural resource and environmental education program involves educators, resource professionals, and citizen groups in developing skills and techniques for teaching others about their environment. Information and involvement programs aim to familiarize the public about natural re-source matters on national and local levels. The Forest Service's Woodsy Owl symbolizes its environmental awareness programs and offers solutions for environmental problems. The fanciful creature, known for his request, "Give a Hoot, Don't Pollute," has been America's environmental champion since 1970 (U.S. Forest Service, 2001). Woodsy visits schools and after-school centers, providing handout materials for children participating in the Conservation Education programs, as well as Teacher Education Guides for use with elementary school programs. As he helps to guide stewardship activities, Woodsy has taken on a new motto, "Lend a Hand, Care for the Land."

PROFESSIONAL EDUCATION

Another responsibility of education is to serve the professional who will act as leader, organizer, interpreter, manager, and/or administrator in outdoor settings. It can be difficult to prescribe specific qualifications for the outdoor education/recreation professional, but there are some qualifications that may be expected of all employees working in outdoor-related programs (Ford, 1985). These include the following:

1. The ability to understand all types of people and to understand their psychological needs.
2. The ability to understand basic physiological needs such as food, liquid, rest, health, exercise, warmth, and shelter from wind, rain, heat, and cold.
3. A knowledge of basic natural resource understanding such as reading signs of changing weather and basic concepts of ecology including the interrelationships of plants, animals, rocks, water, air, and humidity.
4. An understanding of one or more of the following: trees, flowers, mammals, birds, insects, reptiles, or rocks.
5. A knowledge of minimum-impact camping.
6. A knowledge of how to help prevent accidents and administer first aid.
7. An ability to lead songs, tell stories, teach games, express a sense of humor, display high energy, and possess an attitude of professionalism.

In summary, the leader needs the ability to see the world and interpret it to others who do not have the knowledge and, at the same time, to teach the skills necessary for safe and successful enjoyment of activities in the out-of-doors. The following are examples of organizations and schools that offer professional development opportunities.

American Leisure Academy

The American Leisure Academy serves as a forum for promoting advancement of the quality of life of Americans through creative and meaningful leisure and recreation experiences. It was established to advance knowledge related to leisure and leisure service delivery systems, to serve as a forum for networking and exchanging ideas related to leisure, and to recognize and acknowledge the contribution of professional educators, prac-

titioners, and others credited with advancing leisure and recreation concepts and ideas including outdoor education/recreation.

American Association for Physical Activity and Recreation

The American Association for Physical Activity and Recreation (AAPAR) is a national nonprofit membership association serving over 8,000 professionals, and one of several associations that makes up the American Alliance for Health, Physical Education, Recreation, and Dance (AAHPERD), now called SHAPE America. Members include practitioners, educators, volunteers, and students who are dedicated to enhancing the quality of life by promoting active lifestyles through meaningful recreation, physical activity, and fitness experiences across the lifespan predominantly through community-based programs (AAHPERD, 2005). Its Council of Adventure and Outdoor Education (CAOER) is involved in partnerships and sponsors an outdoor education conference (AAHPERD, 2006). AAPAR maintains its position as a leading professional resource for cutting-edge training, high-quality programs, and establishment of standards in this growth area for all people (Gehris, 2007).

American Camping Association

Founded in 1910, the American Camping Association (ACA), originally named Camp Directors Association of America, is the largest association serving the camping industry. The nonprofit educational organization's more than 7,000 members are composed of all segments of the camp profession who help people experience the out-of-doors, including camp owners, directors, executives, students, businesses, day and resident camps, private and not-for-profit camps, travel and trip camps, school programs, environmental education centers, special emphasis camps, and agency camps. The association's mission is to enhance the quality of the experience for youth and adults in organized camping. To do so, ACA promotes high professional practices in camp administration and interprets the values of organized camping to the public. ACA is the only organization that accredits all types of summer camps based on up to 300 national standards for health and safety that are recognized by courts of law and government regulations. ACA accreditation is a voluntary process with a 50-year history (ACA, 2007). Through the accreditation process, it educates camp owners and directors in administering camp operations and assists the public in selecting camps that meet recognized standards (ACA, 2001).

The ACA offers education and training through conferences, educational events, study materials, and mentors. *Camping Magazine,* which debuted in 1926, is published seven times a year. It offers ACA professional development courses, and the Leave No Trace Center on Outdoor Ethics is dedicated to inspire responsible outdoor recreation through education, research, and partnerships while building awareness, appreciation, respect for wilderness through program offerings, and curriculum for children (ACA, 2007).

National Outdoor Leadership School

Since 1965, the National Outdoor Leadership School (NOLS, 2015a) has taught wilderness skills, conservation, and leadership to over 120,000 graduates worldwide and is the largest backcountry permit holder in the United States. Each area of study provides the fundamental knowledge, skills, and experiences essential for leave-no-trace use and enjoyment of a wilderness environment by emphasizing safety, judgment, leadership, teamwork, outdoor skills, and environmental analyses. Instructors provide hands-on personal instruction that help students develop leadership abilities along with their physical skills. No matter what the topic—group dynamics, risk management, environmental ethics, leadership, managing groups in the outdoors, or natural history—educators will be immersed in the field of outdoor education.

Educator courses are offered for outdoor recreation specialists, classroom teachers looking for new approaches, or persons who would like to become wilderness edu-

cators. Courses extend unique opportunities for professionals to share ideas and to teach approaches and skills with colleagues and peers in an expedition setting. Ideas are exchanged, and students are encouraged to teach a class in an area of expertise. With the assistance of instructors, students alternate functioning as leaders. Classes offer expedition planning, equipment selection, student evaluation processes, and college credit. Instructor courses are offered to people interested in working as field instructors. The NOLS professional training curriculum includes custom courses, leadership training, leave-no-trace courses, and risk management training, all designed to fit unique needs including the U.S. Naval Academy, Cornell's Graduate School of Management, and the National Aeronautics and Space Administration (NOLS, 2015b).

National Recreation and Park Association

The National Recreation and Park Association (NRPA) is an independent nonprofit organization established in 1965. It originated as the Playground Association of America in 1911 and became the National Recreation Association in 1926. The association promotes the wise use of leisure, the conservation of natural and human resources, and the extension of the social, health, cultural, and economic benefits of parks and recreation for all Americans. NRPA's (2007) 19,000 members include park and recreation professionals, educators, citizens, and students who are actively involved on all levels with its numerous branches and sections of specialized interest in the park and recreation field. Their outreach activities can reach professionals and others informed about national affairs that could impact their work and leisure activities. Their annual congress and exposition is held each fall, and the organization's main publication is *Parks and Recreation.*

National Wildlife Federation

The National Wildlife Federation (NWF) offers outdoor educational opportunities for K–12 teachers, administrators, and outdoor educators. The focus is a multidisciplinary approach to environmental education. Education programs, interpretive activities, and indoor/outdoor adventures are taught by skilled training coordinators from one of the NWF Field Offices. Each program demonstrates how nature studies can be readily incorporated into existing classes in the arts and humanities, global issues and current events, and science by bringing the natural world into the classroom and the classroom out into nature. Continuing education and/or graduate-level credits are available. After school is finished, students receive an NWF tote bag and kit filled with classroom materials and lesson plans, regular program updates, and a quarterly electronic newsletter. Workshop topics include information about habitats, endangered species, wetlands, the arctic environment, the northern forest, prairies, wolves, smart growth, water quality, activities for persons with disabilities, and schoolyard habitats (NWF, 2001).

In addition, the NWF offers an inclusive class, called Access Nature, for all audiences, including students with disabilities. Children and adolescents learn about nature as members of their community-based conservation clubs, known as Ranger Rick's Earth-Savers (elementary), Teen Adventure (middle school), and Earth Tomorrow (high school). In partnership with the Wilderness Education Institute, NWF offers educational summer camps for youth and teens at Rocky Mountain National Park in Colorado. Family Summit, their weeklong environmental discovery program, has unique opportunities available for the entire family. And NWF's educational outdoor adventure program offers participants a chance to see wild places and wildlife from around the world.

Wilderness Education Association

The Wilderness Education Association (WEA), located in Bloomington, Indiana, is a not-for-profit organization committed to educating the general public and leaders in the appropriate use of wildlands and protected areas by developing and implementing educational curricula, programs forming strategic alliances with federal agencies,

conservation groups, and all organizations that benefit from wildlands, outdoor leadership as a profession, adventure travel, and the conservation of the wild outdoors (WEA, 2001).

Founded in 1977, the WEA believes that professional outdoor leaders must possess knowledge and skills based on sound judgment and decision-making ability and be able to appraise their competencies and weaknesses candidly. Their 18-point curriculum for outdoor leadership certification is designed to be used in different courses offered to professional wilderness leaders through the WEA. The 18-point curriculum includes decision making and problem solving, leadership, expedition behavior and group dynamics, environmental ethics, basic camping skills, nutrition and rations planning, equipment and clothing selection and use, weather, health and sanitation, travel techniques, navigation, safety and risk management, emergency procedures and treatment, natural and cultural history, specialized travel and adventure activities, group processing and communication, trip planning, and teacher and transference. WEA also offers a Wilderness Education workshop to provide children, adults, and professionals an opportunity to explore the basics of outdoor travel. Their annual conference impacts people from all areas of outdoor education and leadership (WEA, 2001).

Student Conservation Association

The Student Conservation Association (SCA) is a nonprofit, educational organization and the oldest provider of national and community service opportunities in conservation, outdoor education, and career training for students and volunteers in the stewardship of public lands and natural resources. Founded in 1957, the SCA offers conservation internships for thousands of people 18 years and older. These 3- to 12- month, expense-paid internships are available in all 50 states in more than 50 professional fields with the National Park Service, the U.S. Forest Service, the Bureau of Land Management, the U.S. Fish and Wildlife Service, the U.S. Geological

Survey, and state and local agencies, among others. Academic credit is also available (SCA, 2007). Those in high school can volunteer on weekends for the Conservation Leadership Corps or during the summer for the Conservation Commuter Crew. Many join and find future work with the agencies or the SCA.

INTERNATIONAL PROGRAMS

International outdoor education is probably best characterized by a great diversity in outdoor adventures. The diversity of programs is influenced by the immediate environment, time, and philosophy. Although Americans may marvel at schools allowing 5-day camp experiences, Bavarian codes endorse camp experiences of 2 weeks or more. Philosophical goals vary from country to country and may take on a social emphasis, a conservation emphasis or a physical fitness emphasis.

As a result of a partnership between the Canadian Space Agency, the Canadian Wildlife Service of Environment Canada, the Canadian Wildlife Federation and National Resources, and Canada Center for Remote Sensing, a Web-based project linking space age technology to the conservation of endangered species was launched in 2000 (Canadian Space Agency, 2001). The goal of the Space for Species program is to allow students in Canada to become actively engaged with the struggles of these special animals by connecting participating classrooms to four at-risk species: the leatherback turtle, polar bear, caribou, and eider duck. Monitoring their migratory cycle online, it is hoped that students will learn the threats of their existence by tracking a leatherback turtle in its search for jellyfish prey or by following a pregnant polar bear as she searches for a den (Government of Canada, 2015).

Global, Environmental, and Outdoor Education Council

The Global, Environmental, and Outdoor Education Council of the Alberta Teacher's Association believes that young people yearn for more from education than simply preparing for a career. Finding that desirable goals lead to desirable outcomes, they strive to teach toward a vision of the world in which "the environment is cared for; human development is sustainable; human rights are protected; cultural diversity is valued and a culture of peace is the norm" (Coumantarakis, 1999, pp. 1–2). Their mission is, then, to promote quality professional development in the area of global, environmental, and outdoor education by providing workshops and free lesson plans (Global, Environmental, and Outdoor Education Council, 2007).

North American Association for Environmental Education

North American Association for Environmental Education (NAAEE) members believe that education must go beyond consciousness-raising to prepare people for environmental stewardship and working together to try to solve environmental problems. This network of professionals, students, and volunteers working in environmental education throughout North America and 55 other countries believes that to be effective, environmental issues must be integrated into all aspects of the curriculum and into all types of educating institutions for the widest array of audiences (Ocwieja, 2006). Since 1971, NAAEE, based in Rock Spring, Georgia, has integrated environmental groups and organizations dedicated to improving education into a balanced approach through its annual conference, publications, and online services.

SUMMARY

Outdoor education has a multitude of objectives, including to help people live in harmony with the natural environment, to establish a basic understanding of others, to use an interdisciplinary approach to education, to learn to use all of the senses, to learn in the natural laboratory, and to arouse the natural curiosity of the student. Outdoor education is commonly defined as education in, about, and for the out-of-doors.

In America, outdoor education goes back to the 18th and 19th centuries when it began to expand in reaction to the industrialization of North America. Among the early advocates were Joseph Cogswell, George Bancroft, Ernest Thompson Seton, Lloyd Burgess Sharp, and Julian Smith. Their efforts resulted in formal offerings such as Round Hill School and informal ones through youth organizations. Traditional schools became involved in outdoor education through interdisciplinary programs and planned instruction.

As a self-conscious movement in American education, outdoor education experiences have moved from elementary school camping to all age levels and outdoor settings. Preschoolers to adults are enriched by outdoor education courses. No longer a middle-class phenomenon, outdoor education has moved to a greater class-spread and to special groups. Schools without camps seek local settings within walking distance. Farms, forests, and gardens offer increasing possibilities. At the college level, centers for outdoor education have been established and extracurricular programs with outdoor orientation bring opportunities to students, staff, and the community. Academic credit is given for students who are planning careers in recreation or education through undergraduate and graduate institutions.

A number of nonprofit organizations, such as the National Audubon Society and the YMCA, became involved in providing outdoor education experiences, and other organizations, such as the American Camping Association, are concerned with the education and training of staff. Outward Bound offers courses around the world to those who want to learn about practical outdoor skills, self-discovery, and the natural environment. The approaches used to teach outdoor/environmental education can be shared with others at conferences put on by professional organizations. One organization, the North American Association for Environmental Education, serves professionals, students, and volunteers from more than 55 countries throughout the world.

REFERENCES

American Alliance for Health, Physical Education, Recreation, and Dance. (2005, May/June). Its official! AALF and AALR unite. *Update, 2005.*

American Alliance for Health, Physical Education, Recreation, and Dance. (2006). AAPAR ends the way to life long fitness and fun. *Update, 2006,* 30.

American Camping Association. (2001). ACA fact sheet. Retrieved from http://www.acacamps.org/media/factset.htm

American Camping Association (2007). ACA fact sheet. Martinsville, IN: Author.

Association for Experiential Education. (2013). Frequently asked questions. Retrieved July 9, 2013, from http://www.aee.org/membership/FAQs

Bennett, B. (1974). Camping and outdoor education began at Round Hill School. In G. Donaldson & O. Goering (Eds.), *Perspectives on outdoor education* (pp. 33–37). Dubuque, IA: Wm. C. Brown.

Boy Scouts of America. (2001). *Passport to high adventure.* Retrieved from http://www.scouting.org/pubs/ptha/index.html

Brown, R. (1998). Outdoor learning centers: Realistic social studies experience for K–6 students. *The Social Studies, 89*(5), 199–204.

Canadian Space Agency. (2001). Kids, space, and species: Leading the way in wildlife conservation. Ottawa, Canada: Media Relations Office.

Christie, E. (2001). Girl Scouts and the Environmental Protection Agency collaborate on new badge. Retrieved from http://www.girlscouts.org/news/epa.html

Chung, A. (2004). *After school programs: Keeping children safe and smart.* Washington, DC: U.S. Department of Education.

Cogswell, J., & Bancroft, G. (1823). *Prospects of a school to be established at Round Hill.* Northampton, MA: Cambridge University Press.

Coles, R. (2000). *Careers in recreation.* Reston, VA: American Association for Leisure and Recreation.

Conrad, L. (1974). Lloyd B. Sharp's philosophy of education. In G. Donaldson & O. Goering (Eds.), *Perspectives on outdoor education* (pp. 16–20). Dubuque, IA: Wm. C. Brown.

Coumantarakis, S. (1999). Why global education? Retrieved from http://www.rockies.ca/eoec/about/why-global.html

Council on Outdoor Education. (1989). Outdoor education—Definition and philosophy. *Journal of Physical Education, Recreation, and Dance, 60*(2), 31–34.

Crawford, S. (1998). Should outdoor education be a regular part of physical education programs addressing national standards? *Journal of Physical Education, Recreation, and Dance, 69*(6), 11.

Donaldson, G. (1974). Julian W. Smith. In G. Donaldson & O. Goering (Eds.), *Perspectives on outdoor education* (pp. 59–61). Dubuque, IA: Wm. C. Brown.

Educational Directories Unlimited. (2001). Outdoor education graduate schools in the United States. Retrieved from http://www.gradschools.com/listings/all/edu_outdoor.html

Ford, P. (1985). Outdoor education/recreation. In *American Association for Leisure and Recreation career information.* Reston, VA: American Alliance for Health, Physical Education, Recreation, and Dance.

Ford, P. (1987). *Outdoor education: Definition and philosophy.* Retrieved from ERIC. (ED267941)

Ford, P. (1989a). *The inseparable links of outdoor education or you can't divide a mobius* [Julian Smith lecture]. Reston, VA: The Council on Outdoor Education (American Alliance for Health, Physical Education, Recreation, and Dance).

Ford, P. (1989b, February). Outdoor education. *Journal of Physical Education, Recreation, and Dance, 60*(2), 30.

Gehris, J. (2007). American Association for Physical Activity and Recreation Councils: Council for Adventure and Education/Recreation. Retrieved from http://www.aahperd.org/aapar/template.cfm?template=councils_societies.html

Global, Environmental, and Outdoor Education Council. (2007). About the Global, Environmental, and Outdoor Education Council. Edmonton, Canada: Author.

Government of Canada. (2015). Government related initiatives program: Space for species. Retrieved May 6, 2015, from http://www4.asc-csa.gc.ca/AUOT-EOAU/eng/GRIP/Projects/72515.aspx

Lappin, E. (2000). Outdoor education for behavior disordered students. Retrieved from http://www.kidsource.com/kidsource/content2/outdoor.education.1d.k12.3.html

Los Angeles Schools. (1961). *Outdoor education & school camping.* Los Angeles, CA: Division of Instructional Services, Youth Services Section.

Maine Audubon Society. (2007). Todd Audubon Sanctuary. Retrieved from http://www.maineaudubon.org/explore/centers/hogisle.shtml

Martin, B., Cashel, C., Wagstaff, M., & Breunig, M. (2006). *Outdoor leadership theory and practice.* Champaign, IL: Human Kinetics.

McManus, R. (2001, May/June). Happy trails. *Sierra, 86*(3), 40–42.

Nash, R. (1970). *The call of the wild: 1900–1916.* New York, NY: George Braziller.

National Outdoor Leadership School. (2015a). NOLS history. Retrieved May 6, 2015, from http://www.nols.edu/about/history/nols_history.shtml

National Outdoor Leadership School. (2015b). NOLS professional training. Retrieved May 6, 2015, from http://www.nols.edu/nolspro/

National Recreation and Park Association. (2007). Membership. Ashburn, VA: Author.

National Wildlife Federation. (2001). Workshop topics. Retrieved from http://www.nwf.org/schoolyardhabitats/workshoptopics.cfm

Neill, J. (2004). Outward bound: History of an innovative educational movement. Retrieved from http://wilderdom.com/outwardbound/ob.html

Ocwieja, M. (2006). Welcome to NAAEE. Washington, DC: North American Association for Environmental Education.

Pullias, E. (1974). Better education for modern man. In G. Donaldson & O. Goering (Eds.), *Perspectives on outdoor education* (pp. 9–15). Dubuque, IA: Wm. C. Brown.

Pumula, E. (1973). The San Diego California community school camp. In D. Hammerman & W. Hammerman (Eds.), *Outdoor education: A book of readings.* Minneapolis, MN: Burgess.

Rillo, T. (1985). *Outdoor education: Beyond the classroom walls.* Bloomington, IN: Phi Delta Kappa Educational Foundation.

Rose, T. (2001). Incorporating the outdoors in physical education. *Journal of Physical Education, Recreation, and Dance, 72*(6), 17–18.

Ruiz-Kohn, J. (2004). Sierra Club inside the outdoors. Retrieved from http://www.aeoe.org/news/newsletter/articles.sc_ito.html

San Diego County Office of Education. (1999). Images from the past. Retrieved from http//www.sdcoe.k12.ca.us/outdoored/past/past.html

Shepard, C., & Caruso, V. (1988, January). Kid's play in the great outdoors. *Camping Magazine, 60*(3), 28–30.

Sierra Club. (1997, November/December). Last words. *Sierra, 1997,* 1–3. Retrieved from http://www.sierraclub.org/sierra/199711/last.asp

Sierra Club. (2001). What is inner city outings? Retrieved from http://www.sierraclub.org/education/programs.asp

Sierra Club. (2006). *Building bridges to the outdoors.* San Francisco, CA: Author.

Smith, J. (1974a). Where we have been—What we will become. In G. Donaldson & O. Goering (Eds.), *Perspectives on outdoor education.* Dubuque, IA: Wm. C. Brown.

Smith, J. (1974b). Words, words, words. In G. Donaldson & O. Goering (Eds.), *Perspectives on outdoor education* (pp. 23–24). Dubuque, IA: Wm. C. Brown.

Student Conservation Association. (2007). Conservation internships. Charlestown, NH: Author.

U.S. Forest Service. (2001). Woodsy owl. Retrieved from http://www.fs.fed.us/spf/woodsy

Vinal, W. (1974). Still more outdoor leaders I have known. In G. Donaldson & O. Goering (Eds.), *Perspectives on outdoor education* (pp. 45–49). Dubuque, IA: Wm. C. Brown.

Wilderness Education Association. (2001, February). *National conference on outdoor leadership: Shaping the wave of the profession.* Wilderness Education Association Program, San Diego, CA.

Wilson, R. (1999). What can I teach my young child about the environment? Retrieved from http//www.sierraclub.org/education/eear1299.asp

Witt, P. (2001, July). Re-examining the role of recreation and parks in after-school programs. *Parks & Recreation, 36*(7), 20, 22, 24–28.

Young Men's Christian Association. (2000). YMCA Camp Cosby. Retrieved from http://www.campcosby.org/history.htm

Young Men's Christian Association. (2007). YMCA Camp Cosby. Retrieved from http://eeingeorgia.org/net/org/info.aspx?se50890.0.0.4863

Chapter 15

Outdoor Recreational Activities

America's landscapes include mountains, deserts, woodlands, wetlands, prairies, swamps, and tundras. Its waterways form a web over most of the continent, and its coastline, if stretched, would reach halfway around the world. Its wildlife refuges are unparalleled, and its panoramic vistas are a source of American pride. Approximately 28% of the total land area in the United States is in federal ownership, and more than a third of this land comprises federal, state, regional, county, and municipal property (Betz, English, & Cordell, 1999; President's Commission on Americans Outdoors, 1987). Although some of this land is not conducive to recreational pursuits, much of it is open to recreational use. The land available is a living testament of America's commitment to the outdoors, and recreational use provides precious benefits.

Today, 77% of Americans say outdoor recreation plays an important role in their lives (American Whitewater, 2014b). In fact, about half of all Americans engage in some type of outdoor recreation. In 2012, Americans took 12.4 billion outdoor excursions, almost 1 billion more than taken the previous year. Stand up paddling has the highest number of new participants (Outdoor Foundation, 2013). Please refer to Figure 15.1. It is estimated that leisure technology is impact-

ing participation, especially among younger adults (aged 18 to 29). Because those who participate in outdoor recreation consistently report higher satisfaction with their lives, this is likely to have broad societal benefits (Roper Starch, 2003). Because the public lands are available to all Americans at little cost, if any, it is important that the public sector have up-to-date information detailing demand trends to discern if recreational opportunities are expanding in the right direction to meet increasing public needs.

In an analysis, well-known researcher H. Ken Cordell (Cordell, Bergstrom, Hartmann, & English, 1990) explained that the demand for outdoor recreation grew after World War II, when the economy grew to support it. At the same time, many new families were started, and the population rapidly increased. The quality of automobiles and roads improved, fuel became cheaper, and the average workweek declined to 40 hours over 5 days. Outdoor recreational opportunities became increasingly available to middle- and low-income groups. Use of the public recreational lands expanded. By the mid-1950s it burgeoned, but many federal recreational sites were deteriorating. Park Service Director Newton Drury responded with Mission 66, a program to rehabilitate facilities and build new ones by 1966. Conservationists,

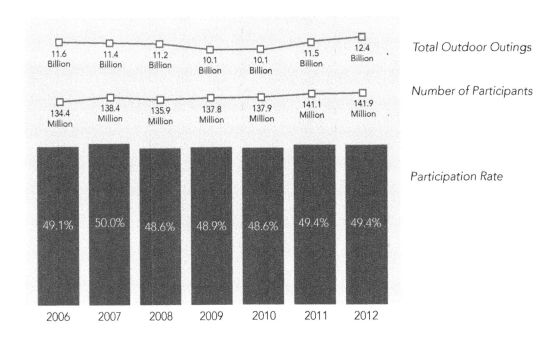

Figure 15.1. Outdoor participation over time. From *Outdoor Participation Report*, by Outdoor Foundation, 2013, http://www.outdoorfoundation.org/pdf/ResearchParticipation2013.pdf, p. 8.

led by Joseph Penfold of the Izaak Walton League, recommended additional action to meet the nation's outdoor recreational needs. The result was congressional action in 1958 establishing the Outdoor Recreation Resources Review Commission (ORRRC). The ORRRC was charged with addressing the nation's outdoor recreational needs to the year 2000 and recommending programs to address those needs. Information was gathered by the commission over 3 years.

The ORRRC found that outdoor recreation was a major leisure activity growing in importance and that outdoor recreational opportunities were most urgently needed near metropolitan areas. Although considerable land was available for outdoor recreation, it was not effectively meeting the need. The ORRRC's recommendations led to the creation of the Bureau of Outdoor Recreation in 1963 (reorganized into the Heritage Conservation and Recreation Service by the Carter administration) to coordinate national

recreation policy and programs, and they influenced the development of the Land and Water Conservation Fund (1965), the Wilderness Preservation System (1964), the National Wild and Scenic Rivers System (1968), and the National Trails System (1968; see Chapter 7).

In the 1960s and early 1970s, demand for outdoor recreational opportunities dramatically increased again. Government at all levels responded to the demands. With money from the Land and Water Conservation Fund, states, cities, and counties expanded their park and open-space systems. Meanwhile, American society changed significantly. Its population increased by 63 million people and shifted southward and westward; the average American became older; the nation shifted from dependence on traditional heavy industry to high technology, communication, and services; and government, business, and residences became less centralized.

The 1980s brought major changes in the demand for and the supply of outdoor recreational opportunities (see Table 15.1). Participation in many activities had surpassed the projections of the ORRRC. A growing population put increased pressure on recreational lands, and residential development took away available open space in and near cities and towns. Technology spawned a host of new activities, from hang gliding, to driving rugged vehicles off-road, to snowmobiling. The population changed toward an older citizenry, more working women, and more single parents. The federal government and many states were finding it difficult to pay for many programs, including outdoor recreation.

A consortium of interest groups went to Laurance Rockefeller, the chairman of the 1960 ORRRC, and urged that he take the lead in stimulating a new ORRRC-like assessment of outdoor recreational trends and needs. He convened with a small group of conservation and recreation leaders. Rockefeller's Outdoor Recreation Policy Review Group concluded that there was evidence that outdoor recreational opportunities were contracting rather than expanding. These findings led the group to recommend that a comprehensive federal reappraisal of the nation's recreation policy and resources be made by a new commission patterned after the ORRRC (Cordell et al., 1990).

When efforts to have Congress enact legislation creating the commission stalled, President Ronald Reagan established, by executive order, the President's Commission on Americans Outdoors in 1985, although the Heritage Conservation and Recreation Service was abolished and with it the outdoor recreation planning process (Betz, 1999). President Reagan then directed the commission to look ahead to determine what Americans wanted to do outdoors and what was needed to ensure that they have the necessary opportunities. The commission's report, *Americans Outdoors: The Legacy, the Challenge* (1987), although not as extensive as that of the ORRRC, contained more than 60 specific recommendations. It urged the establishment of greenways, described as corridors of private and public lands and waters to provide people with access to open spaces closest to where they live; it urged communities to shape growth so they could remain attractive places to live and work; and it recommended intensified efforts to maintain the quality of national resources and to increase recreation opportunities on federal lands. Partnerships between government agencies and the private sector were seen as a key to expanding outdoor opportunities. Finally, the commission recommended that Congress establish a dedicated trust fund to provide a minimum of $1 billion a year for outdoor recreation (Cordell et al., 1990).

ORRRC's recommendation that a national survey about outdoor recreation be conducted every 5 years resulted in a series of general-population surveys coordinated by the National Park Service. These National Recreation Surveys, which began in 1960, resulted in a series of periodic updates to 1982–1983. The survey process continued in 1994–1995 with a new name, the National Survey on Recreation and the Environment; a new coordinating sponsor, the Forest Service; other federal sponsors; and a private sponsor, the Sporting Goods Manufacturers Association. In addition, the Forest Service has been conducting assessments since Congress passed the Forest and Rangeland Renewable Resources Planning Act (RPA) in 1974, directing the secretary of agriculture to prepare a Renewable Resources Assessment in 1975, 1979, and every 10 years thereafter. Although not intended to be a national plan, the RPA assessment is highly valued as the most reliable and scientifically sound assessment of outdoor recreation and wilderness in the United States and for its future projections (Betz, 1999). The 1998 national outdoor recreation assessment, for instance, was conducted by Forest Service scientists at the Southern Research Station along with many collaborators and contributors. These findings were published by Sagamore Publishing in a volume entitled *Outdoor Recreation in American Life: A National Assessment of Demand and Supply Trends* (Cordell, 1999). Some of the findings included the following (Betz, 1999; Society of Park and Recreation Educators, 1999):

Table 15.1

Maximum Preferred Demand for Recreational Trip Away From Home and Indices of Future Demand Growth to 2040

Resource category and activity	Trips demand (millions) 1987	Estimated trips as percentage of 1987 demand 2000	2010	2020	2030	2040
Land						
Wildlife observation and photography	69.5	116	131	146	162	174
Camping in primitive campgrounds	38.1	114	127	140	154	164
Backpacking	26.0	134	164	196	230	255
Nature study	70.8	105	113	120	131	138
Horseback riding	63.2	123	141	160	177	190
Day hiking	91.2	131	161	196	244	293
Photography	42.0	123	143	165	188	205
Visiting prehistoric sites	16.7	133	160	192	233	278
Collecting berries	19.0	113	126	143	166	192
Collecting firewood	30.3	112	124	138	157	178
Walking for pleasure	266.5	116	131	146	164	177
Running/jogging	83.7	133	163	197	234	262
Bicycle riding	114.6	125	148	173	202	222
Driving vehicles or motorcycles off-road	80.2	105	111	118	125	130
Visiting museums or information centers	9.7	118	136	153	174	188
Attending special events	73.7	114	127	141	157	168
Visiting historic sites	73.1	112	143	169	203	241
Driving for pleasure	421.6	115	128	142	157	167
Family gatherings	74.4	119	135	152	170	182
Sightseeing	292.7	118	136	156	183	212
Picnicking	262.0	108	117	126	136	144
Camping in developed campgrounds	60.6	120	137	155	173	186
Water						
Canoeing/kayaking	39.8	113	126	140	157	169
Stream/lake/ocean swimming	238.8	105	110	117	124	129
Rafting/tubing	8.9	111	136	164	215	255
Rowing/paddling/other boating	61.8	112	124	136	150	159
Motor boating	219.5	106	111	117	123	127
Water skiing	107.5	111	121	131	141	148
Pool swimming	221.0	137	169	205	242	269
Snow and Ice						
Cross-country skiing	9.7	147	177	199	212	195
Downhill skiing	64.3	153	197	247	298	333

Note. From *An Analysis of the Outdoor Recreation and Wilderness Situation in the United States: 1989–2040*, by H. K. Cordell, L. Bergstrom, L. Hartmann, and D. English, 1990, Fort Collins, CO: U.S. Forest Service, p. 44.

1. Outdoor recreational opportunities in the United States have increased.
2. Growth in the acreage among the federal estate has been limited, but special designations such as wilderness areas and national scenic rivers have increased appreciably.
3. State park systems and local park and recreation systems continue to supply increasing numbers of sites.
4. Rural private land available for outdoor recreational use has declined significantly, and public–private partnerships have enabled greenways, scenic byways, and watchable wildlife programs to burgeon.
5. The changing and evolving nature of outdoor recreation guarantees that relevant research on experience preferences and motivations will continue.

Each year since 1994 a national study has been conducted by Roper Starch Worldwide for the Recreation Roundtable, which represents many of the country's expert recreation-oriented companies, but who will provide a nationwide recreation plan for the future as outdoor recreation continues to evolve in this century? The renewal of the Bureau of Outdoor Recreation (abolished in 1987) is recommended by many recreation professionals (Crysdale, 2002) for the following reasons:

1. To provide a beacon for trends and standards.
2. To holistically address problems and issues.
3. To assist and provide recreation experience to agencies when needed.

To increase awareness about the many outdoor activities available, a few examples of them are classified in this chapter according to their natural features including land, snow, water, and air. The activities selected are also intended to represent popular, growth, high-risk, or high-tech adventures that cross a variety of income levels. A spe-

cial section, representing viewing and learning activities, follows. The activity section ends with orienteering and camping activities, which are associated with many of the selected activities. Although a few safety tips are included in the activities section, this is not within the scope of this book. A number of courses and books specialize in more specific first aid advice, outdoor survival skills, and instruction. Anyone who is interested in participating in the activities in this chapter should turn to these books and related organizations for the latest specifics.

When low-impact suggestions are given, adventurers should always follow the low-impact advice of the local area management officials. Two not-for-profit organizations, Leave No Trace and Tread Lightly!, offer educational materials that are used by outdoor recreation enthusiasts who want to do their part to diminish their impact on the backcountry while continuing to enjoy their activities in it. Each of these programs, launched by the Forest Service, was based on the same type of premise as their Smoky the Bear and Woodsy Owl programs, which were designed to reduce the impacts of fire and litter.

The Leave No Trace (LNT) education program, developed as an outdoor ethics program for nonmotorized users, went into partnership with the National Outdoor Leadership School (NOLS) in 1991 before the program grew into its present model. Tread Lightly!, conceived by a Forest Service task force in 1985, provides a focus for educational messages geared toward motorized visitors. Through the years, this program steadily added new dimensions to meet the needs of all types of outdoor adventurers. To maximize its effectiveness, the program was transferred in 1990. There tends to be a strong association between outdoor recreation and environmental awareness, and virtually all Americans agree (95%) that outdoor recreation is a good way to increase people's appreciation for the environment (Roper Starch, 2001). Those who want to minimize their impact on the land and water can contact the programs listed at the end of this chapter.

A hiker peers down the world-famous Grand Canyon.

ADVENTURES ON LAND

Land adventures are activities that occur primarily on land as opposed to snow, ice, or water. Together these adventures constitute the largest single category of outdoor recreation participation in the country. Providing a foundation for numerous other outdoor experiences, this volume highlights hiking and backpacking. Mountain bicycling is also included in this section.

Hiking

Trails for day hikers go through beautiful scenic areas throughout the United States. A hike may simply break up a lengthy vacation drive, lead to another recreational activity, or provide recreation in and of itself. Whatever the purpose, hiking is an outdoor activity for

Soft packs are better for bushwhacking, scrambling over rock fields, climbing, and skiing.

Backpacking trips are usually planned well ahead of time so camping reservations and permits can be arranged and maps can be ordered and studied.

almost everyone. For instance, a 2-mile city trail, the Freedom Trail in Boston, attracts 2 million to 3 million people each year. Trails are also designed for those with visual and physical impairments. Other than transportation to a trailhead and appropriate footwear, little else is needed to participate.

A hike often occurs in a natural setting and is generally longer and more vigorous than a walk. For instance, in the United States, there is no doubt that walking is the single most popular activity and that hiking is among the most popular outdoor recreational activities. Over 34 million people are hiking (Centers for Disease Control and Prevention, 2014; Statista, 2014). Hiking is projected to increase marginally faster than the population growth by 2050 (Bowker, English, & Cordell, 1999). At little cost, it provides a setting for social interaction with friends, with family, or in an organized group. Although it can be done alone, it is not recommended for safety reasons. Likewise, groups larger than eight or 10 are not recommend-ed either for environmental reasons. Because hiking provides many diversions along the trail that occupy the mind, it is known for reducing stress and building self-esteem. Most hikers will say each trail leads to a unique experience.

One of the best cardiovascular exercises, hiking, promotes fitness and strengthens muscles. It places less strain on bones and joints than most other aerobic activities, and it is an excellent way to lose weight and guard against osteoporosis. Although rugged terrains provide excellent conditions for cardiovascular development, hills can be strenuous for beginners or for those who do not walk or hike regularly. For instance, as much energy is needed to hike 2 miles an hour up a 10% grade as hiking 4 miles an hour on a level trail (McKinney, 1998). Hikers try to maintain a steady, comfortable pace. For more useful horizontal energy, hikers can try lengthening their stride to increase speed by allowing the hips to turn so the forward leg advances farther and the rear leg swings farther back.

Everyone on the hike ought to be aware of the destination, and whenever there is a fork or change along the trail, all members of the party gather for directions. No one leaves the trail without asking a member of the party to wait. Off-trail hiking, however, is only done where permissible and with a topographical map and compass (see Orienteering section). When hiking off-trail in wilderness, with the exception of the desert, a group should spread out width-wise rather than marching single file. This keeps everyone from tramping over the same ground, which creates undesirable trails. As such, the general rule is to stay on trails. This is always important in the desert because delicate cryptogamic soil is damaged from even the slightest disturbance.

Prior to departure, hikers should leave a note at the trailhead, in the car, or with a ranger or friend to provide the intended destination and the expected time of return, but first they should prepare for weather, terrain, and altitude changes. Even the most healthy and physically fit hikers (backpackers and skiers) need to become acclimated. Regardless of fitness level, altitude can cause discomfort, including shortness of breath, headache, nausea, and dehydration above 5,000 feet. Altitude sickness, also called acute mountain sickness, may begin at 8,000 feet and become more intense at higher levels (McKinney, 1998). Beach hiking calls for knowledge of tide changes. Desert monsoons can lead to disaster when hiking in ravines, which are capable of transforming into running rapids with little notice.

Although required equipment varies according to the length of the hike and the other variables mentioned (see Table 15.2), the day hiker should always carry water or must plan to treat water found en route with purification tablets or a filter. Food packed in is always packed out, and trail mix is really great to take along! It is recommended that day hikers bring an extra meal in case it is necessary to spend the night. A hiking stick is desirable for balance in hilly or rough terrain; some turn to their cross-country ski poles or ultralight trekking poles. The soft frameless day pack should be firmly padded at the shoulder straps and have a pocket large enough for a water bottle. A waist or hip band helps to keep the pack stabilized.

Clothing made of natural fibers suitable to existing weather conditions is recommended. Light colors are best in warm climates, and layering is helpful for day hikes. Special precautions are necessary to protect against ultraviolet rays of the sun including protective lotions, hats, sunglasses with UV protection, and a handkerchief around the neck. Loose pants, tucked into the boots or socks, and long-sleeved shirts provide protection in all climates and guard against brambles and brush, poison oak and poison ivy, and insects. For damp, rainy, and cool environments, breathable, high-tech fabric laminates are hiker friendly, but a water-resistant jacket or poncho accommodates the conditions. Gaiters, attached to the bottom of the boot by a cord, protect boots and lower leggings against rain and snow.

Lightweight hiking boots that have been broken in provide the best protection and traction and are advantageous for longer hikes. Socks that will not bunch or wrinkle help to prevent blisters. Two pairs are recommended. The lighter inside pair moves with the foot and protects the heel. With only one pair of socks, the boots and the socks tend to move together and rub against the heel. Because tennis shoes absorb heat, they can be particularly uncomfortable in warmer climates, but exercise-walking shoes or running shoes can get the novice started.

Safety. Blisters are the hiker's most common problem. Caused by improperly sized shoes, new or stiff shoes, or temperature extremes, blisters can cause incapacitation. Early signs and symptoms are hot spots or sore areas. Treatment involves changing to dry socks and readjusting the boot lacing. The hiker keeps pressure off of a smaller blister to help prevent it from breaking by covering with an adhesive bandage and covering a large one with a plastic-coated gauze pad that absorbs moisture and breathes. If the blister is too painful and there are no health problems, it should be washed and drained before applying antibiotic ointment with a bandage or gauze pad. To drain the large

Table 15.2
Essentials for Hiking and Backpacking

Ten Essentials:

- Compass
- First aid kit (including moleskin, Nu-skin, tape)
- Clothing (enough to survive most probable adverse conditions)
- Sunglasses (goggles or clip on)
- Extra food/water
- Pocket knife, whistle
- Flashlight/headlamp
- Map (USGS topographic)/notebook, pencil (navigation)
- Fire starter (candle, heat lamp, etc.)
- Waterproof matches (or matches in water-proof container)

Clothing:

- Socks/sockliners, two pair
- Weather-appropriate jackets (wind and water resistant)
- Boots
- Shirts and/or sweater (have several including a wool or pile one to utilize the layer) system
- Long pants (weather appropriate)
- Gloves/mittens (wool, pile, GTX)
- Hat/cap

Additional Items for Day Trips:

- Pack (lashcord/straps)
- Plastic bags
- Additional food/water
- Tissue and/or toilet paper
- Emergency shelter (tube tent, space blanket)
- Litter bag
- Insect repellent
- Watch
- Ice axe or walking stick/poles
- Poncho, rain chaps, gaiters, or other rain gear
- Sitting pad (ensolite, etc.)
- Hiking shorts/light shirt
- Insulated cup
- Sunscreen, lip balm
- Handkerchief, bandana/headband
- Camera and film

Additional Equipment for Overnight Trips:

- Shelter (tent or tarp)/poles, stakes
- Extra flashlight battery and bulb
- Ground cloth
- Pot gripper, trowel
- Sleeping bag in waterproof stuff bag
- Eating utensils
- Sleeping pad
- Bag for hanging food
- Stove and fuel
- Nylon cord, sewing kit
- Cooking pot/pans (nesting)
- Personal toilet items, medication
- Water filter or purification kit
- Biodegradable soap and detergent
- Long underwear
- Rain cover for pack

Other Things:

- Swimsuit
- Pack towel
- Camp shoes
- Notebook and pencil (journal)
- Binoculars

Note. Adapted from "Backpacking Checklist," REI, http://www.rei.com/learn/expert-advice/backpacking-checklist.html, and "Summer Backpacking Gear Checklist," NPS, http://www.nps.gov/romo/planyourvisit/upload/summer_backpacking_gear_checklist.pdf. Reprinted with permission.

blister, a sterilized clean needle is inserted under the skin just inside the edge of the blister (Mayo Clinic, 2014).

The spread of Lyme disease makes it more important for hikers to occasionally check their clothes and skin for small, dark ticks when in infested areas. This is easier to do when light-colored fabrics are worn. The skin and hair can be checked before bathing. If a tick is still moving when found, it likely has not fed. If embedded, it is slowly lifted by pulling straight out of the skin with tweezers, trying not to crush the body. The area is washed and an antiseptic is applied. Lyme disease, a bacterial infection, is usually spread by the nymph deer tick. Symptoms include an expanding red rash that may resemble a bull's-eye, fever, headache, fatigue, stiff neck, or muscle and joint pain. A vaccine is available for individuals who spend a good amount of time in infected areas. Other means of prevention include pulling socks over pant legs, wearing a hat and long-sleeved shirt, staying in the middle of the trail, and applying DEET or recommended repellent to exposed areas or to clothing. The tick is saved in a jar for tests if symptoms develop (Kemper, The Healthwise Staff, & The Physicians and Staff of Kaiser Permanente, 2005).

Backpacking

Backpackers can hike deep into the wilderness, carrying essentials in a backpack allowing for overnight outings. The hiker, carrying a lighter day pack, can cover more ground but must return to shelter by nightfall. The increased distance and freedom from civilization can make the burden of the heavier pack worthwhile, but backpacking trips are usually more difficult to arrange on the spur of the moment. Reservations for camping are generally required before, during, and after the trip. It is important to order and study maps, elevations, and current weather conditions before attempting a trip in the backcountry (see Orienteering in this chapter). Beginners may prefer guided trips, which can be arranged by local outfitters, the American Forestry Association, The Wilderness Society, or the Sierra Club, for example.

A packer's hiking speed should be the same throughout the day. The weight is balanced over the feet or slightly ahead; a bent-over posture is only advisable for steep inclines. When going uphill, the stride may be shortened and should be lengthened when going downhill. Steady, even breathing will help to keep the heart beating at an even pace. Resting is important, but for brief stops the pack is not removed. Instead, the waist belt is simply released so the packer can bend at the waist until the pack is parallel to the ground. Hands placed on slightly bent knees help relieve strain on the shoulders. Since these stops only last a couple of minutes, the muscles will not stiffen as the body cools down. For longer stops, the backpack is removed.

In addition to day-hiker supplies, the typical backpacker carries other equipment (see Table 15.2). It is advisable for backpackers to underestimate the weight that can be carried and to test their abilities with short trips before an extensive one is undertaken, or a rule of thumb is to carry no more than one third of the body weight when in good condition and no more than one fourth otherwise. The ideal weight to carry for comfort and agility is no more than one fifth of the body weight (Meier, 1980). A well-ventilated poncho, readily available in the pack, is recommended because it protects not only the packer but also the pack. Excess water weight weighs down the pack. Raingear typically consists of a poncho or rain jacket and pants.

Backpacks generally have external or internal frames. External frames distribute the load more evenly over the back, and the frame allows air to pass between the back and the load. It is suited fine for carrying gear when traveling mostly on trails, but it can throw the packer off balance if there is a need to climb or travel in rough terrain. Internal frames, sometimes called soft packs, have a lower center of gravity and can be worn tighter to the body, making it easier to keep balanced. While they are not as comfortable for carrying heavy loads, the balance and upper body mobility make them better for bushwhacking, scrambling over rock fields, climbing, and skiing. There are also frameless packs that need to be packed just right to fit the body and provide stability. With varying degrees of adjustability, they can be checked as luggage. Light sleeping bags that compress easily and small ultralightweight tents aid in keeping the weight down.

Backpacks arranged so the weight rests on the hips in a balanced fashion are put on by tightening the shoulder straps until the pack is comfortable against the back. While fastening the waist belt, the shoulders are hunched so the waist belt is clinched tightly until the weight of the pack is held directly on the hips. The shoulders simply lend stability. Outside pockets carry items used throughout the day. Other items can be stored at the bottom of the pack or in an inside compartment. Heavier items are placed high and as close to the body as possible. This method allows for the heavier equipment to align with the center of gravity, and it keeps the pack from pulling off the shoulders. All equipment is packed inside to prevent snagging trees. To protect items from moisture and make them more accessible, they may be packed together in plastic bags according to their general use.

Safety. Carrying a pack can certainly be depleting on hot summer days. This is true especially when it is humid. As the body heats, the heat is displaced by perspiration, increased respiration, and dissipation through the skin. Hotter conditions make it more difficult for the body to keep cool. Heat stroke and heat exhaustion are disorders that transpire when the body's capability of removing heat is surpassed by the rate at which heat is being generated.

Heat exhaustion transpires when the body cannot sweat enough to keep cool. Signs and symptoms of heat exhaustion include a weak, rapid pulse, headache, muscle cramps, dizziness, nausea, and general weakness. The whole body may feel cool and clammy from perspiration and appear pale, red, or flushed. Since heat exhaustion can lead to heat stroke, a much more serious and life-threatening condition, it is important to terminate the activity, move to a cooler loca-

tion, drink water, sponge the body with cold water, and lie down if nauseated or dizzy (Kemper, 1999; WebMD, 2014).

Heat stroke occurs when the heat-regulating mechanism fails, putting the circulatory system under great strain. In this case, the body stops sweating and the temperature continues to rise, often to 105 degrees or higher. Some symptoms include confusion, delirium, or unconsciousness. The skin is red or flushed and dry, even under the armpits. While waiting for medical help, the backpacker needs emergency treatment to lower the body temperature quickly by fanning and applying cold, wet cloths all over the body, especially to armpits, groin, neck, and back, or by immersion in cold water (WebMD, 2014). Care is given, however, not to overcool the body if it falls to 102 degrees. Both heat exhaustion and heat stroke can generally be prevented by drinking eight to 10 glasses of water per day or more when exercising in hot weather, drinking more liquid than a person's thirst requires when exercising strenuously, avoiding strenuous outdoor physical activity during the hottest part of the day, resting often in cool areas on hot days, refraining from sudden changes in temperature, and wearing loose-fitting, light-colored clothing that reflects the sun (Kemper, 1999).

As with all outdoor activities, the importance of current first aid knowledge and an adequate first aid kit cannot be emphasized enough. Packers must take care to disinfect water by vigorously boiling for 2 minutes, adding eight drops of household chlorine bleach to 1 gallon, adding 20 drops of iodine to 1 gallon, or following directions on commercial products such as purification tablets or filters.

Low-impact. Hikers and backpackers can help to protect the environment by doing the following (also see Camping):

1. Blending in.
2. Staying on the trail.
3. Moving off the trail only when meeting less mobile trail users.
4. Spreading out when hiking cross-country to avoid creating trails, and

walking carefully on rocks or snow when possible.

5. Following one another's footsteps when there is no way to avoid cryptobiotic soil or microbiotic crusts that are unique to arid regions.

5. Selecting campsites that will reduce impact.

6. Packing out what was packed in.

7. Disposing of solid bodily waste properly.

Mountain Bicycling

With upright handlebars, wide tires, and low gearing, mountain bikes provide cyclists with a nonmotorized ability to leave the pavement and enter a world of beauty. Few activities exploded on the scene like mountain bicycling. Estimated participation increased, according to the Sporting Goods Manufacturers Association, more than 100% between 1987 and 1989 from 1.5 million to 3.2 million total user days (Chavez, 1999). About 5% of American adults claimed to mountain bike (Roper Starch, 2003).

Many of the mountain biking events held in the past few years have attracted hundreds of participants and thousands of viewers. Where allowed, night riding, when done with care and with companions, may provide a new and different experience. Additionally, a number of recreational sites that are open to other activities are open to mountain bicyclists. For instance, downhill skiing facilities open to mountain bikes during the off-season. Almost overnight, mountain bikers discovered roads, trails, and slickrock. Some of the best riding in the world is seen on public lands administered by the Bureau of Land Management in southern Utah. Besides the Moab Slickrock Bike Trails, which caught international attention, thousands of miles of old mining and ranching roads in the area provide access to some of the most amazing backcountry anywhere. When bikers use no-trace etiquette, these and other trails remain open.

The popularity of mountain bicycling, however, has also led to user conflicts, and threats to the environment cause trails to close to bikers. This rising concern has led many mountain bikers to join clubs and organizations that represent their interests and can help them gain access to sites. These developments also spurred the establishment of the International Mountain Bicycling Association (IMBA), a nonprofit, public-supported organization that promotes mountain bicycling opportunities that are environmentally sound and socially responsible. Working to keep trails open and in good condition for everyone, the IMBA publicized their six Rules of the Trail in 1988 for land managers to post at trailheads. These rules are recognized around the world as the standard code of conduct for mountain bikers (see Low-Impact below).

Safety. It is always best to ride with two or three riders in backcountry in case of an accident or breakdown. Essential items for backcountry riding include water, containers, pump tube, patch kit, light, appropriate tools, and first aid kit. They also carry along the same items as the hiker, such as a whistle, candle, and extra food. Because trail descriptions cannot list every turn, a map and compass are necessary. Before leaving, it is wise to check the weather and prepare accordingly by bringing along necessary clothing. Cyclists generally wear cycling shorts or tights, gloves, jersey or light cycling jacket, sturdy shoes, sunglasses, helmet, and appropriate safety gear. Low streams are crossed slowly at a 90-degree angle. Because bottoms are slippery, walking is preferable. By following the IMBA standard code of conduct below, mountain bicyclers protect their safety, their environment, and their opportunity to use the trails.

Low-impact. The IMBA National Mountain Bike Patrol establishes mountain bikers as land stewards, a much-needed help to overworked and underbudgeted land managers who are overwhelmed by recreational demands. Their standard code of conduct encourages mountain bicyclists to do the following:

1. Ride on open trails only (by obtaining permits and avoiding closed areas).
2. Leave no trace (by practicing low-impact cycling, considering other riding options when trails are wet and muddy, staying on existing trails, and packing out at least as much as was packed in).
3. Control bicycles (by paying attention and obeying all bicycle speed regulations and recommendations).
4. Always yield the trail (by slowing down, establishing communication, stopping if needed).
5. Never scare animals (by making sudden movements or loud noises— they need extra room and time to adjust; special care when passing; gates left as they were found).
6. Plan ahead (by knowing and preparing equipment, keeping it in good repair; carrying extra supplies, and wearing a helmet and appropriate safety gear).

For low-impact camping information, please see Backpacking and Camping sections.

ADVENTURES ON SNOW

Trail adventures continue after leaves have fallen when clean, fresh snow transforms the most humble terrain into a beautiful area ideal for snowshoeing or ski touring and other winter activities. With simple equipment, the adventures below can take place as a brisk outing or as a weeklong journey into challenging backcountry, where crowds begin to vanish and the presence of nature intensifies the spirit.

Snowshoeing

By strapping on snowshoes, outdoor adventurers gain access to a winter wonderland of crisp, fresh air and may reach winter wilderness lands that are otherwise inaccessible to skiers because of underbrush or rough terrain. Snowshoes also present a great way to take a look at wildlife from a safe distance. When snowshoers keep an appropriate distance, animals are not forced to waste precious energy to run away.

Although invigorating, snowshoeing is not to be overly strenuous. Even so, the low-impact aerobic activity can burn more calories, 400 to 1,000 per hour, than running or cross-country skiing (Lohr, 1999; Potter, 1998). The 2,000-year-old activity originated in the subarctic region of what is now Canada among the Inuit (once called Eskimo) and spread to trappers, hunters, loggers, farmers, ice fishers, mountaineers, and snowshoe-clad adventurers, who tote their packs into the backcountry. Through the years, modern technology has made the shoes user-friendly. Today's lightweight snowshoes are durable and easy to walk on and maintain. As the saying goes, "If you can walk, you can snowshoe." This does not necessarily mean that everyone can do it well, or that they are in condition for it. It does mean that nearly everyone can do it, making it an excellent group activity. If someone seeks a greater challenge, the lead position is a good place to find it. As groups travel single file, leaders take turns doing the more strenuous work of breaking in the trail. Taller leaders usually need to shorten their normal stride to accommodate anyone shorter following behind.

Snowshoes are tailored for walking, hiking, and running with different sizes in the walking and hiking lines capable of handling anyone from a child to a person over 300 pounds. When a pack is added, it can make a difference, so trying out rented shoes is helpful before buying. Ski poles can be carried for balance and for maneuvering in tight spots. The left pole is placed in the snow ahead while the right shoe is carried forward just high enough to lift the front two thirds of the snowshoe off the snow, dragging the tail behind. The tail then pushes the shoe ahead slightly when stepping down for more momentum until a rhythmic, rolling gait is established. Other skills include learning to travel on slopes, turning, and recovering from a fall.

For outdoor wear, garments designed for cross-country skiing work well. Layering allows for weather changes during longer outings and adjustments as the body warms up.

Heavy perspiration can cause a quick chill-down later. To transport perspiration away from the body, the first layer, or wicking layer, is composed of long underwear made of synthetic fibers and newer fabric designed to wick the moisture away. Natural fabrics, used in low-exertion activities, do not transport moisture away from the body as readily. The middle layer of clothing, or insulating layer, is composed of wool, fleece, down, or treated materials that trap air around the body to provide warmth. In warmer conditions, the legs do not need this layer. A breathable, waterproof outer layer is best for blocking wind and snow. It should provide enough room for the insulating layer, but not be so big that it allows heat loss. An extra layer of clothing can be carried in a day pack for added warmth when stopping for lunch. Hats, gloves, neck gaiters, balaclava hoods, and headbands add comfort. On shorter stints, to accommodate for the generation of body heat from activity, some simply incorporate the "25-degree rule," that is, dressing 25 degrees lighter than the weather would normally call for. This does not account for emergencies, however.

For the feet, lighter, flexible waterproof boots make it easier to snowshoe. Too many socks tend to cut off circulation, impeding the body's efforts to warm the feet. Wool or blended socks work well with a synthetic liner to help wick away moisture. Gaiters are worn around leggings and boots to help keep the powdery snow from getting inside around the socks.

Snowshoe rentals generally cost less than a lift ticket and have become popular means to travel on snow. Guided tours, some offering gourmet lunches, are also available. Meanwhile, cross-country ski centers have become a mecca for snowshoeing, and when ski trails become buried under 2 feet or more of snow, cross-country skiers may switch to their snowshoes. In parks, such as Adirondack State Park in upstate New York, more than 2,000 miles of snowshoe hiking trails go through forests of spruce, fir, and hardwoods; marshes; swamps; and lakes, rivers, and streams from mid-December until mid-March. At Indian Peaks Wilderness Area in the Rocky Mountains of Colorado in the Arapaho and Roosevelt National Forests, snowshoers choose from more than 28 trails of varying difficulty, length, and scenery that pass along mountain lakes, streams, elk, and deer on the way to camping sites or to peak zones, where elevation ranges from 10,000 to 13,500 feet.

Cross-Country Skiing

Many crowded national parks, such as Yellowstone and Yosemite, are advocating that the outdoor adventurer take up cross-country skiing for a pristine winter nature experience. The trails are far less crowded in winter and the parks are more peaceful. Cross-country, or Nordic, skiing is exhilarating and far easier to learn than Alpine, or downhill, skiing. Although comparatively new in North America, it originated many centuries ago. In fact, a crude ski unearthed by archaeologists from a Swedish peat bog is estimated to be over 5,000 years old.

Cross-country skiing may take place on prepared or unprepared trails at parks, at golf courses, and at many Alpine ski developments. Bushwhacking, skiing in deep woods and up and down hills, requires precision skills to avoid trees. Wilderness schools offer excellent instruction for backcountry skiing and how to make quick-fix repairs when in the field. They generally provide lessons in orienteering, snow camping/backpacking, and bushwhacking.

Recreational touring on cross-country skis is in essence an extension of walking with the addition of two basic moves: the kick and the glide. The kick occurs as the skier pushes down on one ski, which causes it to grip the snow as the other ski slides or glides forwaRoad The arms swing as if walking, but poles are carried and placed in the snow in a manner similar to snowshoeing. Poles aid power. As the knee drives ahead, the skier pushes back with the arm and pole on the same side. Other touring skills include turning, recovering from a fall, sidestepping, climbing in a herringbone pattern, moving downhill, and stopping. None of these skills are too difficult, but practice is needed for

Cross-country skiing offers an alternative to the typical summer exploration of crowded parks.

achieve the grip and glide effect. Because the waxable ski can be adjusted to the weather conditions, they can provide the best performance. Waxless skis use a synthetic base to achieve the grip and glide, and they are convenient because they function well in varying snow conditions. For a better glide, glide wax can be applied to the tip and tail sections of the ski. These skis are best suited to soft, new snow or spring snow and in areas where temperatures vary.

In general, longer skis are more stable, but the right length is determined by the skier's weight, height, ability, and the ski design. Providing a hinge between the foot and the ski are the boots. Comfort is the most important feature of the boot. They should flex at the same point where the toes flex. Boots are designed for touring, mountaineering, and racing. As with snowshoeing, clothing is layered. Pants that do not restrict leg motion are best. Skiers benefit from technological advances in clothing, ski equipment, and ski facilities.

A nationwide survey projected that about 3,307,000 Americans participate in ski touring (Snocountry, 2013). Several commercial cross-country ski areas reach out to snowshoers and other trail users as well. As such, the industry has constructively worked on trail courtesies that encourage shared trail use. Snowshoers, for example, unknowingly interfere with machine-prepared ski track grooves in the snow.

Safety. Ski centers create comparatively safe alternatives for snow enthusiasts as the refined trails help them to develop skills, confidence, and preparedness before heading off to local parks, wilderness trails, and the backcountry. Snowmobile trails can be dangerous for snowshoers and cross-country skiers, however, and should not be used unless they are marked for shared trail use. In these cases, great care is necessary, especially among quiet, quick cross-country skiers, who run the risk of collisions with snowmobiles at intersections and corners.

Touring safely in the mountains lies in learning how to choose the safest route. It is important to always travel with a companion, and it is best to find a companion who has

them to become natural. Lessons are available through recreational centers, schools, and colleges; at ski resorts; and through outfitters. As with snowshoeing, it is possible to learn the basic skills by studying an instructional manual, but the advice of an expert always helps beginners to develop technique and skiers with more experience to excel. Learning on groomed trails also leads to greater success and the chance that the adventurer will develop cross-country skiing as a lifetime sport.

Most skiers select equipment for general touring in groomed areas, but specialized skis, boots, bindings, and poles are available for backcountry and Alpine ski touring, telemarking, skate skiing, or racing. Touring skis come in waxable or waxless models. Depending on snow conditions, a varying hardness of wax is used on waxable skis to traveled the same or similar terrain before. And it is best to always gather as much information about the proposed route of travel as possible. Land managers can usually provide information about avalanche conditions that range from low, to moderate, to high, to extreme. A low rating means that the route may be taken, although that does not mean there will not be an avalanche. Moderate conditions require extra care, especially on steep snow-covered open slopes and gullies. During high and extreme conditions, the route is not to be taken (Tilton, 1997; U.S. Forest Service, 1994).

Before leaving, skiers must know what to do if caught in an avalanche and how others can be helped by taking an avalanche course. An itinerary with information regarding who to contact for search and rescue action is given to someone who will know when and if the traveler returned on time. It is important to pay attention to weather and warnings. Traveling with a group is best. Even on a day trip, extra food, water, and clothing are taken along, and a sleeping bag can save a life. Essential avalanche equipment is taken when in avalanche territory as well as a first aid kit, matches in a waterproof container, candle, fire starter, knife, wide tape for repairs, map, compass, and extra food and water (Tilton, 1997; Trailpeak, 2006).

Because safety always precedes adventure, if dangerous conditions occur, it is best to turn back. Large area slides, called *slab avalanches,* are often started by victims, and loose snow slides that trap victims are usually triggered by other members of the party if not by natural causes. Dangerous slopes are not traversed, and cornices are not to be disturbed. If dangerous slopes must be crossed, it is advisable to stay high and to avoid fracture lines and similar snow areas. They are crossed by one person at a time with all party members watching the traveler. The traveler removes ski pole straps and ski safety straps, loosens equipment, and puts on and fastens all clothing. Prudent travelers always watch for evidence of old avalanche paths, recent activity, and unusual weather conditions, and they listen for sounds of hollow snow or cracks. Although an avalanche can occur in other areas, they are more common at higher elevations, on slopes from 30 to 45 degrees, on convex slopes, and on smooth, open slopes. Wind, storms, snowfall, warmer temperature, temperature inversions, and wet snow create dangerous conditions (U.S. Forest Service, 1994).

Low-impact. Snowshoers and cross-country skiers can help to maintain their trails by following these guidelines:

1. Snowshoers stay off of ski tracks.
2. Skiers stay to the right side and yield to faster skiers and those coming downhill.
3. Skiers get out of the track by lifting their skis parallel and off without disturbing the track.
4. When breaking trail, skiers keep skis wider apart than normal as the trail will narrow with use.
5. Both fill and smooth the trail after a fall.
6. On roads, make the ski track near the edge so snowmobiles can avoid it.

ADVENTURES IN WHITE-WATER RIVERS

For thousands of years, the earth's rivers have served as thoroughfares for transportation, exploration, and commerce. Log canoes, reed boats, and crude rafts traversed the rivers past mountains and deserts. The three most common river sport vessels today—the canoe, kayak, and inflatable raft—are descendants of early river history. Each has its own special features and requires independent skills. These modern crafts made of metal, fiberglass, and synthetic material can hit river boulders by the force of currents with less serious damage. As gear and skills improve, advanced paddlers have the thrill of running harder white water on rivers just as different as the settings they traverse.

Viewing nature from the river offers the enthusiast a unique perspective of the land, wildlife, and rare birds. White-water boating continues to attract new participants because it offers a degree of risk that challenges the physical and mental skills of the individual and the opportunities to work in groups. Some rivercraft can be used to explore lakes and wilderness areas or to reach otherwise impossible terrain for backpacking and for fishing. Outfitters run tours, teach skills, and rent equipment, but the future of white-water activities depends on the quality and quantity of available opportunities. Overcrowding is a concern on popular white-water rivers such as the Ocoee in Tennessee, the Lower Youghiogheny in Pennsylvania, and the South Fork American in California. Overcrowding can result in quotas and lower the quality of the experience (Cordell et al., 1999). Growing more popular, white-water paddling is an activity in which 28% of Americans participate—or intend to participate (Roper Starch, 2003).

Canoeing

The modern canoe with its fine sturdy workmanship and graceful lines is a descendant of the North American Indian birch bark canoe (see Figure 15.2). Used for many purposes, the versatile craft is the most popular muscle-powered boat in North America with about 19.7 million canoeists (American Whitewater, 2014b). A good river canoe is designed differently than a lake canoe. River canoes generally have higher sides and lack keels, which catch on rocks and reduce maneuverability. A shorter, wider canoe is slower but more maneuverable.

Lakes are the safest way to introduce families to water adventures and skills, and lessons can be arranged at local clubs or recreation organizations such as the YMCA and the Red Cross. For the more challenging adventures on rivers, wise novices join outfitters on a tour. To control and guide a canoe successfully in white water, it takes keen concentration and strength for a firm and steady hand. Navigating with a partner is an exercise in teamwork, concentration, and skill. In the slender craft, paddlers fight for control of the river's force by finding safe, exhilarating runs and by battling crosscurrents to keep the boat from upsetting. The experienced stern paddler in the back of the canoe is responsible for steering and is the master of the *J*

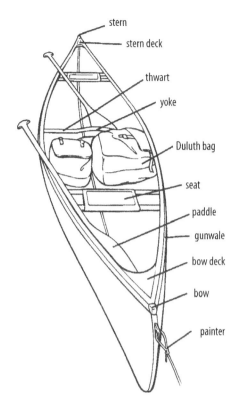

Figure 15.2. Diagram of the components of a typical canoe.

stroke, which is used to keep the canoe on a straight course. The bow paddler paddles on the opposite side, setting the rhythm of the stroke while looking out for rocks or snags. On some trips, it is necessary to portage or carry the canoe past shallow or rough waters.

To the joy of paddlers, the route of the Lewis and Clark National Historic Trail includes designated water trail segments where the expeditioners traveled by canoe, keelboat, or pirogue on the Missouri, Yellowstone, Snake, and Columbia Rivers and their tributaries. Although travelers cope with a series of dams and impounded lakes in some areas, these segments can be retraced today. In Montana, the Bureau of Land Management administers the 149-mile Upper Missouri National Wild and Scenic River, where a section of the Lewis and Clark route has changed very little since the Corps of Discovery's exploration. Also exhibiting the river's dynamic character are two stretches—one

Successful river trips are dependent on the river runner's ability to read hazards and select routes that avoid danger.

from Ponca State Park in Nebraska to Gavins Point Dam near Yankton, South Dakota, and a second above Lewis and Clark Lake—administered by the Army Corps of Engineers through a cooperative effort with the National Park Service (Cordes, 1999).

Kayaking

The kayak is traced back to the Aleutian Inuit of the high Arctic, who built their kayaks by stretching sealskins over driftwood or whalebone frames before rubbing the skins with animal fat to waterproof them. Sleek modern kayaks are designed for challenging white water and wilderness touring. They are also used for slalom and river racing and for lake and ocean adventures. The kayak's exceptional buoyancy allows it to handle fiercer white water. Although faster than a canoe, the longer craft is more difficult to turn. It lacks the same viewing opportunities provided by the canoe because of the low seating. The low seat, on the other hand, presents outstanding opportunities to view birds and shoreline wildlife. On longer tours, "kayakers" may regret that they do not have as much room for storing camping supplies. They do have the option to travel on their own in a single kayak or with a buddy in a double.

Kayaks are outfitted with seats, foot braces, knee pads, thigh braces, back straps, and grab loops for both bow and stern. The paddler sits in a small cockpit, uses a double-bladed paddle, and is held to the vessel by foot, thigh, and knee braces. A waterproof spray skirt seals in the paddler, protecting against water spray. This can cause the beginner some uncomfortable moments. When the kayak tips, the paddler hangs upside down under the water. For this reason, proper and adequate training is necessary. Progressing in both directions from either canoe to kayak or kayak to canoe is common, but the skills are different, making lessons and practice sessions essential before rapids are navigated. For instance, control can be tricky in rapids, which seem like waves to the kayaker who sits so close to the water. Because the kayak is so agile, the paddler must be in complete control. Skill refinements come only after serious effort and practice.

The Nantahala Outdoor Center in Bryson City, North Carolina, offers some 200 clinics for kayakers and canoeists of various skill and experience levels. Local outfitters schedule lessons and tours as well.

Unlike the designs of a river boat, the newer generation ocean kayak is not designed for speed or maneuverability, but rather for stability and comfort. This larger sea-worthy craft rarely tips over even in moderate to heavy waves. And if it does turn over, the kayaker, who often sits unrestrained in an open deck, is not stuck inside. Recovery by climbing back on board is reportedly easy. Suited for younger or older paddlers alike, as well as people with physical challenges, these kayaks are billed as unsinkable and self-bailing, meaning that water will automatically drain out. The saying here is that "anyone who can swim can kayak." Surprisingly, ocean kayaking, also known as sea kayaking or bluewater kayak touring, is as different to river kayaking as cross-country is to downhill skiing.

Besides presenting an excellent cardiovascular workout, kayaking strengthens the arms, shoulders, back, and abdominal muscles, which are important for low back strength and stability. In turn, isometric pushing of the legs works the hamstrings and thigh muscles. Kayaking also improves balance and coordination. From a carryover perspective, many of the skills drawn upon for white-water paddling are similar to the edge-to-edge turning and carving techniques used for snowboarding and skiing. Also, the upper body strength and conditioning required for paddling improves upper body endurance for using poles in snowshoeing or cross-country skiing and overall endurance for mountain biking.

Rafting

Inflatable river rafts, the descendants of life rafts developed for World War II sea rescues, are relatively newer vessels for use with white-water river running. Today, raft tours provide beginners and others the luxury of traveling through churning rapids with little exertion or any great demands. Rafts are limiting because they only travel downstream, and transportation must be arranged to carry rafters up the river for another run. Ranging in style from inflatables suited for two to larger pontoons capable of holding numerous passengers and equipment, rafts offer a variety of experiences. Exceptionally buoyant, they bounce off boulders and waves that would demolish other boats. Made of puncture-resistant material, the raft is composed of small air chambers that link together. If one chamber is damaged, the remaining flotation chambers retain their buoyancy. A diagram of the typical components of a river raft is shown in Figure 15.3. Rafting is probably safer and easier than other white-water activities.

Commercial raft trips provide an excellent means to experience river running. Professionals pilot the craft while passengers take a turn at the oars or shift their weight according to command. Guides often prepare meals at rest stops along the river, which provides the guests with additional time for hiking, photography, swimming, and exploration. Because plastic bags are inadequate protection for cameras, most people use army surplus ammo boxes, pelican-style camera boxes, and plastic products that enclose cameras. In Yellowstone, float trips down the Yellowstone River provide tourists with outstanding opportunities to view wildlife. A trip in Canyonlands National Park floats past ancient Anasazi ruins and petroglyphs carved in rock. The Upper Gauley in West Virginia races passengers through thrilling, swirling Class V river challenges, not meant for beginners or the faint-of-heart.

River safety. Successful river trips are dependent on the river runner's ability to read hazards and select routes that avoid danger. Guidebooks, U.S. Geological Survey maps, rangers, and wilderness outfitters are consulted before a downriver adventure is attempted. The ability to swim is essen-

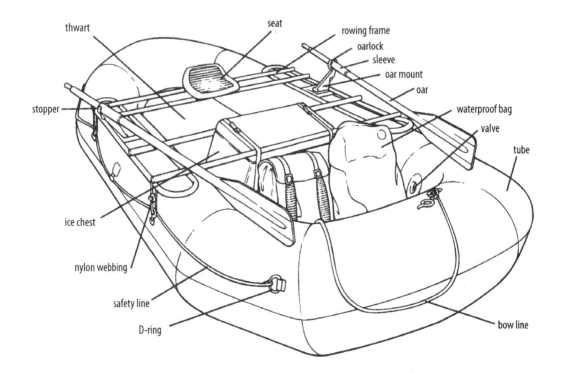

Figure 15.3. Diagram of the typical components of a river raft.

tial, life jackets or personal flotation devices (PFDs) are a must, and skillful boat handling is important but not enough—the adventurer needs to know how to read water and weather. Rivers have common features such as wide V-patterns, known as tongues, which point the way downstream between rocks. V-patterns pointing upstream warn of submerged boulders, and a horizontal line indicates that a dam or vertical drop lies ahead. Dangerous water traps called suckholes form when water flows over an obstacle with force, causing the flow to reverse at the base of the obstacle. These currents may form a hole that can trap a boat. Eddies or pools of calm water that tend to collect debris can be found in the midst of raging streams. They can provide a refuge, a place to relax and judge the next set of rapids (David & Moran, 1983). Even before entering the craft, rafters should make efforts to identify rough water, boulders, and other obstacles from shore.

Small dams are responsible for over 8% of river fatalities, and accidents could have been prevented by wearing a life vest. Extremes are avoided including high flows and cold temperatures (American Whitewater, 2014a).

River running is an exciting risk activity. Life jackets, boating helmets, and protective sport shoes are worn. Wet suits provide protection against hypothermia if the wearer is thrown into cold waters. When capsized, the general rule is to stay with the craft because it should be able to support the passengers even when filled with water. Ropes attached to the craft allow the boater to hang on with one hand while paddling to shore with the other. Containers for boiling water, safety lines for rescues, extra flotation devices, emergency rations, first aid kits, and extra paddles are carried along. Clothing items may include a wool hat, wool or synthetic sweater, wool socks, gloves, windbreaker, rain parka or paddling jacket, swimsuit, sunglasses, a change of clothes, and broad-brimmed hat for after river running. Other items include a hat for shore, suntan lotion, and bug repellent. Equipment is always checked to be sure that it is in good repair,

and appropriate repair materials are taken along. Supplies should be placed in waterproof protectors that are strapped to the craft. A person should never boat alone. A minimum of three boats and boaters should travel together and maintain visual communication. Local rules are followed.

A river trip is not attempted until the necessary skills are mastered in calm water. Rivers of higher levels are attempted only after lower grades are mastered. A shortened version of the standard rating system used to compare difficulty throughout the world, called the International Rating Scale for Whitewater Rivers, follows:

- **Class I: Easy.** Fast-moving water with a few riffles and small waves. Few or no obstructions with slight risk to swimmers.
- **Class II: Novice.** Easy rapids with obvious channels. Rocks and waves are easily missed by trained paddlers. Some maneuvering is required, but no scouting is necessary. Swimmers are seldom injured.
- **Class III: Intermediate.** Rapids with moderate, irregular waves are capable of swamping an open canoe. Fast currents in narrow passages require complex maneuvers. Large waves or strainers can be easily avoided. The inexperienced should scout. Injuries to swimmers are rare, and self-rescue is possible. Group assistance may be required, however, to avoid long swims.
- **Class IV: Advanced.** Intense, powerful but predictable rapids with constricted passages that often require precise maneuvering in turbulent waters. There may be large, unavoidable waves and holes. Scouting from shore is necessary. Risk of injury to swimmers is moderate to high, and rescue may be difficult.
- **Class V: Expert.** Extremely long, obstructed, or very violent rapids expose a paddler to added risk. Drops may contain large, unavoidable

364 OUTDOOR RECREATION Enrichment for a Lifetime

waves and holes or steep, congested chutes with complex, demanding routes. Rapids may continue for long distances between pools, demanding a high level of fitness. What eddies exist may be small, turbulent, or hard to reach. Rescue is difficult, and there is significant hazard to life. Scouting is recommended but may be difficult. Swims are dangerous, and rescue is often difficult even for experts. Proper equipment, extensive experience, and practiced rescue skills are essential.

- **Class VI: Extreme and Exploratory.** These runs have almost never been attempted and often exemplify the extremes of difficulty, unpredictability, and danger. The consequences of errors are very severe, and rescue may be impossible. This class is for teams of experts only, at favorable water levels, after close personal inspection, and after taking all precautions. After a Class VI rapid has been run many times, the rating may be changed to an appropriate Class V rating.

Low-impact. Each river has different guidelines to follow for minimum-impact techniques that should be observed. On some rivers, campsites are assigned. When a choice may be made, camps are made on nonvegetated sites. Some areas stress making camp below the waterline so any possible trace is washed away with later floods. The following guidelines can help keep campsites in good shape:

1. Everything packed in is packed out.
2. Because open fires result in ashes, charcoal, partially burnt garbage, and blackened fire rings, pack stoves are used.
3. Dishwashing is done at least 200 feet away from any side streams with small amounts of biodegradable soap. The water is then strained and scattered.

4. Where there are no toilets, there are several commercially available portable toilet-type devices that solve human waste problems. Otherwise, leak-resistant methods to pack out solid human waste can be devised from ammo cans and heavy-duty plastic bags. Aqua Chem or bleach should be used.
5. By camping only on durable surfaces in remote areas and staying in well-established campsites in popular areas, campers can minimize changes to the landscape and prevent the proliferation of unnecessary campsites.
6. If there is no established campsite or no suitable sandy beach for a site, campers camp at least 100 feet from the river and 200 feet from side streams and springs. They take alternate paths to the river and between tent sites. This will help protect the fragile riverside ecosystem known as the riparian area. Wildlife depend on this zone for food, water, cover, and shelter, and it is a natural travel route for migratory birds and animals.
7. Avoid sites for camping that show slight use. With time and rest, these sites may revert back to their natural appearance if left alone. If not left alone, a certain trampling threshold may be reached from which the area may become barren. This can occur after only a couple tramplings in one season. Then the site expands and deteriorates rapidly, and nonnative and noxious weeds may be encouraged to grow that provide poor forage for wildlife.
8. Prior to leaving, the camper naturalizes the area by covering up scuffed up areas with native materials such as pine needles and rakes matted grassy areas with a stick to help recovery.
9. The Camping section of this chapter offers general low-impact camp techniques.

ADVENTURES IN THE OCEAN

The ocean can invade the senses with its unique environment, its own geology, and its life forms. The ocean's mystery is intensified by its moods and contrasts between its wild nature and serenity. It may even be this very characteristic that induces people to explore its depths and its tidepools and to exhilarate in its challenges.

Skin Diving and SCUBA Diving

Diving underwater dates back to the earliest of times. Human lungs were eventually aided by air-filled animal bladders, and then the development of the air compressor in the early 1800s opened the way for the modern era of underwater sea diving. By 1819, Augustus Siebe of England developed the forerunner of the modern diving outfit. In 1943, Jacques-Yves Cousteau and Emile Gagnan introduced the aqualung, which regulated air automatically in relation to the depth of the diver. By the 1960s, SCUBA diving (that is, diving with a Self-Contained Underwater Breathing Apparatus) had become the fastest growing American activity, and by the 1970s, an estimated 10% of the population owned some type of diving gear (Fisher & Brown, 1979). Today's bright array of equipment allows the underwater adventurer to explore a unique, fascinating, and peaceful world. In the United States, 3% of American adults scuba dive or snorkel (Roper Starch, 2003).

Supervised lessons are essential. Many enthusiasts start by trying the older, simpler, and inexpensive skindiving (also called snorkeling, free diving, or breath-hold diving). Snorkeling, a popular family activity, teaches valuable SCUBA skills, including breathing through a mouthpiece with a snorkel and using a mask and fins. By diving down, a snorkeler can explore a reef from top to bottom, much like a SCUBA diver. Free divers, however, can explore only as long as they can hold their breath. The snorkel is not useful for breathing unless the snorkeler returns to the surface of the water where the breathing activity takes place.

Many SCUBA divers prefer shallow dives as well because that is where the light and color are better. They build slowly to deeper depths under the supervision of a teacher, generally on guided dives. SCUBA lessons are available at many ocean resorts, schools and colleges, recreational centers, community organizations, and SCUBA clubs and organizations. Certification is necessary to go on a dive, rent equipment, or fill up an air tank. Participants that decide to pursue certification (or C card) must be at least 12 years old to enroll in a SCUBA course. Organizations that certify divers and train instructors have similar requirements for certification, although classroom time, philosophy, and teacher training differ. Most require a physical examination, swim test, and about 16 to 24 hours of classroom and pool use followed by 4 or 5 hours of open-water dives (Berger, 2000). Some classes are intensive, and others run over a stretch of time. Some courses do open-water dives at tropical destinations. Without appropriate attention and reassurance at this phase, divers tend to drop out, finding the ocean dive a traumatic experience. For this reason, it is wise to do research first and/or to interview instructors to find out the ratio of pupils per teacher at open-water dives. Once certification is obtained, it is important to keep up with skills and/or take a refresher course. Advanced courses are available, and lessons in photography, wreck diving, and night diving are offered through several diving shops and clubs. Cave and ice diving are a few of the diving activities done today. Truth Aquatics sends dive boats to the Channel Islands National Park, and Cave Excursions offers trips in Florida.

Safety. Before diving, it is important to be in good physical health. A medical examination is highly recommended. All divers should be competent swimmers. For instance, a 1974 Los Angeles County SCUBA diving ordinance required that new divers demonstrate the ability to swim continuously for 200 yards without swimming aids, swim 50 feet underwater without swimming aids, swim 50 yards towing another person without swimming aids, float and/or tread water with minimal movement for 10 minutes, and tread water with legs only for 20 seconds (Fisher & Brown, 1979).

Using rental gear is generally satisfactory when taking classes or when limited to a few dives a year. Caution is applied particularly when renting SCUBA gear in some countries, where faulty equipment has led to unfortunate mishaps. To avoid accidents, participants may be required to wear inflatable snorkeling vests and plant dive flags within 50 feet of them and at locations that mark the location of a diver. Diving suits provide protection against sunburn and accidental coral encounters and are handy for long swims, when snorkelers become cooler than they realize. Weights worn with a quick-release belt to aid diving are correctly weighted to allow buoyancy at the surface. Before descending, a few breaths are taken prior to holding the breath. Too many, though, can cause hyperventilation. Ascents are made looking up to the surface for boats and other objects. Snorkelers should be aware that a mask on the forehead means distress.

SCUBA instruction includes coverage of many safety measures. For example, how to react to an emergency situation such as an air shortage or what to do if another diver is stricken in the water. Divers know the location of the nearest decompression chamber, the local rescue telephone numbers, and how to use a diver's flag and underwater distress signals. Signals are listed in the *U.S. Navy Diving Manual*. Divers should not go beyond their experience or wear gear that they have not been trained to use. In addition, all divers check weather conditions, check local tides and currents, and inspect their equipment. Observing the buddy system and joining a diver who knows the local waters is important in unfamiliar areas. Many resorts, charter boats, and SCUBA clubs offer convenient trips with locals who are familiar with the waters. First aid and repair kits are assembled, and divers know how to prevent and respond to hyperthermia, dehydration, heat exhaustion, and heatstroke. They attempt to stay in good shape, and avoid alcohol, cigarettes, and drugs, which are especially hazardous before a dive.

The fear of a shark attack is often exaggerated. Among the roughly 360 shark species, only a score appear to attack humans. Humans are a greater danger to sharks, threatening some with extinction. Shark aggression is not consistent, but attacks are generally more frequent in tropical and subtropical seas and whenever water temperatures are over 70 degrees. Sharks may alter their normal habits and become dangerous when attracted by blood, flashing lights, colored materials, or splashing water. They tend to sneak up from behind, attacking a nonmoving part (Cahill, 1990). Cousteau equipped his divers with shafts of wood or aluminum over 3 feet long. Small nails were placed in one end in circular formation. The nails were long enough to be felt, but not so long or sharp as to injure the shark or to aggravate an attack. Cousteau's divers also pioneered the use of cages that divers could climb into if threatened. They also operated in pairs, back-to-back, if an attack seemed probable. Some chemical repellents have received negligible success. Air bubbling from a diver's aqualung has deterred some sharks (Steel, 1985). Shark attack tips should be studied.

Other dangerous creatures include the great barracuda, octopus, and the orca, known also as the killer whale. Groupers swim around rocks, caverns, and old wrecks; the moray eel may lurk beneath rocks and coral; and jellyfish and sea urchins are found in the deep. The stingray can inject a venom. Divers must always be aware and cautious. If dangerous predators are seen, it is advisable to keep away and get out of the water. With the proper precautions, diving provides a lifetime activity.

The Florida Department of Natural Resources (n.d.) recommends the following safeguards:

1. Never dive alone.
2. Participate in appropriate training.
3. Display a diver-down flag when in the water.
4. Be aware of other boats and diver-down flags.

5. Do not dive in narrow channels where you are a hazard to navigation.
6. Avoid direct contact with corals. Contact may kill them or cause infection or disease, and divers risk an allergic reaction.
7. Do not feed fish because it often attracts predators such as sharks and barracuda. Certain foods eaten by humans can be unhealthy and often fatal to fish.
8. Be aware of potentially dangerous sea life.
9. A boat operator should remain on board when divers are in the water. Divers should begin the dive by proceeding upcurrent from the boat. Strong currents can carry divers far from the boat.

Low-impact. The Divers Alert Network offers a responsible Diver's Code. In this case, "divers take nothing but pictures, and leave nothing but bubbles." Divers can help protect the underwater environment in the following ways (National Oceanic and Atmospheric Administration & Professional Association of Diving Instructors, 1993):

1. Dive carefully in fragile ecosystems, such as coral (and avoid silting up the bottom).
2. Be aware of body equipment placement when diving.
3. Keep diving skills sharp with continuing education.
4. Be considerate of aquatic life.
5. Understand and respect underwater life.
6. Resist the urge to collect souvenirs.
7. All hunting laws and restrictions are obeyed. Do not spearfish in areas that other divers are using.
8. Report environmental disturbances or destruction.
9. Be a role model for others.
10. Get involved in local environmental activities and issues.

Windsurfing

Windsurfing or sailboarding quickly developed into a popular outdoor activity throughout the world, and it is estimated that 1.6 million individuals in the United States participate in windsurfing and boardsailing. A combination of sailing, surfing, water skiing, and hang gliding, its early beginnings are difficult to attribute. The ancient Polynesians and the early surfers deserve credit, but sailor and aeronautical engineer Jim Drake and surfer Hoyle Schweitzer are the 1968 inventors of the Windsurfer that drew their two activities together into a new hybrid. Pioneered in the United States, it was first popularized in Europe, where Europeans produced their own designs. By the 1980s, windsurfing underwent extraordinary growth. Equipment development progressed, racing participation increased, the World Cup tour was initiated, and, as a sport, it was awarded Olympics status at the Los Angeles Games in 1984. Now there are destination resorts all over the world and prime locations, including premier destinations in Aruba, Hawaii, Florida, and North Carolina.

Windsurfing is not confined to the ocean. In fact, calmer waters are recommended for beginners before progressing to wavesailing. The Hood River Event Site on the Columbia River in Oregon is the site of international windsurfing events. The park is also available to amateurs. With appropriate instruction and equipment, beginners can learn to windsurf in a few hours. The skills are not too difficult to master and are easy to remember. Certified instructors offer individual and group lessons. Lessons are available through local windsurfing shops and schools across the country. Top professionals also conduct nationwide clinic tours at the prime windsurfing beaches. Because equipment has become much lighter, easier to use, and more reliable, learning has only gotten easier. Requiring finesse more than strength has made windsurfing attractive to all ages and to girls and women. To the surprise of many, a good, basic setup is relatively inexpensive, and it can be used for a lifetime of general light-wind sailing.

Light-wind windsurfing takes place in winds of 10 knots or under. Cruising from point to point is the simplest and most popular form. Freestyle involves putting the board and sail through a series of turns, spins, and maneuvers and is done by all levels of sailors. *High-wind windsurfing,* done in winds over 10 knots and generally at a range from 15 to 25 knots, appeals to some advanced sailors. A popular style is slalom sailing, where exhilarating runs and high speed are done on slalom boards at speeds up to 40 miles per hour. *Bump-and-jump-sailing* is accomplished when the winds are good and the waters are choppy, and sailors can make spectacular jumps, turns, and loops. The spectacular and difficult *wavesailing* is practiced on open swells breaking parallel to the beach and when the wind is blowing along the beach or sideshore (windsurfer.com, 2000a).

For any wind conditions, windsurfing equipment is composed of five primary pieces: board, sail, mast, boom, and mast base. When put together, it is called a *rig.* The board carries a universal joint capable of swinging completely around, and the universal joint carries the mast to which the sail is attached. Sailors hold on to the boom. Longboards are used for light-wind windsurfing and longboard racing, and smaller more maneuverable boards are used for high-wind windsurfing. Smaller boards go faster, but require more agility and quicker reflexes to handle. Bigger sails are used in lighter wind. Smaller sails with their smaller area to collect wind are needed for strong winds so the sailor can hang on. Beginners use a smaller sail to learn. Most boards have footstraps, which are used by experts to keep them aboard when traveling at high speeds or for wave jumping and fun boarding. Tandem windsurfing is done on a board for two. A board built for three is called a tridem. Windsurfing boards have also been adapted for use on land, ice, and snow.

Safety. A progress chart is available for windsurfers to match their abilities with skill level, including the beginner, novice, intermediate, advanced, expert, and professional. Because one of the greatest dangers is colliding with commercial vessels and swimmers, windsurfers stay clear of motorboats, learn right-of-way rules, avoid swimmers, and avert waves that break on the beach. Windsurfers must swim well; learn self-help techniques, including how to recognize hypothermia; sail with others; tell someone where they are; and avoid sailing in poor conditions, including night hours. Some safety rules follow (U.S. Sailing, 2014; windsurfer.com, 2000b):

1. In the rare event that the board and rig are separated, stay with the board for flotation.
2. Check gear and prepare for the conditions by wearing a wetsuit, drysuit, buoyancy aid, visor, booties, sunscreen, and life jacket with whistle.
3. Know the sailing site, including boat traffic patterns and weather conditions that will likely be encountered. Check tides and other dangers, and know correct surf rescue techniques. This includes drinking water in sunny, humid conditions and returning to shore after a shiver.
4. Learn the international distress signal. If in serious need of help while on the water, sit on the board and raise and lower your arms above your head and down to your sides.
5. Before sailing, learn to read the wind by looking at a flag, tossing sand, and so forth.

ADVENTURES IN THE AIR

Humans have always envied birds' ability to fly. Outdoor enthusiasts can achieve the feeling of conquering gravity by taking part in adventures in the air. A new world awaits those who dare to soar above. Vistas sweep far below and off to the horizon, and gentle breezes beckon. For those who prefer to have their feet on the ground, gliders, hot air balloons, and parachutes provide a relaxing backdrop for picnics or as the focus at an outdoor festival or event.

Hang Gliding

According to legend, Daedalus, held in exile on the island of Crete, fashioned a set of wings to suspend himself in the air. King Mi-

Certified instructors teach this high-risk activity at schools certified by the United States Hang Gliding Association.

nos told him he would never be permitted to travel by land or sea, but the air was free, so he studied the flight of birds. After devising a set of wings for himself and his son, they flew into the air. His son Icarus flew higher and higher trying to reach the sun, until the wax holding the feathers began to melt. Disaster came when the feathers detached and Icarus fell into the sea (Oiney, 1976).

Today, the dream of flying is accomplished by hang gliders, who launch from mountaintops, ski slopes, and sand dunes. The majority of pilots fly their entire careers without sustaining a serious injury, but great care is required (Mackey & Leonard, 1995). Aviation is not very forgiving if a careless judgment is made in error. For this reason, beginners should, under no conditions, try this high-risk activity without the supervision of a competent certified instructor. The United States Hang Gliding Association (USHGA) certifies hang gliding instructors and schools. This program consists of a stan-

dardized set of flying skills corresponding to a series of pilot proficiency rates (Beginner through Master), each carrying a set of recommended operating limitations.

Hang gliders can launch from just about any slope that is relatively free from obstructions, is steeper than about 6 to 1, and faces into the wind. Depending on the flight sight, ideal winds for launching and landing vary from 5 to 20 miles per hour, but pilots can safely launch, fly, and land in winds from 0 to 30 (Mackey & Leonard, 1995). Attached to the underside of the wings of gliders, which look like large triangles, pilots provide the energy for launching and landing with their legs. To launch, they hold on to the control bar and quickly run downhill into the wind. Thus, the expression, "If you can jog while balancing a 50- to 70-pound weight on your shoulders, you can learn to fly!" In actuality, flying does not require great strength because the straps, not the pilot's arms, hold the pilot up. Long flights in turbulent conditions require a moderate degree of upper body endurance that generally develops as the pilot progresses through training (Mackey & Leonard, 1995).

Once a glider is airborne, wind speed is less important because the pilot controls the speed of the glider. Speed is increased or decreased by pulling the bar forward or backward, respectively. Riding underneath the glider, the pilot hangs from a harness (thus the name "hang" glider) and is capable of controlling the wing with the trapeze, a triangle of tubing that extends straight down under the wing structure in front of the pilot's body. By moving the body to one side, the glider will tilt and turn to the desired direction. To go up and ride an air draft, the pilot pushes back. Landing judgments are instantaneous as hesitations can prove fatal. For a perfect landing, the glider is in a stall the moment the feet touch the ground. Even so, pilots must start running immediately to prevent the forward momentum from pulling them off balance (Dean, 1982; Fisher & Brown, 1979).

On good days, pilots land when the sun goes down, but flight time is all a matter of conditions and altitude. In summers in the western United States, pilots typically reach altitudes of 5,000 to 10,000 feet and fly over 100 miles, but flights in excess of 300 miles in length and altitudes of well over 17,999 feet have been recorded. Because air temperature tends to fall by about four degrees for every 1,000 foot gain in elevation, high altitude pilots that expect to fly over 12,000 to 14,000 feet in the summer will generally require warm clothing to protect them against exposure (Mackey & Leonard, 1995). Safety gear includes high shoes to protect the ankles, knee and elbow protectors, long pants, and a crash helmet. Gliders in the United States are certified for airworthiness by the Hang Glider Manufacturers Association.

Although time required for training varies with the student's innate skills and the type of training conditions, most students obtain the first two United States Hang Gliding and Paragliding Association (USHPA) ratings, Beginner and Novice, after taking five to 10 lessons for 3 to 6 months. In 1 day, a student learns the rudiments of flight. By the end of the primary training process, students are usually flying in moderate altitudes from several hundred to a few thousand feet in relatively mild conditions (USHPA, 2014).

Because flying depends more on balance and endurance than brute strength, hang glider pilots range in age from teens to octogenarians. About 10% to 15% of the pilots in the United States are women. Because most pilots range in weight from 90 to 250 pounds, it can be difficult for anyone beyond this range to find equipment, although heavier pilots may use specially designed tandem gliders. Harness and glider modification may be necessary for individuals outside the range of 5 to 6.5 feet tall (Mackey & Leonard, 1995). One veteran finds that hang gliding appeals to the person who wants to be detached and free to enjoy nature.

Safety. Instructors usually provide training equipment through the Beginner rating as part of their package. Part of preparation is understanding weather conditions. More advanced students obtain their own equipment, a serious and costly endeavor. Instructors generally offer sound advice to get started on the search. If used equipment is purchased as a cost-saving measure, it is critical that an experienced pilot familiar with equipment goes along for inspection and approval. Some will have degraded sails, dented or bent frame parts, kinked wires, or rust on the hardware or are simply difficult to fly safely. Because current aircraft are more nimble and forgiving, purchasing a new glider in the pilot's class and weight range is recommended. These glides are also pretuned and test flown to ensure that the glider will fly like the one that the customer test flew (Meadows, 1994). Likewise, seeking a good price when selecting a school is secondary to looking for professionalism and skill. Rated pilots do not fly beyond their proficiency rating. Progression to more difficult flying conditions continues under the supervision of more experienced pilots or Observers/Advanced Instructors (Hamilton, 2007; Mackey & Leonard, 1995).

Hot Air Ballooning

Hot air ballooning began in France in 1782 when two paper makers, Joseph and Etienne Montgolfier, launched the first hot air balloon. They had noticed burning pieces of paper flying up the chimney and tried to float small bags over the kitchen fire. Later they constructed a much larger bag of paper and linen, filled it with smoke from burning straw, and watched it drift away. By 1783, the first balloonist was lifted from earth. Today's hot air balloons are highly maneuverable, allowing more adventurers to float in the sky and create a brightly colored scene for viewers below.

Hot air balloon rallies are held in beautiful locations that allow spectacular views. The world's largest ballooning event, the Albuquerque International Balloon Fiesta, is held in New Mexico every October. As the official ballooning branch of the United States National Aeronautic Association, the Balloon Federation of America (BFA) organizes and operates the United States National Balloon Championships, as well as other competitions, and selects United States representative pilots for participation in the World Championships and the world's most prestigious gas balloon race, the Coupe Aéronautique Gordon Bennett, also referred to as the Gordon Bennett Cup. The first Women's World Hot Air Balloon Championships were held in 2014.

Rallies present opportunities for the beginning enthusiast to learn about piloting skills because volunteers are frequently needed to offer services (and respond to orders) when the balloons are being prepared for inflation and launching. Preparations begin before sunrise to avoid dangerous air turbulence caused later in the day as the sun begins to heat wind currents in the atmosphere. Sunset flights are also popular. Formal rides can be arranged through balloon companies and tours. The balloons carry from four to eight passengers. Commercial pilots should be licensed by the Federal Aviation Administration (FAA) and have many hours of flying experience. Balloons have also been used for air safaris in Africa as a means to observe the

Hot air balloons fly over the Temecula Valley wine country in California.

animals and by risk-taking bungee jumpers who have taken their leap from balloons.

Ballooning equipment is expensive, but once acquired, the only cost remaining is the propane used for an average flight of 2 hours. Balloon shapes are generally spheres, oblate spheroids, and aerodynamic configurations. The envelope, or bag, is made of thin, very light but very strong material. The basket, or gondola, is made of wicker. Burners put out the equivalent of over 5,000 horse power. The crew members, ideally consisting of the pilot, crew chief, and three other members, work together throughout the flight on the assembly, launch, chase, and landing. After clearing the launch site, they pull the heavy envelope and basket out of the trailer for the *assembly* and help the pilot install upright poles and set the burner unit in place. Only the pilot can make connections to propane tanks (Carlton, 2000a). Helping with the *launch,* crew place their weight on the basket, keeping one foot on the ground at all times. After releasing the tie-off rope, the balloon begins its ascent.

Basically, a balloon drifts with the wind. The pilot adjusts the altitude by regulating the temperature of the air within the envelope, and higher or lower altitudes may offer wind currents of different directions. The crew chief directs operations on the ground, which starts with the *chase.* The chase involves driving in front of the balloon to look for and get permission for the landing. Most landowners are obliging, but it may be necessary for the crew chief to explain the necessity of an unplanned landing. On a rare occasion that a landowner is especially concerned, this is communicated to the pilot who may elect to fly on. Crew members keep eye contact with the balloon. The pilot can land the balloon without the crew, but they can be very helpful provided that they do not get in front of it. During the *landing* and recovery, crews catch the balloon by the sides or the back as it hits the ground and place their weight on the basket until the pilot tells them to gather in the envelope. Landowners, crew, passengers, and pilot often celebrate the landing together with champagne and soft drinks. Crews are not to help a pilot who has had anything alcoholic within 8 hours of the flight (BFA, 1999).

Lessons may be arranged through balloon touring companies, schools, or manufacturers. Training includes practical and theoretical experience. The school's safety record should be checked before lessons begin. Balloons used for lessons and rental need to be FAA certified. In many countries, instructor ratings are awarded to pilots of sufficient skill and experience. Examiners are appointed by the balloon club on behalf of the national aviation authority to certify that a student has achieved a safe level of competence in practical and theoretical instruction. Flying hours are required to qualify for a license. Medical standards for ballooning are much lower than for aircraft licenses (Wirth, 1980). Attire is cotton based and casual to include long pants and long sleeves, hiking boots, jacket or sweater, and leather gloves (crews also wear gloves because oil from the hands will deteriorate nylon). Warmer clothes are generally not needed because the propane burners, which heat the air inside the balloon, keep the passengers warm in the gondola.

Safety. The BFA provides a long list of crew advice and safety information as much needs to be done to provide a safe trip. Some tips follow (Carlton, 2000b):

1. Do not smoke.
2. Be careful around ropes, and never wrap them around any part of you.
3. Keep hair and loose items away from the fan.
4. Pay attention at all times to your surroundings.
5. Do not get in front of a moving basket.
6. Always keep one foot on the ground unless in the basket.
7. Know where and how to use fire extinguishers.
8. Have a lost balloon phone number.
9. Be aware of hot burners.
10. Follow the pilot's directions.

Skydiving

Panoramic views are enjoyed by skydivers, who claim that the experience of jumping from aircraft is more like flying than falling. Leonardo da Vinci is credited with the design of a parachute that was dropped off the Tower of Pisa in Italy. Because a skydive requires aircraft, this probably did not occur until the 18th century when Frenchman Andre Garnerin jumped out of an air balloon.

It should be noted that although some skydivers have become *fixed-object* jumpers using similar equipment, it is a separate and distinct activity. By the early 20th century, "barnstormers" began stunt flying, which eventually included jumping out of airplanes with parachutes. After World War II, many of the trained ex-paratroopers who wanted to continue jumping organized jumping clubs for small groups of enthusiasts. A jump made from a small airplane for fun was soon known as sport parachuting. A few of these pioneers proved that parachuting was not limited to low-altitude jumps, with parachutes that automatically opened by a static line attached to the departure aircraft. This led to *skydiving*, a term that appeared later to define the experience of jumping from an aircraft in flight to enjoy the experience of falling free prior to pulling the chute for a safe landing. In 1960, Colonel Joseph Kittinger, Jr. jumped from a balloon at 102,000 feet to make the longest freefall. In 2012, Felix Baumgartner was the first to break the speed of sound in freefall from the stratosphere.

The United States Parachute Association (USPA, 2014) estimates that more than 1 million jumps have been made each year since 2010. There are many reasons for skydiving's popularity. Many Americans are looking for more adventurous sports, motion pictures have used skydiving as an underlying theme, and the ability to take air-to-air videos shows how skydiving can be. More important, the advancements in equipment and techniques have made parachuting safer. Automatic activation devices reduced fatal accidents, and ram-air parachutes, developed in the 1960s, made landings soft and fun. Traditional round parachutes, often referred to as canopies, offer a slow vertical descent, but it was discovered in the 1950s that jumpers could move laterally if holes were cut in the back of the canopy. Ram parachutes, shaped like an aircraft wing or *airfoil*, retain a slow descent and generate lift that makes steering possible when the skydiver distorts the airfoil with special steering lines. When the skydiver pulls down on both rear steering lines, for example, the "angle of attack" of the canopy could be raised to the relative wind. Because it also increases drag, which slows the skydiver while momentarily increasing lift, the jumper is allowed to land slowly and gently. Schools and camps use older, round canopies for supervised children's exercises and games, but they are getting harder to find.

Freefall time depends on the height of the jump or the exit from the airplane to the point where the jumper ends the freefall by pulling the ripcord or cable that holds the parachute pack together, thereby causing the parachute to release. This action prompts a tug to the shoulders as the jumper begins the float to the ground, but landings can be so soft that the jumper remains standing. The higher the airplane, the longer the freefall opportunity. Experienced jumpers, sometimes working in groups, make formations in the sky during the freefall. Group jumping is more difficult and dangerous because there is always a chance that the parachute lines could become entangled. Group skydivers must allow themselves time to move away from each other after the formation to open their parachutes.

Despite the inherent dangers, people are attracted to skydiving due to the excitement and adventure. They also find the adventure satisfying because it provides a feeling of accomplishment in overcoming gravity and the basic human fear of falling (Benson, 1979). As with hang gliding, sessions are scheduled at parachuting schools and clubs with skilled instructors and sound equipment. Parachute clubs and centers offering lessons are located throughout the United States. Those associated with the USPA are likely to be a good choice because the courses are taught by certified instructors who must follow basic safety regulations. USPA rules allow minors as young as 16 to skydive with written parental or guardian consent, but schools may set their own standards.

The *static line* or *instructor-assisted deployment*, where the student jumps and the parachute opens right away automatically, and *harness-hold*, where two USPA Accelerated Freefall Jumpmasters go alongside in freefall holding on until the student opens the parachute, are part of progressive multiple-jump training courses. Instruction for this package commonly includes an orientation, information regarding use of equipment and the inspection of equipment, parachute packing, instructions for malfunction, and drills in emergency procedures. Skill instruction ordinarily entails appropriate techniques for the jump, steering and control, landing preparation, and proper landing falls. Most people who just make one jump make the *tandem* jump, where the student and the instructor jump out, freefall, and land together under the same parachute system. For a tandem jump, the amount of preparation time varies from a few minutes to a full course, depending on the student's objectives and the school's administration strategy. Because more training is needed for multiple-jump training, students pay a heftier price. One solo jump can also be accomplished after a day of lessons. Each drop zone sets its own jump training prices based upon its operating costs and the school's objectives. Lessons usually include equipment, and some lessons may include the cost of an airplane for the jump. Students should be prepared for possible delays due to weather conditions or other factors. Typical clothes and sneakers worn for outdoor activities are appropriate. Generally, those wishing to purchase equipment start the process with the drop zone's instructional staff or the pro shop at the school or center.

Safety. Skydiving is a self-regulated activity, meaning that skydivers voluntarily follow a set of basic safety requirements set by the USPA. The FAA has established federal rules, but most apply to the aircraft from which skydivers jump. Just as SCUBA diving can become more dangerous at lower depths, skydiving risks can increase with altitude. During 2013, the number of fatalities was 0.0075 per 1,000 jumps. Tandem skydiving had about 0.003 student fatalities per 1,000 tandem jumps (USPA, 2014). Injuries are more difficult to estimate because there is no requirement that they be reported or that parachute malfunctions be reported. It is estimated that in 600 to 1,000 random main parachute openings, one will result in malfunction, requiring the reserve parachute. Jumpers can help to control this by design choice, study, inspection and maintenance, packing, putting parachute on properly, being careful with gear in the airplane, and stability on opening (USPA, 2003). One of the greatest dangers comes from overconfidence, which leads to carelessness.

VIEWING AND LEARNING ACTIVITIES

Viewing and learning activities include bird-watching, rock hounding, tidepooling, plant identification, and photography. They include trips to park nature centers, visitor centers, traditional and outdoor museums, planetariums, and aquariums. They include visits to archaeological and historic sites, such as ancient American Indian mounds, battlefields, canals, and other sites that are important to preserving and understanding the nation's culture and heritage. Sightseeing, a loosely defined activity, is also a part of this type of participation, which includes driving on a scenic byway or traveling to a city to see the sights.

Birding

The numbers of people actively bird-watching increased a dramatic 155% from the mid-1980s to the mid-1990s (Cordell et al., 1999). Today, there are some 47 million people in the United States who watch birds, making it the number one outdoor activity in America. About 41 million of these are *residential* or backyard birders. Of the 18 million who ventured to other sites, most used public land (Carver, 2013). The age distribution of the participants is shown in Table 15.3. Seeking a wide range of experiences, birders in one study were ranked into four groups corresponding with their distinct characteristics. In order of declining behavior interest, they were called undifferentiated birders, outdoor recreationists, generalists and water seekers, and heritage recreationists and comfort seekers (Cordell et al., 1999). Altogether, American bird-watchers, according to a U.S. Fish and Wildlife report, spent almost $41 billion for travel, binoculars, wildbird seed, and the like (Carver, 2013), more than sports fans spent that same year on professional sports (Reilly, 2012).

Some bird-watching field trips are taken to wild and remote places, especially when in search of exotic species. A *pelagic trip* is an ocean or gulf trip where participants go out to sea to find oceanic species. It is also possible to identify, attract, and become absorbed by a surprising variety of birds in the backyaRoad This is where individuals can often learn to key in on details for species identification, which with practice, generally become more apparent just as the sounds

Table 15.3

Age Distribution of the U.S. Population and Birders

Age	U.S. population	Number of birders	Participation rate
16 to 24	34,169	1,939	6%
25 to 34	41,613	4,767	11%
35 to 44	40,779	6,799	17%
45 to 54	46,167	10,396	23%
55 plus	76,586	22,840	30%

Note. Population 16 years of age and older. Numbers in thousands. From *Birding in the United States: A Demographic and Economic Analysis*, by E. Carver, 2013, Arlington, VA: U.S. Fish and Wildlife Service, p. 4.

become more distinct. Local clubs or Audubon chapters also schedule field trips that are especially helpful for newcomers. These organizations are located through telephone directories, local natural history museums, nature centers, or outdoor stores specializing in bird-feeding equipment. The National Audubon Society can advise of the nearest local Audubon chapter. Ornithology classes on the science of bird study are also available in many areas.

If there appears to be no organization in the area, birding can be self-taught. Basic abilities include looking and listening. The observer learns to identify distinct characteristics of the bird being watched. Birds are identified by certain markings or by their behavior, song, size, or shape. Observations are recorded in a notebook and looked up later. Studying a field guide before participating in an excursion is helpful. When birding in a group, someone is usually able to offer an identification when simple descriptions are given. Checklists are often available to keep records of sightings.

Along with the field guide, checklist, and notebook, hiking boots or tennis shoes and binoculars are essential. Birds are usually found with the naked eye. Binoculars are then brought forward for a sharper, closer look by keeping the eyes on the biRoad Sweeping an open area or body of water with binoculars is also helpful. To find the right binoculars, quality optical equipment is matched to particular characteristics of the individual's eyes. It is best to try several binoculars before buying. The buyer usually knows when the chemistry is right, but it is generally better not to sacrifice quality to save a few dollars (Brandt, 1997).

Standard-sized binoculars are generally used, but when bird-watching while hiking or biking, compact or mini binoculars may be favorable. Standard and compact binoculars are also available with a rubber coating to help withstand shock and in some cases water. The basic measure of binoculars is a formula such as 7 x 35. The first number represents the magnification. With 7x binoculars objects appear to be 7 times closer. For most beginners, 6x, 7x, or 8x is adequate and 10 is the maximum. The greater the magnification, the narrower the field of view and the greater the image shakes as the unavoidable result of heartbeat and hand shaking. The second number indicates the objective lens diameter in millimeters. The larger the opening, the more light that is collected; better binoculars are for low-light use. For example, dividing the first number into the second will result in the binoculars' brightness, or exit pupil. The pair that is 7 x 35 has an exit pupil of 5, which is acceptable for most conditions. An 8 x 20 has an exit pupil of only 2.5, which would tend to be dark even in bright daylight.

For bird identification, true birders need to see detail, and this is aided by a good pair of binoculars that have high resolution or clarity. Resolution is tested by focusing on an object that has detail or lines. The details should be sharp both near the middle and at the edge of the viewer's field of vision. Another important factor in maximum optical quality is depth of view. Because birds move around, birders do not want to have to constantly refocus. And because birders tend to be very hard on equipment, binoculars should be light but strong and rugged. Waterproof and fogproof is best. A growing line of compact models is also available. More experienced birders sometimes invest in powerful spotting scopes set up on tripods to zero in on birds at long range. On birding trips, leaders will usually have one or two scopes. To care for binoculars, they are cleaned with lens tissues, not with clothes or facial tissue.

Bird-watching is a good daybreak activity, and photographers also find it an excellent time to photograph the birds in their natural surroundings. More experienced birders enjoy capturing birds on film. Hiking, backpacking, bicycling, and boating can be enhanced by a search for various bird species. For instance, people from all over the nation and world flock to Everglades National Park in Florida, a paradise, especially for those who want to watch wading birds. On the Platte River, cranes are seen near Grand Island, Nebraska. Other popular sites include the Cape May, New Jersey, migrations and the raptor migrations to Hawk Mountain, Pennsylvania and to High Island, Texas. Biologists, however, attribute a decline in migratory species such as western bluebirds and wood thrushers to loss of vital habitat throughout the western hemisphere. If the popular songbird species continues to decline, an important segment of the bird-watching population will be at risk. Presently, it is expected that wildlife watching observation and photographing, including birding, is expected to rise by 61% for participants and 97% for total participation days by 2050 (Cordell et al., 1999).

Safety. Birders must follow the same safety precautions as other adventurers, depending on the mode of transportation and length of the trip. According to one authority,

the bird-watcher on a forest trail must keep one eye on the treetops and the other eye on the ground (Lotz, 1987). Admittedly impossible, the advice calls for watching ahead for snakes, wild animals, puddles, rocks, and other hazards.

Low-impact. Those interested in birding can volunteer as observers for the annual Christmas Bird Count, Breeding Bird Survey, or Project Feederwatch sponsored locally and nationally by the National Audubon Society, the Fish and Wildlife Service, and other organizations. Birders can help with conservation and education programs, and reduce waste and energy use by reusing and recycling materials. When viewing wildlife experts advise the following:

1. Wear natural colors and fade into the scenery.
2. Be considerate by keeping your distance from wildlife and nests and by letting them be themselves.
3. Leave pets at home.
4. Respect the space of other viewers.
4. Carry out trash.
5. Use existing roads and trails.
6. Report wildlife or environmental abuse.

Rock Art

Archaeological and historic sites are important to preserving and understanding the nation's heritage. When available for the public to visit and experience personally, they can spark wonder, delight, and reflection. Finding these sites can also be physically demanding. For example, only able hikers can locate some of the rock art sites found in remote desert areas. Some of the nation's best rock art museums are found on federal lands, where canyon walls, caves, and rock faces have depictions of ancient hunting scenes, stars, wildlife, and humanlike figures. Archaeologists interpret the figures as cultural, religious, or ceremonial symbols; astronomical observations; and expressions of the supernatural.

When the drawing is etched onto a rock or chipped away by bone chisels and rock hammers, it is known as a *petroglyph*. More

A natural protective coating on desert boulders called desert varnish once attracted ancient artists who pecked away at the dark surface to create lighter images as seen in the rock pictured. The technique of painting came later.

than 15,000 prehistoric and historic American Indian and Hispanic petroglyphs stretch along 17 miles of Albuquerque's West Mesa escarpment at Petroglyph National Monument in New Mexico. Pictures on rock, known as *pictographs,* may display many colors. Pigments formed by the American Indians were made by crushing minerals. When the minerals were mixed with water, red, black, yellow, white, and blue paints could be created. These paints were applied with plant fibers or by spreading the pigment onto a rock by hand. Negative-image pictographs were also created by painting around an object such as a hand (Browning, 1989). Well-known examples of pictographs are found in El Morro National Monument in New Mexico and in the Virgin Islands National Park. Canyonlands National Park in Utah is known for several striking polychromatic, or multicolored,

pictographs. Park interpreters lead day and overnight trips to some of the sites. Some sites can only be viewed after a hard climb up a bed of rocks, but sometimes rock art is reached after a short walk or through a good pair of binoculars.

Safety. Care must be taken when climbing to avoid injuries and site damage. Refer to Hiking, Backpacking, Camping, and Birding sections for tips.

Low-impact. When it comes to visiting archaeological and historic sites, the fragile and irreplaceable settings demand care and protection. Unauthorized collecting or digging for artifacts is illegal on federal land and many other public lands, as well as on private land without permission. To prevent vandalism at some rock art sites, several archaeologists refused to disclose site locations until more recent years when attitudes among modern archaeologists began to shift toward a belief that greater public awareness of the art's frailty and historical significance is a better means of preservation (Browning, 1989). Unfortunately, some rock art sites have fallen to housing developments and natural wear by flash floods, rock exfoliation, natural erosion, and acid rain. Rock art should only be appreciated by viewing, photographing, or sketching. Direct contact such as chalking, rubbing, tracing, or touching slowly causes it to disappear, and it can make it impossible to use new dating techniques. It is strictly prohibited for a person to take it home or to add art, and substantial fines and penalties are authorized. Other information to remember when visiting archaeological and historic resources follows:

1. Stay on the trail and off of middens (trash piles left by original occupants) and still-standing structures.
2. Leave artifacts where they lie.
3. Camp, sleep, cook, and gather wood well away from sites.
4. Report violators.

ORIENTEERING AND CAMPING

Orienteering is a form of navigation that is used by outdoor travelers who enjoy hiking, backpacking, snowshoeing, cross-country skiing, canoeing, kayaking, cycling, and nature study. When day turns into night, these same adventurers find that a night spent away from the comforts of home can be as refreshing and rewarding as the day's activities. Whether hiking in the mountains, rafting down a white-water river, or snorkeling in the ocean, the night stars, the howls of the coyotes, a warm meal, and a place to rest offer a welcome respite from the activities of the day. These skills can also be basic to survival in the out-of-doors.

Orienteering and Navigation

Nature provides several means of navigation. Before the development of the compass, the North Star, the sun, the winds, moving clouds, and ocean currents served as guides. About 2500 B.C., the Chinese observed that when lodestone was placed on drifting wood that it consistently rotated to the same direction. From this finding, the compass needle, a strip of magnetized steel balanced on a pivot free to swing in any direction, came into being. The Arabs and Vikings used a simple magnetic compass to help them navigate their vessels, but the compass probably did not become widely used by Western civilization until the 13th century. Eventually, the map and compass became invaluable aids to the adventurer. Putting map and compass skills to use to find the correct path is called orienteering. Developing effective orienteering techniques requires hands-on experience. By acknowledging that nobody has a perfect "sense of direction," there is less chance of becoming lost. Whenever a person is in unfamiliar surroundings, a map and compass are invaluable, and the same basic skills can be used for land navigation at any time of the year. Precautions are taken when noting landmarks, and topographical maps are excellent aids.

The U.S. Geological Survey (USGS) began topographic and geologic mapping in 1879. Today, more than 2 million natural and man-made features are identified in topographic map series available from the USGS. These features make topographic maps extremely useful to professional and recreational map users alike. The first step in reading a map includes learning what the lines, symbols, and colors mean. Colors, for example, depict the work of humans, water, or the contours of hills and valleys. The shape and steepness of hillsides appear as contour lines—the closer the lines, the steeper the hill. Several forms of measurement may be offered on the scale found on the map. For instance, the degree or percent of slope is a good indicator of the degree of difficulty in traversing the area by foot, ski, or bicycle. It is also a good indicator for snow avalanche hazaRoad Information on the types of maps produced by the USGS can be found in the USGS *Catalog of Maps*. The *Index Circular*, a reference book in which each state is divided into sections or quadrangles, is useful in identifying which maps are applicable. Separate maps exist for each quadrangle, which often means that the purchase of more than one map may be necessary. National Forest recreation maps are available from the district ranger, forest supervisor, or regional offices of the Forest Service, and several outdoor recreation and conservation organizations also make useful maps.

A compass is a necessary tool for orienting the map to determine direction of travel. The most versatile compass for backcountry travel is the orienteering compass (Figure 15.4) with its rotating transparent plastic base plate allowing for more effortless use with a map. Care is taken that no nearby metallic objects disturb the needle, causing a false reading. The needle points to magnetic north, not true north. To identify true north, it is necessary to understand *declination*. Declination is the angle between magnetic north and true north. The difference between magnetic north and true north (the declination angle) varies according to geographic location. For example, the declination angle in New Hampshire can be 15 degrees west and in Montana 20 degrees east.

The declination for a given area is generally printed on the map margin adjacent to the north arrow. True north, magnetic north, and declination are shown in Figure 15.5. Not knowing the effect of declination (or variation) could cause travelers to miss their destination point by a wide margin. To travel by map and compass, the map must be oriented to the terrain. The magnetic north arrow on the map points the same direction as the magnetic needle on the compass. The compass is then placed on the map with one long edge of the base plate touching a line between the starting point and the destination. The direction-of-travel arrow on the compass should be pointing in the direction of the destination point. Holding the base plate firmly, the traveler rotates the compass housing until the orienting arrow is in line with the north portion of the compass needle. To begin the venture, the traveler looks up to see where the direction-of-travel arrow is pointed and finds a landmark that is out as far as the terrain will allow and is in direct line with the travel arrow. From this point, it is the map, not the compass, that is the important tool.

Orienteering clubs set up local competitions open to everyone for a nominal fee. Orienteers bring a compass and water bottle and wear hiking boots, long pants, and light layers. The challenge lies in how quickly the competitor can find, in correct order, a series

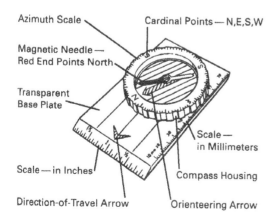

Figure 15.4. Orienteering compass.

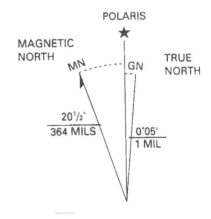

Figure 15.5. Declination marker.

Using observation skills from a high vantage point, this hiker can benefit from orienteering skills when exploring the inhospitable desert.

of preset control points in a wilderness setting, usually finishing at the point of origin. Cards are punched with unique pin-punches found hanging at the control point. To miss a control spells doom. The sport, which began in Sweden in the early 1900s as a military exercise, was developed in the United States in the 1940s by outdoor enthusiasts. Orienteering events (O-meets) have several courses that are arranged from novice to expert levels. Beginner courses are usually a mile long. An advanced course could take about 2 or 3 hours, with orienteers following contour lines, ridgelines, gullies, bodies of water, stone walls, and other features, all detailed on specially made topographic maps. After the standard 3-hour time limit, organizers go after anyone who has not finished while everyone else is checking out their time and where they placed on the results board. International championships include World Orienteering Championships, Junior World Orienteering Championships, World Masters Championships, and the International Orienteering Federation's World Cup. In addition, there are more than 100 world ranking events and regional championships in Europe, Asia, North America, South America, and Oceania. Orienteering is also part of multisport games such as The World Games, the World Masters Games, and the Winter Military World Games. There is World Military Orienteering, World University Orienteering Championships, and World University Ski Orienteering Championships (International Orienteering Federation, 2011). Orienteering USA supports a number of teams that represent the U.S. at international competitions. These include the U.S. Trail Orienteering Team, Ski Orienteering Team, Mountain

Bike Orienteering Team, Senior Foot Orienteering Team, Junior Foot Orienteering Team, University Foot Orienteering team, and Deaf Orienteering Team.

Safety. By following the trail and carrying a map and compass, hikers will not likely get lost. If they do, there are techniques used with the map and compass to backtrack and to find where they are by selecting two landmarks. On longer wilderness treks, observing nature is more than pleasure. Landmarks are canvassed from the front and back. There is a surprising difference in the appearance of landmarks when backtracking. Making notes mentally and on the map can save wilderness travelers anguish later. Nature also provides direction. For example, although the sun and moon only rise in the east and west twice a year, during the equinoxes, they do travel in a general east–west direction. Moss, on the other hand, does not always grow on the north side of a tree, as many people believe. Stars tend to rise in the east and set in the west and move toward the hiker's right when facing south and to the left when the hiker is facing north. The North Star aligns with Ursa Major, the bright star in the Big Dipper. And then, of course, the hiker can always pick up a Global Positioning System (GPS) unit. GPS units lock on to high-frequency radio signals from some of the GPS satellites and calculate the exact location of the user through triangulation. Geocaching makes use of GPS receivers on "hide-and-seek hunts." An event cache is a gathering for events. Geocaching (caching) and orienteering share some common methods and goals and are sometimes combined.

Survival emergencies occur more often when the backcountry orienteer or traveler has been pushing too hard and energy is low or if the individual has not bothered to take preventative measures to avoid distress situations (see Camping Safety). The backpacker, for example, should remember that storms and lightning can come on suddenly and unexpectedly. Once signs of lightning appear, the packers drop their packs, remove metal objects, descend high points, get out of water, and stay away from solitary trees and objects. Surprisingly, a forest of shorter trees surrounded by taller trees can be a relatively safer refuge. A dry, low-lying area is another choice, but it is important to crouch down on heels with the head between the knees and ears covered. This minimizes contact with the ground (Wild Backpacker, 2014).

In response to an emergency, panic wastes energy, and there will most likely be other travelers, campers, or rangers in the local area. Resting and waiting is ordinarily the best plan. A good night's sleep is more likely to be beneficial than taking a chance on aimless travel. Rescuers will respond to the lapsing of the planned return time and generally begin to search during daylight. They are attracted to signals that make the wilderness traveler larger, louder, and more colorful than usual. The universal distress signal is any signal repeated three times. For example, blasting a whistle three times signals distress. Aircraft can be signaled by using colors that contrast with the natural terrain. An *X* indicates distress and can be made from bright clothing or by lining stones. Flashing a mirror, tin foil, or a tin lid can be seen miles away. While waiting, the traveler must drink enough water to remain healthy and do everything possible to prevent the loss of moisture through perspiration. Necessary activities are accomplished in cool hours. During the day, it can be important to stay in the shade, and if in the desert, it is necessary to move above the desert floor.

Low-impact. Orienteers can follow low-impact suggestions for hikers and backpackers. They should be sure to do the following (Drury & Holmlund, 1997):

1. Keep noise levels down.
2. Stay on trails.
3. Avoid cutting switchbacks.
4. Walk on durable surfaces, such as open rocks, sand, and gravel, to minimize trail erosion.
5. Spread out to walk cross-country to avoid creating pathways.
6. Do not crowd wildlife.

Camping

Camping is as old as human existence. In the United States, recreational camping in the great outdoors can probably be traced to the early 1800s when some Americans began to see wilderness for its beauty and as a source of inspiration (McEwen, 1999). Later that century, devoted men and women organized outings for young people, which became organized camping (Meier & Mitchell, 1993). After World War II as new technology and increases in disposable income and leisure time improved, people began to flock to the backcountry (Drury & Holmlund, 1997). By the 1960s, the majority of the 13 million people 12 years of age and older who reported camping one or more times during the previous 12 months had done so mainly in tents at developed campgrounds with their families. By the mid-1990s, the more than 58 million people, also 12 years of age and older, who had participated in camping in the previous 12 months camped in tents, recreational vehicles, and motor homes. Developed camping grew about 42%, and others with weather-resistant tents and RVs turned to more primitive settings, creating a 72% growth in primitive camping (Cordell et al., 1999). About 15% of Americans over age 6 participate in campground camping at this time (Outdoor Foundation, Coleman, Kampgrounds of America, 2012). Tent camping is addressed below.

The best way to enjoy a night spent under the stars is to be prepared. The first step in setting up camp requires finding the natural advantages of a location. It is preferable to use existing sites when possible. When it is not, the camper tries to anticipate the unexpected and plans for dangers such as high winds or floods. Some of the questions to be considered are as follows:

- Is there an established site?
- Is the site close to water?
- Will the site provide shelter?
- Is the land flat?
- Is the area protected; could it flood?
- Are there any dead trees next to the campsite?
- Is the site aesthetically pleasing?
- Does the site offer privacy and interesting scenery?

After the site is selected, each member of the party takes on different duties, such as clearing a place for the tent, setting it up, getting the water, and cooking. If the camp is laid out properly, an overnight fire will not be missed, and the use of single-burner cookstoves can minimize the negative effects of campfires. Before pitching the tent, sticks and small stones are cleared from the tent site, but leaves, pine needles, or humus remain in place. They serve as a cushion and improve drainage. The tent is pitched on a waterproof ground layering to form a tent floor that will, when combined with a foam pad, protect the bed from moisture. When possible, the back of the tent is positioned on the wind side with the door facing toward the rising sun. This positioning will help to dry the tent and gear better. When it rains, the humidity inside the tent is very high and the outside temperature is cool. Because moisture will condense on nonbreathable surfaces, it is helpful to ventilate by leaving vents, windows, and doors open as much as possible. When bugs are not a problem, the netting is opened as well because anything that increases air circulation will decrease condensation. On dry days, the sleeping bag is unrolled as early as possible to restore it to its original loft. The dining area may be centrally located if bears are not a threat. The cooking area needs to be level to prevent stove tip-over, away from pine needles or other inflammable materials, and protected from the wind.

Safety. If bears are around, they can smell food from more than 2 miles away. By learning proper food-storage techniques and following procedures of land managers, backpackers and campers can help protect bears and themselves. Because they are unpredictable, however, there are no hard-and-fast rules about how adventurers can protect themselves. Sites are avoided that are obviously used by bears, such as sites near ripe berry patches and less obvious avalanche chutes where bears like to graze. Tents are pitched at least 150 feet upwind from the cooking area. Food is eaten in one spot, and any spills are cleaned. Food is never eaten or stored in a tent, and cooking clothes

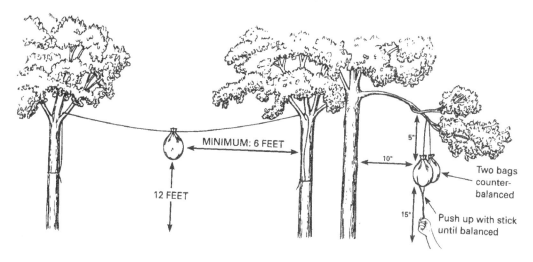

Figure 15.6. Diagram of a suspended food bag.

are stored like food (Cordes, 2001). Local procedures are carefully followed, but typically food is placed in waterproof bags and hung at least 12 feet up and at least 6 feet out in a tree (see Figure 15.6). One recommendation is to place tents near climbable trees, but experts provide varying recommendations for bear encounters. According to one old tale, you can tell a grizzly from a black bear by sneaking up behind the bear and giving it a swift kick. If the bear knocks the tree over and eats you, it's a grizzly. If it climbs up the tree and eats you, it's a black bear ("Our Favorite Animal Stories," 1990). Obviously this old tale should not be tested, and information about bear encounters needs to be studied before entering bear country.

It is believed best to stay odor-free by keeping personally clean but shunning scented lotions, soaps, deodorants, and cosmetics. Even before the trip, it is important not to use scented water softeners, whose strong, sweet smell attracts bears. And needless to say, carrying dried or freeze-dried food is much safer than food with odors. Noisemakers and flashlights make handy deterrents, and when on the trail, noise is made at blind corners, in thick brush, on

windy days, and near running water, where it may be more difficult for a bear to sense human presence. Before and after camping, especially in grizzly country, it is advisable for backpackers to travel in large groups during the middle of the day.

Camps are also not set up near plants with three leaflets, including poison ivy and poison oak. To avoid snakes and poisonous insects, the camper (and hiker) does not sit or step where it is impossible to see clearly (this includes stepping over logs); put hands inside holes in logs, trees, or rocks; or wander around the camp at night without a flashlight. Boots and clothing are inspected in the morning before putting them on. If a rattler's buzz is heard, the camper stops, finds out where the noise came from, and then retreats carefully. Normally rattlesnakes strike moving objects. Because they seldom strike very high, leather hiking boots provide protection. Although there are several hundred varieties of snakes in the United States, only four are poisonous. These are the coral, the rattler, the copperhead, and the cottonmouth, but there are several varieties of each. Corals are found in the South, copperheads in the eastern and southern states, cottonmouth moccasins or water moccasins in swamps, and various varieties of rattlers in nearly all of the 50 states.

Winter Camping

With modern equipment designed to function for below-freezing or even in sub-zero weather, winter can be one of the best times to visit the outdoors. The camper does not need to fight crowds or insects, but there are special challenges. A solid foundation in basic camping and survival techniques is essential, as well as advanced cold-weather skills.

Winter campers need to become familiar with cold-weather techniques, equipment, and local conditions. For instance, with night arriving earlier in the winter, camps are set up by midafternoon. Cold wind is avoided as much as possible by selecting a shielded site near shorter, younger trees or building a snow windbreak on the weather side of the tent site. A tree can provide additional protection, but snow-laden trees are bypassed because the snow can fall on the tent. It is important to be aware of avalanche conditions and to avoid locations near hills with a gradient of over 20 degrees, and taking avalanche gear along and knowing how to use it is a must. Downed needles may furnish excellent ground covering around the packed snow site and may prevent the tent from freezing to the ground. If freezing does occur, a tent may be detached with boiling water to help keep it from ripping. Moutaineering tents should be waterproof, condensation-resistant, and sturdy in design. Hoop and dome tents are often preferred by winter campers. Snow shelters such as snow domes, snow caves, and igloos can be made and will provide greater insulation than tents. Building methods are discussed in books focused on camping and winter survival.

Equipment can be carried in backpacks or by pulling a sled or toboggan. Clothes that wick perspiration and dry quickly are worn next to the skin in two layers. A middle layer follows and is designed to insulate, such as fleece in a goose down jacket. The outer layer is a breathable wind and waterproof laminate or alternative. Hats, gloves, mittens, socks, boots, garters, goggles, and glasses are also key (Recreational Equipment, Inc., 2014). Pine needles are collected to insulate the bed. Mummy bags with built-in hoods add protection on cold nights. With down bags, less clothing leads to more comfort and less perspiration, which makes the night and early morning even colder. Down provides the excellent insulation per carried pound, but it is ineffective insulation when wet. Some bags, insulated with high-tech materials, may be preferable in wet weather. Even if a fire is not intended, wood, tinder, and kindling are collected for emergencies. Fuel is placed on plastic and kept inside the tent to help it to dry out. Any fires must be carefully planned and tended. Tent heaters are a hazaRoad Winter camping accidents can occur from asphyxiation.

Winter campers tend to drink less than they should. It is important to drink more fluids to avoid dehydration. Hot liquids warm the body better than hot foods. Water may be collected from streams flowing too swiftly to freeze or by cutting through ice with a hammer and chisel. To melt snow, a few cups of water are placed at the bottom of a pot to create steam. More water results from melting chunks of ice and slab snow than from melting powdered snow. After water is collected, it must be purified. To make life easier, local outfitters provide organized tours and special equipment to meet the challenges of cold weather. With the advances in high-tech materials, gear, and technology, more and more enthusiasts are expanding their camping adventures into a year-round activity. The national and state parks, in an effort to provide relief from the crowded summer months, have launched public relations campaigns encouraging winter camping.

Safety. Two of the most common hazards are frostbite and hypothermia. Frostbite, caused by prolonged exposure to cold, is similar to a burn. The body parts most commonly affected by frostbite are ears, nose, hands, and feet. Signs and symptoms may involve a tingling sensation, pain followed by numbness. There is a white or purplish appearance to the skin. To avoid frostbite, the camper stays dry and out of wind in extremely cold temperatures. Layered clothing is worn as described previously in this chapter. Exposed areas of the skin are covered, and smoking and alcohol is bypassed in extreme cold. Chemical heat packs also help keep the body warm and to avoid frostbite. To treat frostbite, the camper should go inside or seek shelter from the wind, check for signs of hypothermia, and treat it first (to be discussed). Small areas are warmed with warm breath, and hands or feet are placed next to bare skin. The skin is not rubbed, and every effort is made to avoid walking on frostbitten feet. The frostbitten part is elevated and wrapped with blankets or soft material. If possible, it is immersed in warm water from 99 to 104 degrees. Using fire to thaw for speedy recovery can increase injury. If blisters appear, they are not broken and a doctor is called. A doctor is also called and careful rewarming and antibiotic treatment is needed when the skin is white or blue, hard, and cold. Aspirin or acetaminophen may be required if the skin turns red, burns, tingles, or becomes very painful (Kemper, 2005; Recreational Equipment, Inc. 2014).

When the body loses so much heat that it can no longer warm itself, *hypothermia* has occurred. *Hypo* means *low*, and *thermia* means *heat*. Untreated conditions will result in a continual drop in the body's core temperature until bodily functions cease. Hypothermia can happen at temperatures of 45 degrees or higher when in wet and windy weather or to frail and inactive people if not dressed warmly indoors. Signs and symptoms involve shivering, cold and pale skin, slurred speech, slow breathing, apathy, and impaired judgment. Physical and mental deterioration will continue until the advanced stages, which include cold abdomen, slow pulse and slow breathing, weakness or drowsiness, and confusion. Shivering may stop if body temperature drops below 96 degrees.

Treatment must be immediate for this emergency situation, which can lead to unconsciousness and death, so the camper must first call for emergency assistance. The victim is taken out of the cold or wind, and wet clothing is replaced with a dry covering.

Warm compresses are applied to the center of the body and head, but not to the arms and legs. This could be fatal because heat to the extremities forces cold back to the heart, lungs, and brain (Mayo Clinic, 2014b).

Low-impact. Campers are quiet and considerate of others and adhere to the following guidelines:

1. When possible, use existing campsites.
2. Observe all fire restrictions, and use outdoor camp stoves for cooking when possible. They are generally preferable to a campfire in terms of impact on the land. Use only fallen timber for a fire, and gather it well away from the camp. Let a fire burn down to a fine ash and ensure it is completely extinguished.
3. Carry water containers to reduce traffic at campsites. Do not wash in streams or lakes. Detergents, toothpaste, and soap harm fish and other aquatic life.
4. Do not use evergreen boughs for shelter or beds. Do not cut standing trees.
5. Plan to stay for as few nights as possible to avoid waste accumulation and injury to plants. One night in each campsite is best to avoid impact.
6. Try to leave the site in better condition than it was originally found by restoring the natural appearance of pristine sites and packing everything out that was packed in.

Camping With Pack Animals

Many adventurers enjoy horse packing in backcountry areas. Pack stock groups must be equally conscientious about leaving no trace of their visit. Proper trip planning, selection of camp location, and containment of animals once in camp demand special attention. In general, the same type of planning is used for a pack stock trip as for a backpacking trip. It is important to check with local officials for trail conditions and to find out if stock is allowed. Some areas are closed to

It is our duty to exercise responsible outdoor practices while enjoying outdoor activities.

pack animals due to overuse or fragile environments. The fewer animals taken, the less impact on the land. The group should be kept small, and campers should carry lightweight equipment to reduce the number of animals needed. On the trail, campers try to keep stock in single file.

For the horsepacker, the first rule of campsite selection is to think of the stock. The campsite should be able to accommodate the animals without damage to the area. After riding into a potential campsite, the packer must decide if there is enough feed. The packer should also consider the wildlife in the area. If the area is overgrazed, pack stock may remove feed otherwise needed by deer and elk during winter months. If grazed, it should be on north or east slopes, which will be snow-covered during the winter, leaving forage for wildlife on exposed south and west slopes. Stock water is another important consideration. A place downstream from camp in a gravelly area where the stream

bank can withstand hard use lowers impact, or use buckets. Hitchlines, hobbles, and pickets are methods of containing pack animals. Hitchlines need to be erected in rocky areas and on good stout trees using tree saver straps. Hobbles prevent horses from moving too fast, and pickets confine them to an area that is only as long as the rope or chain. Pickets should be moved at least twice daily to prevent overgrazing. Temporary corrals are an excellent method of containing pack animals for several days but should be moved frequently. They can be built out of natural timbers, rope, or portable electric fence. Stock should be tied to trees and brush only for short periods of time, if at all. They may paw up roots or strip the bark by gnawing and fighting the ropes, which can kill the brush or trees. Nylon tree saver straps help.

Feeding pack animals can cause a negative impact on an area. Spreading loose hay on the ground could introduce exotic plant species to an area. Instead, processed weed-seed-free feed is packed in, and feed bags are used. This helps prevent overgrazing. Begin feeding stock the weed-seed-free feed (try to say that three times) 72 hours before the trip to avoid leaving seeds in the manure. National Park Service areas do not allow grazing of stock.

Safety. The nature of traveling with stock requires the utmost care and continual attention to safety precautions. The latest procedures and the local procedures need to be followed at all times. Basic safety precautions include the following:

1. Check all riding gear for need of repair prior to departure.
2. Carry a first aid kit for riders and stock.
3. Know the ability of the stock and any limitations.
4. Know the ability of the riders and any limitations.
5. Practice backcountry techniques at home.
6. Familiarize the horses with llamas and backpackers prior to departure.
6. Travel single file and do not run the animals.
7. If hikers or bikers are encountered, they should yield the trail, but horses yield to pack strings and horses going uphill. ATV riders come to a stop and turn off engines.

Low-impact. The National Leadership School (NOLS) offers Leave No Trace courses in cooperation with major federal agencies. A few of these techniques follow (NOLS, 2007; U.S. Forest Service, 1993):

1. Follow all local regulations and permit requirements for use of stock in the backcountry.
2. Try to camp only one night in each location to protect the area from overuse. If a stay is more than 1 night at a destination camp, considerable determination and commitment are needed to keep the area of disturbance from growing larger. Picket pins and fences have to be moved

again and again to prevent overgrazing and trampling. It is best if extra horses can be sent out of base camp with a friend or member of the party for the length of the extended stay.

3. The general rule is the greater the confinement of horses, the greater the impact. Free-roaming horses grazing on good grassy areas cause little long-term impact. Ideally, the horses will only be in the immediate camp area long enough to load and unload. Hobbling of horses causes little environmental impact. Tree saver straps are needed if a highline is used, and grazing areas should be as large as possible.
4. Pack in weed-seed-free feed to avoid introducing exotic plants and weeds. Use feed bags, and water the stock at established fords, in low rocky spots, or in gravel-protected areas. Buckets are an alternative to avoid damage to delicate riparian areas.
5. It takes extra time to naturalize an area from the impact of pack animals. Manure piles need to be scattered to aid decomposition and discourage flies, and as a courtesy to other users. Areas dug up by animal hooves will need to be filled and trampled areas made to look natural.

SUMMARY

Americans' love of nature is reflected in the type, as well as the amount, of outdoor activities they partake. We provided a glimpse of these activities in this chapter. Participation equipment, and possible dangers, were often included. Adventures on land include hiking, backpacking, and mountain biking. Activities in the snow include snowshoeing and cross-country skiing. The white-water rivers of America provide ample opportunities for leisure pursuits, such as canoeing, kayaking, and rafting. On the other hand, the ocean is used for SCUBA diving and windsurfing. In the air, Americans enjoy hang gliding, hot air ballooning, and skydiving. Bird-watching and rock art visits are viewing and educational activities that were described in detail. Orienteering and navigation are necessary for many outdoor pursuits, and camping is an activity that is enjoyed in winter and summer and that can be accompanied by pack animals.

We briefly described safety techniques and low-impact techniques, but these should be updated before participation begins. Safety must always be a priority in planning and during the activity, and minimizing impact helps to protect the environment by leaving no sign of visitation. Despite overcrowding in wilderness areas, the recreationist can prevent adverse impact by practicing the no-trace ethic. The low-impact ethic advocates leaving wilderness areas in better condition than before they were visited. By practicing no-trace and low-impact techniques, wilderness visitors can enjoy these beautiful and pristine environments today and tomorrow.

ORGANIZATIONS

Many organizations that support outdoor recreation are shown in Appendix B. The following organizations provide excellent resources for learning proper techniques for the activities cited.

Ballooning

Balloon Federation of America, PO Box 400, 1601 North Jefferson, Indianola, IA 50125, Ph: (515) 961-8809, Fax: (515) 961-3537, www.bfa.net

Bicycling

Adventure Cycling Association, 150 East Pine Street, Missoula, MT 59807, Ph: (800) 755-2453, (406) 721-1776, Fax: (406) 721-8754, www.adventurecycling.org

International Mountain Bicycling Association, PO Box 20280, Boulder, CO 80306, Ph: (303) 545-9011, Fax: (303) 545-9026, www.imba.com

Birding

National Audubon Society, 700 Broadway, New York, NY 10003, Ph: (212) 979-3000, Fax: (212) 979-3188, www.audubon.org

Cornell Laboratory of Ornithology, 159 Sapsucker Woods Road, Ithaca, NY 14850, Ph: (607) 254-2473, www.birds.cornell.edu

Camping

American Camping Association, Bradford Woods, 5000 State Road 67 North, Martinsville, IN 46151-7902, Ph: (765) 342-8456, Fax: (765) 342-2065, www.acacamps.org

Association of Independent Camps, 10331 Tarpan Drive, Indianapolis, IN 46256-9792, Ph: (317) 596-8701, Fax: (317) 596-8703, www.independentcamps.com

Christian Camping International, PO Box 62189, Colorado Springs, CO 80962-2189, Ph: (719) 260-9400, http://cci-worldwide.org

National Camp Association, 610 Fifth Avenue, PO Box 5371, New York, NY 10185, Ph: (800) 966-CAMP (2267), (212) 645-0653, Fax: (845) 354-5501, www.summercamp.org

Family Campers and RVers Association, 74 West Genesee Street, Skanteles, NY 13152, www.fcrv.org

Canoeing, Kayaking, and Rafting

American Canoe Association, 7432 Alban Station Boulevard, Suite B-232, Springfield, VA 22150, Ph: (703) 451-0141, Fax: (703) 451-2245, www.americancanoe.org

American Whitewater Association, 1430 Fenwick Lane, Silver Spring, MD 20910, Ph: (866) BOAT4AW, Fax: (301) 589-6121, www.americanwhitewater.org

National Organization for Rivers, 212 West Cheyenne Mountain Boulevard, Colorado Springs, CO 80906, Ph: (719) 579-8759, Fax: (719) 576-6238, www.nationalrivers.org

United States Canoe Association, 606 Ross Street, Middletown, OH 45042, www.uscanoe.com

Cross-Country Skiing and Snowshoeing

Cross Country Ski Areas Association, 259 Bolton Road, Winchester, NH 03470, Ph: (603) 239-4341, Fax: (603) 239-6387, www.xcski.org

Far West Ski Association, 3021 NE 72nd Drive, Suite 9, Box #207, Vancouver, WA 98661, www.fwsa.org

Professional Ski Instructors of America (PSIA), 133 S. Van Gordon, Suite 101, Lakewood, CO 80228, Ph: (303) 988-0545, (303) 988-3005, www.thesnowpros.org

The North American Telemark Organization, Box 44, Waitsfield, VT 05673, Ph: (800) 835-3404, Fax: (802) 496-5515, www.telemarknato.com

The Sierra Club, 85 Second Street, Second Floor, San Francisco, CA 94105-3441, Ph: (415) 977-5500, Fax: (415) 977-5799, www.sierraclub.org

Hang Gliding

Hang Glider Manufacturers Association (HGMA), 137 Oregon Street, El Segundo, CA 90245, http://hgma.net

United States Hang Gliding and Paragliding Association (USHPA), PO Box 1330, Colorado Springs, CO 80901, Ph: (719) 632-8300, Fax: (719) 632-6417, www.ushpa.org

Hiking/Backpacking

American Hiking Society, 1422 Fenwick Lane, Silver Spring, MD 20910, Ph: (301) 565-6704, Fax: (301) 565-6714, www.americanhiking.org

American Trails, 21750 Rolling Hills Road, Palo Cedro, CA 96073, Ph: (530) 547-2060, www.americantrails.org

Appalachian Trail Conservancy, 799 Washington Street, Harpers Ferry, WV 25425, Ph: (304) 535-6331, Fax: (304) 535-2667, www.atconf.org

Appalachian Mountain Club AMC Main Office, 5 Joy Street, Boston, MA 02108, Ph: (617) 523-0636, Fax: (617) 523-0722, www.outdoors.org

Rails-to-Trails Conservancy, 1100 17th Street NW, 10th Floor, Washington, DC 20036, Ph: (202) 331-9696, Fax: (202) 331-9680, www.railstotrails.org

Orienteering

National Outdoor Leadership School, 284 Lincoln Street, Lander, WY 82520-3148, Ph: (307) 332-5300, Fax: (307) 332-1220, www.nols.edu/NOLSHome.html

Outward Bound, 910 Jackson Street, Suite 140, Golden, CO 80401, Ph: (866) 467-7651, www.outwardbound.org

Orienteering USA, PO Box 505, Riderwood, MD 21139, Ph: (410) 802-1125, www.us.orienteering.org

United States Orienteering Federation, PO Box 1444, Forest Park, GA 30051, www.us.orienteering.org

Map Information U.S. Geological Survey, USGS Information Services, PO Box 25286, Denver, CO 80225. A free Topographical Map Index Circular for any state east or west of the Mississippi River can be requested at (888) ASK-USGS (1-888-275-8747), www.usgs.gov

U.S. Geological Survey, 12201 Sunrise Valley Drive, Reston, VA 20192, Ph: (888) 275-8747, www.usgs.gov

Parachuting

United States Parachute Association (USPA), 5401 Southpoint Centre Boulevard, Fredericksburg, VA 22047, Ph: (540) 604-9740, Fax: (540) 604-9741, www.uspa.org

Rock Art

American Rock Art Research Association (ARARA), Arizona State Museum University of Arizona, Tucson, AZ 85721-0026, Ph: (520) 621-3999, Fax: (520) 621-2976, www.arara.org

National Pictographic Society, PO Box 94, Copperton, UT 84006

SCUBA Diving

Underwater Society of America, 1701 Lake Avenue, Glenview, IL 60025, http://underwater-society.org

For Diver Certification:

Handicapped Scuba Association (certification agency for persons with disabilities), 1104 El Prado, San Clemente, CA 92672, Ph: (714) 498-6128, Fax: (714) 498-6128, www.hsascuba.com

IDEA (International Diving Education Association), PO Box 8427, Jacksonville, FL 32239, Ph: (904) 744-5554, Fax: (904) 743-5425

NAUI (National Association of Underwater Instructors), 9942 Currie Davis Drive, Ste H, Tampa, FL 33619-2667, Ph: (813) 628-6284, Fax: (813) 628-8253, www.naui.org

PADI (Professional Association of Diving Instructors), 30151 Tomas, Rancho Santo Margarita, CA 92688, Fax: (949) 267-1263, www.padi.com

PDIC (Professional Diving Instructors Corporation, International), PO Box 3633, 1554 Gardner Avenue, Scranton, PA 18505, Ph: (717) 342-1480, Fax: (717) 342-1276, www.pdic-intl.com

SSI (Scuba Schools International—SSI merged with the National Association of SCUBA Diving Schools and collaborates the YMCA of the USA), 2619 Canton Ct., Ft. Collins, CO 80525, Ph: (800) 892-2702, (970) 482-0883, Fax: (970) 482-6157, www.divessi.com

Windsurfing

International Windsurfing Association, Mengham Cottage, Mengham Lane, Hayling Island, Hampshire PO11 9JX United Kingdom, www.internationalwindsurfing.com

United States Windsurfing Association, 8211 Sun Spring Cir., Apt. 73, Orlando, FL 32825, Ph: (877) 386-8708, www.uswindsurfing.org

REFERENCES

American Whitewater. (2014a). AW's safety program. Retrieved from http://www.americanwhitewater.org/content/Safety/view/

American Whitewater. (2014b). Risk, safety, and personal responsibility. Retrieved from http://www.americanwhitewater.org/content/Wiki/stewardship:risk

Balloon Federation of America. (1999). Crew and safety tips. Retrieved from http://www.bfa-jr-balloonist.com/crew.htm

Benson, R. (1979). *Skydiving.* Minneapolis, MN: Turner Publications.

Berger, K. (2000). *SCUBA diving: A trailside guide.* New York, NY: W.W. Norton.

Betz, C. (1999, January). National outdoor recreation assessments. *Parks & Recreation, 34*(1), 22–31.

Betz, C., English, D., & Cordell, H. K. (1999). Outdoor recreation resources. In H. K. Cordell (Ed.), *Outdoor recreation in American life: A national assessment of demand and supply trends* (pp. 39–182). Champaign, IL: Sagamore.

Bowker, J., English, D., & Cordell, H. K. (1999). Projections of outdoor recreation participation to 2050. In H. K. Cordell (Ed.), *Outdoor recreation in American life: A national assessment of demand and supply trends* (pp. 323–351). Champaign, IL: Sagamore.

Brandt, A. (1997, January). Crane spotting. *Sky, 1997,* 62–63.

Browning, T. (1989, September/October). Spirits in stone. *National Parks, 63,* 9–10.

Cahill, T. (1990, October). Swimming with sharks. *Reader's Digest, 137,* 822.

Carlton, D. (2000a). Assembly. Retrieved from http://www.heritagedevelop.com/crewing/assembly.htm

Carlton, D. (2000b). Safety. Retrieved from http://www.heritagedevelop.com/crewing/safety.htm

Carver, E. (2013). *Birding in the United States: A demographic and economic analysis* (Report 2011-1). Arlington, VA: U.S. Fish and Wildlife Service.

Centers for Disease Control and Prevention. (2013, August). More people walk to better health. Retrieved from http://www.cdc.gov/VitalSigns/Walking/

Chavez, D. (1999). Mountain biking: A rapidly growing sport. In H. K. Cordell (Ed.), *Outdoor recreation in American life: A national assessment of demand and supply trends* (pp. 245–246). Champaign, IL: Sagamore.

Cordell, H. K. (Ed.). (1999). *Outdoor recreation in American life: A national assessment of demand and supply trends.* Champaign, IL: Sagamore.

Cordell, H. K., Bergstrom, L., Hartmann, L., & English, D. (1990). *An analysis of the outdoor recreation and wilderness situation in the United States: 1989–2040* (Gen. Tech. Rep. RM-189). Fort Collins, CO: U.S. Forest Service.

Cordell, H. K., McDonald, B., Teasley, R., Bergstrom, J., Martin, J., Bason, J., & Leeworthy, V. (1999). Outdoor recreation participation trends. In H. K. Cordell (Ed.), *Outdoor recreation in American life: A national assessment of demand and supply trends* (pp. 219–322). Champaign, IL: Sagamore.

Cordes, K. (1999). *America's national historic trails*. Norman: University of Oklahoma Press.

Cordes, K. (2001). *America's national scenic trails*. Norman: University of Oklahoma Press.

Crysdale, D. (2002, November), ORRRC at 40! *Parks and Recreation, 37*(11), 74–77.

David, A., & Moran, T. (1983). *River thrill sports*. Minneapolis, MN: Lemer Publications.

Dean, A. (1982). *Wind sports*. Philadelphia, PA: Westminster Press.

Drury, J., & Holmlund, E. (1997). *The camper's guide to outdoor pursuits*. Champaign, IL: Sagamore.

Fisher, R., & Brown, L. (Eds.). (1979). *Fodors outdoors America*. New York, NY: David McKay.

Florida Department of Natural Resources. (n.d.). *Reef guide*. Tallahassee, FL: Author.

Hamilton, P. (2007). All about hang gliding. Retrieved from http://www.all-about-hang-gliding.com

International Orienteering Federation. (2011). About orienteering. Retrieved from http://orienteering.org

Kemper, D. (1999). *Kaiser Permanente healthwise handbook*. Boise, ID: Healthwise.

Kemper, D., The Healthwise Staff, & The Physicians and Staff of Kaiser Permanente. (2005). *Kaiser Permanente healthwise handbook*. Boise, ID: Healthwise.

Leave No Trace. (1997, July). *Leave no trace outdoor skills & ethics backcountry horse* (Vol. 3.2). Lander, WY: National Outdoor Leadership School.

Lohr, R. (1999, October). Dashing through the snow. *Parks & Recreation, 34*(10), 85–87.

Lotz, A. (1987). *Birding around the world*. New York, NY: Dodd, Mead.

Mackey, B., & Leonard, R. (1995). Frequently asked questions about hang gliding and paragliding. Retrieved from http://www.ushga.org/faq.asp

Mayo Clinic. (2014a). Blisters: First aid. Retrieved from http://www.mayoclinic.org/first-aid/first-aid-blisters/basics/art-20056691

Mayo Clinic. (2014b). Hypothermia: First aid. Retrieved from http://www.mayoclinic.org/first-aid/first-aid-hypothermia/basics/ART-20056624

McEwen, D. (1999). Camping facilities on public land. In H. K. Cordell (Ed.), *Outdoor recreation in American life: A national assessment of demand and supply trends* (pp. 89–92). Champaign, IL: Sagamore.

McKinney, J. (1998). *Day hiker's guide to southern California*. Santa Barbara, CA: Olympus Press.

Meadows, G. (1994, September). How to buy a used entry-level hang glider. *USHGA Hang Gliding Magazine, 1994*, 1–4. Retrieved from http://www.ushga.org/article05.asp

Meier, J. (1980). *Backpacking*. Dubuque, IA: Wm. C. Brown.

Meier, J., & Mitchell, A. (1993). *Camp counseling*. Dubuque, IA: WCB Brown & Benchmark.

National Oceanic and Atmospheric Administration & Professional Association of Diving Instructors. (1993). *Ten ways a diver can protect the underwater environment* [Brochure]. Washington, DC: U.S. Government Printing Office.

Oiney, R. (1976). *Hang gliding*. New York, NY: Putnam's Sons.

Outdoor Foundation. (2013). *Outdoor participation report*. Retrieved from http://www.outdoorfoundation.org/pdf/ResearchParticipation2013.pdf

Outdoor Foundation, Coleman, & Kampgrounds of America. (2012). *2012 American camper report*. Retrieved from http://www.outdoorfoundation.org/pdf/research.camping.2012.pdf

Our favorite animal stories. (1996, October). *Backpacker, 18*(2).

Potter, E. (1998, February, 1). Snowshoein' it. *The San Diego Union-Tribune,* p. F-12.

President's Commission on Americans Outdoors. (1987). *Americans outdoors: The legacy, the challenge.* Washington, DC: Island Press.

Recreational Equipment, Inc. (2014). Winter camping and backpacking tips. Retrieved from http://www.rei.com/learn/expert-advice/winter-camping.html

Reilly, L. (2012, July 17). By the numbers: How Americans spend their money. *Mental_Floss.* Retrieved from http://mentalfloss.com/article/31222/numbers-how-americans-spend-their-money

Roper Starch. (2001). *Outdoor recreation in America 1999: The family and the environment.* A report prepared for the Recreation Roundtable, Washington, DC.

Roper Starch. (2003). *Outdoor recreation in America 2003: Recreation's benefits to society challenges by trends.* Washington, DC: The Recreation Roundtable.

Snocountry. (2013, August 2). Overview of 2013 cross country skiing statistics; 23 percent decline [Blog post]. Retrieved from http://www.snocountry.com/en/news/entry/overview-of-2013-cross-country-skiing-statistics-23-percent-decline

Society of Park and Recreation Educators. (1999, January). Research into action: What's hot in outdoor recreation. *Parks & Recreation, 34*(1), 28.

Statista. (2014). Most popular outdoor activities in the United States from 2009 to 2013, by number of participants (in millions). Retrieved from http://www.statista.com/statistics/190202/number-of-participants-in-outdoor-activities-in-the-us-2009/

Steel, R. (1985). *Sharks of the world.* New York, NY: Blanford Press.

Tilton, B. (1997). Avalanche safety: Choosing the safest route. *Continental Divide Trail News, 2*(1), 5.

Trailpeak. (2006). *Getting ready to ski.* Vancouver, Canada: Trailpeak.

United States Hang Gliding and Paragliding Association. (2014). Frequently asked questions about hang gliding. Retrieved from http://www.ushpa.aero/faq.asp

United States Parachute Association. (2003). Accident statistics. Retrieved from http://www.uspa.org/about/page2/relative_safety.htm.

United States Parachute Association. (2014). Sky diving safety. Retrieved from http://www.uspa.org/AboutSkydiving/SkydivingSafety/tabid/526/Default.aspx

U.S. Forest Service. (1993). *Horse sense* (Pamphlet R1-93-23). Washington, DC: Author.

U.S. Forest Service. (1994). *Winter safety guide* (R1 94-1). Washington, DC: U.S. Government Printing Office.

U.S. Sailing. (2014). Start windsurfing right: The windsurfing safety code. Retrieved from http://www.ussailing.org/resources/start-windsurfing-right-the-windsurfing-safety-code/

WebMD. (2014). Heat stroke: Symptoms and treatment. Retrieved from http://www.webmd.com/a-to-z-guides/heat-stroke-symptoms-and-treatment?page=3

Wild Backpacker. (2014). Surviving a lightning storm. Retrieved from http://www.wildbackpacker.com/wilderness-survival/articles/surviving-a-lightning-storm/

Windsurfer.com. (2000). Basic lesson. Retrieved from http://www.windsurfer.com/newsite/biginners/lesson.cfm

Windsurfer.com. (2000). Many spects. Retrieved from http://www.windsurfer.com/newsite/beginners/aspects.cfm

Wirth, D. (1980). *Ballooning.* New York, NY: Random House.

Chapter 16

The Environment

Today, most people no longer possess outdoor survival skills. The hostile natural environment once feared by the pioneers has been developed and industrialized, generally eliminating the need for use of outdoor skills on a daily basis. Wilderness survival instincts are satisfied by outdoor enthusiasts in wilderness and nature preserves. The return to these skills by recreationists tends to stimulate sensitivity to the protection of nature and its survival. One survey shows that an overwhelming 95% of the respondents who spend time outdoors and participate in outdoor recreational activities understand the importance of environmental protection (Roper Starch, 2000). Three aspects of this relationship follow (Atkinson, 1990):

1. Leisure activities that are focused on appreciating the natural (nature walking, canoeing, outdoor photography) appear to have a greater impact on a person's environmental concern and likelihood to behave in a pro-environmental fashion when contrasted with activities that are more consumptive of energy or natural resources.
2. Recreationists may possess stronger attitudes about aspects of the environment on which their leisure activity is dependent (clean water for fishing, clean air for ballooning, etc.).
3. Pro-environmental attitudes of recreationists do not always translate into sound environmental behavior. Some recreationists in their enthusiasms and efforts to see and experience remote or desirable public lands are guilty of damaging some of the most fragile ecosystems.

Increasingly, chemicals, agriculture, and urban development place tremendous pressure on natural resources. Because it is difficult to measure the state of the natural environment, and because many environmental issues seem invisible and distant, Americans are increasingly dependent on conservation groups, public laws, the media, museums, zoos, parks, and nature centers for information regarding the condition of the natural world. Outdoor enthusiasts, for instance, experience nature firsthand, thereby giving them a unique opportunity to share their knowledge, experiences, and interpretations with their recreational societies to keep them abreast of environmental issues affecting their activity. The American Hiking Society finds that the longer multiple environmental impacts go unobserved, the more likely they will accelerate ecological damage.

In recognizing that trails offer the potential to act as indicators of a community's ecological health, the society recommends that trail managers assign dependable volunteer hikers to observe the ecosystems in their regions. Any changes observed are reported to trail managers who will then describe the changes to scientists and environmental advocates.

Outdoor leaders must understand basic concepts of environmental conservation. Not only do they teach others to enjoy the wonders of the natural world, they also teach them how to preserve nature and to develop outdoor ethics. According to the National Environmental Education Training Foundation and Roper Starch Worldwide, the average American's environmental knowledge of essential aspects is limited (Coyle, 2005; Environmental Protection Agency [EPA], 1999). When people at leisure interact with the natural environment, three ingredients characterize the interaction, especially when they are simultaneously exposed to the leadership of a role model (Chase, 1990):

1. *Direct experience* provides a reference point to view the effect of leisure on the natural environment and may nurture empathy for other users and an environmental conscience.
2. *Cognition,* enhanced by direct experience, provides for short-term and long-term betterment of the environment due to a strengthened knowledge base.
3. *Ethics,* positively influenced by cognition, produce an immediate betterment in the form of awareness of the aesthetic appeal of a natural environment that is free of debris and other traces of the user. Long-term betterment results through responsible management grounded in an ethical framework.

THE ENVIRONMENTAL MOVEMENT

Early environmentalists, such as Henry David Thoreau, George Perkins Marks, and John Muir, provided the foundation for the environmental movement (Sessions, 1995). And President Theodore Roosevelt propelled the first wave of the conservation campaign when he announced in his first State of the Union address that natural resource issues were "the most vital international problems of the United States." A second wave resulted when President Franklin D. Roosevelt set up the Civilian Conservation Corps and encouraged scientists to think holistically. The conservation-minded scientists, such as Aldo Leopold, influenced the public to look at the broader picture of the interaction between people and the environment. When Rachel Carson's 1962 book *Silent Spring* came out, it served as a mandate for a cause that was waiting to happen. Adding fuel to the fire, Stewart L. Udall, secretary of the interior from 1961 to 1969, predicted an environmental crisis in his 1963 book *The Quiet Crisis.* When a series of environmental accidents followed, such as a fire on the polluted Cuyahoga River in Cleveland and an oil spill off California in the Santa Barbara Harbor, a third wave took place. Citizens were aroused into action, and environmental laws such as the Federal Clean Air Act of 1963, Wilderness Act of 1964, Land and Water Conservation Fund Act of 1965, National Wildlife Refuge System Administration Act of 1966, Wild and Scenic Rivers Act of 1968, and the National Environmental Policy Act of 1969 were passed (Weiss, 2005; G. Williams, 2000).

On April 22, 1970, environmentalists led by Senator Gaylord Nelson, called the father of Earth Day, were drawn together for a series of environmental teach-ins across the nation that were coordinated by Denis Hayes, who serves as the head of the Earth Day Network. The next year President Richard Nixon signed the law creating the EPA. In 1973, Congress passed the Endangered Species Act, one of the most comprehensive laws ever enacted to prevent the extinction of imperiled life. That same year the debate over the last frontier in Alaska began. The Alaska Lands Act was signed in December 1980 as one of President Jimmy Carter's last official acts, although oil drilling in the Alaska National Wildlife Refuge is still debated today. During the 1980s, memberships in environmental and conservation organizations soared. By the 1990s, there were more than 10,000 non-profit environmental groups in the United States, according to The Conservation Fund. They ranged from traditional land and wild-life conservation or nature education groups to hybrids of health and pollution control organizations (Weiss, 2005).

When more than 200 million people in 184 countries participated in Earth Day 1990, Hayes (2000) announced that he believed that the environmental movement was the most successful social movement in the United States. With support from 95% of all Americans and 96% of parents, environmental education in schools became the norm (EPA, 1999). By 1996, President William Clinton protected 1.9 million acres of Utah red rock as the Grand Staircase-Escalante National Monument. In his second term, he proposed permanent protection for more than 58 million acres of wild, roadless national forests and before leaving office had designated or expanded by presidential proclamation more than 22 national monuments. Earth Day 2000 attracted an estimated 500 million people—25 times the number of those who took part in the first Earth Day in 1970—to activities that were focused on the roots of environmental awareness in America, which began with the American Indians (Pope, 2001). Today, Earth Day activities are celebrated by more than 1 billion people, making it the largest civic observance in the world (Cassie, 2015).

Environmental Approaches

Environmentalists are often divided into two basic philosophical groups. *Reformists* believe that environmental problems are resolved through technology, increased governmental and industrial expenditures, and ceaseless public vigilance and legal action. Their critics maintain that they do not reach the root causes of the ecocrisis, thereby failing to turn the tide of global environmental destruction. These *deep environmentalists* do not believe in a technological fix, but instead focus on an entirely new social and economic value system that they believe will

help prevent environmental deterioration. Concluding that a decrease in the consumption of the earth's resources is essential, they support a move from an anthropocentric to a spiritual/ecocentric value orientation (Capra, 1995; Sessions, 1995).

In *anthropocentric* orientation, also known as *shallow* ecology, humans are viewed as above or outside of nature. Under this orientation, the wilderness is preserved in a piecemeal fashion based on rationales such as aesthetics and recreation. The motivation to protect entire ecosystems and maintain ecosystem integrity was fundamentally ignored, and compromises became the norm (Sessions, 1995). In the holistic *ecocentric* orientation, wilderness areas are much more than aesthetic or recreational spaces. They are also seen as essential components in the newer ecological concept of an unfinished system of interconnected nature preserves that will provide habitat for wide-ranging or sensitive wilderness-dependent species (Foreman, 1995; Sessions, 1995). Like the American Indians, these environmentalists believe that society must live in harmony with all living things (Capra, 1995). They hold contrasting positions on issues such as pollution, resources, human overpopulation, cultural diversity and appropriate technology, land and sea ethics, and education and the scientific enterprise. For example, in the shallow approach, conservation of resources is viewed as for future generations of humans, whereas in the *deep* approach, this is taken a step further. Although they recognize the need to use resources to satisfy vital needs, they will not come into conflict with the vital needs of nonhumans to satisfy nonvital needs. Although it is believed that the deep ecology approach will last well throughout the 21st century, one question looms in the horizon: How much irreversible global ecological destruction will result before existing trends can be significantly reversed (Sessions, 1995)? Critics of the deep movement insist that no matter how a person feels about the environment, it is the political actors who will make the decision to destroy or protect it (Slater, 2001). This would indicate that voters must take time to understand issues and politicians' records before casting a ballot.

At the Department of the Interior's 2001 Conference on the Environment, The Path Before Us: Environmental Stewardship for the 21st Century, participants were exposed to both philosophies. Technological training was offered and American Indians detailed their view of the earth and the environment (Mathews, 2001). Whichever philosophy or combination of philosophies is endorsed, solutions to environmental problems are vital. Worldwatch Institute, an environment research group, warned government officials that many global ecosystems are in danger (Dunphy, 2001). According to ecological footprint studies, humans have gone 60% beyond the planet's ecological capacity. This means that globally, according to the Worldwatch Institute (2013), humans must reduce total resource use to a level below the natural threshold. Several environmental issues affecting outdoor recreation follow, but further study of these issues will be required. Future leaders will be expected to educate others and sensitize the public to problems related to the use and enjoyment of nature.

THE NATURE OF ECOSYSTEMS

All organisms share an evolutionary history and an ecological kinship. An *ecosystem* is a community of all living organisms that function together in a particular environment. This includes every plant, insect, aquatic animal, bird, or land species (including humans) and forms a complex web of interdependency. An action taken at any level in the food chain has a potential domino effect on every other occupant of that system. This includes the use of pesticides, for example. Ecology is the study of these relationships within the environment (EPA, 1996).

Ecological relationships are manifested in physiochemical settings of nonliving, or *abiotic,* environmental substances and gradients. These groups consist of basic inorganic elements and compounds such as oxygen, water, carbon dioxide, and an array of organic compounds, the by-products of organism activity. Physical factors and gradients such as moisture, winds, currents, tides, and solar radiation are also included. *Biotic* components, or the living components, such as plants, animals, and microbes, interplay against the abiotic backdrop (EPA, 1996; Kormondy, 1984). These relationships are so intricate, however, that only the most obvious mysteries have been unraveled. The following cycles exhibit noteworthy relationships:

1. **The food chain cycle:** A sequence of organisms, each of which uses the next, lower member of the sequence as a food source. Plants flourish by receiving energy from the sun and nutrients from the soil. Smaller animals consume the plants, larger animals feed on the smaller, and so on. Upon their deaths the bodies decompose and return to the soil, where plants absorb the fresh nutrients, thus completing the chain.

2. **The oxygen–carbon cycle:** Similar to the food chain cycle, the oxygen–carbon cycle generates life. Animals consume oxygen and exhale carbon dioxide. Carbon dioxide is also produced when plants and animals decay and when fuels are burned. Plants use carbon dioxide to produce oxygen. Sunlight, the source of all energy, works with the photosynthetic pigments such as green chlorophyll in plants to combine carbon from the air with water to originate sugars that plants use for food. This process, *photosynthesis,* or making something from light, allows for the production of oxygen.

3. **The water cycle:** Plants and animals depend on water, which permits foods and gases to pass through the cells of plants and animals. Relying on the sun for power, water circulates through the environment in a cycle. The sun's heat evaporates water from the aquatic ecosystems. The vapors form clouds, and when the air cools or becomes filled with moisture, the vapor falls as rain, snow, sleet, or hail.

Plants use the water soaked into the soil. Some water becomes part of the groundwater supply, forming springs and wells, which eventually returns to lakes and oceans where it can evaporate, continuing the cycle.

In general, there are two major ecosystems: aquatic and terrestrial with subdivisions that will be discussed in this chapter. *Aquatic ecosystems* are distinguished as freshwater, estuarine, and marine ecosystems, and *terrestrial ecosystems* include forests, tundra, savanna, grasslands, and desert. Very large ecosystems are sometimes referred to as ecoregions. In recent years, policymakers have become more cognizant of the significance of preserving the natural diversity in these physical environments (Loomis, Bonetti, & Echohawk, 1999). And because ecosystems do not stop at traditional boundary lines, active partnerships between the federal agencies and the federal, state, and public agencies with private industry have become extremely important.

Ecosystem management is an environmentally sensitive, socially responsible, and scientifically sound way to manage the nation's public land so the environment will be healthy, diverse, and productive. Ecosystem management also means trying to restore damaged resources to a healthy condition. When healthy, ecosystems provide clean, clear water; furnish habitat for fish, wildlife, and plants; offer way stations for migratory birds; help purify the air and prevent soil erosion; supply rich, fertile, and productive soils; turn over higher water tables; afford greener streamside areas; allow for more songbirds; clean streambanks; create buffers for flooding; present better fishing and hunting; result in a more resilient mix of native plants; produce healthier livestock; and encourage disease-free forests. Healthy ecosystems also help to ensure that future generations will have the opportunity to draw social, aesthetic, and spiritual benefits from the land.

NATURE CHANGING

Nature changes constantly, and these alterations are essential for living things to thrive. For example, a forest matures gradually, taking hundreds or even thousands of years to develop. In an area starting as a pond, soil washes in from hillsides and collects along the edges. Wind carries grass seeds, which take root in the soil. As the grass grows and dies, it mats and decays, producing a nutrient-rich bed for larger plants. Frogs and fish find protection among the plants, and insects lay eggs on the leaves. These plants and animals eventually expire, decay, and build a more fertile soil, which ultimately becomes home to bushes and small trees. As the plants decay, they form additional earth for larger trees, which gradually grow into a stand or forest. The pond disappears and the forest, which has developed through the long process of succession, has a vast number of plants and animals within it. Diversity in the forest acts as a buffer against drastic change, allowing an area to adjust slowly to new conditions. If one tree species is destroyed, for instance, another may take over. Should a solitary species exist in an area, any threat would endanger the entire forest.

Rapid natural changes also occur from forest fires or volcanic eruptions. Destruction by forest fire allows for a continuing process of succession. Humans, too, have the ability to alter the earth. They may suit their needs, rather than adapting their needs to existing conditions. Although they do not intend to harm the environment, outdoor recreationists have an impact. Steps taken to minimize this impact such as the no-trace ethic were addressed in Chapter 15.

Climate Change

Never free from change, the earth's atmosphere varies in composition and temperature. In the last two centuries, though, the composition of the atmosphere has undergone disturbing changes. A dramatic increase in carbon dioxide (CO_2), most likely caused by the burning of fossil fuels, smoke stacks, and the clearing and burning of forests for agriculture (Revkin, 2006), has been released in greater quantities than can be removed by photosynthesis on land or by diffusion in the oceans. Scientists are concerned that the growing burden of carbon dioxide and other gases will enhance a warming trend. Carbon dioxide, for instance, has increased more than 35% since the beginning of the Industrial Revolution. This is one of the strongest pieces of evidence for human-induced climate change (National Center for Atmospheric Research and University Corporation for Atmospheric Research, 2014a). Over the past 30 years, the earth has warmed about 1.53 degrees and over that past 100 years since modern records began more than a century ago (National Center for Atmospheric Research and University Corporation for Atmospheric Research, 2014b). The average global surface temperature will increase 2 to 11.5 degrees by 2100 or at least twice as much as it has for the last 100 years (EPA, 2014b).

Climate change, commonly used interchangeably with *global warming* and the *greenhouse effect,* refers to the buildup of human-made gases in the atmosphere that trap the sun's heat, causing changes in weather patterns on a global scale. The effects include changes in rainfall pattern, sea level rise, potential droughts, habitat loss, and heat stress. The greenhouse gases of most concern are carbon dioxide, methane, and nitrous oxide (EPA, 1996, 1998b). Atmospheric concentrations of carbon dioxide are responsible for about 84% of greenhouse gases. Methane (CH_4) results from agricultural activities, landfills, and other sources. Nitrous oxide (NO_4), known as laughing gas, includes everything from nitrogen-based fertilizer to manure from farm animals (Kelly & Vergano, 2006; Watson & Weisman, 2001). Climate change is primarily due to human activities. Human-induced warming is superimposed on naturally varying climates, so it is not uniform (Melillo, Richmond, & Yohe, 2014).

Climatologists forecast that continued temperature rises will continue to disrupt the climate with increasingly severe weather. The seas are expected to rise, glaciers will continue to melt, and other unpredictable consequences are expected to result. If global rainfall patterns shift, it could cause deserts to expand, rich farmland to suffer droughts, heavier flooding, ice sheets to melt, oceans to expand, loss of habitat, the disappearance of endangered species, heat-related deaths, and the increase of infectious diseases such as malaria (Melillo et al., 2014; Weise, 2006).

To help stabilize the climate, humanity needs to cut greenhouse gas emissions (Gelbspan, 2001). On the question of global warming and the nation's responsibility, 75% of respondents polled in a nationwide survey favor regulating carbon dioxide (Romm, 2012). Even with continued compelling evidence, change is uncertain and difficult to pin down. Climate skeptics find it questionable that humans are pushing matters beyond the natural variability that already exists and for the need for alarm (Revkin, 2004). As one geoscientist cautioned, though, "We have only one world to play with" (Lemonick, 2006, pp. 58–59). How emission levels determine temperature rises is shown in Figure 16.1.

Taking Initiative

Approaches for tackling global warming and air pollution follow.

Kyoto Protocol. In 1992, 150 countries signed the Framework Convention on Climate Change (FCCC), which has the objective of stabilizing the concentration of greenhouse gases in the atmosphere at levels that would prevent dangerous interference with the climate system. Parties to the FCCC formulated the *Kyoto Protocol* at a 1997 conference held in Kyoto, Japan. The Kyoto Protocol reduced greenhouse gas emission targets for industrialized countries for 2008–2012. The protocol also provided for measures, such as international emissions trading with other countries, to help them meet their commitments at the lowest possible cost. Supporters of the proposal believed that the United States' compliance costs are modest and would be offset by savings from sharply de-

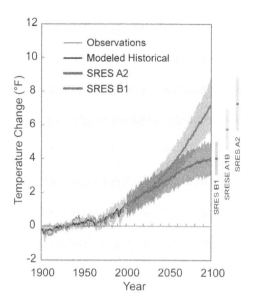
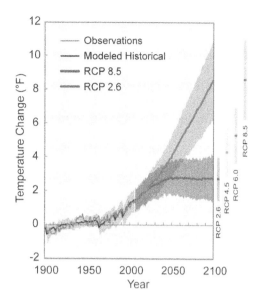

Figure 16.1. Emission levels determine temperature rises. Different amounts of heat-trapping gases released into the atmosphere by human activities produce different projected increases in earth's temperature. In the figure, each line represents a central estimate of global average temperature rise (relative to the 1901–1960 average) for a specific emissions pathway. Shading indicates the range (5th to 95th percentile) of results from a suite of climate models. Projections in 2099 for additional emissions pathways are indicated by the bars to the right of each panel. In all cases, temperatures are expected to rise, although the difference between lower and higher emissions pathways is substantial. (Left) The panel shows the two main scenarios (SRES – Special Report on Emissions Scenarios) used in this report: A2 assumes continued increases in emissions throughout this century, and B1 assumes much slower increases in emissions beginning now and significant emissions reductions beginning around 2050, though not due explicitly to climate change policies. (Right) The panel shows newer analyses, which are results from the most recent generation of climate models (CMIP5) using the most recent emissions pathways (RCPs – Representative Concentration Pathways). Some of these new projections explicitly consider climate policies that would result in emissions reductions, which the SRES set did not. The newest set includes both lower and higher pathways than did the previous set. The lowest emissions pathway shown here, RCP 2.6, assumes immediate and rapid reductions in emissions and would result in about 2.5 °F of warming in this century. The highest pathway, RCP 8.5, roughly similar to a continuation of the current path of global emissions increases, is projected to lead to more than 8 °F warming by 2100, with a high-end possibility of more than 11 °F. (Data from CMIP3, CMIP5, and NOAA NCDC). From *Climate Change Impacts in the United States: The Third National Climate Assessment,* by J. M. Melillo, T. Richmond, and G. W. Yohe (Eds.), 2014, Washington, DC: U.S. Global Change Research Program, p. 26. Available at http://nca2014.globalchange.gov/report/our-changing-climate/future-climate-change

clining energy use. Opponents believed that compliance would be too costly and that similar demands should be placed on developing nations (Watson & Weisman, 2001). In 2005, the Kyoto Protocol passed, in which 163 nations, including 55 industrialized nations—not the United States—agreed to reduce emissions of greenhouse gases.

Climate Action Plan. The United States adopted a *Climate Action Plan (CCAP)* in 1993 to reduce greenhouse gas emissions. Thousands of companies and nonprofit organizations worked together to effectively reduce emissions. By 1997, these voluntary programs reduced greenhouse gas emissions by more than 15 million tons of carbon, and partners saved over $1 billion from energy bill savings (EPA, 1998). In 2006, the PEW Center on Global Climate Change produced the first plan, the *Agenda for Climate Action,* to reduce greenhouse gas emissions in the United States with a call for technology and policy actions. In 2013, President Barack Obama announced a series of executive actions to reduce carbon pollution in the United States and encouraged other countries to take action at the United Nations September Climate Summit.

Clean Air Act. The Clean Air Act of 1970 is the comprehensive federal law that regulates air emissions from area, stationary, and mobile sources. This law authorizes the EPA to establish National Ambient Air Quality Standards (NAAQS) to protect public health and the environment. The goal of the act was to set and achieve NAAQS in every state by 1975. The setting of maximum pollutant standards was coupled with directing the states to develop state implementation plans applicable to appropriate industrial sources in the state. In 1977, the act was amended primarily to set new dates for achieving attainment of NAAQS because many areas of the country had failed to meet the deadlines (EPA, 1996). The 1990 amendments to the Clean Air Act in large part were intended to address problems such as acid rain, ground-level ozone, stratospheric ozone depletion, and air pollutants, commonly called toxic air pollutants. In recent action, the United States announced new limits on soot, an important part of the Clean Air Act, helping to save 15,000 people a year from premature asthma attacks. This was the first time in the EPA's 36-year history, however, that it rejected the tougher standards recommended by its scientific advisors and agency staff experts in setting health-based air quality standards (Associated Press, 2006).

AIR POLLUTION AND ACID RAIN IN RECREATION AREAS

When travelers were asked if they had ever been adversely affected by air quality at a vacation destination, 47% of the respondents to one survey answered yes (Mark Clements Research, 1996). Visitors should not assume that air quality in treasured national parks is better than in surrounding towns and cities. Park service officials at dozens of national parks, monuments, and wilderness areas have been monitoring air quality since an amendment was added to the Clean Air Act in 1977. Some national parks have even experienced high air pollution concentrations as a result of pollutants being transported many miles from their original source. Ground-level ozone concentrations in remote locations of the Great Smoky Mountains National Park in Tennessee and North Carolina, for example, are among the highest in the East and have exceeded levels that threaten human health. Park plants are also threatened by ozone pollution. These effects can significantly decrease the natural beauty of national parks, forests, and recreation areas.

Ozone, an odorless, colorless gas, can be good or bad depending on where it is found. In the earth's upper atmosphere—10 to 12 miles above the earth's surface—it forms a protective layer that shields people from the damaging ultraviolet rays of the sun. Because this *good ozone* is gradually being destroyed by human-made chemicals, humans are more susceptible to sunburn and skin cancers when they participate in outdoor activities. As such, suntan lotion and sunglasses are highly recommended. Near ground level, in the lower atmosphere, *bad ozone* forms when pollutants react chemically in the presence of sunlight. This can happen frequently when outdoor adventurers go to natural areas in summer. Ozone exposure irritates the respiratory system and can become painful, especially for those who actively participate in outdoor recreational activities. If this condition occurs frequently, the lung may change permanently in a way that could cause long-term health effects and a lower quality of life.

In the western United States, the typical visual range has decreased from 140 miles to 35 to 90 miles due to human-made air pollution. In most of the East, the typical visual range is reduced from 140 miles under natural conditions to 15 to 25 miles. The *haze* is caused when sunlight encounters tiny pollution particles in the air. Some of the light is absorbed by particles, and other light is scattered away before it reaches an observer. More pollutants mean more absorption and scattering of light, which reduces the clarity and color of what is seen (EPA, 2012a). From the rim of the Grand Canyon in Arizona, colors sometimes appear faded and rock formations can become indistinguishable to the dismay of outdoor nature photographers and other visitors. Natural sources of air pollution come from sources such as windblown dust and soot from wildfires. Human-made sources come from motor vehicles, electric utilities, industrial fuel burning, manufacturing operations, and other sources.

Some haze-causing particles are directly emitted to the air, and others are formed when gases emitted to the air form particles as they are carried many miles from the source of pollutants. Air pollution caused by distant power plants, smelters, and automobiles obscures views in some of America's most scenic national parks, forests, and wilderness areas, attesting that smog has been creeping into some of the most cherished lands in the nation. *Smog,* literally a blend of smoke and fog, from the Los Angeles basin is blamed for muddying views and crippling plants in Joshua Tree National Monument, 120 miles away. In 1997, the EPA proposed a new regional haze program to address visibility impairment in national parks and wilderness areas. Where such impairment is caused by numerous sources located over broad regions, states are encouraged to coordinate with each other to develop strategies to improve visibility.

Meanwhile, acid deposition, blamed for visibility in the Okefenokee National Wildlife Area in Florida, Boundary Waters Canoe Area in Minnesota, and Upper Buffalo Wilderness Area, places severe stress on many ecosystems. Lakes and bodies of water have increased in acidity, a special concern for anglers. Many of the forests enjoyed by recreationists have been damaged, particularly in the Northeast and at high elevations. *Acid deposition* occurs when emissions of sulfur and nitrogen compounds and other substances form acid compounds. These compounds fall to the earth in either dry (gas and particles) or wet (rain, snow, and fog) forms known as *acid rain.* Some of these substances are carried by the wind across state lines and national borders (EPA, 2012e). Before falling to the earth, they contribute to the poor visibility and impact public health. Besides raising the acid levels in soils and various bodies of water, acid rain also speeds the decay of buildings, statues, and sculptures that are part of the national heritage.

Soil degradation, which causes slower growth, injury, or death of forests, impacts Shenandoah and Great Smoky Mountain National Parks. Because the thinner soils cannot buffer or neutralize the acid rainwater, nutrients and minerals are washed away before trees and other plants can use them to grow. At the same time, the acid rain causes the release of substances that are toxic to trees and plants. These substances are washed into the watershed. Acidification has taken place in the lakes and streams in Adirondack Park and Catskill Forest Preserve in New York, Shenandoah National Park in the Appalachian Mountains in Virginia, and other recreation areas. A National Surface Water Survey shows that acid rain has caused acidity in 75% of the lakes and about 50% of the acid streams surveyed. The Canadian government estimates that 14,000 lakes in eastern Canada are acidic (EPA, 2012b). High acidic levels cause declines in the fish population and species diversity. Some acid lakes have no fish. In higher elevations—even where soil is buffeted—acid clouds and fog blanket trees and strip them of their leaves and needles. The goal of EPA's Acid Rain Program, established by the Clean Air Act, is to reduce levels of sulfates, nitrates, and ground-level ozone to improve health, benefit water quality in lakes and streams, reduce damage to trees, and enhance the beauty of the country's scenic vistas, including those in national parks and forests.

AQUATIC ECOSYSTEMS AND OUTDOOR RECREATION

Water, an odorless, tasteless, substance, covers more than 70% of the earth's surface, making *aquatic ecosystems* the earth's most dominant feature. Distinguished on the basis of their salt content, they include freshwater, estuarine, and marine systems. Only about 2.5% of earth's water is fresh, with more than half of that in solid form found in ice caps and glaciers. Because most of the earth's water, about 97%, is salt water found in oceans, that means only about 1% of the water is available for use by people and land animals (U.S. Geological Survey, 2014). This fresh water is acquired in streams, rivers, ponds, and lakes and in the ground. A small amount is found as vapor in the atmosphere.

Water that returns to earth as precipitation runs off the surface of the land, flowing downhill into streams, rivers, ponds, and lakes to eventually reach the ocean or larger lake. A *watershed* is a region in which a common set of streams and rivers work together to do this. Because a watershed includes the larger river and all of its tributaries, a watershed may be large or small. Smaller watersheds are usually part of larger ones. The Mississippi River watershed, for example, covers much of the Midwest and some of the West, including the Rockies. On the way to the ocean, the larger river carries not only the water that runs into streams and rivers from the surface, but also the water that has filtered through soil and drains into the same streams and rivers. These processes of *surface runoff* and *infiltration* are important to aquatic ecosystems because the water supplies

them. Anything that is not a natural element of the system is a type of pollution. Some water pollution can be traced directly to a particular factory or industrial plant. Other types are more difficult to monitor because they come from widespread sources. These include fertilizers spread on fields, runoff of livestock wastes, soil resulting from erosion, pesticides sprayed on lawn and crops, and materials washed from streets into storm drains (Evergreen Project, 1998). These pollutants choke the rivers and streams, which should be healthy sources of life.

Freshwater Ecosystems

Some lakes are the source for some rivers, and some rivers end in lakes. Because both are freshwater and flow in and out of each other, they share similar characteristics. These characteristics allow some aquatic life to move in and out of both habitats, whereas others prefer only one environment. Freshwater ecosystems are distinguished as *lotic* or *lentic*, with running water or still water, respectively. Waterfalls are associated with lotic ecosystems. Running freshwater streams (springs, creeks, brooks) and rivers may vary on their course from narrow and shallow and relatively rapid to increasingly broad, deep, and slow moving. Most streams are characterized by a repeating sequence of rapids and pools (lentic systems) that decrease in frequency downstream. Chemically, lentic environments are rich in oxygen upstream. Downstream, where the water becomes more sluggish, oxygen level tends to drop. With a continual addition of nutrients en route, there is also an increase of nutrient levels downstream. Lentic ecosystems, including pools, ponds, bogs, and lakes, vary considerably in their physical, chemical, and biological characteristics (Kormondy, 1984).

Human-made dams across rivers control their flow, improve navigation, regulate flooding, or produce hydroelectric power. Water is also used to dilute and remove municipal and industrial waste, for irrigation, for cooling purposes, for transportation, and for recreation. With each use, there is also opportunity for abuse. For example, some municipalities and industries have polluted freshwater lakes chemically and thermally. After water is used to irrigate fields, it is frequently returned with chemical residues from fertilizers. Oil and refuse is left behind by ships. And recreational users commonly ignore basic sanitary and antipollution practices to the detriment of the waters enjoyed. Others believe that public waters can be used as they see fit. To improve water pollution, the Federal Water Pollution Control Act of 1972 set the basic structure for regulating discharges of pollutants into waters. The Clean Water Act (CWA) followed as a 1977 amendment to the Federal Water Pollution Control Act. The law, focusing on toxic substances, gave the EPA the authority to set effluent standards on an industry-by-industry basis and continued the requirements to set water quality standards for all contaminants in surface waters. It also makes it unlawful to discharge any pollutant into navigable waters without a permit. A federal agency report on Appalachian Surface mining, for example, found that 724 miles of stream had been buried by mining spoils with more in danger (O'Connell, 2004). In 1987, when the CWA was reauthorized, it condoned citizen suit provisions and funded sewage treatment plants (EPA, 1998). The CWA provides for the EPA to delegate many permitting, administrative, and enforcement aspects of the law to state governments.

Inevitably, environmental choices will have to be made as sources of water are exploited. Poor water quality has vastly affected recreational pursuits. One of every 3 lakes in the United States and nearly a quarter of the rivers contain enough pollution that people should limit and avoid eating fish caught there (Associated Press, 2004). In fact, one survey disclosed that more than half of the respondents had to forego swimming at a vacation destination because of the water quality (Mark Clements Research, 1996). For the continuation of water recreation activities, recreation and park professionals are becoming more knowledgeable and defensive of the resource, and they educate others about the resource to modify behaviors and attitudes. Managers are making long-term plans, remembering that they are working with a living system whose health is at risk from human factors. These plans address water quality, habitat health and capacity, commercial and residential development, economic impact, and recreation use.

Environmental impacts on freshwater sportfishing. Nearly 20% of the Bass Club respondents, composed primarily of anglers, identified pollution as a constraint to participation (Cordell, 1997). The Bass Club is one of the seven market segments defined by the National Survey on Recreation and the Environment. In an attempt to ensure environmental safety of fish habitats, fishing organizations, such as the Bass Anglers Sportsman Society (BASS), have made this a primary goal. BASS resurrected the 1899 Refuse Act in 1970, filing lawsuits against more than 200 polluters. They created Anglers for Clean Water, and they organized affiliated clubs into 25 federations that work with state agencies on pollution problems.

Working together, fishing organizations lobbied to pass and protect key provisions to the 1984 Wallop–Breaux Amendment to the Dingell–Johnson Sportfish Restoration Act. This brought more than $1 billion from additional taxes on motorboat fuel and fishing tackle into state fish and wildlife agencies for management programs, including safeguarding endangered species, catching poachers and polluters, protecting birds and marine life from oil spills, stocking streams, and staving off commercial development in animal habitats (Cordell, 1999). Anglers are also looking for ways to help species that are hurt by dams when using rivers to spawn.

Dams on rivers provide clean, pollution-free energy, but they can harm the environment. For years, salmon have been fighting dams and other diversions built on rivers. Some dams have even taken on names such as "Fish-Killer" dam because swirling waters and backwash have disoriented their delicate homing mechanisms. In the Northwest, sockeye salmon and trout populations dropped from 16 million to 2.5 million after hydroelectric plants were built on the Columbia River (Evergreen Project, 1998), with about 5% to 14% of the active salmon population killed at each of the eight large dams they pass while swimming upriver (Miller, 2000). Salmon, for instance, leave the ocean to return to the freshwater stream where they were first hatched to breed, lay their eggs, and die. About the same time that they are traveling upstream, young salmon, called smolts, are trying to make it down the Columbia River to the ocean. When human-made fish ladders—concrete waterways that guide the salmon above the dam—are available, only a small percentage of the adults headed upstream are stopped by the dam. After the trip, however, some are too tired to spawn. Others are taken by predators who take advantage of the situation by waiting to feed on them at the bottom of the dam. More lethal are the turbines that kill smolts headed downstream. As they are forced through the powerhouses at high pressure and speed, their swim bladders explode. Moreover, reservoirs flood the gravel bars where salmon spawn, thereby increasing the time it takes smolts to move from streams to the ocean. This also gives predators more time to attack. Heat upstream increases mortality as well (Montaigne, 2001). As salmon disappear, hatcheries have bred the wildness out of them, inhibiting genetic diversity. Anglers complain that beautiful fish have been replaced with "just another dumb fish." Likewise, some of the fish caught off the Columbia at a Willamette River Superfund site show high levels of deformity that may result from agricultural and industrial pollutants.

Experts agree that the only real safeguard against extinction is to restore the salmon's natural spawning grounds and stream dynamics. One free-flowing stretch of the Columbia on the Hanford Ranch, where an estimated 30,000 salmon spawn, was protected from development when it was declared a national monument. Furthermore, a passionate commitment among citizen groups and anglers is helping to heal streams and restore some fish runs. Courts have recognized the salmon's need for water as equal to human need. The Northwest Power Planning Council was established in 1980 to help coordinate conservation efforts. Fish and power were given equal priority, causing a modest salmon recovery on the Columbia River. Fish ladders were added and turbine intakes screened. Deflectors were fitted on spillways, helping to speed young salmon downstream around some dams (Montaigne, 2001). To lower death rates, the National Marine Fisheries Service (NMFS) and the Army Corps of Engineers began barging three quarters of all salmon and steelhead smolts to release points in the 1970s. Unfortunately, only about 1% make their way back to spawn (Thomas, 2004).

It is debated if some of the dams should be dismantled to create a free-flowing lower Snake River to rebuild commercial and sport-fishing industries. A new economy based on tourism, angling, and recreation could be worth hundreds of millions annually and create jobs for some but eliminate or restrict those who depend on dams for their livelihood, including farmers and barge operators. One seventh grade class discussed the complicated issues and decided to breach each of the eight dams after they followed the salmon's plight by rafting, boogie boarding, and jet boarding along the river (Thomas, 2004). In 2012, 1,544,600 salmon passed Bonneville Dam. Improvements have helped. It is expected people will need to protect salmon forever (Bonneville Power Administration, 2013).

Likewise, California populations of steelhead trout have dropped by more than 90%. Born in freshwater streams, they also migrate to the ocean to live as adults. Unlike salmon, they make numerous trips to their freshwater origins to spawn. By the mid-1960s, dams had blocked access to tributary spawning beds and dried some streams. Other streams were uninhabitable due to logging, mining, agriculture, and other developments. Many waters were simply overfished. To anglers, they represent the pinnacle of freshwater fishing, and they want to save them. The turnabout came when anglers became concerned that wild strains of trout were disappearing. Where southern coast populations have been listed as endangered, many anglers and concerned citizens called for the removal of Rindge Dam at Malibu Canyon to free eight miles of prime spawning habitat for steelhead and to benefit Pacific lamprey, another anadromous fish. The closure of the dam is touted as an environmentally responsible move by California state park officials (Sawicki, 2014).

Working with state biologists, small groups of anglers have helped to develop management programs that protect remaining wild trout populations. Some states have developed wild trout programs, setting restrictions on tackle and catch limits, including *catch-and-release programs* or the gentle handling to resuscitate and release fish back into the waters. *Resuscitation* includes sweeping the fish back and forth through the water to restore oxygen to its gills after its long struggle on the line. Few states, however, have laws to protect designated wild trout streams from poor land-use practices, and existing laws are not broad enough.

Preservation is possible when the public demands it. In Nueltin Lake in central Canada on the border between Manitoba and the Northwest Territories, one trend-setting law increased clientele. Here the "big one" must be returned. This departure from standard angling ethics allows anglers to keep most of the big fish caught, but requires them to return the little ones. Unless participating in catch-and-release programs, the vast majority of anglers still follow this standard ethic, assuming that the small fish will replace the larger ones, but this has not proven to be true. Part of the practice revolves around sportsmanship: Smaller fish are easier to catch, and the larger fish is smarter and more worthy. Minimum-size regulations, however, added to the rapid depletion of large native fish in the more popular freshwater lakes and streams.

Additional safeguards at Nueltin include allowing only the trained guides to resuscitate the fish. Anglers may not pose too long for trophy shots or use any lure except live bait. All multiple hooks must be removed and replaced with a barbless single hook to ensure a quick and easy release. No fish may be weighed with the traditional, damaging jaw scale. Instead, the length–girth conversion system is used to calculate the weight. Following the experiment, Manitoba became the first province or state in North America to pass a law requiring barbless hooks for all of its sportfishing. Many of its lakes and rivers follow either *no-trophy* or *one-trophy* rules. Several states and provinces are basing most of their sportfishing laws or policies to protect big fish. New moral pressures can help to establish a new code so future generations can go fishing in North America. In the oceans, there is an overall decrease in predators, large fish, and variety. They become less resilient when they lose larger fish that can better survive change to their habitat (Liberman, 2006d).

Estuaries and Wetlands

An *estuary* is a complex ecosystem defined more by salinity than geographical boundaries. The partially enclosed body of water is formed where fresh water from rivers and streams flows into the ocean, mixing with the salty seawater. Estuaries and lands surrounding them are places of transition from land to sea and from fresh to salt water. Although influenced by the tides, they are protected from the full force of ocean waves, winds, and storms by the reefs, barrier islands, or fingers of land, mud, or sand that define an estuary's seaward boundary. Estuaries come in all shapes and sizes and are often known as bays, lagoons, harbors, inlets, sounds, and sloughs (EPA, 2001a). Nonetheless, not all bodies by those names are estuaries. It is the mixing of waters, not the name, that defines an estuary. Familiar examples include San Francisco Bay (California), South Slough (Oregon), Indian River Lagoon (Florida), Galveston Bay (Texas), North Inlet/Winyah Bay (South Carolina), Boston Harbor (Massachusetts), and Long Island Sound (New York and Connecticut).

The tidal-sheltered waters of estuaries support unique communities of plants and animals that are especially adapted for life at the margin of the sea. These estuarine environments are among the most productive on earth, creating more organic matter each year than comparably sized areas of forest, grassland, or agricultural land. Many habitat types are found in and around estuaries, including shallow open waters, freshwater and salt marshes, sandy beaches, mud and sand flats, rocky shores, oyster reefs, mangrove forests, river deltas, tidal pools, sea grass and kelp beds, and wooded swamps (EPA, 2001b). The productivity and variety of estuarine habitats foster an abundance and diversity of wildlife, including shore birds, fish, crabs and lobsters, clams and shellfish, reptiles, and marine mammals that make their homes in and around estuaries. These animals are linked to one another and to an assortment of specialized plants and microscopic organisms through complex food webs and other interactions. Estuarine environments also provide ideal spots for migratory birds to rest and protected places for species of fish and shellfish to spawn.

These critical living resources also provide Americans with vast aesthetic, recreational, economical opportunities while reducing polluted runoff and controlling flooding. Photography, swimming, boating, bird-watching, and fishing are just a few of the outdoor activities enjoyed. In fact, one third of all Americans visit the coast each year, spending about $44 billion on recreation, including resorts, outfitters, and cruiselines (EPA, 2012c). To illustrate, estuaries provide habitat for 80% to 90% of the country's recreational fish catch and more than 75% of the nation's commercial catch.

As the population grows around these already populated coastal areas, where roughly over half of the U.S. population lives, and where 910 million take trips to the beach annually (Harrison, 2006), the demands imposed on the estuarine and marine ecosystems have increased tremendously. Decisions to convert natural resource wetlands to real estate by filling them to create waterfront lots or dredging them to make canals or otherwise interfering with normal tidal circulation by draining, impounding, or diking are the subject of extensive controversy. Additionally, abundant pollution from discharges of domestic and industrial wastes can cause serious deterioration of their functions. Stresses caused by overuse and unchecked land use have resulted in unsafe drinking water, beach and shellfish bed closings, harmful algal blooms, unproductive fisheries, fish kills, wildlife loss, excessive

nutrient pollution, and loss of habitat (EPA, 2001b). Louisiana's estuaries lose about 24 square miles of wetlands each year due to natural and human causes (National Wildlife Federation, 2014).

The National Estuary Program (NEP) is designed to restore and protect America's nationally significant estuaries. Through its approach of inclusive, community-based planning and action on the watershed level, the NEP is an important initiative toward conserving estuarine resources. Under the Coastal Zone Management Act of 1972, as amended, the National Oceanic and Atmospheric Administration (NOAA) protects and studies estuarine areas through a network of 28 reserves. The National Estuary Program, administered by the EPA, was established in 1987 by amendments to the Clean Water Act. This program encourages federal, state, and local communities to work together to maintain estuaries as a whole system, protecting their chemical, physical, biological, economic, recreational, and aesthetic properties and values. In the future, communities will need to make every effort to prevent or limit disruptive activities, control pollution, restore former saltwater wetlands if possible, and define the boundaries of their natural resources.

Wetlands, a collective term for marshes, swamps, bogs, prairie potholes, and similar areas found in generally flat vegetated areas, in depressions in the landscape, and between dry land and water along the edges of streams, rivers, lakes, and, of course, coastline, vary widely because of regional and local differences in soils, topography, climate, hydrology, water chemistry, vegetation, and other factors, including human disturbance. They can be large or very small, wet at all times or completely dry most of the time. Overall, they fall into two general categories, the coastal or tidal wetlands already mentioned and inland or nontidal wetlands (EPA, 2001b).

The coastal wetlands that fringe many estuaries provide crucial habitat for wildlife and perform other valuable services. As the water drained from the uplands flows through fresh and salt marshes, much of the sediments, nutrients, and other pollutants that were carried in the water are filtered out. This filtration process creates cleaner and clearer water, which benefits people and marine life. Wetland plants and soils also act as a natural buffer between the land and ocean, absorbing floodwaters and dissipating storm surges. This protects upland organisms as well as valuable real estate from storm and flood damage. Salt marsh grasses and other estuarine plants also help prevent erosion and stabilize the shoreline. The wetland vegetation removes silt, toxic chemicals, and nutrients from coastal water. If wetland vegetation were eliminated, the food supply, and thus the carrying capacity of the coastal ecosystem, would be greatly reduced. Restoration of the tidal ebb flow at the Bolsa Chica Wetlands in California is expected to replenish marshes, which could attract more species, introduce new plants, and gradually eliminate invasives. The project, which took 30 years to complete, corrects the result of over a century of damming and is now expected to provide habitat for endangered birds.

Besides the *coastal wetlands,* which include unvegetated mud flats or sand flats, tidal salt marshes with grasses and grass-like plants, and mangrove swamps with salt-loving shrubs or trees that are linked to the nation's estuaries, some tidal freshwater wetlands form beyond the upper edges of tidal salt marshes (EPA, 2001b). This is where the influence of salt water ends and inland wetlands begin. Inland wetlands are most common on floodplains along rivers (riparian wetlands), in isolated depressions surrounded by dry land (e.g., playas, basins, and potholes), along the margins of lakes and ponds, and in other low-lying areas where the groundwater intercepts the soil surface or where precipitation sufficiently saturates the soil (vernal pools and bogs).

Inland wetlands include marshes and wet meadows dominated by herbaceous plants, swamps dominated by shrubs, and wooded swamps dominated by trees. Certain types of inland wetlands are common to particular regions of the country. These include bogs and fens of the Northeast and North Central states and Alaska; wet meadows or wet prairies in the Midwest; inland saline and alkaline marshes and riparian wetlands of the arid and semiarid West; prairie potholes of Iowa, Minnesota, and the Dakotas; alpine meadows of the West; playa lakes of the Southwest and Great Plains; bottomland hardwood swamps of the South; pocosins and Carolina Bays of the Southeast coastal states; and tundra wetlands of Alaska (EPA, 2001b). Many of these are seasonal or wet only periodically, particularly in the arid and semiarid West. The quantity of water and the timing of its presence in part determine the functions of a wetland.

Found from the tundra to the tropic and on every continent except Antarctica, wetlands are among the most productive ecosystems in the world, comparable to rain forests and coral reefs. Yet because they have been regarded as wastelands, sources of mosquitos, odors, and disease, more than half of America's original wetlands have been destroyed since the days that European settlement began. In the United States, an estimated 220 million acres of wetlands that existed in the lower 48 during the 1600s fell to an estimated 103.3 million acres of wetlands by the mid-1980s and continue but only at a loss of 10.3 square miles per year (America's Wetland Foundation, 2013). In Alaska, there is an estimated 170 million to 200 million acres of wetlands, and Hawaii has another 52,000 acres (EPA, 2001b). The years from the mid-1950s to the mid-1970s brought much of the loss—about 458,000 acres a year—as wetlands were drained, filled, or used to dispose of household and industrial waste (Watson, 1999).

Realizing that these losses helped lead the way to declining bird populations, for example, and increased flood and drought damages, humans now know that wetlands provide values that no other ecosystem can. These include natural water quality improvement, natural products for human use, flood and shoreline erosion control, habitat protection for wildlife, and opportunities for outdoor recreation and aesthetic gratifications. Wetlands, particularly on America's National Wildlife Refuges, offer wildlife and plant life observation, birding, photography, hunting, fishing, canoeing, sightseeing, and hiking on trails and boardwalks. Wetland management districts were created in 1962 as the Fish and Wildlife Service's land acquisition program accelerated because of increasing Duck Stamp sales (Chapter 7). Wetland management staff also manage wetland easements and work with willing private landowners who protect their wetlands. Protecting wetlands also protects human welfare and saves money. Without the Congaree Bottomland Hardwood Swamp, a national monument in South Carolina, the area would need to spend billions on a wastewater treatment plant. In addition to improving water quality through filtering, some wetlands maintain stream flow during dry periods, and several replenish groundwater that many depend on for drinking. They store carbon within their plant communities and soil instead of releasing it to the atmosphere as carbon dioxide, thereby helping moderate global climate.

The federal government protects wetlands through regulations (e.g., Section 404 of the Clean Water Act and watershed protection initiatives), economic incentives and disincentives, cooperative programs, and acquisitions for national wildlife refuges. Beyond the federal level, a number of states have enacted laws to regulate activities in wetlands, and some counties and towns have adopted local wetlands protection ordinances or have changed the way development is permitted. Most coastal states have significantly reduced losses of coastal wetlands through protective laws. Fewer states have laws specifically regulating activities in inland wetlands, although some states and local governments have nonregulatory programs that help protect wetlands.

Partnerships to manage whole watersheds have developed among federal, state, tribal, and local governments; nonprofit organizations; and private landowners. The goal of these partnerships is to implement comprehensive, integrated watershed protection approaches that recognize the interconnectedness of water, land, and wetlands resources for more complete solutions to wetland degradation (see Using Technology for Habitat Restoration in this chapter). Finally, public efforts in conjunction with states, local governments, and private citizens to educate the public are helping (EPA, 2001b). Though wetland loss is slowing, many environmentalists believe that much more needs to be done. On the international level, the Convention on Wetlands of International Importance held in Ramsar, Iran, in 1971 provides a framework for conserving wetlands worldwide.

Marine Ecosystems

On the bluffs above any ocean there is beautiful, vast, seemingly limitless water. At its deepest spot, the Mariana Trench reaches a depth of 36,198 feet. Nonetheless, the concentration of nutrients in the ocean is low. Its salt content if dried would cover all of the continents to a depth of about 5 feet. Unlike land and freshwater ecosystems, the sea is continuous and is in circulation via the major surface currents. Waves cause the water to oscillate. The rise and fall of the water level is caused by tides that are related to the gravitational effects of the moon and the sun.

As boundless as they seem, oceans, accounting for more than 70% of the earth's surface (Leinbach, 2005), receive enough of the world's waste to have raised public alarm concerning safety of outdoor activities, such as swimming, surfing, and fishing. Shifting sands, foul water, and human-made follies present threats to coasts. With more people living near and visiting beaches, tons of trash make their way into the ocean. Most trash left on beaches is from beachgoers who do not use trash cans. Worldwide, 60% to 80% of coastal debris that finds its way into the marine environment comes from land rather than ships and boats at sea (Rogers, 2006a). Each year the International Coastal Clean-Up volunteers scavenge surf and shoals for litter. They found 8,282 syringes and over 100 animals entangled in debris. In Peru alone, they picked up 38,100 plastic bottles. In Egypt, volunteers removed more than 1 million cigarette butts. Some beaches in the United States have begun to ban smoking (B. Williams, 2006).

Standing on the bluffs above any ocean, people can see a beautiful, vast, seemingly limitless water.

Environmentalists have identified the nation's most significant marine debris problem to be so-called "offshore icebergs." Upon closer inspection, these icebergs are collages of discarded cups, containers, bottles, and straws. This plastic trash is posing serious problems to wildlife. Indigestible plastic bags are confused for jellyfish and are eaten by whales, dolphins, and turtles. Gulls and other birds eat broken foam cups, eventually choking. Fish have become wedged in the plastic rings used for beer and soda cans, which sliced them as they grew. Sprawling icebergs, perhaps more aptly termed "trashbergs," are caused by collections of trash flushed into oceans from storm drains, creeks, and rivers. Great volumes of sewage pollute beaches. Storm drains bring motor oil, garbage, pesticides, and untreated animal waste directly to beaches. Swimming near drains has resulted in skin rashes and eye and ear infections. Wastewater flow has endangered several bird species and led to warnings not to eat bottom-dwelling fish caught off ocean piers.

Problems worsen with the oil spills from old shore tankers. When 37,000 tons of crude oil spilled, it affected marine life through western Prince William Sound just below Valdez, Alaska, the Gulf of Alaska, and lower Cook Inlet, passing Kenai Fjords National Park on its way south to contaminate Katmai National Park. Pristine coastlines off Africa, Asia, Europe, and South America and those near the earth's poles have been sadly blighted. Oil continues to clog the ocean. In addition to oil from accidents, tankers dump oil into seas, mostly from flushing oily residue from empty tanks. The toll on wildlife is tragic. Although much remains unknown about the possible long-term effects of spills, it is estimated 3,500 to 5,500 sea otters may have died as a direct consequence of the grounding of the Exxon Valdez (Fair & Becker, 2000). The Gulf of Mexico oil spill in 2010, the largest marine spill in history, is thought

Beach homes with their own individual ladders mar the natural scenery and encourage cliff erosion.

to have released roughly 5 million barrels, with about 4.2 million pouring into the Gulf of Mexico and leaving an oil slick the size of South Carolina. Oil came ashore in Louisiana, Mississippi, Alabama, and Florida, creating wildlife fatalities, potentially impacting 32 national wildlife refuges, and causing a fishing ban in 36% of federal waters. Other contaminants include industrial chemicals, toxic algal blooms, metals, and pesticides (Cleveland, 2013).

Chronic stress effects from environmental contaminants have caused widespread concern, particularly as mass mortalities are on the rise. Coastal waters are nearing their capacity to absorb civilian waste. Starfish appear to be diseased in various areas along the Pacific Coast. More than 700 dolphins died mysteriously along the Atlantic coast. Many that washed ashore had snouts, flippers, and tails pocked with blisters and craters. In the Gulf of Maine, harbor seals were rated with the highest pesticide level of any U.S. mammal on land or water. From Portland, Maine, to Morehead City, North Carolina, lobsters and crabs were found with gaping holes in their shells. Fish have been reported with rotted fins and ulcerous lesions. Fragile kelp beds, rivaled only by coral reefs and tropical forests for their biological diversity, are yielding to a hybrid of pollution, dredging, overfishing, and natural change. Coral reefs, habitation to one third of the world's marine species, are rapidly succumbing to pollution. Bottom-trawling for fish and other human activities are also responsible. Sophisticated electronic devices are used to spot fast, larger boats, impacts of hatchery-destroying pollution, and loss of coastal habitat, yet marine species in 15 of the world's 17 largest fisheries are in trouble ("The Dirty Seas," 1988; Fair & Becker, 2000; Johnson, 2000; Larkin, 1999; Lord, 1998; PBS Newshour, 2014).

Other mortalities come from indirect threats. Dolphins are entangled in tuna nets, and noise and acoustic influences range from ship traffic, to ocean experimentation, to recreational whale watching. The broadest attack to sea creatures could come from global warming. As seawater warms, its volume increases with thermal expansion ac-counting for approximately one third of the current sea-level rise. Global sea level, which has risen 8 inches since 1900, could continue to rise another 3 feet or more by 2100. The unknown factor is the future of ice sheets. The current sea level is rising twice as fast as it did a few decades ago. Presently, it is rising an eighth of an inch per year and accelerating (Folger, 2013). Past and projected changes in global sea level rise are shown in Figure 16.2 (Papciak, 2001). There could also be increasing sea-surface temperatures as inferred from ancient corals found on Palmyra Island south of Hawaii, which shows that rising ocean surface temperatures at the island are the highest recorded during the past 1,100 years (Liberman, 2003). Condensation of water evaporated from warm seas provides energy for hurricanes. Greater precipitation would lead to more runoff of pollution and nutrient-laden soil and water into coastal waters. An increasing ultraviolet-B radiation caused by ozone depletion may damage or kill fish eggs and larvae. This would reduce the productivity of plankton (collection of minute organisms on which animals feed), the source of 70% of oxygen on earth (Lord, 1998; National Geographic Society, 2005). Some bodies of water have already been almost totally depleted of oxygen—a huge dead zone is adrift in the Gulf of Mexico.

With problems lying miles from the ocean where contaminants enter streams and rivers, corrective action is needed on a national scale. Six-pack rings are now made of substances that decompose. Previously unregulated storm drains are regulated in some regions. Where sewage disposal has undergone upgraded treatment, scientists have measured a concurrent drop in the pollution level on beaches even though sewage is dumped in greater volume. Other positive steps toward diminishing marine pollution include legislation that places cleanup costs of oil spills on oil companies rather than on taxpayers and bars offshore drilling, particularly where environmental risks outweigh potential energy benefits. The Clean Air Act impacts ocean vessels, cruise ships, and sewage discharges. And as stewards of the ocean, NOAA researches, monitors, and as-

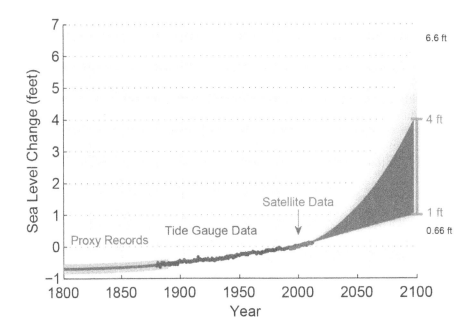

Figure 16.2. Past and projected changes in global sea level rise. Estimated, observed, and possible future amounts of global sea level rise from 1800 to 2100, relative to the year 2000. Estimates from proxy data1 (for example, based on sediment records) are shown in red (1800-1890, pink band shows uncertainty), tide gauge data are shown in blue for 1880-2009,2 and satellite observations are shown in green from 1993 to 2012.3 The future scenarios range from 0.66 feet to 6.6 feet in 2100.4 These scenarios are not based on climate model simulations, but rather reflect the range of possible scenarios based on other scientific studies. The orange line at right shows the currently projected range of sea level rise of 1 to 4 feet by 2100, which falls within the larger risk-based scenario range. The large projected range reflects uncertainty about how glaciers and ice sheets will react to the warming ocean, the warming atmosphere, and changing winds and currents. As seen in the observations, there are year-to-year variations in the trend. Adapted from *Global Sea Level Rise Scenarios for the United States National Climate Assessment, by* Parris et al., 2012, Silver Spring, MD: National Oceanic and Atmospheric Administration, p.12, with input from NASA Jet Propulsion Laboratory. Available at http://nca2014.globalchange.gov/report/our-changing-climate/sea-level-rise

sesses toxic red tides, damaging storms, pollution, and coastal development; works on environmental issues with experts in other countries and forms international agreements; makes efforts to balance competing public needs and interests while preserving biological integrity; protects national marine sanctuaries; and works with partners and volunteers on projects that will embrace their ocean ethic—to preserve, protect, and respect the nation's marine environment. As a result of the Oceans Act of 2000, the Commission on Ocean Policy (2006) recommended in its final report that a coordinated national ocean policy on all government levels be established. The EPA (2014c) works with U.S. government agency partners, foreign nations, industry, and nongovernmental organizations to ensure that international decisions and management of marine pollution issues protect human health and safeguard the natural environment.

Coral Reefs and Human Activity

The nation's most extensive living coral reef and third longest barrier reef in the world is adjacent to the island chain of the Florida Keys. To protect some of the world's northernmost coral reefs, the nation's and world's first undersea park was established in 1960. The boundaries of John Pennekamp Coral Reef State Park were changed at a later date, placing most of the reefs within an adjacent federal preserve referred to as the Sanctuary. After three freighters ran aground in the area within 17 days in 1989, this, and previous concerns for the environment, led to a proposal that all of the reefs from Biscayne to Dry Tortugas National Park be designated the Florida Keys National Marine Sanctuary in 1990.

Although all ships were off-limits, the initial influx of recreational boats, divers, and swimmers put pressure on the underwater environment. With five of its most popular reefs attracting nearly 3,000 people a day to generate about $1.6 billion from recreational uses, it had become one of the most popular recreational destinations in the world (Jameson, Erdmann, Karr, Gibson, & Potts, 2000). With the popularity came destruction. Incompetent boat operators crashed into reefs and coral. Portions of reef were broken by impact of boat anchors, and boaters polluted the water with litter, sewage, and petroleum products. They dragged hooks, fishing line, and nets across the coral reefs. Lobster traps were placed on reefs and recovered from them. Boats running through shallow water disturbed and suspended silts with their propellers, and snorkelers and divers kicked up sediment that blocked essential sunlight. Thousands of swimmers, snorkelers, and divers routinely bumped, scraped, and stood on coral. Their suntan oil inadvertently harmed and killed sensitive corals. Souvenir specimen collecting and spearfishing continued, even where unlawful. Overfishing removed important species that ate the algae growing on corals, causing it to overgrow. More than 4 million domestic and foreign visitors drive, fly, or cruise to the area, especially "during season" from November to April (NOAA, 2002).

Besides recreational and commercial fishing activities taking a toll, nature can intrude on coral as well. Waves stirred by hurricanes may cause damage, as will fluctuations in water temperatures. Reefs usually recover from these natural disturbances, but there is concern that global warming has and will increase hurricane action that can rip coral reefs apart. Likewise, destruction from human-made pollution can be devastating. Coral reefs, the largest constructions formed by living organisms, are developed by small marine animals called polyps. After a polyp dies, it leaves deposits of calcium carbonate behind for other polyps to build upon. When nutrient levels surge from improperly treated sewage, atmospheric deposition, agricultural and urban runoff, and cleaning products high in phosphate, they overstimulate the growth of aquatic plants and algae. The algae eventually overcome and in turn impact the fish and other aquatic organisms, leading to a decrease in biodiversity and alterations in the use of the water for fishing and swimming.

Coral reefs are also vulnerable to the acidification caused by human-generated carbon dioxide. This can reduce coral's ability to form skeletons as well as other marine organisms that also need to make calcium carbonate shells (Liberman, 2006a). Additionally, the introduction of toxic substances from runoff, mining activities, organic chemicals, metals, pesticides, and herbicides cause scarring, death, or reproductive failure in fish, shellfish, and other marine organisms. Because of this pollution, some water quality experts believe that the Florida Reef Tract could become the first in the world to be killed by humans. Worldwide if present conditions continue, NOAA predicts that 70% of the coral reefs will disappear by 2050 (Hymon, 2001).

Among other responses to the difficulties, NOAA called for the designation of an ecological reserve. A no-take ecological reserve went into effect July 1, 2001, in the westernmost waters of the Florida Keys National Marine Sanctuary. The sanctuary's network of *no-take zones*, established in 1997, excludes fishing to increase the natural production of the marine habitat (NOAA, 2002). The Tortugas Ecological Reserve is broken into two sections. Tortugas North, west of Dry Tortugas National Park, contains some of the most spectacular coral reefs in North America. Tortugas South, located southwest of the park, includes critical spawning grounds. Besides regulations that prohibit the taking of all marine life, the reserve in Tortugas North, for example, restricts vessel discharges and engine exhaust and prohibits anchoring and the use of mooring buoys by vessels more than 100 feet in combined length. Snorkeling and diving is permitted, but these activities require a simple no-cost, phone-in permit to ensure that all vessels have access to mooring buoys, to ease enforcement, and to assist in monitoring visitor impacts (NOAA, 2002).

It is believed that reserves also help scientists evaluate what is happening outside of the reserve. After receiving overwhelming support, the National Park Service (NPS) designated 42% of the waters in the park a research natural area, which prohibits fishing and limits public access. This is the first time that action was taken to protect marine habitat in a national park (Daerr, 2001). The plan to protect coral reefs, fish, and sea grasses does not impact recreational fishing and other uses in a large portion of the park. It also demonstrates how states and national parks can work together to protect coral reefs. Additionally, studies on the worldwide marine-protected areas, commonly called no-take areas, show that within the sanctuaries, fish increase in size and number and that the overall diversity of marine life flourishes. Fishers, in theory, will benefit from the spillover of fish into areas outside of the reserve (Rogers, 2006b).

Other sources of protection are found in the Clean Water Act, the River and Harbors Act, and the Coastal Zone Management Act. The EPA and other federal agencies also developed guidance programs for runoff of pollutants, marine debris monitoring, discharge regulation, and water quality standards. The International Coral Reef Initiative (ICRI) coordinates information, bringing higher visibility to the need for coral reef ecosystem preservation throughout the world. As a result of the International Year of the Ocean in 1998, Executive Order 13089 on Coral Reef Protection was issued to direct federal agencies to protect coral reef ecosystems to the extent feasible and to instruct particular agencies to develop coordinated, science-based plans to restore damaged reefs as well as mitigate current and future impacts on reefs in the United States and the world. Though coral reefs are difficult to repair, coral reef biologists are collecting living coral colonies surrounding damaged ones. They are grown in a controlled environment until they can be returned to a natural environment. Due to slow growth, it can take 10 to 15 years to return some rescued coral. It's worth it; although coral reefs account for less than 1% of the surface of the earth, they house 70% of marine organisms on earth (Kirkwood, 2006a).

TERRESTRIAL ECOSYSTEMS

Terrestrial ecosystems, which may be divided into forests, savannas, grasslands, tundra, and desert, are generally distinguished on the basis of the predominant type of vegetation, such as trees or grass. An interaction of temperature and rainfall is significant to the type of vegetation that grows. For example, grasslands may be sustained in regions with low rainfall coupled with low temperatures or with high rainfall combined with higher temperatures. Soil and vegetation are intimate parts of the same ecosystem. *Forests* found in humid climates feature trees that form a canopy over the ground. A *savanna* consists of a mixture of forest and grassland associated with a tropical climate. *Grasslands* are dominated by grass and found in semiarid climatic zones. *Tundra* is limited to herbs and shrubs and is located in cold climates, including arctic, subarctic, and high mountains. The *desert* originates in arid regions where generally low herbs and shrubs form a disconnected cover. Each is a resource to be protected and enjoyed. Some are discussed in more detail.

Forests

Tropical forests play a vital role in regulating the global climate. Disappearance of forests is regarded by many environmental experts as one of the most serious global environmental problems today. They believe that carbon dioxide must be kept in balance to help prevent a significant warming of the earth this century. Major carbon dioxide emissions are created by the burning of trees and vegetation from cut forests as well as the burning of fossil fuels. Forests have the capacity to absorb huge quantities of carbon dioxide through photosynthesis. Yet statistics show that climate change is increasing the vulnerability of forest ecosystem changes and tree mortality through fire, insect infestation, drought, and disease outbreaks (Joyce et al., 2014). A conceptual analysis of forest vulnerability in climate parameters is shown in Figure 16.3. The following are increasing globally:

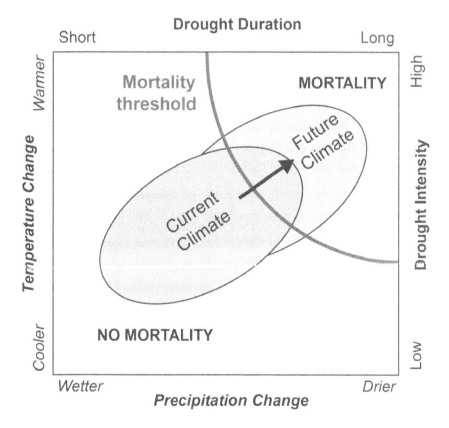

Figure 16.3. Forest vulnerability to changing climate. The figure shows a conceptual climate envelope analysis of forest vulnerability under current and projected future ranges of variability in climate parameters (temperature and precipitation, or alternatively drought duration and intensity). Climate models project increasing temperatures across the U.S. in coming decades, but a range of increasing or decreasing precipitation depending on region. Episodic droughts (where evaporation far exceeds precipitation) are also expected to increase in duration and/or intensity (see Ch. 2: Our Changing Climate). The overall result will be increased vulnerability of forests to periodic widespread regional mortality events resulting from trees exceeding their physiological stress thresholds. From "A Global Overview of Drought and Heat-Induced Tree Mortality Reveals Emerging Climate Change Risks for Forests," by C.D. Allen, et al., 2010, Forest Ecology and Management, 259, 660–684. Available from http://nca2014.globalchange.gov/report/sectors/forests

1. **Global emissions of carbon dioxide are reaching new highs.** Emissions in the United States have grown at an alarming rate of 18% since 1990, and the Department of Energy predicts they will increase by another 37% by 2030 (PEW Center, 2006).
2. **Forest fires appear to be happening more frequently and with greater intensity due to unfavorable weather conditions and land-use practices.** In Indonesia, fires burned for several months in 1997. The Wallow Fire in Arizona and New Mexico in 2011 was the largest in the history of the Southwestern United States.
3. **The world has lost 80% of its original forests.** Remaining old-growth forests found primarily in the Amazon rain forest, Central Africa, Southeast Asia, Canada, and the Russian Federation are in jeopardy from logging, mining, and development (Lee, 2006).

If the world continues to warm, tropical forests are expected to shrivel and possibly turn into grasslands. As the trees die, they will release more carbon dioxide through decomposition and fires that are more prevalent during warm, dry conditions. In turn, the more carbon dioxide released, the warmer the world may become as heat becomes trapped by the rising levels of atmospheric carbon dioxide. With fewer trees to absorb the carbon, global warming could escalate by, ironically, turning the forests into major emitters of carbon dioxide (Lee, 2006).

To start restoring damaged habitat, there is a need to bring back naturally functioning ecosystems. The Brazilian State of Acre has launched a project to reforest previously cleared land that was used for ranching in the Amazon. Nursery trees will be issued to large landowners who will be required to reforest up to 30% of their property with the intent to shift from ranching to sustainable logging and producing nuts, rubber, and medicinal plants (Liberman, 2006b). Meanwhile Brazil's Mamiraua Reserve, the first to be based on a sustainable development model, provides opportunities for visitors to stay in floating jungle lodges. The reserve helps locals manage their forestry, farming, and grazing in an environmentally sound manner so they do not become dependent on tourism.

Preservation of the world's largest trees. Environmental groups convinced 400 corporations and several cities to phase out the sale or use of wood from old-growth forests. As consumer pressure mounted, the government of British Columbia announced an immediate moratorium on logging in the 3.5 million-acre Great Bear Rainforest, thereby devising the largest rain forest conservation measure in North American history (Sierra Club, 2001). Classic old-growth forests contain redwoods, cedars, Douglas fir, hemlock, and spruce. At a minimum, these forests contain eight large trees that are older than 300 years or are more than 40 inches in diameter at chest height per acre.

In the United States, more than 95% of the old growth has been logged. About one third of the approximately 43 million acres remaining are protected in designated public lands ("Protect One Hundred Million Acres," 2006). Originally, redwoods composed the greatest old-growth forest on earth. Today, much like the loss of old-growth Douglas fir, only about 5% remain (Save the Redwoods League, 2014). These lingering redwood giants are found mostly in parks, such as Redwood National Park in northern California. Towering over all other trees in the world, the coastal redwoods, cousin to the giant sequoia, grow larger in diameter and bulk. The tree that once grew all over North America is protected in central California in Yosemite, Sequoia, and Kings Canyon National Parks and Giant Sequoia National Monument, where hikers, campers, horseback riders, skiers, and anglers can gaze up at their majesty. If left to grow, sequoias reach heights of 300 feet and live 500 to 700 years. That is only a portion of the potential age of the coastal redwood, which can survive to be 2,000 years old.

California redwoods are the tallest living things on earth.

With most of the old growth cut by companies on lands they owned in the 1960s, public sources were needed to meet high demands for lumber.

In 1850, redwood "gold," however, lured loggers away from the depleted eastern forest. In an expanding nation, the need for wood products grew rapidly. With new machinery, chain saws, large trucks, and the bulldozer, logging activity accelerated even further after World War II. The old-growth or "virgin" forests began to disappear with alarming speed during the 1950s and 1960s, leaving behind overcut, eroding landscapes. Sensing the need for protection of the rapidly diminishing redwood forest, concerned citizens became active in setting aside redwood lands as local, state, and national parks. Redwood National Park was established in 1968 to preserve superlative prime coastal redwood forests along the coastline and rivers of northern California. After park establishment, however, extensive logging continued on private timberlands around this narrow corridor. Large-scale logging of the unstable, highly erosive Redwood Creek watershed increased landsliding and surface erosion far above pre-logging levels. Besides directly altering the landscape and causing soil compaction, loss of topsoil, destruction of ground cover, elimination of shade, and massive changes to small drainages, the logging activities also produced cumulative downstream impacts. These included increased streamside landslides, elevated and wild streambeds, greater bank erosion, higher winter stream discharge, and lower summer discharge. These physical changes of the stream system jeopardized the associated plant and animal communities, and a heightened water table directly threatened the Tall Trees Grove and other trees growing on alluvial terraces adjacent to Redwood Creek.

As a result of these problems, in March 1978 Congress expanded the existing 58,000-acre Redwood National Park by an additional 48,000 acres. Realizing that land-use practices adjoining the park can damage resources within, Congress made a landmark decision by establishing a 30,000-acre Park Protection Zone upstream in the Redwood Creek watershed. Of the 48,000 acres of new parklands, only about 9,000 acres were old-growth redwoods. Because most of the area was recently logged land, Congress authorized $33 million for Redwood National Park to rehabilitate overcut forestlands, with a major emphasis on erosion control as part of the expansion of the park. This watershed rehabilitation program has a long-term goal of speeding the recovery of natural forest, stream systems, and life communities as well as protecting park values and outdoor recreational opportunities.

Rehabilitation begins with reducing excessive erosion and creek siltation resulting from past timber harvesting and road building and with replanting forests and shaping their regrowth. Years will pass before evidence of logging disappears and streams are fully recovered, but in Redwood National Park lies the unique challenge and opportunity to perpetuate and restore one of nature's most majestic natural systems.

Clear-cutting and the spotted owl. Clear-cutting is the practice of removing all standing timber from a given area, typically 80 to 120 acres. Multiple clear-cuts are separated by narrow strips of timber several hundred feet in width. The consequences of clear-cutting vary according to terrain, soil conditions, weather patterns, and species. When all trees are cleared, there are no nutrients from dead rotting trees to benefit the soil. New growth is often weak and spindly as a result. Clear-cuts also tend to spoil rivers and destroy fisheries. One specialist claimed,

> After a clear-cut it takes two or three years for the soil-supporting rootlet to rot away. Then the headwalls just

fall into the rivers, sluice them out and settle into the lower reaches, sending the water braiding over or under wide, fish-proof deltas. (T. Williams, 1990, p. 7)

One such deluge of forest soil slid out from under a clear-cut at the source of Gwynn Creek in Oregon's Siuslaw National Forest's Mapleton District, the district containing the best public steelhead and salmon water south of Alaska. Sliding for 4 miles, the soil merged with the sea. It instantly obliterated fish habitat and abolished fish life (T. Williams, 1990).

Several creatures depend on original, uncut ancient forest. In the Pacific Northwest, the northern spotted owl dwells in the old and dead trees of the rain forests. When it was announced on July 23, 1990, that the spotted owl was listed as threatened, it came under the protection of the federal Endangered Species Act. A heated debate among environmentalists and the timber industry followed. To environmentalists, who were opposed to overharvesting and the unalterable loss of old-growth forests, the spotted owl was seen as a barometer to determine the integrity and health of the ancient forest ecosystem and the hundreds of species dependent on it for all or part of their needs. It became a symbol of an era when acres of primeval forest blanketed much of the continent and natural events were the controlling fate of the forest and its creatures. The spotted owl's listing brought public attention to the 95% decline of these forests (Forests Forever, 1990). To the timber industry, the spotted owl's protection meant loss of work as prime timberland was set aside as protected habitat by the Forest Service. With most of the old growth cut by companies on lands they owned in the 1960s, these public sources were needed to meet high demands for lumber (Yuskavitch, 2001). They saw trees as a renewable resource, noting that Americans rely on thousands of wood products daily.

With the spotlight on the owl, the issue of impacts to fisheries stayed in the background. Even if a forest that is unfit for a spotted owl is unfit for wild salmonoid, it was believed that there would be less public sympathy for an owl that few had seen or ever heard of than for fish and water (T. Williams, 1990). For many, though, economic issues were outweighed by the ecological survival, and the northern spotted owl became an endearing mascot in the struggles to save the old-growth forest in the Northwest.

In seeking to find a solution to the controversies surrounding forest management, President Clinton held a 1993 Forest Conference in Portland, Oregon. After a Forest Ecosystem Management Assessment Team was established to develop options for managing federal forest ecosystems, a revolutionary plan was selected. The plan conserves not only the owls, but also all species found in old-growth forests on federal lands within the range of spotted owls. According to the habitat-based conservation strategy, much of the land—some 7.5 million acres—was designated as late-successional reserves. In those areas, federal land managers from the Forest Service and the Bureau of Land Management take a hands-off approach, with the goal of nurturing remaining stands of old growth by working together to preserve ecosystems common to their jurisdictions (Yuskavitch, 2001). Although logging restrictions were imposed, in part because of the northern spotted owl, the regional economy began booming. Three years after curtailment of logging in federal forests, Oregon posted its lowest unemployment rate in a generation (U.S. Fish and Wildlife Service, 1998a). As for the owl, its struggle for life continues. Restoring forest health is a key goal to its survival.

Although loggers saw mill jobs disappear and environmentalists watched hundreds of thousands of acres of forest in the Northwest disappear, both parties agreed that Americans needed to be concerned about consumption and to explore new ways to minimize the use of trees. Georgia-Pacific (1990) reported that the United States had the world's highest rate of paper use. Today, recycled paper accounts for the 69 million tons of paper and paperboard used in the United States (EPA, 2014a). If waste is cut and trees are saved, more trees will be left behind for outdoor recreation.

Forest fires. Fire is important and necessary to a wide range of natural ecosystems. The chaparral and giant sequoias of California, prairies of the Midwest, the bogs of the Southeast, and the lodgepole pines of Yellowstone National Park depend on periodic fires. One type of lodgepole cone opens and releases its seed only after exposure to heat. Other environmental conditions are created by burns: Dead branches and pine needles are cleared; sunlight and nutrients allow new trees to grow and flourish; and grasses and herbs grow, providing new food sources for wildlife. In the spring that follows a fire, wildflowers bloom profusely, and by summer, the vegetation is well on its way to recovery so deer can feed on nutritious, succulent new shoots and grasses.

For years, the Forest Service, Bureau of Land Management, the NPS, and state parks believed that fires should be prevented at all costs to preserve the nation's forests. In 1945, the creation of Smokey the Bear played a vital role in the U.S. Forest Service's fire prevention campaign. When Smokey's messages began, hundred of thousands of acres of American forests were consumed by human-caused wildfires every year. Since that time, it has been estimated that this message helped reduce these fires by as much as 97% (U.S. Forest Service, 1998). Smokey's communiqué did not distinguish between natural and human-made fires, however. In time, it became apparent that wildland fires were getting larger and burning hotter, faster, and more frequently. Overgrown vegetation that had accumulated unnaturally in areas where fire was kept out provided fuel for unprecedented, raging fires (U.S. Department of Agriculture, 2005). Researchers soon learned that all fires are not evil. In stark contrast, *fire suppression* was perceived as unnatural by the 1970s. Instead, *natural fires* in remote locations that did not threaten life, property, or critical natural and cultural resources were allowed to burn when weather conditions were right. Under the right conditions, *let-it-burn* practices in wildlands preserve natural systems and allow for higher biological diversity. Because fires tend to jump rather than to burn cleanly over the landscape, interesting variety and diversity can result.

True natural wildfire occurrences, such as those caused from lightning, happen infrequently. These fires, referred to as *prescribed natural fires,* may be allowed to burn when communities are not at risk. In contrast, unwanted or unplanned fires, including those resulting from improper campfire care, cigarettes, or motorcycles without spark arresters are contained immediately because they burn outside of prescribed guidelines. *Prescribed burns* are small fires that are deliberately set in a particular forest area by foresters and wildfire managers to reduce fuel buildup, stimulate wildlife habitat and runoff, and control large-scale wildfires. Prescribed burns are particularly important to recreational areas of parks and forests where human use is high, thereby thwarting the risk of a large unnatural fire that could cause harm to persons and property. These "friendly fires" generally do not exceed the natural fire frequency, intensity, and seasonality, as determined by replicate studies on the ecosystem involved, or the impacts could be harmful. In Crater Lake National Park in Oregon, where decades of fire suppression led to unnatural fuel accumulations, prescribed fire has been used to restore the ponderosa pine ecosystem and reduce dangerous fuel loads (NPS, 2003).

Prescribed burns can become wildfires that burn out of control. The 2000 Cerro Grande wildfire started as a prescribed burn at Bandelier National Monument in New Mexico and burned more than 48,000 acres of the Santa Fe National Forest. In process, it also destroyed 200 homes (National Parks and Conservation Association, 2000). In 1988, the great fire in Yellowstone increased awareness of fuel loads and values at risk. As a result of years of fire suppressions, drought-like conditions, high winds, and high temperatures, fires continued for weeks. Controversy mounted when the wind-driven flames moved in on the historic Old Faithful Inn and the towns of West Yellowstone, Cooke City, and Silver Gate by late summer.

Notwithstanding the efforts of some 10,000 civilian and military firefighters, nearly a million acres of the entire Yellowstone territory burned, and timber and homes worth billions of dollars were destroyed (Jeffery, 1989). In the charred areas, a lush carpet of green with young pines took root after the lodgepoles' cones exploded in the intense heat. Nonetheless, after each of these firestorms, fire management policies in wilderness environments were reviewed.

Among other recommendations, interagency coordination, stronger public input, and careful planning and preparation around high-value developments and recreational resources took on high priorities. It also became clear that remaining tracts of wilderness are small in comparison to the times when fires moved freely, making it compelling for humans, not nature, to be the primary managers (Romme & Despain, 1989). During the investigation of Bandelier National Monument–Santa Fe National Forest wildfire, it was recommended that once a prescribed fire becomes a wildfire, the blaze be suppressed as quickly as possible even if it requires mechanical means.

The 2001 National Fire Plan is an interagency plan to reduce hazardous fires and create conditions where prescribed fire in combination with other treatments returns balance to diverse plant communities much like it was when the American Indians used fire as a land management tool. Traditionally, policy that dictates action after fires varies between the Forest Service and the NPS. Customarily, the Forest Service will respond by rapidly clearing fire-killed trees and planting new ones. The park service generally responds as it would to any other natural forest process; that is, the remains are best left alone for scientists and park visitors to study and observe unless the damage requires rehabilitation. The Forest Service and other big land management agencies must consider the production of resources such as timber on their lands, except in wilderness areas, and the national parks are managed under policies that protect and preserve all native species in their natural habitat. In Arizona, Kaibab National Forests Pumpkin Fire Self-

Guiding Auto Tour highlights fire effects on the landscape and firefighting techniques.

Grasslands

Familiar garden lawns and grassy urban parks are human-made, but the world's fast-disappearing native grasslands are as natural as forests or deserts. Generally requiring a moisture level somewhere between the humid climate that supports a forest and the dry climate that supports a desert, grasslands are most often found in semiarid climates. Summer drought is long enough to prevent most tree and shrub growth, but not severe enough to prohibit growth of bounteous grass and forbs (broad-leaf herbs). Sometimes given other names in other countries, grasslands are found on all continents except Antarctica.

In the United States, grasslands extend west from the Appalachians to the Rocky Mountains through a relatively flat land known as the Interior Plains. These grasslands of central North America are divided into three major types, including the *tallgrass prairie* toward the east and the *shortgrass prairie* in the west. Between them is a middle section comprising both types. This *mixed prairie* is found in most of the Dakotas, much of Nebraska and Kansas, the central part of Oklahoma, and parts of north central Texas. The transition from tall to short grass correlates with an increased aridity, reduced rainfall, and increased evaporation. Other grassland varieties exist in the Southwest, the Far West, and the East. Collectively, these grassland ecosystems, which once covered more than half of the land surface of the contiguous United States, provide homes to more than 7,500 plant and animal species (Hoofnagle, 2001).

Boundaries between the various grassland types were difficult to define because they were bordered by transition zones. Influenced by precipitation, the transition zone between tallgrass and mixed-grass prairie, for instance, could retreat from tallgrass to mixed prairie during years of decreased precipitation. During the great drought of 1933 to 1939, scientists documented an eastward retraction of 100 to 150 miles on the tallgrass prairie's western border (Brown, 1997). Roughly, tallgrass prairie once stretched from Ohio and Michigan across large portions of the Midwest to the eastern edges of Kansas, Nebraska, South Dakota, and North Dakota, where it extended northward into Canada and south over northern Texas.

Nutrients from the grasses produced a dark, rich soil that was perfect for agriculture. Victims of their own lushness, grasslands vanished from many states due to farms, roads, industry, and development. Some of the native grasses were replaced with other species, including corn on the tallgrass prairie and wheat on the mixed prairie, known as the Great Plains. Where the grasslands were too dry for crop production, they were eaten by sheep and cows. This was particularly the case in the shortgrass prairie, which was never considered to be attractive for agriculture in the way that the other prairie systems were. Because only portions of this land were plowed, shortgrass prairie remains less altered (Brown, 1997). Countless acres have suffered from overgrazing, however. Some areas have been permanently degraded, yet others still have the capacity to recover. The shortgrass prairie, also known as the Great Plains and the High Plains, occupies eastern Wyoming, much of Montana, eastern Colorado, western Kansas, the Oklahoma panhandle, northern Texas, and eastern New Mexico.

North American prairies are thought to date back to Miocene times beginning 35 million years ago. Vast areas had grass so thick and tall that pioneers on horseback feared getting lost in them. They were full of bobcats, wolves, deer, elk, rabbits, prairie dogs, and bison. Swarms of birds hovered above in search of food, and winds encouraged the spread of fire. Within a relatively short span, pioneers changed this wild, native land to a country of farms, ranches, railroads, and towns, but conservationists are mobilizing to save remaining grasslands. Tallgrass prairie is preserved in the Flint Hills region of Kansas in Tallgrass Prairie National Preserve and in Nebraska's Homestead National Monument of America.

Other smaller regions are scattered throughout the Midwest. When a 1-acre swatch of virgin grassland was going to be destroyed to mine gravel, for instance, an experimental transplant was made by the Illinois chapter of The Nature Conservancy in an attempt to preserve it. The cooperative effort emphasizes the rarity of the once prodigious prairies and increased society's awareness of the need to save the endangered environment and ecosystem in the Prairie State and elsewhere. In an unlikely partnership, the Sierra Club joined the National Rifle Association to protect the Texas Katy Prairie, the winter home for millions of waterfowl. Furthermore, grasses are also conserved by the Bureau of Land Management at Fort Meade Recreation Area in South Dakota, and prairie landscaping along highways and around homes has resulted in the restoration and recreation of tallgrass prairies. A pocket of shortgrass prairie is reserved in Canada's Grasslands National Park in Saskatchewan.

National grasslands. Today's national grasslands, administered by the Forest Service, present a scene of quiet beauty. Culminating more than two decades of conservation, these public lands were given permanent status as the National Grasslands system on June 20, 1960. Prior to that these lands were known as Land Utilization Projects, or LU lands. They were purchased by the federal government from homesteaders who were facing bankruptcy and foreclosure due to drought and depression in America's heartland during the 1930s. Continual cultivation, excessive grazing, recurrent dry years, and relentless wind had changed sod to dust. The land purchase program brought about a basic change in land use that was better suited to the dry, windy plains. Farms and ranches that remained had been, in general, larger and better able to operate economically. The areas purchased were slowly rehabilitated and became summer pastures. Sheep and cattle became the chief agricultural product in grass country, and grass resumed its rightful place as the dominant resource in the western plains.

Under leadership of the Soil Conservation Service, grazing associations and soil conservation districts were organized who leased the new public ranges under controls guaranteeing range improvement and conservation. Land Utilization Project managers led the way in demonstrating conservation techniques and practices toward a fully restored range. Now, the Land Utilization Projects on the plains have become the National Grasslands and a part of the National Forest System. These lands continue to support stable grassland agriculture and support other resources such as outdoor recreation in a manner that will blend and remain beneficial for generations. Just one of 20 national grassland sites, the Little Missouri National Grassland in North Dakota offers trails with special programs for hikers, campgrounds, canoeing, hunting, fishing, and wildlife and scenic tours. In Colorado, Comanche National Grassland has hiking and horseback riding, prairie chicken viewing, wildflowers, picnicking, camping, and 22 miles of the Santa Fe National Historic Trail.

Deserts

For many people, deserts conjure an image of lifeless sand dunes shimmering in waves of heat. Appearing barren, deserts seem to be forsaken. Yet the clear skies, the distant horizons, and the starry nights may represent the same appeal that oceans or mountains bring to others. Deserts, covering about one third of the earth's land area, occur from vicinities close to the poles down to expanses near the equator. These arid regions may be hot or cold, but they are always dry. Surprisingly, sand covers only about 20% of the earth's deserts. Nearly 50% of desert surfaces are plains where wind and runoff have removed the fine-grained material, leaving exposed loose gravel. The remaining surfaces of arid lands comprise uncovered bedrock outcrops, desert soils, and fluvial deposits including alluvial fans, playas, desert lakes, and oases (U.S. Geological Survey, 1996). Some of these features can be seen in Guadalupe Mountains and Arches National Parks in Texas and Utah, at Anza-Borrego Desert State Park in California, along the Pyramid Lake National Scenic Byway through Pyramid Lake Indian Reservation in Nevada, and at numerous other desert parks and recreational lands.

Giant saguaro cacti, unique to the Sonoran Desert, sometimes reach a height of 50 feet in the cactus forest of Saguaro National Monument near Tucson, Arizona.

In the harshest *dry desert*, such as the Atacama of northern Chile, the terrain is essentially barren. Only a few small, isolated plants are able to survive. The *shrub deserts* of the American West are a different story. In fact, the Sonoran Desert, the home of Saguaro National Park near Tucson, Arizona, has the most complex desert vegetation on earth. Although the living conditions are still severe, the shrub desert is far from uninhabited. Its plants and animals possess highly specialized abilities and mechanisms for survival. The diverse plant life, which covers roughly 10% to 20% of the ground (more around dry riverbeds), varies from cactus with their shallow root systems to plants with long tap roots that can anchor the soil and control erosion. Some plants have evolved into water-storing succulents,

and others have developed reduced leaf size or drop them altogether in dry conditions. Overall, the stems and leaves of plants help lower the surface velocity of winds that carry sand away. Most of the desert mammals are nocturnal, burrowing during the day.

Deserts also contain valuable mineral deposits that were formed in the arid environment or that were exposed by erosion. A paved trail in Death Valley National Park in California passes the old refinery and one of the famous "20-mule team" borax wagons used to haul loads of the precious material across the desert. Balance between preservation and use, including mining, ranching, and landfills, is an important factor for desert properties such as Grand Canyon-Parashant National Monument in Arizona, Grand Staircase-Escalante National Monument in Utah, and Joshua Tree National Park in California. And because deserts are dry, they present ideal places for human artifacts and fossils to be preserved, such as the fossils of gigantic fish dinosaurs found at Berlin-Ichthyosaur State Park in Nevada.

Misuse of these fragile environments is a serious and growing problem (U.S. Geological Survey, 1996), especially in the transition zone from the arid desert to more humid environments. These delicate areas are easily stressed by overgrazing and the hooves of livestock, which causes the desertification of productive land. As vegetation is lost, local arid climates are encouraged. The same problem can occur far from natural deserts if the land is not properly managed. This is the same process that occurred when parts of the grasslands of the Great Plains turned into a "Dust Bowl" in the 1930s. Greatly improved methods of agriculture and land and water management have prevented that disaster from recurring, but increased pressure on marginal lands and desert environments encourages erosion and loss. Overgrazing made the Rio Puerco Basin of central New Mexico one of the most eroded river basins of the American West. Overgrazing is the leading cause of desertification in China. Traditional herders graze their animals on ecologically fragile hills and steppes where they uproot and eat vast swathes of grass-

An intaglio or geoglyph, in the Mojave Desert near Blyth, California, is marred by dirt bikes that rode over the ancient sand drawings a few years ago. Tread Lightly! (2015) encourages leave-no-trace principles and inspires trail etiquette.

land. When strong winds blow the loosened topsoil away, the resulting massive sandstorms batter their cities, reaching South Korea, Japan, and the west coast of North America. China's developing dust bowl represents the largest conversion of productive land to desert in the world. As their deserts expand due also to drought, indiscriminate use of groundwater, and rampant logging, they are fighting back with reforestation on the fringes, herding restrictions, and other innovations. Near cities, "sand parks" have been developed where children ride camels, ride toboggan dunes, and drive SUVs (Pocha, 2006).

Desert running. Recreationally, off-road vehicle activity (ORV) significantly increases soil loss in the delicate desert environment. In just a few seconds, soils that took hundreds of years to develop are destroyed (U.S. Geological Survey, 1996). Because the desert is a fragile ecosystem, when abused it is dam-

aged long term. Desert ecologists estimate that it can take up to 200 years for some of the destroyed habitat to recover (Lance, 2001). Recreationists traveling on dirt bikes and off-road vehicles scar the desert and can kill the plants and animals. The compacted soil erodes rapidly and will not absorb water or insulate the roots against temperature extremes. The loss of plant life in turn devastates other dependent life forms. It is important, then, that appropriate space be provided for these activities and that other areas are protected. In the Mojave Desert, for instance, scientists reported a 90% drop in small-mammal populations after a race on Bureau of Land Management land. The noise of approximately 1,200 motorcycles and all-terrain vehicles (ATV) were found to be extremely damaging to animal life. After the race, kangaroo rats were found weaving in circles; their bleeding ears burst from the noise pollution. Other animals were found crushed or buried alive in their burrows ("Vanishing California," 1989). Tracks were seen on the cracked shells of desert tortoises, which were placed on the federal list of endangered species in 1989 on emergency status.

When the annual race was canceled for environmental reasons, over 100 motorcyclists demonstrated for the American right to use the nation's public lands (Warren, 1990). Now ATV enthusiasts from across the Southwest converge on the state's Imperial Sand Dunes Recreation Area, making the dunes the most-used public land in the nation on Thanksgiving weekend—the beginning of the 8-month season.

One survey conducted for the Bureau of Land Management after Utah's Moab Easter Jeep Safari found that 62% of the participants listed four-wheelers going off established trails as a major management problem (Reiter, Blahna, & Von Koch, 1997). In 1999, the state received funding from the Recreation Trails Program administered by the Federal Highway Administration for trails construction. Funds were used to form the Off-Road PALs Program, which promotes safe, responsible off-road riding and opportunities for at-risk youth to off-road in state parks. With the state's vehicular recreation areas located in varied and unique settings, other more sensitive regions were restricted. Tread Lightly!, originally launched by the Forest Service in 1985 to help protect public and private land, was transferred to the private sector to maximize its effectiveness. Now a nonprofit organization, Tread Lightly! educates the public on "low-impact" principles related to outdoor recreational activities, including ATV and four-wheeling. Hikers, campers, and people on mountain bicycles are also advised to stay on trails to avoid damaging delicate desert soil.

NOISE POLLUTION

Besides the noise pollution impacts on desert animals cited above, humans suffer from noise pollution. The peacefulness and quietude that many visitors seek in parks are lost to low-flying military jets, helicopters, au-tomobiles, and ORVs. Sailors complain about motorboats and personal watercraft, also known as jet skis. Cross-country skiers barely tolerate noisy snowmobiles. Hikers and anglers contend with noise from swamp buggies, airboats, and other mechanized equipment. Each seeks its own space. A report presented to the President's Commission on Americans Outdoors (D. Williams & Jacobs, 1986) noted psychological annoyance depends on many factors: the extent of interference with communication, relaxation, and sleep; the settings in which the noise occurs; the importance of the activities interrupted; and the time of exposure. A standard of 70 decibels is sufficient to protect hearing loss. However, about half of the people exposed to noise at this level over time became highly dissatisfied.

After measuring sound in a number of the national parks, researchers defined two primary types of intrusive noises. Sudden loud noises, such as those from cell phones, cause immediate disturbances and distractions. Background noise, including motorized vehicles, airplanes, and oil pumps, disrupt the overall soundscape. Animals who depend on their hearing for hunting, mating calls, and so forth may also be affected (Marquis, 2006). Zion National Park in Utah bans private cars for much of the year in favor of the public transport system, cutting traffic noise disruptive to wildlife and visitors. Because attitudes of the perceiver affect the assessment of annoyance, noise levels are likely to be evaluated much more critically in outdoor recreation settings than in urban settings where adaptations to noise levels have been made. Complaints mount when noisy equipment is also linked to more conspicuous and measurable disturbances such as air or water pollution, wildlife disruption, environmental destruction, property loss, or personal injury.

Restrictions, stricter guidelines, permits, and bans are being applied, but when too soft, damages may result that might otherwise have been controlled. ORV users suffer the public relations loss that comes with the repercussions. Hunters reported that mosaic scars covered the fragile land in Big Cypress

National Preserve. Funds for patrols needed to prevent future illegal incursions are often required after extreme occurrences. In the meantime, ORV lobbies demand access to public lands, and managers strive to find low-impact ways to allow high-impact activity that will not disturb others. The nonprofit organization American Trails helps all trail groups resolve discord by working together. Educational materials to help visitors understand how they can help control noise are needed. To encourage a more enjoyable acoustic environment, the NPS is encouraging information exchanges with private companies, nonprofits, and governmental agencies. In turn, these conferences may help spark interest in cutting-edge policies and the cutting-edge science of noise control.

WILDLIFE

No one knows exactly why some animals and plants flourish for thousands of years and others vanish within a relatively short time. But those species that survive exhibit a common trait: adaptability. The animal or plant that is able to change its requirements to fit changes in its environment holds the vital key to survival. Conversely, animals and plants that are highly specialized can be more vulnerable to extinction. The black-footed ferret of the Great Plains, for instance, feeds almost entirely on the prairie dog, making it precariously dependent on an extremely narrow resource or habitat. In some cases, plants and animals will become extinct for reasons not fully understood by science. Others may die out regardless of what is done for them (U.S. Fish and Wildlife Service, 1998b). Extinction remains a fact of life on earth, but the species of the world are becoming increasingly endangered. It is estimated that the rapid loss of species is between 150 and 200 species every 24 hours. This mass extinction is greater than experienced in the past 65 million years (United Nations Environmental Programme, 2010). The greatest causes of extinction legally related to human activity are the loss of habitat and fragmentation, pollution, commercial exploitation, edifica-

tion, the introduction of exotic species, and global warming.

Loss of habitat. Destruction, degradation, and the fragmentation of habitat are leading causes of extinction for plants and animals. Clear-cutting forests near rivers can cause excessive erosion, and the increased silt in the waterways can suffocate fish. This caused the Michigan grayling, a trout-like sport fish, to become extinct in the 1920s. Habitat protection on federal and private lands may enhance recovery efforts for the red-cockaded woodpecker. Once abundant throughout the Southeast, it began a rapid decline as humans altered its pine forest habitat. In 1970, the species was listed as endangered under a precursor to the 1978 endangered species law. Their current population is fragmented into isolated islands of populations. Working closely with the U.S. Fish and Wildlife Service, the Forest Service is striving to preserve colonies, and the Georgia-Pacific Company established a landmark conservation agreement with the Fish and Wildlife Service to help save the woodpecker on some of their acres. It is still on the endangered species list.

Pollution. Endangered species often serve as indicators of environmental problems that may also affect people. A good example is freshwater mussels. Several mussels are endangered in large part due to pollution of the waterways where they live. Contamination commonly results from agricultural pesticide runoff, municipal sewage disposal, and industrial waste discharge. Because people depend on the nation's waterways for sources of food and water, and as these are popular places for recreational activities, health and well-being are in jeopardy when these areas become polluted. Interest in opening up the Arctic National Wildlife Refuge in northern Alaska to oil drilling has resulted in the mobilization of thousands of Americans who fear that, despite new technology, the distinctive wildlife nursery for polar bears and caribou herds; wetland nesting grounds for millions of snow geese, sandhill cranes, red-throated loons, and other bird species; and the year-round home of musk oxen, grizzlies, wolves, foxes, golden eagles, and snowy owls will be turned into a polluted oil field with potential for oil spills. Wildlife is also vulnerable to climate change (Defenders of Wildlife, 2014). In January 2015, the U.S. Fish and Wildlife Service released the final comprehensive plan (CCP) for the Arctic National Wildlife Refuge. This plan will guide the refuge's management and recommends that three Wilderness Study Areas be designated as Wilderness and recommends four rivers for designation as Wild and Scenic Rivers.

Commercial exploitation. Many early laws passed to protect animals and plants were poorly written and inadequately enforced. They made it relatively easy for rare, native plants such as some cacti, carnivorous plants, orchids, and others to pass into commercial trade. The demand for exotic pets, such as parrots and other wild birds, has caused many of these species to become endangered. In the early 1900s, there were reported sightings of flocks of thick-billed parrots numbering in the thousands in the Chiricahua Mountains of Arizona. Although their range once spanned from Venezuela in South America to Arizona and New Mexico, they are now clinging to existence in northwest Mexico. Captive-breeding programs hope to reintroduce them into the wild. Additionally, some Asian cultures consider animal parts, such as those of bear species, rhinoceros, and tiger, to have medicinal powers. The illegal wildlife trade is a lucrative business, and the demand for these animal parts is a growing threat to their survival. Elephants and sea turtles are also endangered due in large part to the demand for ivory and turtle shell for jewelry and other wildlife products. Poaching has caused African elephants to decline by at least 2% each year since 2010. With at least 100,000 dead in just the last 3 years, they could go extinct in a few decades (Biello, 2014).

Edification. Some animal species have joined humans in a population explosion. Human-made edifices (structures of especially imposing appearance) such as agricultural developments, dams, reservoirs, drainage schemes, interstate highways, and buildings have aided the evolution. Certain species that adapt well to these structures are known as edification species. Edification species have had a negative effect on general wildlife diversity by causing species turnover and replacement. In New England's coastal islands, herring gull eggs were once collected to near extinction. The gulls began to make a comeback in the 1950s when their central edifice became the sanitary landfill. They grew as they fed in cities and dumps. Nesting on offshore islets, they ate the eggs and chicks of smaller species and crowded out larger ones. Biological diversity tumbled until gull population control became mandatory. In the 1960s, their nests were eradicated and greater control of landfills and fish-processing practices reduced their food base. Afterward, other seabirds began nesting in greater numbers on coastal islets (Lazell, 1989). Besides reducing habitat for native life, they diminish the recreation experience, make some campsites unusable, and limit river access. Similarly, buildings offer sanctuary for raccoons. Expanding its regional range to lakes and shores in the north where wildlife are unaccustomed to the marauders, the raccoons eat summer garbage and winter under summer cottages. Capable of living off their fat during winter, they have consumed the eggs and chicks of nesting loons in the spring.

Exotic species. Invasive species have been purposefully, carelessly, and unwittingly introduced around the globe since Polynesian seafarers began transporting rats to Pacific islands via dugout canoes more than 1,500 years ago. In the Hawaiian Islands, rats introduced by sailing ships have played havoc with nesting birds. When mongooses were imported to control the rats, they turned on the nesting birds instead and were a serious factor in bringing the nene goose to near extinction. Second only to habitat destruction, nonnative species can, if uncontrolled, increase and become a threat to other species of wildlife. During the 19th century, more than 4,500 foreign species established a foothold in the United States (The Nature Conservancy, 1999). In addition, diseases and parasites, introduced by international trade, have caused disasters in U.S. forests. Since its introduction into Massachusetts from Europe in 1869, the gypsy moth has spread to the entire Northeast and is still spreading. This major threat to hardwoods costs the economy millions in damages and the resulting deforestation impacts reproductive success of forest-dwelling birds. Carrying out a policy to eradicate noxious or exotic plant and animal species on public lands is not always easy. Physically, for instance, weeds spread like wildfire and approximately 3.5 million acres of national forestland are infested (U.S. Department of Agriculture, 2005). Politically in the Grand Canyon National Park, burros released by early prospectors had almost completely displaced the desert bighorn sheep by overgrazing. Because park managers were charged with protecting the habitat, they ordered that the burros be shot. Associated with preservation and not destruction, the action led to public outcry. As a result, the Wild Free-Roaming Horses and Burros Act of 1971 directs the Bureau of Land Management to offer excess wild horses and burros for adoption to those who meet adoption requirements (Bureau of Land Management, 2004).

Endangered Species Act

In early 1973, an international conference on endangered species took place in Washington, DC. The meeting resulted in the formation of the Convention on International Trade in Endangered Species of Wild Fauna and Flora (CITES), a 130-nation agreement designed to prevent species from becoming endangered or extinct because of international trade. To meet some of the agreement's provisions, the United States needed new legislation. By the end of that year, one of the most comprehensive laws ever enacted by any country to prevent the extinction of imperiled life was enacted (Hogan, 1999). Upon passing the Endangered Species Act (ESA, 1973), Congress recognized a concern not only that many of the nation's native plants and animals were in decline, but also that the rich natural heritage was of "esthetic, ecological, educational, recreation, and scientific value to the Nation and its people."

The ultimate goal of the ESA is to conserve the ecosystems upon which endangered and threatened species are dependent and to conserve and recover species so they no longer need protection under the act. *Endangered* means a species is in danger of extinction throughout all or a significant portion of its range. *Threatened* means a species is likely to become endangered within the foreseeable future. All species of plants and animals, except pest insects, are eligible for listing, based on the best scientific and commercial data available. After a species is listed, it becomes protected by federal law. Of the 1,561 United States species listed, 1,214 are endangered and 347 are threatened (U.S. Fish and Wildlife Service, 2014). Groups with the most listed species are (in order) plants, birds, fishes, mammals, and clams/mussels (U.S. Fish and Wildlife Service, 2006). A listed species cannot be taken, which includes killing, harming, or harassing. The law also provides species protection by requiring federal agencies to ensure activities that they conduct, authorize, or fund do not jeopardize the continued existence of listed species. When prudent, this includes the designation of critical habitat. Federal agencies, in turn, consult with the U.S. Fish and Wildlife Service and the National Marine Fisheries Service (the two federal agencies responsible for administering the law) to allow their projects to go forward at the same time species are protected. This action alone is sometimes enough to save a species from extinction and start it back on the road to recovery. As such, the law has been a catalyst in the way Americans approach land-use decisions.

Still, the number of listed species continue to grow, creating controversy between economic growth and preserving imperiled wildlife and its habitat. As the human population grows and spreads, there is less room for plants and animals. Opponents complain that since its inception only a few species have recovered enough to no longer need protection. Since passage of the ESA, conservation actions carried out have been successful in preventing the extinction of 99% of the species listed (U.S. Fish and Wildlife

Service, 2005). Supporters credit the law, then, with blocking the extinction of species, finding that just as it takes time for species to become endangered, it also takes time for them to recover. When the Northwest Forest Plan was implemented, for example, the object was to prevent the acceleration of the decline of the spotted owl by preserving old-growth forests on federal lands within its range. The decline will continue until the new growth in clear-cut areas of the old-growth forests reach sufficient stature to allow for a possible recovery. This could take years, but the newly planted stands may begin to support juvenile owls, just as they did years ago when fires burned some areas of the forest.

Supporters of the act, in turn, are concerned about a backlog of candidate species that are losing their habitat while the U.S. Fish and Wildlife Service reviews an overwhelming number of petitions for the list. It is believed that each day of delay increases the possibility of extinction. Other laws to protect species include the Marine Mammal Protection Act, the Migratory Bird Treaty Act, and the Anadromous Fish Conservation Act. The Lacey Act makes it a federal crime for any person to import, export, transport, sell, receive, acquire, possess, or purchase any fish, wildlife, or plant taken, possessed, transported, or sold in violation of any federal, state, foreign, or Indian tribal law, treaty, or regulation. Species protection has also been achieved through partnerships with states and nonfederal landowners.

Habitat Protection

The greatest protection of biological diversity is in preserving habitats or ecosystems. Here various species draw upon resources available in the ecosystem to which they also contribute. A holistic habitat protection approach helps protect species before they reach critical stages, requiring the individual attention of a species-by-species approach. The theory holds that when habitats are saved, more species, in the long run, can be saved and that when the listing process is scaled down, more resources are available to protect habitats (Norton, 1987). The Northwest Forest Plan was considered revo-

lutionary because it did not seek to manage the lands just for the threatened spotted owl, but for all species found in old-growth forests on federal lands within the range of the threatened species (Yuskavitch, 2001).

Some animals who venture outside park boundaries require habitat protection. For example, hunters shoot bison that wander out of Yellowstone National Park, home of the last free-roaming herd in the nation. National attention came when a harsh winter in 1989 drove 800 of the herd over the park's northern boundary to find grass to eat, thereby providing ranchers and hunters with the opportunity to kill more than half of the celebrated northern herd. Critics cite this case to illustrate the arbitrary nature of national park and public lands borders, which often ignore natural boundaries, such as ridgelines and watersheds, slicing through the natural boundaries of animal habitats.

Artificial Habitats

Zoos, wild animal parks, wildlife research centers, and marine mammal research centers contribute to animal comebacks. Zoos, sometimes criticized for capturing and exploiting animals, have rescued some species from extinction, such as the California condor, black-footed ferret, Arabian oryx, and red wolf. Others, such as the bighorn sheep, would be rapidly declining if it were not for contributions from Species Survival Plans (SSP). The SSP is a cooperative breeding and conservation program designed to preserve endangered species through captive breeding and gene pool management. The program, established and maintained by the American Zoo and Aquarium Association (AZA), brings together accredited zoos and aquariums to manage species of mammals, birds, amphibians, reptiles, fish, and invertebrates. If AZA decides that a captive-breeding program can aid the recovery of an endangered species, an SSP is established, and participating programs manage and exchange their animals in the best interest of the species, including selecting a mate, determining the desired number of offspring, and creating strategies for habitat preservation in the wild. SSPs also support

These red mangroves with massive exposed root systems fringe the waterways of the Everglades and filter material washed from the land, trapping debris and sediment. Mangrove roots provide nursery grounds to many species of fish and invertebrates, and near Key Largo, are the habitat for the endangered American crocodile.

public education, supportive research, and reintroduction to the wild. Barasingha deer, tree kangaroos, clouded leopards, and giant pandas are just some of the species the AZA is working to save from extinction.

Using Technology for Habitat Restoration

Nearly one third of the nation's endangered and threatened species live only in wetlands, and nearly half use them at some point in their lives. Many other animals and plants depend on wetland habitats for survival (EPA, 2012d). For instance, some fish and shellfish, various birds, and certain mammals must have coastal wetlands to survive. Yet in California, 90% of the state's coastal wetlands have been lost in just 150 years (Lafee, 2001). The rare restoration of the 387-acre Bolsa Chica tidal wetlands in Huntington Beach discussed in the Estuaries and Wetlands section may serve as an example for future proj-

ects. The return of the natural ebb and flow after damming should replenish marshes that provide nesting habitat for endangered birds and chase out invasive species.

Inland wetlands are needed by many animals and plants such as wood ducks, muskrat, and swamp rose. For others, including striped bass, peregrine falcon, and black bears, wetland habitats provide important food, water, or shelter. Song birds and hawks use them to feed, nest, and raise their young. Migratory waterfowl use coastal and inland wetlands as resting, feeding, or nesting grounds for at least part of the year. For these reasons, an international agreement to protect wetland habitats of international importance was developed. In some cases, migratory birds are so completely dependent on certain wetlands that they would become extinct if they were destroyed (EPA, 2001b). Nationally, H.R. 5539 reauthorizes the North American Wetland Conservation Act to protect wetlands and associated habitat (Liberman, 2006c).

Although restoring a fully functional ecosystem is difficult, technology and scientific innovations are helping. The vital water system of southern Florida consists of three essential elements: the Kissimmee River, Lake Okeechobee, and the Everglades. About a century ago, the freshwater system of Florida nurtured an ecosystem unique to the earth. Water flowed from a chain of lakes into the Kissimmee River. It carried water through the savanna to Lake Okeechobee, an area higher than the expanse to the south. The lake would periodically overflow, moving south across the saw grass of the Everglades, over the then-undrawn boundaries of Big Cypress National Preserve and Everglades National Park. This flowing water in part evaporated, contributing moisture for rain in a constantly renewing cycle. But after the Civil War, an environmental onslaught began as efforts were undertaken to contain the flood-prone lake. By the turn of the 19th century, a network of locks, dams, and canals was established for flood control. Farming was tried, but the topsoil dried to a powder or decomposed. Nutrients that were released flowed into the Everglades. The U.S. Army Corps of Engineers strengthened dikes and dug more channels to tame the flooding water system. Finally, plumbing projects of the 1940s changed the water wilderness. As the population grew, water was further tapped for human needs, greatly affecting nesting and wading birds, whose numbers declined dramatically. High concentrations of mercury were found in fish, egrets, and Florida panthers. Cattails began to take over thousands of acres of former saw grass marsh. Alligator nests flooded when excess summer water could no longer spread over larger areas. During dry periods, the region was parched. Indicator species—the Florida panther and the alligator—almost became extinct as a result of the environmental degradation (Cordes, 2001).

By the 1980s, polluted Lake Okeechobee had burst into blooms of blue-green algae, just as other forms of life in the lake were threatened. To save the unusual ecosystem, a commitment to restore a more natural flow of water was necessary. A computer program was designed to imitate seasonal rainfall conditions. Annual water deliveries were made for the appropriate distribution of water allotments. A levee was breached to assist the restoration of natural water flow. After successful rehabilitation of the Kissimmee was effected by engineers, waterfowl began to return. Other changes were devised to keep manure nutrients from Lake Okeechobee, and laws were enacted for pollution reduction and environmental restoration (Cordes, 2001). The experiment is still in progress. Meanwhile, hikers pass through Big Cypress National Preserve and visit the marshes on the Florida National Scenic Trail.

Partnerships Protecting Wildlife

Approximately one third of all federally listed species dwell on national forests and grasslands. And more than 2,500 sensitive species, those requiring special management to prevent their loss, are also found on these lands. This means that the national forests and grasslands harbor the greatest diversity of wildlife under any single ownership nationwide. The Forest Service believes that partnerships are critical in their effort to maintain the ecosystems essential for supporting healthy populations of wildlife. Their Challenge Cost-Share Program provides the means for the Forest Service and the private sector to share management and financial costs for projects in the national forests that help to restore wildlife and fish habitat. Anglers, hunters, birders, off-highway vehicle users, ranchers, miners, utility companies, educational institutions, conservation groups, and other recreation users are among the thousands of partners working with the Forest Service in programs to aid wildlife and their habitats (G. Williams, 2000). With cooperative efforts, there is hope that the decline in forest habitat will cease. Programs such as Get Wild, Every Species Counts, Rise to the Future, and NatureWatch help the Forest Service to inventory and improve habitats; recover and conserve rare species; coordinate aquatic habitat management goals, plans, and programs; and provide enhanced recreational opportunities for the public.

NIGHT SKIES

Two thirds of Americans cannot see the Milky Way from their backyards, and 99% of the population live in an area that scientists consider light-polluted. The rate at which light pollution is increasing will leave almost no dark skies in the contiguous United States by 2025 (NPS, 2007). Although people have been taught that bright light leads to safety, improper lighting can threaten security by casting harsh shadows and by inducing glare. Moreover, poor outdoor lighting is making natural darkness a rarity in urban settings, and the unnatural illumination is spreading into remote parklands. "Light pollution" generated by an upward glow from poorly designed lights also creates waste.

Lowering bulb wattage and shielding lights are easy ways to help reduce light pollution and expenses. It is estimated that 30 % of street lights, for instance, waste light by shining upward. When calculating this percentage in the United States alone, it is estimated that approximately 22,000 gigawatt-hours a year are wasted. At a conservative average of $0.10 per kilowatt-hour, the cost of wasted energy totals approximately $2.2 billion a year. Besides the financial waste, 3.6 tons of coal or 12.9 million barrels of oil are wasted every year to produce lost light as well International Dark-Sky Association, 2014). Not only does this misdirected light cause people to lose view of the stars that their ancestors once admired, but also astronomical research is being threatened.

Bad lighting negatively impacts animals as well. Using the stars and sun as guides, migrating birds often mistake the distant glow for sunrise or sunset. As a result, they stray from their course or wander into the ocean and parish. Thousands crash into multistory buildings left unnecessarily illuminated at night. Along the eastern seaboard, newly hatched marine turtles mistake lights for moonlight, causing them to lose their way to the sea. To help protect nocturnal animals and preserve the night sky for visitors, the National Park's Night Skies program released its Vanishing Night Skies report that grew from a survey of NPS superintendents. They recommend seven ways to enjoy natural darkness (NPS, 2012):

1. Conquer fears by walking in the dark with a flashlight available.
2. Make a night-vision friendly flashlight by covering your small flashlight with red cellophane or a red filter.
3. Stargaze through telescopes and learn about the cosmos.
4. Go for a moonlit hike after letting eyes fully adjust.
5. Awaken nocturnal senses by giving eyes 20 minutes to adjust and by listening to the night sounds.
6. Watch nocturnal wildlife.
7. Be inspired and find ways to connect with humankind's celestial companion.

To do their part, parks are going beyond the traditional evening campground programs. The astute can sign up early in the day for ranger-led moon hikes at night where the flashlight is taboo. Eyes adjust during information talks before the small group takes off with the guide. Radiant cliffs, spiraling towers, and giant hoodoos take shapes on the moonlit Fairyland Loop Trail in Utah's Bryce Canyon National Park, one of the darkest parks in the system. Some parks also offer nocturnal wildlife viewing and stargazing in the natural lightscape. Volunteers set up their telescopes so visitors can enjoy the rings of Saturn, the moon's craters, and nebulas. To encourage their visitors to follow suit, the NPS is trying to model behavior by improving its own lighting habits in anticipation that every camper will be able to delight in the spectacular views once enjoyed by their ancestors on dark clear nights.

HARMONY WITH NATURE

With over 6 billion inhabitants in the world, tremendous demands are placed on the environment. Humanity can hardly afford to waste, pollute, or abuse it. Still, the

Future Stewards of Nature

One innovative outdoor environmental program takes children and youth, Grades 3 to 12, on an environmental journey. Passionate about reconnecting this "digital generation" with nature, the nonprofit Santa Rosa Plateau Nature Education Foundation serves over 8,000 students from 10 school districts in southwest Riverside County in California. The education program began in 1994 with a focus on third grade and since has brought 85,000 third graders into the natural environment for educational experiences. Fifth graders develop an awareness of public land and what restoration means. They specialize in native and nonnative plants, conduct a "seed bank study," and learn how to grow native plants. Middle school students discover how environments and habitats become altered and endangered. They develop a restoration plan and do restorative work on an altered habitat. During this process, they learn field biology/ecology techniques and terminology. High school students build on these experiences, monitor habitats, analyze results, make conclusions, and mentor younger students. As skills and knowledge grow, their awareness of the environment deepens from firsthand experience in the unique, protected public land of the Santa Rosa Ecological Plateau Reserve and in diverse watershed areas surrounding the reserve.

The hills of this beautiful reserve offer wind-rippled grasses, swaying poppies, and more than 450 native plants among ancient Engelmann oaks. Once widespread throughout the western United States, these oaks are now found only between San Diego and Santa Barbara. Most stands contain only a few specimens capable of re-generation, but here they are healthy. Some of the state's last vernal pools are also found at the reserve. In late winter or early spring, much needed rains cause the pools to form and seemingly blossom from dry land. For a brief time here, endangered fairy shrimp thrive, but only when the water allows the dormant crustaceans to emerge. During damp mornings, children can observe sparkling dew collections on large circles of web left by tunnel spiders over old gopher holes. This exquisite home to about 60 sensitive species of plants and animals is a perfect setting in which to teach children how fragile natural life is. Rare and endangered plants such as chocolate lilies, San Diego button celery (coyote thistle), and Santa Rosa Basalt brodiaea are discovered. The ecological treasure at the plateau has been recognized by UNESCO as a biosphere reserve.

In 1984, The Nature Conservancy of California purchased the first 3,100 acres. Later in partnership with the Metropolitan Water District of Southern California, the County of Riverside and the California Department of Fish and Game/Wildlife Conservation Board acquired more land and now manage nearly 10,000 acres. Trails wind through chaparral and oak woodlands. Some pass what Spanish *vaqueros* called *tenajas* or deep holes in creek beds that hold pools of water year-round that sustain western pond turtles and red-legged frogs. The landscape, much like it was when the Luiseño people came to the area to collect acorns from the oaks, has large granite boulders with small wells that were created when the women rubbed pestles over the seeds repeatedly. In a later time, the Moreno adobe and Machado adobe were built and are now preserved.

Foundation board and members take their volunteer work seriously, pairing the outdoor fieldwork with classroom instruction. Programs are integrated with new Common Core objectives, EEI and NCLI (Environmental Education and No Child Left Inside) initiatives as well as NGSS (Next Generation Science Standards) and STEM (Science, Technology, Engineering, and Math). In time, it is hoped that their students will share experiences with others and become future stewards of nature. As author Richard Louv (2008) explained, "If we are going to save environmentalism and the environment, we must also save an endangered indicator species: the child in nature" (p. 159).

signs of environmental abuse are all around. Sometimes no one understands how the environment will respond to human actions. Nonetheless, landfills are choking with the tons of garbage dumped every day. Acid rain caused by automobile and factory emissions is killing forests and polluting lakes. Sewage and industrial pollution are fouling rivers and oceans. Inappropriate methods of farming, mining, logging, and manufacturing are eroding land, poisoning water, and threatening wildlife.

With technology, consideration, diligence, partnerships, and mindful management, humans can slow and perhaps even reverse much of the damage. In many instances, tourism dollars are replacing older economies as outdoor adventurers and nature enthusiasts make new and often improved demands of the environment. And the more time spent outside, the more is learned about the need to live in harmony with nature. With the passage of the National Environmental Policy Act of 1969, the enhancement of harmony between people and their environment became a national policy. As a direct result, the Council on Environmental Quality was established, which required that all federal agencies prepare reports on the environmental impact of all major planned programs. A growing number of Americans are finding that the earth is sacred. The majority of respondents to a nationwide poll, 71%, believe the country should do whatever it can to protect the environment (Romm, 2011). One of the most powerful orations addressing the environment that has ever been made follows. In his 1854 address to the American people who had offered to buy a large portion of American Indian land, Chief Seattle stressed ecological values and harmony with nature:

How can you buy or sell the sky, the warmth of the land? The idea is strange to us.

If we do not own the freshness of the air and the sparkle of the water, how can you buy them?

THE EARTH IS SACRED

Every part of this earth is sacred to my people. Every shining pine needle, every sandy shore, every mist in the dark woods, every clearing and humming insect is holy in the memory and experience of my people. The sap which courses through the trees carries the memories of the red man.

The white man's dead forget the country of their birth when they go to walk among the stars. Our dead never forget this beautiful earth, for it is the mother of the red man.

We are part of the earth and it is part of us. The perfumed flowers are our sisters; the deer, the horse, the great eagle, these are our brothers. The rocky crests, the juices in the meadow, the body heat of the pony, and man—all belong to the same family.

THINGS TO REMEMBER

So, when the Great Chief in Washington sends word that he wishes to buy our land, he asks much of us. The Great Chief sends word he will reserve us a place so that we can live comfortably to ourselves.

He will be our father and we will be his children. So we will consider your offer to buy our land.

But it will not be easy. For this land is sacred to us.

This shining water that moves in the streams and rivers is not just water but the blood of our ancestors.

If we sell you land, you must remember that it is sacred, and you must teach your children that it is sacred and that each ghostly reflection in the clear water of the lakes tells of events and memories in the life of my people.

The water's murmur is the voice of my father's father.

GIVE THE RIVERS KINDNESS

The rivers are our brothers, they quench our thirst. The rivers carry our canoes, and feed our children. If we sell you our land, you must remember, and teach your children that the rivers are our brothers, and yours, and you must henceforth give the rivers the kindness you would give any brother.

We know that the white man does not understand our ways. One portion of land is the same to him as the next, for he is a stranger who comes in the night and takes from the land whatever he needs.

The earth is not his brother, but his enemy, and when he has conquered it, he moves on.

He leaves his father's grave behind, and he does not care. He kidnaps the earth from his children, and he does not care.

His father's grave, and his children's birthright, are forgotten. He treats his mother, the earth, and his brother, the sky, as things to be bought, plundered, sold like sheep or bright beads.

His appetite will devour the earth and leave behind only a desert.

I do not know. Our ways are different from your ways.

The sight of your cities pains the eyes of the red man. But perhaps it is because the red man is a savage and does not understand.

There is no quiet place in the white man's cities. No place to hear the unfurling of leaves in spring, or the rustle of an insect's wings.

But perhaps it is because I am a savage and do not understand.

The clatter only seems to insult the ears. And what is there to life if a man cannot hear the lonely cry of the whippoorwill or the arguments of the frogs around a pond at night? I am a red man and do not understand.

The Indian prefers the soft sound of the wind darting over the face of a pond and the smell of the wind itself, cleaned by a midday rain, or scented with the pinon pine.

THE AIR SHARES ITS SPIRIT
The air is precious to the red man, for all things share the same breath—the beast, the tree, the man, they all share the same breath.

The white man does not seem to notice the air he breathes. Like a man dying for many days, he is numb to the stench.

But if we sell you our land, you must remember that the air is precious to us, that the air shares its spirit with all the life it supports. The wind that gave our grandfather his first breath also receives his last sigh.

And if we sell you our land, you must keep it apart and sacred, as a place where even the white man can go to taste the wind that is sweetened by the meadow's flowers.

TREAT THE BEASTS AS BROTHERS
So we will consider your offer to buy our land. If we decide to accept, I will make one condition: The white man must treat the beasts of this land as his brothers.

I am a savage and I do not understand any other way.

I have seen a thousand rotting buffaloes on the prairie, left by the white man who shot them from a passing train.

I am a savage and I do not understand how the smoking iron horse can be more important than the buffalo that we kill only to stay alive.

What is man without the beasts? If all the beasts were gone, man would die from a great loneliness of spirit.

For whatever happens to the beasts, soon happens to man. All things are connected.

TEACH YOUR CHILDREN
You must teach your children that the ground beneath their feet is the ashes of your grandfathers. So that they will respect the land, tell your children that the earth is rich with the lives of our kin.

Teach your children what we have taught our children, that the earth is our mother.

Whatever befalls the earth befalls the sons of the earth. If men spit upon the ground, they spit upon themselves.

This we know: The earth does not belong to man; man belongs to the earth. This we know.

All things are connected like the blood which unites one family. All things are connected.

Whatever befalls the earth befalls the sons of the earth. Man did not weave the web of life: He is merely a strand in it. Whatever he does to the web, he does to himself.

Even the white man, whose God walks and talks with him as friend to friend, cannot be exempt from the common destiny.

We may be brothers after all.

We shall see.

One thing we know, which the white man may one day discover—our God is the same God. You may think now that you own Him as you wish to own our land; but you cannot. He is the God of man, and His compassion is equal for the red man and the white.

This earth is precious to Him, and to harm the earth is to heap contempt on its Creator. The whites too shall pass; perhaps sooner than all other tribes. Contaminate your bed, and you will one night suffocate in your own waste. But in your perishing you will shine brightly, fired by the strength of the God who brought you to this land and for some special purpose gave you dominion over this land and over the red man.

That destiny is a mystery to us, for we do not understand when the buffalo are all slaughtered, the wild horses are tamed, the secret corners of the forest heavy with scent of many men, and the view of the ripe hills blotted by talking wires.

Where is the thicket? Gone.

Where is the eagle? Gone.
The end of living and the beginning of survival.

If we sell you our land, love it as we have loved it. Care for it as we have cared for it. Hold in your mind the memory of the land as it is when you take it. And with all your strength, with all your mind, with all your heart, preserve it for your children and love it . . . as God loves us all.

SUMMARY

Human activities, including outdoor recreation, impact the environment. Air pollution causes havoc in national parks, even after the passage of the Clean Air Act. The destruction to the freshwater aquatic system is seen in the extinction and near extinction of many fish. This has impacted fishing and fishing ethics. Other areas affected by human activities are the estuarine and marine systems. Changes in the ocean's circulation produce climate change. Coral reefs along the Florida Keys could become the first in the world to be killed by humans.

Forests and trees are disappearing at an alarming rate, the recreational values of which are gone forever. But most important is the impact of unwise timber harvesting on the environment, which results in the loss of wildlife and helps to create a potentially dangerous level of global warming. Ancient forests support established ecosystems.

Prairie lands may be the most endangered terrestrial ecosystem, and the desert is extremely fragile. Steps are being taken to reduce damage.

REFERENCES

America's Wetland Foundation. (2013). America's wetland in a nutshell-FAQs. Retrieved from http://www.americaswetlandresources.com/background_facts/basicfacts/FAQs.html

Associated Press. (2004, August 25). Polluted fish warnings. *San Diego Union-Tribune*, p. 1A.

Associated Press. (2006, September 22). EPA's new soot standards are weaker than panel suggested. *San Diego Union-Tribune*, p. A7.

Atkinson, G. (1990, April). Outdoor recreation's contribution to environmental attitudes. *Leisure Today*, 14-16.

Biello, D. (2014, August 18). Poaching could drive elephants extinct in decades [Blog post]. Retrieved from http://blogs.scientificamerican.com/observations/2014/08/18/poaching-could-drive-elephants-extinct-in-decades/

Bonneville Power Administration. (2013, March). The amazing journey of Columiba River salmon [Poster]. Retrieved from http://www.bpa.gov/PublicInvolvement/Community Education/CurriculumActivities/CurriculumDocuments/Amazing%20Journey%20of%20Columbia%20River %20Salmon%20-WEB-%20POSTER.pdf

Brown, L. (1997). *Grasslands*. New York, NY: National Audubon Society.

Bureau of Land Management. (2004). *Adopting a wild horse or burro* (USGPO 2004-675-048). Washington, DC: U.S. Department of the Interior.

Capra, R. (1995). Deep ecology: A new paradigm. In G. Sessions (Ed.), *Deep ecology for the 21st century* (pp. 19–25). Boston, MA: Shambhala Publications.

Cassie, R. (2015, April 22). The first Earth Day: a brief history. *Baltimore*. Retrieved from http://www.baltimoremagazine.net/2015/4/22/the-first-earth-day-a-brief-history

Chase, C. (1990). Cognition, ethics, and direct experience. *Journal of Physical Education, Recreation, and Dance, 61*(4), 55–56.

Cleveland, C. J. (2013). Deepwater Horizon oil spill. In *Encyclopedia of Earth*. Retrieved from http://www.eoearth.org/view/article/161185/

Commission on Ocean Policy. (2006). About the Committee on Ocean Policy. Retrieved from http://oceans.ceq.gov/about/welcome.html

Cordell, H. K. (1997, April). *Emerging markets for outdoor recreation in the United States: A report to the Sporting Goods Manufacturers Association and the Outdoor Products Council*. Athens, GA: USDA Forest Service.

Cordell, H. K. (1999). Outdoor recreation participation trends. In H. K. Cordell (Ed.), *Recreation in American life: A national assessment of demand and supply trends* (pp. 219–321) Champaign, IL: Sagamore.

Cordes, K. (2001). *America's national scenic trails*. Norman: University of Oklahoma Press.

Coyle, K. (2005). *Environmental literacy in America*. Washington, DC: The Environmental Education and Training Foundation.

Daerr, E. (2001). Regional report. *National Parks, 75*(9-10),16.

Defenders of Wildlife. (2014). Arctic National Wildlife Refuge. Retrieved from https://www.defenders.org/arctic-national-wildlife-refuge

The dirty seas. (1988, August 1). *Time, 132*(5), 44–50.

Dunphy, H. (2001, January 14). Environment group warns of worldwide ecological decline. *The San Diego Union-Tribune*, p. 25.

Endangered Species Act of 1973, 16 U.S.C. § 1531.

Environmental Protection Agency. (1996). *Guide to environmental issues* (EPA-520/B-94-001 9/1996). Washington, DC: Author.

Environmental Protection Agency. (1998, December). Highlights. Washington, DC: EPA Office of Air & Radiation.

Environmental Protection Agency. (1999, January). *Key findings of America's environmental knowledge, attitudes, and behaviors* (EPA-171-F-98-019). Washington, DC: Author.

Environmental Protection Agency. (2001a). About estuaries. Retrieved from http://www.epa.gov/OWOW/estuaries/about1.htm

Environmental Protection Agency. (2001b). America's wetlands. Retrieved from http://www.epa.gov/OWOW/wetlands/vital/people.html

Environmental Protection Agency. (2012a). Basic information. Retrieved from http://www.epa.gov/visibility/what.html

Environmental Protection Agency. (2012b). Effect of acid rain – Surface waters and aquatic animals. Retrieved from http://www.epa.gov/acidrain/effects/surface_water.html

Environmental Protection Agency. (2012c). *Liquid assets 2000: America's water resources at a turning point*. Retrieved from http://water.epa.gov/lawsregs/lawsguidance/cwa/economics/liquidassets/business.cfm

Environmental Protection Agency. (2012d). Wetlands and people. Retrieved from http://water.epa.gov/type/wetlands/people.cfm

Environmental Protection Agency. (2012e). What is acid rain? Retrieved from http://www.epa.gov/acidrain/what/index.html

Environmental Protection Agency. (2014a). Frequent questions. Retrieved from http://www.epa.gov/epawaste/conserve/materials/paper/faqs.htm

Environmental Protection Agency. (2014b). Future climate change. Retrieved from http://www.epa.gov/climatechange/science/future.html

Environmental Protection Agency. (2014c). Protecting the marine environment. Retrieved from http://www2.epa.gov/international-cooperation/protecting-marine-environment

Evergreen Project. (1998). What is a watershed? Retrieved from http://mbgnet.mobot.org/fresh/index.htm

Fair, P., & Becker, P. (2000). Review of stress in marine mammals. *Journal of Aquatic Eco-System Stress and Recovery, 7*, 335–354.

Folger, T. (September 2013). Rising seas. *National Geographic, 224*(3), 30–43.

Foreman, D. (1995). The new conservation movement. In G. Sessions (Ed.), *Deep ecology for the 21st century* (pp. 50–56). Boston, MA: Shambhala Publications.

Forests Forever. (1990). *California forest facts*. Ukiah, CA: Author.

Gelbspan, R. (2001). A modest proposal to stop global warming. *Sierra, 86*(3). Retrieved from http://vault.sierraclub.org/sierra/200105/globalwarm.asp

Georgia Pacific Corporation. (1990). *A natural Partnership: Georgia Pacific and the environment*. Atlanta,GA: Author.

Harrison, D. (2006, June 6). It's no day at the beach. *Parade*.

Hayes, D. (2000). Earth Day. Retrieved from http//www.pollutionissues.com-Ea/Earth-Day.html

Hogan, D. (1999, January 3). Endangered Species Act at 25. *The San Diego Union-Tribune*, p. G-5.

Hoofnagle, S. (2001). America's grasslands. *Habitats, 4*(3), 1.

Hymon, S. (2001). Bringing up coral. *National Parks, 75*(9-10), 19–22.

International Dark-Sky Association. (2014). Light pollution and energy. Retrieved from http//www.darksky.org/education/311

Jameson, S. C., Erdmann, M. V., Karr, J. R., Gibson, G. R., Jr., & Potts, K. W. (2000). *Charting a course toward diagnostic monitoring: A continuing review of coral reef attributes and a research strategy for creating coral reef indexes of biotic integrity.* The Plains, VA: Coral Seas.

Jeffery, D. (1989, February). Yellowstone: The great fires of 1988. *National Geographic, 175,* 2.

Johnson, C. (2000, February 13). Disappearing forest. *North County Times,* pp. G-1, G-2.

Joyce, L. A., Running, S. W., Breshears, D. D., Dale, V. H., Malmsheimer, R. W., Sampson, R. N., . . . Woodall, C. W. (2014). Forests. In J. M. Melillo, T. Richmond, & G. W. Yohe (Eds.), *Climate change impact in the United States* (pp. 175–194). Retrieved from http://nca2014.globalchange.gov/downloads

Kelly, S., & Vergano, D. (2006, May 30). How the greenhouse effect works. *USA Today,* p. 5-D.

Kirkwood, S. (2006a). Lost at sea. *National Parks, 80*(2), 70–71.

Kirkwood, S. (2006b). Star struck. *National Parks, 80*(3), 8–10.

Kormondy, E. (1984). *Concepts of ecology.* Englewood Cliffs, NJ: Prentice Hall.

Lafee, S. (2001, May). True Lagoon. *San Diego Union-Tribune,* p. F1.

Lance, V. (2001). Disease in desert tortoises: Is it affecting long-term survival? *ZooNooz, 74*(9), 8–9.

Larkin, P. (Ed.). (1999). *Sustainable seas expeditions.* Santa Barbara, CA: National Oceanic and Atmospheric Administration.

Lazell, J., Jr. (1989). Wildlife. *National Parks, 65,* 9–10.

Lee, M. (2006, September 21). Warming. *San Diego Union-Tribune,* pp. E1, E8.

Leinbach, A. (2005, Spring). Sanctuary in the sea. *National Parks, 79*(2), 22.

Lemonick, M. (2006, February). Has the meltdown begun? *Time, 167*(9), 58–59.

Liberman, B. (2003, July 17). Weather cycle studied by Scrhipps. *San Diego Union-Tribune,* p. B1–4.

Liberman, B. (2006a, September 14). Acid test. *San Diego Union-Tribune,* p. E1, E8.

Liberman, B. (2006b, October 5). Amazon reforestation. *San Diego Union-Tribune,* p. E3.

Liberman, B. (2006c, October 15). Wetlands Conservation Act renewed for six more years. *San Diego Union-Tribune,* p. C13.

Liberman, B. (2006d, October 20). Fish population at risk, study warns. *San Diego Union-Tribune,* p. B2.

Loomis, J., Bonetti, K., & Echohawk, C. (1999). Demand for and supply of wilderness. In H. K. Cordell (Ed.), *Outdoor recreation in American life: A national assessment of demand and supply trends* (pp. 351–376). Champaign, IL: Sagamore.

Lord, N. (1998). Our only ocean. *Sierra, 83*(4), 35–39.

Louv, R. (2008). *Last child in the woods: Saving our children from nature-deficit disorder.* Chapel Hill, NC: Algonquin Books.

Mark Clements Research. (1996, September). Readers poll: Travel and the environment. *Conde Nast Traveler, 1996,* 22.

Marquis, A. (2006). A sound resolution. *National Parks, 80*(2), 14–16.

Mathews, A. (2001). The 2001 Conference on the Environment: Practicing what we preach. *People, Land, and Water, 8*(3),8.

Melillo, J. M., Richmond, T., & Yohe, G. W. (Eds.). (2014). *Climate change impact in the United States: The third national climate assessment.* Retrieved from http://nca2014.globalchange.gov/downloads

Miller, K. (2000, August). A call for review of large dams. *River Monitor, 1*(4), 3.

Montaigne, F. (2001). A river dammed. *National Geographic, 199*(4), 1–33.

National Audubon Society. (1997). Whither the spotted owl. *Audubon, 99*(2), 18–19.

National Center for Atmospheric Research and University Corporation for Atmospheric Research. (2014a). How much carbon dioxide (and other kinds of greenhouse gas) is already in the atmosphere? Retrieved from https://www2.ucar.edu/news/how-much-carbon-dioxide-and-other-kinds-greenhouse-gas-already-atmosphere

National Center for Atmospheric Research and University Corporation for Atmospheric Research. (2014b). How much has the global temperature risen in the last 100 years? Retrieved from https://www2.ucar.edu/news/how-much-has-global-temperature-risen-last-100-years

National Geographic Society. (2005). *Ocean literacy* [Pamphlet]. Washington, DC: Author.

National Oceanic and Atmospheric Administration. (2006). No-take zones. Retrieved from http://www.csc.noaa.gov/magazine/2002/06/flkeys.html

National Park Service. (2003). Different places, different strategies. *Prescribed Fire in Pacific West Parks, 2003*, 5.

National Park Service. (2007). *National lightscopes*. Washington, DC: Author.

National Park Service. (2012). Enhance your nighttime experience. Retrieved from http://www.nature.nps.gov/night/enhance.cfm

National Parks and Conservation Association. (2000). Los Alamos causes fire policy change. *National Parks, 74*(9-10), 13.

National Parks and Conservation Association. (2001). Energy and environment. *National Parks, 75*(9-10), 12.

National Wildlife Federation. (2014). Mississippi River delta. Retrieved from http://nwf.org/Wildlife/Wild-Places/Mississippi-River-Delta.aspx

The Nature Conservancy. (1999). Pathways of invasion. *Nature Conservancy, 49*(4).

Norton, B. (1987). *Why preserve natural variety?* Princeton, NJ: Princeton University Press.

O'Connell, K. (2004). *National Parks, 78*(3), 24.

Papciak, M. (2001). Endless bummer. *Sierra, 86*(3), 82–83.

Parris, A., Bromirski, P., Burkett, V., Cayan, D., Culver, M., Hall, J. . . . Weiss, J. (2012). *Global sea level rise scenarios for the United States national climate assessment* (NOAA Tech Memo OAR CPO-1). Silver Spring, MD: National Oceanic and Atmospheric Administration.

PBS Newshour. (2014, January 30). Mysterious epidemic devastates starfish population off the Pacific Coast. Retrieved from http://www.pbs.org/newshour/bb/mysterious-epidemic-devastates-starfish-population-pacific-coast/

PEW Center. (2006, February 8). *First comprehensive approach to climate change.* Arlington, VA: PEW Center on Global Climate Change.

Pocha, J. (2006, September 28). China's growing deserts having impact around the globe. *San Diego Union-Tribune*, p. E8.

Pope, C. (2001). The new conquerors. *Sierra, 86*(4), 16–17.

Protect one hundred million acres. (2006). *Sierra, 91*(6), 56.

Reiter, D., Blahna, D., & Von Koch, R. (1997). *Off-highway vehicle four-wheeler survey of 1997 Moab Easter Jeep Safari participants.* Logan, UT: Institute for Outdoor Recreation and Tourism.

Revkin, A. (2004, March 28). Climate debate gets its icon: Mountain Kilimanjaro. *North County Times*, G-1.

Revkin, A. (2006, June 1). Arctic ocean used to be toasty. *San Diego Union-Tribune*, p. A-3.

Rogers, T. (2006a, September 3). Trashing the beach. *San Diego Union-Tribune*, p. O6.

Rogers, T. (2006b, September 17). Troubled waters. *San Diego Union-Tribune*, p. A22.

Romm, J. (2011, May 9). Pew: 71% of Americans say this country should do whatever it takes to protect the environment. Retrieved from http://thinkprogress.org/climate/2011/05/09/208054/pew-poll-protect-the-environment/

Romm, J. (2012). Poll: 75 percent of Americans support regulating CO2 as a pollutant, 60 percent support revenue-neutral carbon tax. Retrieved from http://thinkprogress.org/climate/2012/04/26/471840/poll-75-americans-support/

Romme, W., & Despain, D. (1989, November). The Yellowstone fires. *Scientific American, 261*, 5.

Roper Starch. (2000). *Outdoor recreation in America 2000: Addressing key societal concerns.* Washington, DC: Author.

Save the Redwoods League. (2014). Coast redwoods. Retrieved from http://www.savetheredwoods.org/redwoods/coast-redwoods/

Sawicki, E. (2014, August 22). California State Parks shuts down Malibu's Rindge Dam. *The Malibu Times.* Retrieved from http://www.malibutimes.com/news/article_ac40b16e-2899-11e4-8c79-0019bb2963f4.html

Sessions, G. (Ed.). (1995). *Deep ecology for the 21st century.* Boston, MA: Shambhala Publications.

Sierra Club. (2001). Strange bedfellows or natural allies? *Sierra, 86*(4), 60–61.

Slack, G. (1998, Winter). Dammed if we don't. *Headwaters, 1998,* 6–7.

Slater, D. (2001). Moments of truth. *Sierra, 86*(4), 48–57.

Thomas, M. (2004, October 8). Follow the way of the salmon. *Idaho Mountain Express,* p. A1.

Tread Lightly! (2015). *Dirt biking: Tread Lightly!'s responsible recreation tips* [Brochure]. Retrieved from http://www.treadlightly.org/wp-content/uploads/2015/03/dirtbike_tips_sm.pdf

United Nations Environmental Programme. (2010, June 5). The state of the planet's biodiversity. Retrieved from http://www.unep.org/wed/2010/english/biodiversity.asp

U.S. Department of Agriculture. (2005, February). Fire fuels USDA Forest Service Southwest District. Washington, DC: Author.

U.S. Fish and Wildlife Service. (1998a). Endangered species general information. Retrieved from http://www.fws.gov

U.S. Fish and Wildlife Service. (1998b). Myths and realities of the Endangered Species Act. Retrieved from http://www.fws.gov/r9endspplendspp.html

U.S. Fish and Wildlife Service. (2001). ESA basics. Retrieved from http://www.fws.gov/endangered/esa-library/pdf/ESA_basics.pdf

U.S. Fish and Wildlife Service. (2005). *Why save endangered species?* Arlington, VA: Author.

U.S. Fish and Wildlife Service. (2006, February 11). Threatened and endangered species system. Retrieved from http://eco.fws.gov/tess_public/boxscore.do

U.S. Fish and Wildlife Service. (2014, October 24). Summary of listed species: Listed populations and plans. Retrieved from http://www.fws.gov/ecos/ajax/tess_public/pub/boxScore.jsp

U.S. Fish & Wildlife Service. (2015, April 3). *USFWS 2015 comprehensive plan and final environmental impact statement.* Retrieved from http://www.fws.gov/home/arctic-ccp/

U.S. Forest Service. (1998). *Rx fire!* Washington, DC: Author.

U.S. Forest Service. (2000). *America's forests: 1999 health update.* Washington, DC: Author.

U.S. Geological Survey. (1996). *Deserts: Geology and resources.* Washington, DC: Author.

U.S. Geological Survey. (2014). The world's water. Retrieved from http://water.usgs.gov/edu/earthwherewater.html

Vanishing California. (1989, December). *California Magazine, 1989,* 105.

Walsh, J., Wuebbles, D., Hayhoe, K., Kossin, J., Kunkel, K., Stephens, G. . . . Somerville, R. (2014). Our changing climate. In J. M. Melillo, Terese (T.C.) Richmond, & G. W. Yohe (Eds.), *Climate change impacts in the United States: The third national climate assessment* (pp. 19–67). Washington, DC: U.S. Global Change Research Program. doi:10.7930/J0KW5CXT

Warren, J. (1990, November 25.). Bikers kick up dust over canceled desert run. *Los Angeles Times,* p. A3.

Watson, T. (1999, June 8). Wetlands preservation plan draws a groundswell of support, Critics. *USA Today,* p. 12A.

Watson, T., & Weisman, J. (2001, July 16). Six ways to combat global warming. *USA Today,* pp. 1A–2A.

Weise, E. (2006, May 30). Alaska the "poster state" for climate concerns. *USA Today,* p. 4A.

Weiss, D. (2005). Environmental movement. Retrieved from http://www.ectotopia.org/ehof/timeline.html.

Williams, B. (2006, September 3). Volunteers comb coast. *San Diego Union-Tribune,* p. B1.

Williams, D., & Jacobs, G. (1986). Off-site resource development conflicts. in The President's Commission on Americans Outdoors, *A literature review* (p. M20). Washington, DC: U.S. Government Printing Office.

Williams, G. (2000). *The USDA Forest Service: The first century.* Washington, DC: Author.

Williams, T. (1990, March). Clearcutting spoils rivers, destroys fisheries. *Forest Voice, 2,*1.

Worldwatch Institute. (2013, May 21). Getting to one-planet living. Retrieved from http://www.worldwatch.org/getting-one-planet-living

*Youtz, G. (1987). *If we sell you our land.* Tacoma, WA: Pacific Lutheran University.

Yuskavitch, J. (2001, March/April). Bye bye birdie? *Forest Magazine, 2001,* 41–45.

Note: According to Gregory Youtz (*If We Sell You Our Land,* Tacoma, WA: Pacific Lutheran University, 1987), Chief Seattle is also referred to as Chief Sealth of the Puget Sound area. Dr. Henry Smith published his version of the speech in the *Seattle Sunday Star* in 1877, 30 years after it was made. Smith reported that the speech was given to Governor Isaac Stevens at the beginning of treaty negotiations. It is unclear exactly who took notes at the speech, but it is possible that Seattle's native tongue, Lushootseed, had to be translated into Chinook, and then into English. Smith may have reconstructed the speech over 30 years after the fact from his notes or Stevens' notes. Thus, the exact words may have been lost (Youtz, 1987, pp. 1–3).

Epilogue

Climb the mountains and get their good tidings. Nature's peace will flow into you as sunshine flows into trees. The winds will blow their own freshness into you, and the storms their energy, while cares will drop off like autumn leaves.
~ John Muir

Nature provided us with plants and wildlife, which became the source for our primary need for protection and survival. A new picture emerged and contemporary psychology showed us that there is more to life than mere survival and safety. For instance, belonging is an important human need, so is the need for expression. Outdoor pursuits encourage a sense of belonging and creative expression in the natural world. This volume begins with a description of the relationship between outdoor pursuits and human needs along with the work of those who helped us understand the importance of that relationship.

It is important to remember that the earth's natural resources are not limitless, even if some of these resources are renewable. Many of the earth's resources have been exhausted in our quest for survival and safety. The additional quest for outdoor pursuits also causes impacts. Mindful human–nature interaction can be achieved through the wise management of outdoor recreation resources as well as through formal and informal education. Only then will the future of outdoor recreation be protected.

Appendix A

State Agencies Involved in Outdoor Recreation

State	Agencies With Principal Responsibilities in Outdoor Recreation	Agencies With Limited Responsibilities in Outdoor Recreation
Alabama	Department of Conservation Division of Water Safety Division of State Parks, Monuments, and Historical Sites Division of Game and Fish Division of Seafoods Division of Outdoor Recreation	Mound State Monument Department of Highways
Alaska	Department of Natural Resources	
Arizona	Game and Fish Commission State Parks Board Outdoor Recreation Coordinating Commission	Highway Commission Economic Planning Development Board
Arkansas	State Planning Commission Game and Fish Commission Parks, Recreation, and Travel Commission	Ozarks Regional Commission (joint federal–state agency) Geological Commission Forestry Commission Industrial Development Commission State Highway Department
California	Resources Agency Department of Parks and Recreation Division of Beaches and Parks Division of Recreation Division of Small Craft Harbors Department of Conservation Division of Forestry Department of Fish and Game Department of Water Resources	Department of Public Works Bureau of Health Education, Physical Education, and Recreation State Lands Commission Water Pollution Control Department of Health

State	Agencies With Principal Responsibilities in Outdoor Recreation	Agencies With Limited Responsibilities in Outdoor Recreation
Colorado	Department of Natural Resources Division of Game, Fish, and Parks	State Historical Society Department of Highways State Board of Land Commissioners
Connecticut	Park and Forest Commission Board of Fisheries and Game	State Highway Department State Department of Health Water Resources Commission State Development Commission
Delaware	Board of Game and Fish Commissioners State Park Commission	State Archives Commission State Forestry Department State Highway Department State Developmental Department State Board of Health Water and Air Resources Commission Soil and Water Conservation Commission
Florida	Outdoor Recreational Development Council Board of Parks and Historical Memorials Game and Fresh Water Fish Commission	Board of Forestry Board of Conservation State Road Department Development Commission Trustees of the Internal Improvement Fund Board of Archives and History
Georgia	Department of State Parks State Game and Fish Commission Jekyll Island State Park Authority	Stone Mountain Memorial Association State Highway Department Lake Lanier Islands Development Authority North Georgia Mountains Commission

Hawaii	Department of Land and Natural Resources
	   State Parks Division
	   Fish and Game Division
	   Forestry Division
		Marinas and Small Boat Harbors

Idaho	State Park Board Fish and Game Commission	State Forestry Department Department of Highways Department of Aeronautics State Department of Commerce and Development State Historical Society State Land Department

Illinois	Department of Conservation
	   Division of Parks and Memorials
	   Division of Game
	   Division of Fisheries
	   Division of Forestry
		Department of Public Works and Buildings
		Department of Registration and Education
		Department of Public Health
		Illinois State Youth Commission
		Department of Business and Economic
		   Development

State	Agencies With Principal Responsibilities in Outdoor Recreation	Agencies With Limited Responsibilities in Outdoor Recreation
Indiana	Department of Natural Resources Division of Fish and Game Division of Forestry Division of State Parks Division of Reservoir Management	State Highway Department Department of Recreation Great Lakes Park Training Institute State Health Department State Commission on Aging and the Aged and the Governor's Youth Council Wabash Valley Commission Department of Commerce and Public Relations Indiana Flood Control-Water Resources Commission Governor's Advisory Committee on Recreation
Iowa	State Conservation Commission Division of Administration Division of Fish and Game Division of Land and Waters	State Soil Conservation Committee Iowa Development Commission State Highway Commission Office of Planning and Programming
Kansas	State Park and Resources Authority Forestry, Fish, and Game Commission Joint Council on Recreation	State Highway Commission State Recreation Commission State Historical Society Department of Economic Development Water Resources Board
Kentucky	Department of Conservation Division of Forestry Division of Soil and Water Resources Division of Strip Mining and Reclamation Flood Control and Water Usage Board Department of Fish and Wildlife Resources	Department of Public Safety Department of Public Information Kentucky Highway Department State Historical Society
Louisiana	State Parks and Recreation Commission Wildlife and Fisheries Commission	Department of Highways Department of Public Works Department of Commerce and Industries State Land Office Louisiana Tourist Development Commission
Maine	Department of Inland Fisheries and Game State Park Commission Baxter State Park Authority Maine Forest Service	Atlantic Sea Run Salmon Commission Department of Sea and Shore Fisheries Water Improvement Commission Department of Economic Development State Highway Commission Department of Health and Welfare
Maryland	Board of Natural Resources Department of Forests and Parks Department of Game and Inland Fish Department of Tidewater Fisheries Department of Research and Education	Department of Geology, Mines, and Water Resources Water Pollution Control Commission State Roads Commission Department of Economic Development

State	Agencies With Principal Responsibilities in Outdoor Recreation	Agencies With Limited Responsibilities in Outdoor Recreation

Massachusetts	Department of Natural Resources
	    Division of Fisheries
	    Division of Water Resources
	    Division of Forests and Parks
	    Division of Marine Fisheries
	    Division of Law Enforcement
	Metropolitan District Commission
	    Parks Engineering Division
	Department of Public Works
		Department of Public Health
		Department of Commerce
		Department of Correction
		Youth Service Board

Michigan	Department of Natural Resources
	    Office of Administration
	    Field Administration Division
	    Fish and Fisheries Division
	    Forestry Division
	    Game Division
	    Geological Survey Division
	    Lands Division
	    Parks and Recreation Division
	State Waterways Commission
	Huron-Clinton Metropolitan Authority
	Mackinac Island State Park Commission
		Michigan Tourist Council
		State Highway Department
		Department of Health
		Department of Social Welfare
		Michigan Water Resources Commission
		Department of Public Instruction

Minnesota	Department of Conservation
	    Division of Forestry
	    Division of Game and Fish
	    Division of Parks and Recreation
	    Division of Enforcement and Field Service
		Department of Highways
		Historical Society
		Iron Range Resources and Rehabilitation
		    Commission
		Pollution Control Agency
		State Planning Agency
		Minnesota Resources Commission
		Minnesota–Wisconsin Boundary Area
		    Commission
		Department of Economic Development

Mississippi	Mississippi Game and Fish Commission State Park Commission	Highway Department State Board of Health Mississippi Forestry Commission Pearl River Valley Water Supply District Water Resources Board Yellow Creek Watershed Authority Pearl River Industrial Commission
Missouri	State Conservation Commission State Park Board	State Highway Commission Division of Commerce and Industrial Development Bi-State Development Agency

State	Agencies With Principal Responsibilities in Outdoor Recreation	Agencies With Limited Responsibilities in Outdoor Recreation
Montana	State Fish and Game Commission State Highway Commission Park Division	Board of Land Commissioners Office of State Forester State Highway Department Board of Health State Historical Society State Water Conservation Board
Nebraska	Game and Parks Commission	Department of Health Department of Roads State Historical Society
Nevada	Department of Conservation and Natural Resources Fish and Game Commission	Department of Economic Development Department of Highways State Museum Division of Forestry

New Hampshire	Department of Resources and Economic
	    Development
	    Division of Parks
	Fish and Game Department
	State Advisory Commission
		Natural Resources Council
		Water Resources Board
		Water Pollution Commission
		State Historical Commission
		Department of Public Works and Highways

New Jersey	Department of Conservation and
	    Economic Development
	        Division of Fish and Game
	        Division of Resource Development
	        Division of Water Policy and Supply
	        Division of State and Regional Planning
		State Department of Health
		Department of Highways

New Mexico	Department of Game and Fish State Park and Recreation Commission State Planning Office	State Highway Department Department of Development Department of Public Health and Welfare Museum of New Mexico Department of Education

New York	Department of Conservation
	    Division of Lands and Forests
	    Division of Parks
	    Division of Saratoga Springs Reservation
	    New York State Historic Trust
	    Division of Fish and Game
	    Division of Water Resources
	    Division of Motor Boats
	    Division of Conservation Education
	    Lake George Park Commission
	    Water Resources Commission
		Department of Health
		Department of Public Works
		Department of Education

State	Agencies With Principal Responsibilities in Outdoor Recreation	Agencies With Limited Responsibilities in Outdoor Recreation

North Carolina	State Recreation Commission
	Department of Conservation and Development
	    State Parks Division
	    Travel and Promotion Division
	Wildlife Resources Commission
	Department of Archives and History
	    Historical Sites Division
	State Planning Task Force on Recreation
		Kerr Reservoir Development Commission
		State Highway Commission
		Department of Water and Air Resources
		Coastal Plains Regional Commission
		Appalachian Regional Commission
		Department of Conservation and Development
		    Community Planning Division
		    Forestry Division
		Seashore Commission
		State Board of Health

North Dakota	State Outdoor Recreation Agency State Park Service State Game and Fish Department	State Water Commission State Health Department State Historical Society State Soil Conservation Committee State Highway Department State Travel Department Economic Development Commission

Ohio	Department of Natural Resources
	    Division of Parks and Recreation
	    Division of Wildlife
	    Division of Watercraft
	    Division of Forestry and Reclamation
		Department of Highways
		Department of Industrial and Economic
		    Development
		Department of Health
		Department of Correction
		Department of Public Works
		Historical Society
		Muskingum Conservancy District

Oklahoma	Oklahoma Planning and Resources Board Wildlife Conservation Commission	State Highway Department Grand River Dam Authority
Oregon	State Highway Commission State Parks and Recreation Division State Game Commission State Committee on Natural Resources State Fish Commission State Department of Forestry	Department of Geology and Mineral Industries State Water Resources Board State Marine Board State Engineer Sanitary Authority Columbia River Gorge Commission
Pennsylvania	Department of Forests and Water Water and Power Resources Board State Fish Commission State Game Commission	Department of Commerce Department of Health Department of Internal Affairs Military Reservation Commission Department of Highways Historical and Museum Commission

Rhode Island	Department of Natural Resources
	    Division of Parks and Recreation
	    Division of Forestry
	    Division of Fish and Game
	    Division of Harbors and Rivers
		Department of Health
		State Developmental Council

State	Agencies With Principal Responsibilities in Outdoor Recreation	Agencies With Limited Responsibilities in Outdoor Recreation
South Carolina	Wildlife Resources Department Forestry Commission Department of Parks, Recreation, and Tourism	Highway Department State Board of Health Water Pollution Control Authority State Development Board State Budget and Control Board Public Service Authority

South Dakota	Department of Game, Fish, and Parks
	    Game Division
	    Fisheries Division
	    Parks Division
	    Custer State Park
		Commissioner of School and Public Lands
		Department of Highways
		Department of History
		Water Resources Commission
		State Planning Commission

Tennessee	Department of Conservation
	    Division of Parks
	    Division of Information and Tourist Promotion
	Game Commission
	Fish Commission
		State Planning Commission
		Department of Highways

Texas	State Parks and Wildlife	The Daughters of the Republic of Texas Battleship Texas Commission State Highway Department

Utah	Department of Natural Resources
	    Division of Parks and Recreation
	    Division of Fish and Game
	    Outdoor Recreation Assistance Agency
		State Road Commission
		Tourist and Publicity Council
		Utah National Guard
		State Land Division

Vermont	Department of Forests and Parks Fish and Game Department Natural Resources Interagency Committee State Recreation Commission	Department of Highways State Health Department Water Conservation Board State Development Corporation

Virginia	Department of Conservation and Economic
	    Development
	        Division of Forestry
	        Division of Parks
	Commission of Game and Inland Fisheries
	Commission of Outdoor Recreation
	Interagency Committee on Recreation
		Department of Highways
		Breaks Interstate Park Commission
		Water Control Board
		Department of Health
		Commission of Fisheries
		Agencies Administering Historic Sites
		Historic Landmark Commission

Washington	Department of Natural Resources State Parks and Recreation Commission Department of Game Interagency Committee for Outdoor Recreation Department of Fisheries	Highway Department Department of Health Pollution Control Commission Department of Commerce and Economic Development Department of Water Resources

State	Agencies With Principal Responsibilities in Outdoor Recreation	Agencies With Limited Responsibilities in Outdoor Recreation

West Virginia	Department of Natural Resources
	   Division of Game and Fish
	   Division of Forestry
	   Division of Parks and Recreation
	   Division of Water Resources
	   Division of Reclamation
	Public Lands Corporation
		State Road Commission
		Department of Commerce
		Office of Federal–State Relations

Wyoming	Department of State Parks and Cultural Resources Wyoming Game and Fish Department Wyoming Wildlife and Natural Resources Trust	Department of Environmental Quality Department of Family Services Wyoming Retirement System

Appendix B

Organizations Involved in Outdoor Recreation

Access Fund
PO Box 17010
Boulder, CO 80308
www.accessfund.org

Adirondack Mountain Club
814 Goggins Road
Lake George, NY 12845
www.adk.org

America Outdoors Association
PO Box 10847
Knoxville, TN 37939
www.americaoutdoors.org

American Alpine Club
710 10th Street
Suite 100
Golden, CO 80401
www.americanalpineclub.org

American Blind Skiing Foundation
610 South William Street
Mount Prospect, IL 60056
www.absf.org

American Camping Association
Bradford Woods
Martinsville, IN 46151
www.acacamps.org

American Canoe Association
7432 Alban Station Boulevard
Suite B-232
Springfield, VA 22150
www.americancanoe.org

The American Canyoneering Academy
2625 South Plaza Drive
Suite 400
Tempe, AZ 85282
www.canyoneering.net

American Casting Association
1773 Lance End Lane
Fenton, MO 63026
www.americancastingassoc.org

American Cross Country Skiers
PO Box 604
Bend, OR 97709
www.xcskiworld.com

American Forests
PO Box 2000
Washington, DC 20013
www.americanforests.org

American Hiking Society
1422 Fenwick Lane
Silver Spring, MD 20910
www.americanhiking.org

American Sportfishing Association
1033 North Fairfax Street #200
Alexandria, VA 22314
www.asafishing.org

American Trails
PO Box 491797
Redding, CA 96049
www.americantrails.org

American Whitewater
1430 Fenwick Lane
Silver Spring, MD 20910
www.americanwhitewater.org

Association for Challenge Course Technology
PO Box 970
Purcellville, VA 20134
www.acctinfo.org

Association for Experiential Education
2305 Canyon Boulevard
Suite 100
Boulder, CO 80302
www.aee.org

Association of Outdoor Recreation and Education
PO Box 1829
Boulder, CO 80306
www.aore.org

Blue Water Sportfishing Association
PO Box 611997
Port Huron, MI 48061
www.bluewatersportfishing.net

Boy Scouts of America
PO Box 152079
Irving, TX 75015
www.scouting.org

Botanical Society of America
Missouri Botanical Garden
Saint Louis, MO 63166
www.botany.org

Canadian Parks and Recreation Association
216-1600 James Naismith Drive
Gloucester, ON K1B 5N4
www.cpra.ca

Christian Camping International
PO Box 62189
Colorado Springs, CO 60189
http://cciworldwide.org/

Coalition for Education in the Outdoors
PO Box 2000
Cortland, NY 13045
www.cortland.edu

Ducks Unlimited
One Waterfowl Way
Memphis, TN
www.ducks.org

Family Campers and RVers
74 West Genessee Street
Skanteles, NY 13152
www.fcrv.org

Foundation for Jewish Camp
253 West 35th Street, 4th Fl
New York, NY 10001
www.jewishcamp.org

Greater Yellowstone Coalition
PO Box 1874
Bozeman, MT 59715
www.greateryellowstone.org

Handicapped Scuba Association
1104 El Prado
San Clemente, CA 92672
www.hsascuba.com

International Game Fish Association
300 Gulf Stream Way
Dania Beach, FL
www.igfa.org

International Hunter Education Association
800 East 73rd Avenue, Unit 2
Denver, CO 80229

www.ihea.com

International Hunting Land Association
PO Box 416
Johnstown, PA 15907
www.ihea.com

International Mountain Bicycling Association
PO Box 7578
Boulder, CO 80306
www.imba.com

International Windsurfing Association
Mengham Cottage
Mengham Lane
Hayling Island
Hampshire
PO11 9JX
United Kingdom
www.internationalwindsurfing.com

The Izaak Walton League of America
IWLA Conservation Center
707 Conservation Lane
Gaithersburg, MD 20807
www.iwla.org

Girl Scouts of the USA
830 Third Avenue and 51st Street
New York, NY 10022
www.gsusa.org

Leave No Trace
PO Box 997
Boulder, CO 80306
www.lnt.org

National Association of Competitive

Mounted Orienteering
503 171st Avenue SE
Tenino, WA 98589
www.nacmo.org

National Association of Conservation Districts
509 Capitol Court NE
Washington, DC 20002
www.nacdnet.org

National Association of State Foresters
444 North Capitol Street NW
Suite 540
Washington, DC 2001
www.stateforesters.org

National Association of State Outdoor Recreation
Liaison Officers
NASORLO, 105 H, ABNR Building
University of Missouri
Columbia, MO 65211
www.nasorlo.org

National Association of State Park Directors
9894 East Holden Place
Tucson, AZ 85748
www.NASPD.org

National Association of Therapeutic
Wilderness Camps
4270 Hambrick Way
Stone Mountain, GA 30083
www.natwc.org

National Association of Underwater Instructors
NAUI Worldwide Headquarters
9030 Camden Field Parkway
Riverview, FL 33578
www.naui.org

National Audubon Society
950 Third Avenue
New York, NY 10003
www.audubon.org

National Camp Association
610 5th Avenue
PO Box 5371
New York, NY 10185
www.summercamp.org

National Center for Therapeutic Riding
PO Box 434
Burtonsville, MD 20866
www.nchpad.org

National Organization for Rivers
212 West Cheyenne Mountain Boulevard
Colorado Springs, CO 80906
www.nationalrivers.org

National Outdoor Leadership School
288 West Main Street
Lander, WY 82520
www.nols.edu

National Park Foundation
1101 17th Street NW
Suite 1102
Washington, DC 20036
www.nationalparks.org

National Parks Conservation Association
1300 19th Street NW
Washington, DC 20036
www.npca.org

National Recreation and Park Association
22377 Belmont Ridge Road
Ashburn, VA 20148
www.nrpa.org

National Society for Experiential Education
1703 North Beauregard Street
Suite 400
Alexandria, VA 22311
www.nsee.org

National Speleological Society
2813 Cave Avenue
Huntsville, AL
www.caves.org

National Trust for Historic Preservation
1785 Massachusetts Avenue NW
Washington, DC 20036
www.nationaltrust.org

National Wildlife Federation
1400 10th Street NW
Washington, DC 20036
www.nwf.org

National Wildlife Refuge Association
1010 Wisconsin Avenue NW
Suite 200
Washington, DC 20007
refugeassociation.org

Natural Areas Association
PO Box 1504
Bend, OR 97709
naturalareas.org

The Nature Conservancy
4245 Fairfax Drive
Suite 100
Arlington, VA 22203
www.nature.org

North American Association for
Environmental Education
1825 Connecticut Avenue NW
Washington, DC 20009
www.naaee.org

North American Gamebird Association
1214 Brooks Avenue
Raleigh, NC 27607
www.mynaga.org

North American Telemark Organization
PO Box 44
Waitsfield, VT 05673
www.telemarknato.com

Orienteering USA
PO Box 1444
Forest Park, GA 30051
www.us.orienteering.org

Outdoor Industry Association
PO Box 1319
Boulder, CO 80304
outdoorindustry.org

Outdoor Writers Association of America
27 Fort Missoula Road
Suite 1
Missoula, MT 59804
www.owaa.org

Outward Bound
100 Mystery Point Road
Garrison, NY 10524
www.outwardbound.org

PATH International
PO Box 33150
Denver, CO 80233
www.pathintl.org

Professional Association of Diving Instructors
30151 Thomas
Rancho Santa Margarita, CA 92688
www.padi.com

Rails-to-Trails Conservancy
1100 17th Street NW
10th Floor
Washington, DC 20037
www.railstotrails.org

SHAPE America
1900 Association Drive
Reston, VA 20191
www.shapeamerica.org

Sierra Club
85 2nd Street, 2nd Floor
San Francisco, CA 94105
www.sierraclub.org

Society of American Foresters
5400 Governor Lane
Bethesda, MD 20814
www.safnet.org

Sportsmen for Fish and Wildlife
PO Box 95970
South Jordon, UT 84095
sfw.net

The Student Conservation Association
PO Box 550
Charlestown, NH 03603
www.thesca.org

Trout Unlimited
1500 Wilson Boulevard
Suite 310
Arlington, VA
www.tu.org

Underwater Society of America
1701 Lake Avenue
Glenview, IL 60025
underwater-society.org

United States Canoe Association
606 Ross Street
Middletown, OH 45055
www.uscanoe.com

United States Equestrian Federation
4047 Iron Works Parkway
Lexington, KY 40511
www.equestrian.org

United States Hang Gliding
and Paragliding Association
PO Box 1330
Colorado Springs, CO 80901
www.ushga.org

United States Parachute Association
1440 Duke Street
Alexandria, VA 22314
www.uspa.org

United States Snowshoe Association
678 County Route 25
Corinth, NY 12822
www.snowshoeracing.com

United States Sportsmen's Alliance
801 Kingsmill Parkway
Columbus, OH
www.ussportsmen.org

United States Windsurfing Association
PO Box 978
Hood River, OR 97031
www.uswindsurfing.org

U.S. Sportsmen's Alliance
801 Kingsmill Parkway
Columbus, OH 43229
www.ussportsmen.org

Wilderness Education Association
PO Box 158897
Nashville, TN 37215
www.weainfo.org

Wilderness Inquiry
808 14th Avenue SE
Minneapolis, MN 55414
www.wildernessinquiry.org

Wilderness Medical Society
3595 East Fountain Boulevard
Suite A-1
Colorado Springs, CO 80910
www.wms.org

The Wilderness Society
900 17th Street NW
Washington, DC 20006
www.wilderness.org

Wilderness Watch
PO Box 9175
Missoula, MT
www.wildernesswatch.org

Wildlife Management Institute
1101 14th Street NW
Suite 801
Washington, DC 20005
www.wildlifemanagementinstitute.org

The Wildlife Society
5410 Grosvenor Lane
Bethesda, MD 20814
www.wildlife.org

Women Outdoors
55 Talbot Avenue
Medford, MA 02155
www.womenoutdoors.org

Wooden Canoe Heritage Association
PO Box 226
Blue Mountain Lake, NY 12812
www.wcha.org

Young Men's Christian Association
101 North Wacker Drive
Chicago, IL 60606
www.ymca.net

Young Women's Christian Association
Empire State Building
350 Fifth Avenue
Suite 301
New York, NY 10118
www.ywca.org

Appendix C

Federal Agencies Involved in Outdoor Recreation

DEPARTMENT OF AGRICULTURE

USDA Forest Service
Sidney R. Yates Federal Building
201 14th Street, SW at Independence Avenue SW
Washington, DC 20250

Regional Offices
Northern (Montana, Northern Idaho, North Dakota,
and Northwestern South Dakota)
Federal Building
PO Box 7669
Missoula, MT 59807

Rocky Mountain (Colorado, Kansas, Nebraska,
South Dakota, and Wyoming)
PO Box 25127
Lakewood, CO 80225;
740 Simms Street
Golden, CO 80401

Southwestern (Arizona and New Mexico)
333 Broadway, SE
Albuquerque, NM 87102

Intermountain (Southern Idaho, Nevada, Utah,
and Western Wyoming)
Federal Building 324
25th Street
Ogden, UT 84401

Pacific Southwest (California, Hawaii, Guam, and
Trust Territories of the Pacific Islands)
1323 Club Drive
Vallejo, CA 94592

Pacific Northwest (Oregon and Washington)
333 SW First Avenue
Portland, OR 97204

Southern (Alabama, Arkansas, Florida, Georgia,
Kentucky, Louisiana, Mississippi, NorthCarolina,
Oklahoma, Puerto Rico, South Carolina,
Tennessee, Texas, Virgin Islands, and Virginia)
1720 Peachtree Road NW
Atlanta, GA 30309

Eastern (Illinois, Indiana, Iowa, Maine, Maryland,
Massachusetts, Michigan, Minnesota, Missouri,
New Hampshire, New Jersey, New York, Ohio, Penn-
sylvania, Rhode Island, Vermont, West Virginia,
Wisconsin)
310 W. Wisconsin Avenue
Milwaukee, WI 53203

Alaska
Federal Office Building
709 W. 9th Street
Anchorage, AK 99801-1807

DEPARTMENT OF THE ARMY

Army Corps of Engineers
Office of the Chief of Engineers
441 G Street NW
Washington, DC 20314

Divisions
Mississippi Valley
PO Box 80
Vicksburg, MS 39181
North Atlantic
302 General Lee Avenue
Fort Hamilton Military Community
Brooklyn, NY 11252

Great Lake and Ohio River
PO Box 1159
Cincinnati, OH 45201

Pacific Ocean
Building 230,
Fort Shafter, HI 96858

South Atlantic
Room 9M15
60 Forsyth Street SW
Atlanta, GA 30303

Southwestern
1100 Commerce Street
Dallas, TX 75242

DEPARTMENT OF COMMERCE

National Oceanic and Atmospheric Administration
Sanctuaries and Reserves Division
1305 East-West Highway, 12th Floor
Silver Spring, MD 20910

National Marine Fisheries Service
Office of Constituent Services
1315 East-West Highway, 14th Floor
Silver Spring, MD 20910

DEPARTMENT OF THE INTERIOR

Bureau of Indian Affairs
Office of Public Affairs
1849 C Street NW
Washington, DC 20240

Bureau of Land Management
Recreation Group
1849 C Street NW
Washington, DC 20240

Denver Service Center
Center Federal Center, Building 50
Denver, CO

State Directors:
Alaska
222 West 7th Avenue #13,
Anchorage, AK 99513

Arizona
222 North Central Avenue
Phoenix, AZ 85004

California
Room E-2841
2800 Cottage Way
Sacramento, CA 95825

Colorado
2850 Youngfield Street
Lakewood, CO 80215

Idaho
1387 South Vinnell Way
Boise, ID 83709

Montana
5001 Southgate Drive
Billings, MT 59101

New Mexico (including Kansas, Oklahoma, and Texas)
1474 Rodeo Road, Santa Fe, NM 87505

Oregon and Washington
333 SW First Avenue
Portland, OR 97204

Utah
324 South State Street, 4th Floor
Salt Lake City, UT 84111

Wyoming
5353 Yellowstone
Cheyenne, WY 82003

Eastern States Office
7450 Boston Boulevard
Springfield, VA 22153

Bureau of Reclamation
1849 C Street NW
Washington D.C. 20240-0001

Regional Offices:
Great Plains
PO Box 36900
Billings, MT 59107-6900

Lower Colorado
400 Railroad Avenue
Boulder City, NV 89005-2422

Mid Pacific
Federal Office Building
2800 Cottage Way
Sacramento CA 95825-1898

Pacific Northwest
1150 North Curtis Road
Suite 100
Boise, Idaho 83706-1234
Upper Colorado
125 South State Street, Room 6107
Salt Lake City, UT 84138-1102

National Park Service
1849 C Street NW
Washington, DC 20240

Regional Offices:
Alaska Area Region
2525 Gambell St. RM 107
Anchorage, AK 99503

Midwest Region
1709 Jackson Street
Omaha, NE 68102

Intermountain Region
12795 Alameda Parkway
Denver, CO 80225

Pacific West Region
One Jackson Center
1111 Jackson Street, Suite 700
Oakland, CA 94607

Northeast Region
U.S. Custom House
200 Chestnut Street, Fifth Floor
Philadelphia, PA 19106

National Capital Region
1100 Ohio Drive, SW
Washington, DC 20242

Southeast Region
100 Alabama Street SW
1924 Building
Atlanta, GA 30303

U.S. Fish and Wildlife Service
1849 C Street, NW
Washington, DC 20240

Regional Offices:
Region 1: Washington, Oregon, California, Nevada,
Idaho, Hawaii
911 NE 11th Avenue
Portland, Oregon 97232-4181

Region 2: New Mexico, Arizona, Oklahoma, Texas
PO Box 1306
Albuquerque, NM 87103

Region 3: Minnesota, Indiana, Missouri, Michigan,
Wisconsin, Ohio, Illinois, Iowa
Federal Building, Fort Snelling
Twin Cities, MN 55111

Region 4: Kentucky, Arkansas, Tennessee, North
Carolina, South Carolina, Georgia, Alabama,
Mississippi, Louisiana, Florida, Virgin Islands, Puerto
Rico
1875 Century Boulevard
Atlanta, GA 30345

Region 5: Virginia, West Virginia, Maryland,
Pennsylvania, New York, Delaware, New Jersey,
Connecticut, Maine, Massachusetts, Vermont, New
Hampshire, Rhode Island
300 Westgate Center Drive
Hadley, MA 01035

Region 6: Colorado, Montana, Nebraska, Utah,
Wyoming, Kansas, North Dakota, South Dakota
PO Box 25486
Denver, CO 80025

Region 7: Alaska
1011 East Tudor Road
Anchorage, AK 99503

DEPARTMENT OF TRANSPORTATION

Federal Highway Administration
National Scenic Byways Program
400 Seventh Street, SW
Room 3222, HEPM
Washington, DC 20590

INDEPENDENT AGENCY

Tennessee Valley Authority
400 West Summit Hill Drive
Knoxville, TN 37902-1499
Phone: 865-632-2101

Appendix D

Federal Laws Related to Outdoor Recreation

Forest Reserve Act (Creative Act of National Forests) ch. 561	1891 USFS	

Organic Administration Act-National Forests
ch. 2 — 1897 USFS

Weeks Law
ch. 186 — 1911 USFS

Multiple-Use Sustained-Yield Act
P.L. 86-517 — 1960 USFS

Forest and Rangeland Renewable Resources Planning Act
P.L. 93-378 — 1974 USFS

Eastern Wilderness Act
P.L. 93-622 — 1975 USFS

National Forest Management Act
P.L. 94-388 — 1976 USFS

Yellowstone National Park Act
ch. 24 — 1897 NPS

Antiquities Act
ch. 3060 — 1906 NPS

National Park Service Act
ch. 408 — 1916 NPS

Historic Sites Act
ch. 593 — 1935 NPS

Bureau of Outdoor Recreation Organic Act
P.L. 88-29 — 1963 NPS

Land and Water Conservation Fund Act
P.L. 88-578 — 1965 NPS

National Historic Preservation Act
P.L. 89-665 — 1966 NPS

Golden Gate National Recreation Area Act
P.L. 92-589 — 1972 NPS

National Historic Preservation Fund (Title II of Land and Water Conservation Fund Act Amendments)
P.L. 94-422 — 1976 NPS

Omnibus Parks and Public Lands Management Act
P.L. 104-333 — 1996 NPS

Migratory Bird Conservation Act
ch. 257 — 1929 FWS

Migratory Bird Hunting Stamp Act
ch. 71 — 1934 FWS

Federal Aid to Wildlife Restoration Act
ch. 899 — 1937 FWS

Fish Restoration and Management Projects Act
ch. 658 — 1950 FWS

Fish and Wildlife Act (Fish and Wildlife Service Establishment)
ch. 1036 — 1956 FWS

Refuge Recreation Act
P.L. 87-714 — 1962 FWS

National Wildlife Refuge System
Administration Act (Organic Act)   1966
    P.L. 93-205   FWS

National Wildlife Refuge System
Administration Act   1997
    P.L. 105-57   FWS

O&C Sustained Yield Forestry Act   1937
    ch. 876 (P.L. 405 of 75th Congress)   BLM

Federal Property and Administrative
Services Act (Surplus Property Act)
(first passed 1926)   1954
    ch. 263 (P.L. 387)   BLM

Federal Land Policy and Management Act
(BLM Organic Act)   1976
    P.L. 94-579   BLM

National Marine Sanctuaries Act   1972
    Title III   NOAA

National Marine Sanctuaries Act   1996
    P.L. 104-283   NOAA

National Marine Sanctuaries
Amendment Act   2000
    P.L. 106-513   NOAA

Intermodal Surface Transportation
Efficiency Act (ISTEA)   1996
    P.L. 102-240   FHWA

Transportation Equity Act for the
21st Century (TEA-21)   1991
    P.L. 105-178   FHWA

Housing and Community
Development Act   1974
    P.L. 93-383   HUD

Watershed Protection and Flood
Prevention Act   1954
    P.L. 566   SCS

Federal Water Projects Recreation Act   1965
    P.L. 89-72   COE, B. Recl.

Federal Water Pollution Control Act
Amendments   1972
    P.L. 92-500

Coastal Zone Management Act   1972
    P.L. 92-583

Wilderness Act   1964
    P.L. 88-577

National Trails System Act   1968
    P.L. 90-543, P.L. 98-11   1983

Wild and Scenic Rivers Act   1968
    P.L. 90-542

National Environmental Policy Act   1969
    P.L. 91-190

Environmental Education Act   1970
    P.L. 91-516

Alaska Native Claims Settlement Act   1971
    P.L. 92-203

Alaska National Interest Lands
Conservation Act   1980
    P.L. 96-487

Endangered Species Act   1973
    P.L. 93-205   1983

Public Lands-Local Government Funds
Act or "Payment In Lieu of Taxes" Act   1976
    P.L. 94-579   USFS, BLM

California Desert Protection Act   1994
    P.L. 104-333   NPS, BLM, USFS, FWS

ALIVE Outdoors, Inc.
30 Elmsdale Road
Toronto, ON, M4J 3M4
www.aliveoutdoors.com

Alpine Club of Canada
201 Indian Flats Road
PO Box 8040, Station Main
Canmore, AB, T1W 2T8
www.alpineclubofcanada.ca

Association of Canadian Mountain Guides
ACMG office
Box 8341
Canmore, AB, T1W 2V1
www.acmg.ca

Avalanche Canada
Box 560, 110 MacKenzie Avenue
Revelstoke, BC, V0E 2S0
www.avalanche.ca

Bird Studies Canada
PO Box 160, 115 Front Street
Port Rowan, ON, N0E 1M0
www.bsc-eoc.org

Canadian Camping Association
100-180 Duncan Mill Road
Toronto, ON, M3B 1Z6
www.ccamping.org/about/

Canadian Forestry Association
PO Box 99
6905 Hwy 17 West
Mattawa, ON, P0H 1V0
www.canadianforestry.com

Canadian Parks and Wilderness Society
National Office
506-250 City Centre Avenue
Ottawa, ON, K1R 6K7
www.cpaws.org

Canadian Wildlife Federation
350 Michael Cowpland Drive
Kanata, ON, K2M 2W1
www.cwf-fcf.org

International Mountain Bicycling
Association Canada
PO Box 23034
Kitchener, ON, N2B 3V1
www.imbacanada.com

Leave No Trace Canada
151 Boulevard Sainte-Rose
Laval, QC, H7L 1L2
www.leavenotrace.ca

National Outdoor Leadership School,
Yukon Territory
12 Burns Road
Whitehorse, YT, Y1A 4Y9
www.nols.edu/locations/nols-yukon

Nature Conservancy of Canada
36 Eglinton Avenue West, Suite 400
Toronto, ON, M4R 1A1
www.natureconservancy.ca

Ontario Rock Climbing Access Coalition
Toronto, ON
www.ontarioaccesscoalition.com

Outward Bound Canada
550 Bayview Avenue, Building 1, Suite 201
Toronto, ON, M4W 3X8
www.outwardbound.ca

Paddle Canada
PO Box 126, Station Main
Kingston, ON, K7L 4V6
www.paddlingcanada.com

Parks Canada
30 Victoria Street
Gatineau, QC, J8X 0B3
www.pc.gc.ca

Trans Canada Trail
321 de la Commune West, Suite 300
Montréal, QC, H2Y 2E1
www.tctrail.ca

Tree Canada
470 Somerset Street West
Ottawa, ON, K1R 5J8
www.treecanada.ca

Index

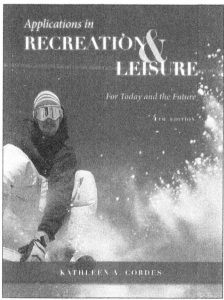